# Arabic Military Dictionary

# Arabic Military Dictionary

ENGLISH - ARABIC

ARABIC - ENGLISH

Compiled by Multi-Lingual International Publishers Ltd

under the general editorship of

Ernest Kay

Routledge & Kegan Paul

London, Boston and Henley

Words which the authors, editors and publishers have reason to believe constitute registered trade marks have been labelled as such, using the abbreviation TM. However, neither the presence nor the absence of such designation should be regarded as affecting in any way the legal status of any trademark.

*First published in 1986*
*by Routledge & Kegan Paul plc*

*14 Leicester Square, London WC2H 7PH, England*

*9 Park Street, Boston, Mass. 02108, USA and*

*Broadway House, Newtown Road,*
*Henley-on-Thames, Oxon RG9 1EN, England*

*Printed in Great Britain*
*by T.J. Press (Padstow) Ltd*
*Padstow, Cornwall*



*ISBN 0-7102-0458-2*

# CONTENTS

# INTRODUCTION

THIS translation dictionary has been compiled for use by military personnel and by anyone who is directly or indirectly involved in military technology. It is essentially a practical dictionary, containing words and terms in everyday use in the field or in headquarters, and avoids definitions — it is assumed that those using a particular word will know the meaning of that word.

Technical coverage of the dictionary extends throughout the sphere of the Armed Forces and Military Technology, including the armed forces of the world, arms and armaments, land-based weapons and equipment, including tanks, missiles, combat and reconnaissance aircraft, helicopters, warships including submarines, naval aviation, communications and training.

Not only have translation requirements featured prominently during the compilation of this dictionary, but careful consideration has been given to the problems associated with the pronunciation of Arabic script so frequently encountered by English-speaking people. Because of these difficulties, each word in Arabic script is accompanied by its own pronunciation aid — a transliteration which has been proved successful over the years. A short guide to the use of this transliteration follows this introduction.

As the first Military Dictionary of its kind, it will be an essential tool for anyone in or connected with the armed forces, whether engaged in armed conflict in the field or in headquarters, or acting in a peace-keeping capacity. Because of its extensive subject coverage, those associated with military activities in any way, including those manufacturing or supplying arms and equipment to the armed forces, will find the dictionary useful. Teachers and students of military strategy and tactics in technical colleges, universities and military academies will find the dictionary very helpful, as will translators, interpreters and anyone charged with the task of providing an equivalent Arabic word or term.

In order to keep the dictionary to a manageable size words have been selected carefully — and in many cases words have been presented as part of a term or phrase which is in frequent use — but some omissions will have occurred. Certain omissions have been deliberate because the words are in such common use that they occur in most general dictionaries. Others are not intended and constructive comments are welcome to help improve subsequent editions.

# NOTES ON TRANSLITERATION

Arabic is written from right to left using an alphabet of 29 letters. There are no capitals, but some letters (when joined together) change their shape slightly, as shown in brackets. The alphabet is set out below with the corresponding transliteration for each letter.

| Letter | Joined form | Transliteration | Letter | Joined form | Transliteration |
|---|---|---|---|---|---|
| أ | | *a* | ط | | *ṭ* |
| ب | (بـ) | *b* | ظ | | *ẓ* |
| ت | (تـ) | *t* | ع | (عـ) | ʿ |
| ث | (ثـ) | *th* | غ | (غـ) | *gh* |
| ج | (جـ) | *j* | ف | (فـ) | *f* |
| ح | (حـ) | *ḥ* | ق | (قـ) | *q* |
| خ | (خـ) | *kh* | ك | (كـ) | *k* |
| د | | *d* | ل | | *l* |
| ذ | | *dh* | م | (مـ) | *m* |
| ر | | *r* | ن | (نـ) | *n* |
| ز | | *z* | هـ | (ﻬ) | *h* |
| س | (سـ) | *s* | و | | *w* |
| ش | (شـ) | *sh* | ي | (يـ) | *y* |
| ص | (صـ) | *ṣ* | ء | | ʾ |
| ض | (ضـ) | *ḍ* | | | |

The following letters are pronounced like their English equivalents:

بـ = *b*, تـ = *t*, ثـ = *th* (as in *thin*), جـ = *j*
د = *d*, ر = *r*, ز = *z*, سـ = *s*, ذ = *dh* (as in *the*)
شـ = *sh*, فـ = *f*, كـ = *k*, لـ = *l*, مـ = *m*
نـ = *n*, هـ = *h*, و = *w*, يـ = *y*.

The following sounds need special attention:

- حـ transliterated *(ḥ)*, is a throaty sound like *h* in a loud whisper;
- خـ transliterated *(kh)* is another throaty sound as in the Scottish word *loch*;
- ء transliterated (ʾ). This is a glottal stop. It can be heard in Cockney English, e.g. *"bread and bu-ʾer";*
- عـ transliterated (ʿ). This is a throaty sound. To produce it, make a long sound *aaa* while pressing on the throat;
- غـ transliterated *(gh)* is a gargling sound like a long *r*;
- قـ transliterated *(q)*. It sounds like a *k* pronounced in the back of the throat.

ص (*ṣ*), ض (*ḍ*), ط (*ṭ*), and ظ (*ẓ*) are emphatic counterparts of
س (*s*), د (*d*), ت (*t*), and ذ (*dh*).

Pronounce each strongly as if it was followed by the Arabic vowel *u*, thus *ṣu* for ص. (The *u* part of the sound is not included in the transliteration).

There are three short vowels in Arabic: *a* as in *fat, i* as in *fit,* and *u* as in *pull.* These are not written in the Arabic but they are transliterated. Corresponding to the short vowels are three long vowels indicated by a dash placed above them: *ā* like the American *'a'* in *path, ī* as in *feet, ū* as in *pool.*

There are two diphthongs in Arabic: *ay* as in *may* and *aw* as in *how.*

Short vowels must be pronounced short, and long ones pronounced long; double consonants must be emphasised as double. If this is not done the meaning may change, e.g.:
*malik* = king, *mālik* = owner,
*darasa* = to learn, *darrasa* = to teach.

# ENGLISH - ARABIC

# انكليزي - عربي

A-class submarine — غواصة « ابتو »
*ghawwāṣa ṭirāz ayy*

A1-20 turboprop — طائرة بمحرك مروحي تربيني « ايه ١-٢٠ »
*ṭāʾira bi-muḥarrik mirwaḥī turbīnī ayy-wāḥid ʿishrīn*

A-4 bomber — طائرة قاذفة « ايه - ٤ »
*ṭāʾira qādhifa ayy arbaʿa*

A-4EH aircraft — طائرة « ايه-٤ ئي إتش »
*ṭāʾirat ayy arbaʿa ī itsh*

A-4H bomber — طائرة قاذفة « ايه - ٤ إتش »
*ṭāʾira qādhifa ayy arbaʿa itsh*

A-4 M bomber — طائرة قاذفة « ايه - ٤ إم »
*ṭāʾira qādhifa ayy arbaʿa imm*

A-6E bomber — طائرة قاذفة « ايه - ٦ ئي »
*ṭāʾira qādhifa ayy sitta ī*

A-7 bomber — طائرة قاذفة « ايه - ٧ »
*ṭāʾira qādhifa ayy sabʿa*

A-7D fighter — طائرة مقاتلة « ايه - ٧ دي »
*ṭāʾira muqātila ayy sabʿa dī*

A-7E aircraft — طائرة « ايه - ٧ ئي »
*ṭāʾirat ayy sabʿa ī*

A-10A attack aircraft — طائرة مهاجمة « ايه - ١٠ ايه »
*ṭāʾira muhājima ayy ʿashara ayy*

A-18 fighter — طائرة مقاتلة « ايه - ١٨ »
*ṭāʾira muhājima ayy thamānyata ʿashar*

A-37B fighter — طائرة مقاتلة « ايه - ٣٧ بي »
*ṭāʾira muhājima ayy sabʿa wa thalāthīn bī*

A41 tank — دبابة « ايه ٤١ »
*dabbābat ayy wāḥid wa arbaʿīn*

A 80 pistol — مسدس « ايه ٨٠ »
*musaddas ayy thamānīn*

A-109 helicopter — طائرة عمودية « ايه ١٠٩ »
*ṭāʾira ʿamūdīya ayy miʾa wa tisʿa*

A-129 helicopter — طائرة عمودية « ايه ١٢٩ »
*ṭāʾira ʿamūdīya ayy miʾa wa tisʿa wa ʿishrīn*

AA-1 AAM — صاروخ جو - جو « ايه ايه - ١ »
*ṣārūkh jaww-jaww ayy ayy wāḥid*

AA-2 AAM — صاروخ جو - جو « ايه ايه - ٢ »
*ṣārūkh jaww-jaww ayy ayy ithnayn*

AA-2-2 AAM — صاروخ جو - جو « ايه ايه ٢ - ٢ »
*ṣārūkh jaww-jaww ayy ayy ithnayn ithnayn*

AA-3 AAM — صاروخ جو - جو « ايه ايه - ٣ »
*ṣārūkh jaww-jaww ayy ayy thalātha*

AA-3-2 AAM — صاروخ جو - جو « ايه ايه - ٣ - ٢ »
*ṣārūkh jaww-jaww ayy ayy thalātha ithnayn*

AA-4 AAM — صاروخ جو - جو « ايه ايه - ٤ »
*ṣārūkh jaww-jaww ayy ayy arbaʿa*

AA-5 AAM — صاروخ جو - جو « ايه ايه - ٥ »
*ṣārūkh jaww-jaww ayy ayy khamsa*

AA-6 AAM — صاروخ جو - جو « ايه ايه - ٦ »
*ṣārūkh jaww-jaww ayy ayy sitta*

AA-7 AAM — صاروخ جو - جو « ايه ايه - ٧ »
*ṣārūkh jaww-jaww ayy ayy sabʿa*

AA-8 AAM — صاروخ جو - جو « ايه ايه - ٨ »
*ṣārūkh jaww-jaww ayy ayy thamānya*

AA-9 AAM — صاروخ جو - جو « ايه ايه - ٩ »
*ṣārūkh jaww-jaww ayy ayy tisʿa*

AA gun — مدفع مضاد للطائرات
*midfaʿ muḍādd liṭ-ṭāʾirāt*

AAM صاروخ جو ـ جو
*ṣārūkh jaww-jaww*

AAM-1 صاروخ جو ـ جو « ١ ـ »
*ṣārūkh jaww-jaww wāḥid*

AAM-2 صاروخ جو ـ جو « ٢ ـ »
*ṣārūkh jaww-jaww ithnayn*

AA-X-9 AAM صاروخ جو ـ جو « ايه ايه ـ اكس ـ ٩ »
*ṣārūkh jaww-jaww ayy ayy iks tisʿa*

AA-X-10 AAM صاروخ جو ـ جو « ايه ايه ـ اكس ـ ١٠ »
*ṣārūkh jaww-jaww ayy ayy iks ʿashara*

AA-XP-1 AAM صاروخ جو ـ جو « ايه ايه ـ اكس پى ـ ١ »
*ṣārūkh jaww-jaww ayy ayy iks pī wāḥid*

AA-XP-2 AAM صاروخ جو ـ جو « ايه ايه ـ اكس پى ـ ٢ »
*ṣārūkh jaww-jaww ayy ayy iks pī ithnayn*

AB-47 helicopter طائرة عمودية « ايه بى ـ ٤٧ »
*ṭāʾira ʿamūdīya ayy bī sabʿa wa arbaʿīn*

AB-204 helicopter طائرة عمودية « ايه بي ٢٠٤ »
*ṭāʾira ʿamūdīya ayy bī miʾatayn wa arbaʿa*

AB-204 B helicopter طائرة عمودية « ايه بي ٢٠٤ بي »
*ṭāʾira ʿamūdīya ayy bī miʾatayn wa arbaʿa bī*

AB-205 helicopter طائرة عمودية « ايه بي ٢٠٥ »
*ṭāʾira ʿamūdīya ayy bī miʾatayn wa khamsa*

AB-212 helicopter طائرة عمودية « ايه بي ـ ٢١٢ »
*ṭāʾira ʿamūdīya ayy bī miʾatayn wa ithnata ʿashara*

AB-412 helicopter طائرة عمودية « ايه بي ـ ٤١٢ »
*ṭāʾira ʿamūdīya ayy bī arbaʿ miʾa wa ithnata ʿashara*

Abbey Hill أبي هيل
*abi hil*

Abbot gun مدفع أبت
*midfaʿ abat*

Abdiel supply ship سفينة تموين « أبديل »
*safīnat tamwīn abdīl*

ABM-1B missile صاروخ « ايه بي ام ـ ١ بي »
*ṣārūkh ayy bī imm wāḥid bī*

about turn! « الى الوراء ـ در »
*ilal warāʾ durr*

above establishment اكثر من المقرر
*akthar min al-muqarrar*

Abrams tank دبابة « ابرامز »
*dabbābat abrāmz*

absent without leave تغيب بدون إذن
*taghayyub bidūn idhn*

Abtao submarine غواصة « طراز ايه »
*ghawwāṣat abtū*

Abu Dhabi أبو ظبي
*abū ẓabī*

accelerate عجل . تسارع
*ʿajjala · tasāraʿa*

access hatch باب دخول
*bāb dukhūl*

accessible to tanks منفتح للدبابات
*munfatiḥ lid-dabbābāt*

accident report تقرير حادث
*taqrīr ḥādith*

acclimatization room غرفة التأقلم
*ghurfat at-taʾaqlum*

accommodation سكن . إيواء . تكييف
*sakan · īwāʾ · takyīf*

accommodation deck طابق المسكن (في سفينة)
*ṭābiq al-maskan (fī-safīna)*

acoustic صوتي . سمعي
*ṣawtī · samʿī*

acoustical effects تأثيرات صوتية
*taʾthīrāt ṣawtīya*

acoustic data معطيات صوتية
*muʿṭayāt ṣawtīya*

acquire اكتسب
*iktasaba*

acquisition اكتساب
*iktisāb*

acquisition unit وحدة احراز
*wiḥdat iḥrāz*

acquisition window نافذة احراز
*nāfidhat iḥrāz*

Acrid AAM صاروخ جو ـ جو « أكريد »
*ṣārūkh jaww-jaww akrid*

ACRV مركبة قيادة واستطلاع مدرعة
*markabat qiyāda wa istiṭlāʿ mudarraʿa*

action اجراء . عمل . معركة
*ijrāʾ · ʿamal · maʿraka*

action information system نظام بيانات القتال
*niẓām bayānāt al-qitāl*

activating agent عامل تنشيط
*ʿāmil tanshīṭ*

active countermeasures اجراءات مضادة فعالة
*ijrāʾāt muḍādda faʿʿāla*

active duty خدمة فعلية
*khidma fiʿlīya*

active jamming تشويش فعال
*tashwīsh faʿʿāl*

active radar
*rādār faʿʿāl*
رادار فعال

active radar homing
*tawjīh rādārī faʿʿāl*
توجيه راداري فعال

active radar seeker
*bāḥith rādārī faʿʿāl*
باحث راداري فعال

active satellite
*qamar ṣināʿī faʿʿāl*
قمر صناعي فعال

active service
*khidma ʿāmila · khidma fiʿlīya*
خدمة عاملة . خدمة فعلية

active sonar
*sūnār faʿʿāl*
سونار فعال

actuator
*mushaghghil · nāqil al-ḥaraka*
مُشغل . ناقل الحركة

ACV
*markaba bi-wisāda hawāʾīya*
مركبة بوسادة هوائية

ADAC radar seeker
*bāḥith rādārī ayy dī ayy sī*
باحث راداري « ايه دي ايه سي »

Adams destroyer
*mudammirat ādamz*
مدمرة آدمز

adapter shoe
*naʿl al-munaẓẓim*
نعل المنظم

ADATS
*niẓām muḍādd lid-dabbābāt lid-difāʿ al-jawwī*
نظام مضاد للدبابات للدفاع الجوي

ADAWS
*nāʾib mudīr al-khadamāt al-ijtimāʿīya bil-jaysh (al-mamlaka al-muttaḥida)*
نائب مدير الخدمات الاجتماعية بالجيش (المملكة المتحدة)

Aden cannon
*midfaʿ hāwun aydan*
مدفع هاون « أيدن »

ADG-6-30 CIWS
*niẓām asliḥat al-ishtibāk (burj baḥrī muḍādd liṭ-ṭāʾirāt) ayy dī jī sitta-thalāthīn*
نظام أسلحة الاشتباك (برج بحري مضاد للطائرات) ايه دي جي ٦-٣٠

adjustment of fire
*ḍabṭ an-nīrān*
ضبط النيران

adjutant
*musāʿid · ḍābiṭ musāʿid lil-qāʾid*
مساعد . ضابط مساعد للقائد

Adjutant minesweeper
*kāsiḥat alghām ājutant*
كاسحة ألغام اجوتنت

administration
*idāra · ḥukūma*
إدارة . حكومة

administrative officer
*ḍābiṭ idārī*
ضابط إداري

administrator
*mudīr · ḍābiṭ tanfīdhī*
مدير . ضابط تنفيذي

adopt a ready position
*yuttakhidh waḍʿ al-istiʿdād*
يتخذ وضع الاستعداد

Adour Mk 104 turbofan
*mirwaḥa turbīnīya adūr ṭirāz miʾa wa arbaʿa*
مروحة تربينية « أدور » طراز ١٠٤

ADS
*shabakat difāʿ jawwī*
شبكة دفاع جوي

advance!
*lil-amān · taqaddam*
للأمام ـ تقدم !

Advanced Anab AAM
*ṣārūkh jaww-jaww anab mutaqaddim*
صاروخ جو ـ جو « اناب » متقدم

Advanced Atoll AAM
*ṣārūkh jaww-jaww atūl mutaqaddim*
صاروخ جو ـ جو « أتول » متقدم

Advanced Attack Helicopter
*ṭāʾira ʿamūdīya muhājima mutaqaddima*
طائرة عمودية مهاجمة متقدمة

advance detachment
*mafraza mutaqaddima*
مفرزة متقدمة

Advanced Intercept AAM
*ṣārūkh jaww-jaww iʿtirāḍī mutaqaddim*
صاروخ جو ـ جو اعتراضي متقدم

advanced radar processing system
*niẓām taḥlīl rādārī mutaqaddim*
نظام تحليل راداري متقدم

advance guard
*al-muqaddima*
المقدمة

advance in force
*taqaddum bil-qūwa*
تقدم بالقوة

advance information
*maʿlūmāt mutaqaddima*
معلومات متقدمة

advance post
*markaz mutaqaddim*
مركز متقدم

advance to contact
*taqaddam lit-tamās*
تقدم للتماس

adverse terrain
*arḍīya ghayr mulāʾima*
أرضية غير ملائمة

AEGIS radar
*rādār ayjis*
رادار « ايجيس »

aerial attack
*hujūm jawwī*
هجوم جوي

aerial bomb
*qunbula jawwīya*
قنبلة جوية

aerial bombing
*qadhf qanābil jawwīya*
قذف قنابل جوية

aerial photography
*taṣwīr jawwī*
تصوير جوي

aerial reconnaissance استطلاع جوي
*istiṭlāʿ jawwī*
aerial scout helicopter طائرة عمودية للاستطلاع الجوي
*ṭāʾira ʿamūdīya lil-istiṭlāʿ al-jawwī*
aerial spotter مراقب جوي . راصد جوي
*murāqib jawwī · rāṣid jawwī*
aerial target هدف جوي
*hadaf jawwī*
Aeritalia (Co) شركة « أيريتاليا »
*sharikat ayritālya*
Aermacchi (Co) شركة « أيرماكي »
*sharikat ayrmākī*
aerodynamic brakes مكابح ايروديناميكية
*makābiḥ ayrūdīnāmīkīya*
aerodynamic control تحكم ايروديناميكي
*taḥakkum ayrūdīnāmīkī*
aerodynamic noise ضجيج ايروديناميكي
*ḍajīj ayrūdīnāmīkī*
aerofoil سطح انسيابي رافع
*saṭḥ insīyābī rāfiʿ*
aerofoil boat زورق بسطح انسيابي
*zawraq bi-saṭḥ insīyābī*
aerojet نفاثة بالضغط الهوائي
*naffātha biḍ-ḍaghṭ al-hawāʾī*
aeronautical chart خريطة الملاحة الجوية
*kharīṭat al-milāḥa al-jawwīya*
aerosol bomb قنبلة إيروسول
*qunbulat īrūsūl*
aerospace motor محرك جوي
*muḥarrik jawwī*
Aérospatiale (Co) شركة أيروسباسيال
*sharikat ayrūspasyāl*
Aero Vodochody (Co) شركة إيرو فودوشودي
*sharikat ayrū fūdū shūdī*
AEW نظام تحذير مبكر محمول جواً
*niẓām taḥdhīr mubakkir maḥmūl jawwan*
Afghanistan أفغانستان
*afghānistān*
aft مؤخرة السفينة ذيل الطائرة
*muʾakhkharat as-safīna · dhayl aṭ-ṭāʾira*
afterburner حارق لاحق
*ḥāriq lāḥiq*
afterburner nozzle فوهة الحارق اللاحق
*fūhat al-ḥāriq al-lāḥiq*
afterburning thrust دفع احتراق لاحق
*dafʿ iḥtirāq lāḥiq*
afterburning turbojet طائرة نفاثة بالاحتراق اللاحق
*ṭāʾira naffātha bil-iḥtirāq al-lāḥiq*
after casing تغليف لاحق
*taghlīf lāḥiq*
after end طرف المؤخرة
*ṭaraf al-muʾakhkhara*
aft-facing مواجه للمؤخرة
*muwājih lil-muʾakhkhara*
aft superstructure الانشاء الاساسي للمؤخرة
*al-inshāʾ al-asāsī lil-muʾakhkhara*
AG 15 data link جهاز إرسال المعطيات « ايه جي ١٥ »
*jihāz irsāl al-muʿṭayāt ayy jī khamsata ʿashar*
Agave radar رادار أجاف
*rādār agāv*
aggresive minesweeper كاسحة ألغام عدائية
*kāsiḥat alghām ʿidāʾīya*
aggressor معتد . باغي
*muʿtadi · bāghī*
agility رشاقة المناورة
*rashāqat al-munāwara*
AGM صاروخ جو - أرض
*ṣārūkh jaww-arḍ*
AGM-12 صاروخ جو - أرض « - ١٢ »
*ṣārūkh jaww-arḍ ithnata ʿashar*
AGM-28 صاروخ جو - أرض « - ٢٨ »
*ṣārūkh jaww-arḍ thamānya wa ʿishrīn*
AGM-45 صاروخ جو - أرض « - ٤٥ »
*ṣārūkh jaww-arḍ khamsa wa arbaʿīn*
AGM-53 صاروخ جو - أرض « - ٥٣ »
*ṣārūkh jaww-arḍ thalātha wa khamsīn*
AGM-62 صاروخ جو - أرض « - ٦٢ »
*ṣārūkh jaww-arḍ ithnayn wa sittīn*
AGM-65 صاروخ جو - أرض « - ٦٥ »
*ṣārūkh jaww-arḍ khamsa wa sittīn*
AGM-69 صاروخ جو - أرض « - ٦٩ »
*ṣārūkh jaww-arḍ tisʿa wa sittīn*
AGM-69A SRAM صاروخ جو - أرض « ٦٩ ايه - اس آر ايه إم »
*ṣārūkh jaww-arḍ tisʿa wa sittīn ayy is ār ayy imm*

AGM-78 صاروخ جو ـ أرض « ـ ٧٨ »
*ṣārūkh jaww-arḍ thamānya wa sabʿīn*

AGM-83 صاروخ جو ـ أرض « ٨٣ »
*ṣārūkh jaww-arḍ thalātha wa thamānīn*

AGM-84A صاروخ جو ـ أرض « ـ ٨٤ ايه »
*ṣārūkh jaww-arḍ arbaʿa wa thamānīn ayy*

AGM-86 صاروخ جو ـ أرض « ـ ٨٦ »
*ṣārūkh jaww-arḍ sitta wa thamānīn*

AGM-86B ALCM صاروخ جو ـ أرض « ـ ٨٦ بي ـ ايه ال سي إم »
*ṣārūkh jaww-arḍ sitta wa thamānīn bī-ayy il sī imm*

AGM-88 صاروخ جو ـ أرض « ـ ٨٨ »
*ṣārūkh jaww-arḍ thamānya wa thamānīn*

Agosta submarine غواصة « أجوستا »
*ghawwāṣat agusta*

AGSS submarine غواصة « ايه جي اس اس »
*ghawwāṣat ayy jī is is*

AGT-1500 engine محرك « ايه جي تي ـ ١٥٠٠ »
*muḥarrik ayy jī tī alf wa khamsa miʾa*

AH-1 helicopter طائرة عمودية « ايه إتش ـ ١ »
*ṭāʾira ʿamūdīya ayy itsh wāḥid*

AH-1G helicopter طائرة عمودية « ايه إتش ـ ١ جي »
*ṭāʾira ʿamūdīya ayy itsh wāḥid jī*

AH-1S helicopter طائرة عمودية « ايه إتش ـ ١ اس »
*ṭāʾira ʿamūdīya ayy itsh wāḥid is*

AH-15 helicopter طائرة عمودية « ايه اتش ـ ١٥ »
*ṭāʾira ʿamūdīya ayy itsh khamsata ʿashar*

AH-56 helicopter طائرة عمودية « ايه إتش ـ ٥٦ »
*ṭāʾira ʿamūdīya ayy itsh sitta wa khamsīn*

AH-64 helicopter طائرة عمودية « ايه إتش ـ ٦٤ »
*ṭāʾira ʿamūdīya ayy itsh arbaʿa wa sittīn*

AH-IT helicopter طائرة عمودية « ايه إتش ـ آي تي »
*ṭāʾira ʿamūdīya ayy itsh āyy tī*

AIDC (Co) شركة « ايه أى دي سي »
*sharikat ayy āyy dī sī*

ailerons جنيحات
*junayḥāt*

aim تسديد . تصويب
*tasdīd · taṣwīb*

AIM قذيفة اعتراضية جوية
*qadhīfa iʿtirāḍīya jawwīya*

AIM-4 قذيفة اعتراضية جوية « ايه آي ام ـ ٤ »
*qadhīfa iʿtirāḍīya jawwīya arbaʿa*

AIM-7 قذيفة اعتراضية جوية « ايه آي ام ـ ٧ »
*qadhīfa iʿtirāḍīya jawwīya sabʿa*

AIM-9 قذيفة اعتراضية جوية « ايه آي ام ـ ٩ »
*qadhīfa iʿtirāḍīya jawwīya tisʿa*

AIM-26 قذيفة اعتراضية جوية « ايه آي ام ـ ٢٦ »
*qadhīfa iʿtirāḍīya jawwīya sitta wa ʿishrīn*

AIM-47 قذيفة اعتراضية جوية « ايه آي ام ـ ٤٧ »
*qadhīfa iʿtirāḍīya jawwīya sabʿa wa arbaʿīn*

AIM-54 قذيفة اعتراضية جوية « ايه آي ام ـ ٥٤ »
*qadhīfa iʿtirāḍīya jawwīya arbaʿa wa khamsīn*

AIM-120 AAM قذيفة اعتراضية جوية « ايه آي ام ـ ١٢٠ ايه ايه ام »
*qadhīfa iʿtirāḍīya jawwīya miʾa wa ʿishrīn ayy ayy im*

aiming post شاخص التصويب
*shākhiṣ at-taṣwīb*

aiming telescope تلسكوب التصويب
*talskūb at-taṣwīb*

aiming unit وحدة تصويب
*wiḥdat taṣwīb*

aim-off تصحيح أمام الهدف
*taṣḥīḥ amām al-hadaf*

air جو . هواء
*jaww · hawāʾ*

AIR-2A صاروخ « ايه آي آر ـ ٢ ايه »
*ṣārūkh ayy āyy ār - ithnayn ayy*

air arm القوات الجوية
*al-qūwāt al-jawwīya*

air assault brigade لواء اقتحام جوي
*liwāʾ iqtiḥām jawwī*

air assault division فرقة اقتحام جوي
*firqat iqtiḥām jawwī*

air attack هجوم جوي
*hujūm jawwī*

air base قاعدة جوية
*qāʿida jawwīya*

airborne منقول جواً
*manqūl jawwan*

airborne assault gun — مدفع اقتحام منقول جواً
*midfaʿ iqtiḥām manqūl jawwan*

Airborne Battlefield Command — قيادة معارك جند الجو
*qiyādat maʿārik jund al-jaww*

Airborne Command — قيادة جند الجو
*qiyādat jund al-jaww*

airborne division — فرقة محمولة جواً
*firqa maḥmūla jawwan*

airborne drop — إسقاط جوي . قذف جوي
*isqāṭ jawwī · qadhf jawwī*

airborne early warning — إنذار مبكر محمول جواً
*indhār mubakkir maḥmūl jawwan*

airborne forces — القوات المحمولة جواً
*al-qūwāt al-maḥmūla jawwan*

airborne-interception radar — رادار اعتراضي محمول جواً
*rādār iʿtirāḍī maḥmūl jawwan*

airborne-interception rocket — صاروخ اعتراضي محمول جواً
*ṣārūkh iʿtirāḍī maḥmūl jawwan*

airborne platform — منصة جوية
*minaṣṣa jawwīya*

airborne radar — رادار جوي
*rādār jawwī*

airborne stand-off radar — رادار محمول جواً عن بعد
*rādār maḥmūl jawwan ʿan buʿd*

airborne surveillance — إستطلاع جوي
*istiṭlāʿ jawwī*

airborne technician — فني جوي
*fannī jawwī*

airborne troops — جند الجو
*jund al-jaww*

airborne unit — وحدة محمولة جواً
*wiḥda maḥmūla jawwan*

airborne warning and control system — نظام مراقبة وانذار جوي
*niẓām murāqaba wa indhār jawwī*

airbrake — مكبح هوائي
*mikbaḥ hawāʾī*

air-burst nuclear warhead — رأس مقذوف نووي ينفجر في الجو
*raʾs maqdhūf nawawī yanfajir fil-jaww*

airbus — طائرة اير باص
*ṭāʾirat ayrbāṣ*

air-conditioned — مكيف الهواء
*mukayyaf al-hawāʾ*

air conditioning system — نظام تكييف بالهواء
*niẓām takyīf bil-hawāʾ*

air controller — مراقب جوي
*murāqib jawwī*

air-cooled — مُبرد بالهواء
*mubarrad bil-hawāʾ*

air corridor — ممر جوي
*mamarr jawwī*

air cover — حماية جوية
*ḥimāya jawwīya*

aircraft belly — بطن الطائرة
*baṭn aṭ-ṭāʾira*

aircraft carrier — حاملة طائرات
*ḥāmilat ṭāʾirāt*

aircraft complement — عدد كامل للطائرات
*ʿadad kāmil liṭ-ṭāʾirāt*

aircraft data link — جهاز ارسال معطيات الطائرة
*jihāz irsāl muʿṭayāt aṭ-ṭāʾira*

aircraft elevator — مصعد الطائرة
*miṣʿad aṭ-ṭāʾira*

aircraft fuel — وقود الطائرات
*wuqūd aṭ-ṭāʾirāt*

aircraft hangar — حظيرة الطائرات
*ḥaẓīrāt aṭ-ṭāʾirāt*

aircraft movements — تحركات الطائرات
*taḥarrukāt aṭ-ṭāʾirāt*

aircraft velocity — سرعة الطائرة
*surʿat aṭ-ṭāʾira*

air cushion vehicle — مركبة بوسادة هوائية
*markaba bi-wisāda hawāʾīya*

air-data sensor probe — مسبار حساس البيانات الجوية
*misbār ḥassās al-bayānāt al-jawwīya*

air defence — دفاع جوي
*difāʿ jawwī*

Air Defence Command — قيادة الدفاع الجوي
*qiyādat ad-difāʿ al-jawwī*

Air Defence Force — قوات الدفاع الجوي
*qūwāt ad-difāʿ al-jawwī*

air defence missile system — شبكة صواريخ الدفاع الجوي
*shabakat ṣawārīkh ad-difāʿ al-jawwī*

air defence suppression missile — صاروخ ابطال الدفاع الجوي
*ṣārūkh ibṭāl ad-difāʿ al-jawwī*

air defence system شبكة دفاع جوي
*shabakat difāʿ jawwī*
air drop قذف جوي
*qadhf jawwī*
air-dropping إسقاط جوي
*isqāṭ jawwī*
air extractor system نظام طرد الهواء
*niẓām ṭard al-hawāʾ*
airfield مطار
*maṭār*
Air Force القوات الجوية
*al-qūwāt al-jawwīya*
Air Force Reserve إحتياطي القوات الجوية
*iḥtiyāṭī al-qūwāt al-jawwīya*
airframe هيكل الطائرة
*haykal aṭ-ṭāʾira*
air intake مدخل الهواء
*madkhal al-hawāʾ*
air-interception equipment معدات اعتراض جوي
*muʿaddāt iʿtirāḍ jawwī*
air-interception missile قذيفة اعتراضية جوية
*qadhīfa iʿtirāḍīya jawwīya*
air launch إنطلاق جوي
*inṭilāq jawwī*
air-launched cruise missile صاروخ كروز يطلق من الجو
*ṣārūkh krūz yuṭlaq min al-jaww*
air-launched guided missile صاروخ موجه يطلق من الجو
*ṣārūkh muwajjah yuṭlaq min al-jaww*
airlift جسر جوي
*jisr jawwī*
airlifter طائرة نقل
*ṭāʾirat naql*
airliner طائرة نقل الركاب
*ṭāʾirat naql ar-rukkāb*
airline traffic مرور الطائرات
*murūr aṭ-ṭāʾirāt*
airman طيار . ملاح جوي
*ṭayyār · mallāḥ jawwī*
airmobile brigade فرقة جنود قابلة للنقل جواً
*firqat junūd qābila lin-naql jawwan*
Air National Guard الحرس الجوي الوطني
*ḥaras al-jawwī al-waṭanī*
air-portable قابل للنقل الجوي
*qābil lin-naql al-jawwī*
air pressure ضغط الهواء
*ḍaghṭ al-hawāʾ*
air search radar رادار استكشاف جوي
*rādār istikshāf jawwī*
air self-defence force قوة الدفاع الذاتي الجوية
*qūwat ad-difāʿ adh-dhātī al-jawwīya*
air sickness دوار الجو
*dawār al-jaww*
air slew دوران جوي
*dawarān jawwī*
air space مجال جوي
*majāl jawwī*
airstrip مهبط طائرات
*mihbaṭ ṭāʾirāt*
air superiority تفوق جوي
*tafawwuq jawwī*
air supply إمداد الهواء
*imdād al-hawāʾ*
air support دعم جوي
*daʿm jawwī*
air supremacy إمتياز جوي . تفوق جوي
*imtiyāz jawwī · tafawwuq jawwī*
air surface zone منطقة السطح الجوي
*minṭaqat as-saṭḥ al-jawwī*
air-surveillance radar رادار استطلاع جوي
*rādār istiṭlāʿ jawwī*
air threat تهديد جوي
*tahdīd jawwī*
air-to-air missile صاروخ جو ـ جو
*ṣārūkh jaww-jaww*
air-to-ground missile صاروخ جو ـ أرض
*ṣārūkh jaww-arḍ*
air-to-surface missile صاروخ جو ـ سطح
*ṣārūkh jaww-saṭḥ*
air-to-surface ranging تحديد مسافة الهدف من الجو
*taḥdīd masāfat al-hadaf min al-jaww*
air traffic control مراقبة المرور الجوي
*murāqabat al-murūr al-jawwī*
air transport نقل جوي
*naql jawwī*
air-transportable قابل للنقل الجوي
*qābil lin-naql al-jawwī*
Air Transport Force قوات النقل الجوي
*qūwāt an-naql al-jawwī*
air wing جناح جوي
*janāḥ jawwī*
air worthiness صلاحية الطيران
*ṣalāḥīyat aṭ-ṭayarān*
Aist hovercraft حوامة « ايست »
*ḥawwāmat ayst*

AJ-37 aircraft طائرة « ايه جيه ٣٧ »
*ṭā'irat ayy jayy sab'a wa thalāthīn*
AK-47 rifle بندقية « ايه كيه ٤٧ »
*bunduqīyat ayy kayy sab'a wa arba'īn*
AKM rifle بندقية « ايه كيه إم »
*bunduqīyat ayy kayy imm*
AKS-74 rifle بندقية « ايه كيه إس - ٧٤ »
*bunduqīyat ayy kayy is arba'a wa sab'īn*
AL-21-3 turbojet نفاثة تربينية « إيه إل - ٢١ - ٣ »
*naffātha turbīnīya ayy il wāḥid wa 'ishrīn-thalātha*
alarm إنذار
*indhār*
alarm flare cartridge خرطوشة مشعل إنذار
*kharṭūshat mish'al indhār*
Albania الألبانية
*al-albānya*
Albanian ألباني
*albānī*
Albany cruiser طرادة الباني
*ṭarrādaṭ albani*
Albatross fighter طائرة مقاتلة ألباتروس
*ṭā'ira muqātila albatrūs*
Albatross helicopter طائرة عمودية ألباتروس
*ṭā'ira 'amūdīya albatrūs*
Albatross SAM صاروخ سطح - جو ألباتروس
*ṣārūkh saṭḥ-jaww albatrūs*
Alcatel dipping sonar سونار غاطس ألكاتل
*sūnār ghāṭis alkatil*
ALE-40 countermeasurers dispenser مطلق التدابير المضادة ايه ال ئي - ٤٠
*muṭliq at-tadābīr al-muḍādda ayy il ī arba'īn*
alert حالة طوارىء
*ḥālat ṭawāri'*
Alesha ship سفينة أليشا
*safīnat alīsha*
Alfa submarine غواصة ألفا
*ghawwāṣat alfa*
Algeria الجزائر
*al-jazā'ir*
Algerian جزائري
*jazā'irī*
Alizé aircraft طائرة أليزيه
*ṭā'irat alīzay*
Alkali AAM صاروخ جو - جو ألكالي
*ṣārūkh jaww-jaww alkalī*
Alligator vessel سفينة اليچايتور
*safīnat aligaytar*
all-nuclear task force قوات واجب ذرية بالكامل
*qūwāt wājib dharrīya bil-kāmil*
allow to approach السماح بالاقتراب
*as-samāḥ bil-iqtirāb*
all present and correct الكل موجود وصحيح
*al-kull mawjūd wa ṣaḥīḥ*
all-purpose weapon سلاح لجميع الأغراض
*silāḥ li-jamī' al-aghrāḍ*
all-weather avionics إلكترونات طيران لجميع الأجواء
*iliktrūnīyāt ṭayarān li-jamī' al-ajwā'*
all-weather capability إمكانيات الاستخدام في جميع الأجواء
*imkānīyāt al-istikhdām fi jamī' al-ajwā'*
all-weather interceptor طائرة اعتراضية لجميع الأجواء
*ṭā'ira i'tirāḍīya li-jamī' al-ajwā'*
all-welded ملحوم بأكمله
*malḥūm bi-akmalih*
all-welded turret برج ملحوم بأكمله
*burj malḥūm bi-akmalih*
Alouette helicopter طائرة عمودية « ألويت »
*ṭā'ira 'amūdīya alwīt*
Alpha Jet aircraft طائرة « ألفا جيت »
*ṭā'irat alfajīt*
Alpha submarine غواصة « ألفا »
*ghawwāṣat alfa*
ALQ-99 E W نظام انذار مبكر « ايه ال - كيو ٩٩ »
*niẓām indhār mubakkir ayy il kyū tis'a wa tis'īn*
ALQ-131 ECM تدابير مضادة الكترونية « ايه ال كيو - ١٣١ »
*tadābīr muḍādda iliktrūnīya ayy ill kyū mi'a wa wāḥid wa thalāthīn*
ALR-69 ECM تدابير مضادة الكترونية « ايه ال آر - ٦٩ »
*tadābīr muḍādda iliktrūnīya ayy il ār tis'a wa sittīn*
Altair III radar رادار « ألتأير ٣ »
*rādār altayr thalātha*
aluminium ألومنيوم
*aluminyūm*
AM-39 SSM صاروخ سطح - سطح « ايه ام ٣٩ »
*ṣārūkh saṭḥ-saṭḥ ayy im tis'a wa thalāthīn*
amagnetic equipment معدات غير مغنطيسية
*mu'addāt ghayr mugnaṭīsīya*
Amal أمل
*amal*

Amazon frigate فرقاطة « أمازون »
*firqāṭat amāzūn*
ambient temperature درجة الحرارة المحيطة
*darajat al-ḥarāra al-muḥīṭīya*
ambulance عربة اسعاف
*ʿarabat isʿāf*
ambush كمين
*kamīn*
AMD-1000 mine لغم « ايه إم دي - ١٠٠٠ »
*lughm ayy im dī alf*
America aircraft carrier حاملة الطائرات « أمريكا »
*ḥāmilat aṭ-ṭāʾirāt amrīka*
American Forces القوات الأمريكية
*al-qūwāt al-amrīkīya*
Amga ship سفينة « أمجا »
*safīnat amga*
amidships في وسط السفينة
*fī wasaṭ as-safīna*
Amit training aircraft طائرة تدريب « أميت »
*ṭāʾirat tadrīb amit*
AML-90 armoured car عربة مدرعة « ايه ام ال - ٩٠ »
*ʿaraba mudarraʿa ayy im il tisʿīn*
ammunition ذخيرة
*dhakhīra*
ammunition belt حزام الذخيرة
*ḥizām adh-dhakhīra*
ammunition box صندوق الذخيرة
*ṣundūq adh-dhakhīra*
ammunition dump مخزون الذخيرة
*makhzūn adh-dhakhīra*
ammunition mix خلط الذخيرة
*khalṭ adh-dhakhīra*
ammunition store مخزن ذخيرة
*makhzan dhakhīra*
ammunition stowage مخزون ذخيرة
*makhzūn dhakhīra*
ammunition supply تموين ذخيرة
*tamwīn dhakhīra*
ammunition temperature درجة حرارة الذخيرة
*darajat ḥarārat adh-dhakhīra*
ammunition trailer مقطورة الذخيرة
*maqṭūrat adh-dhakhira*
ammunition type نوع الذخيرة
*nawʿ adh-dhakhīra*
amphibious برمائي
*barmāʾī*
amphibious air cushion vehicle مركبة برمائية بوسادة هوائية
*markaba barmāʾīya bi-wisāda hawāʾīya*
amphibious assault هجوم برمائي
*hujūm barmāʾī*
amphibious assault vessel سفينة هجوم برمائي
*safīnat hujūm barmāʾī*
amphibious beach unit وحدة شواطىء برمائية
*wiḥdat shawāṭiʾ barmāʾīya*
amphibious boat زورق برمائي
*zawraq barmāʾī*
amphibious cargo ship سفينة بضائع برمائية
*safīnat baḍāʾiʿ barmāʾīya*
Amphibious Command قيادة القوات البرمائية
*qiyādat al-qūwāt al-barmāʾīya*
Amphibious Command ship سفينة قيادة القوات البرمائية
*safīnat qiyādat al-qūwāt al-barmāʾīya*
amphibious detachment كتيبة برمائية
*katība barmāʾīya*
amphibious helicopter assault ship سفينة اقتحام برمائية مجهزة بطائرات عمودية
*safīnat iqtiḥām barmāʾīya mujahhaza bi-ṭāʾirāt ʿamūdīya*
amphibious light tank دبابة برمائية خفيفة
*dabbāba barmāʾīya khafīfa*
amphibious operation عملية برمائية
*ʿamalīya barmāʾīya*
amphibious reconnaissance vehicle مركبة استطلاع برمائية
*markabat istiṭlāʿ barmāʾīya*
amphibious transport dock حوض نقل برمائي
*ḥawḍ naql barmāʾī*
amphibious vehicle مركبة برمائية
*markaba barmāʾīya*
amphibious warfare حرب برمائية
*ḥarb barmāʾīya*
amphibious warfare ship سفينة حربية برمائية
*safīna ḥarbīya barmāʾīya*
amplifier مضخم
*muḍakhkhim*
ampoule أمبولة قارورة صغيرة
*umbūla · qārūra ṣaghīra*
AMRAAM صاروخ جو -جو « ايه إم آر »
*ṣārūkh jaww-jaww ayy im ār*
am receiving انا استقبلك
*ana astaqbiluk*
AMX-10P vehicle مركبة « ايه إم إكس - ١٠ بي »
*markabat ayy im iks ʿashara pī*

AMX-10RC tank — دبابة « ايه إم إكس ـ ١٠ أرسي »
*dabbābat ayy im iks ʿashara ār sī*

AMX-13 light tank — دبابة خفيفة « ايه إم إكس ـ ١٣ »
*dabbāba khafīfa ayy im iks thalāthataʿashar*

AMX-30D recovery tank — دبابة اصلاح « ايه إم إكس ـ ٣٠ دي »
*dabbābat iṣlāḥ ayy im iks thalāthīn dī*

AMX-30 DCA gun — مدفع « ايه ام اكس ـ ٣٠ دي سي ايه »
*midfaʿ ayy im iks thalāthīn dī sī ayy*

AMX-30 MBT — دبابة معارك رئيسية « ايه ام اكس ـ ٣٠ »
*dabbābat maʿārik raʾīsīya ayy im iks thalāthīn*

AMX-32 MBT — دبابة معارك رئيسية « ايه ام اكس ـ ٣٢ »
*dabbābat maʿārik raʾīsīya ayy im iks ithnayn wa thalāthīn*

AM-X fighter — طائرة مقاتلة « ايه إم ـ اكس »
*ṭāʾira muqātila ayy im - iks*

AMX gun — مدفع « ايه إم إكس »
*midfaʿ ayy im iks*

An-12 airtransporter — طائرة نقل « ايه إن ـ ١٢ »
*ṭāʾirat naql ayy in ithnata ashar*

An-14 airtransporter — طائرة نقل « ايه إن ـ ١٤ »
*ṭāʾirat naql ayy in arbaʿatʿashar*

An-22 airtransporter — طائرة نقل « ايه إن ـ ٢٢ »
*ṭāʾirat naql ayy in ithnayn wa ʿishrīn*

An-26 airtransporter — طائرة نقل « ايه إن ـ ٢٦ »
*ṭāʾirat naql ayy in sitta wa ʿishrīn*

An-28 airtransporter — طائرة نقل « ايه إن ـ ٢٨ »
*ṭāʾirat naql ayy in thamānya wa ʿishrīn*

AN52 nuclear bomb — قنبلة نووية « ايه إن ـ ٥٢ »
*qunbula nawwawīya ayy in ithnayn wa khamsīn*

An-72 airtransporter — طائرة نقل « ايه إن ـ ٧٢ »
*ṭāʾirat naql ayy in ithnayn wa sabʿīn*

AN/AAR-38 radar — رادار « ايه إن/ايه ايه أر ـ ٣٨ »
*rādār ayy in ayy ayy ār thamānya wa thalathīn*

AN/AAS-18 radar — رادار « ايه إن/ايه ايه إس ـ ١٨ »
*rādār ayy in ayy ayy is thamānyata ʿashar*

Anab AAM — صاروخ جو ـ جو « أناب »
*ṣārūkh jaww-jaww anab*

AN/ALA-6 radar — رادار « ايه إن/ايه إل ايه ـ ٦ »
*rādār ayy in ayy il ayy sitta*

AN/ALD-51 radar — رادار « ايه إن/ايه إل دي ـ ٥١ »
*rādār ayy in ayy il dī wāḥid wa khamsīn*

AN/ALE-5 radar — رادار « ايه إن/إيه إل ئي ـ ٥ »
*rādār ayy in ayy il ī-khamsa*

AN/ALH-46 radar — رادار « ايه إن/ايه إل إتش ـ ٤٦ »
*rādār ayy in ayy il itsh sitta wa arbaʿīn*

AN/ALM-166 radar — رادار « ايه إن/ايه إل إم ـ ١٦٦ »
*rādār ayy in ayy il im miʾa wa sitta wa sittīn*

analogue computer — حاسبة نسبية
*ḥāsiba nisbīya*

AN/ALQ-52 radar — رادار « ايه ان/ايه ال كيو ـ ٥٢ »
*rādār ayy in ayy il kjū ithnayn wa khamsīn*

AN/ALQ-63 radar — رادار « ايه ان/ايه ال كيو ـ ٦٣ »
*rādār ayy in ayy il kjū thalātha wa sittīn*

AN/ALQ-119 — رادار « ايه ان/ايه ال كيو ـ ١١٩ »
*rādār ayy in ayy il kjū miʾa wa tisʿataʿashar*

AN/ALQ-161 radar — رادار « ايه ان/ايه ال كيو ـ ١٦١ »
*rādār ayy in ayy il kjū miʾa wa wāḥid wa sittīn*

AN/ALR-46 EWS — نظام انذار مبكر « ايه ان/ايه ال أر ـ ٤٦ »
*niẓām indhār mubakkir ayy in / ayy il ār sitta wa arbaʿīn*

AN/ALR-54 EWS — نظام انذار مبكر « ايه ان/ايه ال أر ـ ٥٤ »
*niẓām indhār mubakkir ayy in / ayy il ār arbaʿa wa khamsīn*

analyser system — نظام محلل
*niẓām muḥallil*

analysis centre — مركز تحليل
*markaz taḥlīl*

AN/APG-63 radar — رادار « ايه إن/ايه پي جي ـ ٦٣ »
*rādār ayy in ayy pī jī thalātha wa sittīn*

AN/APG-67 radar — رادار « ايه إن/ايه پي جي ـ ٦٧ »
*rādār ayy in ayy pī jī sabʿa wa sittīn*

AN/APM-83 radar — رادار « ايه إن/ايه پي إم ـ ٨٣ »
*rādār ayy in ayy pī imm thalātha wa thamānīn*

AN/APR-17 radar — رادار « ايه إن/ايه پي أر ـ ١٧ »
*rādār ayy in ayy pī ār-sabʿata ʿashar*

AN/APR-38 EWS — نظام انذار مبكر « ايه ان/ايه بي آر ـ ٣٨ »
*niẓām indhār mubakkir ayy in / ayy pī ār thamānya wa thalathīn*

AN/APS-82 radar — رادار « ايه إن/ايه پي اس ـ ٨٢ »
*rādār ayy in ayy pī īs ithnayn wa thamānīn*

AN-APS-118 radar — رادار « ايه إن ـ ايه پي إس ـ ١١٨ »
*rādār ayy in ayy pī īs mi'a wa thamānyata ʿashar*

AN/ASD-5 radar — رادار « ايه إن/إيه إس دي ـ ٥ »
*rādār ayy in ayy is dī khamsa*

AN/ASQ-18 EWS — نظام انذار مبكر « ايه ان/ايه اس كيو ـ ١٨ »
*niẓām indhār mubakkir ayy in / ayy is kjū thamānyata ʿashar*

AN/ASR-5 radar — رادار ايه إن/ايه اس آر ـ ٥ »
*rādār ayy in ayy is ār khamsa*

AN/ASS-2 radar — رادار « ايه إن/ايه اس اس ـ ٢ »
*rādār ayy in ayy is is ithnayn*

AN/AYH-1 radar — رادار « ايه إن/ايه واي إتش ـ ١ »
*rādār ayy in ayy wāyy itsh-wāḥid*

Anchorage class ship — سفينة طراز « أنكوراج »
*safīna ṭirāz ankurij*

Andover aircraft — طائرة « أندوڤر »
*ṭā'irat andūvar*

Andrea Doria cruiser — طرادة « أندريا دوريا »
*ṭarrādat andrīya dūrīya*

anechoic tiles — بلاط لا صدي
*balāṭ lā ṣaddī*

AN/FPS warning system — نظام تحذير ايه إن/اف پي اس
*niẓām taḥdhīr ayy in if pī is*

angled deck — سطح زاوي
*saṭḥ zāwī*

angled flight deck — سطح طيران زاوي
*saṭḥ ṭayarān zāwī*

angled muzzle attachment — وصلة فوهة زاويّة
*waṣlat fūha zāwīya*

angle of approach — زاوية الاقتراب
*zāwīyat al-iqtirāb*

angle of attack — زاوية الهبوب
*zāwīyat al-hubūb*

angle of impact — زاوية الاصطدام
*zāwīyat al-iṣṭidām*

angle of sight — زاوية التسديد
*zāwīyat at-tasdīd*

angle of view — زاوية الرؤية
*zāwīyat ar-ru'ya*

Angola — أنغولا
*angūla*

Angolan — أنغولي
*angūlī*

angular deviation — إنحراف زاوي
*inḥirāf zāwī*

angular scan — مسح زاوي
*masḥ zāwī*

animal transport — نقل الحيوانات
*naql al-ḥayawānāt*

annual leave — اجازة سنوية
*ijāza sanawīya*

annular blast/fragmentation warhead — رأس قذيفة شظايا/انفجار مستدير
*ra's qadhīfa shaẓāya/infijār mustadīr*

Anshan destroyer — مدمرة « أنشان »
*mudammirat anshān*

AN/SPQ-11 radar — رادار « ايه إن/اس پي كيو ـ ١١ »
*rādār ayy in is pī kjū-aḥada ʿashar*

AN/SPS-48 radar — رادار «ايه إن/اس پي اس ـ ٤٨ »
*rādār ayy in is pī is-thamānya wa arbaʿīn*

AN/SPS 503 radar — رادار «ايه ان/اس پي اس ٥٠٣ »
*rādār ayy in is pī is-khams mi'a wa thalātha*

Antarctic — قطبي جنوبي
*quṭbī janūbī*

antenna — هوائي
*hawā'ī*

antenna array — صف هوائيات
*ṣaff hawā'īyāt*

antenna complex — مجمع هوائيات
*mujammaʿ hawā'īyāt*

antenna coupler — مقرنة هوائيات
*miqranat hawā'īyāt*

antenna sidelobes — نتوءات جانبية للهوائي
*nutū'āt jānibīya lil-hawā'ī*

antenna system — نظام الهوائي
*niẓām al-hawā'ī*

Anteo rescue ship — سفينة انقاذ «أنتيو »
*safīnat inqād antyū*

anti- — مضاد مقاوم
*muḍādd · muqāwim*

anti-aircraft — مضاد للطائرات
*muḍādd liṭ-ṭā'irāt*

anti-aircraft armament — سلاح مضاد للطائرات
*silāḥ muḍadd liṭ-ṭā'irāt*

anti-aircraft artillery battalion — كتيبة مدفعية مضادة للطائرات
*katībat midfaʿīya muḍādda liṭ-ṭāʾirāt*

anti-aircraft defence — دفاع مضاد للطائرات
*difāʿ muḍādd liṭ-ṭāʾirāt*

anti-aircraft gun — مدفع مضاد للطائرات
*midfāʿ muḍādd liṭ-ṭāʾirāt*

anti-aircraft machine gun — رشاش مضاد للطائرات
*rashshāsh muḍadd liṭ-ṭāʾirāt*

anti-armour missile — صاروخ مضاد للمدرعات
*ṣārūkh muḍādd lil-mudarraʿāt*

anti-ballistic missile system — نظام دفاعي ضد الصواريخ البالستية
*niẓām difāʿī ḍidd aṣ-ṣawārīkh al-bālistīya*

antibiotic — مضاد حيوي (للجراثيم)
*muḍādd ḥayawī (lil-jarāthīm)*

antidote — ترياق
*tiryāq*

anti-gangrene — مضاد الغنغرينا
*muḍādd lil-ghanghrīna*

anti-gas cape — قناع واقي من الغاز
*qanāʿ wāqī min al-ghāz*

anti-ice — مانع للجليد
*māniʿ lil-jalīd*

anti-missile — مضاد للصواريخ
*muḍadd liṣ-ṣawrīkh*

anti-overheating equipment — معدات مانعة لفرط الاحماء
*muʿaddāt māniʿa li-farṭ al-aḥmāʾ*

anti-personnel — مضاد للأفراد
*muḍādd lil-afrād*

anti-personnel grenade — قنبلة يدوية مضادة للأفراد
*qunbula yadawīya muḍadda lil-afrād*

anti-radar missile — صاروخ مضاد للرادار
*ṣārūkh muḍādd lir-rādār*

anti-radiation seeker — باحث مضاد للاشعاع
*bāḥith muḍādd lil-ishʿāʿ*

anti-satellite hunter missile — صاروخ قانص مضاد للأقمار الصناعية
*ṣārūkh qāniṣ muḍādd lil-aqmār aṣ-ṣināʿīya*

anti-satellite killer missile — قذيفة قاتلة مضادة للأقمار الصناعية
*qadhīfa qātila muḍādda lil-aqmār aṣ-ṣināʿīya*

anti-satellite weapon system — نظام حربي مضاد للأقمار الصناعية
*niẓām ḥarbī muḍādd lil-aqmār aṣ-ṣināʿīya*

antiseptic — مطهر · مانع للعفونة
*muṭahhir · maniʿ lil-ʿafūna*

antiseptic dressing — ضمادة مطهرة
*ḍimāda mutahhira*

anti-ship — مضاد للسفن
*muḍādd lis-sufun*

anti-ship missile — صاروخ مضاد للسفن
*ṣārūkh muḍādd lis-sufun*

anti-ship missile attack — هجوم بالصواريخ المضادة للسفن
*hujūm biṣ-ṣawārīkh al-muḍādda lis-sufun*

anti-ship missile defence — دفاع بالصواريخ المضادة للسفن
*difāʿ biṣ-ṣawārīkh al-muḍādda lis-sufun*

anti-ship surveillance — إستطلاع مضاد للسفن
*istiṭlāʿ muḍādd lis-sufun*

anti-submarine armament — سلاح مضاد للغواصات
*silāḥ muḍādd lil-ghawwāṣāt*

anti-submarine helicopter — طائرة عمودية مضادة للغواصات
*ṭāʾira ʿamūdīya muḍādda lil-ghawwāṣāt*

anti-submarine missile — صاروخ مضاد للغواصات
*ṣārūkh muḍādd lil-ghawwāṣāt*

anti-submarine torpedo — طوربيد مضاد للغواصات
*ṭūrbīd muḍādd lil-ghawwāṣāt*

anti-submarine warfare — حرب ضد الغواصات
*ḥarb ḍidd al-ghawwāṣāt*

anti-submarine warfare vessel — سفينةحربية مضادة للغواصات
*safīna ḥarbīya muḍādda lil-ghawwāṣāt*

anti-submarine weapon — سلاح مضاد للغواصات
*silāḥ muḍādd lil-ghawwāṣāt*

anti-surface capability — إمكانيات مضادة لاهداف سطحية
*imkānīyāt muḍādda li-ahdāf saṭḥīya*

anti-surface vessel — سفينة مضادة لاهداف سطحية
*safīna muḍādda li-ahdāf saṭḥīya*

anti-tank — مضاد للدبابات
*muḍādd lid-dabbābāt*

anti-tank cannon — مدفع هاون مضاد للدبابات
*midfaʿ hāwun muḍādd lid-dabbābāt*

anti-tank guided weapon — سلاح موجه مضاد للدبابات
*silāḥ muwajjah muḍādd lid-dabbābāt*
anti-tank guided weapon brigade — لواء أسلحة موجه مضادة للدبابات
*liwā᾽ asliḥa muwajjaha muḍādda lid-dabbābāt*
anti-tank gun — مدفع مضاد للدبابات
*midfaʿ muḍādd lid-dabbābāt*
anti-tank helicopter — طائرة عمودية مضادة للدبابات
*ṭā᾽ira ʿamūdīya muḍādda lid-dabbābāt*
anti-tank mine — لغم مضاد للدبابات
*lughm muḍādd lid-dabbābāt*
anti-tank missile — صاروخ مضاد للدبابات
*ṣārūkh muḍādd lid-dabbābāt*
anti-tank operation — عملية ضد الدبابات
*ʿamalīya ḍidd ad-dabbābāt*
anti-tank platoon — فصيلة مضادة للدبابات
*faṣīla muḍādda lid-dabbābāt*
anti-tank regiment — كتيبة مضادة للدبابات
*katība muḍādda lid-dabbābāt*
anti-tattletale escort — مفرزة مضادة للواشي
*mafraza muḍādda lil-wāshī*
anti-tetanus — مضاد للكزاز
*muḍādd lil-kuzzāz*
anti-toxin — أنتيتكسين
*antitaksīn*
AN/UAS-4 radar — رادار « ايه ان/يو ايه اس ـ ٤ »
*rādār ayy in yū ayy is - arbaʿa*
AN/ULA-2 radar — رادار «ايه ان/يو ال ايه ـ ٢ »
*rādār ayy in yū il ayy - ithnayn*
AN/USD-7 — نظام بيانات «ايه ان/يواس دي ـ ٧ »
*niẓām bayānāt ayy in/yū is dī - sabʿa*
AN/USR-1 radar — رادار «ايه ان/يو اس آر ـ ١ »
*rādār ayy in yū is ār - wāḥid*
AN/UXD-1 data system — نظام بيانات «ايه ان/يو اكس دي ـ ١ »
*niẓām bayānāt ayy in/yū iks dī - wāḥid*
AN/UYK-7 computer — كومبيوتر «ايه ان/يو واي كيه ـ ٧ »
*kumbyūtar ayy in/yū wāyy kayy - sabʿa*
AN/UYK-20 computer — كومبيوتر «ايه ان/يو واي كيه ـ ٢٠ »
*kumbyūtar ayy in/yū wāyy kayy - ʿishrīn*
AN/UYK-21 radar — رادار «ايه ان/يو واي كيه ـ ٢١ »
*rādār ayy in yū wāyy kayy - wāḥid wa ʿishrīn*
AOP-9 aircraft — طائرة ايه اوه پي ـ ٩
*ṭā᾽irat ayy aw pī - tisʿa*
AP-32Z grenade — قنبلة يدوية ايه پي ـ ٣٢ زد
*qunbula yadawīya ayy pī - ithnayn wa thalāthīn zid*
APA-171 antenna — هوائي ايه پي ايه ـ ١٧١
*hawā᾽ī ayy pī ayy - mi᾽a wa wāḥid wa sabʿīn*
Apache helicopter — طائرة عمودية «اباتشي »
*ṭā᾽ira ʿamūdīya apatshī*
APC — حاملة جنود مدرعة
*ḥāmilat junūd mudarraʿa*
Apex AAM — صاروخ جو ـ جو «أبيكس »
*ṣārūkh jaww-jaww aypiks*
APFSDS — قذيفة متوازنة بالزعانف خارقة للمدرعات
*qadhīfa mutawāzina biz-zaʿānif khāriqa lil-mudarraʿāt*
APG-63 radar — رادار «ايه پي جي ـ ٦٣ »
*rādār ayy pī jī - thalātha wa sittīn*
APG-66 radar — رادار «ايه پي جي ـ ٦٦ »
*rādār ayy pī jī - sitta wa sittīn*
Aphid AAM — صاروخ جو ـ جو «أفيد »
*ṣārūkh jaww-jaww afīd*
apply safety-catches! — تثبيت سقاطة الأمان
*tathbīt saqqāṭat al-amān*
approach lights — أضواء الاقتراب
*aḍwā᾽ al-iqtirāb*
approach radar — رادار الاقتراب
*rādār al-iqtirāb*
approving authority — سلطة التصديق
*ṣulṭat at-taṣdīq*
APR-39 radar — رادار «ايه پي آر ـ ٣٩ »
*rādār ayy pī ār - tisʿa wa thalathīn*
apron — ممر طيران
*mamarr ṭayarān*
APS-124 radar — رادار «ايه پي اس ـ ١٢٤ »
*rādār ayy pī is - mi᾽a wa arbaʿa wa ʿishrīn*
APY-1 radar — رادار « ايه پي واي ـ ١ »
*rādār ayy pī wāyy - wāḥid*
aquatic training — تدريب مائي
*tadrīb mā᾽ī*
AR-3D radar — رادار «ايه آر ـ ٣ دي »
*rādār ayy ār - thalātha dī*

AR-15 rifle بندقية «ايه آر ـ ١٥ »
*bunduqīyat ayy ār khamsata ʿashar*

AR-18 rifle بندقة «ايه آر ـ ١٨ »
*bunduqīyat ayy ār thamānyata ʿashar*

AR70 rifle بندقية «ايه آر ٧٠ »
*bunduqīyat ayy ār sabʿīn*

Arab Gulf الخليج العربي
*al-khalīj al-ʿarabī*

Arab neighbours الجيران العرب
*al-jīrān al-ʿarab*

Arauca patrol craft سفينة خفر السواحل «اراوكا»
*safīnat khafar as-sawāḥil arawka*

Arctic منطقة القطب الشمالي
*minṭaqat al-quṭb ash-shamālī*

area bombing قصف منطقة
*qaṣf minṭaqa*

area of operations منطقة العمليات
*minṭaqat al-ʿamalīyāt*

area of responsibility مجال المسؤولية
*majāl al-masʾūlīya*

ARES cannon مدفع هاون «أريس »
*midfaʿ hāwun arīz*

Arethuse submarine غواصة «أريثيوز »
*ghawwāṣat arīthjūz*

Argentina الأرجنتين
*al-arjantīn*

Argentine ارجنتيني
*arjantīnī*

armament سلاح
*silāḥ*

armament factory مصنع حربي
*maṣnaʿ ḥarbī*

armband إشارة ذراع
*ishārat dhirāʿ*

armed combat قتال مسلح
*qitāl musallaḥ*

armed conflict نزاع مسلح
*nizāʿ musallaḥ*

armed division فرقة مسلحة
*firqa musallaḥa*

armed forces قوات مسلحة
*qūwāt musallaḥa*

armed helicopter battalion كتيبة طائرات عمودية مسلحة
*katībat ṭāʾirāt ʿamūdīya musallaḥa*

armed intervention تدخل مسلح
*tadakhkhul musallaḥ*

armed militia ميليشيا مسلحة
*mīlīshya musallaḥa*

armed reconnaissance mission بعثة استطلاع مسلحة
*baʿthat istiṭlāʿ musallaḥa*

ARM missile صاروخ «ايه آر إم »
*ṣārūkh ayy ār im*

armour درع
*dirʿ*

armoured body suit بزة واقية مدرعة
*bizza wāqīya mudarraʿa*

armoured branch سلاح المدرعات
*silāḥ al-mudarraʿāt*

armoured brigade لواء مدرعات
*liwāʾ mudarraʿāt*

armoured car عربة مدرعة
*ʿaraba mudarraʿa*

armoured car squadron سرية عربات مدرعة
*sarīyat ʿarabāt mudarraʿa*

armoured command/ reconnaissance vehicle مركبة قيادة / استطلاع مصفحة
*markabat qiyāda istiṭlāʿ muṣaffaḥa*

armoured division فرقة مدرعات
*firqat mudarraʿāt*

armoured engineer vehicle مركبة مهندسين مدرعة
*markabat muhandisīn mudarraʿa*

armoured personnel carrier حاملة جنود مدرعة
*ḥāmilat junūd mudarraʿa*

armoured recovery vehicle عربة اصلاح مدرعة
*ʿarabat iṣlāḥ mudarraʿa*

armoured troop carrier ناقلة جنود مدرعة
*nāqilat junūd mudarraʿa*

armoured turret برج مدرع
*burj mudarraʿ*

armoured unit وحدة مدرعة
*wiḥda mudarraʿa*

armour-piercing خارق للدروع
*khāriq lid-durūʿ*

Armour-Piercing Fin-Stabilised Discarding Sabot قذيفة متوازنة بالزعانف خارقة للمدرعات
*qadhīfa mutawāzina bi-zaʿānif khāriqa lil-mudarraʿāt*

armour-piercing projectile مقذوف خارق للدروع
*maqdhūf khāriq lid-durūʾ*

armour-piercing shell قذيفة خارقة للدروع
*qadhīfa khāriqa lid-durūʿ*

armour plating تدريع تصفيح
*tadrīʿ · taṣfīḥ*

armour protection وقاية بالدروع
*wiqāya bid-durūʿ*
arms depot مستودع أسلحة
*mustawdaʿ asliḥa*
arms drill تدريب بالأسلحة
*tadrīb bil-asliḥa*
army جيش
*jaysh*
army aviation battalion كتيبة طيران الجيش
*katībat ṭayarān al-jaysh*
army aviation command قيادة طيران الجيش
*qiyādat ṭayarān al-jaysh*
army general لواء في الجيش
*liwāʾ fil-jaysh*
army group مجموعة جيوش
*majmūʿat juyūsh*
army inventory جرد عسكري
*jard ʿaskarī*
army training school مدرسة التدريب العسكري
*madrasat at-tadrīb al-ʿaskarī*
army universal gun مدفع حربي عام
*midfaʿ ḥarbī ʿām*
army weapons أسلحة الجيش
*asliḥat al-jaysh*
array صف . مجموعة مرتبة
*ṣaff · majmūʿa murattaba*
arrester gear جهاز الايقاف
*jihāz al-īqāf*
arrester hook خطاف كمح السرعة
*khuṭṭāf kamḥ as-surʿa*
arrester net شبكة الايقاف
*shabakat al-īqāf*
arrester wire سلك الايقاف
*silk al-īqāf*
arrow read firing system نظام رمي قارىء للسهم
*niẓām ramī qāriʾ lis-sahm*
ARS-12U decontamination جهاز التطهير «ايه أر اس ـ ١٢ يو »
*jihāz at-taṭhīr ayy ār is - ithnata ʿashar yū*
arsenal مخزونات / مصنع أسلحة
*makhzūnāt/maṣnaʿ asliḥa*
artificer صانع ماهر
*ṣāniʿ māhir*
artificial obstacle عائق اصطناعي
*ʿāʾiq iṣṭināʿī*
artificial stability إتزان اصطناعي
*ittizān iṣṭināʿī*
artillery battalion كتيبة مدفعية
*katībat midfaʿīya*
artillery battery سرية مدفعية
*sarīyat midfaʿīya*
artillery rocket قذيفة مدفعية
*qadhīfat midfaʿīya*
artillery support دعم المدفعية
*daʿm al-midfaʿīya*
AS-1 ASM صاروخ جو ـ سطح «ايه اس ـ ١ »
*ṣārūkh jaww-saṭḥ ayy is wāḥid*
AS-2 ASM صاروخ جو ـ سطح «ايه اس ـ ٢ »
*ṣārūkh jaww-saṭḥ ayy is ithnayn*
AS-2L ASM صاروخ جو ـ سطح «ايه اس ـ ٢ ال »
*ṣārūkh jaww-saṭḥ ayy is ithnayn il*
AS-3 ASM صاروخ جو ـ سطح «ايه اس ـ ٣ »
*ṣārūkh jaww-saṭḥ ayy is thalātha*
AS-4 ASM صاروخ جو ـ سطح «ايه اس ـ ٤ »
*ṣārūkh jaww-saṭḥ ayy is arbaʿa*
AS-5 ASM صاروخ جو ـ سطح «ايه اس ـ ٥ »
*ṣārūkh jaww-saṭḥ ayy is khamsa*
AS-6 ASM صاروخ جو ـ سطح «ايه اس ـ ٦ »
*ṣārūkh jaww-saṭḥ ayy is sitta*
AS-7 ASM صاروخ جو ـ سطح «ايه اس ـ ٧ »
*ṣārūkh jaww-saṭḥ ayy is sabʿa*
AS-8 ASM صاروخ جو ـ سطح «ايه اس ـ ٨ »
*ṣārūkh jaww-saṭḥ ayy is thamānya*
AS-11 ASM صاروخ جو سطح «ايه اس ـ ١١ »
*ṣārūkh jaww-saṭḥ ayy is aḥada ʿashar*
AS-12 ASM صاروخ جو ـ سطح «ايه اس ـ ١٢ »
*ṣārūkh jaww-saṭḥ ayy is ithnata ʿashar*
AS-15 ASM صاروخ جو ـ سطح «ايه اس ـ ١٥ »
*ṣārūkh jaww-saṭḥ ayy is khamsata ʿashar*
AS-15TT ASM صاروخ جو ـ سطح «ايه اس ـ ١٥ تي تي »
*ṣārūkh jaww-saṭḥ ayy is khamsata ʿashar tī tī*
AS-20 ASM صاروخ جو ـ سطح «ايه اس ـ ٢٠ »
*ṣārūkh jaww-saṭḥ ayy is ʿishrīn*
AS-30 ASM صاروخ جو ـ سطح «ايه اس ـ ٣٠ »
*ṣārūkh jaww-saṭḥ ayy is thalāthīn*
AS-30L ASM صاروخ جو ـ سطح «ايه اس ـ ٣٠ إل »
*ṣārūkh jaww-saṭḥ ayy is thalāthīn il*

AS-37 radar — رادار «ايه اس ـ ٣٧»
*rādār ayy is sabʿa wa thalāthīn*

AS-39 ASM — صاروخ جو ـ سطح «ايه اس ـ ٣٩»
*ṣārūkh jaww-saṭḥ ayy is tisʿa wa thalāthīn*

AS-244/S torpedo — طوربيد «ايه اس ٢٤٤/اس»
*ṭūrbīd ayy is miʾtayn wa arbaʿa wa arbaʿīn is*

AS-332B helicopter — طائرة عمودية «ايه اس ـ ٣٣٢ بي»
*ṭāʾira ʿamūdīya ayy is thalātha miʾa wa ithnayn wa thalāthīn bī*

AS-350B helicopter — طائرة عمودية «ايه اس ـ ٣٥٠ بي»
*ṭāʾira ʿamūdīya ayy is thalātha miʾa wa khamsīn bī*

AS-365N helicopter — طائرة عمودية «ايه اس ـ ٣٦٥ ان»
*ṭāʾira ʿamūdīya ayy is thalātha miʾa wa khamsa wa sittīn in*

Ash ASM — صاروخ جو ـ سطح «أش»
*ṣārūkh jaww-saṭḥ ash*

Asheville class ship — سفينة من طراز «أشيڤيل»
*safīna min ṭirāz ashvil*

ASM-1 missile — صاروخ «ايه اس ام ـ ١»
*ṣārūkh ayy is im wāḥid*

ASMP ASM — صاروخ جو ـ سطح «ايه اس ام پي»
*ṣārūkh jaww-saṭḥ ayy is im pī*

Aspide SAM — صاروخ سطح ـ جو «اسپيد»
*ṣārūkh saṭḥ-jaww aspid*

ASRAAM — صاروخ جو ـ جو متقدم قصير المدى
*ṣārūkh jaww-jaww mutaqaddim qaṣīr al-mada*

ASROC — طوربيد صاروخي بالتوجيه الراداري مضاد للغواصات
*ṭūrbīd ṣārūkhī bit-tawjīh ar-rādārī muḍādd lil-ghawwāṣāt*

Assad corvette — سفينة حراسة صغيرة «أسد»
*safīnat ḥirāsa ṣaghīra asad*

assault — هجوم
*hujūm*

assault carrier — ناقلة هجومية
*nāqila hujūmīya*

assault course — ميدان الاقتحام
*maydān al-iqtiḥām*

assault crossing — عبور انقضاضي
*ʿubūr inqiḍāḍī*

assault group headquarters — مقر جماعة الاقتحام
*maqarr jamāʿat al-iqtiḥām*

assault line — خط الاقتحام
*khaṭṭ al-iqtiḥām*

assault operations room — غرفة عمليات الاقتحام
*ghurfat ʿamalīyāt al-iqtiḥām*

assault over the beach — إقتحام على الشاطىء
*iqtiḥām ʿalash-shāṭiʾ*

assault rifle — بندقية اقتحام
*bunduqīyat iqtiḥām*

assault squadron — سرية اقتحام
*sarīyat iqtiḥām*

assault support patrol boat — زورق حراسة لدعم الاقتحام
*zawraq ḥirāsa li-daʿm al-iqtiḥām*

assault support ship — سفينة دعم الاقتحام
*safīnat daʿm al-iqtiḥām*

assault troop carrier — ناقلة جنود الاقتحام
*nāqilat junūd al-iqtiḥām*

assault troops — جند الاقتحام
*jund al-iqtiḥām*

assault unit — وحدة الاقتحام
*wiḥdat al-iqtiḥām*

assembly point — نقطة التجمع
*nuqṭat at-tajammuʿ*

AST-1228 missile — صاروخ «ايه اس تي ـ ١٢٢٨»
*ṣārūkh ayy is tī alf wa miʾatayn wa thamānya wa ʿishrīn*

Aster SAM — صاروخ سطح ـ جو أستر
*ṣārūkh saṭḥ-jaww astir*

AS torpedo — طوربيد «ايه اس»
*ṭūrbīd ayy is*

astro-inertial navigation — ملاحة بالجمود الفلكي
*milāḥa bil-jumūd al-falakī*

astronaut — ملاح فضائي
*mallāḥ faḍāʾī*

ASU-57 gun — مدفع «ايه اس يو ٥٧»
*midfaʿ ayy is yū sabʿa wa khamsīn*

ASU-85 gun — مدفع «ايه اس يو ـ ٨٥»
*midfaʿ ayy is yū khamsa wa thamānīn*

ASW — حرب ضد الغواصات
*ḥarb ḍidd al-ghawwāṣāt*

ASW aircraft — طائرة حرب ضد الغواصات
*ṭāʾirat ḥarb ḍidd al-ghawwāṣāt*

ASW navigation system — نظام ملاحة للحرب ضد الغواصات
*niẓām milāḥa lil-ḥarb ḍidd al-ghawwaṣāt*

| | |
|---|---|
| ASW sensor<br>*jihāz iḥsās lil-ḥarb al-muḍadda lil-ghawwāṣāt* | جهاز احساس للحرب المضادة للغواصات |
| ASW Stand-off Weapon<br>*silāḥ iṭlāq ʿan buʿd lil-ḥarb al-muḍādda lil-ghawwāṣāt* | سلاح اطلاق عن بعد للحرب المضادة للغواصات |
| ASW torpedo<br>*ṭūrbīd ḥarb ḍidd al-ghawwāṣāt* | طوربيد حرب ضد الغواصات |
| ASW torpedo tube<br>*masūrat ṭūrbīd al-ḥarb ḍidd al-ghawwāṣat* | ماسورة طوربيد الحرب ضد الغواصات |
| ASW torpedo tube mounting<br>*qāʿidat māsurat ṭūrbīd al-ḥarb ḍidd al-ghawwāṣāt* | قاعدة ماسورة طوربيد الحرب ضد الغواصات |
| ASW unit<br>*wiḥdat al-ḥarb ḍidd al-ghawwāṣāt* | وحدة الحرب ضد الغواصات |
| AS-X-9 ASM<br>*ṣārūkh jaww-saṭḥ ayy is iks tisʿa* | صاروخ جو ـ سطح « ايه اس ـ اكس ـ ٩ » |
| AS-X-10 ASM<br>*ṣārūkh jaww-saṭḥ ayy is iks ʿashara* | صاروخ جو ـ سطح « ايه اس ـ اكس ـ ١٠ » |
| as you were!<br>*kamā kunt* | « كما كنت ! » |
| AT-1 ATM<br>*ṣarūkh muḍādd lid-dabbābāt ayy tī - wāḥid* | صاروخ مضاد للدبابات « ايه تي ـ ١ » |
| AT-2 ATM<br>*ṣarūkh muḍādd lid-dabbābāt ayy tī - ithnayn* | صاروخ مضاد للدبابات « ايه تي ـ ٢ » |
| AT-3 ATM<br>*ṣarūkh muḍādd lid-dabbābāt ayy tī - thalātha* | صاروخ مضاد للدبابات « ايه تي ـ ٣ » |
| AT-4 ATM<br>*ṣarūkh muḍādd lid-dabbābāt ayy tī - arbaʿa* | صاروخ مضاد للدبابات « ايه تي ـ ٤ » |
| AT-5 ATM<br>*ṣarūkh muḍādd lid-dabbābāt ayy tī - khamsa* | صاروخ مضاد للدبابات « ايه تي ـ ٥ » |
| AT-6 ATM<br>*ṣarūkh muḍādd lid-dabbābāt ayy tī - sitta* | صاروخ مضاد للدبابات « ايه تي ـ ٦ » |
| Atar 8K50 turbojet<br>*naffātha turbīnīya atār thamānya kayy khamsīn* | نفاثة تربينية « أتار ٨ كيه ٥٠ » |
| Atlantic<br>*al-muḥīṭ al-aṭlasī* | المحيط الأطلسي |
| Atlantic aircraft<br>*ṭāʾirat aṭlantik* | طائرة « أطلنتيك » |
| at launch<br>*ʿind al-iṭlāq* | عند الاطلاق |
| atmosphere<br>*al-jaww* | الجو |
| at my command!<br>*taḥta qiyādatī* | تحت قيادتي |
| Atoll AAM<br>*ṣarūkh jaww-jaww atūl* | صاروخ جو ـ جو « أتول » |
| atomic bomb<br>*qunbula dharrīya* | قنبلة ذرية |
| AT-S artillery tractor<br>*jarrār midfaʿīya ayy tī is* | جرار مدفعية « ايه تي ـ اس » |
| Atsiumi amphibious vessel<br>*safīna barmāʾīya atsiyūmī* | سفينة برمائية « أتسيومي » |
| attachment<br>*ilḥāq · waṣl* | إلحاق . وصل |
| attack<br>*hujūm - hājama* | هجوم هاجم |
| attack aircraft<br>*ṭāʾirat muhājima* | طائرة مهاجمة |
| attack base<br>*qāʿidat al-hujūm* | قاعدة الهجوم |
| attack equipment<br>*muʿaddāt hujūm* | معدات هجوم |
| attack force<br>*qūwāt al-hujūm* | قوات الهجوم |
| attack in force<br>*hujūm wāsiʿ* | هجوم واسع |
| attack mission<br>*muhimma hujūmīya* | مهمة هجومية |
| attack patrol boat<br>*zawraq ḥaras sawāḥil hujūmī* | زورق حرس سواحل هجومي |
| attack squadron<br>*sirb hujūm · sarīyat hujūm* | سرب هجوم سرية هجوم |
| attack submarine<br>*ghawwāṣa hujūmīya* | غواصة هجومية |
| attention!<br>*intibāh* | إنتباه |
| at the double!<br>*harwil* | هرول ! |
| attitude-hold autopilot<br>*jihāz ṭayarān tilqāʾī li-tathbīt waḍʿ aṭ-ṭayarān* | جهاز طيران تلقائي لتثبيت وضع الطيران |
| attitude reference system<br>*niẓām isnād al-waḍʿ* | نظام اسناد الوضع |
| AT-T tractor<br>*jarrār ayy tī tī* | جرار « ايه تي ـ تي » |

Audace destroyer مدمرة « اوداس »
*mudammirat awdas*
audible alarm إنذار مسموع
*indhār masmū'*
auger مثقاب
*mithqāb*
AUG rifle بندقية « ايه يو جي »
*bunduqīya ayy yū jī*
Augusta (Co) شركة « اوجاستا »
*sharikat awgusta*
Aurora ASW aircraft طائرة الحرب ضد الغواصات « اورورا »
*ṭā'irat al-ḥarb ḍidd al-ghawwāṣāt awrūrā*
Austin transport ship سفينة نقل « اوستن »
*safīnat naql awstin*
Australia أستراليا
*ustrālya*
Australian استرالي
*ustrālī*
Austria النمسا
*an-nimsā*
Austrian نمساوي
*nimsāwī*
authorization ترخيص . تفويض
*tarkhīṣ · tafwīḍ*
authorize (to) فوّض . خوّل
*fawwaḍa · khawwala*
auto-approach إقتراب اوتوماتي
*iqtirāb awtūmātī*
auto-gather جمع اوتوماتي
*jam' awtūmātī*
auto-gathering device جهاز جمع اوتوماتي
*jihāza jam' awtūmātī*
automated يعمل اوتوماتيكياً
*ya'mal awtūmātīkīyan*
automatic آلي . اوتوماتيكي
*ālī · awtūmātīkī*
automatically تلقائياً أوتوماتيكياً
*tilqā'īyan · awtūmātīkīyan*
automatically homing بتوجيه راداري تلقائي
*bi-tawjīh rādārī tilqā'ī*
automatic blade folding طي آلي للأرياش
*ṭayy ālī lil-ariyāsh*
automatic data transmission نقل البيانات اوتوماتيكيا
*naql al-bayānāt awtūmātīkīyan*
automatic feed تلقيم اوتوماتي
*talqīm awtūmātī*
automatic fire إطلاق نيران اوتوماتيكي
*iṭlāq nīrān awtūmātīkī*
automatic flare launcher قاذفة مشاعل آلية
*qādhifat mashā'il ālīya*
automatic grenade launcher قاذفة قنابل يدوية آلية
*qādhifat qanābil yadawīya ālīya*
automatic information processing معالجة البيانات اوتوماتيكياً
*mu'ālajat al-bayānat awtūmātīkīyan*
automatic laser tracker معقب ليزر آلي
*mu'aqqib layzar ālī*
automatic loader ملقّم آلي
*mulaqqim ālī*
automatic loading تلقيم آلي
*talqīm ālī*
automatic programming برمجة اوتوماتيكية
*barmaja awtūmātīkīya*
automatic rifle بندقية آلية
*bunduqīya ālīya*
automatic transmission نقل اوتوماتيكي
*naql awtūmātīkī*
automatic weapon سلاح آلي
*silāḥ ālī*
automation تشغيل آلي . اوتوماتية
*tashghīl ālī · awtūmātīya*
Autonoc (Co) شركة اوتونوك
*sharikat awtūnūk*
autopilot جهاز طيران تلقائي
*jihāz ṭayarān tilqā'ī*
autopilot guidance هداية جهاز الطيران التلقائي
*hidāyat jihāz aṭ-ṭayarān at-tilqā'ī*
auto-stabilization إتزان اوتوماتيكي
*ittizān awtūmātīkī*
auto-stabilization system نظام موازنة اوتوماتيكي
*niẓām muwāzana awtūmātīkī*
auxiliary barrack ship سفينة ايواء مساعدة
*safīnat īwā' musā'ida*
auxiliary power unit وحدة طاقة مساعدة
*wiḥdat ṭāya musā'ida*
AV-8A Harrier طائرة « هارير ايه ڤي - ٨ ايه »
*ṭā'irat hāryar ayy vī thamānya ayy*
AV-8B fighter طائرة مقاتلة « ايه ڤي - ٨ بي »
*ṭā'ira muqātila ayy vī thamānya bī*

AVDS-1790-2A diesel engine محرك ديزل « ايه ڤي دي اس ـ ١٧٩ ١-٢ ايه »
*muḥarrik dīzl ayy vī dī is alf wa sab‘a mi’a wa tis‘īn - ithnayn ayy*
Avenger aircraft طائرة أڤينجر
*ṭā’irat avinjar*
Avenger cannon مدفع هاون « أڤينجر »
*mifda‘ hāwun avinjar*
aviation army جيش الطيران
*jaysh aṭ-ṭayarān*
aviation fuel وقود الطائرات
*wuqūd aṭ-ṭā’irāt*
aviation gasoline بنزين الطائرات
*banzīn aṭ-ṭā’irāt*
aviation staff أركان الطيران
*arkān aṭ-ṭayarān*
aviation weapon سلاح الطائرات
*silāḥ aṭ-ṭā’irāt*
Aviocar aircraft طائرة « أڤيوكار »
*ṭā’irat avyūkār*
Aviojet trainer طائرة « أڤيوجيت »
*ṭā’irat avyūjit*
avionics إلكترونيات الطيران
*iliktrūnīyāt aṭ-ṭayarān*
AWACS طائرة الاستطلاع « اواكس »
*ṭā’irat al-istiṭlā‘ awaks*
AWAC Wing جناح نظام « اواك »
*janāḥ niẓām awak*
AWG-9 Radar رادار « ايه دبليو جي ـ ٩ »
*rādār ayy dablyū jī - tis‘a*
Awl AAM صاروخ جو ـ جو « أول »
*ṣārūkh jaww-jaww awl*
awning ظُلة
*ẓulla*
AW-X gun مدفع « ايه دبليو ـ إكس »
*midfa‘ ayy dablyū iks*
azimuth سمت . توجيه
*samt · tawjīh*

# B

206B helicopter — طائرة عمودية « ٢٠٦ بي »
*ṭā'ira ʿamūdīya mi'atayn wa sitta bī*

B gun — مدفع « بي »
*midfaʿ bī*

B-turret — برج « بي »
*burj-bī*

B-1B bomber — طائرة قاذفة « بي ـ ١ بي »
*ṭā'ira qādhifa bī - wāḥid bī*

B-52 bomber — طائرة قاذفة « بي ـ ٥٢ »
*ṭā'irat qādhifa bī-ithnayn wa khamsīn*

B-52G aircraft — طائرة « بي ـ ٥٢ جي »
*ṭā'irat bī - ithnayn wa khamsīn jī*

B-52H aircraft — طائرة « بي ـ ٥٢ إتش »
*ṭā'irat bī - ithnayn wa khamsīn itsh*

B-300 rocket launcher — قاذفة صواريخ « بي ـ ٣٠٠ »
*qādhifat ṣawārīkh bī-thalātha mi'a*

BAC 145 aircraft — طائرة « بي ايه سي ١٤٥ »
*ṭā'irat bī ayy sī mi'a wa khamsa wa arbaʿīn*

BAC-167 air transport — طائرة نقل « بي ايه سي ـ ١٦٧ »
*ṭā'irat naql bī ayy sī mi'a wa sabʿa wa sittīn*

backfire — إشتعال خلفي
*ishtiʿāl khalfī*

Backfire bomber — طائرة قاذفة « باك فاير »
*ṭā'ira qādhifa bakfāyr*

Back Net radar — رادار باك نيت
*rādār bak nit*

Backscatter radar — رادار باك سكاتر
*rādār bak skatar*

backsight — مسددة خلفية . موجه خلفي
*musaddida khalfīya · muwajjih khalfī*

back-up centre — مركز الدعم
*markaz ad-daʿm*

bacterial contamination — تلوث بكتيري
*talawwuth baktīrī*

bacteriological warfare — حرب الجراثيم
*ḥarb al-jarāthīm*

badge — شارة . شعار
*shāra · shiʿār*

badge of rank — شارة الرتبة
*shārat ar-rutba*

Badger bomber — طائرة قاذفة « بادجر »
*ṭā'ira qādhifa bajar*

Badger G bomber — قاذفة قنابل « بادجر جي »
*qādhifat qanābil bajar jī*

Badger helicopter — طائرة عمودية « بادجر »
*ṭā'ira ʿamūdīya bajar*

Badger night vision system — نظام الرؤية الليلية « بادجر »
*niẓām ar-ru'ya al-laylīya bājar*

bad visibility — سوء الرؤية
*sū' ar-ru'ya*

bad-weather — جو سيء
*jaww sayyi'*

Bahrain — البحرين
*al-baḥrayn*

Bailey bridge — جسر « بيلي »
*jisr baylī*

Bainbridge cruiser — طرادة « بينبريدج »
*ṭarrāda baynbrij*

balaclava — رخمار
*rakhmār*

balance of power — ميزان القوة
*mīzān al-qūwa*

Balao submarine — غواصة « بالاو »
*ghawwāṣat balaw*

ballast tank — خزان حصى الرصف
*khazzān ḥaṣṣa ar-raṣf*

ballistic computer — كومبيوتر قذفي بالستيك
*kumbyūtar qadhfī balīstīk*

B

ballistic missile صاروخ قذفي
*ṣārūkh qadhfī*
ballistic missile submarine غواصة صواريخ قذفية
*ghawwāṣat ṣawārīkh qadhfīya*
ballistic re-entry programme برنامج إعادة دخول قذيفي
*barnāmij iʿādat dukhūl qadhīfī*
ballistic stability استقرار قذيفي
*istiqrār qadhīfī*
balloon منطاد
*munṭād*
ball powder بارود الذخيرة
*bārūd adh-dhakhīra*
Baltic بلطيقي
*balṭīqī*
Baltic Fleet أسطول بحر البلطيق
*usṭūl baḥr al-balṭīq*
bandage ضمادة
*ḍimāda*
Bandkanon gun مدفع « باندكانون »
*midfaʿ bandkanun*
bandolier جراب الطلقات
*jirāb aṭ-ṭalaqāt*
Band Stand radar رادار « باند ستاند »
*rādār band stand*
Bangladesh بانغلاديش
*banghladīsh*
Bantam missile صاروخ « بانتام »
*ṣārūkh bantām*
Barak missile صاروخ « باراك »
*ṣārūkh barāk*
Baranquilla river gunboat سفينة نهرية مزودة بالمدافع « برنكيلا »
*safīna nahrīya muzawwada bil-madāfiʿ barankīla*
bar armour تدريع قضيبي
*tadrīʿ qaḍībī*
barbed wire سلك شائك
*silk shāʾik*
barbed wire cutter قطاعة سلك شائك
*qaṭṭāʿat silk shāʾik*
Barbel submarine غواصة « باربيل »
*ghawwāṣat bārbil*
Bar Lock radar رادار « بارلوك »
*rādār bār lūk*
barrack ثكنة
*thukna*
barrack equipment معدات الثكنات
*muʿaddāt ath-thuknāt*
barracks ثكنات
*thuknāt*
barrack square ميدان الثكنات
*maydān ath-thuknāt*
Barracuda revolver مسدس « باراكودا »
*musaddas barakūda*
barrage balloon منطاد مضاد للطائرات
*munṭād muḍādd lit-ṭāʾirat*
barrel ماسورة
*māsūra*
barrel wear بلى الماسورة
*balī al-māsūra*
barricade متراس . حصن
*mitrās · ḥiṣn*
bases قواعد
*qawāʿid*
basic training تدريب أساسي
*tadrīb asāsī*
Bassej volunteer متطوع « باسج »
*mutaṭawwiʿ bāsij*
Bass Tilt radar رادار « بيس تيلت »
*rādār bays tilt*
BATES processing معالجة « باتس »
*muʿālajat bayts*
bath حوض . مغطس حمام
*ḥawḍ · maghṭas ḥammān*
batman مرسال
*mirsāl*
Batral landing ship سفينة إنزال « باترال »
*safīnat inzāl batrāl*
battalion كتيبة
*katība*
battery سرية مدفعية . بطارية
*sarīya midfaʿīya · baṭṭārīya*
battery charger شاحن بطاريات
*shāḥin baṭṭārīyāt*
Battery Control Centre مركز مراقبة السرية
*markaz murāqabat as-sarīya*
battle activity نشاط المعركة
*nashāṭ al-maʿraka*
battle area منطقة المعركة
*minṭaqat al-maʿraka*
battle experience خبرة قتالية
*khibra qitālīya*
battlefield ساحة القتال
*sāḥat al-qitāl*
battlefield helicopter طائرة عمودية لساحة المعركة
*ṭāʾira ʿamūdīya li-sāḥat al-maʿraka*
battlefield interdiction قطع ساحة المعركة
*qaṭʿ sāḥat al-maʿraka*

B

battlefield radar رادار ساحة المعركة
*rādār sāḥat al-maʿraka*
battlefield support missile صاروخ دعم ساحة المعركة
*ṣārūkh daʿm sāḥat al-maʿraka*
battlefield surveillance إستطلاع ساحة المعركة
*istiṭlāʿ sāḥat al-maʿraka*
battlefield target هدف ساحة المعركة
*hadaf sāḥat al-maʿraka*
battle fleet أسطول قتال
*usṭūl qitāl*
battle formation تشكيل المعركة
*tashkīl al-maʿraka*
battleground أرض المعركة
*arḍ al-maʿraka*
Battle Group مجموعة قتال
*majmūʿat qitāl*
battle honours أوسمة القتال
*awsimat al-qitāl*
battle staff أركان حرب
*arkān ḥarb*
battle stations! خذ أوضاع القتال !
*khudh awḍāʿ al-qitāl*
bayonet حربة . سنان البندقية
*ḥarba · sinān al-bunduqīya*
bayonet scabbard غمد الحربة
*ghimd al-ḥarba*
bayonets fix! ركب الحربة
*rakkib al-ḥarba*
bazooka launcher قاذفة بازوكا
*qādhifat bāzūka*
BCQ-4 fire control نظام السيطرة على الرمي « بي سي كيو ـ ٤ »
*niẓām as-sayṭara ʿalar-ramī bī sī kyū arbaʿa*
Be-12 aircraft طائرة « بي ئي ـ ١٢ »
*ṭāʾira - bī ī ithnata ʿashar*
beach head رأس الشاطىء
*raʾs ash-shāṭiʾ*
beacon receiver مستقبل المرشد اللاسلكي
*mustaqbil al-murshid al-lā-silkī*
beam شعاع . عتبة
*shuʿāʿ · ʿataba*
beam angle زاوية الشعاع
*zāwīyat ash-shuʿāʿ*
beam of energy حزمة طاقة
*ḥuzmat ṭāqa*
Bear D surveillance aircraft طائرة استطلاع « بيردي »
*ṭāʾirat istiṭlāʿ bayr dī*
Bear E surveillance aircraft طائرة استطلاع « بيرئي »
*ṭāʾirat istiṭlāʿ bayr ī*
bearing محمل . كرسي تحميل . اتجاه
*maḥmil · kursī taḥmīl · ittijāh*
bear left! لليسار ـ در !
*lil-yasār durr*
bear right! لليمين ـ در !
*lil-yamīn durr*
Bear Trap نظام حط على السطح للطائرات العمودية البحرية
*niẓām ḥaṭṭ ʿalas-saṭḥ liṭ-ṭāʾirāt al-ʿamūdīya al-baḥrīya*
Beaver aircraft طائرة « بيڤر »
*ṭāʾirat bīvar*
Bedezina ship سفينة « بدزينا »
*safīnat badzīna*
Beech (Co) شركة بيتش
*sharikat bītsh*
Bee Hind radar رادار « بي هايند »
*rādār bī hāynd*
beehive projectile مقذوف نخروبي
*maqdhūf nukhrūbī*
Belgian بلجيكي
*baljīkī*
Belgium بلجيكا
*baljīka*
Belknap cruiser طرادة « بلناپ »
*ṭarrādat belnap*
Bell (Co) شركة بل للطائرات
*sharikat bil liṭ-ṭāʾirāt*
Bell-206 helicopter طائرة عمودية « بل ٢٠٦ »
*ṭāʾira ʿamūdīya bil miʾatayn wa sitta*
Bell-209 helicopter طائرة عمودية « بل ـ ٢٠٩ »
*ṭāʾira ʿamūdīya bil miʾatayn wa tisʿa*
Bell-214ST helicopter طائرة عمودية « بل ٢١٤ اس تي »
*ṭāʾira ʿamūdīya bil miʾatayn wa arbaʿata ʿashar is tī*
Bell AH-1S helicopter طائرة عمودية « بل ايه إتش ـ ١ اس »
*ṭāʾira ʿamūdīya bil ayy itsh - wāḥid is*
Bell Clout ECM تدابير مضادة الكترونية « بل كلوت »
*tadābīr muḍādda iliktrūnīya bil klawt*
belligerent محارب
*muḥārib*
Bell Shroud ECM تدابير مضادة الكترونية « بل شرود »
*tadabīr muḍādda iliktrūnīya bil shrawd*
Bell Slam ECM تدابير مضادة الكترونية « بل سلام »
*tadabīr muḍādda iliktrūnīya bil slām*

Bell Squat ECM تدابير مضادة الكترونية « بل سكوات »
*tadabīr muḍādda iliktrūnīiya bil skwāt*

Bell Tap ECM تدابير مضادة الكترونية « بل تاب »
*tadabīr muḍādda iliktrūnīya bil tāb*

belly-wheel عجلة بطنية
*ʿajala baṭnīya*

below strength غير كامل العدد
*ghayr kāmil al-ʿadad*

belt حزام . شريط
*hizām · sharīṭ*

belted ammunition ذخيرة في شريط
*dhakhīra fī-sharīṭ*

Bendix sonar سونار « بنديكس »
*sūnār bandiks*

Benin البنين
*al-banīn*

Benina craft سفينة « بنينا »
*ṣafīnat banīna*

Beretta 84 pistol مسدس « بريتا ٨٤ »
*musaddas birīta arbaʿa wa thamānīn*

Beretta 92S pistol مسدس « بريتا ٩٢ اس »
*musaddas birīta ithnayn wa tisʿīn is*

beyond visual range خارج مدى البصر
*khārij madda al-baṣar*

BGM-109G missile صاروخ « بي جي إم - ١٠٩ جي »
*ṣārūkh bī jī im miʾa wa tisʿa jī*

Biber bridge layer ممددة جسور « بيبر »
*mumaddidat jusūr bībar*

Big Bar radar رادار « بيج بار »
*rādār bīg bār*

Big Bird satellite قمر صناعي « بيج بيرد »
*qamar ṣināʿī bīg bird*

Big Bulge radar رادار « بيج بالج »
*rādār bīg balj*

Big Fred radar رادار « بيج فريد »
*rādār bīg farīd*

Big Mesh radar رادار « بيج ميش »
*rādār bīg mish*

Big Net radar رادار « بيج نت »
*rādār bīg nit*

Big Nose radar رادار « بيج نوز »
*rādār bīg nūz*

bilge pump مضخة جوف المركب
*miḍakhkha jawf al-markab*

Billboard antenna هوائي « بلبورد »
*hawāʾī bilbūrd*

billet مأوى
*maʾwā*

billeting officer ضابط الاسكان
*ḍābiṭ al-iskān*

binoculars منظار ثنائي العينية
*minẓār thunāʾī al-ʿaynīya*

binocular sight جهاز تسديد مزدوج العينين
*jihāz tasdīd muzdawij al-ʿaynayn*

bipod حامل ذو ساقين
*ḥāmil dhū sāqayn*

bipod legs قوائم الحامل
*qawāʾim al-ḥāmil*

Bison aircraft طائرة « بيسون »
*ṭāʾirat baysun*

BK 117 helicopter طائرة عمودية « بي كيه ١١٧ »
*ṭāʾira ʿamūdīya bī kayy miʾa wa sabʿata ʿashar*

BL 755 cluster bomb قنبلة عنقودية « بي ال ٧٥٥ »
*qunbula ʿunqūdīya bī il sabʿa miʾa wa khamsa wa khamsīn*

Blackbird aircraft طائرة « بلاك بيرد »
*ṭāʾirat blakbīrd*

Black-Com 1 cruiser طرادة « بلاك ـكوم ١ »
*ṭarrādat blak kum wāḥid*

Black Hawk helicopter طائرة عمودية « بلاك هوك »
*ṭāʾira ʿamūdīya blak hūk*

black light IR ضوء أسود بالأشعة دون الحمراء
*ḍawʾ aswad bil-ashiʿʿa dūn al-ḥamrāʾ*

blacklist قائمة سوداء
*qāʾima sawdāʾ*

blackout إطفاء الأنوار
*iṭfāʾ al-anwār*

Black Sea البحر الأسود
*al-baḥr al-aswad*

Black Sea Fleet أسطول البحر الأسود
*usṭūl al-baḥr al-aswad*

black smoke دخان أسود
*dukhān aswad*

Black Swan frigate فرقاطة « بلاك سوان »
*firqāṭat blak sawān*

blank ammunition ذخيرة خلبية
*dhakhīra khullabīya*

blank cartridge خرطوشة خلبية
*kharṭūsha khullabīya*

blast إنفجار
*infijār*

blast effect تأثير الانفجار
*taʾthīr al-infijār*

blast-fragmentation تفجير تشظية
*tafjīr-tashẓīya*
blasting gelatine هلام متفجر
*hulām mutafajjir*
Blinder bomber طائرة قاذفة « بلايندر »
*ṭā'ira qādhifa blāyndar*
blind launching إطلاق عشوائي
*iṭlāq ʿashwā'ī*
blister نفطة . بثرة
*nafṭa · bathra*
blistering agent عوامل التنفط
*awāmil at-tanaffuṭ*
blockade حصار
*ḥiṣār*
blockade duties مهام الحصار
*mahām al-ḥiṣār*
blockade runner مخترق الحصار
*mukhtariq al-ḥiṣār*
block and tackle بكرة وحبل
*bakara wa ḥabl*
blood agent عامل الدم
*ʿāmil ad-damm*
Bloodhound SAM صاروخ سطح -جو « بلودهاوند »
*ṣārūkh saṭḥ–jaww blūd-hawnd*
bloodless battle معركة بيضاء
*maʿraka bayḍā'*
bloodshed إراقة الدم
*irāqat ad-damm*
blood test فحص الدم
*faḥṣ ad-damm*
blood transfusion نقل الدم
*naql ad-damm*
blowback system نظام يعمل بدفع الغاز
*niẓām yaʿmal bi-dafʿ al-ghāz*
Blowpipe missile صاروخ سطح -جو بلوبايب
*ṣārūkh saṭḥ-jaww blūbāyb*
blow up (to) انفجر
*infajara*
Blue Fox radar رادار « بلوفوكس »
*rādār blū fuks*
Blue Kestrel radar رادار « بلوكستريل »
*rādār blū kistril*
Blue Ridge vessel سفينة « بلو ريدج »
*safīnat blū rij*
blue smoke دخان أزرق
*dukhān azraq*
BM-21 craft سفينة « بي إم - ٢١ »
*safīnat bī im wāḥid wa ʿishrīn*
BM-21 rocket launcher قاذفة صواريخ « بي إم - ٢١ »
*qādhifat ṣawārīkh bī im wāḥid wa ʿishrīn*
BM-24 rocket launcher قاذفة صواريخ « بي إم - ٢٤ »
*qādhifat ṣawārīkh bī im arbaʿa wa ʿishrīn*
BM-25 rocket launcher قاذفة صواريخ « بي إم - ٢٥ »
*qādhifat ṣawārīkh bī im khamsa wa ʿishrīn*
BMD rocket launcher قاذفة صواريخ « بي إم دي »
*qādhifat ṣawārīkh bī im dī*
BMG-109 cruise missile صاروخ كروز « بي إم جي - ١٠٩ »
*ṣārūkh krūz bī im jī mi'a wa tisʿa*
BMP personnel carrier ناقلة جنود « بي إم بي »
*nāqilat junūd bī im pī*
BO 105 helicopter طائرة عمودية « بي اوه ١٠٥ »
*ṭā'ira ʿamūdīya bī aw mi'a wa khamsa*
Boat Sail radar رادار « بوت سيل »
*rādār būt sayl*
body guard حرس خاص
*ḥaras khāṣ*
body of men مجموعة رجال
*majmūʿat rijāl*
Boeing بوينج
*buwing*
Bofors A/S rocket launcher قاذفة صواريخ « بوفورز ايه/اس »
*qādhifat ṣawārīkh būfūrz ayy/is*
Bofors gun مدفع « بوفورز »
*midfaʿ būfūrz*
bogged down عاجز
*ʿājiz*
bogie عربة نقل منخفضة
*ʿarabat naql munkhafiḍa*
bogie wheel عجلة الدرجان
*ʿajalat ad-darajān*
boiler مرجل . مغلاة
*mirjal · ghallāya*
Bolivia بوليفيا
*būlīvya*
Bolivian بوليفي
*būlīvī*
bolt action حركة الرتاج
*ḥarakat ar-ritāj*
bolt-assist plunger كبّاس مقوّى بالرتاج
*kabbās muqawwa bir-ritāj*
bolt cam كامة الرتاج
*kāmat ar-ritāj*

bolt closure device وسيلة غلق رتاجية
*wasīlat ghalq ritājīya*
bolt group مجموعة الرتاج
*majmūʿat ar-ritāj*
bomb قنبلة
*qunbula*
bomb (to) قصف . قذف بالقنابل
*qaṣf · qadhf bil-qanābil*
Bombardier truck شاحنة « بومباردير »
*shāhinat bumbārdīyar*
bombardment قذف قنابل
*qadhf qanābil*
bomb damage assessment تقدير خسائر القذف
*taqdīr khasāʾir al-qadhf*
bomb door باب القنابل
*bāb al-qanābil*
bomb drop قذف القنابل
*qadhf al-qanābil*
bomber command قيادة القاذفات
*qiyādat al-qādhifāt*
bomber defense missile صاروخ دفاعي للقاذفات
*ṣārūkh difāʿī lil-qādhifāt*
bomber regiment فوج قاذفات
*fawj qādhifāt*
bomb sight جهاز تصويب القنابل
*jihāz taṣwīb al-qanābil*
booby trap شرك
*sharak*
booby trapped ملغم
*mulaghgham*
boom هدير صعيق
*hadīr · ṣaʿīq*
booster معزز
*muʿazziz*
booster motor محرك تعزيز
*muḥarrik taʿzīz*
booster rocket engine محرك صاروخي معزز
*muḥarrik ṣārūkhī muʿazziz*
boost motor ignition إشعال المحرك المعزز
*ishʿāl al-muḥarrik al-muʿazziz*
boot حذاء الجندي
*ḥidhāʾ al-jundī*
border guard حرس الحدود
*ḥaras al-ḥudūd*
border patrol دورية مراقبة الحدود
*dawrīyat murāqabat al-ḥudūd*
Border Tribal Militia حرس قبلي للحدود
*ḥaras qabalī lil-ḥudūd*
Boris Chilikin ship سفينة « بوريس تشيليكين »
*safīnat būrīs tshilikin*
boron armour درع « بورون »
*dirʿ burūn*
Botswana بوتسوانا
*būtswānā*
bottle cap opener فتاحة زجاجات
*fattāḥat zujājāt*
bottleneck عنق الزجاجة
*ʿunq az-zujāja*
bottom-bounce mode وضع الارتداد السفلي
*waḍʿ al-irtidād as-suflī*
bottom mine لغم أعماق
*lughm aʿmāq*
Bouchard mine-sweeper كاسحة ألغام « بوشار »
*kāsiḥat alghām būshār*
bow مقدمة السفينة
*muqaddimat as-safīna*
bow door باب مقدمة السفينة
*bāb muqadimmat as-safīna*
bow launch position وضع الاطلاق الأمامي
*waḍʿ al-iṭlāq al-amāmī*
bowser شاحنة صهريجية
*shāḥina ṣihrījīya*
bow sonar سونار المقدمة
*sūnār al-muqaddima*
box hangar حظيرة صندوقية
*ḥazīra ṣundūqīya*
Boxina patrol craft سفينة حراسة « بوكسينا »
*safīnat ḥirāsa buksīna*
box magazine خزنة ذخيرة صندوقية
*khaznat dhakhīra ṣundūqīya*
box-type launcher قاذفة صندوقة
*qādhifa ṣundūqīya*
BPDMS نقطة الأساس لنظام الصواريخ الدفاعية
*nuqṭat al-asās li-niẓām aṣ-ṣawārīkh ad-difāʿīya*
BQQ-2 sonar سونار « بي كيو كيو - ٢ »
*sūnār bī kyū kyū ithnayn*
BQQ-5 sonar سونار . « بي كيو كيو - ٥ »
*sūnār bī kyū kyū khamsa*
BQR-7 sonar سونار « بي كيو آر - ٧ »
*sūnār bī kyū ār sabʿa*
BQS-4 sonar سونار « بي كيو اس - ٤ »
*sūnār bī kyū is arbaʿa*
BQS-6 sonar سونار « بي كيو اس - ٦ »
*sūnār bī kyū is sitta*
Br.1150 aircraft طائرة « بي ار ١١٥٠ »
*ṭāʾirat bī ār alf wa miʾa wa khamsīn*

B

bracing plate — لوح تكتيف
*lawḥ taktīf*
Bradley combat vehicle — مركبة قتال « برادلي »
*markabat qitāl bradlī*
braked bomb — قنبلة بمكبح
*qunbula bi-mikbaḥ*
Bravo trainer — طائرة تدريب « براڤو »
*ṭā'irat tadrīb brāvū*
Brazil — البرازيل
*al-brāzīl*
Brazilian — برازيلي
*brāzīlī*
BRDM-1 vehicle — مركبة« بي أر دي ام - ١ »
*markaba bī ār dī im - wāḥid*
BRDM-2 vehicle — مركبة . بي أر دي ام - ٢ »
*markaba bī ār dī im - ithnayn*
breach (to) — خرق
*kharq*
break a code — حل الشفرة
*ḥall ash-shifra*
breakaway — تشتت . إنفكاك
*tashattut · infikāk*
break camp — تقويض الخيام
*taqwīḍ al-khayām*
breakdown — عطل . توقف
*ʿaṭl · tawaqquf*
break off — قطع . توقف
*qaṭʿ · tawaqquf*
break step! — « الخطوة - أترك ! »
*al-khuṭwa utruk*
breakthrough — خرق . ثغرة
*kharq · thughra*
Breda AA gun — مدفع مضاد للطائرات « بريدا »
*midfaʿ muḍādd liṭ-ṭā'irāt brīdā*
breech — مغلاق
*mighlāq*
breech block — بدن المغلاق
*badan al-mighlāq*
breech-locking system — نظام قفل المغلاق
*niẓām qafl al-mighlāq*
Brick Pump ESM — تدابير دعم الكترونية « بريك پمپ »
*tadābīr daʿm iliktrūnīya brik pamp*
Brick Split ESM — تدابير دعم الكترونية « بريك سپليت »
*tadābīr daʿm iliktrūnīya brik split*
bridge — جسر
*jisr*
bridge crossing — عبور الجسر
*ʿubūr al-jisr*
bridgehead — رأس الجسر
*ra's al-jisr*
bridgelayer — ممددة الجسر
*mumaddidat al-jisr*
briefing — إعطاء التعليمات
*iʿṭā' at-taʿlīmāt*
brigade — لواء
*liwā'*
brigadier — عميد
*ʿamīd*
Breguet (Co) — شركة « بريجيه »
*sharikat brigayy*
bring fire to bear — رمى بناره
*rama bi-nārih*
bring into action — أربض
*arbaḍa*
bring up reserves — إستدعاء الاحتياطي
*istidʿā' al-iḥtiyāṭī*
Britain — بريطانيا
*barīṭānya*
British — بريطاني
*barīṭānī*
British Aerospace (Co) — شركة بريتش ايروسپيس
*sharikat brītish ayrūspays*
Broadsword frigate — فرقاطة « برودس ورد »
*firqāṭat brūdsūrd*
broken terrain — أرض مجزأة
*arḍ mujazzā'a*
Bronco aircraft — طائرة « برونكو »
*ṭā'irat brūnkū*
Bronstein frigate — فرقاطة « برونستين »
*firqāṭat brūnstīn*
Brooke frigate — فرقاطة « بروك »
*firqāṭat brūk*
Broussard trainer — طائرة تدريب « بروسار »
*ṭā'irat tadrīb brūsār*
Brown Boveri gas turbine — تربين غازي « براون بوڤري »
*tūrbīn ghāzī brawn buvarī*
Browning 50 machine gun — رشاش « براونينج ٥٠ »
*rashshāsh brawning khamsīn*
Brunei — بريوني
*baryūnī*
BTM-TMG trench digger — حفار خنادق « بي تي ام - تي ام جي »
*ḥaffār khanādiq bī tī im - tī im jī*
BTR-40 APC — حاملة جنود مدرعة « بي تي آر - ٤٠ »
*ḥāmilat junūd mudarraʿa bī tī ār arbaʿīn*
BTR-50 APC — حاملة جنود مدرعة « بي تي آر - ٥٠ »
*ḥāmilat junūd mudarraʿa bī tī ār khamsīn*

BTR-60 APC حاملة جنود مدرعة « بي تي آر ـ ٦٠ »
*ḥāmilat junūd mudarraʿa bī tī ār sittīn*
BTR-70 APC حاملة جنود مدرعة « بي تي آر ـ ٧٠ »
*ḥāmilat junūd mudarraʿa bī tī ār sabʿīn*
BTR-152 APC حاملة جنود مدرعة « بي تي آر ـ ١٥٢ »
*ḥāmilat junūd mudarraʿa bī tī ār miʾa wa ithnayn wa khamsīn*
bubble canopy غطاء منزلق شفاف
*ghitāʾ munzaliq shafāf*
Buccaneer aircraft طائرة « بكانير »
*ṭāʾirat bakanīr*
buddy refuelling التزويد بالوقود اثناء الطيران
*at-tazwīd bil-wuqūd athnāʾ aṭ-ṭayarān*
Buffalo aircraft طائرة « بافالو »
*ṭāʾirat bafalū*
built-in مبيت . مدمج
*mubayyat · mudmaj*
Bulgaria بلغاري
*bulghārya*
Bulgarian بلغاريا
*bulghārī*
bulges نتوءات
*nutūʾāt*
bulls-eye النقطة السوداء
*an-nuqta as-sawdāʾ*
Bulldog AGM صاروخ جو ـ أرض « بولدوج »
*ṣārūkh jaww-arḍ būldūg*
Bulldog trainer طائرة تدريب « بولدوج »
*ṭāʾirat tadrīb būldūg*
bullet-proof لا يخرقه الرصاص
*lā yakhriquhu ar-raṣāṣ*
bullet-proof glass زجاج لا يخرقه الرصاص
*zujāj lā yakhriquhu ar-raṣāṣ*
bullet-proof vest صدرة صامدة للرصاص
*ṣudra ṣāmida lir-raṣāṣ*
Bullpup AGM صاروخ جو ـ أرض « بولپاپ »
*ṣārūkh jaww-arḍ bulpap*
bull's eye مركز الهدف
*markaz al-hadaf*
bunker مخزن وقود
*makhzan wuqūd*
buoyancy قابلية الطفو
*qābilīyat aṭ-ṭafw*
buoyant طاف
*ṭāfi*
buoyant canister علبة طافية
*ʿulba ṭāfīya*
burial ground أرض المدافن
*arḍ al-madāfin*
Burkina Faso بركينا فاسو
*būrkīna fāsū*
Burma بورما
*būrmā*
burn حرق . أحرق
*ḥarq · aḥraqa*
burn dressing kit أدوات تضميد الحروق
*adawāt taḍmīd al-ḥurūq*
burn time زمن الاحتراق
*zaman al-iḥtirāq*
burst دفعة نيران
*dafʿat nīrān*
burst (to) إنفجار . تفجير
*infijār · tafjīr*
Burundi بوروندي
*būrūndī*
butt عقب البندقية
*ʿaqb al-bunduqīya*
buttplate لوحة عقب البندقية
*lawḥat ʿaqb al-bunduqīya*
butts ميدان رمي
*maydān rami*
bypass ممر فرعي . تفرع
*mamarr farʿī · tafarruʿ*
bypass ratio نسبة التحويل
*nisbat at-taḥwīl*

C

# C

250-C20B turboshaft عمود ادارة تربيني « ٢٥٠ ـ سي ٢٠ بي »
*ʿamūd idāra turbīnī miʾtayn wa khamsīn sī ʿishrīn bī*

C-1 submarine غواصة « سي ـ ١ »
*ghawwāṣat sī wāḥid*

C-2A aircraft طائرة « سي ـ ٢ ايه »
*ṭāʾirat sī ithnayn ayy*

C-5A airtransporter طائرة نقل « سي ـ ٥ ايه »
*ṭāʾirat sī khamsa ayy*

C-12A aircraft طائرة « سي ـ ١٢ ايه »
*ṭāʾirat sī ithna ʿashar ayy*

C-107 landing craft زورق إنزال « سي ـ ١٠٧ »
*zawraq inzāl sī miʾa wa sabʿa*

C-130 aircraft طائرة « سي ـ ١٣٠ »
*ṭāʾirat sī miʾa wa thalāthīn*

C130 B/H airtransporter طائرة نقل « سي ١٣٠ بي/اتش »
*ṭāʾirat naql sī miʾa wa thalāthīn bī itsh*

C-130H transporter طائرة نقل « سي ـ ١٣٠ اتش »
*ṭāʾirat naql sī miʾa wa thalāthīn itsh*

C-135 airtransporter طائرة نقل « سي ـ ١٣٥ »
*ṭāʾirat naql sī miʾa wa khamsa wa thalāthīn*

C-141 airtransporter طائرة نقل « سي ـ ١٤١ »
*ṭāʾirat naql sī miʾa wa wāḥid wa arbaʿīn*

C-212A airtransporter طائرة نقل « سي ـ ٢١٢ ايه »
*ṭāʾirat naql sī miʿatayn wa ithna ʿashar ayy*

cable كبل . أبرق
*kabl · abraqa*

cablegram برقية
*barqīya*

cable grip مقبض كلابي لمد الكبلات
*miqbaḍ kullābī li-madd al-kablāt*

Cactus SAM صاروخ سطح ـ جو كاكتوس
*ṣārūkh saṭḥ-jaww kaktus*

cadet طالب عسكري
*ṭālib ʿaskarī*

Caesar tank دبابة « سيزر »
*dabbābat sīzar*

Cake Series radar رادار « كيك سيريز »
*rādār kayk sīrīz*

calibration test إختبار المعايرة
*ikhtibār al-muʿāyara*

calibre قطر داخلي . عيار
*quṭr dākhilī · ʿīyār*

California cruiser طرادة « كاليفورنيا »
*ṭarrādat kalifūrnya*

call sign رمز النداء
*ramz an-nidāʾ*

call signal إشارة النداء
*ishārat an-nidāʾ*

call-up notice إشعار الاستدعاء
*ishʿār al-istidʿāʾ*

camber نسبة الاحديداب
*nisbat al-iḥdīdāb*

Cambodia كمبوديا
*kambūdya*

camel جمل
*jamal*

camel corps battalion كتيبة جند الهجانة
*katībat jund al-hajāna*

camera unit وحدة تصوير
*wiḥdat taṣwīr*

Cameroon الكميرون
*al-kāmīrūn*

camouflage تمويه
*tamwīh*

camouflaged مموّه
*mumawwah*

camouflaged target هدف مموّه
*hadaf mummawah*

C

camouflage paint دهان للتمويه
*dihān lit-tamwīh*

camp معسكر
*muʿaskar*

Canada كندا
*kanada*

Canadian كندي
*kanadī*

Canadian (Co) شركة كناديان
*sharikat kanaydyan*

canard جنيح مساعد
*junayḥ musāʾid*

canard configuration شكل الجنيحات المساعدة
*shakl al-junayḥāt al-musāʾida*

Canberra طائرة « كانبيريا »
*ṭāʾirat kanbīra*

Candid airtransporter طائرة نقل « كانديد »
*ṭāʾirat naql kandīd*

canister علبة
*ʿulba*

canister grouping مجموعة علب
*majmūʿat ʿulab*

cannon مدفع هاون
*midfaʿ hāwun*

canteen cover غطاء كانتين
*ghiṭāʾ kantīn*

canvas قماش القنب
*qumāsh al-qunnab*

canvas bag كيس من قماش القنب
*kīs min qumāsh al-qunnab*

cap غطاء . كبسولة
*ghiṭāʾ · kabsūla*

capacity سعة . أهلية
*siʿa · ahlīya*

capsule كبسولة
*kabsūla*

captain قبطان . قائد الطائرة
*qubṭān · qāʾid aṭ-ṭāʾira*

captive firing إطلاق مقيد للنيران
*iṭlāq muqayyid lin-nīrān*

capture أسر . غنيمة
*asr · ghanīma*

captured equipment معدات مغتنمة
*muʿaddāt mughtanama*

Caravelle airtransporter طائرة نقل « كارڤيل »
*ṭāʾirat naql kārāvīl*

carbine بندقية قصيرة
*bunduqīya qaṣīra*

Carcara ASM صاروخ جو ـ سطح « كاركرا »
*ṣārūkh jaww-saṭḥ kārkarā*

cargo شحنة . حمولة
*ḥumūla*

cargo carrier ناقلة بضائع
*nāqilat baḍāʾiʿ*

cargo chassis هيكل نقل بضائع
*haykal naql baḍāʾiʿ*

cargo hook خطاف نقل البضائع
*khaṭṭāf naql al-baḍāʾiʿ*

cargo transport نقل البضائع
*naql al-baḍāʾiʿ*

cargo vehicle سيارة شحن
*sayyārat shaḥn*

Carl Gustav sub-machine gun رشاش قصير « كارل غوستاف »
*rashshāsh qaṣīr kārl ghūstāf*

carrier حاملة . ناقلة
*ḥāmila · nāqila*

carrier-based موجود بالحاملة
*mawjūd bil-ḥāmila*

carrierborne محمول على الحاملة
*maḥmūl ʿalal-ḥāmila*

carrierborne aircraft طائرة منقولة على الحاملة
*ṭāʾira manqūla ʿalal-ḥāmila*

carrier-controlled radar رادار محكوم من الحاملة
*rādār maḥkūm min al-ḥāmila*

carrier escort حرس الحاملة
*ḥaras al-ḥāmila*

carrier force قوة الحاملة
*qūwat al-ḥāmila*

carrier landing إنزال بالحاملة
*inzāl bil-ḥāmila*

carrier onboard delivery تسليم على متن الحاملة
*taslīm ʿala matn al-ḥāmila*

carry on! « داوم ! »
*dāwim*

carry out نفذ . أنجز
*naffaḍha · anjaza*

cartridge خرطوشة
*kharṭūsha*

cartridge bag كيس الخرطوشة
*kīs al-kharṭūshāt*

cartridge revolver مسدس خرطوشة
*musaddas kharṭūsha*

Casa (Co) شركات كاسا
*sharikat kāsā*

Cascavel armoured car عربة مدرعة « كاسكاڤيل »
*ʿaraba mudarraʿa kāskavīl*

Cascavel vehicle سيارة « كاسكاڤيل »
*sayyārat kāskāvīl*

caseless ammunition ذخيرة سائبة
*dhakhīra sā'iba*
casevac role مهمة اخلاء المصابين
*muhimmat ikhlā' al-muṣābīn*
Caspian Sea بحر قزوين
*baḥr qazwīn*
Cassegrain Optics بصريات « كاسجرين »
*baṣarīyāt kasgrīn*
cast قذف . رتب . صب
*qadhafa · rattaba · ṣabba*
Castor radar رادار « كاستور »
*rādār kastūr*
Castor stand-off radar رادار كاستور يعمل عن بعد
*rādār kastūr ya'mul 'an bu'd*
casualties مصابون . خسائر
*muṣābūn · khasā'ir*
casualty خسارة . قتيل . جريح
*khasāra · qatīl · jarīḥ*
casualty evacuation إخلاء المصابين
*ikhlā' al-muṣābīn*
casualty litter حمالة المصابين
*ḥammālat al-muṣābīn*
catapult منجنيق
*manjanīq*
catering officer ضابط الاعاشة
*ḍābiṭ al-i'āsha*
cathode-ray tube أنبوب أشعة كثود
*unbūb ashi''a kathūd*
Cat House radar رادار « كات هاوس »
*rādār kāt haws*
cavalry سلاح الفرسان
*silāḥ al-fursān*
cavalry squadron سرية الفرسان
*sarīyat al-fursān*
cavitating target هدف مجوّف
*hadaf mujawwaf*
cavitation تجويف . تجوف
*tajwīf · tajawwuf*
cease fire وقف إطلاق النار . هدنة
*waqf iṭlāq an-nār · hudna*
cemetery مقبرة . مدفن
*maqbara · madfan*
censor مراقب . رقيب
*murāqib · raqīb*
Central African Republic جمهورية أفريقيا الوسطى
*jumhūrīyat afrīqya al-wusṭa*
Central Air Force القوات الجوية المركزية
*al-qūwāt al-jawwīya al-markazīya*
central command القيادة المركزية
*al-qiyāda al-markazīya*
central computer كومبيوتر مركزي
*kumbyūtar markazī*
central container خزان مركزي
*khazzān markazī*
Central Intelligence Agency وكالة المخابرات المركزية
*wakālat al-mukhābarāt al-markazīya*
central search radar رادار استكشاف مركزي
*rādār istikshāf markazī*
Centurion tank دبابة « سنتيوريون »
*dabbābat sintyūriyūn*
ceramic خزفي . فخاري
*khazafī · fukhārī*
ceramic armour درع خزفي
*dir' khazafī*
ceremonial إحتفال
*iḥtifāl*
ceremonial dress بزة المراسم
*bizzat al-marāsim*
ceremonial step خطوة المراسم
*khuṭwat al-marāsim*
Cessna aircraft طائرة « سيسنا »
*ṭā'irat sisna*
Cessna (Co) شركة سيسنا
*sharikat sisna*
Cetme rifle بندقية سيتمي
*bunduqīyat sitmi*
CF-101 aircraft طائرة « سي إف ـ ١٠١ »
*ṭā'irat sī if mi'a wa wāḥid*
CGN cruiser طرادة « سي جي إن »
*ṭarrādat sī jī in*
CH-46 helicopter طائرة عمودية « سي اتش ٤٦ »
*ṭā'ira 'amūdīya sī itsh sitta wa arba'īn*
CH-47 helicopter طائرة عمودية « سي اتش ـ ٤٧ »
*ṭā'ira 'amūdīya sī itsh sab'a wa arba'īn*
CH-47C helicopter طائرة عمودية « سي اتش ـ ٤٧ سي »
*ṭā'ira 'amūdīya sī itsh sab'a wa arba'īn sī*
CH47D helicopter طائرة عمودية « سي اتش ٤٧ دي »
*ṭā'ira 'amūdīya sī itsh sab'a wa arba'īn dī*
CH-53 helicopter طائرة عمودية « سي اتش ـ ٥٣ »
*ṭā'ira 'amūdīya sī itsh thalātha wa khamsīn*
CH-54 helicopter طائرة عمودية « سي اتش ـ ٥٤ »
*ṭā'ira 'amūdīya sī itsh arba'a wa khamsīn*

Chad تشاد
*tshad*

chaff شرائح تشويش
*sharāʾiḥ tashwīsh*

chaff and flare dispenser موزع شرائح التشويش والمشاعل
*muwazziʿ sharāʾiḥ at-tashwīsh wal-mashāʿil*

chaff launcher قاذفة شرائح التشويش
*qādhifat sharāʾiḥ at-tashwīsh*

chaff penetration aid معين اختراق شرائح التشويش
*muʿīn ikhtirāq sharāʾiḥ at-tashwīsh*

chain gun مدفع سلسلي
*midfaʿ silsilī*

chain of command سلسلة القيادة
*silsilat al-qiyāda*

Challenger tank دبابة « تشالينجر »
*dabbābat tshalinjar*

chamber غرفة
*ghurfa*

chamber temperature درجة حرارة الغرفة
*darajat ḥarārat al-ghurfa*

change course تغيير السير
*taghyīr as-sayr*

change location تغيير الموقع
*taghyīr al-mawqiʿ*

change of position تغيير الوضع
*taghyīr al-waḍʿ*

channel قناة
*qanāh*

Chaparral ADS نظام دفاع جوي « شاپارال »
*niẓām difāʿ jawwī shābārāl*

Chaparral SAM صاروخ سطح ـ جو « شابارال »
*ṣārūkh saṭḥ-jaww shabarāl*

chaplain قسيس
*qissīs*

charge! إهجم
*ihjim*

charges عناصر الاتهام
*ʿanāṣir al-ittihām*

charge temperature درجة حرارة الشحن
*darajat ḥarārat ash-shaḥn*

Charleston cargo ship سفينة نقل « تشارلستون »
*safīnat naql tshārlshtūn*

Charlie submarine غواصة « تشارلي »
*qhawwāṣat tshārlī*

chart خارطة مخطط
*khāriṭa · mukhaṭṭaṭ*

check point نقطة الفحص
*nuqṭat al-faḥṣ*

cheek-rest سناد الشكيمة
*sinād ash-shakīma*

Cheese Cake radar رادار « تشيزكيك »
*rādār tshīz kayk*

chemical كيماوي
*kīmāwī*

chemical absorption gas analyser محلل غازي بالامتصاص الكيماوي
*muḥallil ghāzī bil-imtiṣāṣ al-kīmāwī*

chemical bomb قنبلة كيماوية
*qunbula kīmāwīya*

chemical defence troops قوات الدفاع الكيماوي
*qūwāt ad-difāʿ al-kīmāwī*

chemical projectile مقذوف كيماوي
*maqdhūf kīmāwī*

chemical shell قذيفة كيماوية
*qadhīfa kīmāwīya*

chemical warfare حرب كيماوية
*ḥarb kīmāwīya*

chemical warhead رأس قذيفة كيماوية
*raʾs qadhīfa kīmāwīya*

chemosphere طبقة جوية ذات نشاط كهربائي ضوئي
*ṭabaqa jawwīya dhāt nashāṭ kahrabāʾī ḍawʾī*

Chengdu frigate فرقاطة « تشينجدو »
*firqāṭat tshingdū*

Cherokee jeep عربة جيب « تشيروكي »
*ʿarabat jīb tshirūkī*

Chevaline missile صاروخ « شاڤالين »
*ṣārūkh shavālīn*

Cheverton tender مقطورة « شيڤرتون »
*maqṭūrat shivartūn*

chief marshal المشير الأعلى
*al-mushīr al-aʿlā*

chief of battle staff رئيس أركان الحرب
*raʾīs arkān al-ḥarb*

chief of staff رئيس الأركان
*raʾīs al-arkān*

Chieftain tank دبابة « تشيفتاين »
*dabbābat tshīftan*

Chikugo frigate فرقاطة « تشيكوجو »
*firqāṭat tshikūgū*

Chile تشيلي
*tshīlī*

China الصين
*aṣ-ṣīn*

Chincul (Co) شركة تشينكول
*sharikat tshinkūl*

chine حافة . عطف
*ḥāffa · ʿiṭf*

Chinese صيني
*ṣīnī*
Chinook helicopter طائرة عمودية « تشينوك »
*ṭā'ira ʿamūdīya tshīnūk*
Chipmunk aircraft طائرة « تشيبمونك »
*ṭā'irat tshibmūnk*
chlorination معالجة بالكلور
*muʿālaja bil-klūr*
chlorine كلور
*klūr*
Chobham armour درع « تشوبام »
*dirʿ tshubām*
cholera كوليرا
*kūlīrā*
Chonburi gun boat سفينة مجهزة بالمدافع « تشونبوري »
*safīna mujahhaza bil-madāfiʿ shūnbūrī*
Christian مسيحي
*masīḥī*
chromed bore ماسورة بندقية مطلية بالكروم
*māsurat bunduqīya maṭlīya bil-krūm*
Churchill submarine غواصة تشرشل
*ghawwāṣat tsharshil*
Churchill tank دبابة تشرشل
*dabbābat tshārshil*
Ciacio-S torpedo طوربيد . كياسيو ـ اس
*ṭūrbīd kiyasyu - is*
Cinchan frigate فرقاطة « سينشان »
*firqāṭat sīntshān*
cipher شفرة
*shifra*
cipher code نظام شفري
*niẓām shifrī*
ciphering ترامز
*tarāmuz*
circular hatch باب دائري
*bāb dā'irī*
Citation aircraft طائرة « سايتيشن »
*ṭā'irat sāytīshn*
civil defence دفاع مدني
*difāʿ madanī*
Civil Defence Force قوات الدفاع المدني
*qūwāt ad-difāʿ al-madanī*
civilian aircraft طائرة مدنية
*ṭā'ira madanīya*
civilian clothes ملابس مدنية
*malābis madanīya*
civilian military training organisation هيئة التدريب العسكري المدني
*hay'at at-tadrīb al-ʿaskarī al-madanī*
civil transport نقل مدني
*naql madanī*
civil war حرب أهلية
*ḥarb ahlīya*
CJ-5 trainer طائرة تدريب « سي جيه ـ ٥ »
*ṭā'irat tadrīb sī jayy khamsa*
Clam Shell radar رادار « كلام شل »
*rādār klām shil*
clandestine operation عملية سرية
*ʿamalīya sirrīya*
class 1010 gun مدفع طراز ١٠١٠
*midfaʿ ṭirāz alf wa ʿashara*
class 1015 gun مدفع طراز ١٠١٥
*midfaʿ ṭirāz alf wa khamsata ʿashar*
class 1055 launcher قاذفة طراز ١٠٥٥
*qādhifa ṭirāz alf wa khamsa wa khamsīn*
Classification and Analysis Centre مركز التصنيف والتحليل
*markaz at-taṣnīf wat-taḥlīl*
classification centre مركز التصنيف
*markaz at-taṣnīf*
classified information معلومات سرية
*maʿlūmāt sirrīya*
cleaning kit أدوات النظافة
*adawāt an-naẓāfa*
cleared of mines منزوعة الألغام
*manzūʿat al-alghām*
clearing تنظيف . تطهير
*tanẓīf · taṭhīr*
clearing operation عملية تطهير
*ʿamalīyat taṭhīr*
Clemenceau aircraft carrier حاملة طائرات « كليمانصو »
*ḥāmilat ṭā'irāt klīmānṣū*
clerk كاتب
*kātib*
cliff مخدر شاهق
*munhaddar shāhiq*
climb rate معدل التسلق
*muʿaddal at-tasalluq*
clip مشبك . مشط ذخيرة
*mishbak · mushṭ dhakhīra*
clip-on مشبوك
*mashbūk*
close-arrest ايقاف شديد
*īqāf shadīd*
close combat قتال متلاحم
*qitāl mutalāḥim*
close-combat dogfight اشتباك جوي متلاحم
*ishtibāk jawwī mutalāḥim*
close formation تشكيل منضم
*tashkīl munḍamm*

C

close-in عن قرب
*ʿan qurb*
close-in weapon system (CIWS) نظام أسلحة الاشتباك (برج بحري مضاد للطائرات)
*niẓām asliḥat al-ishtibāk (burj baḥrī muḍādd liṭ-ṭāʾirāt)*
close-range مدى قصير
*madda qaṣīr*
close-support سند مباشر
*sanad mubāshir*
close-support aircraft طائرة السند المباشر
*ṭāʾirat as-sanad al-mubāshir*
close-up عن قرب
*ʿan qurb*
closure إغلاق . إقفال
*ighlāq · iqfāl*
clothing allowance بدل ملابس
*badal malābis*
clothing store مخزن ملابس
*makhzan malābis*
cloud سحاب . غيم
*saḥāb · ghaym*
cloud height إرتفاع السحاب
*irtifāʿ as-saḥāb*
cluster bomb قنبلة عنقودية
*qunbula ʿunqūdīya*
clutter تداخل إنعكاسات الموجات الرادارية
*tadākhul inʿikāsāt al-mawjāt ar-rādārīya*
CM-60 gun مدفع « سي ام ـ ٦٠ »
*midfaʿ sī im sittīn*
CM-170 aircraft طائرة « سي ام ١٧٠ »
*ṭāʾirat sī im miʾa wa sabʿīn*
coast ساحل شاطىء
*sāḥil · shāṭiʾ*
coastal ساحلي
*sāḥilī*
coastal artillery مدفعية سواحل
*midfaʿīyat sawāḥil*
coastal defence دفاع ساحلي
*difāʿ sāḥilī*
coastal defence unit وحدة دفاع ساحلي
*wiḥdat difāʿ sāḥilī*
coastal force build-up تعاظم قوة الدفاع الساحلي
*taʿāẓum qūwat ad-difāʿ as-sāḥilī*
coastal patrol دورية حراسة السواحل
*dawrīyat ḥirāsat as-sawāḥil*
coastal patrol craft زورق خفر السواحل
*zawraq khafr as-sawāḥil*
coastal strike هجوم ساحلي
*hujūm sāḥilī*
coastal waters مياه ساحلية
*miyah sāḥilīya*
coast artillery مدفعية سواحل
*midfaʿīyat sawāḥil*
coastguard حرس سواحل
*ḥaras sawāḥil*
coastguard cutter زورق حرس السواحل
*zawraq ḥaras as-sawāḥil*
coastline خط ساحلي
*khaṭṭ sāḥilī*
coaxial متحد المحور
*muttaḥid al-miḥwar*
coaxial rotors دوارات متحدة المحور
*dawwārāt muttaḥidat al-miḥwar*
COBELDA fire control نظام السيطرة على الرمي « كوبلدا »
*niẓām as-sayṭara ʿalar-ramī kūbilda*
Cobra Dane radar system نظام راداري « كوبرا دين »
*niẓām rādārī kūbra dayn*
Cobra fighter طائرة مقاتلة « كوبرا »
*ṭāʾira muqātila kūbra*
Cobra helicopter طائرة عمودية « كوبرا »
*ṭāʾira ʿamūdīya kūbra*
Cobra-Judy radar رادار « كوبرا - جودي »
*rādār kūbra jūdī*
Cobra missile صاروخ « كوبرا »
*ṣārūkh kūbra*
Cobra tracked vehicle عربة مجنزرة « كوبرا »
*ʿaraba mujanzara kūbra*
Cock airtransport طائرة نقل « كوك »
*ṭāʾirat naql kūk*
Cockerill gun مدفع « كوك ريل »
*midfaʿ kukrīl*
cocking handle مقبض القدح
*miqbaḍ al-qadḥ*
cocking lever عتلة القدح
*ʿutlat al-qadḥ*
cockpit حجرة الطيار
*ḥujrat aṭ-ṭayyār*
cockpit display أجهزة العرض بحجرة الطيار
*ajhizat al-ʿarḍ bi-ḥujrat aṭ-ṭayyār*
cock the hammer قدح الزناد
*qadḥ az-zinād*
code رموز
*rumūz*
coder جهاز وضع الرموز
*jihāz waḍʿ ar-rumūz*

CODfish aircraft طائرة « كودفيش »
*ṭāʾirat kūdfīsh*
coding ترامز . كتابة بالرموز
*tarāmuz · kitāba bir-rumūz*
coding room غرفة الترامز
*ghurfat at-tarāmuz*
coil spring نابض لولبي
*nābiḍ lawlabī*
Colbert cruiser طرادة « كولبير »
*ṭarrādat kūlbīr*
cold-launch إطلاق بارد
*iṭlāq bārid*
cold launch capability إمكانية الاطلاق البارد
*imkānīyat al-iṭlāq al-bārid*
cold store مخزن مبرد
*makhzan mubarrid*
cold type launch إطلاق بارد
*iṭlāq bārid*
collaboration تعاون
*taʿāwun*
collaborator متعاون . مشترك
*mutaʿāwun · mushtarik*
collapsible boat قارب يطوى
*qārib yaṭwī*
collector for spent cases مجمع العلب الفارغة
*mujammiʿ al-ʿulab al-fārigha*
collision إصطدام تصادم
*iṣṭidām · taṣādum*
collision course مسار الاصطدام
*masār al-iṣṭidām*
colonel عقيد
*ʿaqīd*
colonel-general عميد
*ʿamīd*
Colossus carrier حاملة « كولوسوس »
*ḥāmilat kulūsūs*
coloured smoke grenade قنبلة دخان ملون يدوية
*qunbulat dukhān mulawwan yadawīya*
Colt commando rifle بندقية فدائي « كولت »
*bunduqīyat fidāʾī kūlt*
Columbia كولومبيا
*kūlūmbya*
Columbian كولومبي
*kūlūmbī*
column leader قائد الطابور
*qāʾid aṭ-ṭābūr*
combat قتال . معركة
*qitāl · maʿraka*

combat activity نشاط المعركة
*nashāṭ al-maʿraka*
combat aircraft طائرة قتال
*ṭāʾirat qitāl*
combat air patroller طائرة دورية مقاتلة
*ṭāʾira dawrīya muqātila*
combatant مقاتل
*muqātil*
combat controls مضابط قتال
*maḍābiṭ qitāl*
combat development تطور المعركة
*taṭawwur al-maʿraka*
combat dress بزة القتال
*bizzat al-qitāl*
combat engineer مهندس قتال
*muhandis qitāl*
combat engineer tractor جرار مهندس قتال
*jarrār muhandis qitāl*
combat engineer vehicle مركبة مهندس قتال
*markabat muhandis qitāl*
combat helicopter طائرة عمودية مقاتلة
*ṭāʾira ʿamūdiya muqātila*
combat information centre مركز بيانات المعركة
*markaz bayānāt al-maʿraka*
combat operations centre مركز عمليات القتال
*markaz ʿamalīyāt al-qitāl*
combat radius نصف قطر القتال
*niṣf quṭr al-qitāl*
combat readiness الاستعداد للقتال
*al-istiʿdād lil-qitāl*
combat salvage boat سفينة انقاذ مقاتلة
*safīnat inqādh muqātila*
combat sortie هجوم معاكس فجائي
*hujūm muʿākis fujāʾī*
Combattante patrol boat زورق حرس سواحل « كومباتانت »
*zawraq ḥaras as-sawāḥil kūmbatānt*
combat training تدريب على القتال
*tadrīb ʿalal-qitāl*
combat troops جند القتال
*jund al-qitāl*
combat wing جناح مقاتل
*janāḥ muqātil*
combat zone منطقة المعركة
*minṭaqat al-maʿraka*
combined launcher قاذفة مشتركة
*qādhifa mushtarika*
combined operations عمليات مشتركة
*ʿamalīyāt mushtaraka*

combustible cartridge case ظرف خرطوشة قابل للاحتراق
*ẓarf kharṭūsha qābil lil-iḥtirāq*

combustion chamber حجرة الاحتراق
*ḥujrat al-iḥtirāq*

command قيادة . أمر
*qiyāda · amr*

command and control boat سفينة القيادة والمراقبة
*safīnat al-qiyāda wal-murāqaba*

command and control centre مركز القيادة والمراقبة
*markaz al-qīyāda wal-murāqaba*

command and control helicopter طائرة قيادة ومراقبة عمودية
*ṭāʾirat qiyāda wa murāqaba ʿamūdīya*

commandant أمر . قائد
*āmir · qāʾid*

command buffer system نظام أمن القيادة
*niẓām amn al-qiyāda*

command-detonated mine لغم ينفجر بالأمر
*lughm yanfajir bil-amr*

commander قائد
*qāʾid*

commander-in-chief القائد العام
*al-qāʾid al-ʿām*

command facilities تسهيلات القيادة
*tashīlāt al-qiyāda*

command guidance إرشاد قيادي
*irshād qiyādī*

command-guided موجّه قيادياً
*muwajjah qiyādīyan*

command headquarters مقر القيادة
*maqarr al-qiyāda*

commanding officer قائد وحدة
*qāʾid wiḥda*

commando فدائي
*fidāʾī*

commando assault helicopter طائرة عمودية للهجوم الفدائي
*ṭāʾira ʿamūdīya li-hujūm al-fidāʾī*

commando brigade لواء صاعقة
*liwāʾ ṣāʿiqa*

commando group مجموعة صاعقة
*majmūʿa ṣāʿiqa*

commando unit وحدة صاعقة
*wiḥda ṣāʿiqa*

command post مركز قيادة
*markaz qiyāda*

command post vehicle مركبة مركز القيادة
*markabat markaz al-qiyāda*

command structure هيكل القيادة
*haykal al-qiyāda*

command transmitter جهاز الارسال بالقيادة
*jihāz al-irsāl bil-qiyāda*

command vehicle مركبة قيادة
*markabat qiyāda*

commercial traffic مرور تجاري
*murūr tijārī*

commission تفويض . مهمة
*tafwīḍ · muhimma*

commissioned officer ضابط مقلد
*ḍābiṭ muqallad*

communication إتصال
*ittiṣāl*

communication antenna هوائي مواصلات
*hawāʾī muwāṣalāt*

communication equipment معدات الاتصال
*muʿaddāt al-ittiṣāl*

communication facilities تسهيلات الاتصال
*tashīlāt al-ittiṣāl*

communication liaison ربط الاتصالات
*rabṭ al-ittiṣālāt*

communications إتصالات . مواصلات
*ittiṣālāt · muwāṣalāt*

communications buoy عائمة الاتصالات
*ʿāʾimat al-ittiṣālāt*

communications centre مركز الاتصالات
*markaz al-ittiṣālāt*

communications controller مراقب الاتصالات
*murāqib al-ittisālāt*

communications-gathering aircraft طائرة تجميع الاتصالات
*ṭāʾirat tajmīʿ al-ittiṣālāt*

communications intelligence إستخبارات الاتصالات
*istikhbārāt al-ittiṣālāt*

communications operator عامل المواصلات
*ʿāmil al-muwāṣalāt*

communications satellite قمر الاتصالات
*qamr al-ittiṣālāt*

communications squadron سرية اتصالات
*sarīyat ittiṣālāt*

Comoran boat زورق « كوموران »
*zawraq kūmūrān*

co-mounted مركب مع
*murakkab maʿa*

compact gun-mount قاعدة مدفع صغير
*qā'idat midfa' ṣaghīra*
company جماعة
*jamā'a*
compass بوصلة
*būṣala*
compass case علبة البوصلة
*'ulbat al-būṣala*
compassionate leave إجازة خاصة
*ijāza khaṣṣa*
complement عدد كامل
*'adad kāmil*
composite blade نصل مركب
*naṣl murakkab*
compound helicopter طائرة عمودية مركبة
*ṭā'ira 'amūdīya murakkaba*
compressor ضاغط
*ḍāghiṭ*
computer-assisted معان بالكومبيوتر
*mu'ān bil-kumbyūtar*
computer control مراقبة الكومبيوتر
*murāqabat al-kumbyūtar*
computer controlled مراقب بالكومبيوتر
*murāqab bil-kumbyūtar*
computerized يعمل بالكومبيوتر
*ya'mal bil-kumbyūtar*
computerized data-processing معالجة البيانات بالكومبيوتر
*mu'ālajat al-bayānāt bil-kumbyūtar*
concealed مستور . مخفي
*mastūr · makhfī*
concentration حشد . تركيز
*ḥashd · tarkīz*
concrete shelter ملجأ خرساني
*malja' kharasānī*
concussion grenade القنبلة اليدوية الصدمية
*al-qunbula al-yadawīya aṣ-ṣadmīya*
condensor مُكثف
*mukaththif*
Condor AGM صاروخ جو ـ أرض « كوندور »
*ṣārūkh jaww-arḍ kūndūr*
Condor power pack مولد طاقة « كوندور »
*muwallid ṭāqa kūndūr*
conduct سلوك . إدارة . وصل
*sulūk · idāra · waṣl*
confined to barracks حجز في الثكنة
*ḥajz fith-thukna*
confined to quarters حجز في الغرفة
*ḥajz fil-ghurfa*

Congo الكنغو
*al-kunghū*
conquer يفتح . يقهر
*yaftaḥ · yaqhar*
conscript مجند
*mujannad*
conscription تجنيد
*tajnīd*
console خزانة أجهزة
*khizānat al-ajhiza*
consolidate a beach head تعزيز رأس الساحل
*ta'zīz ra's as-sāḥil*
construction إنشاء . تركيب
*inshā' · tarkīb*
construction troops جنود الانشاءات
*junūd al-inshā'āt*
contact fuse فاصمة تماسية
*fāṣima tamāsīya*
contagious مُعد
*mu'di*
contagious disease مرض مُعد
*maraḍ mu'di*
container وعاء . صندوق . حاوية
*wi'ā' · ṣundūq · ḥāwīya*
containerized محفوظ في حاويات
*maḥfūẓ fi-ḥāwīyāt*
container-launcher علبة حاوية قاذفة
*ḥāwīyā qādhifa*
container-launcher box حاوية ـ علبة قاذفة
*'ulbat ḥāwīya qādhifa*
container-launcher unit وحدة حاوية قاذفة
*wiḥdat hāwīya·qādhifa*
container weapon system نظام أسلحة الحاويات
*niẓām asliḥat al-ḥāwīyāt*
containing the enemy تطويق العدو
*taṭwiq al-'adūw*
contaminated area منطقة ملوثة
*minṭaqa mulawwatha*
contamination تلوث
*talawwuth*
contamination area منطقة التلوث
*minṭaqat at-talawwuth*
continental قاري
*qārī*
contingent وحدة
*wiḥda*
continuous fighter support تعزيز مستمر للمقاتلات
*ta'zīz mustamirr lil-muqātilāt*
continuous flight operation عمليات طيران مستمر
*'amalīyāt ṭayarān mustamirr*

continuous wave موجة مستمرة
*mawja mustamirra*
continuous wave acquisition radar رادار اكتساب بموجات مستمرة
*rādār iktisāb bi-mawjāt mustamirra*
continuous wave emission إبتعاث موجي مستمر
*ibtiʿāth mawjī mustamirr*
continuous wave illuminator مصباح مضيء مستمر الموجة
*misbāḥ muḍī mustamirr al-mawja*
continuous wave transmission نقل بموجة مستمرة
*naql bi-mawja mustamirra*
contour كنتور
*kuntūr*
contour flying طيران كنتوري
*ṭayarān kuntūrī*
contraband مهرّبات
*muharrabāt*
contra-rotating turbine تربين دائر في اتجاه معاكس
*turbīn dāʾir fi-ittijāh muʿākis*
contrary to orders مخالف للأوامر
*mukhālif lil-awāmir*
control رقابة . تحكم
*raqāba · taḥakkum*
control cable كبل التحكم
*kabl at-taḥakkum*
control capacity سعة التحكم
*siʿat at-taḥakkum*
control centre مركز المراقبة
*markaz al-murāqaba*
control command قيادة المراقبة
*qiyādat al-murāqaba*
control desk مكتب المراقبة
*maktab al-murāqaba*
control device وسيلة مراقبة
*wasīlat murāqaba*
control facilities تسهيلات مراقبة
*tashīlāt murāqaba*
control headquarters رئاسة المراقبة
*riʾāsat al-murāqaba*
control post مركز مراقبة
*markaz murāqaba*
control room غرفة مراقبة
*ghurfat murāqaba*
control squadron سرية مراقبة
*sarīyat murāqaba*
control system نظام التحكم . نظام التوجيه
*niẓām at-taḥakkum · niẓām at-tawjīh*
control tower برج المراقبة
*burj al-murāqaba*
convalescent متماثل للشفاء
*mutamāthil lish-shifāʾ*
conventional munition ذخيرة غير نووية
*dhakhīra ghayr nawawīya*
conventional stand-off weapon سلاح تقليدي يطلق عن بعد
*silāḥ taqlīdī yuṭlaq ʿan buʿd*
convergence-zone mode نمط منطقة التقارب
*namaṭ minṭaqat at-taqārub*
conversion kit أدوات التحويل
*adawāt at-taḥwīl*
convex hyperboloid sub-dish صحن فرعي مكافئ السطح مقعّر
*ṣaḥn farʿī mukāfiʾ as-saṭḥ muqaʿʿar*
conveyor belt سير الناقلة
*sayr an-nāqila*
convoy قافلة . حرس مرافق
*qāfila · ḥaras murāfiq*
convoy leader قائد القافلة . قائد الحرس
*qāʾid al-qāfila · qāʾid al–ḥaras*
cook طباخ . طاه
*ṭabbākh · ṭāhin*
cooling system نظام تبريد
*niẓām tabrīd*
Coontz destroyer مدمرة « كونتس »
*mudammirat kūnts*
co-ordinated attack هجوم منسق
*hujūm munassaq*
Coot A aircraft طائرة « كوت ايه »
*ṭaʾirat kūt ayy*
co-pilot مساعد طيار
*musāʿid ṭayyār*
Coquelet teleprinter طابعة عن بعد « كوكليه »
*ṭabiʿa ʿan buʿd kūklay*
Cormoran craft سفينة كورموران
*safīnat kūrmūrān*
corporal عريف
*ʿarīf*
corps فيلق
*faylaq*
Corps Radar رادار كور
*rādār kūr*

correction for wind تصحيح للرياح
*taṣḥīḥ lir-riyāḥ*
correct laying offset حيدان التصويب الصحيح
*ḥayadān at-taṣwīb aṣ-ṣaḥīḥ*
Corsair bomber طائرة قاذفة « كورسأير »
*ṭāʾira qādhifa kūrsayr*
Corvette aircraft طائرة « كورفيت »
*ṭāʾirat kūrvīt*
Corvus chaff launcher قاذفة شرائح التشويش « كوفوس »
*qādhifat sharāʾiḥ at-tashwīsh kūrvūs*
cosmonaut رائد فضاء
*rāʾid faḍāʾ*
Costa Rica كوستاريكا
*kūsta rīkā*
cost-effective معتدل السعر إقتصادي
*muʿtadil as-siʿr · iqtiṣādī*
COTAC FCS نظام السيطرة على الرمي « كوتاك »
*niẓām as-sayṭara ʿalar-ramī kūtāk*
council of war مجلس الحرب
*majlis al-ḥarb*
count-down عد تنازلي
*ʿadd tanāzulī*
counteraction مضادة
*muḍadda*
counter-ambush vessel سفينة انقضاض مضاد
*safīnat inqiḍāḍ muḍādd*
counter-attack هجوم مضاد
*hujūm muḍādd*
counter-bombardment قصف مضاد
*qaṣf muḍādd*
counter-espionage مضاد للتجسس
*muḍādd lit-tajassus*
counter-insurgency مضاد للعصيان
*muḍādd lil-ʿiṣyān*
counter-intelligence مقاومة مخابرات العدو
*muqāwamat mukhābarāt al-ʿadūw*
counter-measure تدابير مضادة
*tadābīr muḍādda*
counter-measures dispenser موزع التدابير المضادة
*muwazziʿ at-tadābir al-muḍādda*
counter-offensive هجوم مضاد
*hujūm muḍādd*
counter-terrorist unit وحدة رد الارهابيين
*wiḥdat radd al-irhābīyīn*
coupled-cavity تجويف متقارن
*tajwīf mutaqārin*

court-martial محكمة عسكرية
*maḥkama ʿaskarīya*
covering تغطية . تغليف
*taghṭīya · taghlīf*
covering fire نيران التغطية
*nīrān at-taghṭīya*
covert force قوة سرية
*qūwa sirrīya*
CP-140 aircraft طائرة « سي بي ـ ١٤٠ »
*ṭaʾirat sī pī miʾa wa arbaʿīn*
crane مرفاع
*mirfāʿ*
crash إصطدام . سقوط
*iṣṭidām · suqūṭ*
crash-resistant features مميزات مقاومة الارتطام
*mumayyizāt muqāwimat al-irtiṭām*
crate قفص
*qafaṣ*
crew طاقم
*ṭāqim*
crew compartment حجرة الطاقم
*ḥujrat aṭ-ṭāqim*
crewmen ملاحو السفينة أو الطائرة
*mallāḥū as-safīna aw aṭ-ṭāʾira*
crew trainer طائرة تدريب الملاحين
*ṭāʾirat tadrib al-mallāḥīn*
cross-country عبر الضواحي والحقول
*ʿabr aḍ-ḍawāḥī wal-ḥuqūl*
cross-country performance الأداء خارج الطرق
*al-adāʾ khārij aṭ-ṭuruq*
cross-fire نيران متقاطعة
*nīrān mutaqāṭaʿa*
cross hairs خيوط متصالبة
*khuyūt mutaṣāliba*
cross wind ريح معترضة
*rīḥ muʿtariḍa*
Crotale SAM صاروخ سطح ـ جو « كروتال »
*ṣārūkh saṭḥ-jaww krūtāl*
cruciform صليبي الشكل
*ṣalībī ash-shakl*
cruciform rear fins زعانف خلفية صليبية
*zaʿānif khalfīya ṣalībīya*
cruciform-wing weapon سلاح ذو اجنحة صليبية الشكل
*silāḥ dhū ajniḥa ṣalībīyat ash-shakl*
cruise missile صاروخ كروز
*ṣārūkh krūz*
cruise-missile submarine غواصة صواريخ كروز
*ghawwāṣat ṣawārīkh krūz*

cruise phase — مرحلة السير نحو الهدف
*marḥalat as-sayr nahwal-hadaf*

cruiser — طرادة
*ṭarrada*

cruise speed — سرعة التطاوف
*surʿat at-taṭāwuf*

cruising speed — السرعة التطاوفية
*as-surʿa at-taṭāwufīya*

Crusader fighter — طائرة مقاتلة « كروسيدر »
*ṭāʾira muqātila krusīdar*

CRV7 rocket — صاروخ « سي آر ڤي ٧ »
*ṣārūkh sī ār vī sabʿa*

cryogenically cooled — مبرد بغاز أو سائل التبريد
*mubarrad bi-ghāz aw sāʾil at-tabrīd*

cryogenic system — نظام التبريد
*niẓām at-tabrīd*

Cryptacec 80 telephone — هاتف « كريبتاسيك ٨٠ »
*hātif krībtasīk thamānīn*

cryptoanalyst — حلاّل الرموز
*ḥallāl ar-rumūz*

CSS-1 SSM — صاروخ سطح ـ سطح « سي اس اس ـ ١ »
*ṣārūkh saṭḥ-saṭḥ sī is is wāhid*

CSS-2 SSM — صاروخ سطح ـ سطح « سي اس اس ـ ٢ »
*ṣārūkh saṭḥ-saṭḥ sī is is ithnayn*

CSS-3 SSM — صاروخ سطح ـ سطح « سي اس اس ـ ٣ »
*ṣārūkh saṭḥ-saṭḥ sī is is thalātha*

CSS-5 SSM — صاروخ سطح ـ سطح « سي اس اس ـ ٥ »
*ṣārūkh saṭḥ-saṭḥ sī is is khamsa*

CSS-NX-4 missile — صاروخ « سي اس اس ـ ان اكس ـ ٤ »
*ṣārūkh sī is is in iks arbaʿa*

CSS-X-4 SSM — صاروخ سطح ـ سطح « سي اس اس ـ اكس ـ ٤ »
*ṣārūkh sạtḥ-sạtḥ sī is is iks arbaʿa*

Cuba — كوبا
*kūba*

Cub airtransporter — طائرة نقل « كوب »
*ṭāʾirat naql kūb*

Cuban — كوبي
*kūbī*

Cummins diesel — محرك ديزل « كومينز »
*muḥarrik dīzl kūmīnz*

cupola — قبة . سطح مقبب
*qubba · saṭḥ muqabbab*

Curl transporter — طائرة نقل كيرل
*ṭāʾirat naql kīrl*

curtain of fire — ساتر نيران
*sātir nīrān*

CVN nuclear powered aircraft carrier — حاملة طائرات نووية « سي ڤي ان »
*ḥamilat ṭāʾirāt nawawīya sī vī in*

CWI radar — رادار « سي دبليو آي »
*rādār sī dablyū āyy*

cyanide — سيانيد
*sīyānīd*

cycle — دورة . حلقة . شوط
*dawra · ḥalaqa · shawṭ*

cyclic rate of fire — المعدل النظري للرمي
*al-muʿaddal an-naẓarī lir-ramī*

Cyclope IR system — نظام أشعة دون الحمراء « سايكلوب »
*niẓam ashiʿʿa dūn al-ḥamrāʾ sāyklūb*

Cylinder Head radar — رادار سليندر هيد
*rādār silindar hīd*

cypher telegram — برقية بالشفرة
*barqīya bish-shifra*

Cyprus — قبرص
*qubruṣ*

Cyrano radar — رادار سيرانو
*rādār sīrānū*

cytographic equipment — أجهزة رسم الخلايا
*ajhizat rasm al-khalāyā*

Czech — تشيكوسلوڤاكي
*tshīkūslūvākī*

Czechoslovakia — تشيكوسلوڤاكيا
*tshīkūslūvākīya*

D

# D

D-III submarine — غواصة « دي ـ ٣ »
*ghawwāṣat dī thalātha*
D2G reactor — مفاعل « دي ٢ جي »
*mufāʿil dī ithnayn jī*
D-5X aircraft — طائرة « دي ـ ٥ اكس »
*ṭāʾirat dī khamsa iks*
D-10T rifle gun — مدفع محلزن « دي ـ ١٠ تي »
*midfaʿ muḥalzan dī ʿashara tī*
D-20 howitzer — مدفع هاوتزر « دي ـ ٢٠ »
*midfaʿ hāwitsar dī ʿishrīn*
D-30 field howitzer — مدفع هاوتزر ميداني « دي ـ ٣٠ »
*midfaʿ hāwitsar maydānī dī thalāthīn*
D-44 gun — مدفع « دي ـ ٤٤ »
*midfaʿ dī arbaʿa wa arbaʿīn*
D-56T gun — مدفع « دي ـ ٥٦ تي »
*midfaʿ dī sitta wa khamsīn tī*
D-74 gun — مدفع « دي ـ ٧٤ »
*midfaʿ dī arbaʿa wa sabʿīn*
D95 supply ship — سفينة تموين دي ٩٥
*safīnat tamwīn dī khamsa wa tisʿīn*
D1280 radar — رادار « دي ١٢٨٠ »
*rādār dī alf wa miʾtayn wa thamānīn*
DA-02 radar — رادار « دي ايه ـ ٠٢ »
*rādār dī ayy ṣifr ithnayn*
DA 140 pistol — مسدس « دي ايه ـ ١٤٠ »
*musaddas dī ayy miʾa wa arbaʿīn*
Dabur patrol craft — سفينة خفر السواحل « دابور »
*safīnat khafr as-sawāḥil dābūr*
Dagaie anti-missile decoy — شرك مضاد للصواريخ « داجاي »
*sharāk muḍādd liṣ-ṣawārīkh dagāy*
Dagger fighter — طائرة مقاتلة . داجر »
*ṭāʾira muqātila dagar*

daily allowance — بدل يومي
*badal yawmī*
damage — خسارة . أذى . تلف
*khasāra · adhan · talaf*
damage assessment officer — ضابط تقدير الخسائر
*ḍābiṭ taqdīr al-khasāʾir*
DANA howitzer — مدفع هاوتزر « دانا »
*midfaʿ hāwitsar dānā*
danger — خطر
*khaṭr*
Danish — دانمركي
*dānmarkī*
Daphné submarine — غواصة « دافني »
*ghawwāṣat dāfnī*
Dardo fire control — جهاز السيطرة على الرمي « داردو »
*jihāz as-sayṭara ʿalar-ramī dārdū*
dart — قذف . سهم مريش
*qadhf · sahm murayyash*
Darter submarine — غواصة « دارتر »
*ghawwāṣat dārtar*
Dassault-Breguet (Co) — شركة « داسو ـ بريجيه »
*sharikat dasū-brīgay*
data delay — تعويق البيانات
*taʿwīq al-bayānāt*
data handling — تحليل البيانات
*taḥlīl al-bayānāt*
data link — توصيل البيانات
*tawṣīl al-bayānāt*
data link system — نظام توصيل البيانات
*niẓām tawṣīl al-bayānāt*
data-processing system — نظام تحليل البيانات
*niẓam taḥlīl al-bayānāt*
data transmission — نقل البيانات
*naql al-bayānāt*
Dauphin helicopter — طائرة عمودية « دوفين »
*ṭāʾira ʿamūdīya dūfīn*
DAVID battery computer — كومبيوتر بطارية « ديفيد »
*kumbyūtar baṭṭārīya dīvīd*

David Brown (Co) شركة ديفيد براون
*sharikat dīvīd brawn*
davits نياط القوارب
*niyāṭ al-qawārib*
dawn patrol دورية الفجر
*dawrīyat al-fajr*
daylight ضوء النهار
*ḍaw' an-nahār*
day operation عملية نهارية
*ʿamalīya nahārīya*
DCB مجلس اتصالات الدفاع
*majlis ittiṣālāt ad-difāʿ*
DD 280 destroyer مدمرة « دي دي ٢٨٠ »
*mudammirat dī dī mi'tayn wa thamānīn*
DDG destroyer مدمرة « دي دي جي »
*mudammirat dī dī jī*
DE 1160 sonar سونار « دي ئي ١١٦٠ »
*sūnār dī alf wa mi'a wa sittīn*
Dead Duck IFF نظام تمييز الصديق العدو « ديد داك »
*niẓām tamyīz aṣ-ṣadīq wal-ʿadūw dīd dak*
deadly قاتل . مميت
*qātil · mumayyit*
death certificate شهادة وفاة
*shihādat wafāh*
Decatur destroyer مدمرة « ديكاتور »
*mudammirat dīkātūr*
decay grenade قنبلة يدوية انحلالية
*qunbula yadawīya inḥilālīya*
Decca radar رادار « ديكا »
*rādār dīkā*
Decca RM 416 radar رادار « ديكا آر ام ٤١٦ »
*rādār dīkā ār im arbaʿa miʿa wa sit ʿashar*
decipher (to) حل الرموز
*ḥall ar-rumūz*
decipherer وحدة حل الرموز
*wiḥdat ḥall ar-rumūz*
deck crane مرفاع ظهر المركب
*mirfāʿ ẓahr al-markab*
deck crane equipment معدات مرفاع ظهر المركب
*muʿaddāt mirfāʿẓahr al-markab*
deckhouse حجرة السطح
*ḥujrat as-saṭḥ*
deck landing الهبوط على السطح
*al-hubuṭ ʿalas-saṭḥ*
deck machinery آلات السطح
*ālāt as-saṭḥ*
deck park موقف السطح
*mawqif as-saṭḥ*
decode يحل الشفرة
*yaḥall ash-shifra*
decoding حل الشفرة
*ḥall ash-shifra*
decompression chamber غرفة تخفيف الانضغاط
*ghurfat takhfīf al-inḍighāṭ*
decontamination إزالة التلوث
*izālat at-talawwuth*
decontamination bowser شاحنة إزالة التلوث
*shāḥinat izālat at-talawwuth*
decontamination chamber غرفة إزالة التلوث
*ghurfat izālat at-talawwuth*
decontamination equipment معدات إزالة التلوث
*muʿaddāt izālat at-talawwuth*
decoy شرك . خدعة
*sharak · khudʿa*
decoy flare مشعل خادع
*mashʿal khādiʿ*
decoy missile صاروخ خادع
*ṣārūkh khādiʿ*
decoy penetration aid معين إختراق الشرك
*muʿīn ikhtirāq as-sharak*
Dedalo ASW carrier حاملة « ديدالو ايه اس دبليو »
*ḥāmilat dīdālū ayy is dablyū*
deep diving capability إمكانية الغوص العميق
*imkānīyat al-ghawṣ al-ʿamīq*
deep-submergence rescue vehicle مركبة انقاذ عميقة الغوص
*markabat inqādh ʿamīqat al-ghawṣ*
DEFA 552 gun مدفع « دي ئي اف ايه ٥٥٢ »
*midfaʿ dī ī if ayy khamsa mi'a wa ithnayn wa khamsīn*
DEFA cannon مدفع هاون « دي ئي اف ايه »
*midfaʿ hāwun dī if ayy*
defeat هزيمة
*hazīma*
defect (to) يغادر
*yughādir*
defector مغادر
*mughādir*
defence دفاع . حماية
*difāʿ · ḥimāya*
defence expenditure مصروفات الدفاع
*maṣrūfāt ad-difāʿ*
defence force قوات دفاعية
*qūwāt difāʿ īya*

|  |  |  |
|---|---|---|
| defence minister | *wazīr ad-difāʿ* | وزير الدفاع |
| defence network | *shabakat ad-difāʿ* | شبكة الدفاع |
| defence role | *muhimmat ad-difāʿ* | مهمة الدفاع |
| defences | *taḥṣīnāt* | تحصينات |
| defence system | *shabakat difāʿ* | شبكة دفاع |
| defend | *dāfiʿ ʿan · ḥamā* | دافع عن . حمى |
| Defender helicopter | *ṭāʾira ʿamūdīya difindar* | طائرة عمودية « دفيندر » |
| defending radar | *rādār mudāfiʿ* | رادار مُدافع |
| Defense Aid Program | *barnāmij maʿūnat ad-difāʿ* | برنامج معونة الدفاع |
| defensive action | *ijrāʾ difāʿī* | إجراء دفاعي |
| defensive battle | *maʿraka difāʿīya* | معركة دفاعية |
| defensive operations | *ʿamalīyāt difāʿya* | عمليات دفاعية |
| defensive positions | *mawāḍiʿ difāʿīya* | مواضع دفاعية |
| defensive reinforcement | *taʿzīzat difāʿīya* | تعزيزات دفاعية |
| defensive support vest | *ṣudrat daʿm difāʿīya* | صدرة دعم دفاعية |
| defensive zone | *minṭaqa difāʿīya* | منطقة دفاعية |
| deflection angle | *zāwiyat al-inḥirāf* | زاوية الانحراف |
| deflector | *ḥārifa* | حارفة |
| 360 degrees coverage | *taghṭīyat thalātha miʾa wa sittīn daraja* | تغطية ٣٦٠ درجة |
| de Havilland (Co) | *sharikat dī hāvilānd* | شركة دي هاڤيلاند |
| de-icer | *muzīl al-jalīd* | مزيل الجليد |
| delay | *ʿawq · amhala* | عوق . أمهل |
| delayed action | *fiʿl muʿawwaq* | فعل معوق |
| delayed jump | *qafz muʿawwaq* | قفز معوق |
| delay mechanism | *ālīyat at-taʾkhīr* | آلية التأخير |
| delay time | *zaman at-taʿwīq* | زمن التعويق |
| Delco fire-control computer | *kumbyūtar as-sayṭara ʿalar-rami dīlkū* | كومبيوتر السيطرة على الرمي « ديلكو » |
| Delfinen submarine | *ghawwāṣat dalfīnīn* | غواصة دلفينين |
| Delfin L-29 aircraft | *ṭāʾirat dalfīn il tisʿa wa ʿishrīn* | طائرة « دلفين ال ـ ٢٩ » |
| de-lousing equipment | *muʿaddāt izālat al-qaml* | معدات إزالة القمل |
| Delta Dart interceptor | *tāʾirat iʿtirāḍ diltā dārt* | طائرة اعتراض « دلتا دارت » |
| Delta submarine | *ghawwāṣat diltā* | غواصة « دلتا » |
| delta wing | *janāḥ muthallathī* | جناح مثلثي |
| demarcation | *taḥdīd · takhṭīṭ al-ḥudūd* | تحديد . تخطيط الحدود |
| 25 de Mayo aircraft carrier | *ḥāmilat aṭ-ṭāʾirāt khamsa wa ʿishrīn di māyū* | حاملة الطائرات ٢٥ دي مايو |
| demobilization | *tasrīḥ* | تسريح |
| Democratic People's Republic of Korea | *jumhurīyat kūryā ad-dīmuqrāṭīya ash-shaʿbīya* | جمهورية كوريا الديمقراطية الشعبية |
| demolition | *tadmīr · hadm* | تدمير . هدم |
| demolition blasting | *nasf lil-hadm* | نسف للهدم |
| demonstration | *bayān ʿamalī · muẓāhara* | بيان عملي . مظاهرة |
| demoralize | *awhana al-ʿazīma* | أوهن العزيمة |
| demountable bridge | *jisr qābil lil-fakk* | جسر قابل للفك |
| Denmark | *ad-dānmark* | الدانمرك |
| dentistry room | *ghurfat ṭubb al-asnān* | غرفة طب الأسنان |
| Department of Defense | *wizārat ad-difāʿ* | وزارة الدفاع |
| deployment | *nashr · tawzīʿ · intishār* | نشر . توزيع . انتشار |
| deployment area | *minṭaqat intishār* | منطقة انتشار |
| deployment capability | *imkānīyat intishār* | إمكانية انتشار |

depot مستودع . مخزن
*mustawdaʿ · makhzan*
depth charge قذيفة أعماق
*qadhīfat aʿmāq*
depth of penetration عمق التغلغل
*ʿamq at-taghalghal*
DERBV 23B radar رادار « دي ئي اربي ڤ ٢٣ بي »
*rādār dī ī ar bī vī thalātha wa ʿishrīn bī*
derrick crane مرفاع برج الحفر
*mirfāʿ burj al-ḥafr*
Descubierta corvette سفينة حراسة صغيرة « ديسكو بييرتا »
*safīnat ḥirāsa ṣaghīra diskūbyirta*
desert صحراء
*ṣaḥrāʾ*
desert cavalry battalion كتيبة فرسان الصحراء
*katībat fursān aṣ-ṣaḥrāʾ*
deserter هارب من الجندية
*hārib min al-jundīya*
desert guard حرس الصحراء
*ḥaras aṣ-ṣaḥrāʾ*
desert troops جنود الصحراء
*junūd aṣ-ṣaḥrāʾ*
designation تخصيص . تعيين
*takhṣīṣ · taʿyīn*
D'Estienne d'Orves frigate فرقاطة « ديستيين دورڤ »
*firqāṭat distyīn dūrv*
destroy دمر . خرب
*dammara · kharraba*
destroy تدمر . تخرب
*tadammur · takharrub*
destroyer مدمرة
*mudammira*
detachment مفرزة
*faṣl · infiṣāl · mafraza*
detail تفصيل . إسهاب . فريق
*tafṣīl · ishāb · farīq*
detect إكتشف . كشف
*iktishāf · kashf*
detection device وسيلة كشف
*wasīlat kashf*
detection equipment معدات كشف
*muʿaddāt kashf*
detection range مدى الكشف
*mada al-kashf*
detection system نظام كشف
*niẓām kashf*
detector كاشف . مكشاف
*kāshif · mikshāf*

deterrence value ميزّة الردع
*mīzat ar-radʿ*
deterrent رادع
*rādiʿ*
deterrent force قوة الردع
*qūwat ar-radʿ*
detonate فجر . تفجير
*fajjara · tafjīr*
detonating cord سلك التفجير
*silk at-tafjīr*
detonating device وسيلة التفجير
*wasīlat at-tafjīr*
detonation تفجير
*tafjīr*
detonator مفجر . كبسولة تفجير
*mufajjir · kabsūlat tafjīr*
detonator circuit دائرة المفجر
*dāʾirat al-mufajjir*
detonator delay تعويق المفجر
*taʿwīq al-mufajjir*
detour منعطف
*munʿaṭaf*
Detroit engine محرك « ديترويت »
*muḥarrik ditrūwīt*
development aircraft طائرة تطوير
*ṭāʾirat taṭwīr*
DHC-5D transporter طائرة نقل « دي اتش سي ـ ٥ دي »
*ṭāʾirat naql dī itsh sī khamsa dī*
DHC-6 airtransporter طائرة نقل « دي اتش سي ـ ٦
*tāʾirat naql dī itsh sī sitta*
diameter قطر
*quṭr*
dibber weapon أسلحة الحفر
*asliḥat al-ḥafr*
Dicass active sonobuoy طافية صوتية رادارية فعالة « ديكاس »
*ṭāfīya ṣawtīya rādārīya faʿʿāla dikās*
diesel ديزل
*dīzl*
diesel-electric drive إدارة ديزل كهربائية
*idārat dīzl kahrabāʾīya*
diesel-electric submarine غواصة بادارة ديزل كهربائية
*ghawwāṣa bi-idārat dīzl kahrabāʾīya*
diesel engine محرك ديزل
*muḥarrik dīzl*
diesel generator مولد ديزل
*muwallid dīzl*
diesel-powered يعمل بمحرك ديزل
*yaʿmal bi-muḥarrik dīzl*

D

Difar passive sonobuoy طافية صوتية رادارية سلبية « ديفار »
*ṭāfīya sawṭīya rādārīya silbīya dīfār*

dig in (to) تخندق
*takhandaqa*

digital رقمي
*raqmī*

digital computer حاسبة رقمية
*ḥāsiba raqmīya*

digital data link توصيل البيانات الرقمية
*tawṣīl al-bayānāt ar-raqmīya*

digital jamming تشويش رقمي
*tashwīsh raqmī*

3-dimension Multi-Target هدف متعدد ثلاثي الأبعاد
*hadaf mutaʿaddad thullāthī al-abʿād*

dinghy طوف . قارب عريض
*tawf · qārib ʿarīḍ*

dining hall قاعة الطعام
*qāʿat aṭ-ṭaʿām*

dipole ذو قطبين
*dhū quṭbāyn*

dipole emitter مرُسل ثنائي القطب
*mursil thunāʾī al-quṭb*

dipping sonar سونار غمس
*sūnār ghams*

dip point نقطة الميل
*nuqṭat al-mayl*

direct hit إصابة مباشرة
*iṣāba mubāshira*

direction إتجاه . توجيه
*ittijāh · tawjīh*

direction finder مُعين الاتجاه
*muʿayyin al-ittijāh*

direction-finding تعيين الاتجاه
*taʿyīn al-ittijāh*

director aircraft طائرة موجهة
*ṭāʾira muwajjiha*

directors عناصر هوائي اضافية
*ʿanāṣir hawāʾī iḍāfīya*

disarm نزع السلاح . جرد من السلاح
*nazʿ as-silāḥ · jard min as-silāḥ*

disarmed state وضع عدم اصلاء
*waḍʿ ʿadam iṣlāʾ*

disaster كارثة
*kāritha*

disband حل . سرح
*ḥalla · sarraḥa*

discharge فرغ . أعفى . أطلق
*farragha · aʿfā · aṭlaqa*

discharge from army تسريح من الجيش
*tasrīḥ min al-jaysh*

discharge from hospital خروج من المستشفى
*khurūj min al-mustashfa*

disciplinary powers سلطات تأديبية
*sulṭāt taʾdībīya*

discipline ضبط . انضباط
*ḍabṭ · inḍibāṭ*

disease مرض . داء
*maraḍ · dāʾ*

disembark أنزل . فرغ
*anzala · farragha*

disembarked troops جنود مترجلون
*junūd mutarajjalūn*

disengage فصل
*faṣala*

dish antenna هوائي طبقي
*hawāʾī ṭabaqī*

disinfect طهر . أباد
*ṭahhara · abāda*

disinfectant مطهر . مبيد
*muṭahhir · mubīd*

disinfection تطهير . إبادة
*taṭhīr · ibāda*

disinfestation إبادة الحشرات
*ibādat al-ḥasharāt*

disintegration تفتيت . إنحلال
*taftīt · inḥilāl*

dismantle فك
*fakk*

dismiss! اخرج !
*ukhrij*

dismount! انزل !
*inzil*

dispatch إرسال . برقية . رسالة عاجلة
*irsāl · barqīya · risāla ʿājila*

dispatcher مُرسل
*mursil*

dispatch rider ساعٍ راكب
*sāʿin rākib*

dispersion warhead رؤوس حربية منتشرة
*ruʾūs ḥarbīya muntashira*

displacement إزاحة
*izāḥa*

display console خزانة عرض
*khazānat ʿarḍ*

display system نظام عرض
*niẓām ʿarḍ*

disposable load حمل التخلص
*ḥiml at-takhallus*

distortion تشويه . التواء
*tashwīh · iltiwāʾ*
distress signal إشارة استغاثة
*ishārat istighātha*
ditch battle قتال الخنادق
*qitāl al-khanādiq*
dive bombing قذف القنابل أثناء الانقضاض
*qadhf al-qanābil ithnāʾ al-inqiḍāḍ*
dive غطس . غوص . انقضاض
*ghaṭasa · ghawṣ · inqiḍāḍ*
dive limit حدود الانقضاض
*ḥudūd al-inqiḍāḍ*
diver غواص . غطاس
*ghawwāṣ · ghaṭṭās*
diversionary attack هجوم مضلل
*hujūm muḍallil*
diver's suit لباس الغواص
*libās al-ghawwāṣ*
diving depth عمق الغوص
*ʿamq al-ghawṣ*
diving plane مستوى الغوص
*mustawa al-ghawṣ*
division فرقة . قسم
*firqa · qism*
Djibouti جيبوتي
*jībūtī*
DM24 fuse مصهر « دي ام ٢٤ »
*miṣhar dī im arbaʿa wa ʿishrīn*
DM34 fuse مصهر « دي ام ٣٤ »
*miṣhar dī im arbaʿa wa thalāthīn*
DM54 fuse مصهر « دي ام ٥٤ »
*miṣhar dī im arbaʿa wa khamsīn*
DN181 radar رادار « دي ان ١٨١ »
*rādār dī in miʾa wāḥid wa thamāmīn*
DO-27 aircraft طائرة « دي اوه-٢٧ »
*ṭāʾirat dī aw sabʿa wa ʿishrīn*
DO-28 aircraft طائرة « دي اوه-٢٨ »
*ṭāʾirat dī aw thamānya wa ʿishrīn*
DO-28D trainer طائرة تدريب « دي اوه-٢٨ دي »
*ṭāʾirat tadrīb dī aw thamānya wa ʿishrīn dī*
doctor's certificate شهادة طبية
*shahāda ṭubbīya*
documents وثائق . مستندات
*wathāʾiq · mustanadāt*
dogfight اشتباك جوي
*ishtibāk jawwī*
dog handler مدرب كلاب
*mudarrib kilāb*
Dog House radar رادار « دوج هاوس »
*rādār dūg haws*
dog tag صفيحة هوية
*ṣafīḥat hawīya*
Dolfijn submarine غواصة دولفيجن
*ghawwāṣat dūlfijn*
Dolphin helicopter طائرة عمودية « دولفين »
*ṭāʾira ʿamūdīya dūlfīn*
dome قبة
*qubba*
Dominican Republic جمهورية الدومينيكان
*jumhūrīyat ad-dūmīnīkān*
Don-2 radar رادار « دون -٢ »
*rādār dūn ithnayn*
Don Kay radar رادار « دون كيه »
*rādār dūn kayy*
Don ship سفينة « دون »
*safīnat dūn*
doppler beam-sharpening توضيح شعاعي دوپلر
*tawḍīḥ shuʿāʿī dūplir*
Doppler radar رادار « دوپلر »
*rādār dūplir*
dorsal blade aerial هوائي ظهري ريشي
*hawāʾī ẓahrī rīshī*
double action pistol مسدس مزدوج الفعل
*musaddas muzdawij al-fiʿl*
double march! هرول !
*harwil*
double-slotted flap جناح إضافي -مزدوج الشقوق
*janāḥ iḍāfī muzdawij ash-shuqūq*
double-stage مزدوج المرحلة
*muzdawij al-marhala*
Douglas (Co) شركة دوجلاس
*sharikat dūglās*
Dove airtransporter طائرة نقل « دوف »
*ṭāʾirat naql dūv*
down-range مدى تنازلي
*mada tanāzulī*
dozer blade نصل التراكتور
*naṣl at-trāktūr*
DP gun مدفع « دي پي »
*midfaʿ dī pī*
DP gun turret برج مدفع « دي پي »
*burj midfaʿ dī pī*
draft غاطس السفينة
*ghāṭis as-safīna*

drag chute مجرى السحب
*majra as-saḥb*
Dragonfly aircraft طائرة « دراجونفلاى »
*ṭā'irat drāgūnflāyy*
Dragon missile صاروخ « دراجون »
*ṣārūkh drāgūn*
Draken fighter-bomber قاذفة مقاتلة « دراكن »
*qādhifa muqātila drākan*
Draken submarine غواصة « دراكن »
*ghawwāṣat drākan*
draught غاطس السفينة
*ghātis as-safīna*
draw-bridge جسر متحرك
*jisr mutaḥarrik*
draw off fire نيران الانسحاب
*nīrān al-insiḥāb*
DRB 31 radar رادار « دي أربي ٣١ »
*rādār dī ār bī wāḥid wa thalāthīn*
DRBC 31 radar رادار « دي أربي سي ٣١ »
*rādār dī ār bī sī wāḥid wa thalāthīn*
DRBC 32 radar رادار « دي أربي سي ٣٢ »
*rādār dī ār bī sī ithnayn wa thalāthīn*
DRBC 32A FCS نظام السيطرة على الرمي « دي أربي سي ٣٢ ايه »
*niẓām as-sayṭara ʿalar-ramī dī ār bī sī ithnayn wa thalāthīn ayy*
DRBI 10 radar رادار « دي أربي أي ١٠ »
*rādār dī ār bī āyy ʿashara*
DRBI 10D radar رادار « دي أربي أي ١٠ دي »
*rādār dī ār bī āyy ʿashara dī*
DRBN 32 radar رادار « دي أربي ان ٣٢ »
*rādār dī ār bī in ithnayn wa thalāthīn*
DRBR 32C radar رادار « دي أربي أر ٣٢ سي »
*rādār dī ār bī ār ithnayn wa thalāthīn sī*
DRBR 51 radar رادار « دي أربي أر ٥١ »
*rādār dī ār bī ār wāḥid wa khamsīn*
DRBV 20 radar رادار « دي أربي ڤي ٢٠ »
*rādār dī ār bī vī ʿishrīn*
DRBV 20C radar رادار « دي أربي ڤي ٢٠ سي »
*rādār dī ār bī vī ʿishrīn sī*
DRBV 22D radar رادار « دي أربي ڤي ٢٢ دي »
*rādār dī ār bī vī ithnayn wa ʿishrīn dī*
DRBV 23C radar رادار « دي أربي ڤي ٢٣ سي »
*rādār dī ār bī vī thalātha wa ʿishrīn sī*
DRBV 50 radar رادار « دي أربي ڤي ٥٠ »
*rādār dī ār bī vī khamsīn*
Dreadnought submarine غواصة « دريدنوت »
*ghawwāṣat drīdnūt*
dressed overall تراصف كامل
*tarāṣuf kāmil*
drill تدريب . مثقب
*tadrīb · mithqab*
drill (to) درّب
*darraba*
drill instruction تدريب عملي
*tadrīb ʿamalī*
drill movement حركة التدريب
*ḥarikat at-tadrīb*
drill technique أسلوب التدريب
*uslūb at-tadrīb*
drinking device أداة الشرب
*adāt as-shurb*
driver سائق
*sā'iq*
driver training vehicle سيارة تدريب السائقين
*sayyārat tadrīb as-sā'iqīn*
drive sprocket مسننة سلسلة الادارة
*musannanat silsilat al-idāra*
drooped leading edge حافة أمامية ساقطة
*ḥāfa amāmīya sāqiṭa*
drooping aileron جنيح متدلي
*junayḥ mutadallī*
dropping angle زاوية القذف . زاوية السقوط
*zāwīyat al-qadhf · zāwīyat as-suqūṭ*
dropping zone منطقة السقوط
*minṭaqat as-suqūṭ*
drop tank خزان الاسقاط
*khazzān al-isqāṭ*
DRUA 23 radar رادار « دي أريو ايه ٢٣ »
*rādār dī ār yū ayy thalātha wa ʿishrin*
drum magazine خزنة ذخيرة اسطوانية
*khazanat dhakhīra usṭuwānīya*
Drum Tilt radar رادار « درُم تيلت »
*rādār drum tilt*
Druze الدروز
*ad-durūz*
DShK-38 machine gun مدفع رشاش « دي إس اتش كيه ـ ٣٨ »
*rashshāsh dī is itsh kayy - thamānya wa thalāthīn*
DShKM machine-gun رشاش دي إس اتش كيه إم
*rashshāsh dī is itsh kayy im*

| | |
|---|---|
| DSUV 22 sonar<br>*sūnār dī īs yū vī ithnayn wa ʿishrīn* | سونار « دي اس يو ڤي ٢٢ » |
| dual capability<br>*imkānīya muzdawija* | إمكانية مزدوجة |
| dual-control<br>*qiyāda muzdawija*<br>*muzdawija* | قيادة مزدوجة |
| dual-control trainer<br>*ṭāʾirat tadrīb bi-qiyāda muzdawija* | طائرة تدريب بقيادة مزدوجة |
| dual guidance<br>*tawjīh muzdawij* | توجيه مزدوج |
| dual trainer<br>*ṭāʾirat tadrīb muzdawija* | طائرة تدريب مزدوجة |
| Dubai<br>*dubayy* | دبي |
| Dum-Dum bullet<br>*raṣāṣa dam-dam* | رصاصة « دم ـ دم » |
| dummy bomb<br>*qunbulat tamrīn* | قنبلة تمرين |
| Duora patrol craft<br>*safīnat ḥirāsat sawāḥil diyūra* | سفينة حراسة سواحل « ديورا » |
| duplexer<br>*jihāz irsāl wa istiqbāl* | جهاز إرسال واستقبال |
| Durandal ASM<br>*ṣārūkh jaww-saṭḥ dūrāndāl* | صاروخ جو ـ سطح « دور اندال » |
| duty<br>*wājib · muhimma* | واجب . مهمة |
| duty officer<br>*aḍ-ḍābiṭ al-masʾūl* | الضابط المسؤول |
| DUUX 2 sonar<br>*sūnār dī yū yū iks ithnayn* | سونار « دي يو يو اكس ٢ » |
| dynamite<br>*dīnāmīt* | ديناميت |
| dysentery<br>*ishāl · dīzanṭārīya* | إسهال . ديزنطاريا |

E

E-1 submarine غواصة « ئي ـ ١ »
*ghawwāṣat ī wāḥid*
E-II submarine غواصة « ئي ـ ٢ »
*ghawwāṣat ī ithnayn*
E-2 aircraft طائرة « ئي ـ ٢ »
*ṭā'irat ī ithnayn*
E-2C Hawkeye aircraft طائرة « ئي ـ ٢ سي هوكاي »
*ṭā'irat ī ithnayn sī hūkāyy*
E-3A AWACS طائرة أواكس ئي ـ ٣ ايه
*ṭā'irat awaks ī thalātha ayy*
E-4B aircraft طائرة « ئي ـ ٤ بي »
*ṭā'irat ī arbaʿa bī*
E-6A aircraft طائرة « ئي ـ ٦ ايه »
*ṭā'irat ī sitta ayy*
EA-6B aircraft طائرة « ئي ايه ـ ٦ بي »
*ṭā'irat ī ayy sitta bī*
Eagle aircraft طائرة « إيجل »
*ṭā'irat īgl*
early warning انذار مبكر
*indhār mubakkir*
early warning system نظام الانذار المبكر
*niẓām al-indhār al-mubakkir*
earphones مسماع الاذن
*mismāʿ al-udhun*
earth bank قاعدة ترابية
*qāʿida turābīya*
earth penetrator warhead رأس قديفة مخترق للأرض
*ra's qadhīfa mukhtariq lil-arḍ*
East شرق
*sharq*
Eastern Command القيادة الشرقية
*al-qiyāda ash-sharqīya*
East Germany المانيا الشرقية
*almānya ash-sharqīya*
easygrip friction إحتكاك سهل المسك
*iḥtikāk sahl al-mask*
easy scanning مسح هين
*masḥ hayyin*
eavesdropping إختلاس السمع
*ikhtilās as-samʿ*
EC-130 air transporter طائرة نقل « ئي سي ـ ١٣٠ »
*ṭā'irat naql ī sī mi'a wa thalathīn*
EC-135N aircraft طائرة « ئي سي ـ ١٣٥ إن »
*ṭā'irat ī sī mi'a wa khamsa wa thalāthīn in*
echelon نسق
*nasaq*
echo-sounding سبر بالصدى
*sabr biṣ-ṣada*
Echo II submarine غواصة « ايكو ٢ »
*ghawwāṣat ikū ithnayn*
ECM dome قبة رادارية للتدابير الالكترونية المضادة
*qubba radarīya lit-tadābīr al-iliktrūnīya al-muḍādda*
ECM-resistant مقاومة التدابير المضادة الالكترونية
*muqāwim lit-tadābīr al-muḍādda al-iliktrūnīya*
Ecuador الاكوادور
*al-ikwādūr*
Ecuadorean إكوادورى
*ikwādūrī*
Ecureuil helicopter طائرة عمودية « إكورايه »
*ṭā'ira ʿamūdīya ikūrayy*
EDO sonar سونار « ئي دي اوه »
*sūnār ī dī aw*
EE-3 armoured car عربة مدرعة « ئي ئي ـ ٣ »
*ʿaraba mudarraʿa ī ī thalātha*
EE-9 Cascavel armoured car عربة مدرعة « ئي ئي ـ ٩ » كاسكاقل
*ʿaraba mudarraʿa ī ī tisʿa kaskavīl*
EE-11 armoured car عربة مدرعة « ئي ئي ـ ١١ »
*ʿaraba mudarraʿa ī ī aḥada ʿashar*

|  |  |  |
|---|---|---|
| EF-111 aircraft | *ṭāʾirat ī if miʾa wa aḥada ʿashar* | طائرة « ئي اف ـ ١١١ » |
| effective ceiling | *al-irtifāʿ al-aqṣa al-faʿʿāl* | الأرتفاع الأقصى الفعال |
| effective range | *al-mada al-muʾaththir* | المدى المؤثر |
| efflux | *ghāzāt ad-dafʿ aṣ-ṣārūkhī* | غازات الدفع الصاروخي |
| Egg Bowl radar | *rādār ig būl* | رادار « ايج بول » |
| Egg Cup radar | *rādār ig kap* | رادار « ايج كاپ » |
| Egypt | *miṣr* | مصر |
| Egyptian | *miṣrī* | مصري |
| EH-60A helicopter | *ṭāʾira ʿamūdīya ī itsh sittīn ayy* | طائرة عمودية « ئي اتش ـ ٦٠ ايه » |
| EH-101 helicopter | *ṭāʾira ʿamūdīya ī itsh miʾa wa wāḥid* | طائرة عمودية « ئي اتش ـ ١٠١ » |
| eject | *yaqdhif* | يقذف |
| ejection seat | *maqʿad qadhfī* | مقعد قذفي |
| ELAC sonar | *sūnār ī il ayy sī* | سونار « ئي ال ايه سي » |
| elastic cradle | *sarīr marin* | سرير مرن |
| elastomer products | *muntajāt ilastūmīr* | منتجات إلاستومير |
| electrical connections | *tawṣīlāt kahrabāʾīya* | توصيلات كهربائية |
| electrical firing socket | *miqbas iṭlāq an-nār al-kahrabāʾī* | مقبس اطلاق النار الكهربائي |
| electrical generator | *muwallid kahrabāʾī* | مولد كهربائي |
| electrically operated | *mudār kahrabāʾīyan* | مدار كهربائياً |
| electrically propelled | *madfūʿ kahrabāʾīyan* | مدفوع كهربائياً |
| electrically signalled controls | *ḥākimāt bi-ishārāt kahrabāʾīya* | حاكمات باشارات كهربائية |
| electrical signal | *ishāra kahrabāʾīya* | إشارة كهربائية |
| electric battery | *baṭṭārīya kahrabāʾīya* | بطارية كهربائية |
| electric motor | *muḥarrik kahrabāʾī* | محرك كهربائي |
| electric powered | *mudār bil-kahrabāʾ* | مدار بالكهرباء |
| electromagnetic proximity fuse | *ṣimāma taqārubīya kahrū-mughnaṭīsīya* | صمامة تقاربية كهرومغنطيسية |
| electromagnetic radiation | *ishʿāʿ kahrū-mughnaṭīsī* | إشعاع كهرومغنطيسي |
| electromagnetic sensor | *jihāz iḥsās kahrū-mughnaṭīsī* | جهاز إحساس كهرومغنطيسي |
| electro-magnetic spectrum | *ṭayf kahrū-mughnaṭīsī* | طيف كهرومغنطيسي |
| electro-magnetic suitcase | *ḥaqība kahrū-mughnaṭīsīya* | حقيبة كهرومغنطيسية |
| electromagnetic wavelength | *ṭūl mawjī kahrū-mughnaṭīsī* | طول موجي كهرومغنطيسي |
| electron beam | *ḥuzma iliktrūnīya* | حزمة إلكترونية |
| electronic | *iliktrūnī* | الكترونية |
| electronic counter-measures | *tadābīr muḍādda iliktrūnīya* | تدابير مضادة إلكترونية |
| electronic ear | *udhun iliktrūnīya* | أذن إلكترونية |
| electronic eye | *ʿayn iliktrūnīya* | عين إلكترونية |
| electronic image intensifier | *mukaththif shiddat aṣ-ṣūra al-iliktrūnī* | مكثف شدة الصورة الالكتروني |
| electronic intelligence | *istikhbār iliktrūnī* | إستخبار إلكتروني |
| electronic jamming | *tashwīsh iliktrūnī* | تشويش إلكتروني |
| electronic map display | *ʿarḍ kharāʾiṭ iliktrūnī* | عرض خرائط إلكتروني |
| electronics | *iliktrūnīyāt · ʿilm al-iliktrūnīyāt* | إلكترونيات . علم الالكترونيات |
| electronic scanning | *masḥ iliktrūnī* | مسح إلكتروني |
| electronic support | *daʿm iliktrūnī* | دعم إلكتروني |
| electronic support measures | *ijrāʾāt tadʿīm iliktrūnī* | إجراءات تدعيم إلكتروني |
| electronic surveillance measures | *ijrāʾāt istiṭlāʿ iliktrūnī* | إجراءات إستطلاع إلكتروني |

E

electronic warfare حرب إلكترونية
*ḥarb iliktrūnīya*
electronic-warfare aircraft طائرة حرب إلكترونية
*ṭāʾirat ḥarb iliktrūnīya*
electro-optical seeker باحث كهربائي بصري
*bāḥith kahrabāʾī baṣarī*
elevating frame إطار الرفع
*iṭār ar-rafʿ*
elevation إرتفاع . زاوية الارتفاع
*irtifāʿ · zāwīyat al-irtifāʿ*
elevation sensor جهاز الاحساس بالارتفاع
*jihāz al-iḥsās bil-irtifāʿ*
elevator مصعد . سُكان الارتفاع
*miṣʿad · sukkān al-irtifāʿ*
elevon سطح رامغ عاطف
*saṭḥ rāfiʿ ʿāṭif*
ELF antenna هوائي « إلف »
*hawāʾī ilf*
Elint إستخبار إلكتروني
*istikhbār iliktrūnī*
El Salvador السالفادور
*al-salvādūr*
Elta 200 1B radar رادار « إلتا ٢٠٠ ١ بي »
*rādār ilta miʾatayn wāḥid bī*
Elta MN-53 ECM تدابير مضادة إلكترونية « إلتا ام ان ـ ٥٣ »
*tadābīr muḍādda iliktrūnīya ilta im in thalātha wa khamsīn*
EMB-121 aircraft طائرة « ئي ام بي ـ ١٢١ »
*ṭāʾirat ī im bī miʾa wa wāḥid wa ʿishrīn*
EMB-326 aircraft طائرة « ئي ام بي ـ ٣٢٦ »
*ṭāʾira ī im bī thalātha miʾa wa sitta wa ʿishrīn*
embarkation ركوب . تحميل
*rukūb · taḥmīl*
embarkation leave إذن ركوب
*idhn rukūb*
Embraer (Co) شركة إمبراير
*sharikat imbrayyar*
emergency إضطراري . طارىء
*iḍṭirārī · ṭāriʾ*
emergency brake مكبح الطوارىء
*mikbaḥ aṭ-ṭawāriʾ*
emergency drop إسقاط الطوارىء
*isqāṭ aṭ-ṭawāriʾ*
emergency treatment علاج طارىء
*ʿilāj ṭāriʾ*
emission إصدار . إبتعاث
*iṣdār · ibtiʿāth*
empty case ظرف الخرطوشة
*ẓarf al-kharṭūsha*
empty equipped weight الوزن المجهز فارغاً
*al-wazn al-mujahhaz fārighan*
encircle أحاط . طوق
*aḥāṭa · ṭawaqa*
encounter واجه . مجابهة
*wājih · mujābaha*
enemy خصم . عدو
*khaṣm · ʿadūw*
enemy action فعل العدو
*fiʿl al-ʿadūw*
enemy aircraft طائرة معادية
*ṭāʾira muʿādīya*
enemy air space مجال جوي معادي
*majāl jawwī muʿādī*
enemy forces قوات العدو
*qūwāt al-ʿadūw*
enemy-held في قبضة العدو
*fī-qabḍat al-ʿadūw*
enemy-introduced interference تداخل من جانب العدو
*tadākhul min jānib al-adūw*
enemy radar رادار العدو
*rādār al-ʿadūw*
energy طاقة . نشاط
*ṭāqa · nashāṭ*
engagement إشتباك
*ishtibāk*
engine محرك . قاطرة
*muḥarrik · qāṭira*
engine compartment حجرة المحرك
*ḥujrat al-muḥarrik*
engineer مهندس
*muhandis*
engineer vehicle سيارة المهندسين
*sayyārat al-muhandisīn*
engine harmonics توافقات المحرك
*tawāfuqāt al-muḥarrik*
engine room غرفة المحركات
*ghurfat al-muḥarrikāt*
engine silencing system نظام خفت صوت المحرك
*niẓām khaft ṣawt al-muḥarrik*
English Channel بحر المانش . القنال الانجليزي
*baḥr al-mānsh · al-qanāh al-inglīzī*
Enhanced Eagle aircraft طائرة ايجال المحسنة
*ṭāʾirat īgl al-muḥassana*

enhanced image — صورة محسنة
*ṣūra muḥasanna*

enlist — جند . تجند
*janada · tajannada*

Enrico Toti submarine — غواصة « إنريكو توتي »
*ghawwāṣat inrīkū tūtī*

ensign — شارة . راية
*shāra · rāya*

Enterprise carrier — حاملة « إنتربرايز »
*ḥāmilat intarbrāyz*

entrainment area — منطقة ركوب القطار أو تحميله
*minṭaqat rukūb al-qiṭār aw taḥmīluh*

entrenched — مخندق . محصن
*mukhandaq · muḥaṣṣan*

envelopment — إلتفاف . تغليف
*iltifāf · taghlīf*

envoy — مبعوث . رسول
*mabʿūth · rusūl*

epidemic — وباء
*wabāʾ*

epoch — عصر . حقبة
*ʿaṣr · ḥiqba*

Epsilon aircraft — طائرة « إبسيلون »
*ṭāʾirat ibsīlūn*

equipment — عتاد . معدات
*iʿtād · muʿaddāt*

equipment belt — حزام المعدات
*ḥizām al-muʿaddāt*

ERC-90 armoured vehicle — سيارة مدرعة « ئي آر سي ـ ٩٠ »
*sayyāra mudarraʿa ī ār sī tisʿīn*

erector — عامل تركيب
*ʿāmil tarkīb*

erector launcher — معدات إطلاق رافعة
*muʿaddāt iṭlāq rāfiʿa*

Ericsson Giraffe radar — رادار إريكسون جيراف
*rādār iriksūn jirāf*

escape chute — مجرى الهروب
*majra al-hurūb*

escape hatch — كوة النجاة
*kuwwat an-najāh*

escape rocket — صاروخ افلات
*ṣārūkh iflāt*

escort — حرس . حراسة . رافق
*ḥaras · ḥirāsa · rāfiq*

escort carrier — حاملة حراسة
*ḥāmilat ḥirāsa*

escort cruiser — طرادة للحراسة
*ṭarrāda lil-ḥirāsa*

escort duty — مهمة الحراسة
*muhimmat al-ḥirāsa*

escort ship — سفينة الحراسة
*safīnat al-ḥirāsa*

ESD navigational radar — رادار ملاحي ئي اس دي
*rādār mallāḥī ī is dī*

Esmeralda corvette — سفينة حراسة صغيرة « إسميرالدا »
*safīnat ḥirāsa ṣaghīra ismīrāldā*

ESM mast — صاري « ئي اس ام »
*ṣāri ī is im*

España corvette — سفينة حراسة صغيرة « اسبانيا »
*safīnat ḥirāsa ṣaghīra isbanya*

espionage — تجسس . جاسوسية
*tajassus · jāsūsīya*

establish contact — يحقق الاتصال
*yuḥaqqiq al-ittiṣāl*

establishment — إقامه . تشييد . مؤسسة
*iqāma · tasdīd · muʾassasa*

Etendard fighter — طائرة مقاتلة « إتيندارد »
*ṭāʾira muqātila itandārd*

Ethan Allen submarine — غواصة « ايثان ألن »
*ghawwāsat īthān alan*

Ethiopia — إثيوبيا
*ithyūbya*

Euromissile — صاروخ « يوروميسايل »
*ṣārūkh yūrūmisāyl*

evacuation — إخلاء . إجلاء
*ikhlāʾ · ijlāʾ*

evacuation system — نظام الاخلاء
*niẓām al-ikhlāʾ*

Evader ICBM — صاروخ بالستي عابر للقارات « إيڤايدر »
*ṣārūkh bālistī ʿābir lil-qārāt ivaydar*

evade the enemy — تفادى العدو
*tafāda al-ʿadūw*

evasive action — فعل التفادي
*fiʿl at-tafādī*

everyday dress — بزة معتادة
*bizza muʿtāda*

EW device — وسيلة انذار مبكر
*wasīlat indhār mubakkir*

EW operator — مُشغل الانذار المبكر
*mushaghghil al-indhār al-mubakkir*

EW provisions — تدابير الانذار المبكر
*tadābīr al-indhār al-mubakkir*

EWS905 ECM — تدابير مضادة إلكترونية لنظام الانذار المبكر « ئي دبليو اس ٩٠٥ »
*tadābīr muḍādda iliktrūnīya li-niẓām al-indhār al-mubakkir tisʿa miʾa wa khamsa*

E

examination فحص . إختبار
*faḥṣ · ikhtibār*
exercise تدريب . مناورة عسكرية
*tadrīb · munāwara ʿaskarīya*
exhaust gases غازات العادم
*ghāzāt al-ʿādim*
exhaust outlet مخرج العادم
*makhraj al-ʿādim*
Exocet MM38 missile صاروخ « إكسوست إم إم ٣٨ »
*ṣārūkh iksūsit im im thamānya wa thalāthīn*
Exocet MM40 missile صاروخ « اكسوست إم إم ٤٠ »
*ṣārūkh iksūsit im im arbaʿīn*
Exocet SM39 missile صاروخ « اكسوست اس ام ٣٩ »
*ṣārūkh iksūsit is im tisʿa wa thalathīn*
Exocet SSM صاروخ سطح ـ سطح « اكسوست »
*ṣārūkh saṭḥ-saṭḥ iksūsit*
expedition حملة
*ḥamla*
explosion إنفجار
*infijār*
explosive bolt مسامير متفجرة
*masāmīr mutafajjira*
explosive charge شحنة متفجرة
*shaḥna mutafajjira*
exposed position موضع مكشوف
*mawḍiʿ makshūf*
ex-serviceman محارب قديم
*muḥārib qadīm*
extended foil جنيح ممتد
*junayḥ mumtadd*
extended-range guided projectile قذيفة موجهة ذات مدى بعيد
*qadhīfa muwajjaha dhāt mada baʿīd*
extended-range sub-calibre projectile قذيفة مصغرة العيار ذات مدى بعيد
*qadhīfa muṣaghgharat al-ʿiyār dhāt mada baʿīd*
external inspection تفتيش ظاهري
*taftīsh ẓāhirī*
external supply إمداد خارجي
*imdād kharijī*
extractor نازع . مقتلع . منزعة
*nāziʿ · muqtaliʿ · minzaʿa*
extraneous data بيانات خارجية
*bayānāt khārijīya*
extrapolate إستكمل بالاستقراء أو القياس
*istakmil bil-istiqrāʾ aw al-qiyās*
Eyeball sensor جهاز احساس أيبول
*jihāz iḥsās āybūl*
Eye Bowl radar رادار « أيباول »
*rādār āybūl*
eyes left! انظر يساراً
*unẓur yasaran*
eyes right! انظر يميناً
*unẓur yamīnan*

# F

F

F-class submarine غواصة طراز « اف »
*ghawwāṣa ṭirāz if*
F-1 fighter طائرة مقاتلة « اف ـ ١ »
*ṭāʾira muqātila if wāḥid*
F-1C fighter طائرة مقاتلة « اف ١ ـ سي »
*ṭāʾira muqātila if wāḥid sī*
F1 sub-machine gun رشاش قصير « اف ١ »
*rashshāsh qaṣīr if wāhid*
F-4 fighter طائرة مقاتلة « اف ـ ٤ »
*ṭāʾira muqātila if arbaʿa*
F-4G aircraft طائرة « اف ـ ٤ جي »
*ṭāʾira muqātila if arbaʿa jī*
F-5E fighter طائرة مقاتلة « اف ـ ٥ ئي »
*ṭāʾira muqātila if khamsa ī*
F-5F fighter طائرة مقاتلة « اف ـ ٥ اف »
*ṭāʾira muqātila if khamsa if*
F-6 fighter طائرة مقاتلة « اف ـ ٦ »
*ṭāʾira muqātila if sitta*
F-6 bis fighter طائرة مقاتلة « اف ـ ٦ بيس »
*ṭāʾira muqātila if sitta bis*
F-7 fighter طائرة مقاتلة « اف ـ ٧ »
*ṭāʾira muqātila if sabʿa*
F-8 fighter طائرة مقاتلة « اف ـ ٨ »
*ṭāʾira muqātila if thamānya*
F-11 bomber طائرة قاذفة « اف ـ ١١ »
*ṭāʾira qadhifa if aḥada ʿashar*
F-14 fighter طائرة مقاتلة « اف ـ ١٤ »
*ṭāʾira muqātila if arbaʿata ʿashar*
F-14A aircraft طائرة « اف ـ ١٤ ايه »
*ṭāʾira if arbaʿata ʿashar ayy*
F-15 Eagle aircraft طائرة « اف ـ ١٥ ايجال »
*ṭāʾira if khamsata ʿashar īgl*
F-15E fighter طائرة مقاتلة « اف ـ ١٥ ئي »
*ṭāʾira muqātila if khamsata ʿashar ī*
F-16 aircraft طائرة « اف ـ ١٦ »
*ṭāʾirat if sittata ʿashar*
F-16E fighter طائرة مقاتلة « اف ـ ١٦ ئي »
*ṭāʾira muqātila if sittata ʿashar ī*
F-16XL fighter طائرة مقاتلة « اف ـ ١٦ اكس إل »
*ṭāʾira muqātila if sittata ʿashar iks il*
F-18 fighter طائرة مقاتلة « اف ـ ١٨ »
*ṭāʾira muqātila if thamānyata ʿashar*
F-20 fighter طائرة مقاتلة « اف ـ ٢٠ »
*ṭāʾira muqātila if ʿishrīn*
F-27 airtransporter طائرة نقل « إف ـ ٢٧ »
*ṭāʾirat naql if sabʿa wa ʿishrīn*
F-27 600 aircraft طائرة « اف ـ ٢٧ ٦٠٠ »
*ṭāʾirat if sabʿa wa ʿishrīn sitt miʾa*
F-53 fighter طائرة مقاتلة « اف ـ ٥٣ »
*ṭāʾira muqātila if thalatha wa khamsīn*
F-70 fighter طائرة مقاتلة « اف ـ ٧٠ »
*ṭāʾira muqātila if sabʿīn*
F-100 aircraft طائرة « اف ـ ١٠٠ »
*ṭāʾirat if miʾa*
F100-PW-100 turbofan مروحة تربينية « اف ١٠٠ ـ بي دبليو ـ ١٠٠ »
*mirwaḥa turbīnīya if miʾa pī dablyū miʾa*
F-101 fighter طائرة مقاتلة « اف ١٠١ »
*ṭāʾira muqātila if miʾa wa wāḥid*
F103 engine محرك « اف ١٠٣ »
*muḥarrik if miʾa wa thalātha*
F-104 fighter طائرة مقاتلة « اف ـ ١٠٤ »
*ṭāʾira muqātila if miʾa wa arbaʿa*
F-104S fighter طائرة مقاتلة « اف ١٠٤ اس »
*ṭāʾira muqātila if miʾa wa arbaʿa is*
F-106 interceptor طائرة اعتراض « اف ـ ١٠٦ »
*ṭāʾirat iʿtirāḍ if miʾa wa sitta*

|  |  |
|---|---|
| F-2000 frigate<br>*firqāṭat if alfayn* | فرقاطة « اف ـ ٢٠٠٠ » |
| F/A-18A Hornet fighter<br>*ṭāʾira muqātila if ayy thamānyata ʿashar hūrnīt* | طائرة مقاتلة « اف/ايه ـ ١٨ ايه هورنيت » |
| Fairchild (Co)<br>*sharikat fīrtshāyld* | شركة فيرتشايلد |
| fairing<br>*ghiṭāʾ insiyābī* | غطاء انسيابي |
| Falcon aircraft<br>*ṭāʾirat falkūn* | طائرة « فالكون » |
| fall back<br>*taqahqara · tarājaʿa* | تقهقر . تراجعَ |
| fall in!<br>*tajammaʿ* | « تجمع ! » |
| fall out!<br>*tafarraq* | « تفرق ! » |
| false alarm<br>*indhār zāʾif* | إنذار زائف |
| false target<br>*hadaf zāʾif* | هدف زائف |
| FAMAS rifle<br>*bunduqīyat if ayy im ayy is* | بندقية « اف ايه ام ايه إس » |
| Fan Song-E radar<br>*rādār fān sūng ī* | رادار « فان سونج ـ ئي » |
| Fan Tail radar<br>*rādār fān tayl* | رادار « فان تيل » |
| Fantan A fighter<br>*ṭāʾira muqātila fāntān ayy* | طائرة مقاتلة « فانتان ايه » |
| Farmer fighter<br>*ṭāʾira muqātila fārmar* | طائرة مقاتلة « فارمر » |
| Farragut destroyer<br>*mudammirat fārāgūt* | مدمرة « فاراجوت » |
| fast attack craft<br>*zawraq hujūm sarīʿ* | زورق هجوم سريع |
| fast attack unit<br>*wiḥdat inqiḍāḍ sarīʿ* | وحدة انقضاض سريع |
| fast patrol craft<br>*safīnat khafr sawāḥil sarīʿa* | سفينة خفر سواحل سريعة |
| fast strike craft<br>*zawraq hujūm sarīʿ* | زورق هجوم سريع |
| fatal accident<br>*ḥādith mumayyit* | حادث مميت |
| FB-111 bomber<br>*ṭāʾira qādhifa if bī miʾa wa aḥada ʿashar* | طائرة قاذفة « اف بي ـ ١١١ » |
| FCS sonar<br>*sūnār if sī is* | سونار « اف سي اس » |
| Fearless ship<br>*safīnat fīrlis* | سفينة « فيرلس » |

|  |  |
|---|---|
| Fencer aircraft<br>*ṭāʾirat fīnsar* | طائرة « فينسر » |
| Feniks sonar<br>*sūnār finiks* | سونار فنيكس |
| Fero-Z 13 gunsight<br>*mihdāf midfaʿ fīrū thalāthata ʿashar* | مهداف مدفع « فيرو ـ زد ١٣ » |
| Ferranti (Co)<br>*sharikat firāntī* | شركة فرانتي |
| Ferret scout car<br>*sayyārat istiṭlāʿ firit* | سيارة استطلاع « فريت » |
| ferry mission<br>*baʿtha ʿubūr* | بعثة عبور |
| ferry range<br>*mada al-ʿabūr* | مدى العبور |
| Festbrucke Spans for flooding bridge<br>*bāʿāt fistbruka lil-jusūr al-ʿāʾima* | باعات « فستبروكا » للجسور العائمة |
| fever<br>*hummā* | حمّى |
| FFV 890C rifle<br>*bunduqīyat if if vī thamāni miʾa wa tisʿīn sī* | بندقية « اف اف ڤي ٨٩٠ سي » |
| FH-70 howitzer<br>*midfaʿ hāwitsar if itsh sabʿīn* | مدفع هاوتزر « اف إتش ـ ٧٠ » |
| Fiat (Co)<br>*sharikat fīyāt* | شركة فيات |
| Fiat diesel<br>*dīzl fīyāt* | ديزل فيات |
| fibreglass<br>*zujāj līfī* | زجاج ليفي |
| Fiddler fighter<br>*ṭāʾira muqātila fidlar* | طائرة مقاتلة « فيدلر » |
| field ambulance<br>*sayyārat insʿāf al-maydān* | سيارة إسعاف الميدان |
| field cable<br>*kabl al-maydān* | كبل الميدان |
| field conditions<br>*ẓurūf al-maydān* | ظروف الميدان |
| field dress<br>*libās al-maydān* | لباس الميدان |
| field dressing<br>*ḍimādat maydān* | ضمادة ميدان |
| field exercise<br>*tadrīb maydānī* | تدريب ميداني |
| field fortifications<br>*taḥṣīnāt al-maydān* | تحصينات الميدان |
| field gun<br>*mifdaʿ al-maydān* | مدفع الميدان |

field hospital مستشفى الميدان
*mustashfa al-maydān*

field hygiene صحية الميدان
*ṣiḥḥīyat al-maydān*

field kitchen مطبخ الميدان
*maṭbakh al-maydān*

field manual كتاب الميدان
*kitāb al-maydān*

field marshal مشير
*mushīr*

field mine لغم الميدان
*lughm al-maydān*

field of battle ساحة المعركة
*sāḥat al-maʿraka*

field officer ضابط ميدان
*ḍābiṭ maydān*

field of vision مجال النظر
*majāl an-naẓar*

field station مركز ميداني
*markaz maydānī*

field telephone هاتف الميدان
*hātif al-maydān*

fight قتال . صراع
*qitāl · ṣirāʿ*

fighter aircraft طائرة مقاتلة
*ṭāʾira muqātila*

fighter/bomber طائرة مقاتلة/قاذفة
*ṭāʾira muqātila qādhifa*

fighter command قيادة المقاتلات
*qiyādat al-muqātilāt*

fighter squadron سرب مقاتلات
*sirb muqātilāt*

fighting capability إمكانيات قتالية
*imkānīyāt qitālīya*

fighting efficiency قدرة قتالية
*qudra qitālīya*

fighting elements عناصر قتالية
*ʿanāṣir qitālīya*

fighting equipment معدات قتالية
*muʿaddāt qitālīya*

Fighting Falcon fighter طائرة مقاتلة « فايتنج فالكون »
*ṭāʾira muqātila fāyting falkūn*

fighting machine آلة مقاتلة
*ālat muqātila*

fighting strength ملاك القتال
*milāk al-qitāl*

FIM-92A SAM صاروخ سطح ـ جو « اف أي ام ـ ٩٢ ايه »
*ṣārūkh saṭḥ-jaww if āyy im ithnayn wa tisʿīn ayy*

fin زعنفة . جنيح مجموعة الذيل
*ziʿnifa · junayḥ · majmūʿat adh-dhayl*

fin cap غطاء الزعنفة
*ghiṭāʾ az-ziʿnifa*

fine wire سلك دقيق
*silk daqīq*

Finland فنلندة
*finlanda*

Finnish فنلندي
*finlandī*

fin rocket صاروخ ذو جنيحات
*ṣārūkh dhu junayḥāt*

fin-stabilized موازن بجنيحات
*muwāzin bi-junayḥat*

fire رمي . نار
*ramī · nār*

fire and forget أطلق وتناسى
*aṭliq wa tanāsa*

fire-and-update إطلق وجدد
*aṭliq wa jaddid*

firearms أسلحة نارية
*asliḥa nārīya*

Firebar aircraft طائرة « فايربار »
*ṭāʾirat fāyrbār*

Fire Can radar رادار « فايركان »
*rādār fāyrkān*

fire control السيطرة على الرمي
*as-sayṭara ʿalar-ramī*

fire-control computer كومبيوتر السيطرة على الرمي
*kumbyūtar as-sayṭara ʿalar-ramī*

fire control equipment معدات السيطرة على الرمي
*muʿaddāt as-sayṭara ʿalar-ramī*

fire-control radar رادار السيطرة على الرمي
*rādār as-sayṭara ʿalar-ramī*

fire-control sonar سونار مراقبة الرمي
*sūnār murāqabat ar-ramī*

fire-control system نظام السيطرة على الرمي
*niẓām as-sayṭara ʿalar-ramī*

fire extinguishing system نظام اطفاء الحريق
*niẓām iṭfāʾ al-ḥarīq*

fire-fighting مكافحة الحريق
*mukāfaḥat al-ḥarīq*

fire hazard خطر الحريق
*khaṭr al-ḥarīq*

fireman إطفائي
*iṭfāʾī*

fire overhead detector مكشاف حريق معلق
*mikshāf ḥarīq muʿallaq*

F

fire point blank إطلاق مباشر
*iṭlāq mubāshir*
fire power قوة النيران
*qūwat an-nīrān*
fireproof overall رداء سروالي صامد للنار
*ridā' sirwālī ṣāmid lin-nār*
fire selector منتخب الرمي
*muntakhib ar-ramī*
Firestreak AAM صاروخ جو - جو « فاير ستريك »
*ṣārūkh jaww-jaww fāyr strīk*
fire support دعم النيران
*daʿm an-nīrān*
fire-support vehicle سيارة تدعيم النيران
*sayyārat tadʿīm an-nīrān*
Fire Wheel radar رادار « فايرويل »
*rādār fāyr wīl*
firing current تيار النيران
*tayyār an-nīrān*
firing exercise تدريب على اطلاق النار
*tadrīb ʿala iṭlāq an-nār*
firing frequency تردد اطلاق النار
*taraddud iṭlāq an-nār*
firing interval فاصل اطلاق النار
*fāṣil iṭlāq an-nār*
firing mechanism آلية اطلاق النار
*ālīyat iṭlāq an-nār*
firing orders اوامر اطلاق النار
*awāmir iṭlāq an-nār*
firing party مفرزة الرمي مفرزة تنفيذ الاعدام
*mafrazat ar-ramī · mafrazat tanfīdh al-iʿdām*
firing range حقل الرمي
*ḥaql ar-rami*
firing trials تجارب الرمي
*tajārub ar-rami*
firing unit وحدة الرمي
*wiḥdat ar-rami*
Firos field rocket صاروخ ميداني فايروس
*ṣārūkh maydānī fāyrūs*
first aid إسعاف أولي
*isʿāf awwalī*
first aid kit حقيبة الاسعاف الأولي
*ḥaqībat al-isʿāf al-awwalī*
first degree burn حرق من الدرجة الاولى
*ḥarq min ad-daraja al-ūlā*
first-generation الجيل الأول
*al-jīl al-awwal*
first stage المرحلة الاولى
*al-marḥala al-ūlā*
first-stage motor محرك المرحلة الأولى
*muḥarrik al-marḥala al-ūlā*
first-strike probability إحتمالية الهجوم الأول
*iḥtimālīyat al-hujūm al-awwal*
Fishbed fighter طائرة مقاتلة « فيشبيد »
*ṭā'ira muqātila fīshbīd*
fishbone antenna هوائي « فيشبون »
*hawā'ī fīshbūn*
fishery patrol دورية حراسة الصيد
*dawrīyat ḥirāsat aṣ-ṣayd*
Fishpot aircraft طائرة فيشبوت
*ṭā'irat fīshbūt*
fitness certificate شهادة اللياقة
*shihādat al-liyāqa*
Fitter-A fighter طائرة مقاتلة « فيتر - ايه »
*ṭā'ira muqātila fitar ayy*
Fitter-F aircraft طائرة « فيتر اف »
*ṭā'irat fitar if*
Fitter-J aircraft طائرة « فيتر - جيه »
*ṭā'irat fitar jayy*
fitting out تسليح . تجهيز
*taslīḥ · tajhīz*
fix bayonets! « الحراب ركب »
*al-ḥirāb rakkib*
fixed bayonet حربة مركبة
*ḥarba murakkaba*
fixed-pitch propeller مروحة ثابتة الخطوة
*mirwaḥa thābitat al-khuṭwa*
fixed scan مسح ثابت
*masḥ thābit*
fixed tailplane سطح ذيل ثابت
*saṭḥ dhayl thābit*
fixed target هدف ثابت
*hadaf thābit*
fixed ventral inlet مدخل بطني ثابت
*madkhal baṭnī thābit*
fixed-wing جناح ثابت
*janāḥ thābit*
fixed wing aircraft طائرة بجناح ثابت
*ṭā'ira bi-janāḥ thābit*
flag علم . راية
*ʿalam · rāya*
flag at half mast تنكيس العلم
*tankīs al-ʿalam*
flag group جماعة العلم
*jamāʿat al-ʿalam*
Flagon-F aircraft طائرة « فلاجون - اف »
*ṭā'irat flāgūn if*
flagship سفينة القيادة
*safīnat al-qiyāda*

F

flak نيران مدفعية مضادة للطائرات
*nīrān midfaʿīya muḍādda liṭ-ṭāʾirāt*
flamethrower قاذفة لهب
*qādhifat lahab*
Flamingo trainer طائرة تدريب « فلامينجو »
*ṭāʾirat tadrīb flāmīngū*
flank جناح
*janāḥ*
flank attack هجوم جناحي
*hujūm janāḥī*
Flanker fighter طائرة مقاتلة فلانكر
*ṭāʾira muqātila flānkar*
flank guard حراسة الجناح
*ḥirāsat al-janāḥ*
Flap Lid radar رادار « فلاپ ليد »
*rādār flāp līd*
Flap Wheel radar رادار « فلاپ ويل »
*rādār flāp wīl*
flare مشعل . خرطوشة مضيئة
*mishʿal · kharṭūsha muḍīʾa*
flare launcher قاذفة مشاعل
*qādhifat mashāʿil*
flash burn حرق ومضي
*ḥarq wamḍī*
flash hider حاجبة الوميض
*ḥājibat al-wamīḍ*
flashing beacon منارة وماضة
*manāra wammāḍa*
flashing lamp مصباح وماض
*misbāḥ wammāḍ*
flash-suppressor مانع الوميض
*maniʿ al-wamīḍ*
Flat Face radar رادار « فلات فيس »
*rādār flāt fays*
Flat Jack radar رادار « فلات جاك »
*rādār flāt jāk*
flat-plate لوحة مستوية
*lawḥa mustawīya*
flat-plate antenna هوائي ذو لوحة مستوية
*hawāʾī dhū lawḥa mustawīya*
Flat Spin radar رادار « فلات سپين »
*rādār flāt spin*
flat spring نابض مسطح
*nābiḍ musaṭṭaḥ*
flat trajectory مسار باليستي مستوى
*masār bālīstī mustawī*
fleet air force القوات الجوية للاسطول
*al-qūwāt al-jawwīya lil-usṭūl*
fleet command officer قائد الاسطول
*qāʾid al-usṭūl*
fleet-defence دفاع الاسطول
*difāʿ al-usṭūl*
fleet liaison ربط الاسطول
*rabṭ al-usṭūl*
fleet supply ship سفينة تموين الاسطول
*safīnat tamwīn al-usṭūl*
flight-control التحكم في الطائرة
*at-taḥakkum fiṭ-ṭāʾira*
flight-control station مركز التحكم في الطائرة
*markaz al-taḥakkum fiṭ-ṭāʾira*
flight-control system نظام التحكم في الطائرة
*niẓām at-taḥakkum fiṭ-ṭāʾira*
flight crew ملاحو الطائرة
*mallāḥū aṭ-ṭāʾira*
flight deck سطح طيران
*saṭḥ ṭayarān*
flight simulator جهاز محاكاة الطائرة
*jihāz muḥākāt aṭ-ṭāʾira*
flight test إختبار الطيران
*ikhtibār aṭ-ṭayarān*
flight time زمن الطيران
*zaman aṭ-ṭayarān*
flight trial تجربة طيران
*tajribat ṭayarān*
floating antenna هوائي طليق
*hawāʾī ṭalīq*
floating bridge جسر عائم
*jisr ʿāʾim*
floating communication إتصال طليق
*ittiṣāl ṭalīq*
floating dock حوض عائم
*hawḍ ʿāʾim*
Flogger D fighter طائرة مقاتلة « فلوجر دي »
*ṭāʾira muqātila flūgar dī*
Flogger F fighter طائرة مقاتلة « فلوجر اف »
*ṭāʾira muqātila flūgar if*
flotilla أسطول صغير
*usṭūl ṣaghīr*
flotilla leader قائد أسطول صغير
*qāʾid usṭūl ṣaghīr*
FLT fire control system نظام السيطرة على الرمي « اف ال تي »
*niẓām as-sayṭara ʿalar-ramī if il tī*
flush deck سطح متساطح
*saṭḥ mutasāṭiḥ*
fly-by-wire controls حاكمات الطيران بالسلك
*ḥākimāt aṭ-ṭayarān bis-silk*
fly catcher صائد الذباب
*ṣāʾid adh- dhubāb*

F

flygmotor محرك الطائرة
*muḥarrik aṭ-ṭāʾira*
flying طيران
*ṭayarān*
flying-boom refuelling إعادة التزود بالوقود بالذراع الطائر
*iʿādat at-tazawwud bil-wuqūd bidh-dhirāʿ aṭ-ṭāʾir*
flying operations عمليات طيران
*ʿamalīyāt ṭayarān*
fly off lever رافعة الطيران
*rāfiʿat aṭ-ṭayarān*
flypast عرض جوي
*ʿarḍ jawwī*
FMA (Co) شركة « اف ام ايه »
*sharikat if im ayy*
FN FAL rifle بندقية « إف إن إف ايه إل »
*bunduqīyat if in if ayy il*
foe عدو . خصم
*ʿadūw · khaṣm*
Fokker (Co) شركة « فوكر »
*sharikat fūkar*
folding blade ريشة تطوى
*rīsha tuṭwa*
folding butt أخمص قابل للطي
*akhmuṣ qābil liṭ-ṭayy*
folding main rotor دوامة رئيسية قابلة للطي
*duwwāma raʾīsīya qābila liṭ-ṭayy*
folding stock حاضن قابل للطي
*ḥāḍin qābil liṭ-ṭayy*
folding tail ذيل قابل للطي
*dhayl qābil liṭ-ṭayy*
follow me! « اتبعوني ! »
*itabiʿūnī*
follow me truck شاحنة المقدمة
*shāḥinat al-muqaddima*
food طعام . مؤونة
*ṭaʿām · maʾūna*
food supplies تموينات غذائية
*tamwīnāt ghidhāʾīya*
foot bridge جسر مشاة
*jisr mushāh*
foray غزوة . غارة
*ghazwa · ghāra*
forbidden محظور . ممنوع
*maḥẓūr · mamnūʿ*
force commander قائد القوات
*qāʾid al-qūwāt*
forces قوات
*qūwāt*
forces abroad قوات في الخارج
*qūwāt fil-khārij*
fore أمامي . متقدم
*amāmī · mutaqaddim*
forecastle عنبر أمامي للبحارة
*ʿanbar amāmī lil-baḥḥāra*
foredeck سطح مقدم السفينة
*saṭḥ muqaddam as-safīna*
foregrip مقبض أمامي
*miqbaḍ amāmī*
foreign contract military personnel أفراد عسكريون بعقود أجنبية
*afrād ʿaskarīyūn bi-ʿuqūd ajnabīya*
foreign object جسم غريب
*jism gharīb*
fore-see radar رادار للرصد الامامي
*rādār lir-raṣd al-amānī*
foresight مهداف تصويب امامي
*mihdāf taṣwīb amāmī*
fore-sight base قاعدة المهدف الامامي
*qāʿidat al-mihdāf al-amāmī*
forestock حاضن امامي
*ḥaḍin amānī*
forewarn انذار مقدم
*indhār muqaddam*
forged titanium تيتانيوم مطروق
*tītānyūm maṭrūq*
Forger aircraft طائرة « فورجر »
*ṭaʾirat fūrjar*
for inspection, port arms! للتفتيش « عالياً احمل ! »
*lit-taftīsh ʿālīyan iḥmil*
formation تكوين . تشكيل تأسيس
*takwīn · tashkīl · taʾsīs*
form extended line! « انتشار ـ شكل ! »
*intishār – shakkil*
form single rank! « صف واحد ـ شكل ! »
*ṣaff wāḥid – shakkil*
form two ranks! « صفان .. شكل ! »
*ṣaffān – shakkil*
Forrestal carrier حاملة « فوريستال »
*ḥāmilat fūristāl*
Forrest Sherman destroyer مدمرة « فورست شيرمان »
*mudammarat fūrist shīrmān*
fortification تحصين . دفاع
*taḥṣin · difāʿ*
forward! « للأمام ـ سر ! »
*lil-amām – sirr*
forward defence area منطقة الدفاع الأمامية
*minṭaqat ad-difāʿ al-amāmīya*

forward-firing رمي أمامي
*ramī amāmī*
forward fuselage هيكل أمامي للطائرة
*haykal amāmī liṭ-ṭāʾira*
forward gun turret برج مدفع أمامي
*burj midfaʿ amāmī*
forward headquarters القيادة الأمامية
*al-qiyāda al-amāmīya*
forward-looking camera آلة تصوير للرصد الأمامي
*ālat taṣwīr lir-raṣd al-amāmī*
forward looking infra-red sensor جهاز احساس بالأشعة دون الحمراء للرصد الأمامي
*jihāz iḥsās bil-ashiʿʿa dūn al-ḥamrāʾ lir-raṣd al-amāmī*
forward pad منصة أمامية
*minaṣṣa amāmīya*
forward position موضع أمامي
*mawḍiʿ amāmī*
forward sensor turret برج جهاز احساس أمامي
*burj jihāz iḥsās amāmī*
forward thrust دفع أمامي
*dafʿ amāmī*
forward troop concentration حشد الجنود في الجبهة الأمامية
*ḥashd al-junūd fil-jabha al-amāmīya*
four-barrel رباعي الماسورات
*rubāʿī al-māsūrāt*
four-blade rotor دوامة رباعية الشفرات
*duwwāma rubāʿīyat ash-shafarāt*
four-man أربعة رجال
*arbaʿata rijāl*
four-seat رباعي المقاعد
*rubāʿī al-maqāʿid*
Foxbat aircraft طائرة « فوكسبات »
*ṭāʾirat fuksbāt*
fox hole حفرة المناوشة
*ḥufrat al-munāwasha*
Foxhound fighter طائرة « فوكسهاوند »
*ṭāʾirat fukshawnd*
Foxhunter radar رادار « فوكسهنتر »
*rādār fukshantar*
Foxtrot submarine غواصة فوكستروت
*ghawwāṣat fukstrūt*
Fox vehicle سيارة « فوكس »
*sayyārat fuks*
fragmentation تشظية
*tashẓīya*

fragmentation grenade قنبلة يدوية متشظية
*qunbula yadawī mutashshaẓīya*
fragmentation type من نوع متشظي
*min nawʿ mutashshaẓī*
France فرنسا
*fransa*
Franklin submarine غواصة فرانكلين
*ghawwāṣat frānklīn*
FRAS-1 rocket صاروخ « إف ار ايه اس ـ ١ »
*ṣārūkh if ār ayy is wāḥid*
freeboard hull هيكل السفينة الظاهر من الماء
*haykal as-safīna aẓ-ẓāhir min al-māʾ*
Freedom Fighter مجاهد في سبيل الحرية
*mujāhid fi sabīl al-ḥurrīya*
free fall سقوط حر
*suqūṭ ḥurr*
free flight طيران حر
*ṭayarān ḥurr*
Free Lebanese Militia حرس لبنان الحر
*ḥaras lubnān al-ḥurr*
French فرنسي
*fransī*
frequency-agile تغير سريع للتردد
*taghayyur sarīʿ lit-taraddud*
frequency-agile radar رادار بتغير سريع للتردد
*rādār bi-taghayyur sarīʿ lit-taraddud*
frequency band نطاق التردد
*niṭāq at-taraddud*
frequency cable كبل التردد
*kabl at-taraddud*
frequency change تغير التردد
*taghayyur at-taraddud*
frequency converter محول التردد
*muḥawwil at-taraddud*
frequency-domain analysis تحليل مجال التردد
*taḥlīl majāl at-taraddud*
FRESCAN radar رادار « فريسكان »
*rādār frīskān*
Fresco fighter طائرة مقاتلة « فريسكو »
*ṭāʿira muqātila friskū*
friend صديق
*ṣadīq*
friendly ودي
*wadī*
frigate فرقاطة
*firqāṭa*

F

FROG-7 missile صاروخ « فروج ـ ٧ »
*ṣārūkh frūg sabʿa*
FROG-9 missile صاروخ « فروج ـ ٩ »
*ṣārūkh frūg tisʿa*
Frogfoot aircraft طائرة « فروجفوت »
*ṭāʾirat frūgfūt*
from right to left! من اليمين الى اليسار !
*min al-yamīn ilal-yasār*
front واجهة . جبهة
*wājiha · jabha*
frontal attack هجوم جبهي
*hujūm jabhī*
Frontal Aviation Force القوات الجوية الأمامية
*al-qūwāt al-jawwīya al-amāmīya*
frontal thrust دفع أمامي
*dafʿ āmāmī*
frontier guard حرس الحدود
*ḥaras al-ḥudūd*
frontier post مخفر الحدود
*makhfar al-ḥudūd*
front-line service الخدمة في الجبهة
*al-khidma fil-jabha*
front-line submarine غواصة الخط الأمامي
*ghawwāṣat al-khaṭṭ al-amāmī*
front-line unit وحدة الخط الأمامي
*wiḥdat al-khaṭṭ al-amāmī*
Frosch ship سفينة فروش
*safīnat frūsh*
fuel وقود
*wuqūd*
fuel-air explosive warhead رأس قذيفة وقود هواء
*raʾs qadhīfa wuqūd hawāʾ*
fuel bowser شاحنة صهريج للوقود
*shāḥinat ṣihrīj lil-wuqūd*
fuel capacity سعة الوقود
*siʿat al-wuqūd*
fuel dump مستودع الوقود
*mustawdaʿ al-wuqūd*
fuel injection حقن الوقود
*ḥaqn al-wuqūd*
fuel system نظام الوقود
*niẓām al-wuqūd*
fuel tank خزان الوقود
*khazzān al-wūqūd*
fuel tanker ناقلة وقود
*nāqilat wuqūd*
FUG-70 armoured vehicle سيارة مدرعة « اف يو جي ـ ٧٠ »
*sayyāra mudarraʿa if yū jī sabʿīn*
Fuji (Co) شركة فوجي
*sharikat fūjī*
Fulcrum fighter طائرة مقاتلة « فولكروم »
*ṭāʾira muqātila fūlkrūm*
full armament تسليح كامل
*taslīḥ kāmil*
full dress بزة المراسم
*bizzat al-marāsim*
full load حمل كامل
*ḥiml kāmil*
full load displacement إزاحة الحمل الكامل
*izāḥat al-ḥiml al-kāmil*
fully automatic system نظام اوتوماتيكي تماماً
*niẓām awtūmātīkī tamāman*
fully equipped مجهز تماماً
*mujahhaz tamāman*
fully guided موجه بالكامل
*muwajjah bil-kāmil*
fume-extracted bag كيس الدخان المستخلص
*kīs ad-dukhān al-mustakhlaṣ*
fume extractor طارد الدخان
*ṭārid ad-dukhān*
funnel قمع . مدخنة
*qimʿ · madkhana*
fuse مصهر . فاصمة
*miṣhar · fāṣima*
fuselage جسم الطائرة
*jism aṭ-ṭāʾira*
fuselage length طول جسم الطائرة
*ṭūl jism aṭṭāʾira*
fuse option إختيار الفاصمة
*ikhtiyār al-fāṣima*
fuselage pylon عمود بدن الطائرة
*ʿamūd badn at-tāʾira*
FV433 gun مدفع « اف ڤي ٤٣٣ »
*midfaʿ if vī arbaʿa miʾa wa thalātha wa thalāthīn*
FV434 repair vehicle سيارة اصلاح « اف ڤي ٤٣٤ »
*sayyārat iṣlāḥ if vī arbaʿa miʾa wa arbaʿa wa thalāthīn*
FV4201 tank دبابة « اف ڤي ٤٢٠١ »
*dabbābat if vī arbaʿa alāf wa miʾtayn wa wāḥid*
FZ warhead رأس قذيفة اف زد
*raʾs qadhīfa if zid*

# G



G-class submarine — غواصة طراز « جي »
*ghawwāṣa ṭirāz jī*
G3 rifle — بندقية « جي ٣ »
*bunduqīyat jī thalātha*
G3A4 rifle — بندقية « جي ٣ ايه ٤ »
*bunduqīyat jī thalātha ayy arbaʿa*
G11 rifle — بندقية « جي ١١ »
*bunduqīyat jī aḥada ʿashar*
G91R fighter — طائرة مقاتلة « جي ٩١ أر »
*ṭāʾira muqātila jī wāḥid wa tisʿīn ār*
G91Y fighter — طائرة مقاتلة « جي ٩١ واي »
*ṭāʾira muqātila jī wāḥid wa tisʿīn wāyy*
G222 airtransporter — طائرة نقل « جي ٢٢٢ »
*ṭaʾirat naql jī miʾtayn wa ithnayn wa ʿishrīn*
G222VS aircraft — طائرة « جي ٢٢٢ ڤي إس »
*ṭāirat jī miʾtayn wa ithnayn wa ʿishrīn vī is*
GA (Tabun) agent — عنصر غاز تابون جي اي
*ʿunṣur ghāz tābūn jī ayy*
Gabriel 1 missile — صاروخ « جبرييل ١ »
*ṣarūkh gaybriyal wāḥid*
Gabriel 2 missile — صاروخ « جبرييل ٢ »
*ṣārūkh gaybriyal ithnayn*
Gabriel 3 missile — صاروخ « جبرييل ٣ »
*ṣārūkh gaybriyal thalātha*
Gage radar — رادار « جيج »
*rādār gayj*
Gainful SAM — صاروخ سطح ـ جو « جينفول »
*ṣārūkh saṭḥ-jaww gaynfūl*
Galaxy airtransporter — طائرة نقل « چالاكسي »
*ṭaʾirat naql galāksī*
Galeb trainer — طائرة تدريب « جاليب »
*ṭāʾirat tadrīb gālīb*
Galosh missile — صاروخ « جالوش »
*ṣārūkh gālūsh*
Gammon SAM — صاروخ سطح جو « جامون »
*ṣārūkh saṭḥ-jaww gāmūn*
Ganef SAM — صاروخ سطح جو « جانيف »
*ṣārūkh saṭḥ-jaww gānīf*
gantry — حامل قنطري
*ḥāmil qanṭarī*
Garcia frigate — فرقاطة « جارسيا »
*firqāṭa gārsīya*
Garian patrol craft — سفينة خفر سواحل « جريان »
*safīnat khafar as-sawāḥil garīyān*
Garibaldi helicopter carrier — حاملة طائرات عمودية « حارربالدى »
*ḥāmilat ṭāʾirāt ʿamūdīya garībaldī*
gas — غاز
*ghāz*
gas bomb — قنبلة غاز
*qunbulat ghāz*
gas chamber — غرفة الغاز
*ghurfat al-ghāz*
gas cylinder — أسطوانة الغاز
*usṭuwānat al-ghāz*
gas generator system — نظام توليد الغاز
*niẓām tawlīd al-ghāz*
Gaskin SAM — صاروخ سطح جو جاسكين
*ṣārūkh saṭḥ jaww gāskīn*
gas mask — قناع واق من الغاز
*qināʿ wāqi min al-ghāz*
gas-operated — يعمل بالغاز
*yaʿmal bil-ghāz*
gas-pressured — بضغط الغاز
*bi-ḍaghṭ al-ghāz*
gas regulation system — نظام تنظيم الغاز
*niẓām tanẓīm al-ghāz*
gastroenteritis — إلتهاب معدي معوي
*iltihāb maʿidī miʿawī*

| | | |
|---|---|---|
| gas tube | صمام الغاز | *ṣimām al-ghāz* |
| gas turbine | تربين غازي | *turbīn ghāzī* |
| gas turbine engine | محرك بتربين غازي | *muḥarrik bi-turbīn ghāzī* |
| gas-turbine power | قدرة تربين الغاز | *qudrat turbīn al-ghāz* |
| Gatling gun | مدفع جاتلينج | *midfaʿ gātlīng* |
| Gatling turret | برج جاتلينج | *burj gātlīng* |
| GAU-8/A cannon | مدفع هاون « جي ايه يو ـ ٨ / ايه » | *midfaʿ hāwun jī ayy yū thamānya/ayy* |
| Gazelle helicopter | طائرة عمودية « جازيل » | *ṭāʾira ʿamūdīya gazīl* |
| GB (Sarin) agent | عنصر غاز سارين جي بي | *ʿunṣur ghāz sārin jī bī* |
| GBU-15 ASM | صاروخ جو ـ سطح « جي بي يو ـ ١٥ » | *ṣārūkh jaww-saṭḥ jī bī yū khamsata ʿashar* |
| GCT howitzer | مدفع هاوتزر « جي سي تي » | *midfaʿ hāwitsar jī sī tī* |
| GD (Soman) agent | عنصر غاز سومان جي دي | *ʿunṣur ghāz sūmān jī dī* |
| geared steam turbine | تربين بخاري مسنن | *turbīn bukhārī musannan* |
| geared turbine | تربين مسنن | *turbīn musannan* |
| Gearing destroyer | مدمرة « چيرنج » | *mudammarat gīrīng* |
| Gecko SAM | صاروخ سام « جيكو » | *ṣārūkh saṭḥ-jaww gīkū* |
| Geiger counter | عداد « جيجر » | *ʿaddād gāygar* |
| Gem 2 engine | محرك « جيم ٢ » | *muḥarrik jim ithnayn* |
| Gem 41 turboshaft | عمود ادارة تربيني « جيم ٤١ » | *ʿamūd idārat turbīnī jim wāḥid wa arbaʿīn* |
| GE M197 cannon | مدفع هاون « جي ئي ام ١٩٧ » | *midfaʿ hāwun jī ī im miʾa wa sabʿa wa tisʿīn* |
| Gemini boat | زورق « جيمني » | *zawraq jiminī* |
| Gemini radar | رادار « جيمني » | *rādār jiminī* |
| Gendarmerie | الدَّرَك | *ad-darak* |
| general | عام | *ʿāmm* |
| general alert | تنبيه عام | *tanbīh ʿāmm* |
| General Dynamics (Co) | شركة جنرال ديناميكس | *sharikat jinrāl dīnāmīks* |
| General Electric | شركة جنرال الكتريك | *sharikat jinrāl iliktrik* |
| general inspection | تفتيش عام | *taftīsh ʿāmm* |
| general offensive | هجوم عام | *hujūm ʿāmm* |
| general purpose | غرض عام | *gharḍ ʿāmm* |
| general purpose craft | زورق أغراض عامة | *zawraq aghrāḍ ʿāmma* |
| general staff | الأركان العامة | *al-arkān al-ʿāmma* |
| generator | مولد كهرباء | *muwallid kahrabāʾ* |
| Genie AIR | صاروخ اعتراض محمول جواً « جيني » | *ṣārūkh iʿtirāḍ maḥmūl jawwan jīnī* |
| Georges Leygues destroyer | مدمرة « جورج ليج » | *mudammirat jūrj layg* |
| George Washington submarine | غواصة « جورج واشنطن » | *ghawwāṣat jūrj wāshnṭan* |
| Gepard anti-aircraft system | نظام مضاد للطائرات « جيبارد » | *niẓām muḍādd liṭ-ṭāʾirāt gībārd* |
| German Democratic Republic | جمهورية المانيا الديمقراطية | *jumhūrīyat ālmānya ad-dīmuqrāṭīya* |
| German Federal Republic | جمهورية المانيا الاتحادية | *jumhūrīyat ālmānya al-ittiḥādīya* |
| German | الماني | *ālmānī* |
| GFCSI fire control system | نظام السيطرة على الرمي « جي اف سي اس أي » | *niẓām as-sayṭara ʿalar-ramī – jī if sī is āyy* |
| Ghana | غانا | *ghānā* |
| GHN-45 howitzer | مدفع هاوتزر « جي اتش ان ـ ٤٥ » | *midfaʿ hāwitsar jī itsh in khamsa wa arbaʿīn* |
| giant radar | رادار ضخم | *rādār ḍakhm* |

GIAT TS-90 turret برج « جيات تي اس - ٩٠ »
*burj jiyāt tī īs tisʿīn*
gimballed nozzle فوهة مزدوجة المحور
*fūha muzdawijat al-miḥwar*
Giraffe radar رادار « جيراف »
*rādār jīrāf*
Giuseppe Garibaldi carrier حاملة « جيوسيبي جاريبالدي »
*ḥāmilat jiyūsipi gārībaldī*
give your call sign! أذكر اشارة النداء !
*udhkur ishārat an-nidāʾ*
glacis plate لوح منحدر مقابل
*lawḥ munḥadir muqābil*
glass-fibre ألياف زجاجية
*alyāf zujājīya*
glassfibre-reinforced plastic بلاستيك مقوى بالألياف الزجاجية
*blāstik muqawwan bil-alyāf az-zujājīya*
Glenard P. Lipscomb submarine غواصة « جلنارد پي ليپسكم »
*ghawwāṣat glinārd pī lipskam*
global deployment انتشار عالمي
*intishār ʿālamī*
global missile صاروخ كوني
*ṣārūkh kawnī*
global war حرب عالمية
*ḥarb ʿālamīya*
Glover frigate فرقاطة « جلوڤر »
*firqāṭat glūvar*
GMZ minelayer زارعة ألغام « جي ام زد »
*zāriʿat alghām jī im ziḍ*
Gnat fighter طائرة مقاتلة « نات »
*ṭāʾira muqātila nāt*
Gnome turboshaft عمود ادارة تربيني « نوم »
*ʿamūd idārat turbīnī nūm*
Goalkeeper gun مدفع « جول كيبر »
*midfaʿ gūlkībar*
Goa SAM صاروخ سطح - جو « جوا »
*ṣārūkh saṭh-jaww gūwa*
Goblet SAM صاروخ سطح - جو « جوبلت »
*ṣārūkh saṭh-jaww gūblit*
goggles نظارات واقية
*naẓẓārāt wāqiʾa*
Golf missile صاروخ « جولف »
*ṣārūkh gūlf*
Golf submarine غواصة « جولف »
*ghawwāṣat gūlf*
Gomhouria training aircraft طائرة تدريب « جمهورية »
*ṭāʾirat tadrib jumhūrīya*

Gordy destroyer مدمرة « جوردى »
*mudammirat gūrdī*
Gould Ocean System نظام « جولد اوشن »
*niẓām gūld ūshan*
gradient ميل . إنحدار . . درجة الميل
*mayl · inḥidār · darajat al-mayl*
Grail SAM صاروخ سطح - جو « جريل »
*ṣārūkh saṭḥ-jaww grayl*
grapnel كلابة مرساة
*kullāba · mirsāh*
grappling hook خطاف المرساة
*khuṭṭāf al-mirsāh*
graticule شبكة مربعات
*shabakat murabbaʿāt*
graticule sight مهداف مدرج
*mihdāf mudarraj*
gratuity مكافأة . منحة
*makāfaʾa · minḥa*
gravity bomb قنبلة بالثقل
*qunbula bith-thiql*
Grayback submarine غواصة « جرايباك »
*ghawwāṣat graybāk*
Great Britain بريطانيا العظمى
*brītānya al-ʿuẓmā*
greatcoat معطف
*miʿṭaf*
Greece اليونان
*al-yūnān*
Greek يوناني
*yūnānī*
Green Berets القوات البحرية الملكية
*al-qūwāt al-baḥrīya al-malikīya*
Green Knights aircraft طائرة « جرين نايتس »
*ṭāʾirat grīn nāyts*
green smoke دخان أخضر
*dukhān akhḍar*
Greif vehicle عربة « جرايف »
*ʿarabat grāyf*
grenade قنبلة يدوية
*qunbula yadawīya*
grenade flare مشعل قنبلة يدوية
*mashʿal qunbula yadawīya*
grenade launcher قاذفة قنابل يدوية
*qādhifat qanābil yadawīya*
grenade sight مهداف القنابل اليدوية
*mihdāf al-qanābil al-yadawīya*

G

G

grenade surprise مباغتة بالقنابل اليدوية
*mubāghata bil-qanābil al-yadawīya*
Greyhound aircraft طائرة « جراي هوند »
*ṭāʾirat grayhawnd*
grey smoke دخان رمادي
*dukhān ramādī*
Grey Whales helicopter طائرة عمودية « جريه ويلز »
*ṭāʾira ʿamūdīya grayy waylz*
grid شبكة
*shabaka*
grid-modulation تشكيل شبكي
*tashkīl shabakī*
grid system نظام الشبكة
*niẓām ash-shabaka*
Grifon helicopter طائرة عمودية « جريفون »
*ṭāʾira ʿamūdīya grīfūn*
Grisha corvette سفينة حراسة صغيرة « جريشا »
*safīnat ḥirāsa ṣaghīra grīsha*
ground-air data link توصيلة بيانات أرض - جو
*ṭawṣīlat bayānāt arḍ-jaww*
ground arms! « أرضاً - سلاح ! »
*arḍan – silāḥ*
ground-attack هجوم أرضي
*hujūm arḍī*
ground-attack aircraft طائرة هجوم أرضي
*ṭāʾirat hujūm arḍī*
ground-attack squadron سرب هجوم أرضي
*sirb hujūm arḍī*
ground-attack strike aircraft طائرة انقضاض للهجوم الأرضي
*ṭāʾirat inqiḍāḍ lil-hujūm al-arḍī*
ground-based air defence system نظام دفاع جوي أرضي
*niẓām difāʿ jawwī arḍī*
ground-based radar رادار أرضي
*rādār arḍi*
ground clutter تداخل راداري من الارض
*tadākhul rādārī min al-arḍ*
ground fire إطلاق أرضي للنيران
*iṭlāq arḍī lin-nīrān*
ground force قوة أرضية
*qūwa arḍīya*
ground forces قوات أرضية
*qūwāt arḍīya*
ground launch إطلاق أرضي
*iṭlāq arḍī*
ground mine لغم أرضي
*lughm arḍī*
ground radar رادار أرضي
*rādār arḍī*
ground self defence force قوة الدفاع الذاتي الأرضية
*qūwat ad-difāʿ adh-dhātī al-arḍīya*
ground staff أفراد أرضيون
*afrād arḍīyūn*
ground surveillance إستطلاع أرضي
*istiṭlāʿ arḍī*
ground target هدف أرضي
*hadaf arḍī*
group headquarters مقر المجموعة
*maqarr al-majmūʿa*
Grumman (Co) شركة جرومان
*sharikat grūmān*
GSh-23 gun مدفع « جي اس اتش - ٢٣ »
*midfaʿ jī is itsh thalātha wa ʿishrīn*
GTD-3BM turboshaft عمود ادارة تربيني « جي تي دي - ٣ بي ام »
*ʿamūd idārat turbīnī jī tī dī thalātha bī im*
Guarani air transport طائرة نقل « جيوراني »
*ṭāʾirat naql gwarānī*
guard حارس . حماية
*ḥāris · ḥimāya*
guard data بيانات الحرس
*bayānāt al-ḥaras*
guard detail مفرزة الحرس
*mafrazat al-ḥaras*
guard dog كلب حراسة
*kalb ḥirāsa*
guard duty مهمة حراسة
*muhimmat ḥirāsa*
guardroom غرفة الحرس
*ghurfat al-ḥaras*
Guards حرس
*ḥaras*
guards division فرقة الحراسة
*firqat al-ḥirāsa*
guardsman حارس
*ḥāris*
guard-turn out! « الحرس - أخرج »
*al-ḥaras – ikhrij*
Guatemala غواتيمالا
*ghūwātimālā*
guerrilla عصابات
*ʿiṣābāt*
guerrilla activities نشاط العصابات
*nashāṭ al-ʿiṣābāt*
guerrilla faction طائفة العصابات
*ṭāʾifat al-ʿiṣābāt*

guerrilla force قوات العصابات
*qūwāt al-ʿiṣābāt*
guidance إرشاد . توجيه
*irshād · tawjīh*
guidance aerial هوائي إرشاد
*hawāʾī irshād*
guidance beam شعاع إرشاد
*shuʿāʿ irshād*
guidance beam transmitter مرسل شعاع الارشاد
*mursil shuʿāʿ al-irshād*
guidance command أمر التوجيه
*amr at-tawjīh*
guidance correction تصحيح التوجيه
*taṣḥīḥ at-tawjīh*
guidance equipment معدات التوجيه
*muʿaddāt at-tawjīh*
guidance system نظام التوجيه
*niẓām at-tawjīh*
guided missile صاروخ موجه
*ṣārūkh muwajjah*
guided missile cruiser طرادة صواريخ موجهة
*ṭarrādat ṣawārīkh muwajjaha*
guided missile destroyer مدمرة صواريخ موجهة
*mudammirat ṣawārīkh muwajjaha*
guided missile frigate فرقاطة صواريخ موجهة
*firqāṭat ṣawārīkh muwajjaha*
guided missile patrol boat زورق حراسة مجهز بصواريخ موجهة
*zawraq ḥirāsa mujahhaz bi-ṣawārīkh muwajjaha*
guided weapon سلاح موجه
*silāḥ muwajjah*
guideline توجيه
*tawjīh*
Guild SAM صاروخ سطح جو « جيلد »
*ṣārūkh saṭḥ-jaww gild*
Guinea جيني
*gīnī*
Gulf-stream air transport طائرة نقل « جلف - ستريم »
*ṭāʾirat naql galf-strīm*
gun مدفع . بندقية . مسدس
*midfaʿ · bunduqīya · musaddas*
gun armament سلاح المدفعية
*silāḥ al-midfaʿīya*
gun-armed مسلح بمدفع
*musallaḥ bi-midfaʿ*
gunboat زورق مسلح
*zawraq musallaḥ*
gun concentration حشد المدفعية
*ḥashd al-midfaʿīya*
gun cotton قطن البارود
*quṭn al-bārūd*
gun director مدير مدفعية
*mudīr midfaʿīya*
Gun Dish radar رادار « جن ديش »
*rādār gan dīsh*
gun display system نظام عرض المدفع
*niẓām ʿarḍ al-midfaʿ*
gun fire-control system نظام السيطرة على رمي المدفعية
*niẓam as-sayṭara ʿala ramī al-midfaʿīya*
gun gathering جمع المدفعية
*jamʿ al-midfaʿīya*
gunner مدفعي
*midfaʿī*
gunner's sight مهداف التسديد
*mihdāf at-tasdīd*
gunnery training تدريب على رمي المدفعية
*tadrīb ʿala ramī al-midfaʿīya*
gun position موضع المدفع
*mawḍiʿ al-midfaʿ*
gunship helicopter طائرة عمودية مسلحة هجومية
*ṭaʾira ʿamūdīya musallaḥa hujūmīya*
gunsight مهداف المدفع
*mihdāf al-midfaʿ*
gun, single مدفع مفرد
*midfaʿ mufrad*
gun sponson منصة المدفع
*minaṣṣa lil-midfaʿ*
gun-stabilization system نظام موازنة المدفع
*niẓām muwāzanat al-midfaʿ*
gun tractor جرار المدفع
*jarrār al-midfaʿ*
gun, twin مدفع مزدوج
*midfaʿ muzdawij*
Guppy III submarine غواصة « جوبي ٣ »
*ghawwāṣat gūpī thalātha*
Gus ship سفينة « جس »
*safinat gas*
Guyana غايانا
*ghayānā*
GWD30 SAM صاروخ سطح -جو « جي دبليو دي ٣٠ »
*ṣārūkh saṭḥ-jaww jī dablyū dī thalāthīn*
GWS22 radar رادار « جي دبليو اس ٢٢ »
*rādār jī dablyū is ithnayn wa ʿishrīn*

G

gymnasium جمنازيوم
*jimnāzyūm*
gyro جيروسكوب
*jīrūskūb*
gyro rotor دوامة جيروسكوبية
*duwwāma jīrūskūbīya*
gyrostabilized متوازن جيروسكوبيا
*mutawāzan jīrūskūbīyan*
gyro-stabilized optics بصريات متوازنة جيروسكوبيا
*baṣarīyāt mutawāzana jīrūskūbīyan*

G

# H



Hades ACM صاروخ متصل بالجو « هيديز »
*ṣārūkh muttaṣil bil-jaww haydīz*

Haidau craft زورق « هايداو »
*zawraq haydaw*

Haikou craft زورق « هايكو »
*zawraq haykū*

hail of bullets وابل من الرصاص
*wābil min ar-raṣāṣ*

Hainan Class ship سفينة طراز « هاينان »
*safīna ṭirāz haynān*

Hair Net radar رادار « هيرنت »
*rādar hīr nit*

Haiti هاييتي
*hāyītī*

Hai Ying SSM صاروخ سطح - سطح « هاي ينج »
*ṣārūkh saṭḥ-saṭḥ hāyy ying*

HAL Ajeet fighter طائرة مقاتلة « هال أجيت »
*ṭā'ira muqātila hāl ajīt*

Half Bow radar رادار « هاف بو »
*rādār hāf bū*

Halo helicopter طائرة عمودية « هيلو »
*ṭā'ira ʿamūdīya haylu*

halt! « قف ! »
*qiff*

halyard حبل القلع
*ḥabl al-qilʿ*

Hamburg destroyer مدمرة « هامبورج »
*mudammirat hāmbūrg*

hammer مطرقة
*miṭraqa*

Hancock carrier حاملة « هانكوك »
*ḥāmilat hankūk*

handbook كتيب . دليل
*kutayyib · dalīl*

hand flame cartridge launcher قاذفة خرطوشة لهب يدوية
*qādhifat kharṭūshat lahab yadawīya*

hand fuse فتيل يدوي
*fatīl yadawī*

hand grenade قنبلة يدوية
*qunbula yadawīya*

hand-grip مقبض يدوي
*miqbaḍ yadawī*

hand held ممسوك باليد
*mamsūk bil-yad*

hand over يسلم إلى
*yusallim ilā*

hands on throttle and stick اليدين على الخانق والذراع
*al-yadayn ʿalal-khāniq wadh-dhirāʿ*

hand to hand fighting قتال بالسلاح الأبيض
*qitāl bis-silāḥ al-abyaḍ*

hangar حظيرة
*ḥaẓīra*

hangar deck سطح الحظيرة
*saṭḥ al-haẓīra*

Han submarine غواصة « هان »
*ghawwāṣat hān*

harass the enemy إزعاج العدو
*izʿāj al-ʿadūw*

hardened silo صومعة مصلدة
*ṣawmaʿa muṣallada*

hardpoint نقطة تحميل
*nuqṭat taḥmīl*

hardware أجهزة
*ajhiza*

Hare helicopter طائرة عمودية « هير »
*ṭā'ira ʿamūdīya hayr*

Harke helicopter طائرة عمودية « هارك »
*ṭā'ira ʿamūdīya hārk*

HARM ARM صاروخ مضاد للرادار « هارم »
*ṣārūkh muḍādd lir-rādār hārm*

harness rig sling حمالة الأجهزة
*ḥammālat al-ajhiza*

| | |
|---|---|
| Harpoon missile<br>*ṣārūkh hārpūn* | صاروخ هارپون |
| Harrier aircraft<br>*ṭāʾirat hāryar* | طائرة « هارير » |
| Harrier V/STOL aircraft<br>*ṭāʾirat · hāryar vī/istūl* | طائرة « هارير ڤي استول » |
| Haruna destroyer<br>*mudammirat hārūnā* | مدمرة « هارونا » |
| HAS Mk 1 helicopter<br>*ṭāʾira ʿamūdīya itsh ayy is marka wāḥid* | طائرة عمودية « اتش ايه اس ماركة ١ » |
| HAS Mk 2 helicopter<br>*ṭāʾira ʿamūdīya itsh ayy is marka ithnayn* | طائرة عمودية « اتش ايه اس ماركة ٢ » |
| HAS Mk 5 helicopter<br>*ṭāʾira ʿamūdīya itsh ayy is marka khamsa* | طائرة عمودية « اتش ايه اس ماركة ٥ » |
| hatch cover<br>*ghiṭāʾ al-kuwwa* | غطاء الكوة |
| hauldown<br>*inzāl al-ḥibāl* | إنزال الحبال |
| haversack<br>*mizwada · jirāb al-muʾūna* | مزودة . جراب المؤونة |
| Hawk aircraft<br>*ṭāʾirat hūk* | طائرة « هوك » |
| Hawkeye aircraft<br>*ṭāʾirat hūkāyy* | طائرة « هوكاي » |
| Hawk patrol craft<br>*safīnat khafr as-sawāḥil hūk* | سفينة خفر سواحل « هوك » |
| Hawk Screech radar<br>*rādār hūk skrītsh* | رادار « هوك سكريتش » |
| hawser<br>*silk qaṭr · qals* | سلك قطر . قلس |
| Haze helicopter<br>*ṭāʾira ʿamūdīya hayz* | طائرة عمودية « هيز » |
| HE (high explosive)<br>*shadīd al-infijār* | شديدة الانفجار |
| head-down display<br>*ʿarḍ fī ḥujrat aṭ-ṭayyār* | عرض في حجرة الطيار |
| headgear<br>*ghiṭāʾ ar-raʾs* | غطاء الرأس |
| headlamp<br>*miṣbāḥ amāmī* | مصباح أمامي |
| Head Light radar<br>*rādār hīd lāyt* | رادار « هيد لايت » |
| headlight group<br>*majmūʿat al-anwār al-amāmīya* | مجموعة الأنوار الأمامية |
| Head Net-A radar<br>*rādār hīd nit ayy* | رادار « هيد نت ـ ايه » |
| Head Net-C radar<br>*rādār hīd nit sī* | رادار « هيد نت ـ سي » |
| head-on attack<br>*hujūm mubāshir* | هجوم مباشر |
| headquarters<br>*maqarr · riʾāsa* | مقر . رئاسة |
| headset<br>*sammāʿtā ar-raʾs* | سماعتا الرأس |
| head-up display<br>*arḍ bayānāt aṭ-ṭayarān ʿala wāqī ar-rīḥ* | عرض بيانات الطيران على واقي الريح |
| HE ammunition<br>*dhakhīra shadīdat al-infijār* | ذخيرة شديدة الانفجار |
| HEAT<br>*muḍādda lid-dabbābāt shadīdat al-infijār* | مضادة للدبابات شديدة الانفجار |
| HEAT ammunition<br>*dhakhīra muḍādda lid-dabbābāt shādīdat al-infijār* | ذخيرة مضادة للدبابات شديدة الانفجار |
| heat exchanger<br>*mubaddil ḥarārī* | مبدل حراري |
| HEAT fin-stabilized<br>*qadhīfa muḍadda lid-daddābāt shadīdat al-infijār muwāzana bir-riyāsh* | قذيفة مضادة للدبابات شديدة الانفجار موزونة بالرياش |
| heat-insulated<br>*maʿzūl ḥarārīyan* | معزول حرارياً |
| HEAT multi-purpose<br>*qadhīfa muḍādda lid-dabbābāt shadīdat al-infijār mutaʿaddidat al-aghrāḍ* | قذيفة مضادة للدبابات شديدة الانفجار متعددة الأغراض |
| HEAT projectile<br>*qadhīfa mudādda lid-dabbābāt shadīdat al-infijār* | قذيفة مضادة للدبابات شديدة الانفجار |
| heat radiation<br>*ishʿāʿ ḥarārī* | إشعاع حراري |
| heat receiver<br>*mustaqbil ḥarārī* | مستقبل حراري |
| heat-seeking weapon<br>*silāḥ bāḥith ʿan al-ḥarāra* | سلاح باحث عن الحرارة |
| heat-sensitive<br>*ḥisās lil-ḥarāra* | حساس للحرارة |
| heavy armament<br>*taslīḥ thaqīl* | تسليح ثقيل |
| heavy artillery tractor<br>*jarrār midfaʿīya thaqīla* | جرار مدفعية ثقيلة |
| heavy casualties<br>*khasāʾir fādiḥa* | خسائر فادحة |
| heavy-lift<br>*rafʿ thaqīl* | رفع ثقيل |

heavy machine-gun رشاش ثقيل
*rashshāsh thaqīl*
heavy motor brigade لواء آليات ثقيلة
*liwā' āliyāt thaqīla*
HE bomb قنبلة شديدة الانفجار
*qunbula shadīdat al-infijār*
Heckler and Koch (Co) شركة هكْلَرْ اند كوخ
*sharikat hiklar and kūkh*
HE fragmentation تشظية شديدة الانفجار
*tashẓīya shadīdat al-infijār*
height إرتفاع
*irtifā'*
height clearance خلوص الارتفاع
*khulūṣ al-irtifā'*
height-finder معين الارتفاع
*mu'ayyin al-irtifā'*
height-radar مقياس ارتفاع راداري
*miqyās irtifā' rādārī*
helicopter طائرة عمودية
*ṭā'ira 'amudīya*
helicopter carrier حاملة طائرات عمودية
*ḥamilat ṭā'irāt 'amūdīya*
helicopter control bridge جسر مراقبة الطائرات العمودية
*jisr murāqabat aṭ-ṭā'irāt al-'amūdīya*
helicopter deck سطح الطائرات العمودية
*saṭḥ at-ṭā'irāt al-'amūdīya*
helicopter direction radar رادار اتجاه الطائرات العمودية
*rādār ittijāh aṭ-ṭā'irāt al-'amūdīya*
helicopter flightdeck سطح الطيران للطائرات العمودية
*saṭḥ aṭ-ṭayarān liṭ-ṭā'irāt al-'amūdīya*
helicopter hangar حظيرة الطائرات العمودية
*ḥaẓīrat aṭ-ṭā'irāt al-'amūdīya*
helicopter platform منصة الطائرات العمودية
*minaṣṣat aṭ-ṭā'irāt al-'amūdīya*
helicopter squadron سرب طائرات عمودية
*sirb ṭā'irāt 'amūdīya*
Helix helicopter طائرة عمودية « هيلكس »
*ṭā'ira 'amūdīya hīliks*
helix-type من نوع مروحي
*min naw' mirwaḥī*
Hellfire missile صاروخ « هلفاير »
*ṣārūkh hilfāyr*
helmet خوذة
*khūdha*
hemispherical نصف كروي
*niṣf kurawī*
Hen Egg radar رادار « هن إيج »
*rādār hin ig*
Hen House radar رادار « هن هاوس »
*rādār hin haws*
Hen Nest radar رادار « هن نست »
*rādār hin nist*
Hen Roost radar رادار « هن روست »
*rādār hin rūst*
HE projectile قذيفة شديدة الانفجار
*qadhīfa shadīdat al-infijār*
Hercules airtransporter طائرة نقل « ماركيوليز »
*ṭā'irat naql harkyulīz*
Hermes carrier حاملة « هيرميز »
*ḥāmilat hirmīz*
Heroj submarine غواصة « هيروج »
*ghawwāṣat hīrūj*
HE warhead رأس قذيفة شديدة الانفجار
*ra's qadhīfa shadīdat al-infijār*
HF 200 radar رادار « اتش اف ٢٠٠ »
*rādār itsh if mi'atayn*
HH-3E helicopter طائرة عمودية « اتش اتش ـ ٣ ئي »
*ṭā'ira 'amūdīya itsh itsh thalātha ī*
HH-3F helicopter طائرة عمودية « اتش اتش ـ ٣ اف »
*ṭā'ira 'amūdīya itsh itsh thalātha if*
HH-65A helicopter طائرة عمودية « اتش اتش ٦٥ ايه »
*ṭā'ira 'amūdīya itsh itsh khamsa wa sittīn ayy*
HHS-2 helicopter طائرة عمودية « اتش اتش اس ـ ٢ »
*ṭā'ira 'amūdīya itsh itsh is ithnayn*
high acceleration تسارع عالٍ
*tasāru' 'āli*
high altitude إرتفاع عالٍ
*irtifā' 'āli*
high command القيادة العليا
*al-qiyāda al-'ulyā*
high explosive شديد الانفجار
*shadīd al-infijār*
high explosive fragmentation projectile قذيفة تشظية شديدة الانفجار
*qadhīfa tashẓīya shadīdat al-infijār*
high-explosive squash-head رأس مهروس شديد الانفجار
*ra's mahrūs shadīd al-infijār*
high explosive warhead رأس قذيفة شديد الانفجار
*ra's qadhīfa shadīdat al-infijār*
High Fix radar رادار « هاي فيكس »
*rādār hāyy fīks*

|  |  |
|---|---|
| high-frequency hull sonar<br>*sūnār badan as-safīna dhū taraddud ʿālī* | سونار بدن السفينة ذو تردد عالي |
| high-frequency signal<br>*ishāra dhāt taraddud ʿālin* | إشارة ذات تردد عالٍ |
| high-impulse motor<br>*muḥarrik ʿālī an-nabḍāt* | محرك عالي النبضات |
| High Lark radar<br>*rādār hāyy lārk* | رادار « هاي لارك » |
| high-level<br>*mustawa ʿāli* | مستوى عالٍ |
| High Lune radar<br>*rādār hāyy lūn* | رادار « هاي لون » |
| highly-inflammable<br>*sarīʿ al-ishtiʿāl* | سريع الاشتعال |
| highly mobile<br>*mutaḥarrik bi-ṣūra kabīra* | متحرك بصورة كبيرة |
| high performance<br>*adāʾ fāʾiq* | أداء فائق |
| High Pole IFF<br>*tamyīz aṣ-ṣadīq wal-ʿadūw hāyy pūl* | تمييز الصديق والعدو « هاي پول » |
| high-powered jammer<br>*mushawwish ʿālī al-qudra* | مشوش عالي القدرة |
| high power pistol<br>*musaddas ʿālī al-qudra* | مسدس عالي القدرة |
| high-power transmitter<br>*mursil ʿālī al-qudra* | مُرسل عالي القدرة |
| high priority<br>*awlawīya quṣwā* | أولوية قصوى |
| High Sieve radar<br>*rādār hāyy sīf* | رادار « هاي سيف » |
| high-speed<br>*surʿa ʿālīya* | سرعة عالية |
| Hi-liftloader<br>*ḥammāla rāfiʿa hāyy* | حمالة رافعة « هاي » |
| hill<br>*tall · haḍba* | تل . هضبة |
| hi-lo-hi combat<br>*qitāl murtafiʿ-munkhafiḍ-murtafiʿ* | قتال « مرتفع ـ منخفض ـ مرتفع » |
| Hind helicopter<br>*ṭāʾira ʿamūdīya hāynd* | طائرة عمودية « هايند » |
| Hindustan (Co)<br>*sharikat hindūstān* | شركة هندوستان |
| hinged rotor<br>*dawwār mafṣilī* | دوار مفصلي |
| hingeless rotor<br>*dawwār ʿadīm al-mafṣila* | دوار عديم المفصلة |
| Hip-C helicopter<br>*ṭāʾira ʿamūdīya hip-sī* | طائرة عمودية « هيب ـ سي » |
| Hispano-Suiza engine<br>*muḥarrik hispānū swīza* | محرك هيسبانو ـ سويزا « |
| hit<br>*iṣāba · ḍarba* | إصابة . ضربة |
| hit man<br>*muhājim* | مهاجم |
| HK 33 rifle<br>*bunduqīyat itsh kayy thalātha wa thalāthīn* | بندقية « اتش كيه ٣٣ » |
| HKP-7 rifle<br>*bunduqīyat itsh kayy pī-sabʿa* | بندقية « اتش كيه پي ـ ٧ » |
| HMG turret<br>*burj itsh im jī* | برج « اتش ام جي » |
| Hobos ASM<br>*ṣārūkh jaww-saṭḥ hūbūz* | صاروخ جو ـ سطح « هوبوز » |
| Hohlplatte pontoon<br>*ṭawf hūlplata* | طوف هولپلاتا |
| hoist (to)<br>*rafaʿa* | رفع |
| Hoku craft<br>*zawraq hūkū* | زورق « هوكو » |
| Hola craft<br>*zawraq hūlā* | زورق « هولا » |
| holding beam<br>*ḥuzmat istimrār* | حزمة استمرار |
| hold out against<br>*qāwama* | قاوم |
| Hollandse radar<br>*rādār hūlāndza* | رادار هولاندزه |
| hollow-charge rocket<br>*ṣārūkh bi-ḥashwa mufragha* | صاروخ بحشوة مفرغة |
| hollow-charge projectile<br>*qadhīfa bi-ḥashwa mufragha* | قذيفة بحشوة مفرغة |
| hollow-charge warhead<br>*raʾs maqdhūf bi-ḥashwa mufragha* | رأس مقذوف بحشوة مفرغة |
| holster<br>*jirāb lil-musaddas* | جراب المسدس |
| Holy Stone submarine<br>*ghawwāṣat hūlī stūn* | غواصة « هولي ستون » |
| home base<br>*maqarr maḥallī* | مقر محلي |
| home-based<br>*kāʾin maḥallīyan* | كائن محلياً |
| Home Guard<br>*al-ḥaras al-waṭanī* | الحرس الوطني |
| home-on jammer<br>*mushawwish at-tawjīh ar-rādārī* | مشوّش التوجيه الراداري |

homing طيران بالتوجيه نحو الهدف
*ṭayarān bit-tawjīh naḥwal-hadaf*
homing head رأس التوجيه الراداري
*ra's at-tawjīh ar-rādārī*
homing torpedo طوربيد بالتوجيه الراداري
*ṭūrbīd bit-tawjīh ar-rādārī*
Honduras هندوراس
*handūrās*
Honest John SSM صاروخ سطح ـ سطح « اونست جون »
*ṣārūkh saṭḥ-saṭḥ ūnist jūn*
Honggi-2 SAM صاروخ سطح ـ جو « هونجي ـ ٢ »
*ṣārūkh saṭḥ-jaww hūnjī ithnayn*
Hook helicopter طائرة عمودية « هوك »
*ṭā'ira ʿamūdīya hūk*
Hoop helicopter طائرة عمودية « هوپ »
*ṭā'ira ʿamūdīya hūp*
Hoplite helicopter طائرة عمودية « هوپلايت »
*ṭā'ira ʿamūdīya hūplāyt*
Hormone helicopter طائرة عمودية « هورمون »
*ṭā'ira ʿamūdīya hūrmūn*
horn بوق
*būq*
Hornet aircraft طائرة « هورنيت »
*ṭā'irat hūrnit*
Horn Spoon radar رادار « هورن سبون »
*rādār hūrn sbūn*
hose-equipped مجهز بخرطوم
*mujahhaz bi-kharṭūm*
hospital مستشفى
*mustashfa*
hospital treatment علاج بالمستشفى
*ʿilāj bil-mustashfa*
hospital unit وحدة مستشفى عسكرية
*wiḥdat mustashfa ʿaskarīya*
hospital ward جناح المستشفى
*janāḥ al-mustashfa*
hostage رهينة
*rahīna*
hostile عدواني . معادٍ
*ʿudwānī · muʿādin*
hostile aircraft طائرة معادية
*ṭā'ira muʿādīya*
hostile airspace مجال جوي معادي
*majāl jawwī muʿādī*
hostile emitter باعث معادي
*bāʿith muʿādī*
hostile missile صاروخ معادي
*ṣārūkh muʿādī*
hostile signal إشارة عدائية
*ishāra ʿadā'īya*
HOTAS concept مفهوم « هوتاس »
*mafhūm hūtās*
HOT ATM صاروخ مضاد للدبابات « هوت »
*ṣārūkh muḍādd lid-dabbābāt hūt*
hot bleed air هواء تهوية ساخن
*hawā' tahwiya sākhin*
Hot Dog grenade قنبلة يدوية « هوت دوج »
*qunbula yadawīya hūt dūg*
Hotel submarine غواصة « هوتيل »
*ghawwāṣat hūtīl*
hot gun barrel ماسورة مدفع ساخنة
*māsurat midfaʿ sākhina*
hot type launch إطلاق من نوع ساخن
*iṭlāq min nawʿ sākhin*
Hound A helicopter طائرة عمودية « هاوند ايه »
*ṭā'ira ʿamūdīya hawnd ayy*
Hound C helicopter طائرة عمودية « هاوند سي »
*ṭā'ira ʿamūdīya hawnd sī*
Hound-dog AGM صاروخ جو ـ ارض « هوند ـ دوج »
*ṣārūkh jaww-arḍ hawnd dūg*
hours of daylight ساعات النهار
*sāʿāt an-nahār*
hours on station ساعات الخدمة
*sāʿāt al-khidma*
hover حام
*ḥāma*
hovercraft حوامة « هوڤركرافت »
*ḥawwāma · hūvarkrāft*
howitzer مدفع هاوتزر
*midfaʿ hāwitsar*
HSA Reporter radar رادار « اتش اس ايه ـ ريپورتر »
*rādār itsh is ayy ripūrtar*
Hsiung Feng missile صاروخ سيونج فينج
*ṣārūkh syung fing*
HUD unit وحدة عرض بيانات الطيران على واقي الريح
*wiḥdat ʿard bayānāt aṭ-ṭayarān ʿala wāqi ar-rīḥ*
Huey Cobra helicopter طائرة عمودية « هيوي كوبرا »
*ṭā'ira ʿamūdīya hyūwi kūbra*
Hughes (Co) شركة هيوز
*sharikat hyūz*
hull بدن السفينة
*badan as-safīna*
hullborne محمول على الهيكل
*maḥmūl ʿalal-haykal*
Humaita ship سفينة « هيوميتا »
*safīnat hyūmāyta*

H

HU Mk 5 helicopter — طائرة عمودية « اتش يو مارك ٥ »
*ṭā'ira ʿamūdīya itsh yū mārk khamsa*

Hungarian — مجري
*majarī*

Hungary — المجر
*al-majar*

hunter — صياد . قناص
*ṣayyād · qannāṣ*

Hunter fighter — طائرة مقاتلة « هانتر »
*ṭā'ira muqātila hantar*

Hunt frigate — فرقاطة « هانت »
*firqāṭat hant*

hut — كوخ . معسكر خصاص
*kūkh · muʿaskar khiṣāṣ*

HVAP-T shot — قذيفة مخترقة للمدرعات « اتش ڤي ايه پي - تي »
*qadhīfa mukhtariqa lil-mudarraʿāt itsh vī ayy pī tī*

Hybrid propulsion — دفع « هايبريد »
*dafʿ hāybrīd*

hydraulically operated ramp — ممر منحدر هيدرو لي
*mamarr munḥadir hīdrūlī*

hydraulic crane — مرفاع هيدرو لي
*mirfāʿ hīdrūlī*

hydraulic equipment — معدات هيدرولية
*muʿaddāt hīdrūlīya*

hydraulic jack — رافعة هيدرولية
*rāfiʿa hīdrūlīya*

hydraulic shock absorber — مخمد صدمات هيدرو لي
*mukhammid ṣadamāt hīdrūlī*

hydraulic torque-converter — محول عزم هيدرو لي
*muḥawwil ʿazm hīdrūlī*

hydro-electric — هيدروكهربائي
*hīdrū kahrabā'ī*

hydrogas suspension — تعليق هيدروغازي
*taʿlīq hīdrū ghāzī*

hydrogen bomb — قنبلة هيدروجينية
*qunbula hidrūjīnīya*

hydrogen cyanide — سيانيد هيدروجيني
*sīyānīd hīdrujīnī*

hydro-pneumatic suspension — تعليق هوائي سائلي
*taʿlīq hawā'ī sā'ilī*

hydrostatic assistance system — نظام معاونة هيدروستاتي
*niẓām muʿāwana hīdrūstātī*

hydrostatic pressure — ضغط هيدروستاتي
*ḍaghṭ hīdrūstātī*

hypervelocity — السرعة المفرطة
*as-surʿa al-mufriṭa*

Hywema vehicle lift — مرفاع مركبة « هايويما »
*mirfāʿ markaba hāywīma*

HZ-5 aircraft — طائرة « اتش زد ـ ٥ »
*ṭā'irat itsh zid khamsa*

# I

IA-50 air transport — طائرة نقل « أي ايه - ٥٠ »
*ṭāirat naql āyy ayy khamsīn*

I-band monopulse fighter radar — رادار طائرة مقاتلة احادى النبضة ـ نطاق أي
*rādār ṭāʾira muqātila uḥādī an-nabḍa - niṭāq āyy*

ICBM — صاروخ بالستي عابر للقارات
*ṣārūkh bālistī ʿābir lil-qārāt*

icebreaker — سفينة كاسحة جليد
*safīnat kāsiḥat jalīd*

ice reconnaissance — إستطلاع جليدي
*istiṭlāʿ jalīdī*

identification — تمييز . إثبات الهوية
*tamyīz · ithbāt al-huwīya*

Identification, Friend or Foe — نظام تمييز الصديق والعدو
*niẓām tamyīz aṣ-ṣadīq wal-ʿadūw*

identity card — بطاقة هوية
*biṭṭāqat huwīya*

idler — ترس وسيط
*turs wasīṭ*

IFF — نظام تمييز الصديق والعدو
*niẓām tamyīz aṣ-ṣadīq wal-ʿadūw*

IFF interrogator unit — وحدة استجواب لتمييز الصديق والعدو
*wiḥdat istijwab li-tamyiz aṣ-ṣadīq wal-ʿadūw*

IFF radar — رادار تمييز الصديق والعدو
*rādār tamyīz aṣ-ṣadīq wal-ʿadūw*

IFF/SIF transponder — جهاز سائل ومجيب لتمييز الصديق والعدو / لخاصية التمييز الانتقائي
*jihāz sāʾil wa mujīb li-tamyīz aṣ-ṣadīq wal-ʿadūw li-khāṣīyat at-tamyīz al-intiqāʾī*

ignite — أشعل
*ashʿala*

igniter grenade — قنبلة إشعال يدوية
*qunbulat ishʿāl yadawī*

igniter squibs — مفرقعات إشعال
*mufarqiʿāt ishʿāl*

ignition delay — تعويق الاشتعال
*taʿwīq al-ishtiʿāl*

Ikara ASW — سلاح مضاد للغواصات « إيكارا »
*ṣilāḥ muḍādd lil-ghawwāṣāt īkāra*

IKL 540 submarine — غواصة « أي كيه ال ٥٤٠ »
*ghawwāṣat āyy kayy il khams miʾa wa arbaʿīn*

IK V 91 tank — دبابة « أي كيه ڤي ٩١ »
*dabbābat āyy kayy vī wāḥid wa tisʿīn*

IL-14 aircraft — طائرة « إل ـ ١٤ »
*ṭāʾirat il arbaʿata ʿashar*

IL-18 aircraft — طائرة « إل ـ ١٨ »
*ṭāʾirat il thamānyata ʿashar*

IL-28 aircraft — طائرة « إل ـ ٢٨ »
*ṭāʾirat il thamānya wa ʿishrīn*

IL-38 ASW aircraft — طائرة « إل ـ ٣٨ ايه اس دبليو »
*ṭāʾirat il thamānya wa thalāthīn ayy is dabljū*

IL-76 airtransport — طائرة نقل « إل ـ ٧٦ »
*ṭāʾirat naql il sitta wa sabʿīn*

IL-76 AWAC — طائرة « اواك إل ـ ٧٦ »
*ṭāʾirat āwāk il – sitta wa sabʿīn*

IL-86 airtransporter — طائرة نقل « إل ـ ٨٦ »
*ṭāʾirat naql il sitta wa thamānīn*

illuminated — مضاء
*muḍāʾ*

illuminating ammunition — ذخيرة إضاءة
*dhakkīrat iḍāʾa*

illuminating cartridge — خرطوشة إضاءة
*kharṭūshat iḍāʾa*

illumination — إضاءة . إنارة
*iḍāʾa · ināra*

illuminator — مصباح مضيء
*misbāḥ muḍīʾ*

Ilyushin (Co) شركة اليوشين
*sharikat ilyūshin*
image-intensifier مكثف شدة الصورة
*mukaththif shiddat aṣ-ṣūra*
immobilise (to) جمّد
*jammada*
immobilization تجميد . تثبيت
*tajmīd · tathbīt*
immunity to jamming مناعة ضد التشويش
*manāʿʿa ḍidd at at-tashwīsh*
immunization تحصين
*taḥṣīn*
impact صدمة
*ṣadma*
impact fuse صمامة صدمية
*ṣimāma ṣadmīya*
Impala fighter طائرة مقاتلة « إمپالا »
*ṭāʾira muqātila impālā*
impenetrable لا يخترق
*lā yukhtaraq*
implosion إنفجار للداخل
*infijār lid-dākhil*
IMP mine detector كاشف ألغام « أي ام پي »
*kāshif alghām āyy im pī*
improved avionics إلكترونيات طيران محسنة
*iliktrūnīyāt ṭayarān muḥassana*
improved capability إمكانية محسنة
*imkanīya muḥassana*
Improved Hawk AGM صاروخ جو ـ أرض محسّن « هوك »
*ṣārūkh jaww-arḍ muḥassan hūk*
Improved TOW صاروخ تو محسن
*ṣārūkh tū muḥassan*
in action عاملاً
*ʿāmilan*
incendiary ammunition ذخيرة محرقة
*dhakhīra muḥriqa*
incendiary bomb قنبلة محرقة
*qunbula muḥriqa*
incendiary device أداة محرقة
*adāh muḥriqa*
incendiary frangible grenade قنبلة يدوية متشظية محرقة
*qunbula yadawīya mutashaẓẓīya muḥriqa*
incendiary projectile مقذوف محرق
*maqdhūf muḥriq*
incendiary warhead رأس قذيفة محرقة
*raʾs qadhīfa muḥriqa*
in-coming data البيانات الواردة
*al-bayānāt al-wārida*
in concert بانسجام . باتفاق
*bi-insijām · bi-ittifāq*
independently targeted مضبوط على هدف بصورة مستقلة
*maḍbūt ʿala hadaf bi-ṣūra muṣtaqila*
India الهند
*al-hind*
Indian هندي
*hindī*
Indigo SAM صاروخ سطح ـ جو « انديجو »
*ṣārūkh saṭḥ-jaww indīgū*
individual movements, identify تحديد التحركات الفردية
*taḥdīd al-ḥarakāt al-fardīya*
individual training تدريب فردي
*tadrīb fardī*
individual weapon سلاح شخصي
*silāḥ shakhṣī*
indoctrination تلقين
*talqīn*
Indonesia اندونيسيا
*indūnīsya*
Indonesian اندونيسي
*indūnīsī*
inertial guidance توجيه بالقصور الذاتي
*tawjīh bil-quṣūr adh-dhātī*
inertial guidance platform منصة التوجيه بالقصور الذاتي
*minaṣṣat at-tawjīh bil-quṣūr adh-dhātī*
inertial guidance system نظام التوجيه بالقصور الذاتي
*niẓām at-tawjīh bil-quṣūr adh-dhātī*
inertial navigation guidance توجيه ملاحي بالقصور الذاتي
*tawjīh mallāhī bil-quṣūr adh-dhātī*
inertial system نظام قصور ذاتي
*niẓām quṣūr dhātī*
inertial/Tercom guidance توجيه بالقصور الذاتي / تيركوم
*tawjīh bil-quṣūr adh-dhātī/ tīrkūm*
inert pellet كرية خاملة
*kurayya khāmila*
infantry جُند المشاة
*jund al-mushāh*
infantry battalion كتيبة مشاة
*katībat mushāh*
infantry brigade لواء مشاة
*liwāʾ mushāh*

infantry combat vehicle مركبة قتال للمشاة
*markabat qitāl lil-mushāh*
infantry company سرية مشاة
*sarīyat mushāh*
infantry division فرقة مشاة
*firqat mushāh*
infantry fighting vehicle مركبة قتال للمشاة
*markabat qitāl lil-mushāh*
infantry vehicle مركبة مشاة
*markabat mushāh*
infected zone منطقة ملوثة بالجراثيم
*minṭaqa mulawwatha bil-jarāthīm*
infectious مُعدٍ
*muʿdin*
infectious disease داء مُعْدٍ
*dāʾ muʿdin*
infiltrate (to) يتسلل . يتسرب
*yatasallal · yatasarrab*
infiltration تسلل . تسرب
*tasallul · tasarrub*
inflammable سريع الالتهاب
*sarīʿ al-iltihāb*
inflatable air lifting bag كيس رفع جوي قابل للنفخ
*kīs rafʿ jawwī qābil lin-nafkh*
inflatable buoyancy tube أنبوب عوم قابل للنفخ
*unbūb ʿawm qābil lin-nafkh*
inflatable life jacket سترة نجاة قابلة للنفخ
*sutrat najāh qābila lin-nafkh*
inflatable liferaft رمث نجاة قابل للنفخ
*ramath najāh qābil lin-nafkh*
inflatable pontoon طوف قابل للنفخ
*ṭawf qābil lin-nafkh*
inflight adaptable antennae هوائي قابل للتكيف اثناء الطيران
*hawāʾī qābil lit-takayyuf athnāʾ aṭ-ṭayarān*
inflight cocking device أداة للقدح اثناء الطيران
*adāh lil-qadḥ athnāʾa aṭ-ṭayarān*
inflight refuelling تزود بالوقود أثناء الطيران
*tazawwud bil-wuqūd athnāʾa aṭ-tayarān*
inflight refuelling gear جهاز التزود بالوقود أثناء الطيران
*jihāz at-tazawwud bil-wuqūd athnāʾa aṭ-ṭayarān*
inflight refuelling probe مسبار التزود بالوقود أثناء الطيران
*misbār at-tazawwud bil-wuqūd athnāʾ aṭ-ṭayarān*
information معلومات
*maʿlūmāt*

information room غرفة استعلامات
*ghurft istiʿlāmāt*
information system نظام الاستعلامات
*niẓām al-istiʿlāmāt*
informer مخبر . واشي
*mukhbir · wāshi*
infra red دون الحمراء
*dūn al-ḥamrāʾ*
infra-red beacon منارة بالاشعة دون الحمراء
*mināra bil-ashiʿʿa dūn al-ḥamrāʾ*
infra-red decoy شرك بالأشعة دون الحمراء
*sharak bil-ashiʿʿa dūn al-ḥamrāʾ*
infra-red device أداة بالأشعة دون الحمراء
*adāh bil-ashiʿʿa dūn al-ḥamrāʾ*
infra-red driving light ضوء موجه بالأشعة دون الحمراء
*ḍawʾ muwajjih bil-ashiʿʿa dūn al-ḥamrāʾ*
infra-red gathering system نظام تجميع بالأشعة دون الحمراء
*niẓām tajmīʿ bil-ashiʿʿa dūn al-ḥamrāʾ*
infra-red grenade قنبلة يدوية بالأشعة دون الحمراء
*qunbula yadawīya bil-ashiʿʿa dūn al-ḥamrāʾ*
infra-red launcher قاذفة بالأشعة دون الحمراء
*qādhifa bil-ashiʿʿa dūn al-ḥamrāʾ*
infra-red linescan مسح خطي بالأشعة دون الحمراء
*masḥ khaṭṭī bil-ashiʿʿa dūn al-ḥamrāʾ*
infra-red localizer محدد موقع بالأشعة دون الحمراء
*muḥaddid mawqiʿ bil-ashiʿʿa dūn al-ḥamrāʾ*
infra-red night-vision equipment معدات رؤية ليلية بالأشعة دون الحمراء
*muʿaddāt ruʾya laylīya bil-ashiʿʿa dūn al-ḥamrāʾ*
infra-red receiver مُستقبل بالأشعة دون الحمراء
*mustaqbil bil-ashiʿʿa dūn al-ḥamrāʾ*
infra-red search light نور كاشف بالاشعة دون الحمراء
*nūr kāshif bil-ashiʿʿa dūn al-ḥamrāʾ*
infra-red seeker باحث بالأشعة دون الحمراء
*bāḥith bil-ashiʿʿa dūn al-ḥamrāʾ*
infra-red sensor جهاز احساس بالأشعة دون الحمراء
*jihāz iḥsās bil-ashiʿʿa dūn al-ḥamrāʾ*

I

infra-red suitcase حقيبة بالأشعة دون الحمراء
*ḥaqība bil-ashiʿʿa dūn al-ḥamrāʾ*

infra-red terminal homing توجيه آلي طرفي بالأشعة دون الحمراء
*tawjīh ālī ṭarafī bil-ashiʿʿa dūn al-ḥamrāʾ*

infra-red wavelengths أطوال موجية للاشعة دون الحمراء
*aṭwāl mawjīya lil-ashiʿʿa dūn al-ḥamrāʾ*

injection حقن
*ḥaqn*

injury أذى . ضرر . عطل
*adhan · ḍarar · ʿuṭl*

inlet منفذ . مدخل
*manfadh · madkhal*

innoculation تلقيح . تطعيم
*talqīḥ · taṭʿīm*

in-put data بيانات الدخل
*bayānāt ad-dakhl*

in reserve في الاحتياط
*fil-iḥtiyāṭ*

insecticide مبيد حشري
*mubīd ḥasharī*

in service في الخدمة
*fil-khidma*

inshore patrol craft زورق حراسة ساحلية
*zawraq ḥirāsa sāḥilīya*

insignia علامات . شعارات
*ʿalāmāt · shiʿārāt*

inspection تفتيش . فحص
*taftīsh · faḥṣ*

inspection panel لوحة التفتيش
*lawḥat at-taftīsh*

inspection parade إستعراض التفتيش
*istiʿrāḍ at-taftīsh*

inspection workshop ورشة فحص
*warshat faḥṣ*

installation تركيب . إقامة
*tarkīb · iqāma*

instruction تعليم . تدريب . أمر
*taʿlīm · tadrīb · amr*

instruction book دليل . كتيّب تشغيل
*dalīl · kutayyib tashghīl*

insubordination عصيان . تمرد
*ʿiṣyān · tamarrud*

insurgent عاص . متمرد
*ʿāṣi · mutamarrid*

insurrection ثورة . تمرد
*thawra · tamarrud*

integral bayonet حربة مدمجة
*ḥarba mudammaja*

integral reload capability إمكانية إعادة تلقيم مدمجة
*imkānīya iʿādat talqīm mudammaja*

integrated fire control system نظام متكامل للسيطرة على الرمي
*niẓām mutakāmil lis-sayṭara ʿalar-ramī*

integrated naval system نظام بحري متكامل
*niẓām baḥrī mutakāmil*

intelligence إستخبارات
*istikhbārāt*

intelligence agency وكالة استخبارات
*wakālat istikhbārāt*

intelligence agent عميل استخبارات
*ʿamīl istikhbārāt*

intelligence analysis facility تسهيلات تحليل الاستخبارات
*tashīlāt taḥlīl al-istikhbārāt*

intelligence-gathering mission مهمة جمع الاستخبارات
*muhimmat jamʿ al-istikhbārāt*

intelligence information بيانات استخبارات
*bayānāt istikhbārāt*

intelligence organization منظمة استخبارات
*munaẓẓamat istikhbārāt*

intelligence planner مخطط استخبارات
*mukhaṭṭiṭ istikhbārāt*

intelligence report تقرير استخبارات
*taqrīr istikhbārāt*

intensive fire نيران مكثفة
*nīrān mukaththafa*

intercept (to) اعترض
*iʿtaraḍa*

intercepted معترض
*muʿtaraḍ*

interception إعتراض
*iʿtirāḍ*

interception range مدى الاعتراض
*mada al-iʿtirāḍ*

interceptor طائرة اعتراض
*ṭāʾirat iʿtirāḍ*

interceptor squadron سرب طائرات معترضة
*sirb ṭāʾirāt muʿtariḍa*

inter-continental ballistic missile صاروخ بالستى عابر للقارات
*ṣārūkh bālistī ʿābir lil-qārāt*

intercontinental range المدى بين القارات
*al-mada bayn al-qārāt*

interdiction strike ضرب تحريم
*ḍarb taḥrīm*

intermediate-range ballistic missile (IRBM) صاروخ بالستي متوسط المدى
*sārūkh bālistī mutawaṣṣiṭ al-mada*
internal damping كبت داخلي
*kabt dākhilī*
internal fuel وقود داخلي
*wuqūd dākhilī*
internal image intensifier مكثف شدة صورة داخلي
*mukaththif shiddat aṣ-ṣūra dākhilī*
internal mechanism آلية داخلية
*ālīya dakhilīya*
internal volume حجم داخلي
*hajm dakhilī*
internment إعتقال
*iʿtiqāl*
interpolate إستكمل
*istakmala*
interpret (to) فسر . ترجم
*fassara · tarjama*
interpretation ترجمة . تفسير
*tarjama · tafsīr*
interpreter مترجم . مفسر
*mutarjim · mufassir*
interrogate (to) إستجوب
*istajwaba*
interrogation إستجواب
*istijwāb*
interrogator مستجوب
*mustajwib*
intersection تقاطع
*taqāṭuʿ*
intership بين السفن
*bayn as-sufun*
intervention situation حالة التدخل
*ḥālat at-tadākhul*
Intrepid class طراز انتربيد
*ṭirāz intrabīd*
intruder tanker aircraft طائرة صهريجية اقتحامية
*ṭāʾira ṣihrījīya iqtiḥāmīya*
invade (to) غزا . أغار
*ghaza · aghāra*
invader غاز . مكتسح
*ghāzin · muktasiḥ*
invasion غزو . غارة
*ghasū · ghāra*
inventory جرد . بيان الجرد
*jard · bayān al-jard*
inverted-cassegrain antenna هوائي « كاسجرين » مقلوب
*hawāʾī kāsgrīn maqlūb*

investigating board مجلس تحقيق
*majlis taḥqīq*
investigating officer ضابط تحقيقات
*ḍābiṭ taḥqīqāt*
investigation بحث . إستقصاء تحقيق
*baḥth · istiqṣāʾ · taḥqīq*
Invincible cruiser طرادة « إنفينسابل »
*ṭarrādat invīnsibal*
Iowa cruiser طرادة أيووا
*ṭarrādat āyūwa*
IPN 10 data processing جهاز تحليل البيانات « أي پي إن ١٠ »
*jihāz taḥlīl al-bayānāt āyy pī in ʿashara*
Iran ايران
*āyrān*
Iranian ايراني
*āyrānī*
Iraq العراق
*al-ʿirāq*
Iraqi عراقي
*ʿirāqī*
Ireland ايرلندة
*āyrlanda*
Irish ايرلندي
*āyrlandī*
IR-homing missile صاروخ موجه بالأشعة دون الحمراء
*ṣārūkh muwajjah bil-ashiʿʿa dūn al-ḥamrāʾ*
IR linescan مسح خطي بالأشعة دون الحمراء
*masḥ khaṭṭī bil-ashiʿʿa dūn al-ḥamrāʾ*
IR night-vision رؤية ليلية بالأشعة دون الحمراء
*ruʾya laylīya bil-ashiʿʿa dūn al-ḥamrāʾ*
Iroquois destroyer مدمرة إراكوا
*mudammirat irakwā*
IR sources مصادر الأشعة دون الحمراء
*maṣādir al-ashiʿʿa dūn al-ḥamrāʾ*
IR-suppressing كبت بالأشعة دون الحمراء
*kabt bil-ashiʿʿa dūn al-ḥamrāʾ*
IR-suppressing exhaust عادم كبت بالأشعة دون الحمراء
*ʿādim kabt bil-ashiʿʿa dūn al-ḥamrāʾ*
IR telescope تلسكوب بالأشعة دون الحمراء
*talskūb bil-ashiʿʿa dūn al-ḥamrāʾ*
isolation عزل . فصل
*ʿazl · faṣl*

isolation hospital مستشفى العزل
*mustashfa al-ʿazl*

isolation ward جناح العزل
*janāḥ al-ʿazl*

Israel اسرائيل
*isrāʾīl*

Israel Aircraft Industries (Co) شركة مصانع الطائرات الاسرائيلية
*sharikat maṣāniʿ aṭ-ṭāʾirāt al-isrāʾīlīya*

Israeli اسرائيلي
*isrāʾīlī*

issue أصدر . وزع
*aṣdara·wazzaʿa*

ISU-122 gun مدفع « أي اس يو - ١٢٢ »
*midfaʿ āyy is yū miʾa wa ithnayn wa ʿishrīn*

Italian الايطالي
*āyṭālī*

Italy ايطاليا
*āyṭālyā*

Ivan Rogov ship سفينة « ايڤان روجوڤ »
*safīnat āyvan rūgūv*

Ivory Coast ساحل العاج
*saḥil al-ʿāj*

Iwo Jima ship سفينة « ايوا جيما »
*safīnat āywa jīma*

IW XL70E3 rifle بندقية « أي دبليو اكس إل ٧٠ ئي ٣ »
*bunduqīyat āyy dablyū iks il sabʿīn ī thalātha*

# J

J-class submarine — غواصة « طراز جيه »
*ghawwāṣa ṭirāz jī*

J-4 fighter — طائرة مقاتلة « جيه ـ ٤ »
*ṭāʾira muqātila jayy arbaʿa*

J-5 fighter — طائرة مقاتلة « جيه ـ ٥ »
*ṭāʾira muqātila jayy khamsa*

J-6 fighter — طائرة مقاتلة « جيه ـ ٦ »
*ṭāʾira muqātila jayy sitta*

J-7 fighter — طائرة مقاتلة « جيه ـ ٧ »
*ṭāʾira muqātila jayy sabʿa*

J35 aircraft — طائرة « جيه ٣٥ »
*ṭāʾirat jayy khamsa wa thalāthīn*

J52-P-408 turbojet — طائرة نفاثة تربينية « جيه ٥٢ ـ پي ٤٠٨ »
*ṭāʾirat naffātha turbīnīya jayy ithnayn wa khamsīn pī arbaʿ miʾa wa thamānya*

J58 engine — محرك « جيه ٥٨ »
*muḥarrik jayy thamānya wa khamsīn*

J79-17 turbojet — طائرة نفاثة تربينية « جيه ٧٩ ـ ١٧ »
*ṭāʾirat naffātha turbīnīya jayy tisʿa wa sabʿīn – sabʿata ʿashar*

J79-GE-15 turbojet — طائرة نفاثة تربينية « جيه ٧٩ ـ جي ئي ـ ١٥ »
*ṭāʾirat naffātha turbīnīya jayy tisʿa wa sabʿīn – jī ī khamsata ʿashar*

J79-J1E turbojet — طائرة نفاثة تربينية « جيه ٧٩ ـ جيه ١ ئي »
*ṭāʾirat naffātha turbīnīya jayy tisʿa wa sabʿīn – jayy wāḥid ī*

J85-21A turbojet — طائرة نفاثة تربينية « جيه ٨٥ ـ ٢١ ئي »
*ṭāʾirat naffātha turbīnīya jayy khamsa wa thamānīn – wāḥid wa ʿishrīn ayy*

JA37 fighter — طائرة مقاتلة « جيه ايه ٣٧ »
*ṭāʾira muqātila jayy ayy sabʿa wa thalāthīn*

jacket — دثار . غلاف
*dithār · ghilāf*

jacket slot — فرضة الغلاف
*furḍat al-ghilāf*

Jagdpanzer Kanone tank — دبابة ياكت بانتسر كانونة
*dabbābat yakt bantsar kanūna*

Jaguar — جاجوار
*jāgwār*

jam (to) — شوش
*shawwasha*

Jamaica — جامايكا
*jāmāykā*

jammer — مشوّش
*mushawwish*

jammer system — نظام تشويش الكتروني
*niẓām tashwīsh iliktrūnī*

jamming transmission — إرسال تشويش
*irsāl tashwīsh*

Japan — اليابان
*al-yābān*

Japanese — ياباني
*yābānī*

Jararaca armoured car — عربة مدرعة « جاراركا »
*ʿaraba mudarraʿa jārārākā*

Jastreb aircraft — طائرة « جاسترب »
*ṭāʾirat jāstrib*

Jay Bird radar — رادار « جاي بيرد »
*rādār jayy bīrd*

Jeanne d'Arc carrier — حاملة « جاندارك »
*ḥāmilat jandārk*

jet-deflection order — أمر تغيير مسار الطائرة
*amr taghyīr masār aṭ-ṭāʾira*

jet interceptor — طائرة اعتراض نفاثة
*ṭāʾirat iʿtirāḍ naffātha*

jetpipe — أنبوبة نافورية
*unbūba nāfūrīya*

Jet Provost aircraft — طائرة « جيت پروڤوست »
*ṭāʾirat jit prūvūst*

Jet Ranger helicopter — طائرة عمودية « جيت رينجر »
*ṭāʾira ʿamūdīya jit raynjar*

Jetstar aircraft — طائرة « جيتستار »
*ṭāʾirat jit stār*

Jetstream aircraft — طائرة « جيتستريم »
*ṭāʾirat jit strīm*

jettisonable — قابل للتفريغ
*qābil lit-tafrigh*

jettisoned — مفرّغ
*mufarragh*

Jiangdong frigate — فرقاطة « جانج دونج »
*firqāṭat jāngdūng*

Jianghu frigate — فرقاطة « جينغو »
*firqāṭat jāngū*

Jiangnan frigate — فرقاطة « جانج نان »
*firqāṭat jangnān*

Jihan patrol craft — زورق حراسة « جيهان »
*zawraq ḥirāsa jihān*

JJ-4 trainer — طائرة تدريب « جيه جيه ـ ٤ »
*ṭāʾirat tadrīb jayy jayy arbaʿa*

John F. Kennedy carrier — حاملة طائرات « جون ف كنيدي »
*ḥāmilat ṭāʾirat jūn if kinidī*

joint tactical information distribution — توزيع مشترك للمعلومات التكتيكية
*tawzīʿ mushtarak lil-maʿlūmāt at-taktīkīya*

Jolly Green Giant helicopter — طائرة عمودية « جولي جرين جاينت »
*ṭāʾira ʿamūdīya jūlī grīn jāyant*

Jordan — الأردن
*al-urdun*

Jordanian — اردني
*urdunnī*

joystick — ذراع القيادة . عمود الادارة
*dhirāʿ al-qiyāda · ʿamūd al-idāra*

JP-7 fuel — وقود « جيه بي ٧ »
*wuqūd jayy pī sabʿa*

JP-233 bomb — قنبلة « جيه بي ـ ٢٣٣ »
*qunbulat jayy pī miʾatayn wa thalātha wa thalāthīn*

JPzSK-105 gun — مدفع « جيه بي زد اس كيه ـ ١٠٥ »
*midfaʿ jayy pī zid is kayy miʾa wa khamsa*

JT9D engine — محرك « جيه تي ٩ دي »
*muḥarrik jayy tī tisʿa dī*

Juliett submarine — غواصة « جولييت »
*ghawwāṣat jūlyit*

jump! — « إقفز ! »
*iqfiz*

jump seat — مقعد ينطوي
*maʿqad yanṭawī*

junction box — صندوق توصيل . علبة توزيع
*ṣundūq tawṣīl · ʿulbat tawzīʿ*

jungle hat — قبعة الدغل
*qabbaʿat ad-daghal*

junior sergeant — الرقيب الأحدث
*ar-raqīb al-aḥdath*

JZ-6 aircraft — طائرة « جيه زد ـ ٦ »
*ṭāʾirat jayy zid sitta*

J

# K

K9-25 helicopter طائرة عمودية « كيه ٩ ـ ٢٥ »
*ṭā'ira ʿamūdīya kayy tisʿa khamsa wa ʿishrīn*

K-13A missile صاروخ « كيه ـ ١٣ ايه »
*ṣārūkh kayy thalāthata ʿashar ayy*

K60 engine محرك « كيه ٦٠ »
*muḥarrik kayy sittīn*

Ka-6D tanker aircraft طائرة صهريج « كيه ايه ـ ٦ دي »
*ṭā'irat ṣihrīj kayy ayy sitta dī*

Ka-25 helicopter طائرة عمودية « كيه ايه ـ ٢٥ »
*ṭā'ira ʿamudīya kayy ayy khamsa wa ʿishrīn*

Ka-27 helicopter طائرة عموديه « كيه ايه ـ ٢٧ »
*ṭā'ira ʿamudīya kayy ayy sabʿa wa ʿishrīn*

Ka-32 helicopter طائرة عمودية « كيه ايه ـ ٣٢ »
*ṭā'ira ʿamudīya kayy ayy ithnayn wa thalāthīn*

Kaiser radar رادار « كايزر »
*rādār kāyzar*

KAM 9 missile صاروخ « كيه ايه ام ٩ »
*ṣārūkh kayy ayy im tisʿa*

Kaman (Co) شركة كامان
*sharikat kāmān*

Kaman helicopter طائرة عمودية « كامان »
*ṭā'ira ʿamūdīya kāmān*

KAMAZ vehicle مركبة « كاماز »
*markabat kāmāz*

Kamov (Co) شركة كاموف
*sharikat kāmūv*

Kampuchea كمبوتشيا
*kambūtshīya*

Kangaroo ASM صاروخ جو ـ سطح « كانجارو »
*ṣārūkh jaww-saṭḥ kāngārū*

Kanin ship سفينة كانين
*safīnat kānīn*

Kara cruiser طرادة « كارا »
*ṭarrādat kārā*

Kashin destroyer مدمرة « كاشين »
*mudammirat kāshīn*

Kawasaki (Co) شركة كاواسكي
*sharikat kāwāsākī*

KAZ fuse مصهر « كيه ايه زد »
*miṣhar kayy ayy zid*

KBA-B cannon مدفع هاون « كيه بي ايه »
*midfaʿ hāwun kayy bī ayy-bī*

KC-10 tanker aircraft طائرة صهريج « كيه سي ـ ١٠ »
*ṭā'irat ṣihrīj kayy sī ʿashara*

KC-135 tanker aircraft طائرة صهريج « كيه سي ـ ١٣٥ »
*ṭā'irat ṣihrīj kayy sī mi'a wa khamsa wa thalāthīn*

KC-707 air tanker طائرة صهريج « كيه سي ـ ٧٠٧ »
*ṭā'irat ṣihrīj kayy sī sabʿa mi'a wa sabʿ*

KCA cannon مدفع هاون « كيه سي ايه »
*midfaʿ hāwun kayy sī ayy*

keel hatch كوة الصالب
*kuwwat aṣ-ṣālib*

keep step! حافظ على الخطوة !
*ḥāfiẓ ʿalal-khuṭwa*

Keith Nelson patrol craft زورق حراسة « كيث نيلسون »
*zawraq ḥirāsa kīth nilsūn*

Kelt ASM صاروخ جو ـ سطح « كيلت »
*ṣārūkh jaww-saṭḥ kilt*

Kennel ASM صاروخ جو ـ سطح « كنال »
*ṣārūkh jaww-saṭḥ kinal*

Kenya كينيا
*kīnyā*

Kenyan كيني
*kīnī*

kerosene كيروسين
*kīrūsīn*

Kerry ASM صاروخ جو ـ سطح « كيري »
*ṣārūkh jaww-saṭḥ-kirī*

kettledrum طبلة
*ṭabla*
Kfir aircraft طائرة « كفير »
*ṭā'irat kfīr*
KGB border guards حرس الحدود « كيه جي بي »
*ḥaras al-ḥudūd kayy jī bī*
KGB troops قوات « كيه جي بي »
*qūwāt kayy jī bī*
khaki خاكي
*khākī*
Khalid tank دبابة « خالد »
*dabbābat khālid*
Kidd destroyer مدمرة « كيد »
*mudammarat kīd*
Kiev carrier حاملة طائرات « كييف »
*ḥāmilat ṭā'irāt kiyīv*
Kildin ship سفينة « كيلدين »
*safīnat kildin*
kill (to) يقتل
*yaqtul*
killed in action قتيل المعركة
*qatīl al-ma'raka*
killer قاتل
*qātil*
Killer Junior projectile مقذوف « كيلر جونيور »
*maqdhūf kilar jūnyar*
Killer Senior projectile مقذوف « كيلر سنيور »
*maqdhūf kilar sīnyar*
kilometre كيلو متر
*kīlūmitar*
Kilo submarine غواصة « كيلو »
*ghawwāṣat kīlū*
kiloton yield معيار بالكيلوطن
*mi'yār bil-kīlūṭan*
kinematic vehicle مركبة حركية
*markaba ḥarakīya*
kinetic energy طاقة حركة
*ṭāqat ḥaraka*
King Air aircraft طائرة « كينج آير »
*ṭā'irat king ayr*
Kingfish ASM صاروخ جو ـ سطح « كينجفيش »
*ṣārūkh jaww-saṭḥ kingfīsh*
Kingfisher missile صاروخ « كينجفيشر »
*ṣārūkh kingfishar*
kinked main-rotor blade ريشة دوامة رئيسية معقودة
*rīshat duwwāma ra'īsīya ma'qūda*
Kipper ASM صاروخ جو ـ سطح « كيبر »
*ṣārūkh jaww-saṭḥ kipar*

Kirov cruiser طرادة « كيروف »
*ṭarrādat kīrūv*
kit صندوق أدوات · تجهيزات فردية
*ṣundūq adawāt · tajhīzāt fardīya*
kit bag كيس مهمات
*kīs muhimmāt*
Kitchen ASM صاروخ جو ـ سطح « كيتشن »
*ṣārūkh jaww-saṭḥ kitshin*
Kite Screech radar رادار « كايت سكريتش »
*rādār kāyt skrītsh*
kit inspection تفتيش أمتعة
*taftīsh amti'a*
Kitty Hawk carrier حاملة « كيتي هوك »
*ḥāmilat kiti hūk*
Knife Rest radar رادار « نايف ريست »
*rādār nāyf rist*
knife-type سكيني الشكل
*sakīnī ash-shakl*
Knox frigate فرقاطة « نوكس »
*firqāṭat nūks*
Kojak radar رادار « كوجاك »
*rādār kūjāk*
Köln frigate فرقاطة « كولن »
*firqāṭat kūln*
Komar boat زورق « كومار »
*zawraq kūmār*
Koni frigate فرقاطة « كوني »
*firqāṭat kūnī*
Korea كوريا
*kūrya*
Korean كوري
*kūrī*
Kormoran ASM صاروخ جو ـ سطح « كورموران »
*ṣārūkh jaww-saṭḥ kūrmūrān*
Kortenaer frigate فرقاطة « كورتيناير »
*firqāṭat kūrtinayr*
Kotlin SAM destroyer مدمرة مجهّزة بصواريخ سطح ـ جو « كوتلين »
*mudammira mujahhaza bi-ṣawārīkh saṭḥ-jaww kūtlīn*
KPV machine gun رشاش « كيه پي ڤي »
*rashsāsh kayy pī vī*
Krasina cruiser طرادة « كراسينا »
*ṭarrādat krāsīna*
KrAZ-214 vehicle مركبة « كيه ار ايه زد ـ ٢١٤ »
*markabat kayy ār ayy zid mi'atayn wa arba'ata 'ashar*
Kresta cruiser طرادة « كريستا »
*ṭarrādat krista*

Krivak frigate — فرقاطة « كريڤاك »
*firqāṭat krīvak*

KS-92A camera — آلة تصوير « كيه اس - ٩٢ ايه »
*ālat taṣwīr kayy is ithnayn wa tisʿīn ayy*

Kuerassier gun — مدفع « كوراسييه »
*midfaʿ kūrasyayy*

Kuwait — الكويت
*al-kuwayt*

Kuwaiti — كويتي
*kuwaytī*

KV-107 helicopter — طائرة عمودية « كيه ڤي - ١٠٧ »
*ṭāʾira ʿamūdīya kayy vī miʾa wa sabʿa*

Kynda cruiser — طرادة « كيندا »
*ṭarrādat kinda*

# L

| | |
|---|---|
| 474L BMEWS<br>*niẓām indhār mubakkir biṣ-ṣawārīkh al-bālistīya arbaᶜ miʾa wa arbaᶜa wa sabᶜīn il* | نظام انذار مبكر بالصواريخ البالستية « ٤٧٤ إل » |
| 496L BMEWS<br>*niẓām indhār mubakkir bis-sawārīkh al-bālistīya arbaᶜ miᶜa wa sitta wa tisᶜīn il* | نظام انذار مبكر بالصواريخ البالستية « ٤٩٦ إل » |
| L1A1 rifle<br>*bunduqīyat il wāḥid ayy wāḥid* | بندقية « ال ١ ايه ١ » |
| L2A3 sub-machine gun<br>*rashshāsh qaṣir il ithnayn ayy thalātha* | رشاش قصير « ال ٢ ايه ٣ » |
| L7A1 gun<br>*midfaᶜ il sabᶜa ayy wāḥid* | مدفع « ال ٧ ايه ١ » |
| L7A3 gun<br>*midfaᶜ il sabᶜa ayy thalātha* | مدفع « ال ٧ ايه ٣ » |
| L11A5 gun<br>*midfaᶜ il aḥada ᶜashar ayy khamsa* | مدفع « ال ١١ ايه ٥ » |
| L-29 Delfin aircraft<br>*ṭāʾirat il tisᶜa wa ᶜishrīn dilfīn* | طائرة « ال ـ ٢٩ دلفين » |
| L-33 gun<br>*midfaᶜ il thalātha wa thalāthīn* | مدفع « ال ـ ٣٣ » |
| L39D fighter<br>*ṭāʾira muqātila il tisᶜa wa thalāthīn dī* | طائرة مقاتلة « ال ٣٩ دي » |
| L-39ZO trainer<br>*ṭāʾirat tadrīb il tisᶜa wa thalāthīn zid aw* | طائرة تدريب « ال ـ ٣٩ زد اوه » |
| label<br>*biṭāqa · ᶜalāma mumayyiza* | بطاقة . علامة مميزة |
| laboratory<br>*mukhtabar · maᶜmal* | مختبر . معمل |
| lack of discipline<br>*naqṣ aḍ-ḍabṭ* | نقص الضبط |
| La Combattante attack craft<br>*zawraq hujūm lā kūmbātānt* | زورق هجوم « لا كومبتانت » |
| Lafayette submarine<br>*ghawwāṣat lāfāyit* | غواصة « لافاييت » |
| Lama ship<br>*safīnat lāmā* | سفينة « لاما » |
| LAMPS helicopter<br>*ṭāʾira ᶜamūdīya lamps* | طائرة . عمودية « لامبس » |
| Lance SSM<br>*ṣārūkh saṭḥ saṭḥ lāns* | صاروخ سطح ـ سطح « لانس » |
| land (to)<br>*arḍ · barr · nazala · anzala* | أرض . بر . نزل . أنزل |
| land-based<br>*barrī · arḍī* | بري . أرضي |
| land-based fighter<br>*ṭāʾira muqātila barrīya* | طائرة مقاتلة برية |
| land combat<br>*qitāl barrī* | قتال بري |
| landing<br>*inzāl · hubūṭ* | إنزال . هبوط |
| landing aid<br>*muᶜīn hubūt* | معين هبوط |
| landing beam<br>*shuᶜāᶜ hubūṭ* | شعاع هبوط |
| landing craft<br>*zawraq inzāl* | زورق إنزال |
| landing distance<br>*masāfat al-hubūṭ* | مسافة الهبوط |
| landing equipment<br>*muᶜaddāt al-inzāl* | معدات الانزال |
| landing gear<br>*mihbaṭ aṭ-ṭāʾira* | مهبط الطائرة |
| landing platform dock<br>*ḥawḍ minaṣṣat al-inzāl* | حوض منصة الانزال |
| landing ships dock<br>*ḥawḍ sufun al-inzāl* | حوض سفن الانزال |
| landing ships logistics<br>*ḥarakīyāt sufun al-inzāl* | حركيات سفن الانزال |

L

landing ships tank دبابة سفينة الانزال
*dabbābat safīnat al-inzāl*
landing strip مدرج هبوط مؤقت
*madraj hubūt mu'aqqat*
landing team فريق الانزال
*farīq al-inzāl*
landing vehicle مركبة الانزال
*markabat al-inzāl*
landing zone منطقة الهبوط
*minṭaqat al-hubūṭ*
Land Roll radar رادار « لاند رول »
*rādār lānd rūl*
Land Rover سيارة لاند روڤر
*sayyārat lānd rūvar*
Lanze PZ44 weapon سلاح « لانتسا پي زد ٤٤ »
*silāḥ lantsa pī zid arbaʿa wa arbaʿīn*
Laos لأوس
*lā'ūs*
large scale operation عملية واسعة النطاق
*ʿamalīya wāsiʿat an-niṭāq*
Larzac jet engine محرك نفاث « لارزاك »
*muḥarrik naffāth lārzāk*
laser ليزر
*layzar*
laser ceilograph مقياس ليزر لارتفاع السحاب
*miqyās layzar li-irtifāʿ as-saḥāb*
laser display عرض ليزر
*ʿarḍ layzar*
laser equipment معدات ليزر
*muʿaddāt layzar*
laser guidance توجيه بالليزر
*tawjīh bil-layzar*
laser-guided موجه بالليزر
*muwajjah bil-layzar*
laser-guided bomb قنبلة موجهة بالليزر
*qunbula muwajjaha bil-layzar*
laser guided missile صاروخ موجه بالليزر
*ṣārūkh muwajjah bil-layzar*
laser homing توجيه بالليزر
*tawjīh bil-layzar*
laser light إضاءة ليزر
*iḍā'a layzar*
laser rangefinder معين مدى بالليزر
*muʿayyin mada bil-layzar*
laser ranger/marked-target seeker باحث هدف مميز / معين مدى بالليزر
*bāḥith hadaf mumayyaz/ muʿayyin mada bil-layzar*
laser scanning مسح بالليزر
*masḥ bil-layzar*
laser sight line خط تسديد بالليزر
*khaṭṭ tasdīd bil-layzar*
laser target seeker باحث ليزر عن الهدف
*bāḥith layzar ʿanal-hadaf*
laser tracker متعقب بالليزر
*mutaʿaqqib bil-layzar*
laser transmitter مرسل بالليزر
*mursil bil-layzar*
last ditch anti-missile system نظام مضاد للصواريخ بالخندق الأخير
*niẓām muḍādd liṣ-ṣawārīkh bil-khandaq al-akhīr*
lateral outrigger ذراع امتداد جانبي
*dhirāʿ imtidād jānibī*
lateral stub wing جناح أبتر جانبي
*janāḥ abtar jānibī*
lattice mast صاري شبكي
*ṣārī shabakī*
LAU-7 launcher قاذفة « ال ايه يو ـ ٧ »
*qādhifa il ayy yū sabʿa*
launch اطلاق
*iṭlāq*
launch a counter-attack شن هجوم مضاد
*shanna hujūm muḍādd*
launch aircraft طائرة اطلاق
*ṭā'irat iṭlāq*
launch an attack شن هجوماً
*shanna hujūman*
launch control centre مركز مراقبة الاطلاق
*markaz murāqabat al-iṭlāq*
launch control post مركز مراقبة الاطلاق
*markaz murāqabat al-iṭlāq*
launcher قاذفة . جهاز اطلاق
*qādhifa · jihāz iṭlāq*
launcher bin صندوق جهاز الاطلاق
*ṣundūq jihāz al-iṭlāq*
launcher transporter ناقلة القاذفة
*nāqilat al-qādhifa*
launcher tube أنبوبة القذف
*unbūbat al-qadhf*
launching canister علبة القذف
*ʿulbat al-qadhf*
launching pad منصة الاطلاق
*minaṣṣat al-iṭlāq*
launch mode وضع الاطلاق
*waḍʿ al-iṭlāq*
launch pad منصة الاطلاق
*minaṣṣat al-iṭlāq*

L

|  |  |
|---|---|
| launch rail<br>*qaḍīb al-iṭlāq* | قضيب الاطلاق |
| launch tube<br>*unbūbat al-qadhf* | أنبوبة القذف |
| launch vehicle<br>*markabat al-iṭlāq* | مركبة الاطلاق |
| launch weight<br>*wazn ʿindal-itlāq* | وزن عند الاطلاق |
| LAV-25 APC<br>*nāqilat junūd mudarraʿa il ayy vī khamsa wa ʿishrīn* | ناقلة جنود مدرعة « ال ايه ڤي ـ ٢٥ » |
| Lavi strike fighter<br>*ṭāʾira muqātila inqiḍāḍīya lāvī* | طائرة مقاتلة انقضاضية « لاڤي » |
| Law-80 launcher<br>*qādhifat lū thamānīn* | قاذفة « لو ـ ٨٠ » |
| law and order<br>*al-qānūn wan-niẓām* | القانون والنظام |
| layered defence<br>*difāʿ takhaṣṣuṣī* | دفاع تخصصي |
| Lazy Susan ammunition rack<br>*ḥāmil adh-dhakīra layzī sūzān* | حامل الذخيرة « ليزي سوزان » |
| LCM-6 landing craft<br>*zawraq al-inzāl il sī im sitta* | زورق إنزال « ال سي ام ـ ٦ » |
| LCVP<br>*safīnat inzāl markabāt wa afrad* | سفينة إنزال مركبات وأفراد |
| leader<br>*zaʿīm · qāʾid* | زعيم . قائد |
| leadership<br>*zaʿāma · qiyāda* | زعامة . قيادة |
| leading-edge flap<br>*junayḥ qallāba ḥāfat al-mutaqaddima lil-janaḥ* | جنيح قلابة حافة المتقدمة للجناح |
| leading-edge root extensions<br>*tamdīdat jidhr ḥāfat al-mutaqaddima lil-janaḥ* | تمديدات جذر حافة المتقدمة للجناح |
| Leahy cruiser<br>*ṭarrādat līhī* | طرادة « ليهي » |
| Leander frigate<br>*firqāṭat liyāndar* | فرقاطة « لياندر » |
| Learjet air transport<br>*ṭāʾirat naql līr jit* | طائرة نقل « ليرجيت » |
| leave<br>*idhn · ijāza* | إذن . إجازة |
| leave allowance<br>*badal ijāza* | بدل إجازة |
| leave pass<br>*taṣrīḥ ijāza* | تصريح إجازة |
| Lebanese<br>*lubnānī* | لبناني |
| Lebanon<br>*lubnān* | لبنان |
| Lebed hovercraft<br>*ḥawwāmat lībīd* | حوامة « ليبيد » |
| Le Fougeux craft<br>*zawraq li fūgah* | زورق « لي فوجيه » |
| left dress!<br>*yasāran tarāṣaf* | يساراً تراصف ! |
| left flank<br>*janāḥ al-maysara* | جناح الميسرة |
| left turn!<br>*ilal-yasār durr* | إلى اليسار در ! |
| leg<br>*sāq* | ساق |
| leggings<br>*ṭuzluq · lifāfat sāq* | طوزلق . لفافة ساق |
| length<br>*ṭūl · imtidād* | طول . إمتداد |
| length of barrel<br>*ṭul al-māsūra* | طول الماسورة |
| length of service<br>*muddat al-khidma* | مدة الخدمة |
| Leopard IA4 tank<br>*dabbābat lipard āyy ayy arbaʿa* | دبابة « ليپارد أي ايه ٤ » |
| Leopard tank<br>*dabbābat lipard* | دبابة « ليپارد » |
| Le Redoutable submarine<br>*ghawwāṣat li ridūtābl* | غواصة « لي ريدوتابل » |
| lethal dose<br>*jurʿa qātila* | جرعة قاتلة |
| lethal effect<br>*taʾthīr mumayyit* | تأثير مميت |
| level-crossing<br>*taqāṭuʿ sikka maʿa ṭarīq* | تقاطع سكة مع طريق |
| level of command<br>*mustawa al-qiyāda* | مستوى القيادة |
| LF sonar<br>*sūnār il if* | سونار « ال اف » |
| Liason aircraft<br>*ṭāʾirat liyayzan* | طائرة « ليهزن » |
| liberation<br>*taḥrīr* | تحرير |
| Liberia<br>*lāybīriya* | لايبيريا |
| Liberian<br>*lāybīrī* | لايبيري |

Libya لیبیا
*lībiya*
Libyan لیبي
*lībī*
lieutenant ملازم أول
*mulāzim awwal*
lieutenant colonel مقدم
*muqaddam*
lieutenant general فريق
*farīq*
lifeboat قارب نجاة · قارب إنقاذ
*qārib najāh · qārib inqādh*
life jacket صدرة نجاة
*ṣudrat najāh*
life-line حبل نجاة
*ḥabl najāh*
life-raft طوف نجاة
*ṭawf najāh*
life-support system جهاز انعاش
*jihāz inʿāsh*
lift رفع
*rafʿ*
lift-off إنطلاق
*inṭilāq*
lift truck شاحنة لرفع الأثقال ونقلها
*shāḥina li-rafʿ al-athqāl wa naqlaha*
light aircraft carrier حاملة طائرات خفيفة
*ḥāmilat ṭāʾirat khafīfa*
light alloy سبيكة خفيفة
*sabīka khafīfa*
light-amplification تضخيم الضوء
*taḍkhīm aḍ-ḍawʾ*
light anti-tank weapon سلاح خفيف مضاد للدبابات
*silāḥ khafīf mudādd lid-dabbābāt*
light attack هجوم خفيف
*hujūm khafīf*
light freighting نقل خفيف
*naql khafīf*
light gun مدفع خفيف
*midfaʿ khafīf*
light infantry مشاة خفاف
*mushāh khafīf*
lightly armoured مدّرع « خفيفاً »
*mudarraʿ khafīfan*
light machine-gun مدفع رشاش خفيف
*midfaʿ rashshāsh khafīf*
Lightning fighter طائرة مقاتلة « لايتنينج »
*ṭāʾira muqātila lāytnīng*
light portable bridge جسر نقالي خفيف
*jisr naqqālī khafīf*
lights out! أطفيء الأنوار !
*aṭfi al-anwār*
light support weapon سلاح تعزيز خفيف
*silāḥ taʿziz khafīf*
light tactical fighter طائرة مقاتلة تكتيكية خفيفة
*ṭāʾira muqātila taktīkīya khafīfa*
light tank دبابة خفيفة
*dabbāba khafīfa*
light automatic rifle بندقية آلية خفيفة
*bunduqīya ālīya khafīfa*
light weapon سلاح خفيف
*silāḥ khafīf*
light-weight خفيف الوزن
*khafīf al-wazn*
lightweight mortar مدفع هاون خفيف
*midfaʿ hāwun khafīf*
Lightweight Seawolf SAM صاروخ سطح ـ جو « لايتويت سيوولف »
*ṣārūkh saṭḥ-jaww lāytwīt sī wulf*
line of sight خط التسديد
*khaṭṭ at-tasdīd*
lines of communication خطوط الاتصال
*khuṭūṭ al-ittiṣāl*
Link 11 wireless جهاز لاسلكي « لينك ١١ »
*jihāz lā-silkī līnk aḥada ʿashar*
Link 14 teleprinter طابعة عن بعد « لينك ١٤ »
*ṭābiʿa ʿan buʿd līnk arbaʿata ʿashar*
Link data transmission جهاز ارسال البيانات « لينك »
*jihāz irsāl al-bayānāt līnk*
Lion tank دبابة « لايون »
*dabbābat lāyūn*
Lipscomb submarine غواصة ليبسكام
*ghawwāṣat lipskam*
liquidation تصفية
*taṣfīya*
liquid decontaminant سائل مزيل التلوث
*sāʾil muʾzīl at-talawwuth*
liquid-fuel وقود سائل
*wuqūd sāʾil*
liquid-fuel rocket-engine محرك صاروخي بوقود سائل
*muḥarrik ṣārūkhī bi-wuqūd sāʾil*
liquid propellant وقود دفعي سائل
*wuqūd dafʿī sāʾil*
Lirods radar رادار « ليرودز »
*rādār līrūdz*

L

list قائمة . ميلان
*qā'ima · maylān*
listening post مركز تسمع
*markaz tasammu'*
litter نقالة
*naqqāla*
live ammunition ذخيرة حية
*dhakkīra ḥayya*
LLTV unit وحدة تلفزيونية منخفضة الاضاءة
*wiḥdat talfizyūnīya munkhafiḍat al-aḍā'a*
LM2500 gas turbine تربين غازي « ال ام ٢٥٠٠ »
*turbīn ghāzī il im alfayn wa khams mi'a*
LN66 radar رادار « ال ان ٦٦ »
*rādār il in sitta wa sittīn*
LN66HP radar رادار « ال ان ٦٦ اتش بي »
*rādār il in sitta wa sittīn itsh pī*
load! القم !
*alqim*
load (to) القم
*alqama*
loader مُحمل . عامل تحميل
*muḥammil · 'āmil taḥmīl*
loader-transporter vehicle مركبة نقل وتحميل
*markabat naql wa taḥmīl*
loading hatch كوة الملء
*kuwwat al-mil'*
location موقع
*mawqi'*
locked-breech arm ذراع المغلاف المقفل
*dhirā' al-mighlāq al-muqfal*
Lockheed (Co) شركة « لوكهيد »
*sharikat lukhīd*
locking block بدن المغلاق
*badan al-mighlāq*
locking pin مسمار تثبيت
*mismār tathbīt*
lock-on متابعة الهدف بالرادار اوتوماتيكياً
*mutāba'at al-hadaf bir-rādār awtūmātikīyan*
log book سجل السفينة أو الطائرة
*sijill as-safīna aw aṭ-ṭā'ira*
logistics planner مخطط الشؤون الحركية
*mukhaṭṭiṭ ash-shu'ūn al-ḥarakīya*
logistics support تعزيز حركي
*ta'zīz ḥarakī*
logistic support vessel سفينة دعم حركي
*safīnat da'm ḥarakī*

loiter speed سرعة التباطؤ
*sur'at at-tabāṭu'*
loiter time زمن التباطؤ
*zaman at-tabāṭu'*
Long Beach cruiser طرادة « لونج بيتش »
*ṭarrādat lūng bītsh*
Long Bow radar رادار « لونج بو »
*rādār lūng bū*
long-range طويل المدى
*ṭawīl al-mada*
Long-Range Aviation Force قوة جوية طويلة المدى
*qūwa jawwīya ṭawīlat al-mada*
long-range drop tank صهاريج وقود قابلة للاسقاط
*ṣahārīj wuqūd qābila lil-isqāṭ*
long-range eyes عيون بعيدة المدى
*'uyūn ba'īdat al-mada*
long-range operation عملية بعيدة المدى
*'amalīya ba'īdat al-mada*
long-range tank دبابة طويلة المدى
*dabbāba ṭawīlat al-mada*
Long Track radar رادار « لونج تراك »
*rādār lūng trāk*
long-wavelength signals إشارات بأطوال موجية طويلة
*ishārāt bi-aṭwāl mawjīya ṭawīla*
look-down capability قدرة النظر للأسفل
*qudrat an-naẓar lil-asfal*
look-down range مدى النظر للأسفل
*mada an-naẓar lil-asfal*
Look-down/shoot-down potential إمكانية النظر / الاطلاق للأسفل
*imkānīyat an-naẓar/al-iṭlāq lil-asfal*
lookout رصد . مراقبة
*raṣd · murāqaba*
lookout post مركز مراقبة
*markaz murāqaba*
lookout tower برج مراقبة
*burj murāqaba*
Look Two radar رادار « لوك تو »
*rādār lūk tū*
look-up range مدى النظر للأعلى
*mada an-naẓar lil-a'lā*
Loreto gunboat سفينة مجهزة بالمدافع « لوريتو »
*safīna mujahhaza bil-madāfi' lūrītū*
lorry شاحنة
*shāḥina*

Los Angeles submarine — غواصة « لوس انجليز »
*ghawwāṣat lūs anjilīz*

losses — خسائر . مفقودات
*khasāʾir · mafqūdāt*

low altitude — إرتفاع منخفض
*irtifāʿ munkhafiḍ*

low-altitude bombing — قصف من ارتفاع منخفض
*qaṣf min irtifāʿ munkhafiḍ*

low-altitude penetration — إختراق من ارتفاع منخفض
*ikhtirāq min irtifāʿ munkhafiḍ*

Low Blow radar — رادار « لو بلو »
*rādār lū blū*

low-flying aircraft — طائرة طيران منخفض
*ṭāʾirat ṭayarān munkhafiḍ*

low-frequency — ترددات منخفضة
*taraddudāt munkhafiḍa*

low-frequency bow sonar — سونار منخفض التردد مركب في مقدمة السفينة
*sūnār munkhafiḍ at-taraddud murakkab fi muqaddimat as-safīna*

low level — مستوى منخفض
*mustawa munkhafiḍ*

low-level bomber — طائرة قذف من مستوى منخفض
*ṭāʾirat qadhf min mustawa munkhafiḍ*

low-level penetration — إختراق من مستوى منخفض
*ikhtirāq min mustawa munkhafiḍ*

low-level strike — إنقضاض من مستوى منخفض
*inqiḍāḍ min mustawa munkhafiḍ*

low-level strike bomber — طائرة قاذفة للانقضاض من مستوى منخفض
*ṭāʾira qādhifa lil-inqiḍāḍ min mustawa munkhafiḍ*

low-light-level — مستوى اضاءة منخفض
*mustawa iḍāʾa munkhafiḍ*

low-light TV sensor — جهاز احساس تلفزيوني منخفض الاضاءة
*jihāz iḥsās talfizyūnī munkhafiḍ al-iḍāʾa*

low price — سعر منخفض
*siʿr munkhafiḍ*

Low Sieve radar — رادار « لوسيف »
*rādār lū siv*

low-visibility fighter — طائرة مقاتلة للرؤية المنخفضة
*ṭāʾira muqātila lir-ruʾya al-munkhafiḍa*

low yield warhead — رأس مقذوف منخفض العيار
*raʾs maqdhūf munkhafiḍ al-ʿiyār*

lozenge fashion — على شكل المعين
*ʿala shakl al-muʿayyan*

Luchs vehicle — مركبة « لوكس »
*markabat luks*

Lüda destroyer — مدمرة « ليدا »
*mudammirat līda*

Luna SSM — صاروخ سطح - سطح « لونا »
*ṣārūkh saṭḥ-saṭḥ lūnā*

Lupo frigate — فرقاطة « لوبو »
*firqāṭat lūpū*

Lürssen-type attack craft — سفينة انقضاض طراز « ليرسن »
*safīnat inqiḍāḍ ṭirāz līrsan*

Luta destroyer — مدمرة « لوتا »
*mudammirat lūtā*

Luxembourg — اللوكسمبورغ
*al-lūksimbūrgh*

Luz ASM — صاروخ جو - سطح « لوث »
*ṣārūkh jaww-saṭḥ lūth*

LVTP — عربة انزال مجنزرة للافراد
*ʿarabat inzāl mujanzara lil-afrād*

LW-01 radar — رادار « ال دبليو - ٠١ »
*rādār il dablyū ṣīfr wāḥid*

LW-02 radar — رادار « ال دبليو - ٠٢ »
*rādār il dablyū ṣīfr ithnayn*

LW-05 radar — رادار « ال دبليو - ٠٥ »
*rādār il dablyū ṣīfr khamsa*

LW-10 radar — رادار « ال دبليو - ١٠ »
*rādār il dablyū ʿashara*

LW-11 radar — رادار « ال دبليو - ١١ »
*rādār il dablyū aḥada ʿashar*

Lynx 90 turret — برج « لينكس ٩٠ »
*burj links tisʿīn*

Lynx helicopter — طائرة عمودية « لينكس »
*ṭāʾira ʿamūdīya links*

Lyran launcher — قاذفة « لايران »
*qādhifat lāyran*

Lyulka turbojet — طائرة نفاثة تربينية « ليولكا »
*ṭāʾirat naffātha turbīnīya liyulka*

L

# M

| | |
|---|---|
| 500 MD helicopter<br>*ṭā'irat ʿamūdīya khams mi'a im dī* | طائرة عمودية ٥٠٠ إم دي |
| 533-MM torpedo<br>*ṭūrbīd khams mi'a wa thalāthīn im im* | طوربيد ٥٣٣ إم إم |
| M-1 missile<br>*ṣārūkh im wāḥid* | صاروخ « ام ـ ١ » |
| M1 rifle<br>*bunduqīyat im wāḥid* | بندقية « ام ١ » |
| M1 tank<br>*dabbābat im wāḥid* | دبابة « ام ١ » |
| M1A1 rifle<br>*bunduqīyat im wāḥid ayy wāḥid* | بندقية « ام ١ ايه ١ » |
| M2 machine gun<br>*rashshāsh im ithnayn* | رشاش « ام ٢ » |
| M2 MICV<br>*markaba qitālīya lil-mushāh al-ālīya im ithnayn* | مركبة قتالية للمشاة الآلية « ام ٢ » |
| M-2 missile<br>*ṣārūkh im ithnayn* | صاروخ « ام ـ ٢ » |
| M2 rifle<br>*bunduqīyat im ithnayn* | بندقية « ام ٢ » |
| M2HB machine-gun<br>*rashshāsh im ithnayn itsh bī* | رشاش « ام ٢ اتش بي » |
| M3 MICV<br>*markaba qitālīya lil-mushāh al-ālīya im thalātha* | مركبة قتالية للمشاة الآلية « ام ٣ » |
| M3 rifle<br>*bunduqīyat im thalātha* | بندقية « ام ٣ » |
| M3A1 submachine gun<br>*rashshāsh qaṣīr im thalātha ayy wāḥid* | رشاش قصير « ام ٣ ايه ١ » |
| M-4 missile<br>*ṣārūkh im arbaʿa* | صاروخ « ام ـ ٤ » |
| M-12 aircraft<br>*ṭā'irat im ithnata ʿashar* | طائرة « ام ـ ١٢ » |
| M13 link belt<br>*sayr waṣl im thalāthata ʿashar* | سير وصل « ام ١٣ » |
| M14 rifle<br>*bunduqīyat im arbaʿata ʿashar* | بندقية « ام ١٤ » |
| M16 rifle<br>*bunduqīyat im sittata ʿashar* | بندقية « ام ١٦ » |
| M16A1 mine<br>*lughm im sittata ʿashar ayy wāḥid* | لغم « ام ١٦ ايه ١ » |
| M16A1 rifle<br>*bunduqīyat im sittata ʿashar ayy wāḥid* | بندقية « ام ١٦ ايه ١ » |
| M-20 launcher<br>*qādhifa im ʿishrīn* | قاذفة « ام ـ ٢٠ » |
| M22 rifle grenade<br>*qunbula maqdhūfa min bunduqīya - im ithnayn wa ʿishrīn* | قنبلة مقذوفة من بندقية « ام ٢٢ » |
| M22 system<br>*niẓām im ithnayn wa ʿishrīn* | نظام « ام ٢٢ » |
| M29 mortar<br>*midfaʿ hāwun im tisʿa wa ʿishrīn* | مدفع هاون « ام ٢٩ » |
| M41 tank<br>*dabbābat im wāḥid wa arbaʿīn* | دبابة « ام ٤١ » |
| M43A1 grenade<br>*qunbula yadawīya im thalātha wa arbaʿīn ayy wāḥid* | قنبلة يدوية « ام ٤٣ ايه ١ » |
| M44 howitzer<br>*midfaʿ hāwitsar im arbaʿa wa arbaʿīn* | مدفع هاوتزر « ام ٤٤ » |
| M-46 field gun<br>*midfaʿ al-maydān im sitta wa arbaʿīn* | مدفع الميدان « ام ـ ٤٦ » |

M47 tank — دبابة « ام ٤٧ »
*dabbābat im sabʿa wa arbaʿīn*
M48 tank — دبابة « ام ٤٨ »
*dabbābat im thamānya wa arbaʿīn*
M50 diesel — ديزل « ام ٥٠ »
*dīzl im khamsīn*
M52 howitzer — مدفع هاوتزر « ام ٥٢ »
*midfaʿ hāwitsar im ithnayn wa khamsīn*
M53-5 bypass turbojet — محرك تربيني نفاث فرعي « ام ٥٣ ـ ٥ »
*muḥarrik turbīnī naffāth farʿī im thalātha wa khamsīn khamsa*
M60 machine gun — رشاش « ام ٦٠ »
*rashshāsh im sittīn*
M60 tank — دبابة « ام ٦٠ »
*dabbābat im sittīn*
M60A1 tank — دبابة « ام ٦٠ ايه ١ »
*dabbābat im sittīn ayy wāḥid*
M60A2 tank — دبابة « ام ٦٠ ايه ٢ »
*dabbābat im sittīn ayy ithnayn*
M-60A3 conversion kit — مجموعة قطع تبديل « ام ـ ٦٠ ايه ٣ »
*majmūʿat qiṭaʿ tabdīl im sittīn ayy thalātha*
M60A3 tank — دبابة « ام ٦٠ ايه ٣ »
*dabbābat im sittīn ayy thalātha*
M61 cannon — مدفع هاون « ام ٦١ »
*midfaʿ hāwun im wāḥid wa sittīn*
M61A cannon — مدفع هاون « ام ٦١ ايه »
*mifdaʿ hāwun im wāḥid wa sittīn ayy*
M62 rifle — بندقية « ام ٦٢ »
*bunduqīyat im ithnayn wa sittīn*
M67 rifle — بندقية « ام ٦٧ »
*bunduqīyat im sabʿa wa sittīn*
M68 gun — مدفع « ام ٦٨ »
*midfaʿ im thamānya wa sittīn*
M72 rocket — صاروخ « ام ٧٢ »
*ṣārūkh im ithnayn wa sabʿīn*
M72A1 weapon — سلاح « ام ٧٢ ايه ١ »
*silāḥ im ithnayn wa sabʿīn ayy wāḥid*
M72A2 weapon — سلاح « ام ٧٢ ايه ٢ »
*silāḥ im ithnayn wa sabʿīn ayy ithnayn*
M79 grenade launcher — قاذفة قنابل يدوية « ام ٧٩ »
*qādhifat qanābil yadawīya im tisʿa wa sabʿīn*
M88A1 vehicle — مركبة « ام ٨٨ ايه ١ »
*markabat im thamānya wa thamānīn ayy wāḥid*
M101A1 howitzer — مدفع هاوتزر إم ١٠١ ايه ١
*midfaʿ hāwitsar im miʾa wa wāḥid ayy wāḥid*
M102 howitzer — مدفع هاوتزر « ام ١٠٢ »
*midfaʿ hāwitsar im miʾa wa ithnayn*
M-106A2 mortar carrier — حاملة هاون « ام ـ ١٠٦ ايه ٢ »
*ḥāmilat hāwun im miʾa wa sitta ayy ithnayn*
M107 gun — مدفع « ام ١٠٧ »
*midfaʿ im miʾa wa sabʿa*
M109 howitzer — مدفع هاوتزر « ام ١٠٩ »
*midfaʿ hāwitsar im miʾa wa tisʿa*
M110 howitzer — مدفع هاوتزر « ام ١١٠ »
*midfaʿ hāwitsar im miʾa wa ʿashara*
M110A2 projectile — مقذوف « ام ١١٠ ايه ٢ »
*maqdhūf im miʾa wa ʿashara ayy ithnayn*
M113 gun — مدفع « ام ١١٣ »
*midfaʿ im miʾa wa thalāthata ʿashar*
M113A2 personnel carrier — ناقلة جنود « ام ١١٣ ايه ٢ »
*nāqilat junūd im miʾa wa thalāthata ʿashar ayy ithnayn*
M-113 AFV — مركبة قتال مدرعة « ام ـ ١١٣ »
*markabat qitāl mudarraʿa im miʾa wa thalathata ʿashar*
M114 howitzer — مدفع هاوتزر « ام ١١٤ »
*midfaʿ hāwitsar im miʾa wa arbaʿata ʿashar*
M-125A2 mortar carrier — حاملة هاون « ام ـ ١٢٥ ايه ٢ »
*ḥāmilat hāwun im miʾa wa khamsa wa ʿishrīn ayy ithnayn*
M-160 mortar — مدفع هاون « ام ـ ١٦٠ »
*midfaʿ hāwun im miʾa wa sittīn*
M163 gun — مدفع « ام ١٦٣ »
*midfaʿ im miʾa wa thalātha wa sittīn*
M167 gun — مدفع « ام ١٦٧ »
*midfaʿ im miʾa wa sabʿa wa sittīn*

M

M193 cartridge خرطوشة « ام ١٩٣ »
*kharṭūshat im mi'a wa thalātha wa tis'īn*
M198 howitzer مدفع هاوتزر « ام ١٩٨ »
*midfa' hāwitsar im mi'a wa thamānya wa tis'īn*
M203 grenade launcher قاذفة قنابل يدوية « ام ٢٠٣ »
*qādhifat qanābil yadawīya im mi'atayn wa thalātha*
M224 mortar مدفع هاون « ام ٢٢٤ »
*midfa' hāwun im mi'atayn wa arba'a wa 'ishrīn*
M-240 machine gun رشاش « ام ـ ٢٤٠ »
*rashshāsh im mi'atayn wa arba'īn*
M551 tank دبابة « ام ٥٥١ »
*dabbābat im khams mi'a wa wāḥid wa khamsīn*
M577 AFV مركبة قتال مدرعة « ام ٥٧٧ »
*markabat qitāl mudarra'a im khams mi'a wa sab'a wa sab'īn*
M578 vehicle مركبة « ام ٥٧٨ »
*markabat im khams mi'a wa thamānya wa sab'īn*
M727SP Hawk launcher قاذفة « ام ٧٢٧ اس پي هوك »
*qādhifa im sab' mi'a wa sab'a wa 'ishrīn īs pī hūk*
M-901 AFV مركبة قتال مدرعة « ام ـ ٩٠١ »
*markabat qitāl mudarra'a im tis' mi'a wa wāḥid*
M-901 TOW صاروخ ام ٦٠١ تو
*ṣārūkh im tis' mi'a wa wāḥid tū*
M1911A1 pistol مسدس « ام ١٩١١ ايه ١ »
*musaddas im alf wa tis' mi'a wa aḥada 'ashara ayy wāḥid*
M1928A1 sub-machine gun رشاش قصير « ام ١٩٢٨ ايه ١ »
*rashshāsh qaṣīr im alf wa tis' mi'a wa thamānya wa 'ishrīn ayy wāḥid*
M-1937 ammunition ذخيرة « ام ١٩٣٧ »
*dhakhīra im alf wa tis' mi'a wa sab'a wa thalāthīn*
M-1943 gun مدفع « ام ـ ١٩٤٣ »
*midfa' im alf wa tis' mi'a wa thalātha wa arba'īn*
M-1955 gun مدفع « ام ـ ١٩٥٥ »
*midfa' im alf wa tis' mi'a wa khamsa wa khamsīn*
M1973 howitzer مدفع هاوتزر « ام ١٩٧٣ »
*midfa' hāwitsar im alf wa tis' mi'a wa thalātha wa sab'īn*
M1974 howitzer مدفع هاوتزر « ام ١٩٧٤ »
*midfa' hāwitsar im alf wa tis' mi'a wa arba'a wa sab'īn*
Mach ماخ
*mākh*
machine-gun رشاش
*rashshāsh*
machine-gun fire نيران الرشاش
*nīrān ar-rashshāsh*
machine-gun mounting حامل الرشاش
*ḥāmil ar-rashshāsh*
machine-pistol مسدس رشاشة
*musaddas rashshāsha*
machinery noise ضوضاء المكنات
*ḍawḍā' al-makanāt*
machinery quieting system نظام تهدئة ضوضاء المكنات
*niẓām tahdi'at ḍawḍā' al-makanāt*
machine workshop ورشة مكنات
*warshat makanāt*
MAD detector مكشاف « ام ايه دي »
*mikshāf im ayy dī*
Madagascar مدغشقر
*madaghashqar*
Maestrale frigate فرقاطة « ميسترال »
*firqāṭat mīstrāl*
magazine خزنة الذخيرة
*khaznat adh-dhakhīra*
Magic AAM صاروخ جو ـ جو « ماجيك »
*ṣārūkh jaww-jaww mājik*
Magister aircraft طائرة « ماجيستر »
*ṭā'irat mājistar*
magnetic anomaly detector مكشاف ظاهرات مغنطيسية شاذة
*mikshāf ẓāhirāt mughnaṭisīya shādhdha*
magnification تكبير
*takbīr*
Mail aircraft طائرة « ميل »
*ṭā'irat mayl*
main armament تسليح رئيسي
*taslīḥ ra'īsī*
main base facilities تسهيلات القاعدة الرئيسية
*tashīlāt al-qā'ida ar-ra'īsīya*
main battle tank دبابة معارك رئيسية
*dabbābat ma'ārik ra'īsīya*
main body القسم الأكبر
*al-qism al-akbar*

main component الجزء الأساسي
*al-juzʾ al-asāsī*
main defensive position وضع دفاعي رئيسي
*waḍʿ difāʿī raʾīsī*
main force القوة الرئيسية
*al-qūwa ar-raʾīsīya*
main gear المسنن الرئيسي
*al-musannan ar-raʾīsī*
Mainstay AWAC نظام التحذير والمراقبة الجوي « مينستاي »
*niẓām at-taḥdhīr wal-murāqaba al-jawwī maynstayy*
maintenance facilities تسهيلات الصيانة
*tashīlāt aṣ-ṣiyāna*
maintenance parade إستعراض الصيانة
*isitʿrāḍ aṣ-ṣiyāna*
maintenance workshop ورشة الصيانة
*warshat aṣ-ṣiyāna*
major رائد
*rāʾid*
major-general لواء
*liwāʾ*
major refit تجديد شامل
*tajdīd shāmil*
major task مهمة كبرى
*muhimma kubra*
Malafor ASM صاروخ جو ـ سطح « مالفور »
*ṣārūkh jaww-saṭḥ malafur*
Mala submarine غواصة « مالا »
*ghawwāṣat mālā*
Malawi ملاوي
*malāwī*
Malaysia ماليزيا
*mālīzya*
Mali مالي
*mālī*
Malta مالطا
*mālṭā*
Mamba missile صاروخ « مامبا »
*ṣārūkh māmbā*
MAN diesel ديزل « مان »
*dīzl mān*
manned aircraft طائرة يقودها انسان
*ṭāʾira yuqūduha insān*
manoeuvrability سهولة المناورة
*suhūlat al-munāwara*
manoeuvre مناورة
*munāwara*
manoeuvre-by-fire مناورة بالنيران
*munāwara bil-nīrān*
manoeuvre indicator مؤشر المناورة
*muʾashshir al-munāwara*
manoeuvres مناورات
*munāwarāt*
man-portable يحمله إنسان
*yaḥmiluh insān*
manpower قوى عاملة . قدرة بشرية
*quwa ʿāmila · qudra basharīya*
Manta mine لغم « مانتا »
*lughm māntā*
manual loading تلقيم يدوي . تعبئة يدوية
*talqīm yadawī · taʿbiʾa yadawīya*
manual operation تشغيل يدوي
*tashghīl yadawī*
manual transmission تحويل السرعة اليدوي
*taḥwīl as-surʿa al-yadawī*
map خريطة
*kharīṭa*
map watching مطابقة الخرائط
*muṭābaqat al-kharāʾiṭ*
Marada Brigade لواء « مارادا »
*liwāʾ mārādā*
Maranon gunboat زورق مسلح « مارانون »
*zawraq musallaḥ mārānūn*
march زحف
*zaḥf*
Marder chassis هيكل « ماردر »
*haykal mārdar*
Marine Commando unit وحدة فدائية بحرية
*wiḥda fidāʾīya baḥrīya*
marine division فرقة بحرية
*firqa baḥrīya*
Marine Police شرطة بحرية
*shurṭa baḥrīya*
mariner ملاح
*mallāḥ*
maritime بحري . ملاحي
*baḥrī · milāḥī*
maritime helicopter طائرة عمودية بحرية
*ṭāʾira ʿamūdīya baḥrīya*
maritime surveillance إستطلاع بحري
*istiṭlāʿ baḥrī*
marker علامة . واضع الشواخص
*ʿalāma · wāḍiʿ ash-shawākhiṣ*
Markham مركام
*markam*
marksman رام ماهر . هداف
*rāmin māhir · haddāf*

mark time! راوح !
*rāwiḥ*
Maronite Christian مسيحي ماروني
*masīḥī mārūnī*
MAR R24 minehunting sonar سونار بحث عن الألغام « ام ايه آر ار ٢٤ »
*sūnār baḥth ʿanal-alghām im ayy ār ār arbaʿa wa ʿishrīn*
married quarters مساكن المتزوجين
*masākin al-mutazawwijīn*
marshal مشير
*mushīr*
Martel ASM صاروخ جو - سطح « مارتيل »
*ṣārūkh jaww-saṭḥ mārtīl*
Marte missile صاروخ « مارت »
*ṣārūkh mārt*
martial law قانون عرفي
*qānūn ʿurfī*
Marut fighter طائرة مقاتلة « ماروت »
*ṭāʾira muqātila marūt*
MAS 36 rifle بندقية « ام ايه اس ٣٦ »
*bunduqīyat im ayy is sitta wa thalāthīn*
mask قناع . ستار
*qināʿ · sitār*
masked مقنع . محجب
*muqannaʿ · muḥajjab*
mask & filter system نظام القناع والمرشح
*niẓām al-qināʿ wal-murashshiḥ*
mast صاري
*ṣārī*
Mastiff helicopter طائرة عمودية « ماستيف »
*ṭāʾira ʿamūdīya mastif*
mast-mounted sight مهداف مركب على صاري فوق دوامة الطائرة العمودية
*mihdāf murakkab ʿala ṣārī fawqa duwwāmat aṭ-ṭāʾira al-ʿamūdīya*
Masurca SAM صاروخ سطح - جو « مازوركا »
*ṣārūkh saṭḥ-jaww māzurka*
MAT 49 sub-machine gun رشاش قصير « ام ايه تي ٤٩ »
*rashshāsh qaṣīr im ayy tī tisʿa wa arbaʿīn*
Matador aircraft طائرة « ماتدور »
*ṭāʾirat matadūr*
Mathago missile صاروخ « ماثاجو »
*ṣārūkh māthāgū*
Matra Magic ماترا ماجيك
*mātrā mājik*
Matra missile boats زورق صواريخ « ماترا »
*zawraq ṣawārīkh mātrā*
Matra R530 AAM صاروخ جو - جو « ماترا آر ٥٣٠ »
*ṣārūkh jaww-jaww mātrā ār khams miʾa wa thalāthīn*
Matra R550 Magic AAM صاروخ جو - جو « ماترا آر ٥٥٠ ماجيك »
*ṣārūkh jaww-jaww mātrā ār khams miʾa khamsīn majik*
Matra Super R530 AAM صاروخ جو - جو « ماترا سوبر آر ٥٣٠ »
*ṣārūkh jaww-jaww mātrā sūbar ār khams miʾa wa thalāthīn*
Mauritania موريتانيا
*mūrītānya*
Mauser gun مدفع « ماوزر »
*midfaʿ mawzar*
Maverick AGM صاروخ جو - أرض « ماڤريك »
*ṣārūkh jaww-saṭḥ mavrik*
maximum detection range مدى الكشف الأقصى
*mada al-kashf al-aqṣa*
maximum endurance درجة التحمل القصوى
*darajat at-taḥammul al-quṣwa*
maximum range المدى الأقصى
*al-mada al-aqṣa*
maximum permissible load الحمل الأقصى المسموح
*al-ḥiml al-aqṣa masmūḥ*
maximum speed السرعة القصوى
*as-surʿa al-quṣwa*
maximum take-off weight وزن الاقلاع الأقصى
*wazn al-iqlāʿ al-aqṣa*
May aircraft طائرة « مايه »
*ṭāʾirat mayy*
MAZ-537 vehicle مركبة « ام ايه زد - ٧٣٥ »
*markabat im ayy zid khams miʾa wa sabʿa wa thalāthīn*
MAZ-543 vehicle مركبة « ام ايه زد - ٥٤٣ »
*markabat im ayy zid khams miʾa wa thalātha wa arbaʿīn*
MB326 fighter طائرة مقاتلة « ام بي ٣٢٦ »
*ṭāʾira muqātila im bī thalāth miʾa wa sitta wa ʿishrīn*
MB339K fighter طائرة مقاتلة « ام بي ٣٣٩ كيه »
*ṭāʾira muqātila im bī thalāth miʾa wa tisʿa wa thalāthīn kayy*
MBB-223 trainer طائرة تدريب « ام بي بي - ٢٢٣ »
*ṭāʾirat tadrīb im bī bī miʾatayn wa thalātha wa ʿishrīn*
MBU 600 ASW rocket صاروخ مضاد للغواصات « ام بي يو ٦٠٠ »
*ṣārūkh muḍādd lil-ghawwāsāt im bī yū sitt miʾa*

McDonnell Douglas (Co) — شركة « ماكدونل دوجلاس »
*sharikat makdūnal dūglās*
MDK ditching machine — حفار خنادق « ام دي كيه »
*ḥaffār khanādiq im dī kayy*
measuring equipment — معدات القياس
*muʿaddāt al-qiyās*
mechanical steering — توجيه ميكانيكي
*tawjīh mīkānīkī*
mechanized — آلي
*ālī*
mechanized brigade — لواء آلي
*liwāʾ ālī*
mechanized column — رتل آلي
*ratl ālī*
mechanized infantry combat vehicle — مركبة قتال للمشاة الآلية
*markabat qitāl lil-mushāh al-ālīya*
medal — نوط . وسام
*nawṭ · wisām*
medevac — إخلاء طبي
*ikhlāʾ ṭibbī*
medical aid station — محطة إسعاف طبي
*maḥaṭṭat isʿāf ṭibbī*
medical board — اللجنة الطبية
*al-lajna aṭ-ṭibbīya*
medical care tent — خيمة الاسعاف الطبي
*khaymat al-isʿāf aṭ-ṭibbī*
medical centre — مركز طبي
*markaz ṭibbī*
medical examination — فحص طبي
*faḥṣ ṭibbī*
medical inspection — تفتيش طبي
*taftīsh ṭibbī*
medical officer — مسؤول طبي
*masʾūl ṭibbī*
medical orderly — ممرض
*mumarriḍ*
medical post — مركز طبي
*markaz ṭibbī*
medical records — سجلات طبية
*sijillāt ṭibbīya*
medical store — مستودع طبي
*mustawdaʿ ṭibbī*
medical store room — مخزن الامدادات الطبية
*makhzan al-imdādāt aṭ-ṭibbīya*
medical supplies — إمدادات طبية
*imdādāt ṭibbīya*
medical unit — وحدة طبية
*wiḥda ṭibbīya*
medicine — دواء . طب
*dawāʾ · ṭibb*
Mediterranean — البحر الأبيض المتوسط
*al-baḥr al-abyaḍ al-mutawwasiṭ*
medium-frequency — تردد متوسط
*taraddud mutawwasiṭ*
medium range — مدى متوسط
*mada mutawwasiṭ*
medium-range ballistic missile — صاروخ بالستي متوسط المدى
*ṣārūkh bālistī mutawassiṭ al-mada*
Meko destroyer — مدمرة « ميكو »
*mudammirat mīkū*
memory capacity — سعة الذاكرة
*siʿat adh-dhākhira*
men — رجال
*rijāl*
Menon mortar — مدفع هاون « مينون »
*midfaʿ hāwun minūn*
Mepsy system — نظام تحكم بالميكروبروسسور « ميبسي »
*niẓām taḥakkum bil-mīkrubrūsisar mipsi*
mercenary — جندي مرتزق
*jundī murtaziq*
merchant ship — سفينة تجارية
*safīna tijārīya*
Merkava tank — دبابة « مركافا »
*dabbābat mirkava*
mess — مطعم للضباط
*maṭʿam liḍ-ḍubbāṭ*
mess accommodation — أماكن الاطعام
*amākin al-iṭʿām*
message — رسالة
*risāla*
mess expenses — مصروفات المطعم
*maṣrūfāt al-maṭʿam*
messing — إطعام . تغذية
*iṭʿām · taghdhiya*
messing allowance — بدل طعام
*badal ṭaʿām*
meteorological aircraft — طائرة أرصاد جوية
*ṭāʾirat arṣād jawwīya*
methods of instruction — طرق التعليم أو التدريب
*ṭuruq at-taʿlīm aw at-tadrīb*
metre — متر
*mitar*
Mexican — مكسيكي
*miksīkī*

M

Mexico المكسيك
*al-miksīk*
MF sonar سونار « ام اف »
*sūnār im if*
MG3 machine-gun رشاش « ام جي ٣ »
*rashshāsh im jī thalātha*
MGM-31s SSM صاروخ سطح ـ سطح « ام جي ام ـ ٣١ اس »
*ṣārūkh saṭḥ-saṭḥ im jī īm wāḥid wa thalāthīn is*
MGM-52C SSM صاروخ سطح ـ سطح « ام جي ام ـ ٥٢ سي »
*ṣārūkh saṭḥ-saṭḥ im jī im ithnayn wa khamsīn sī*
MGM-118 (MX) ICBM صاروخ عابر للقارات « ام جي ام ـ ١١٨ (ام اكس) »
*ṣārūkh bālistī ʿābir lil-qārāt im jī im miʾa wa thamānyata ʿashar im iks*
Mi-4 helicopter طائرة عمودية « ام اي ـ ٤ »
*ṭāʾira ʿamūdīya im āyy arbaʿa*
Mi-6 helicopter طائرة عمودية « ام اي ـ ٦ »
*ṭāʾira ʿamūdīya im āyy sitta*
Mi-8 helicopter طائرة عمودية « ام اي ـ ٨ »
*ṭāʾira ʿamūdīya im āyy thamānya*
Mi-14 helicopter طائرة عمودية « ام اي ـ ١٤ »
*ṭāʾira ʿamūdīya im āyy arbaʿata ʿashar*
Mi-24 helicopter طائرة عمودية « ام اي ـ ٢٤ »
*ṭāʾira ʿamūdīya im āyy arbaʿa wa ʿishrīn*
Mi-26 helicopter طائرة عمودية « ام اي ـ ٢٦ »
*ṭāʾira ʿamūdīya im āyy sitta wa ʿishrīn*
Mi-29 helicopter طائرة عمودية « ام اي ـ ٢٩ »
*ṭāʾira ʿamūdīya im āyy tisʿa wa ʿishrīn*
microphone ميكروفون
*mīkrūfūn*
microprocessor ميكروبروسسور
*mīkrūbrūsisar*
microprocessor memory ذاكرة الميكروبروسسور
*dhākirat al-mīkrūbrūsisar*
Micro turbo ضاغط هواء ميكرو
*ḍāghiṭ hawāʾ mīkrū*
microwave radiation device أداة إشعاع أمواج دقيقة
*adāt ishʿāʿ amwāj daqīqa*
mid-course نصف المسافة
*niṣf al-masāfa*
mid-course guidance توجيه لنصف المسافة
*tawjīh li-niṣf al-masāfa*

mid-flight نصف الرحلة
*niṣf ar-raḥla*
midget submarine غواصة صغيرة
*ghawwāṣa ṣaghīra*
mid-life refit ترميم منتصف العمر
*tarmīn muntaṣif al-ʿumr*
midshipmen طلاب بحرية
*ṭullāb baḥrīya*
MiG-15 aircraft طائرة « ميج ـ ١٥ »
*ṭāʾirat mīg khamsata ʿashar*
MiG-17 computer كومبيوتر « ميج ـ ١٧ »
*kumbyūtar mīg sabʿaṭa ʿashar*
MiG-19 fighter طائرة مقاتلة « ميج ـ ١٩ »
*ṭāʾira muqātila mīg tisʿata ʿashar*
MiG-21 fighter طائرة مقاتلة « ميج ـ ٢١ »
*ṭāʾira muqātila mīg wāḥid wa ʿishrīn*
MiG-21MF fighter طائرة مقاتلة « ميج ـ ٢١ ام اف »
*ṭāʾira muqātila mīg wāḥid wa ʿishrīn im if*
MiG-21R aircraft طائرة « ميج ـ ٢١ آر »
*ṭāʾirat mīg wāḥid wa ʿishrīn ār*
MiG-23 bomber طائرة قاذفة « ميج ـ ٢٣ »
*ṭāʾira qādhifa mīg thalātha wa ʿishrīn*
MiG-23BN aircraft طائرة « ميج ـ ٢٣ بي إن »
*ṭāʾirat mīg thalātha wa ʿishrīn bī in*
MiG-23MF aircraft طائرة « ميج ـ ٢٣ ام اف »
*ṭāʾirat mīg thalātha wa ʿishrīn im if*
MiG-23S fighter طائرة مقاتلة « ميج ـ ٢٣ اس »
*ṭāʾira muqātila mīg thalātha wa ʿishrīn is*
MiG-23U aircraft طائرة « ميج ـ ٢٣ يو »
*ṭāʾirat mīg thalātha wa ʿishrīn yū*
MiG-25 aircraft طائرة « ميج ـ ٢٥ »
*ṭāʾirat mīg khamsa wa ʿishrīn*
MiG-25M fighter طائرة مقاتلة « ميج ـ ٢٥ ام »
*ṭāʾira muqātila mīg khamsa wa ʿishrīn im*
MiG-25R aircraft طائرة « ميج ـ ٢٥ آر »
*ṭāʾirat mīg khamsa wa ʿishrīn ār*
MiG-27 aircraft طائرة « ميج ـ ٢٧ »
*ṭāʾirat mīg sabʿa wa ʿishrīn*

MiG-29 fighter طائرة مقاتلة « ميج - ٢٩ »
*ṭā'ira muqātila mīg tisʿa wa ʿishrīn*

MiG-31 fighter طائرة مقاتلة « ميج - ٣١ »
*ṭā'ira muqātila mīg wāḥid wa thalāthīn*

Mikoyan-Gurevich (Co) شركة « ميكويان - جوريفيتش »
*sharikat mikūyān gūrīfitsh*

Mil (Co) شركة « ميل »
*sharikat mil*

Milan missile صاروخ « ميلان »
*ṣārūkh mīlān*

mile ميل
*māyl*

military academy كلية عسكرية
*kullīya ʿaskarīya*

military activity نشاط عسكري
*nashāṭ ʿaskarī*

military administration حكومة عسكرية
*ḥukūma ʿaskarīya*

military airlift command قيادة النقل الجوي العسكري
*qiyādat an-naql al-jawwī al-ʿaskarī*

military censorship رقابة عسكرية
*raqāba ʿaskarīya*

military city مدينة عسكرية
*madīna ʿaskarīya*

military consignment إرسالية عسكرية
*irsālīya ʿaskarīya*

military co-ordinating centre مركز تنسيق عسكري
*markaz tansīq ʿaskarī*

military equilibrium توازن عسكري
*tawāzun ʿaskarī*

military helicopter طائرة عمودية عسكرية
*ṭā'ira ʿamūdīya ʿaskarīya*

military honour وسام عسكري
*wisām ʿaskarī*

military intervention تدخل عسكري
*tadakhkhul ʿaskarī*

military justice قضاء عسكري
*qaḍā' ʿaskarī*

military life حياة عسكرية
*ḥayāh ʿaskarīya*

military planner مخطط عسكري
*mukhaṭṭiṭ ʿaskarī*

military radar رادار عسكري
*rādār ʿaskarī*

military region منطقة عسكرية
*minṭaqa ʿaskarīya*

military sealift command قيادة النقل البحري العسكري
*qiyādat an-naql al-baḥrī al-ʿaskarī*

military service خدمة عسكرية
*khidma ʿaskarīya*

military traffic مرور عسكري
*murūr ʿaskarī*

military training تدريب عسكري
*tadrīb ʿaskarī*

military tribunal محكمة عسكرية
*maḥkama ʿaskarīya*

military unit وحدة عسكرية
*wiḥda ʿaskarīya*

militia حرس وطني . ميليشيا
*ḥaras waṭanī · milīshya*

Mil Miz helicopter طائرة عمودية « ميل ميز »
*ṭā'ira ʿamūdīya mil miz*

MIM-8P4 SAM صاروخ سطح - جو « ام أي ام - ٨ پي ٤ »
*ṣārūkh saṭḥ-jaww im āyy im thamānya pī arbaʿa*

MIM-23 SAM صاروخ سطح - جو « ام أي ام - ٢٣ »
*ṣārūkh saṭḥ-jaww im āyy im thalātha wa ʿishrīn*

mine لغم
*lughm*

mine clearance تطهير الألغام
*taṭhīr al-alghām*

mine clearing إزالة الألغام
*izālat al-alghāṃ*

mine countermeasure gear جهاز تدابير مضادة للألغام
*jihāz tadābīr muḍādda lil-alghām*

mine countermeasures helicopter طائرة عمودية للتدابير المضادة للالغام
*ṭā'ira ʿamūdīya lit-tadābīr al-muḍādda lil-alghām*

mine countermeasure ship سفينة تدابير مضادة للألغام
*safīnat tadabīr muḍādda lil-alghām*

minefield حقل ألغام
*ḥaql alghām*

mine hunter قناصة ألغام
*qannāṣat alghām*

minehunting sonar سونار قنص الغام
*sūnār qanṣ alghām*

minelayer زارعة الغام
*zāriʿat alghām*

mine laying زرع ألغام
*zarʿ alghām*

M

mines identification & neutralization system — نظام تمييز الألغام وابطالها
*niẓām tamyiz al-alghām wa ibṭāliha*

minesweeper — كاسحة ألغام
*kāsiḥat alghām*

minesweeping — كسح الغام
*kasḥ alghām*

minesweeping duty — مهمة كسح الألغام
*muhimmat kasḥ al-alghām*

minesweeping equipment — معدات كسح الألغام
*muʿaddāt kasḥ al-alghām*

minesweeping helicopter — طائرة عمودية لكسح الألغام
*ṭāʾira ʿamūdīya li-kasḥ al-alghām*

minesweeping winch — مرفاع كسح ألغام
*mirfāʿ kasḥ alghām*

mini-gun — مدفع صغير
*midfaʿ ṣaghīr*

mini laser — ليزر صغير
*layzar ṣaghīr*

M

Minimi machine gun — رشاش « مينيمي »
*rashshāsh minimī*

minimum interception height — إرتفاع الاعتراض الأدني
*irtifāʿ al-iʿtirāḍ al-adna*

minimum range — المدى الأدني
*al-mada al-adna*

Ministry of Defence — وزارة الدفاع
*wizārat ad-difāʿ*

Minuteman ICBM — صاروخ بالستي عابر للقارات « مينتمان »
*ṣārūkh bālistī ʿābir lil-qārāt minitmān*

Mirage fighter — طائرة مقاتلة « ميراج »
*ṭāʾira muqātila mīrāj*

Mirage III fighter — طائرة مقاتلة « ميراج ٣ »
*ṭāʾira muqātila mīrāj thalātha*

Mirage IIIE fighter — طائرة مقاتلة « ميراج ٣ ئي »
*ṭāʾira muqātila mīrāj thalātha ī*

Mirage IIIEL fighter — طائرة مقاتلة « ميراج ٣ ئي إل »
*ṭāʾira muqātila mīrāj thalātha ī il*

Mirage IV fighter — طائرة مقاتلة « ميراج ٤ »
*ṭāʾira muqātila mīrāj arbaʿa*

Mirage 5 fighter — طائرة مقاتلة « ميراج ٥ »
*ṭāʾira muqātila mīrāj khamsa*

Mirage 5D fighter — طائرة مقاتلة « ميراج ٥ دي »
*ṭāʾira muqātila mīrāj khamsa dī*

Mirage 5E2 fighter — طائرة مقاتلة « ميراج ٥ ئي ٢ »
*ṭāʾira muqātila mīrāj khamsa ī ithnayn*

Mirage 5-50 aircraft — طائرة « ميراج ٥-٥٠ »
*ṭāʾirat mīrāj khamsa - khamsīn*

Mirage 2000 fighter — طائرة مقاتلة « ميراج ٢٠٠٠ »
*ṭāʾira muqātila mīrāj alfayn*

Mirage 2000N fighter — طائرة مقاتلة « ميراج ٢٠٠٠ إن »
*ṭāʾira muqātila mīrāj alfayn in*

Mirage F1 fighter — طائرة مقاتلة « ميراج اف ١ »
*ṭāʾira muqātila mīrāj if wāḥid*

Mirage F-1A — طائرة « ميراج إف - ١ ايه »
*ṭāʾira muqātila mīrāj if wāḥid ayy*

Mirage F-IC interceptor — طائرة اعتراضية « ميراج إف ١ سي »
*ṭāʾira iʿtirāḍīya mīrāj if wāḥid sī*

Mirage F-ICR fighter — طائرة مقاتلة « ميراج إف ١ سي آر »
*ṭāʾira muqātila mīrāj if wāḥid sī ār*

mirror landing sight — مهداف هبوط مرآوي
*mihdāf hubuṭ mirāwī*

misalignment — خطأ التراصف · إختلاف المحاذاة
*khaṭāʾ at-tarʿarṣuf · ikhtilāf al-muḥādhāh*

miscellaneous units — وحدات متنوعة
*wiḥdāt mutanawwaʿa*

miss distance indicator — مؤشر مسافة عدم اصابة
*muʾashshir masāfat ʿadam iṣāba*

missile — صاروخ . قذيفة
*ṣārūkh · qadhīfa*

missile aircraft — طائرة صواريخ
*ṭāʾirat ṣawārīkh*

missile armed — مسلح بالصواريخ
*musallah biṣ-ṣawārīkh*

missile boat — زورق صواريخ
*zawraq ṣawārīkh*

Missile corvette — سفينة حراسة صغيرة مجهزة بالصواريخ
*safīnat ḥirāsa ṣāghīra mujahhaza biṣ-ṣawārīkh*

missile craft — سفينة صواريخ
*safīnat ṣawārīkh*

missile design — تصميم الصواريخ
*taṣmīn aṣ-ṣawārīkh*

missile deviation — إنحراف الصاروخ
*inḥirāf as-ṣārūkh*

missile exhaust عادم الصاروخ
*ʿādim aṣ-ṣārukh*
missile field مجال الصواريخ
*majāl aṣ-ṣawārīkh*
missile fire-control system نظام السيطرة على رمي الصواريخ
*niẓām as-sayṭara ʿala ramī aṣ-ṣawārīkh*
missile forces قوات الصواريخ
*qūwāt aṣ-ṣawārīkh*
missile installation تركيب الصواريخ · منشأة صواريخ
*tarkīb aṣ-ṣawārīkh · munshaʿa ṣawārīkh*
missile-launcher bin صندوق جهاز إطلاق الصواريخ
*ṣundūq jihāz iṭlāq aṣ-ṣawārīkh*
missile length طول الصاروخ
*ṭūl aṣ-ṣārūkh*
missile patrol boat زورق حراسة بالصواريخ
*zawraq ḥirāsa biṣ-ṣawārīkh*
missile regiment كتيبة صواريخ
*katībat ṣawārikh*
missile resupply truck شاحنة اعادة التزويد بالصواريخ
*shāḥinat iʿādat at-tazwīd biṣ-ṣawārīkh*
missile seeker باحث صاروخي
*bāḥith ṣārūkhī*
missile shoe قدم الصاروخ
*qadam aṣ-ṣārūkh*
missile system نظام صواريخ
*niẓām ṣawārīkh*
missile-tracking function وظيفة تعقب الصواريخ
*waẓīfat taʿaqqub aṣ-ṣawārīkh*
missile tube أنبوبة الصاروخ
*unbūbat aṣ-ṣārūkh*
missile weight وزن الصاروخ
*wazn aṣ-ṣārūkh*
mission مهمة
*muhimma*
mission computer كومبيوتر المهمة
*kumbyūtar al-muhimma*
mission crew أفراد المهمة
*afrād al-muhimma*
mission load حمل المهمة
*ḥiml al-muhimma*
Mitsubishi (Co) شركة « ميتسوبيشي »
*sharikat mitsubīshi*
MK32 torpedo طوربيد « ام كيه ٣٢ »
*ṭūrbīd im kayy ithnayn wa thalāthīn*

Mk F3 gun مدفع ماركة اف ٣
*midfaʿ marka if thalātha*
MLMS (Air-Launched Stinger) شبكة صواريخ خفيفة الوزن متعددة الأغراض ستنبجر المقذوفة جواً
*shabakat ṣawārīkh khafīfat al-wazn mutaʿaddidat al-aghrāḍ stingar al maqdhūfa jawwan*
mobile air-defence system شبكة دفاع جوي متحركة
*shabakat difāʿ jawwī mutaḥarrika*
mobile firepower شبكة قوة نيران متحركة
*shabakat qūwat nīrān mutaḥarrika*
mobile kitchen مطبخ متنقل ميداني
*maṭbakh mutanaqqil maydānī*
mobile launcher قاذفة متحركة
*qādhifa mutaḥarrika*
mobile weapon سلاح متحرك
*silāḥ mutaḥarrik*
mobility تنقلية . حركية
*tanaqqulīya · ḥarakīya*
mobilization تعبئة . تجنيد
*taʿbiʾa · tajnīd*
mock-up نموذج بالحجم الطبيعي
*namūdhaj bil-jism aṭ-ṭabīʿī*
model 49 rifle بندقية طراز ٤٩
*bunduqīya ṭirāz tisʿa wa arbaʿīn*
model 84 pistol مسدس طراز ٨٤
*musaddas ṭirāz arbaʿa wa thamānīn*
model 92 pistol مسدس طراز ٩٢
*musaddas ṭirāz ithnayn wa tisʿīn*
model 1911A1 pistol مسدس طراز ١٩١١ ايه ١
*musaddas tirāz alf wa tisʿ miʾa wa aḥada ʿashar ayy wāḥid*
modern حديث . عصري
*ḥadīth · ʿaṣrī*
modern electronic system نظام الكتروني حديث
*niẓām iliktrūnī ḥadīth*
modified معدل
*muʿaddal*
modular action إجراء معياري
*ijrāʾ miʿyārī*
modular facility تسهيلات معيارية
*tashīlāt miʿyārīya*

M

modular operations room غرفة عمليات معيارية
*ghurfat ʿamalīyāt miʿyārīya*
modular system نظام معياري
*niẓām miʿyārī*
modulated laser beam حزمة ليزر مضمنة
*ḥuzmat layzar muḍammana*
Mohawk aircraft طائرة « موهوك »
*ṭāʾirat mūhūk*
Molotov cocktail زجاجة مخلوط « مولوتوف »
*zujājat makhlūṭ mulutuf*
Mongolia منغوليا
*munghūlya*
Mongol trainer طائرة تدريب « مونجول »
*ṭāʾirat tadrīb mungūl*
monitor جهاز مراقبة
*jihāz murāqaba*
monitoring unit وحدة مراقبة
*wiḥdat murāqaba*
monocular sight مهداف وحيد العين
*mihdāf waḥīd al-ʿayn*
monocular telescope تلسكوب وحيد العين
*talskūb waḥīd al-ʿayn*
monopulse وحيد النبضة
*waḥīd an-nabḍa*
monorail أحادي السكة
*uḥādī as-sikka*
monorail system شبكة أحادية السكة
*shabakat uḥādīyat as-sikka*
moored mine لغم راسي
*lughm rāsi*
mooring equipment معدات إرساء
*muʿaddāt irsāʾ*
mopping-up operations عمليات تطهير
*ʿamalīyāt taṭhīr*
Moroccan مغربي
*maghribī*
Morocco المغرب
*al-maghrib*
morse code رموز « مورس »
*rumūz mūrs*
mortar مدفع هاون
*midfaʿ hāwun*
mortar battery سرية مدفعية هاون
*sarīya midfaʿīya hāwun*
mortar bomb قنبلة هاون
*qunbulat hāwun*
mortarman جندي مدفعية هاون
*jundī midfaʿīya hāwun*
mortuary مستودع جثث
*mustawdaʿ juthath*
Moskva cruiser طرادة « موسكفا »
*ṭarrādat muskva*
Mosquito missile صاروخ « موسكيتو »
*ṣārūkh muskītū*
Moss AWAC نظام التحذير والمراقبة المحمول جواً « موس »
*niẓām at-taḥdhīr wal-murāqaba al-maḥmūl jawwan mūs*
mothballed محفوظ في مكان واق
*maḥfūẓ fī makān wāqin*
mother ship سفينة القيادة
*safīnat al-qiyāda*
motor carrier ناقلة آلية
*nāqila ālīya*
motor cycle دراجة نارية
*darrāja nārīya*
motorized منقولة بالسيارات
*manqūla bis-sayyārāt*
motorized infantry مشاة منقولة بالسيارات
*mushāh manqūla bis-sayyārāt*
motorized unit وحدة منقولة بالسيارات
*wiḥda manqūla bis-sayyārāt*
motor-rifle battalion كتيبة بنادق آلية
*katībat banādiq ālīya*
motor-rifle division فرقة بنادق آلية
*firqat banādiq ālīya*
motor-rifle regiment فوج بنادق آلية
*fawj banādiq ālīya*
motor transport نقل بالسيارات
*naql bis-sayyārāt*
Moujik aircraft طائرة « موجيك »
*ṭāʾirat mūjik*
mount قاعدة تثبيت
*qāʿidat tathbīt*
mount! اركب !
*irkab*
mountainous country بلد جبلي
*balad jabalī*
mountainous terrain أرض جبلية
*arḍ jabalīya*
mountain pass ممر جبلي
*mamarr jabalī*
mounting تركيب . تثبيت
*tarkīb · tathbīt*
Mourabitoun Militia ميليشا المرابطون
*mīlīsha al-murābiṭūn*
mouth فم . فوهة
*fam · fūha*

move differentially تحرك تفاضلي
*taḥarruk tafāḍulī*
mover محرك
*muḥarrik*
moving target هدف متحرك
*hadaf mutaḥarrik*
moving target indication بيان الهدف المتحرك
*bayān al-hadaf al-mutaḥarrik*
moving wing جناح متحرك
*janāḥ mutaḥarrik*
Mozambique موزمبيق
*mūzambīq*
MP40 sub-machine gun رشاش قصير « ام بي ٤٠ »
*rashshāsh qaṣīr im pī arbaʿīn*
MP44 rifle بندقية « ام بي ٤٤ »
*bunduqīyat im pī arbaʿa wa arbaʿīn*
MPiKM rifle بندقية « ام بي اي كيه ام »
*bunduqīyat im pī āyy kayy im*
MPQ-49 radar رادار « ام بي كيو - ٤٩ »
*rādār im pī kyū tisʿa wa arbaʿīn*
MR 80 Manta mine لغم « ام آر ٨٠ مانتا »
*lughm im ār thamānīn māntā*
MRBM missile صاروخ « ام آر بي ام »
*ṣārūkh im ār bī im*
MR V warhead رأس قذيفة « ام آر ڤي »
*raʾs qadhīfa im ār vī*
MSC-322 minesweeper كاسحة ألغام « ام اس سي - ٣٢٢ »
*kāsiḥat alghām im is sī thalāth miʾa wa ithnayn wa ʿishrīn*
MT-LB vehicle مركبة « ام تي - ال بي »
*markabat im tī il bī*
M/TR-77 tank دبابة « ام/تي آر - ٧٧ »
*dabbābat im tī ār sabʿa wa sabʿīn*
MTU diesel ديزل « ام تي يو »
*dīzl im tī yū*
Muff Cob radar رادار « ماف كوب »
*rādār maf kūb*
multi-barrel متعدد المواسير
*mutaʿaddid al-mawāsīr*
multi-cannon هاون متعدد
*hāwun mutaʿaddid*
multi-barrel cannon مدفع هاون متعدد المواسير
*midfaʿ hāwun mutaʿaddid al-mawāsīr*

multi-fuel وقود متعدد
*wuqūd mutaʿaddid*
multi-fuel engine محرك يعمل بوقود متعدد
*muḥarrik yaʿmal bi-wuqūd mutaʿaddid*
multi-mission متعدد المهام
*mutaʿaddid al-mahāmm*
multi-mode متعدد الانماط
*mutaʿaddid al-anmāṭ*
multi-mode radar رادار متعدد الأوضاع
*rādār mutaʿaddid al-awḍāʿ*
multiple متعدد . مضاعف
*mutaʿaddid · muḍāʿaf*
multiple rocket launcher قاذفة صواريخ متعددة
*qādhifat ṣawārīkh mutaʿaddida*
multiple rocket system نظام صواريخ متعددة
*niẓām ṣawārīkh mutaʿaddida*
multi-purpose متعدد الأغراض
*mutaʿaddid al-aghrāḍ*
multi-purpose console لوحة التحكم متعددة الأغراض
*lawḥat at-taḥakkum mutaʿaddidat al-aghrāḍ*
multi-purpose tracer ذخيرة خطّاطة متعددة الأغراض
*dhakhīra khaṭṭāṭa mutaʿaddidat al-aghrāḍ*
multi-role متعدد المهام
*mutaʿaddid al-mahāmm*
multi-role fighter طائرة مقاتلة متعددة المهام
*ṭāʾira muqātila mutaʿaddidat al-mahāmm*
multi-role helicopter طائرة عمودية متعددة المهام
*ṭāʾira ʿamūdīya mutaʿaddidat al-mahāmm*
multi-role tracked vehicle عربة مجنزرة متعددة المهام
*ʿaraba mujanzara mutaʿaddidat al-mahāmm*
multi-sensor reconnaissance إستطلاع بأجهزة احساس متعددة
*istiṭlāʿ bi-ajhizat iḥsās mutaʿaddida*
munition deactivation إبطال الذخيرة
*ibṭāl adh-dhakhīra*
munition depot مستودع ذخيرة
*mustawdaʿ dhakhīra*
Mushroom radar رادار « ماشروم »
*rādār mashrūm*
mustard gas غاز الخردل
*ghāz al-khardal*

M

mutiny عصيان . تمرد
*ʿiṣyān · tamarrud*
muzzle فوهة البندقية او المدفع
*fūhat al-bunduqīya aw al-midfaʿ*
muzzle-brake ماسك الفوهة
*māsik al-fūha*
muzzle flash ومض الفوهة
*wamḍ al-fūha*
muzzle velocity السرعة الفوهية
*as-surʿa al-fūhīya*
Mya aircraft طائرة « مايا »
*ṭāʾirat māya*
Myasishchev (Co) شركة « ماياسيتشيف »
*sharikat māyasistshif*
Mystère-Falcon aircraft طائرة « ميستير فالكون »
*ṭāʾirat mistīr-falkan*

# N

NA10 fire-control — نظام السيطرة على الرمي « ان ايه ١٠ »
*niẓām as-sayṭara alar-ramī in ayy ʿashara*

NA30 fire control — نظام السيطرة على الرمي « ان ايه ٣٠ »
*niẓām as-sayṭara alar-ramī in ayy thalāthīn*

Nacken submarine — غواصة « ناكين »
*ghawwāṣat nakan*

Nadge (Nato Air Defence Ground Environment) — البيئة البرية للدفاع الجوي لمنظمة ناتو « نادج »
*al-bīʾa al-barrīya lid-difāʿ al-jawwī li-munaẓẓamat nātū (nāj)*

Nadge radar chain — سلسلة رادار « نادج »
*silsilat rādār nāj*

Nanchang (Co) — شركة « نانتشانج »
*sharikat nāntshāng*

Nanuchka corvette — سفينة حراسة صغيرة « نانوتشكا »
*safīnat ḥirāsa ṣaghīra nānūtshka*

napalm — ناپام
*napām*

napalm bomb — قنبلة ناپام
*qunbulat napām*

Narval submarine — غواصة « نارڤال »
*ghawwāṣat nārvāl*

Narwhal submarine — غواصة « ناروال »
*ghawwāṣat nārwāl*

national air defence troops — قوات الدفاع الجوي الوطنية
*qūwāt ad-difāʿ al-jawwī al-waṭanīya*

National Emergency Airborne Command Post — مركز القيادة الجوية للطوارىء الوطنية
*markaz al-qiyāda al-jawwīya liṭ-ṭawāriʾ al-waṭanīya*

NATO (North Atlantic Treaty Organisation) — منظمة حلف شمال الأطلنطي « ناتو »
*munaẓẓamat ḥilf shamāl al-aṭlanṭī (nātū)*

NATO Air Defence Ground Environment — البيئة البرية للدفاع الجوي لمنظمة ناتو
*al-bīʾa al-barrīya lid-difāʿ al-jawwī li-munaẓẓamat nātū*

NATO cartridge — خرطوشة « ناتو »
*kharṭūshat nātū*

NATO helicopter — طائرة عمودية « ناتو »
*ṭāʾira ʿamūdīya nātū*

NATO inventory — جرد « ناتو »
*jard nātū*

NATO manned — مزود بالرجال « ناتو »
*muzawwad bir-rijāl nātū*

NATO nations — دول منظمة ناتو
*duwal munaẓẓamat nātū*

NATO target — هدف « ناتو »
*hadaf nātū*

natural camouflage — تمويه طبيعي
*tamwīh ṭabīʿī*

natural cover — ساتر طبيعي
*sātir ṭabīʿī*

natural obstacle — عائق طبيعي
*ʿāʾiq ṭabīʿī*

Natya minesweeper — كاسحة الغام « ناتيا »
*kāsiḥat alghām nātya*

nautical mile — ميل بحري
*mīl baḥrī*

navaids — معينات ملاحية
*muʿīnāt mallāḥīya*

naval air force — القوات الجوية البحرية
*al-qūwāt al-jawwīya al-baḥrīya*

naval air surveillance — إستطلاع جوي بحري
*istiṭlāʿ jawwī baḥrī*

Naval Aviation Force — القوات الجوية البحرية
*al-qūwāt al-jawwīya al-baḥrīya*

naval base — قاعدة بحرية
*qāʿida baḥrīya*

N

naval cadet طالب في كلية بحرية
*ṭālib fī kūllīya baḥrīya*
naval commando فدائي بحري
*fidā'ī baḥrī*
naval duty مهمة بحرية
*muhimma bahrīya*
naval exercise مناورات بحري
*munāwarāt baḥrīya*
naval gun mount منصة مدفع بحري
*minaṣṣat midfaʿ baḥrī*
naval helicopter طائرة عمودية بحرية
*ṭā'ira ʿamūdīya baḥrīya*
naval infantry مشاة البحرية
*mushāh al-baḥrīya*
Naval Intelligence Processing System نظام تحليل الاستخبارات البحرية
*niẓām taḥlīl al-istikhbārāt al-baḥrīya*
naval personnel أفراد البحرية
*afrād al-baḥrīya*
naval strike هجوم بحري
*hujūm baḥrī*
navigation ملاحة
*milāḥa*
navigation computer كومبيوتر ملاحي
*kumbyūtar milāḥī*
navigation direction radar رادار توجيه ملاحي
*rādār tawjīh milāḥī*
navigation equipment معدات ملاحية
*muʿaddāt milāḥīya*
navigation radar رادار ملاحة
*rādār milāḥa*
navigation sight مهداف للملاحة
*midhāf lil-milāḥa*
navigation system نظام الملاحة
*niẓām al-milāḥa*
navigation-system output خرج نظام الملاحة
*kharj niẓām al-milāḥa*
navigator ملاّح
*mallāḥ*
NavSat satellite قمر صناعي للملاحة البحرية « ناف سات »
*qamr ṣināʿī lil-milāḥa al-baḥrīya nav sat*
navy inventory جرد البحرية
*jard al-baḥrīya*
Nazario Sauro submarine غواصة « نازاريو ساورو »
*ghawwāṣat nāzāryū sawrū*
NBC system نظام « ان بي سي »
*niẓām in bī sī*
Neiva (Co) شركة « نيڤا »
*sharikat nīva*

Nepal نيبال
*nībāl*
Neptune radar رادار نبتيون
*rādār nibtyūn*
nerve agent عنصر اعصاب
*ʿunṣur aʿṣāb*
nerve gas غاز أعصاب
*ghāz aʿsāb*
Nesher aircraft طائرة « نيشر »
*ṭā'irat nishar*
Netherlands هولندة
*hūlanda*
network شبكة
*shabaka*
neutron bomb قنبلة « نيوترون »
*qunbula nyūtrūn*
Newport ship سفينة « نيوبورت »
*safīnat nyūbūrt*
New Zealand نيوزيلندة
*nyū zīlanda*
next-of-kin أقرب الأقارب
*aqrab al-aqārib*
Nicaragua نيكاراغوا
*nīkārāghwa*
Nicaraguan نيكاراغوي
*nikārāghwī*
Niger نيجاير
*nījayr*
Nigeria نيجيريا
*nījīrya*
Nigerian نيجيري
*nījīrī*
night-action rifle بندقية قتال ليلي
*bunduqīyat qitāl laylī*
night attack هجوم ليلي
*hujūm laylī*
night capability إمكانيات ليلية
*imkanīyāt laylīya*
night operation عملية ليلية
*ʿamalīya laylīya*
night sight مصوبة ليلية
*muṣawwiba laylīya*
night-sighting telescope تلسكوب تصويب ليلي
*talskūb taṣwīb laylī*
night vision رؤية ليلية
*ru'ya laylīya*
night vision equipment معدات الرؤية الليلية
*muʿaddāt ar-ru'ya al-laylīya*
Nike Hercules SAM صاروخ سطح ـجو « نايكي هاركيوليز »
*ṣārūkh saṭḥ-jaww nāykī harkyulīz*

Nimbus turboshaft عمود إدارة تربيني « نيمباص »
*ʿamūd idārat turbīnī nimbaṣ*
Nimitz carrier حاملة « نيميتس »
*ḥāmilat nīmīts*
Nimrod AEW.3 aircraft طائرة « نيمرود ايه ئي دبليو ٣ »
*ṭāʾirat nimrūd ayy ī dablyū thalātha*
nitro-glycerine نتروجليسرين
*nitrūglīsrīn*
no entry ممنوع الدخول
*mamnūʿ ad-dukhūl*
no-flare landing هبوط دون المشاعل
*hubūṭ dūn al-mashāʿil*
noise-level مستوى الضجيج
*mustawa aḍ-ḍajīj*
non-combatant غير مقاتل
*ghayr muqātil*
non-combatant unit وحدة غير مقاتلة
*wiḥda ghayr muqātila*
non-combat troops جنود غير مقاتلين
*junūd ghayr muqātilīn*
non-commissioned officer ضابط صف
*ḍābiṭ ṣaff*
non-metallic material مادة لا معدنية
*mādda lā maʿdinīya*
non-nodal system نظام غير عُقدي
*niẓām ghayr ʿuqdī*
non-serviceable عديم الصيانة
*ʿadīm aṣ-ṣiyāna*
non-strategic cruise missile صاروخ « كروز » لا استراتيجي
*ṣārūkh krūz lā istrātījī*
no overtaking ممنوع التجاوز
*mamnūʿ at-tajāwuz*
no parking ممنوع الوقوف
*mamnuʿ al-wuqūf*
normal combat range مدى القتال المعتاد
*mada al-qital al-muʿtād*
North شمال
*shamāl*
North American (Co) شركة نورث اميريكان
*sharikat nūrth amirikan*
North American Air Defence الدفاع الجوي الأمريكي الشمالي
*ad-difāʿ al-jawwī al-amrīkī ash-shamālī*
northern command القيادة الشمالية
*al-qiyāda ash-shamālīya*
Northern Fleet أسطول الشمال
*usṭūl ash-shamāl*
North Korea كوريا الشمالية
*kūrya as-shamālīya*
Northrop (Co) شركة نورثروپ
*sharikat nurthrūp*
North Yemen اليمن الشمالي
*al-yaman ash-shamālīya*
Norway النرويج
*al-nurwīj*
Norwegian نرويجي
*nurwījī*
nose gun مدفع المقدمة
*midfaʿ al-muqaddima*
nose-hemisphere radar رادار نصف الكرة في المقدّمة
*rādār niṣf al-kura fil-muqaddima*
nose section قطاع المقدمة
*qiṭāʿ al-muqaddima*
November submarine غواصة « نوڤمبر »
*ghawwāṣat nuvimbar*
nozzle فوهة . صنبور
*fūha · ṣunbūr*
NR-23 cannon مدفع هاون « ان آر - ٢٣ »
*midfaʿ hāwun in ār thalātha wa ʿishrīn*
NR8475A1 medium mortar مدفع هاون متوسط « ان آر ٨٤٧٥ ايه ١ »
*midfaʿ hāwun mutawassiṭ in ār thamānyat alāf wa arbaʿ miʿa wa khamsa wa sabʿīn ayy wāḥid*
NRBA landing aid معين الهبوط « ان آر بي ايه »
*muʿīn al-hubūṭ in ār bī ayy*
NTDS equipment معدات نظام البيانات التكتيكية البحرية
*muʿaddāt niẓām al-bayānāt at-taktīkīya al-baḥrīya*
nuclear نووي
*nawawī*
nuclear airburst إنفجار جوي نووي
*infijār jawwī nawawī*
nuclear attack submarine غواصة هجوم نووية
*ghawwāṣat hujūm nawawīya*
nuclear bomb قنبلة نووية
*qunbula nawawīya*
nuclear class طراز نووي
*ṭīrāz nawawī*
nuclear conflict صراع نووي
*ṣirāʿ nawawī*
nuclear contamination تلوث نووي
*talawwuth nawawī*
nuclear energy طاقة نووية
*ṭāqa nawawīya*
nuclear explosion إنفجار نووي
*infijār nawawī*

N

nuclear plant محطة كهرباء نووية
*mahattat kahrabā'ī nawawīya*
nuclear-powered بالطاقة النووية
*biṭ-ṭāqa ān-nawawīya*
nuclear-powered ballistic missile submarine غواصة صواريخ بالستية بالطاقة النووية
*ghawwāṣat ṣawārīkh bālistīya biṭ-ṭāqa an-nawawīya*
nuclear-powered carrier حاملة بالطاقة النووية
*ḥāmila biṭ-ṭāqa an-nawawīya*
nuclear-powered cruiser طرادة بالطاقة النووية
*ṭarrāda biṭ-ṭāqa an-nawawīya*
nuclear projectile مقذوف نووي
*maqdhūf nawawī*
nuclear-propelled مدفوع بالطاقة النووية
*madfūʿ biṭ-ṭāqa an-nawawīya*
nuclear propulsion دفع بالطاقة النووية
*dafʿ biṭ-ṭāqa an-nawawīya*
nuclear propulsion system نظام دفع بالطاقة النووية
*niẓām dafʿ biṭ-ṭāqa an-nawawīya*
nuclear reactor مفاعل نووي
*mufāʿil nawawī*
nuclear shell مقذوف مدفعي نووي
*maqdhūf midfaʿī nawawī*
nuclear stand-off missile صاروخ نووي يطلق عن بعد
*ṣārūkh nawawī yuṭlaq ʿan buʿd*
nuclear strike aircraft طائرة انقضاض نووي
*ṭā'irat inqiḍāḍ nawawī*
nuclear strike force قوات انقضاض نووي
*qūwāt inqiḍāḍ nawawī*
nuclear submarine غواصة نووية
*ghawwāṣat nawawīya*
nuclear-tipped ذو راس قذيفة نووي
*dhū ra's qadhīfa nawawī*
nuclear torpedo طوربيد نووي
*ṭūrbīd nawawī*
nuclear warfare حرب نووية
*ḥarb nawawīya*
nuclear warhead رأس مقذوف نووي
*ra's maqdhūf nawawī*
nuclear weapon سلاح نووية
*silāḥ nawawī*
number 4 rifle بندقية رقم ٤
*bunduqīya raqm arbaʿa*
nylonite نايلونيت
*nāylūnīt*
Nysa C radar رادار « نايسا سي »
*rādār nāysa sī*

N

# O

O-class submarine غواصة « طراز ـ اوه »
*ghawwāṣa ṭirāz aw*
O-2KT warhead رأس مقذوف « اوه ـ ٢ كيه تي »
*ra'š maqdhūf aw ithnayn kayy ti*
Oberon submarine غواصة « اوبرون »
*ghawwāṣat awbirun*
obey (to) يطيع
*yuṭī'*
oblique camera آلة تصوير مائلة
*ālat taṣwīr mā'ila*
oblique frame camera آلة تصوير باطار مائل
*ālat taṣwīr bi-iṭār mā'il*
observation مراقبة . ملاحظة
*murāqaba · mulaḥaẓa*
observation helicopter طائرة عمودية للمراقبة
*ṭā'ira 'amūdīya lil-murāqaba*
observation post مركز مراقبة
*markaz murāqaba*
observer مراقب . راصد
*murāqib · rāṣid*
obsolescent مهجور
*mahjūr*
obstacle clearing إزالة العوائق
*izālat al-'awā'iq*
obstacle course طريق العوائق
*ṭāriq al-'awā'iq*
occupation إحتلال . مهنة
*iḥtilāl · mihna*
October-6 craft سفينة « اكتوبر ـ ٦ »
*safīnat uktūbar sitta*
Oerlikon cannon مدفع هاون « اورليكون »
*midfa' hāwun arlikan*
OE-82 satellite communication نظام اتصال بالقمر الصناعي « اوه ئي ـ ٨٢ »
*niẓām ittiṣāl bil-qamr aṣ-ṣinā'ī aw ī ithnayn wa thamānīn*
Oerlikon/Oto gun مدفع « اورليكون ـ اوتو »
*midfa' arlikan ūtū*
OF-40 tank دبابة « اوه اف ـ ٤٠ »
*dabbāba aw if arba'īn*
off beat شاذ . غريب الأطوار
*shādh · gharīb al-aṭwār*
offensive هجومي . عدواني
*hujūmī · 'udwānī*
offensive capability إمكانيات التعرض
*imkanīyāt at-ta'arruḍ*
offensive operation عملية تعرضية
*'amalīya ta'arruḍīya*
office مكتب . دائرة
*maktab · dā'ira*
office equipment معدات وأجهزة المكاتب
*mu'addāt wa ajhizat al-makātib*
officer ضابط
*ḍābiṭ*
officer cadet طالب في كلية عسكرية
*ṭālib fī kullīya 'askarīya*
officer commanding ضابط قائد . قائد
*ḍābiṭ qā'id · qā'id*
officer in charge ضابط مسؤول
*ḍābiṭ mas'ūl*
officers' mess مطعم الضباط
*maṭ'am aḍ-ḍubbāṭ*
official correspondence مراسلات رسمية
*murāsalāt rasmīya*
OH-6 helicopter طائرة عمودية « اوه اتش ـ ٦ »
*ṭā'ira 'amūdīya aw itsh sitta*
OH-23F helicopter طائرة عمودية « اوه اتش ـ ٢٣ اف »
*ṭā'ira 'amūdīya aw itsh thalātha wa 'ishrīn if*
OH-58A helicopter طائرة عمودية « اوه اتش ـ ٥٨ ايه »
*ṭā'ira 'amūdīya aw itsh thamānya wa khamsīn ayy*
Ohio submarine غواصة « اوهايو »
*ghawwāṣat awhāyū*

oil bottle — زجاجة زيت
*zujāja zayt*
oil-fired boiler — غلاية بنار الزيت
*ghallāya bi-nār az-zayt*
Oliver Hazard Perry frigate — فرقاطة « اوليفر هازارد پيرى »
*firqāṭat awlivar hāzārd piri*
Olympus gas turbine — تربين غاز « اوليمپوس »
*turbīn ghāz ulimpus*
Oman — عُمان
*ʿumān*
Omega inertial navigation system — نظام الملاحة بالقصور الذاتي « اوميجا »
*niẓām al-milāḥa bil-quṣūr adh-dhaṭī ūmiga*
OMERA camera — آلة تصوير « اوميرا »
*ālat taṣwīr ūmīrā*
on-board computer — كومبيوتر على متن
*kumbyūtar ʿala matn*
Ondatra mortar — مدفع هاون « انداترا »
*midfaʿ hāwun andatra*
one-man — رجل واحد
*rajul wāḥid*
on guard! — تأهب !
*taʾahhab*
on my order! — مع صدور أمري !
*maʿa ṣudūr amrī*
on target — على الهدف
*ʿalal-hadaf*
on the move — متحرك . متنقل
*mutaḥarrik · mutanaqqil*
Ooshio submarine — غواصة « وشيو »
*ghawwāṣat ūshiyū*
open country — أرض مكشوفة
*arḍ makshūfa*
open-ended — مفتوح
*maftūḥ*
open fire — افتح النار
*iftaḥ an-nār*
open formation — تشكيل مفتوح
*tashkīl maftūḥ*
open out! — تشكيل مفتوح !
*tashkīl maftūḥ*
operating characteristics — خصائص التشغيل
*khaṣāʾis at-tashghīl*
operating conditions — ظروف التشغيل
*ẓurūf at-tashghīl*
operating room — غرفة العمليات
*ghurfat al-ʿamalīyāt*
operation — تشغيل . عملية
*tashghīl · ʿamalīya*
operational — تشغيلي
*tashghīli*
operational information — بيانات العمليات
*bayānāt al-ʿamalīyāt*
operational status — وضع العمليات
*waḍʿ al-ʿamalīyāt*
operations controller — مراقب العمليات
*murāqib al-ʿamalīyāt*
operations conversion unit — وحدة تحويل العمليات
*wiḥdat taḥwīl al-ʿamalīyāt*
operations planner — مخطط العمليات
*mukhaṭṭiṭ al-ʿamalīyāt*
operation wavelength — الطول الموجي للعمليات
*aṭ-ṭūl al-mawjī lil-ʿamalīyāt*
operator — المشغّل
*al-mushaghghil*
Ophelia helicopter — طائرة عمودية « اوفيليا »
*ṭāʾira ʿamūdīya ūfīlya*
opposing — عارض
*ʿāriḍ*
OPS-9 radar — رادار « اوه پي اس - ٩ »
*rādār aw pī is tisʿa*
OPS-14 radar — رادار « اوه پي اس - ١٤ »
*rādār aw pī is arbaʿata ʿashar*
OPS-16 radar — رادار « اوه پي اس - ١٦ »
*rādār aw pī is sittata ʿashar*
optical beam ride — نظام شعاع بصري للسيطرة على الصواريخ الموجهة
*niẓām shuʿāʿ baṣarī lis-sayṭara ʿalaṣ-ṣawārīkh al-muwajjaha*
optical fire-control — نظام بصري للسيطرة على الرمي
*niẓām baṣarī lis-sayṭara alar-ramī*
optical mode — وضع بصري
*waḍʿ baṣarī*
Optical Seeker Technique — تقنية المتقفي البصري
*taqniyat al-mutaqaffī al-baṣarī*
optical sensor — جهاز احساس بصري
*jihāz iḥsās baṣarī*
optical sight — مصوبة بصرية
*muṣawwiba baṣarīya*
optical sighting — تسديد بصري
*tasdīd baṣarī*
optical telescope — تلسكوب بصري
*talskūb baṣarī*
optical tracker — متقفي بصري
*mutaqaffī baṣarī*
optimum condition — حالة مثالية
*ḥāla mithālīya*

optronic director
*mudīr al-ajhiza al-baṣarīya al-iliktrūnīya*
مدير الاجهزة البصرية الالكترونية

optronic fire control
*as-sayṭara alal-iṭlāq bi-ajhiza baṣarīya iliktrūnīya*
السيطرة على الاطلاق باجهزة بصرية الكترونية

orange smoke
*dukhān burtuqālī*
دخان برتقالي

Orao aircraft
*ṭā'irat awraw*
طائرة « أوراو »

ORB 31 Héraclès I radar
*rādār aw ār bī waḥīd wa thalāthīn hiraklīz wāḥid*
رادار « اوه أربي ٣١ هركليز ١ »

ORB 31W radar
*rādār aw ār bī wāḥid wa thalāthīn dablyū*
رادار « اوه أربي ٣١ دبليو »

ORB 32 Héraclès II radar
*rādār aw ār bī ithnayn wa thalāthīn hiraklīz ithnayn*
رادار « اوه أربي ٣٢ هركليز ٢ »

order arms!
*janban silāḥ*
جنباً سلاح !

orderly
*ḥājib · munawwib*
حاجب . منوب

orderly officer
*ḍābiṭ al-khafar*
ضابط الخفر

orderly-room
*ḥujrat al-munawwibīn*
حجرة المنوبين

order of battle
*niẓām al-maʿraka*
نظام المعركة

ordnance
*muʿaddāt midfaʿīya*
معدّات مدفعية

ordnance magazine
*mustawdaʿ muʿaddāt ḥarbīya*
مستودع معدات حربية

ordnance map
*kharīṭat arkān*
خريطة أركان

ordnance survey
*idārat al-misāḥa*
إدارة المساحة

Orion aircraft
*ṭā'irat arāyan*
طائرة « ارايون »

Orion fire control
*niẓām as-sayṭara ʿalar-ramī arāyan*
نظام السيطرة على الرمي « ارايون »

Osa patrol boat
*safīnat khafar as-sawāḥil awsa*
سفينة خفر السواحل « اوسا »

Oscar submarine
*ghawwāṣat uskār*
غواصة « اوسكار »

oscillating turret
*burj tadhabdhubī*
برج تذبذبي

Otomat ASM
*ṣārūkh jaww-saṭḥ ūtūmāt*
صاروخ جو ـ سطح « اوتومات »

OTO Melara Compact mount
*qā'idat ūtū milāra kumpakt*
قاعدة « اوتو ميلارا كومپاكت »

OTO-Melara gun
*midfaʿ ūtū milāra*
مدفع « اوتو ـ ميلارا »

OTO-Melara turret
*burj ūtū milāra*
برج « اوتو ـ ميلارا »

outboard motor
*muḥarrik zawraq khārijī*
محرك زورق خارجي

outboard pylon
*ʿamūd zawraq khārijī*
عمود زورق خارجي

outer-ring defence
*difāʿ aṭ-ṭawq al-khārijī*
دفاع الطوق الخارجي

outer wing pylon
*ʿamūd al-janāḥ aṭ-ṭarafī*
عمود الجناح الطرفي

outmanoeuvred
*yafūquh barāʿatan*
يفوقه براعة

outnumbered
*yafūquh ʿadadan*
يفوقه عدداً

out of bounds
*maḥẓūr ʿalal-jund*
محظور على الجند

out of line
*munḥarif al-muḥādhāh*
منحرف المحاذاة

out of range
*khārij al-mada*
خارج المدى

outpost
*makhfar amāmī*
مخفر أمامي

outward-facing
*muwājih lil-khārij*
مواجه للخارج

OV-1 aircraft
*ṭā'irat aw vī wāḥid*
طائرة « اوه ڤي ـ ١ »

OV-1D aircraft
*ṭā'irat aw vī wāḥid dī*
طائرة « اوه ڤي ـ ١ دي »

OV-10 aircraft
*ṭā'irat aw vī ʿashara*
طائرة « اوه ڤي ـ ١٠ »

oval
*bayḍawī*
بيضوي

overall
*kāmil · bizzat al-ʿaml*
كامل . بزة العمل

overhead
*ʿalawī · muʿallaq*
علوي . معلق

overhead cable
*kabl muʿallaq*
كبل معلق

overland surveillance
*istiṭlāʿ barrī*
إستطلاع بري

overnight camp
*muʿaskar lil-iqāma al-mu'aqqita*
معسكر للاقامة المؤقتة

override capability إمكانيات التجاوز
*imkanīyāt at-tajāwuz*
overseas خارجي . ما وراء البحار
*khārijī · mā warā' al-biḥār*
overseas deployment انتشار خارجي
*intishār kharijī*
over-the-beach assault هجوم ساحلي
*hujūm sāḥilī*
over-the-horizon radar رادار فوق الأفق
*rādār fawq al-ufuq*
over-the-horizon spotter راصد فوق الأفق
*rāṣid fawq al-ufuq*
overwater فوق الماء
*fawq al-mā'*
overwhelm غلب . سحق
*ghalaba · saḥaqa*
Owl Screech radar رادار أول سكريتش
*rādār awl skrītsh*
oxygen cylinder أسطوانة أكسجين
*usṭuwānat aksijīn*

O

# P

P-class submarine « غواصة « طرازبي
*ghawwāṣa ṭirāz pī*

P-2J aircraft « طائرة « بي ـ ٢ جيه
*ṭā'irat pī ithnayn jayy*

P-3C aircraft « طائرة « بي ـ٣ سي
*ṭā'irat pī thalātha sī*

P4 torpedo boat « زورق طوربيد « بي ٤
*zawraq ṭūrbīd pī arba'a*

P6 torpedo boat « زورق طوربيد « بي ٦
*zawraq ṭūrbīd pī sitta*

P-50 radar « رادار « بي ـ ٥٠
*rādār pī khamsīn*

PA-75 carrier « حاملة « بي ايه ـ ٧٥
*ḥāmilat pī ayy khamsa wa sab'īn*

Pacific متعلق بالمحيط الهادىء
*muta'alliq bil-muḥīṭ al-hādi'*

Pacific Fleet أسطول المحيط الهادي
*usṭūl al-muḥīṭ al-hādi'*

pack حقيبة متاع الجندىء
*ḥaqībat matā' al-jundī*

pack drill تدريب عقابي
*tadrīb 'iqābī*

pack radio جهاز لاسلكي عقابي
*jihāz lā-silki 'iqābī*

padre كاهن عسكري
*kāhin 'askarī*

PAH-1 helicopter « طائرة عمودية « بي ايه اتش ـ ١
*ṭā'ira 'amūdīya pī ayy itsh wāḥid*

Pakistan الباكستان
*al-bākistān*

Pakistani باكستاني
*bākistānī*

Palestine Liberation Organisation (P.L.O) منظمة التحرير الفلسطينية
*munaẓẓamat at-taḥrīr al-filasṭīnīya*

palletized stores مخزونات على منصات نقالة
*makhzūnāt 'ala minaṣṣāt naqqāla*

Palmaria howitzer « مدفع هاوتزر « بالماريا
*midfa' hāwitsar pālmārya*

Palm Frond radar « رادار « بام فروند
*rādār pām frūnd*

Panama باناما
*bānāmā*

Panavia (Co) « شركة « باناڤيا
*sharikat pānāvya*

Panavia Tornado aircraft « طائرة « باناڤياتورنادو
*ṭā'irat pānāvya turnaydū*

Panhard armoured car « عربة مدرعة « بانهارد
*'araba mudarra'a panhārd*

panoramic بانورامي . كامل الرؤية
*bānūrāmī · kāmil ar-ru'ya*

panoramic camera آلة تصوير بانورامية
*ālat taṣwīr bānūrāmīya*

Panzerjäger K tank « دبابة « بانتسر ييجر كيه
*dabbābat panzaryaygar kayy*

PAP 104 underwater vehicle « مركبة تحت مائية « بى اي پى ١٠٤
*markaba taḥta mā'iya pī ayy pī mi'a wa arba'a*

Papa submarine « غواصة « بابا
*ghawwāṣat pāpā*

Papua New Guinea بابوا غيني الجديدة
*bābwa ghīnī al-jadīda*

paraboloid antenna هوائي قطع مكافىء
*hawā'ī qaṭ' mukāfi'*

parachutable vehicle سيارة قابلة للانزال بالمظلة
*sayyāra qābila lil-inzāl bil-miẓalla*

parachute مظلة
*miẓalla*

parachute brigade لواء مظلات
*liwā' miẓallāt*

parachute company سرية مظلات
*sarīyat miẓallāt*

parachute container صندوق مظلي
*ṣundūq miẓallī*
parachute drop إسقاط بالمظلات
*isqāṭ bil-miẓallāt*
parachute harness أحزمة المظلة
*aḥzimat al-miẓalla*
parachute jumping instructor مدرب القفز بالمظلات
*mudarrib al-qafz bil-miẓallāt*
parachutist مظلي
*miẓallī*
parade عرض . إستعراض
*ʿarḍ · istiʿrāḍ*
parade dress بزة الاستعراض
*bizzat al-istiʿrāḍ*
parade ground أرض الاستعراض
*arḍ al-istiʿrāḍ*
Paraguay باراغواي
*barāghwāyy*
parameter معْلم . پارامتر
*maʿlam · pārāmitar*
paramilitary شبه عسكري
*shibh ʿaskarī*
para-military force قوات شبه عسكرية
*qūwāt shibh ʿaskarīya*
paratroop مظلي
*miẓallī*
paratroop unit وحدة مظلات
*wiḥdat miẓallāt*
para version rifle بندقية المظلي
*bunduqīyat al-miẓallī*
parent ship سفينة القيادة
*safīnat al-qiyāda*
PARIS sonar سونار « پاريس »
*sūnār pārīs*
Park Lamp antenna هوائي « پارك لامپ »
*hawāʾī pārk lāmp*
Park Lamp direction finder آلة تحديد الاتجاه « پارك لامپ »
*ālat taḥdīd al-ittijāh pārk lāmp*
partisan موالي
*muwālī*
pass ممر . إجازة مرور
*mamarr · ijāzat murūr*
passenger transport نقل الركاب
*naql ar-rukkāb*
passive سلبي . غير فعال
*salbī · ghayr faʿʿāl*
passive detection system نظام كشف سلبي
*niẓām kashf salbī*

passive-detection system antenna هوائي نظام الكشف السلبي
*hawāʾī niẓām al-kashf as-salbī*
passive intelligence-gathering جمع استخبارات سلبي
*jamʿ istikhbārāt salbī*
passive intercept ESM تدابير دعم الكترونية سلبية الاعتراض
*tadābīr daʿm iliktrūnīya salbīyat al-iʿtirāḍ*
passive ranging sonar سونار تحديد مدى سلبي
*sūnār taḥdīd mada salbī*
passive receiver antenna هوائي مستقبل سلبي
*hawāʾī mustaqbil salbī*
Pat Hand radar رادار « پات هاند »
*rādār pāt hānd*
pathfinder طائرة كشافة
*ṭāʾira kashshāfa*
Patriot SAM صاروخ سطح - جو « پاتريوت »
*ṣārūkh saṭḥ-jaww pātriyūt*
patrol دورية . حراسة
*dawrīya · ḥirāsa*
patrol boat زورق خفر السواحل
*zawraq khafar as-sawāḥil*
patrol craft زورق دورية
*zawraq dawrīya*
patrol gun-boat زورق دورية مسلحة بالمدافع
*zawraq dawrīya musallaḥa bil-madāfiʿ*
patrol mine-sweeper كاسحة ألغام دورية
*kāsiḥat alghām dawrīya*
patrol mission مهمة دورية
*muhimma dawrīya*
patrol pattern نمط الحراسة
*namaṭ al-ḥirāsa*
patrol radius نصف قطر الدورية
*niṣf quṭr ad-dawrīya*
patrol speed سرعة الدورية
*surʿat ad-dawrīya*
patrol submarine غواصة دورية
*ghawwāṣa dawrīya*
patrol vessel سفينة دورية
*safīna dawrīya*
patrol work أعمال الدورية
*aʿmāl ad-dawrīya*
Pauk ship سفينة « پوك »
*safīnat pūk*
Pave Paws radar رادار « پايڤ پوز »
*rādār payv pūz*
Paveway programme برنامج « پايڤويه »
*barnāmij payvwayy*

Paveway-series bomb قنبلة من نوع « بايڤويه »
*qunbula min naw<sup>c</sup> payvwayy*
pay and allowances الراتب والعلاوات
*ar-rātib wal-ʿilāwāt*
pay attention! إنتباه !
*intibāh*
pay clerk كاتب رواتب
*kātib rawātib*
payload وزن الملاحين والآلات
*wazn al-mallāḥīn wal-ālāt*
paymaster أمين الصندوق
*amīn aṣ-ṣundūq*
PBR patrol craft سفينة خفر السواحل « پي بي آر »
*safīnat khafar as-sawāḥil pī bī ār*
PC-7 aircraft طائرة « پي سي ـ ٧ »
*ṭāʾirat pī sī sabʿa*
PCF patrol craft سفينة دورية « پي سي اف »
*safīna dawrīya pī sī if*
PCG-1 corvette سفينة حراسة صغيرة « پي سي جي ـ ١ »
*safīnat ḥirāsa ṣaghīra pī sī jī wāḥid*
Peacekeeper ICBM صاروخ بالستي عابر للقارات « پيسكيپر »
*ṣārūkh bālistī ʿābir lil-qārāt pīskīpar*
peace-keeping force قوات حفظ الأمن
*qūwāt ḥafẓ al-amn*
peacekeeping mission بعثة حفظ الأمن
*baʿthat ḥafẓ al-amn*
peacetime زمن السلم
*zaman as-salm*
peacetime operation عملية في زمن السلم
*ʿamalīya fī zaman as-salm*
peace treaty معاهدة سلام
*muʿāhadat salām*
Peacock patrol craft سفينة خفر السواحل « پيكوك »
*safīnat khafar as-sawāḥil pīkūk*
Pedersen Device أداة « بدرسين »
*adāh pidarsin*
pedestal mount منصة تركيب
*minaṣṣat tarkīb*
Pedro Teixeira ship سفينة « بيدرو تيكسيرا »
*safīnat pīdrū tiksīra*
Peel Group radar رادار « پيل جروپ »
*rādār pīl grūp*
peel-off ينحرف للانقضاض أو الهبوط
*yanḥarif lil-inqiḍāḍ aw al-hubūṭ*
Pegaso vehicle مركبة « پيجاسو »
*markabat pīgāsū*
Pegasus Mk 104 vectored-thrust turbofan مروحة تربينية بالدفع الموجه . پيجاسوس ماركة ١٠٤ »
*mirwaḥa turbinīya bil-dafʿ al-muwajjah pīgasūs marka miʾa wa arbaʿa*
Pelican helicopter طائرة عمودية « پليكان »
*ṭāʾira ʿamūdīya pilikan*
penetration aid معين الاختراق
*muʿīn al-ikhtirāq*
penetration capability إمكانية الاختراق
*imkānīyat al-ikhtirāq*
Penguin ASM صاروخ جو ـ سطح « پينجوين »
*ṣārūkh jaww-saṭḥ pingwīn*
Penguin SSM صاروخ سطح ـ سطح « پينجوين »
*ṣārūkh saṭḥ-saṭḥ pingwīn*
people's army الجيش الشعبي
*al-jaysh ash-shaʿbīya*
People's Liberation Army جيش التحرير الشعبي
*jaysh at-taḥrīr ash-shaʿbī*
percussion revolver مسدس يعمل بالقدح
*musaddas yaʿmal bil-qadḥ*
periscope « بريسكوب »
*biriskūb*
periscope sight مهداف پريسكوبي
*mihdāf piriskūbī*
Permit submarine غواصة « پرميت »
*ghawwāṣat pirmit*
peroxide-powered يعمل بالبيروكسيد
*yaʿmal bil-biruksīd*
Pershing II MRBM صاروخ بالستي متوسط المدى « پرشينج ٢ »
*ṣārūkh bālistī mutawassiṭ al-mada pirshīng ithnayn*
Pershing SRBM صاروخ بالستي قصير المدى « پرشينج ٢ »
*ṣārūkh bālistī qaṣīr al-mada pirshīng*
Persian Gulf الخليج العربي
*al-khalīj al-ʿarabī*
personal cleansing نظافة شخصية
*naẓāfa shakhṣīya*
personal equipment تجهيزات شخصية
*tajhīzāt shakhṣīya*
personal hygiene المحافظة على الصحة الشخصية
*al-muḥāfaẓa ʿalaṣ-ṣiḥḥa ash-shakhṣīya*
personnel carrier ناقلة جنود
*nāqilat junūd*
Peru بيرو
*bīrū*
Pescador ASM صاروخ جو ـ سطح « پيسكادور »
*ṣārūkh jaww-saṭḥ piskādūr*

petrol engine محرك بنزين
*muḥarrik banzīn*
petty officer ضابط صف بحري
*ḍābiṭ ṣaff baḥrī*
Petya ship سفينة « پتيا »
*safīnat pitya*
PFM aircraft طائرة « پي اف ام »
*ṭāʾirat pī if im*
PGG-1 craft سفينة « پي جي جي - ١ »
*safīnat pī jī jī wāḥid*
Phalange الكتائب
*al-katāʾib*
Phantom II fighter طائرة مقاتلة « فانتوم ٢ »
*ṭāʾira mūqatila fantūm ithnayn*
pharmacy صيدلية . مخزن أدوية
*ṣaydalīya · makhzan al-adwīya*
phased-array antenna هوائي مجموعة مشعة
*hawāʾī majmūʿa mushiʿʿa*
phased-array radar رادار بمجموعة عناصر مشعة
*rādār bi-majmūʿat ʿanāsir mushiʿʿa*
phase of signals طور الاشارات
*ṭawr al-ishārāt*
phase shifter مغير أطوار
*mughayyir aṭwār*
Philippine فلبيني
*filibīnī*
Philippines الفلبين
*al-filibīn*
Phoenix AIM صاروخ اعتراض جوي « فينيكس »
*ṣārūkh iʿtirāḍ jawwī fīniks*
phosgene فسجين
*fusjīn*
phosphorus فسفور
*fusfūr*
photoflash cartridge خرطوشة ومضية للتصوير
*kharṭūsha wamḍīya lit-taṣwīr*
photographic image صورة فوتوغرافية
*ṣūra fūtūgrāfīya*
photographic laboratory معمل فوتوغرافي
*maʿmal fūtūgrāfī*
photographic-reconnaissance إستطلاع تصويري
*istiṭlāʿ taṣwīrī*
photography تصوير
*taṣwīr*
photo-interpreter مفسر صور
*mufassir ṣuwar*

physical training رياضة بدنية
*riyāḍa badanīya*
Piaggio (Co) شركة پياجيو
*sharikat piyājū*
Picket ATGW سلاح موجّه مضاد للدبابات « پيكيت »
*silāḥ muwajjah muḍādd lid-dabbābāt pikit*
Pilatus aircraft طائرة « پيلاتوس »
*ṭāʾirat pilātus*
Pilatus (Co) شركة پيلاتوس
*sharikat pilātus*
pillbox مترسة للمدافع
*matrasa lil-madāfiʿ*
pilot مرشد . طيار
*murshid · tayyār*
pilot house برج الملاحة
*burj al-milāḥa*
pilotless aircraft طائرة بدون طيار
*ṭāʾira bidūn ṭayyār*
pilot's night vision system نظام الرؤية الليلية للطيار
*niẓām ar-ruʾya al-laylīya liṭ-ṭayyār*
pincer movement حركة كماشية
*ḥaraka kammāshīya*
pintle-mounted مركب على محور
*murakkab ʿala miḥwar*
Pinzgauer vehicle مركبة « پينتس جاور »
*markabat pintsgawar*
pipelaying مد الأنابيب
*madd al-anābīb*
Piranha vehicle مركبة « پيرانا »
*markabat pirāna*
pistol ammunition ذخيرة المسدس
*dhakhīrat al-musaddas*
pistol cartridge طلقة المسدس
*ṭalqat al-musaddas*
pistol grip قبضة المسدس
*qabḍat al-musaddas*
pitch stability ثبات الترجّح
*thabāt at-tarajjuḥ*
pitch stabilizer jet نفاث موازنة الترجّح
*naffāth muwāzanat at-tarajjuḥ*
PIVADS air defense system نظام الدفاع الجوي « پيڤادز »
*niẓām ad-difāʿ al-jawwī pīvadz*
pivoted locking piece رتاج مغلاق محوري
*ritāj mighlāq miḥwarī*
PKT machine-gun رشاش « پي كيه تي »
*rashshāsh pī kayy tī*

plan position indicator مؤشر الوضع المستوي
*mu'ashshir al-wad' al-mustawī*
PLARK submarine غواصة « پلارك »
*ghawwāṣat plārk*
plastic explosive متفجرات بلاستيك
*mutafajjirāt blāstīk*
plate aerial هوائي لوحي
*hawā'ī lawḥī*
platoon فصيلة
*faṣīla*
Plinth Net radar رادار « پلينث نيت »
*rādār plīnth nīt*
Pluton missile صاروخ « پلوتون »
*ṣārūkh plūtūn*
Pluto radar رادار « پلوتو »
*rādār plūtū*
pneumatic هوائي مضغوط
*hawā'ī maḍghūt*
pneumatically بالهواء المضغوط
*bil-hawā' al-maḍghūṭ*
pocket compass بوصلة الجيب
*būṣalat al-jayb*
point defence system نظام الدفاع النقطي
*niẓām ad-difā' an-nuqṭī*
poisonous gas غاز سام
*ghāz sām*
Poland بولندة
*būlanda*
polar icecap قلنسوة جليدية قطبية
*qalansuwa jalīdīya quṭbīya*
Polaris missile صاروخ « پولاريس »
*ṣārūkh pūlārīs*
Police Air Wing الجناح الجوي للشرطة
*al-janāḥ al-jawwī lish-shurṭa*
Polish بولندي
*būlandī*
Pollux radar رادار « پولكس »
*rādār pūluks*
Polnocny landing ship سفينة إنزال « پولنوكنى »
*safīnat inzāl pūlnūknī*
Poluchat craft سفينة « پوليشات »
*safīnat pūlīshāt*
pontoon رمث . طوف
*ramath · ṭawf*
pontoon causeway section قطاع طريق جسري على اطواف
*qiṭā' ṭarīq jisrī 'ala aṭwāf*
Pop Group radar رادار « پوپ جروپ »
*rādār pūp grūp*
populated area منطقة مأهولة
*minṭaqa ma'hūla*

Porpoise submarine غواصة « پورپويس »
*ghawwāṣat pūrpuwīs*
port ميناء . ميسرة
*mīnā' · maysara*
portable نقالي .
*naqqālī*
port area منطقة الميناء
*minṭaqat al-mīnā'*
port arms! عالياً ـ احمل !
*'ālīyan - iḥmil*
Portugal البرتغال
*al-burtughāl*
Portuguese برتغالي
*burtughālī*
Poseidon missile صاروخ « پوسيدون »
*ṣārūkh pusāydan*
post-boost تعزيز لاحق
*ta'zīz lāḥiq*
post boost vehicle مركبة تعزيز لاحق
*markabat ta'zīz lāḥiq*
Post Lamp radar رادار « پوست لامپ »
*rādār pūst lāmp*
post-mobilization ما بعد التعبئة
*mā ba'd at-ta'bi'a*
post-mobilization training تدريب لاحق على التعبئة
*tadrīb lāḥiq 'alat-ta'bi'a*
post-war ما بعد الحرب
*mā ba'd al-ḥarb*
potassium cyanide سيانيد البوتاسيوم
*siyānīd al-būtāsyūm*
Pot Drum radar رادار « پوت درم »
*rādār pūt dram*
potency فعالية
*fa''ālīya*
Pot Head radar رادار « پوت هيد »
*rādār pūt hīd*
power-assisted مُعان بالطاقة الآلية
*mu'ān biṭ-ṭāqa al-ālīya*
power distribution توزيع الطاقة
*tawzī' aṭ-ṭāqa*
powered-flight طيران بمحرك
*ṭayarān bi-muḥarrik*
power pack مجموعة توليد
*majmū'at tawlīd*
powerplant وحدة طاقة
*wiḥdat ṭāqa*
power supply امدادات الطاقة
*imdādāt aṭ-ṭāqa*
power-to-weight ratio نسبة القدرة الى الوزن
*nisbat al-qudra ilal-wazn*

P

PP Sh41 sub-machine gun — رشاش قصير « بي بي اس اتش ٤١ »
*rashshāsh qaṣīr pī pī is itsh wāḥid wa arbaʿīn*

practice missile — صاروخ تدريب
*ṣārūkh tadrīb*

practice warhead — رأس قذيفة تدريب
*raʾs qadhīfa tadrīb*

Pratt & Whitney (Co) — « شركة پرات اند ويتني »
*sharikat prāt and witnī*

pre-arranged code — رموز مسبقة الإعداد
*rumūz musabbaqat al-iʿdād*

precision flying — طيران بالغ الدقة
*ṭayarān bāligh ad-diqqa*

precision location strike system — نظام هجوم بموقع محدد بدقة
*niẓām hujūm bi-mawqiʿ muḥaddad bi-diqqa*

pre-commissioning — ما قبل بدء التشغيل
*mā qabl badʾ at-tashghīl*

prefabricated bridge — جسر جاهز للتركيب
*jisr jāhiz lit-tarkīb*

pre-fragmented — مسبق التشظية
*musabbaq at-tashẓīya*

pre-heater — مسخن متقدم
*musakhkhin mutaqaddim*

pre-launch — ما قبل الاطلاق
*mā qabl al-iṭlāq*

pre-mobilization — تعبئة متقدمة
*taʿbiʾa mutaqaddima*

prepared position — موقع محصن
*mawqiʿ muḥaṣṣan*

present arms! — سلّم ـ سلاح !
*sallim - silāḥ*

present position — الوضع الحالي
*al-waḍʿ al-ḥālī*

pre-set — مضبوط مقدماً
*maḍbūṭ muqaddaman*

pressure reducing valve — صمام تخفيف الضغط
*ṣimām takhfīf aḍ-ḍaghṭ*

pressurized — مكيف الضغط
*mukayyif aḍ-ḍaghṭ*

pressurized-water cooled — يبرد بالماء المضغوط
*yubarrad bil-māʾ al-maḍghūṭ*

pressurized-water reactor — مفاعل ذري يبرد بالماء المضغوط
*mufāʿil dharrī yubarrad bil-māʾ al-maḍghūṭ*

primary armament — تسليح أساسي
*taslīḥ asāsī*

primary radar target — هدف راداري رئيسي
*hadaf rādārī raʾīsī*

Primorye ship — سفينة « پريموري »
*safīnat prīmūryi*

printed circuit — دائرة مطبوعة
*dāʾira maṭbūʿa*

Prisma radar — رادار « پريزما »
*rādār prizma*

prison — سجن
*sijn*

prisoner — سجين . أسير
*sajīn · asīr*

prisoner of war — أسير الحرب
*asīr al-ḥarb*

private — خصوصي . جندي
*khuṣūṣī · jundī*

private militia — حرس وطني خصوصي
*ḥaras waṭanī khuṣūṣī*

programmed descent — هبوط مبرمج
*hubūṭ mubarmaj*

prohibited area — منطقة محرمة
*minṭaqa muḥarrama*

projectile — قذيفة . مقذوف
*qadhīfa · maqdhūf*

promotion — ترقية . تعزيز
*tarqiya · taʿzīz*

propaganda leaflet — نشرة دعائية
*nashra diʿāʾīya*

propellant — دافع . وقود دفعي
*dāfiʿ · wuqūd dafʿī*

propellant gas — غاز داسر
*ghāz dāsir*

propeller — مروحة
*mirwaḥa*

propulsion — دفع . تسيير
*dafʿ · tasyīr*

propulsion motor — محرك دفعي
*muḥarrik dafʿī*

propulsion plant — وحدة دفعية
*wiḥda dafʿīya*

propulsion system — نظام دفعي
*niẓām dafʿī*

propulsion unit — وحدة دفعية
*wiḥda dafʿīya*

protective clothing — ألبسة واقية
*albisa wāqīya*

protective wire — سلك واق
*silk wāqin*

Proteus gas turbine — تربين غازي « پروتيوس »
*tūrbīn ghāzī prūtyūs*

protocol — مراسيم
*marāsīm*

P

prototype نموذج أولي . طراز بدائي
*namūdaj awwalī · ṭirāz bidā'ī*
protruding device أداة بارزة
*ādāh bāriza*
Province craft سفينة « پروڤينس »
*safīnat prūvins*
Prowler aircraft طائرة « پراولر »
*ṭā'irat prawlar*
proximity fuse صمامة تقاربية
*ṣimāma taqārubīya*
PS7p/R radar رادار « پي اس ٧ پي / آر »
*rādār pī is sabʿa pī/ār*
PS-700 landing craft سفينة إنزال « پي اس - ٧٠٠ »
*safīnat inzāl pī īs - sabʿ mi'a*
PT-76 tank دبابة « پي تي - ٧٦ »
*dabbābat pī tī-sitta wa sabʿīn*
Public Security Force قوات الأمن العام
*qūwāt al-amn al-ʿāmm*
Pucara aircraft طائرة « پوكارا »
*ṭā'irat pūkārā*
Puff Ball radar رادار « پاف پول »
*rādār paf būl*
pull friction إحتكاك السحب
*iḥtikāk as-saḥb*
pulse نبضة . ذبذبة
*nabḍa · dhabdhaba*
pulse acquisition radar رادار كسب الذبذبة
*rādār kasb adh-dhabdhaba*
pulse-compression إنضغاط الذبذبة
*inḍighāṭ adh-dhabdhaba*
pulse-Doppler radar رادار نبضات « دوپلر »
*rādār nabaḍāt dūplar*
pulsed wave emission إبتعاث موجي بالنبضات
*ibtiʿāth mawjī bin-nabaḍāt*
pulse echo صدى النبضات
*ṣada an-nabaḍāt*
pulse repetition frequency تردد تكرار النبضات
*taraddud takrār an-nabaḍāt*
Puma helicopter طائرة عمودية « پيوما »
*ṭā'ira ʿamūdīya pyūma*
pump-jet نفاث مضخة
*naffāth miḍakhkha*
Punch Bowl navigation system نظام الملاحة « پانتش بول »
*niẓām al-milāḥa pantsh būl*
punishment عقاب . عقوبة
*ʿiqāb · ʿuqūba*
punishment battalion كتيبة تأديب
*katībat ta'dīb*
PVO air-defence unit وحدة الدفاع الجوي « پي ڤي اوه »
*wiḥdat ad-difāʿ al-jawwī pī vī aw*
pylon عمود
*ʿamud*
pyrotechnics علم المتفجرات وصناعتها
*ʿilm al-mutafajjirāt wa ṣināʿatiha*
pyrotechnical chains سلاسل صاروخية
*salāsil ṣārūkhīya*
pyrotechnical detonator كبسولة تفجير صاروخية
*kabṣūlat tafjīr ṣārūkhīya*
Python AAM صاروخ جو - جو « پايثون »
*ṣārūkh jaww-jaww pāythan*
PZ 68 tank دبابة « پي زد ٦٨ »
*dabbābat pī zīd thamānya wa sittīn*
PZL Mielec (Co) شركة « پي زد إل ميليك »
*sharikat pī zid il mīlīk*

P

# Q

| | |
|---|---|
| Q-5 fighter<br>*ṭā'ira muqātila kyū-khamsa* | طائرة مقاتلة « كيو ـ ٥ » |
| Qatar<br>*qaṭar* | قطر |
| Qatari<br>*qaṭarī* | قطري |
| Qiang-jiji 5 attack aircraft<br>*ṭā'ira hujūmīya kyang jījī khamsa* | طائرة هجومية « كيانج ـ جيجي ٥ » |
| QRC-334 radar<br>*rādār kyū ār sī - thalāth mi'a wa arbaʿa wa thalāthīn* | رادار « كيو آر سي ـ ٣٣٤ » |
| quad missile box<br>*ṣundūq ṣawārīkh maqṭūr* | صندوق صواريخ مقطور |
| quadricycle landing gear<br>*jihāz hubūṭ rubāʿī al-ʿajalāt* | جهاز هبوط رباعي العجلات |
| quadruple-launcher<br>*qādhifa rubāʿīya* | قاذفة رباعية |
| quad Yagi array<br>*majmūʿat ʿanāṣir hawā'ī yāgī rubā'īya* | مجموعة عناصر هوائي ياجي رباعية |
| quarantine<br>*maḥjar ṣiḥḥī · ḥajr ṣiḥḥī* | محجر صحي . حجر صحي |
| quarter-deck<br>*ṭaraf al-mu'akhkhara · mawqiʿ aḍ-ḍubbāṭ* | طرف المؤخرة . موقع الضباط |
| quartermaster<br>*ḍābiṭ at-tamwīn wal-imdādāt* | ضابط التموين والامدادات |
| quartermaster store<br>*makhzan at-tamwīn wal-imdādāt* | مخزن التموين والامدادات |
| quarters<br>*thukna* | ثكنة |
| Quebec submarine<br>*ghawwāṣat kwibik* | غواصة « كويبك » |
| Queen Air aircraft<br>*ṭā'irat kwīn ayr* | طائرة « كوين اير » |
| quicken step!<br>*khuṭwa - sarīʿa* | خطوة ـ سريعة ! |
| Quick-fix helicopter<br>*ṭā'ira ʿamūdīya kwik fiks* | طائرة عمودية « كويك فيكس » |
| Quick Look II radar<br>*rādār kwik lūk ithnayn* | رادار « كويك لوك ٢ » |
| quick march!<br>*muʿtādan – sirr* | معتاداً ـ سر ! |
| quinine<br>*kīnīn* | كينين |

Q

# R

R-class submarine غواصة « طراز ـ آر »
*ghawwāṣa ṭirāz ār*
R4 helicopter طائرة عمودية آر ٤
*ṭā'ira 'amūdiya ār arba'a*
R-9BF-811 engine محرك آر ـ ٩بي اف ـ ٨١١
*muḥarrik ār - tis'a bī if - thamāni mi'a wa aḥada 'ashar*
R-11 turbojet نفاثة تربينية « آر ـ ١١ »
*naffātha turbīnīya ār - aḥada 'ashar*
R-25 turbojet نفاثة تربينية « آر ـ ٢٥ »
*naffātha turbīnīya ār - khamsa wa 'ishrīn*
R-29B turbojet نفاثة تربينية « آر ـ ٢٩ بي »
*naffātha turbīnīya ār - tis'a wa 'ishrīn bī*
R-31 turbojet نفاثة تربينية « آر ـ ٣١ »
*naffātha turbīnīya ār - wāḥid wa thalāthīn*
R440 missile صاروخ « آر ٤٤٠ »
*ṣārūkh ār arba'a mi'a wa arba'īn*
R-530 AAM صاروخ جو ـ جو « آر ـ ٥٣٠ »
*ṣārūkh jaww-jaww ār khams mi'a wa thalāthīn*
R-550 missile صاروخ « آر ـ ٥٥٠ »
*ṣārūkh ār khams mi'a wa khamsīn*
radar رادار
*rādār*
radar altimeter مقياس ارتفاع راداري
*miqyās irtifā' rādārī*
radar antenna هوائي الرادار
*hawā'ī ar-rādār*
radar blip نقطة رادارية
*nuqṭa rādārīya*
radar-clutter rejection equipment معدات رفض التداخل الراداري
*mu'addāt rafḍ tadākhul ar-rādārī*
radar component جزء الرادار
*juz' ar-rādār*
radar detection كشف راداري
*kashf rādārī*
radar-detection range مدى الكشف الراداري
*mada al-kashf ar-rādārī*
radar dish صحن الرادار
*ṣaḥn ar-rādār*
radar electronics إلكترونيات الرادار
*iliktrūnīyāt ar-rādār*
radar equipment معدات الرادار
*mu'addāt ar-rādār*
radar homing توجيه راداري
*tawjīh rādārī*
radar homing and warning system نظام التوجيه والانذار الراداري
*niẓām at-tawjīh wal-indhār ar-rādārī*
radar horizon أفق الرادار
*ufuq ar-rādār*
radar mast صاري الرادار
*ṣārī ar-rādār*
radar mode نمط الرادار
*namaṭ ar-rādār*
radar monitoring مراقبة رادارية
*murāqaba rādārīya*
radar operator عامل الرادار
*'āmil ar-rādār*
radar performance أداء الرادار
*adā' ar-rādār*
radar proximity fuse صمامة تقاربية رادارية
*ṣimāma taqārubīya rādārīya*
radar receiver مستقبل راداري
*mustaqbil rādārī*

R

radar scan مسح راداري
*masḥ rādārī*
radar scope شاشة الرادار
*shāshat ar-rādār*
radar seeker باحث راداري
*bāḥith rādārī*
radar station محطة رادار
*maḥaṭṭat rādār*
radar target detection كشف راداري عن الهدف
*kashf rādārī ʿanal-hadaf*
radar tracking mode نمط تتبع راداري
*namaṭ tatabbuʿ rādārī*
radar transmitter مرسل راداري
*mursil rādārī*
radar vehicle مركبة رادارية
*markaba rādārīya*
radar warning receiver مستقبل انذار راداري
*mustaqbil indhār rādārī*
radiated noise ضجيج مشع
*ḍajīj mushiʿʿ*
radiating element عنصر مشع
*ʿunṣur mushiʿʿ*
radiation إشعاع
*ishʿāʿ*
radiation-pointing control مراقبة تسديد إشعاعية
*murāqabat tasdīd ishʿāʿīya*
radio altimeter مقياس ارتفاع لاسلكي
*miqyās irtifāʿ lā-silkī*
radio command أمر لاسلكي
*amr lā-silkī*
radio communication مواصلات لاسلكية
*muwāṣalāt lā-silkīya*
radio frequency energy طاقة ترددات لاسلكية
*ṭāqat taraddudāt lā-silkīya*
radio interference تداخل لاسلكي
*tadākhul lā-silkīya*
radio link حلقة اتصال لاسلكي
*ḥalqat ittiṣāl lā-silkī*
radiological إشعاعي
*ishʿāʿī*
radiological warfare حرب إشعاعية
*ḥarb ishʿāʿīya*
radio maintenance men رجال صيانة اللاسلكي
*rijāl ṣiyāna lā-silkīya*
radio-navaid related متعلق باجهزة الملاحة اللاسلكية
*mutaʿallaq bi-ajhizat al-milāḥa al-lā-silkīya*
radio operator عامل لاسلكي
*ʿāmil lā-silkī*
radio silence إسكات لاسلكي
*iskāt lā-silkī*
radio telephone هاتف لاسلكي
*hātif lā-silkī*
radio transmitter مرسل لاسلكي
*mursil lā-silkī*
radome رادوم : قبة هوائي الرادار
*rādūm · qubba hawāʾī ar-rādār*
Rafael gun display system نظام عرض المدفع « رفائيل »
*niẓām ʿarḍ al-midfaʿ rāfāʾīl*
raid غارة
*ghāra*
raiding party جماعة مغيرة
*jamāʿa mughīra*
rain مطر
*maṭar*
Raleigh landing ship سفينة إنزال « رالي »
*safīnat inzāl rāli*
Ramadan frigate فرقاطة رمضان
*firqāṭat ramaḍān*
ramjet محرك نفاث تضاغطي
*muḥarrik naffāth taḍāghutī*
RAM-M aircraft طائرة « آر ايه ام ـ ام »
*ṭāʾirat ār ayy im - im*
ramp مجرى منحدر
*majra munḥadir*
ram-rocket صاروخ تضاغطي
*ṣārūkh taḍāghuṭī*
Rameses radar رادار « رمسيس »
*rādār ramsīs*
RAN 3L 3D radar رادار « آر ايه ان ٣ ال ٣ دي »
*rādār ār ayy in thalātha il thalātha dī*
RAN 10S radar رادار « آر ايه ان ١٠ اس »
*rādār ār ayy in ʿashara is*
range مدى
*mada*
range and bearing launch إطلاق بمدى ومسار
*iṭlāq bi-mada wa masār*
range and intercept sonar سونار تحديد مدى واعتراض
*sūnār taḥdīd mada wa iʿtirāḍ*
range estimation تقدير المدى
*taqdīr al-mada*
range finder معين المدى
*muʿayyin al-mada*
rangefinding قياس المدى
*qiyās al-mada*
range-only radar رادار مدى فقط
*rādār mada faqat*
range-rate معدل سرعة المدى
*muʿaddal surʿat al-mada*

R

ranger battalion كتيبة مغاوير
*katībat maghāwīr*
ranger hat قبعة المغاور
*qubbaʿa al-mughāwir*
ranging and sighting system نظام تحديد المدى والتسديد
*niẓām taḥdīd al-mada wat-tasdīd*
ranging weapon سلاح تحديد المدى
*silāḥ taḥdīd al-mada*
rank رتبه
*rutba*
rapid fire رمي سريع
*ramī sariʿ*
rapid firing إطلاق سريع للنيران
*iṭlāq sarīʿ lin-nīrān*
rapid reload اعادة تلقيم سريع
*iʿādat talqīm sarīʿ*
rapid shift تغير سريع
*taghayyur sarīʿ*
Rapids radar رادار « رابيدز »
*rādār rapidz*
Rapier laserfire اطلاق ليزر لنظام رابيار
*iṭlāq layzar li-niẓām raypyar*
Rapier SAM صاروخ سطح - جو « رابيار »
*ṣārūkh saṭḥ-jaww raypyar*
Rapier system نظام « رابيار »
*niẓām raypyar*
Rapucha landing ship سفينة إنزال « رابوتشا »
*safīnat inzāl rapūtsha*
RAT 31 radar رادار « آر ايه تي ٣١ »
*rādār ār ayy tī wāḥid wa thalāthīn*
RAT 31s radar رادار « آر ايه تي ٣١ اس »
*rādār ār ayy tī wāḥid wa thalāthīn is*
Ratcharit patrol boat سفينة خفر سواحل « راتشاريت »
*safīnat khafar as-sawāḥil ratsharit*
ratchet سقاطة
*saqqāṭa*
rate معدل
*muʿaddal*
rate of fire سرعة الرمي
*surʿat ar-ramī*
ration allowance بدل طعام
*badal ṭaʿām*
raw material مادة خام
*mādda khām*
Raytheon 1900 radar رادار « رايثيون ١٩٠٠ »
*rādār raythyūn alf wa tisʿa miʾa*

RB04 ASM صاروخ جو - سطح « أر بي ٠٤ »
*ṣārūkh jaww-saṭḥ ār bī ṣifr arbaʿa*
RB05 ASM صاروخ جو - سطح « أر بي ٠٥ »
*ṣārūkh jaww-saṭḥ ār bī ṣifr khamsa*
RB08 A missile صاروخ « أر بي ٠٨ ايه »
*ṣārūkh ār bī ṣifr thamānya ayy*
RB 68 SAM صاروخ سطح - جو « أر بي ٦٨ »
*ṣārūkh saṭḥ-jaww ār bī thamānya wa sittīn*
RB-199 turbofan مروحة تربينية « أر بي - ١٩٩ »
*mirwaḥa turbīnīya ār bī miʾa wa tisʿa wa tisʿīn*
RBS 15 missile صاروخ « أر بي اس ١٥ »
*ṣārūkh ār bī is khamsata ʿashar*
RBS-56 missile صاروخ « أر بي اس - ٥٦ »
*ṣārūkh ār bī is sitta wa khamsīn*
RBS 70 SAM صاروخ سطح - جو « أر بي اس ٧٠ »
*ṣārūkh saṭḥ-jaww ār bī is sabʿīn*
RBU 2500 rocket صاروخ « أر بي يو ٢٥٠٠ »
*ṣārūkh ār bī yū alfayn wa khams miʾa*
RBU 6000 ASW rocket launcher قاذفة صواريخ « أر بي يو ٦٠٠٠ ايه اس دبليو »
*qādhifat ṣawārīkh ār bī yū sittat ālāf ayy is dablyu*
RC-12 D aircraft طائرة « أر سي - ١٢ دي »
*ṭāʾirat ār sī ithnata ʿashar dī*
RC-135V aircraft طائرة « أر سي - ١٣٥ في »
*ṭāʾirat ār sī miʾa wa khamsa wa thalāthīn vī*
RDI radar رادار « أردي أي »
*rādār ār dī āyy*
reach وصل الى . بلغ
*waṣala ila · balagha*
reactor core قلب المفاعل
*qalb al-mufāʿil*
reactor shielding حجاب المفاعل
*ḥijāb al-mufāʿil*
ready! إستعد !
*istaʿid*
ready-to-launch جاهز للاطلاق
*jāhiz lil-iṭlāq*
ready-use rack حامل جاهز
*ḥāmil jāhiz*
real-time زمن حقيقي
*zaman ḥaqīqī*

R

rear مؤخرة
*muʾakhkhara*
rear-facing reflector عاكس بمواجهة المؤخرة
*ʿākis bi-muwājahat al-muʾakhkhara*
rear guard حرس المؤخرة
*ḥaras al-muʾakhkhara*
rear guard action قتال المؤخرة
*qitāl al-muʾakhkhara*
re-arming إعادة التسليح
*iʿādat at-taslīḥ*
rear sight base قاعدة المهداف الخلفي
*qāʿidat al-mihdāf al-khalfī*
rebellion ثورة . عصيان
*thawra · ʿiṣyān*
recapture إسترداد . إستعادة
*istirdād · istiʿāda*
recce information معلومات الاستطلاع
*maʿlūmāt al-istiṭlāʿ*
recce party فريق الاستطلاع
*farīq al-istiṭlāʿ*
receiver مستقبل
*mustaqbil*
receiver aerial هوائي المستقبل
*hawāʾī al-mustaqbil*
receiver simulator system نظام حاكي المستقبل
*niẓām ḥākī al-mustaqbil*
reception إستقبال
*istiqbāl*
recharge شحن ثانياً
*shaḥana thānyan*
reciprocal microwave system نظام موجات دقيقة تبادلي
*niẓām mawjāt daqīqa tabādulī*
recoil absorber مخفف إرتدادي
*mukhaffif irtidādī*
recoilless gun مدفع عديم الارتداد
*midfaʿ ʿadīm al-irtidād*
recoilless launcher قاذفة عديمة الارتداد
*qādhifa ʿadīmat al-irtidād*
recoilless rifle بندقية عديمة الارتداد
*bunduqīya ʿadīmat al-irtidād*
recoil pad لينة إرتداد
*laynat irtidād*
recoil spade مجراف إرتدادي
*mijrāf irtidādī*
reconnaissance إستطلاع
*istiṭlāʿ*
reconnaissance mission مهمة إستطلاع
*muhimmat istiṭlāʿ*
reconnaissance satellite قمر إستطلاع
*qamr istiṭlāʿ*
reconnaissance squadron سرية إستطلاع . سرب إستطلاع
*sarīyat istiṭlāʿ · sirb istiṭlāʿ*
reconnaissance training تدريب على الاستطلاع
*tadrīb ʿalal-istiṭlāʿ*
reconnaissance unit وحدة إستطلاع
*wiḥdat istiṭlāʿ*
reconnaissance vehicle مركبة إستطلاع
*markabat istiṭlāʿ*
reconnoitering إستطلاع . استكشاف
*istiṭlāʿ · istikshāf*
record as target! سجل كهدف !
*sajjil ka-hadaf*
record card بطاقة السجل
*biṭṭāqat as-sijill*
record communications operator عامل تسجيل الاتصالات
*ʿāmil tasjīl al-ittiṣālāt*
recording thermometer ثرمومتر مسجل
*thirmūmitar musajjil*
recovery task مهمة استرداد . مهمة اصلاح
*muhimmat istirdād · muhimmat iṣlāḥ*
recovery vehicle عربة اصلاح العطل الطارىء
*ʿarabat iṣlāḥ al-uṭl aṭ-ṭāriʾ*
recruit جندي جديد
*jundī jadīd*
recruit (to) جنَّد
*jannada*
rectangular block حاجز مستطيل
*ḥājiz mustaṭīl*
recuperator مُرجع . مسترجع
*murajjiʿ · mustarjiʿ*
Red Baron radar رادار « ريد بارون »
*rādār rid bārun*
redeploy إعادة انتشار
*iʿādat intishār*
Redeye SAM صاروخ سطح ـ جو « رد آي »
*ṣārūkh saṭḥ-jaww ridāy*
Red Flag SAM صاروخ سطح ـ جو « رد فلاج »
*ṣārūkh saṭḥ-jaww rid flāg*
red smoke دخان أحمر
*dukhān aḥmar*
Red Top AAM صاروخ جو ـ جو « رد توب »
*ṣārūkh jaww-jaww rid tūp*
reduce speed! السرعة ـ خفض !
*as-surʿa – khaffiḍ*
reduction gear ترس تخفيض السرعة
*turs takhfīḍ as-surʿa*

Re'em armoured vehicle عربة مدرعة « رييم »
*ʿaraba mudarraʿa rīm*
re-enlistment إعادة تجنيد
*iʿādat tajnīd*
re-entry package مجموعة الرجعة
*majmūʿat ar-rajʿa*
re-entry vehicle مركبة الرجعة
*markabat ar-rajʿa*
re-equipped مجهز ثانية
*mujahhaz thānyatan*
reference area منطقة إسناد
*minṭaqat isnād*
refined steel فولاذ منقى
*fūlādh munaqqa*
refit إصلاح . تجديد
*iṣlāḥ · tajdīd*
refit programme برنامج التجديد
*barnāmaj at-tajdīd*
reflect (to) عكس . إنعكس
*ʿakasa · inʿakasa*
reflected radiation إشعاع منعكس
*ishʿāʿ munʿakas*
reflector عاكس
*ʿākis*
reflector gun sight مسددة مدفع عاكسة
*musaddidat midfaʿ ʿākisa*
refresher course دورة تجديد المعلومات
*dawrat tajdīd al-maʿlūmāt*
refuelling تزود بالوقود
*tazwīd bil-wuqūd*
refuelling craft سفينة تزويد بالوقود
*safīnat tazwīd bil-wuqūd*
refuelling truck شاحنة تزويد بالوقود
*shāḥinat tazwīd bil-wuqūd*
regiment فرقة . فوج
*firqa · fawj*
regulate نظم . ضبط
*naẓẓama · ḍabbaṭa*
regulations أنظمة
*anẓima*
Regulus I missile صاروخ « ريجيولوس ١ »
*ṣārūkh rigyulus wāḥid*
reheat إعادة التسخين
*iʿādat at-taskhīn*
reinforce (to) عزّز
*ʿazzaza*
reinforcement تعزيز .
*taʿziz*
reinforcements قوات تدعيم
*qūwāt tadʿīm*

relative navigation ملاحة نسبية
*milāḥa nisbīya*
reload (to) إعادة تلقيم
*iʿādat talqīm*
remote control تحكم عن بعد
*taḥakkum ʿan buʿd*
remotely-aimed turret برج مصوب عن بعد
*burj muṣawwab ʿan buʿd*
repair إصلاح . ترميم
*iṣlāḥ · tarmīm*
repair facility تسهيلات الاصلاح
*tashīlāt al-iṣlāḥ*
repair shop ورشة اصلاح
*warshat iṣlāḥ*
replacements بدائل
*badāʾil*
reporter radar رادار مُخبر
*rādār mukhabbir*
report for duty حضور لأداء الواجب
*ḥuḍūr li-adāʾ al-wājib*
reports grenade قنبلة يدوية للبلاغ
*qunbula yadawīya lil-balāgh*
repower-modernization kit لوازم تجديد الطاقة
*lawāzim tajdīd aṭ-ṭāqa*
reprogrammable قابل للبرمجة
*qābil lil-barmaja*
Republican Guard حرس جمهوري
*ḥaras jumhūrī*
request fire support طلب تعزيز النيران
*ṭalab taʿzīz an-nīrān*
rescue hoist مرفاع إنقاذ
*mirfaʿ inqādh*
research and development centre مركز البحوث والتنمية
*markaz al-buḥūth wat-tanmiya*
reserve إحتياطي
*iḥtiyāṭī*
reserve ammunition ذخيرة احتياطية
*dhakhīra iḥtiyāṭīya*
reserve diesel ديزل احتياطي
*dīzl iḥtiyāṭī*
reserve missile صاروخ احتياطي
*ṣārūkh iḥtiyāṭī*
reserves قوات احتياطية
*qūwāt iḥtiyaṭīya*
reserve troop concentration حشد القوات الاحتياطية
*ḥashd al-qūwāt al-iḥtiyāṭīya*
reservists قوات الاحتياط
*qūwāt al-iḥtiyāṭ*

R

Reshaf craft سفينة « ريشاف »
*safīnat rīshāf*
resident مقيم
*muqīm*
Resolution submarine غواصة « ريزولوشن »
*ghawwāṣat rizulūshn*
respirator كمامة . جهاز تنفس اصطناعي
*kimāma · jihāz tanaffus iṣṭināʿī*
respiratory تنفسي
*tanaffusī*
response إستجابة
*istijāba*
restricted area منطقة محظورة . منطقة ممنوعة
*minṭaqa maḥẓūra · minṭaqa mamnūʿa*
resume transmitting! إستأنف الارسال !
*istaʾnif al-irsāl*
retarded bomb قنبلة مؤخرة الانفجار
*qunbula muʾakhkharat al-infijār*
retargeting system نظام تعديل الهدف
*niẓām taʿdīl al-hadaf*
retire إعتزال . تقاعد تراجع
*iʿtizāl · taqāʿud · tarājuʿ*
retractable قابل للطي
*qābil liṭ-ṭayy*
retractable aerial هوائي قابل للطي
*hawāʾī qābil liṭ-ṭayy*
retreat تراجع . تقهقر
*tarājaʿa · taqahqara*
retro-rocket صاروخ كابح
*ṣārūkh kābiḥ*
returning radiation إشعاع مرتد
*ishʿāʿ murtadd*
return rollers دحاريج عودة
*daḥārīj ʿawda*
reusable يستعمل ثانية
*yustaʿmal thānyatan*
reveille إستيقاظ يقظة
*istiqāẓ · yaqẓa*
reverse! الى الوراء ـ در !
*ilal-warāʾdurr*
reverse-pitch خطوة عكسية
*khuṭwa ʿaksīya*
reverse-thrust دفع عكسي
*dafʿ ʿaksī*
review إستعراض . مراجعة . تفتيش
*istiʿrāḍ · murājaʿa · taftīsh*
Revolutionary Guard Corps هيئة الحرس الثوري
*hayʾat al-ḥaras ath-thawrī*

RF-4 aircraft طائرة « أر اف ـ ٤ »
*ṭāʾira ār if arbaʿa*
RF-5 fighter طائرة مقاتلة « أر اف ـ ٥ »
*ṭāʾira muqātila ār if khamsa*
RF-5E aircraft طائرة « أر اف ـ ٥ ئي »
*ṭāʾirat ār if khamsa ī*
R-13F turbojet نفاثة تربينية « آر ـ ١٣ اف »
*naffātha turbīnīya ār thalāthata ʿashar if*
RF-35 aircraft طائرة « أر اف ـ ٣٥ »
*ṭāʾirat ār if khamsa wa thalāthīn*
RF-101 aircraft طائره « أر اف ـ ١٠١ »
*ṭāʾirat ār if miʾa wa wāḥid*
RF-104G Starfighter طائرة مقاتلة « أر اف ـ ١٠٤ جي » ستار فايتر
*ṭāʾira muqātila ār if miʾa wa arbaʿa jī stārfāytar*
RGD-5 grenade قنبلة يدوية « أرجي دي ـ ٥ »
*qunbula yadawīya ār jī dī khamsa*
RGM-84A missile صاروخ « أرجي ام ـ ٨٤ ايه »
*ṣārūkh ār jī im arbaʿa wa thamānīn ayy*
RH-3 helicopter طائرة عمودية « أر اتش ـ ٣ »
*ṭāʾira ʿamūdīya ār itsh thalātha*
RH-53 helicopter طائرة عمودية « أر اتش ـ ٥٣ »
*ṭāʾira ʿamūdīya ār itsh thalātha wa khamsīn*
Rh 202 cannon مدفع هاون « أر اتش ٢٠٢ »
*midfaʿ hāwun ār itsh miʾatayn wa ithnayn*
ribbed bolt برغي مضلع
*burghī muḍallaʿ*
ribbon type braking parachute مظلة كبح من النوع الشريطي
*miẓallat kabḥ min an-nawʿ ash-sharīṭī*
rifle بندقية
*bunduqīya*
rifle division فرقة البنادق
*firqat al-banādiq*
rifle fire نيران البندقية
*nīrān al-bunduqīya*
rifle grenade قنبلة يدوية تطلق بالبندقية
*qunbula yadawīya tuṭlaq bil-bunduqīya*
rifle grenade launcher قاذفة قنابل البندقية
*qādhifat qanābil al-bunduqīya*
rifle sling حمالة البندقية
*ḥammālat al-bunduqīya*

R

Riga patrol ship سفينة حراسة سواحل « ريجا »
*safīnat ḥirāsat sawāḥil rāyga*
right dress! يميناً تراصف !
*yamīnan tarāṣaf*
right turn! إلى اليمين در !
*ilal-yamīn durr*
rigid main rotor دوار رئيسي جاسيء
*dawwār raʾīsī jāsiʾ*
Rigid Raider boat زورق « ريجيد رايدر »
*zawraq rijid raydar*
RIL radar رادار « ار اي ال »
*rādār ār āyy il*
ring laser gyro جيروسكوب ليزر حلقي
*jīrūskūb layzar ḥalaqī*
ripple missile in pairs زوج من الصاروخ التموجي
*zawj min aṣ-ṣārūkh at-tamawwujī*
River frigate فرقاطة « ريڤر »
*firqāṭat rivar*
river crossing عبور الأنهار
*ʿubūr al-anhār*
river gunboat زورق نهري مسلح
*zawraq nahrī musallaḥ*
Riverine warfare vessel سفينة حربية « ريڤرين »
*safīna ḥarbīya rivarāyn*
river patrol craft زورق حراسة نهرية
*zawraq ḥirāsa nahrīya*
RKG-3 grenade قنبلة يدوية « آركيه جي - ٣ »
*qunbula yadawī ār kayy jī - thalātha*
RM6C turbojet نفاثة تربينية « آر ام ٦ سي »
*naffātha turbīnīya ār im sitta sī*
RM7 radar رادار « آر ام ٧ »
*rādār ār im sabʿa*
RM8B turbofan مروحة تربينية « آر ام ٨ بي »
*mirwaḥa turbīnīya ār im thamānya bī*
road block متراس الطريق
*mitrās aṭ-ṭarīq*
road clear طريق مفتوح
*ṭarīq maftūḥ*
road junction تقاطع طرق
*taqāṭuʿ ṭuruq*
road transport نقل بري
*naql barrī*
road wheel دولاب
*dūlāb*
Rock Cake radar رادار « روك كيك »
*rādār ruk kayk*

rocket صاروخ
*ṣārūkh*
rocket-assisted projectile مقذوف معان بالصاروخ
*maqdhūf muʿān biṣ-ṣārūkh*
rocket-assisted shell قذيفة معانة بالصاروخ
*qadhīfa muʿāna biṣ-ṣārūkh*
rocket communications system نظام اتصال صاروخي
*niẓām ittiṣāl ṣārūkhī*
rocket cruiser طرادة صواريخ
*ṭarrādat ṣawārīkh*
rocket-launcher قاذفة صواريخ
*qādhifat ṣawārīkh*
rocket motor محرك صاروخي
*muḥarrik ṣārūkhī*
rocket propulsion دفع صاروخي
*dafʿ ṣārūkhī*
rocket ship سفينة صواريخ
*safīnat ṣawārīkh*
rocket troops جنود صواريخ
*junūd ṣawārīkh*
Rockwell (Co) شركة « روكويل »
*sharikat rukwil*
Rockwell International (Co) شركة « روكويل انترناشيونال »
*sharikat rukwil intarnāshnal*
Roland SAM صاروخ « سطح - جو رولاند »
*ṣārūkh saṭḥ-jaww rūlānd*
Roland vehicle مركبة « رولاند »
*markabat rūlānd*
roll call نداء الحضور
*nadāʾ al-ḥuḍūr*
roll-off operation عملية التفريغ
*ʿamalīyat at-tafrīgh*
roll-on operation عملية التحميل
*ʿamalīyat at-taḥmīl*
roll rocket صاروخ العطوف
*ṣārūkh al-ʿuṭūf*
Rolls-Royce (Co) شركة « رولز - رويس »
*sharikat rūlz ruwīs*
Romania رومانيا
*rūmānya*
Romanian روماني
*rūmānī*
Romb SAM صاروخ سطح - جو « رومب »
*ṣārūkh saṭḥ-jaww rūmb*
Romeo submarine غواصة « روميو »
*ghawwāṣat rūmyū*
roof سقف
*saqf*

R

roof-mounted sight مهداف مركب على السقف
*mihdāf murakkab ʿalas-saqf*
Ropucha landing ship سفينة انزال « روپيتشا »
*safīnat inzāl rupītsha*
Roraima ship سفينة « رورايما »
*safīnat rūrāyma*
rosette scan مسح على شكل وردي
*masḥ ʿala shakl wardī*
rotary-barrel ماسورة دوارة
*māsūra dawwāra*
rotary bolt برغي دوار
*burghī dawwār*
rotary cannon هاون دوار
*hāwun dawwār*
rotary disc قرص دوار
*qurṣ dawwār*
rotary lug bolt برغي ذو اذن لسحب دوار
*burghī dhu udhun li-saḥb dawwār*
rotary type من نوع دوار
*min nawʿ dawwār*
rotary winged aircraft طائرة ذات الأجنحة الدوارة
*ṭāʾira dhāt al-ajniḥa ad-dawwāra*
rotatable nozzle فوهة قابلة للدوران
*fūha qābila lid-dawarān*
rotating دوار . متناوب
*dawwar · mutanāwib*
rotating bolt برغي دوار
*burghī dawwār*
rotating-bolt breech مغلاق برغي دوار
*mighlāq burghī dawwār*
rotating scanner جهاز مسح دوار
*jihāz masḥ dawwār*
Rothesay frigate فرقاطة «روثسي»
*firqāṭat rūthsi*
rotodome aerial هوائي دوار مقبب
*hawāʾī dawwār muqabbab*
rotodome retraction mechanism آلية انكماش هوائي دوار مقبب
*ālīyat inkimāsh hawāʾī dawwār muqabbab*
rotor blades أرياش الدوامة
*aryāsh ad-duwwāma*
rotor diameter قطر الدوامة
*quṭr ad-dawwāra*
rotor disc area مساحة قرص الدوامة
*masāḥat qurṣ ad-dawwāra*
rough sea بحر هائج
*baḥr hāʾij*

rough weather جو عاصف
*jaww ʿāṣif*
round house المبنى الدائري
*al-mabna ad-dāʾirī*
rounds طلقات
*ṭalaqāt*
rounds of ammunition طلقات ذخيرة
*ṭalaqāt dhakhīira*
rounds per minute طلقات في الدقيقة
*ṭalaqāt fid-daqīqa*
route survey مسح الطريق
*masḥ aṭ-ṭarīq*
routine maintenance صيانة معتادة
*ṣiyāna muʿtāda*
RPG-7 grenade launcher قاذفة قنابل يدوية « أر پي جي ـ ٧ »
*qādhifat qanābil yadawīya ār pī jī sabʿa*
RPK gun مدفع « أر پي كيه »
*midfaʿ ār pī kayy*
RPU-14 rocket launcher قاذفة صواريخ « أر پي يو ـ ١٤ »
*qādhifat ṣawārīkh ār pī yū arbaʿata ʿashar*
RPV drone مركبة موجهة « أر پي ڤي »
*markaba muwajjaha ār pī vī*
RS-14 SSM صاروخ سطح ـ سطح « أر اس ـ ١٤ »
*ṣārūkh saṭḥ-saṭḥ ār is arbaʿata ʿashar*
RS-16 SSM صاروخ سطح ـ سطح « أر اس ـ ١٦ »
*ṣārūkh saṭḥ-saṭḥ ār is sittata ʿashar*
RS-18 SSM صاروخ سطح ـ سطح « أر اس ـ ١٨ »
*ṣārūkh saṭḥ-saṭḥ ār is thamānyata ʿashar*
RS-20 SSM صاروخ سطح ـ سطح « أر اس ـ ٢٠ »
*ṣārūkh saṭḥ-saṭḥ ār is ʿishrīn*
RSI tank laser ليزر الدبابة « أر اس أي »
*layzar ad-dabbāba ār is āyy*
RTN-10X radar رادار « أرتي إن ـ ١٠ اكس »
*rādār ār tī in ʿashara iks*
RTN 20X radar رادار « ارتي ان ٢٠ اكس »
*rādār ār tī in ʿishrīn iks*
RTN 30X radar رادار « أرتي ان ٣٠ اكس »
*rādār ār tī in thalāthīn iks*
RU-21 طائرة « أريو ـ ٢١ »
*ṭāʾira ār yū wāḥid wa ʿishrīn*
RU-21J aircraft طائرة « أريو ـ ٢١ جيه »
*ṭāʾira ār yū wāḥid wa ʿishrīn jayy*
rubber bullet طلقة مطاط
*ṭalaqat maṭṭāṭ*

R

rubber tyre إطار مطاط
*iṭār maṭṭāṭ*
Rubis submarine غواصة « روبيس »
*ghawwāṣat rūbis*
rudder دفة . سكان التوجيه
*daffa · sukkān at-tawjīh*
Ruger Mini-14 rifle بندقية « روجر ميني ١٤ »
*bunduqīya rūgar mini arbaʿata ʿashar*

Rum Tub ESM تدبير دعم الكتروني « رام تاب »
*tadābīr daʿm iliktrūnī ram tab*
Russia روسيا
*rūsya*
Russian روسي
*rūsī*
Rwanda رواندة
*ruwānda*

R

# S

2S1 howitzer مدفع هاوتزر « ٢ اس ١ »
*midfaʿ hāwitsar ithnayn is wāḥid*

2S3 gun مدفع « ٢ اس ٣ »
*midfaʿ ithnayn is thalātha*

25 SO-122 gun مدفع « ٢٥ اس اوه - ١٢٢ »
*midfaʿ khamsa wa ʿishrīn is aw - miʾa wa ithnayn wa ʿishrīn*

82 series radar رادار « سلسلة ٨٢ »
*rādār silsilat ithnayn wa thamānīn*

S-2E patrol aircraft طائرة دورية « اس - ٢ ئي »
*ṭāʾira dawrīya is-ithnayn ī*

S-3A aircraft طائرة « اس - ٣ ايه »
*ṭāʾira is-thalātha ayy*

S5G reactor مفاعل « اس ٥ جي »
*mufāʿil is khamsa jī*

S5W reactor مفاعل « اس ٥ دبليو »
*mufāʿil is khamsa dablyū*

S20 turret برج « اس ٢٠ »
*burj is ʿishrīn*

S-23 field gun مدفع ميدان « اس - ٢٣ »
*midfaʿ maydān is-thalātha wa ʿishrīn*

S35E aircraft طائرة « اس ٣٥ ئي »
*ṭāʾirat is khamsa wa thalāthīn ī*

S-60 AA-gun مدفع مضاد للطائرات « اس - ٦٠ »
*midfaʿ muḍādd liṭ-ṭāʾirat is-sittīn*

S-61/H-3 helicopter طائرة عمودية « اس - ٦١/اتش - ٣ »
*ṭāʾira ʿamūdīya is-wāḥid wa sittīn/itsh-thalātha*

S-65/H-53 helicopter طائرة عمودية « اس - ٦٥/اتش - ٥٣ »
*ṭāʾira ʿamūdīya is-khamsa wa sittīn-itsh-thalātha wa khamsīn*

S365 turret برج « اس ٣٦٥ »
*burj is thalātha miʾa wa khamsa wa sittīn*

S530F turret برج « اس ٥٣٠ اف »
*burj is khams miʾa wa thalāthīn if*

SA-1 SAM صاروخ سطح - جو « اس ايه - ١ »
*ṣārūkh saṭḥ-jaww is ayy - wāḥid*

SA-2 SAM صاروخ سطح - جو « اس ايه - ٢ »
*ṣārūkh saṭḥ-jaww is ayy - ithnayn*

SA-3 SAM صاروخ سطح - جو « اس ايه - ٣ »
*ṣārūkh saṭḥ-jaww is ayy - thalātha*

SA-4 SAM صاروخ سطح - جو « اس ايه - ٤ »
*ṣārūkh saṭḥ-jaww is ayy - arbaʿa*

SA-5 SAM صاروخ سطح - جو « اس ايه - ٥ »
*ṣārūkh saṭḥ-jaww is ayy - khamsa*

SA-6 SAM صاروخ سطح - جو « اس ايه - ٦ »
*ṣārūkh saṭḥ-jaww is ayy - sitta*

SA-7 SAM صاروخ سطح - جو « اس ايه - ٧ »
*ṣārūkh saṭḥ-jaww is ayy - sabʿa*

SA-8 SAM صاروخ سطح - جو « اس ايه - ٨ »
*ṣārūkh saṭḥ-jaww is ayy - thamānya*

SA-8B SAM صاروخ سطح - جو « اس ايه - ٨ بي »
*ṣārūkh saṭḥ-jaww is ayy - thamānya bī*

SA-9 SAM صاروخ سطح - جو « اس ايه - ٩ »
*ṣārūkh saṭḥ-jaww is ayy - tisʿa*

SA-10 SAM صاروخ سطح - جو « اس ايه - ١٠ »
*ṣārūkh saṭḥ-jaww is ayy - ʿashara*

S

SA-11 SAM صاروخ سطح - جو « اس ايه - ١١ »
*ṣārūkh saṭḥ-jaww is ayy - aḥada ʿashar*
SA-12 SAM صاروخ سطح - جو « اس ايه - ١٢ »
*ṣārūkh saṭḥ-jaww is ayy - ithnata ʿashar*
SA-13 SAM صاروخ سطح - جو « اس ايه - ١٣ »
*ṣārūkh saṭḥ-jaww is ayy - thalāthata ʿashar*
SA-90 turret برج « اس ايه - ٩٠ »
*burj is ayy-tisʿīn*
SA 316C helicopter طائرة عمودية « اس ايه ٣١٦ سي »
*ṭāʾira ʿamūdīya is ayy thalāth miʾa wa sittata ʿashar sī*
SA 319B helicopter طائرة عمودية « اس ايه ٣١٩ بي »
*ṭāʾira ʿamūdīya is ayy thalāth miʾa wa tisʿata ʿashar bī*
SA 321G helicopter طائرة عمودية « اس ايه ٣٢١ جي »
*ṭāʾira ʿamūdīya is ayy thalāth miʾa wa wāḥid wa ʿishrīn jī*
SA 341F helicopter طائرة عمودية « اس ايه ٣٤١ اف »
*ṭāʾira ʿamūdīya is ayy thalāth miʾa wa wāḥid wa ʿarbaʿīn if*
SA 342M helicopter طائرة عمودية « اس ايه ٣٤٢ ام »
*ṭāʾira ʿamūdīya is ayy thalāth miʾa wa ithnayn wa arbaʿīn im*
SA 360C helicopter طائرة عمودية « اس ايه ٣٦٠ سي »
*ṭāʾira ʿamūdīya is ayy thalāth miʾa wa sittīn sī*
SA 365F helicopter طائرة عمودية « اس ايه ٣٦٥ اف »
*ṭāʾira ʿamūdīya is ayy thalāth miʾa wa khamsa wa sittīn if*
SA 365N helicopter طائرة عمودية « اس ايه ٣٦٥ إن »
*ṭāʾira ʿamūdīya is ayy thalāth miʾa wa khamsa wa sittīn in*
SA 366G helicopter طائرة عمودية « اس ايه ٣٦٦ جي »
*ṭāʾira ʿamūdīya is ayy thalāth miʾa wa sitta wa sittīn jī*
Saab (Co) شركة ساب
*sharikat sāb*
Saab 35 fighter طائرة مقاتلة « ساب ٣٥ »
*ṭāʾira muqātila sāb khamsa wa thalāthīn*
Saab aircraft طائرة « ساب »
*ṭāʾirat sāb*
Saar missile boat زورق صواريخ « زار »
*zawraq ṣawārīkh zār*
SABCA fire control نظام السيطرة على الرمي « سابكا »
*niẓām as-sayṭara ʿalar-ramī sābkā*
Saber missile صاروخ « سيبر »
*ṣārūkh saybr*
sabot نعل القذيفة
*naʿl al-qadhīfa*
sabotage تخريب سري
*takhrīb sirrī*
saboteur مخرب
*mukharrib*
Sabreliner air transport طائرة نقل « سيبر لاينر »
*ṭāʾirat naql saybr lāynar*
safe custody حجز في محل مأمون
*ḥajz fī maḥall maʾmūn*
safety cap غطاء أمان
*ghiṭāʾ amān*
safety catch ممساك أمان
*mimsāk amān*
safety device جهاز الأمان
*jihāz al-amān*
safety factor عامل الأمان
*ʿāmil al-amān*
safety glass زجاج أمان
*zujāj amān*
safety line حد الأمان
*ḥadd al-amān*
safety precautions إحتياطات الأمان
*ihtiyāṭāt al-amān*
safety switch مفتاح الأمان
*miftāḥ al-amān*
safety system نظام الأمان
*niẓām al-amān*
Safir trainer طائرة تدريب « سافير »
*ṭāʾirat tadrīb sāfīr*
Sagger ATM صاروخ مضاد للدبابات « ساجر »
*ṣārūkh muḍādd lid-dabbābāt sāgar*
Sahara brigade لواء الصحراء
*liwāʾ as-ṣaḥrāʾ*
sailer مركب شراعي
*markab shirāʿī*
sailor بحار
*baḥḥār*
Saladin armoured car عربة مدرعة « سالادين »
*ʿaraba mudarraʿa saladin*
SALT (Strategic Arms Limitation Talks) مفاوضات الحد من الأسلحة الاستراتيجية (سالت)
*mufāwaḍāt al-ḥadd min al-asliḥa al-istrātījīya (ṣalt)*
SALT Agreement إتفاقية الحد من الأسلحة الاستراتيجية
*ittifāqīyat al-ḥadd min al-asliḥa al-istrātījīya*

S

salute — تحية . سلام
*taḥīya · salām*

saluting gun — مدفع تحية
*midfaᶜ taḥīya*

salvage — إنقاذ
*inqādh*

salvo attack — رشقة مدفعية
*hujūm bi-rashq midfaᶜīya*

salvo attack — هجوم برشق مدفعية
*hujūm bi-rashq al-midfaᶜī*

SAM — صاروخ سطح ـ جو « سام »
*ṣārūkh saṭḥ-jaww sām*

Samaritan — ساماريتان
*samaritan*

SAM-armed — مسلح بصواريخ سطح ـ جو
*musallaḥ bi-ṣawārīkh saṭḥ-jaww*

Sam Browne — حزام وشريط كتف للضباط
*ḥizām wa sharīṭ katif liḍ-ḍubbāṭ*

SAM launcher — قاذفة صواريخ سطح ـ جو
*qādhifat ṣawārīkh saṭḥ-jaww*

Samlet SAM — صاروخ سطح ـ جو « ساملیت »
*ṣārūkh saṭḥ-jaww samlit*

SAMM S530 turret — برج « اس ايه ام ام اس ٥٣٠ »
*burj is ayy im im is khamsa miʾa wa thalāthīn*

Samson vehicle — مركبة « سامسون »
*markabat sāmsūn*

SA-N-1 SAM — صاروخ سطح ـ جو « اس ايه ـ ان ـ ١ »
*ṣārūkh saṭḥ-jaww is ayy - in - wāḥid*

SA-N-2 SAM — صاروخ سطح ـ جو « اس ايه ـ ان ـ ٢ »
*ṣārūkh saṭḥ-jaww is ayy - in - ithnayn*

SA-N-3 SAM — صاروخ سطح ـ جو « اس ايه ـ ان ـ ٣ »
*ṣārūkh saṭḥ-jaww is ayy - in - thalātha*

SA-N-4 SAM — صاروخ سطح ـ جو « اس ايه ـ ان ـ ٤ »
*ṣārūkh saṭḥ-jaww is ayy - in - arbaᶜa*

SA-N-5 SAM — صاروخ سطح ـ جو « اس ايه ـ ان ـ ٥ »
*ṣārūkh saṭḥ-jaww is ayy - in - khamsa*

SA-N-6 SAM — صاروخ سطح ـ جو « اس ايه ـ ان ـ ٦ »
*ṣārūkh saṭḥ-jaww is ayy - in - sitta*

SA-N-7 SAM — صاروخ سطح ـ جو « اس ايه ـ ان ـ ٧ »
*ṣārūkh saṭḥ-jaww is ayy - in - sabᶜa*

Sandal SSM — صاروخ سطح ـ سطح « صندل »
*ṣārūkh saṭḥ-saṭḥ ṣandl*

sand bag — كيس الرمل
*kīs ar-raml*

Sandbox SSM — صاروخ سطح ـ سطح « ساندبوكس »
*ṣārūkh saṭḥ-saṭḥ sāndbuks*

sand dune — كثيب رملي
*kathīb ramlī*

sanitary conditions — الظروف الصحية
*aẓ-ẓurūf aṣ-ṣiḥḥīya*

sapper — مهندس عسكري
*muhandis ᶜaskarī*

Sapphire fire-control system — نظام السيطرة على الرمي « سافاير »
*niẓām as-saytara ᶜalar-ramī sāfāyr*

Saracen armoured car — عربة مدرعة « ساراسن »
*ᶜaraba mudarraᶜa sarasan*

Saracen tank — دبابة «ساراسن »
*dabbābat sarasan*

SAR helicopter — طائرة عمودية « اس ايه آر »
*ṭāʾira ᶜamūdīya is ayy ār*

SARH homing — توجيه راداري « اس ايه آر اتش »
*tawjīh rādārī is ayy ār itsh*

SAR radar — رادار « اس ايه آر »
*rādār is ayy ār*

SAT Cyclope 160 AT IR linescan — جهاز مسح بالأشعة دون الحمراء « اس اى تي سايكلوپ ١٦٠ ايه تي »
*jihāz masḥ bil-ashiᶜᶜa dūn al-ḥamrāʾ is ayy tī sāyklūp miʾa wa sittīn ayy tī*

satellite — قمر صناعي
*qamr ṣināᶜī*

satellite communications — إتصالات بالقمر الصناعي
*ittiṣālāt bil-qamr aṣ-ṣināᶜī*

satellite communication system — نظام اتصالات بالقمر الصناعي
*niẓām ittiṣālāt bil-qamr aṣ-ṣināᶜī*

satellite reconnaissance — إستطلاع بالقمر الصناعي
*istiṭlāᶜ bil-qamr aṣ-ṣināᶜī*

Saudi Arabia — العربية السعودية
*al-ᶜarabīya as-saᶜūdīya*

Saudi Arabian — سعودي
*saᶜūdī*

Sauer pistol — مسدس « زاور »
*musaddas zawar*

Sauro submarine — غواصة « سورو »
*ghawwāṣat sūrū*

Savage frigate — فرقاطة « سافيج »
*firqāṭat savij*

Savage SSM صاروخ سطح ـ سطح « سافيج »
*ṣārūkh saṭḥ-saṭḥ savij*
Sava submarine غواصة « سافا »
*ghawwāṣat sāvā*
Saxon armoured car عربة مدرعة « ساكسون »
*ʿaraba mudarraʿa saksun*
SC-7 aircraft طائرة « اس سي ـ ٧ »
*ṭāʾirat is sī sabʿa*
SC70 rifle بندقية « اس سي ٧٠ »
*bunduqīyat is sī sabʿīn*
Scaleboard SSM صاروخ سطح ـ سطح « سكايلبورد »
*ṣārūkh saṭḥ-saṭḥ skaylbūrd*
Scamp vehicle مركبة سكامب
*markabat skamp*
Scan Fix رادار سكان فيكس
*rādār skān fiks*
scanner جهاز مسح
*jihāz masḥ*
Scan Odd radar رادار « سكان اود »
*rādār skān ūd*
Scanter 009 search radar رادار باحث « سكانتر ٠٠٩ »
*rādār bāḥith skantar ṣifr ṣifr tisʿa*
Scan Three radar رادار « سكان ثري »
*rādār skān thrī*
Scapegoat SSM صاروخ سطح ـ سطح « سكايبجوت »
*ṣārūkh saṭḥ-saṭḥ skaypgūt*
Scarp SSM صاروخ سطح ـ سطح « سكارب »
*ṣārūkh saṭḥ-saṭḥ skārp*
scatter تبدد . تشتت
*tabaddud · tashattut*
scene! مشهد ! .
*mashhad*
schnorkel أنبوب تهوية تحت الماء
*unbūb tahwiya taḥt al-māʾ*
school ship سفينة تدريب
*safīnat tadrīb*
Scimitar زورق هجوم « سيميتار »
*zawraq hujūm simitar*
scissors bridge جسر على المقص
*jisr ʿalal-miqaṣṣ*
Sclar launcher system قاذفة نظام القذف « سكلار »
*niẓām qādhifa sklār*
Scoop Pair radar رادار « سكوب پير »
*rādār skūp payr*
Score Board radar رادار « سكور بورد »
*rādār skūr būrd*
Scorpion vehicle مركبة « سكورپيون »
*markabat skurpyūn*
Scout AH helicopter طائرة عمودية « سكوت ايه اتش »
*ṭāʾira ʿamūdīya skawt ayy itsh*
scout car عربة استكشاف
*ʿarabat istikshāf*
Scout Defender helicopter طائرة عمودية « سكوت ديفيندر »
*ṭāʾira ʿamūdīya skawt difindar*
Scout helicopter طائرة عمودية « سكوت »
*ṭāʾira ʿamūdīya skawt*
Scrag SSM صاروخ سطح ـ سطح « سكراج »
*ṣārūkh saṭḥ-saṭḥ skrāg*
scramble الالتحاق بالطائرة والاقلاع مباشرة
*al-iltiḥāq biṭ-ṭāʾira wal-iqlāʿ mubāshiratan*
screen armour درع حاجب
*dirʿ ḥājib*
screening smoke حجاب دخان
*ḥijāb dukhān*
Scrooge SSM صاروخ سطح ـ سطح « سكروج »
*ṣārūkh saṭḥ-saṭḥ skrūj*
Scrubber SSM صاروخ سطح ـ سطح « سكرابر »
*ṣārūkh saṭḥ-saṭḥ skrabar*
scuba جهاز مستقل للتنفس تحت الماء
*jihāz mustaqill lit-tanaffus taḥt al-māʾ*
Scud-A SSM صاروخ سطح ـ سطح « سكاد ـ ايه »
*ṣārūkh saṭḥ-saṭḥ skad ayy*
Scud-B SSM صاروخ سطح ـ سطح « سكاد ـ بي »
*ṣārūkh saṭḥ-saṭḥ skad bī*
SD-44 gun مدفع « اس دي ـ ٤٤ »
*midfaʿ is dī - arbaʿa wa arbaʿīn*
SD-510 inertial system نظام بالقصور الذاتي « اس دي ـ ٥١٠ »
*niẓām bil-quṣūr adh-dhātī is dī-khams miʾa wa ʿashara*
SE313B helicopter طائرة عمودية « اس ئي ٣١٣ بي »
*ṭāʾira ʿamūdīya is ī thalāth miʾa wa thalāthata ʿashar bī*
sea بحر
*baḥr*
sea-based fighter طائرة مقاتلة بحرية
*ṭāʾira muqātila baḥrīya*
seaborne force قوات محمولة بحراً
*qūwāt maḥmūla baḥran*
Seacat SAM صاروخ سطح ـ جو « سيكات »
*ṣārūkh saṭḥ-jaww sīkāt*
Sea Chaparral ADS نظام دفاع جوي « سي شاپرال »
*niẓām difāʿ jawwī sī shaprāl*
sea clutter تداخل راداري من البحر
*tadākhul rādārī min al-baḥr*
Sea Cobra helicopter طائرة عمودية « سي كوبرا »
*ṭāʾira ʿamudīya sī kubra*
Sea Dart SAM صاروخ سطح ـ جو « سي ـ دارت »
*ṣārūkh saṭḥ-jaww sī dārt*

S

Sea Devon aircraft طائرة « سي ديفن »
*ṭā'irat sī divn*
Sea Eagle SSM صاروخ سطح ـ سطح « سي ايجل »
*ṣārūkh saṭḥ-saṭḥ sī īgl*
Seafire radar رادار « سي فاير »
*rādār sī fāyr*
seagoing مسافر بحراً . بحري
*musāfir bahran · baḥrī*
seagoing vessel سفينة بحرية
*safīna baḥrīya*
Sea Gull radar رادار « سي ـ جل »
*rādār sī gal*
Sea Harrier aircraft طائرة « سي هارير »
*ṭā'irat sī hāryar*
Seahawk fighter طائرة مقاتلة « سي هوك »
*ṭā'ira muqātila sī hūk*
Sea Heron aircraft طائرة « سي هيرون »
*ṭā'irat sī hiran*
Sea Killer missile صاروخ « سي كيلر »
*ṣārūkh sī kilar*
Sea King helicopter طائرة عمودية « سي كينج »
*ṭā'ira ʿamūdīya sī king*
Sea Knight helicopter طائرة عمودية « سي نايت »
*ṭā'ira ʿamūdīya sī nāyt*
sealed magazine خزنة مختومة
*khaznat makhtūma*
sea level مستوى سطح البحر
*mustawa saṭḥ al-baḥr*
Sea Lines Of Communication خطوط الاتصالات البحرية
*khuṭūt al-ittiṣālāt al-baḥrīya*
Seal Type torpedo طوربيد طراز « سيل »
*turbīd ṭirāz sīl*
search and destroy البحث والتدمير
*al-baḥth wat-tadmīr*
search and find البحث والتعيين
*al-baḥth wat-taʿyīn*
search-and-rescue البحث والانقاذ
*al-baḥth wal-inqādh*
search equipment معدات البحث
*muʿaddāt al-baḥth*
searchlight نور كاشف
*nūr kāshif*
search radar رادار باحث
*rādār bāḥith*
Searchwater radar رادار بحري جو ـ سطح « سيرتشووتر »
*rādār baḥrī jaww-saṭḥ sartshwatar*
Sea Scan aircraft طائرة « سي سكان »
*ṭā'irat sī skān*

Sea Searcher radar رادار « سي سيرتشر »
*rādār sī sartshar*
sea-skimming missile صاروخ يطير فوق سطح البحر
*ṣārūkh yaṭīr fawqa saṭḥ al-baḥr*
Sea Skua ASM صاروخ جو ـ سطح « سي سكيوا »
*ṣārūkh jaww-saṭḥ sī skyūwa*
Seaslug SAM صاروخ سطح ـ جو « سيسلج »
*ṣārūkh saṭḥ-jaww sī slag*
Sea Sparrow missile صاروخ « سي سپارو »
*ṣārūkh sī spārū*
Seaspray radar رادار « سي سپريه »
*rādār sī sprayy*
Seasprite helicopter طائرة عمودية « سي سپرايت »
*ṭā'ira ʿamūdīya sī sprāyt*
Sea Stallion helicopter طائرة عمودية « سي ستاليون »
*ṭā'ira ʿamūdīya sī stalyan*
Sea State 4 حالة البحر ٤
*ḥālat al-baḥr arbaʿa*
Sea State 6 حالة البحر ٦
*ḥālat al-baḥr sitta*
seat معقد . مركز . قاعدة
*maqʿad · markaz · qāʿida*
seating capacity عدد المقاعد
*ʿadad al-maqāʿid*
sea training تدريب بحري
*tadrīb baḥrī*
sea transport نقل بحري
*naql baḥrī*
sea trial تجربة بحرية
*tajriba baḥrīya*
Sea Urchin mine لغم « سي ارتشن »
*lughm sī artshin*
sea water desalination تحلية ماء البحر
*taḥlīya mā' al-baḥr*
Seawolf boat زورق « سي وولف »
*zawraq sī wulf*
Seawolf missile صاروخ « سي وولف »
*ṣārūkh sī wulf*
seaworthy صالح للابحار
*ṣāliḥ lil-ibḥār*
SE bridge جسر « اس ئي »
*jisr is ī*
secondary attack capability إمكانيات الهجوم الثانوي
*imkānīyāt al-hujūm ath-thānawī*
secondary battle zone منطقة المعركة الفرعية
*minṭaqat al-maʿraka al-farʿīya*
secondary emission إبتعاث ثانوي
*ibtiʿāth thānawī*

S

secondary explosion إنفجار ثانوي
*infijār thānawī*
secondary role مهمة ثانوية
*muhimma thānawīya*
secondary-surveillance radar رادار استطلاع ثانوي
*rādār istiṭlā' thānawī*
second degree burn حرق من الدرجة الثانية
*ḥarq min ad-daraja ath-thānya*
second stage المرحلة الثانية
*al-marḥala ath-thānya*
second-stage motor محرك المرحلة الثانية
*muḥarrik al-marḥala ath-thānya*
section مقطع . قسم . فصل
*maqṭa' · qism · faṣl*
security أمن . سلامة
*amn · salāma*
security classification تصنيف الأمن
*taṣnīf al-amn*
security-coded مميز برمز سري
*mumayyaz bi-ramz sirrī*
security force قوات الأمن
*qūwāt al-amn*
security troops جنود الأمن
*junūd al-amn*
security wire سلك أمن
*silk amn*
security work أعمال الأمن
*a'māl al-amn*
seeker جهاز باحث . متقفي
*jihāz bāḥith · mutaqaffī*
seeker cooling system نظام تبريد الباحث
*niẓām tabrīd al-bāḥith*
seeker head رأس الباحث
*ra's al-bāḥith*
selective conscription تجنيد انتقائي
*tajnīd intiqā'ī*
selective fire رمي انتقائي
*ramī intiqā'ī*
selector mechanism آلية الانتخاب
*ālīyat al-intikhāb*
Selenia laser rangefinder معين مدى ليزر « سلينيا »
*mu'ayyin mada layzar silīnya*
Selenia Orion radar رادار « سلينيا ارايون »
*rādār silīnya urāyun*
self-contained مستقل .
*mustaqill*
self-defence دفاع عن النفس
*difā' 'anan-nafs*
self-defence weapon سلاح الدفاع عن النفس
*silāḥ ad-difā' 'anan-nafs*
self-destruct تخريب ذاتي . إتلاف ذاتي
*takhrīb dhātī · ittilāf dhātī*
self-destructed متلوف ذاتياً
*matlūf dhātīyan*
self-homing توجيه آلي ذاتي
*tawjīh ālī dhātī*
self-loading ذاتي التلقيم
*dhātī at-talqīm*
self-loading pistol مسدس ذاتي التلقيم
*musaddas dhātī at-talqīm*
self-projection jammer جهاز تشويش ذاتي الاسقاط
*jihāz tashwīsh dhātī al-isqāṭ*
self-propelled ذاتي الحركة
*dhātī al-ḥaraka*
self-propelled gun مدفع ذاتي الحركة
*midfa' dhātī al-ḥaraka*
self-propelled howitzer مدفع هاوتزر ذاتي الحركة
*midfa' hāwitsar dhātī al-ḥaraka*
semi-active homing missile صاروخ ذو توجيه آلي نصف فعال
*ṣārūkh dhū tawjīh ālī niṣf fa''āl*
semi-active laser ليزر نصف فعال
*layzar niṣf fa''āl*
semi-active radar homing توجيه آلي راداري نصف فعال
*tawjīh ālī rādārī niṣf fa''āl*
semi-active terminal homing توجيه آلي طرفي نصف فعال
*tawjīh ālī ṭarafī niṣf fa''āl*
semi-submerged نصف مغمور
*niṣf maghmūr*
semi-transportable شبه قابل للنقل
*shibh qābil lin-naql*
Senegal السنغال
*as-sinīghāl*
senior officer الضابط الأقدم
*aḍ-ḍābiṭ al-aqdam*
senior sergeant الرقيب الأقدم
*ar-raqīb al-aqdam*
SENIT-2 data system نظام البيانات « سينيت ـ ٢ »
*niẓām al-bayānāt sinit-ithnayn*
Sense and Destroy Armour سلاح احساس المدرعات وتدميرها
*silāḥ iḥsās al-mudarra'āt wa tadmīriha*
sensitive border حدود حساسة
*ḥudūd ḥassāsa*

S

sensitive installations تركيبات حساسة
*tarkībāt ḥassāsa*
sensor جهاز إحساس
*jihāz iḥsās*
sensors أجهزة إحساس
*ajhizat iḥsās*
sensor signature توقيع الكتروني لجهاز الاحساس
*tawqīʿ iliktrūnī li-jihāz al-iḥsās*
sensor system نظام حساس
*niẓām ḥassās*
sentence حُكم بعقوبة . عقوبة
*ḥukm bi-ʿuqūba · ʿuqūba*
sentry حارس . خفير . رقيب
*ḥāris · khafīr · raqīb*
Sentry AWACS طائرة « أواكس سنتري »
*ṭāʾirat āwaks sintri*
sentry box مظلة الحارس
*miẓallat al-ḥāris*
sentry post مركز الحارس
*markaz al-ḥāris*
Sepal SSM صاروخ سطح ـ سطح « سيپال »
*ṣārūkh saṭḥ-saṭḥ sīpal*
separate-loading تلقيم منفصل . تحميل منفصل
*talqīm munfaṣil · taḥmīl munfaṣil*
Sepecat (Co) شركة سيپيكات
*sharikat sipikat*
Sepecat Jaguar جاجوار سيپيكات
*jagwār sipikat*
sequential salvo رشق متتابع
*rashq mutatābiʿ*
sergeant رقيب
*raqīb*
sergeant major رئيس رقباء
*raʾis ruqabāʾ*
serious خطير . جدي
*khaṭīr · jaddī*
Serval turret برج « سرڤال »
*burj sarval*
service خدمة . صيانة
*khidma · ṣiyāna*
serviceable صالح للاستخدام
*ṣāliḥ lil-istikhdām*
service ceiling الارتفاع العملي الاقصى
*al-irtifāʿ al-ʿamalī al-aqṣa*
service delivery توزيع للقوات العسكرية
*tawzīʿ lil-qūwāt al-ʿaskarīya*
serviceman جندي . عسكري
*jundī · ʿaskarī*
service school مدرسة عسكرية
*madrasa ʿaskarīya*
service unit وحدة عسكرية
*wiḥda ʿaskarīya*
servo جهاز مؤازر
*jihāz muʾāzir*
servo motor محرك مؤازر
*muḥarrik muʾāzir*
severe weather جو قاسي
*jaww qāsi*
SF 37 طائرة « اس اف ٣٧ »
*ṭāʾirat is if sabʿa wa thalāthīn*
SF-260 aircraft طائرة « اس اف ـ ٢٦٠ »
*ṭāʾirat is if-miʾatayn wa sittīn*
SF-260M trainer طائرة تدريب « اس اف ـ ٢٦٠ ام »
*ṭāʾirat tadrīb is if-miʾatayn wa sittīn im*
SF-260WL trainer طائرة تدريب « اس اف ـ ٢٦٠ دبليو ال »
*ṭāʾirat tadrīb is if-miʾatayn wa sittīn dablyū il*
SGMT machine-gun رشاش . « اس جي ام تي »
*rashshāsh is jī im tī*
SGR-109 radar رادار « اس جي آر ـ ١٠٩ »
*rādār is jī ar-miʾa wa tisʿa*
SH-2 helicopter طائرة عمودية « اس اتش ـ ٢ »
*ṭāʾira ʿamūdīya is itsh ithnayn*
SH-2F helicopter طائرة عمودية « اس اتش ـ ٢ اف »
*ṭāʾira ʿamūdīya is itsh-ithnayn if*
SH-3 helicopter طائرة عمودية « اس اتش ـ ٣ »
*ṭāʾira ʿamūdīya is itsh-thalātha*
SH-60 helicopter طائرة عمودية « اس اتش ـ ٦٠ »
*ṭāʾira ʿamūdīya is itsh-sittīn*
Shackleton AEW-2 طائرة انذار مبكر « شاكلتون ايه ئي دبليو ـ ٢ »
*ṭāʾirat indhār mubakkir shakltan ayy ī dablyu ithnayn*
Shaddock SSM صاروخ سطح ـ سطح « شادوك »
*ṣārūkh saṭḥ-saṭḥ shadak*
Shafrir 2 AAM صاروخ جو ـ جو « شافرير ٢ »
*ṣārūkh jaww-jaww shafrīr ithnayn*
shaft عمود إدارة
*ʿamūd idāra*
Shahine SAM صاروخ سطح ـ جو « شاهين »
*ṣārūkh saṭḥ-jaww shāhīn*
shakedown flying طيران تجريبي
*ṭayarān tajrībī*

shallow-water operation عملية في الماء الضحل
*ʿamalīya fil-māʾ aḍ-ḍaḥl*
Shanghai attack craft زورق هجوم « شانغ هاي »
*zawraq hujūm shanghāy*
Shark vehicle مركبة « شارك »
*markabat shārk*
Sharland armoured car عربة مدرعة « شارلاند »
*ʿaraba mudarraʿa shārland*
sharp shooter رامي حاذق
*rāmi ḥādhiq*
Sheffield destroyer مدمرة « شفيلد »
*mudammarat shifīld*
shell case ظرف القذيفة
*ẓarf al-qadhīfa*
shell splinter شظية القذيفة
*shaẓīyat al-qadhīfa*
shelter ملجأ . مأوى
*maljāʾ · maʾwan*
shelter-mounted مركب في مأوى
*murrakab fī maʾwan*
Shenyang (Co) شركة « شينيانج »
*sharikat shinyāng*
Sheridan tank دبابة « شيريدان »
*dabbābat shiridan*
Sherman tank دبابة شيرمان
*dabbābat shirman*
Shershen torpedo boat زورق طوربيد « شيرشن »
*zawraq ṭūrbīd shirshin*
SHF DF antenna هوائي « اس اتش اف دي اف »
*hawāʾī is itsh if dī if*
Shillelagh missile صاروخ شيليهلي
*ṣārūkh shilaylī*
Shin Meiwa (Co) شركة « شين ميه وا »
*sharikat shin maywā*
Shin Meiwa flying boat طائرة بحرية شين ميه وا
*ṭāʾira baḥrīya shin may wa*
ship-based helicopter طائرة عمودية للسفن
*ṭāʾira ʿamūdīya lis-sufun*
ship-board operation عملية على متن سفينة
*ʿamalīya ʿala matn safīna*
shipborne محمول على متن السفينة
*maḥmūl ʿala matn as-safīna*
ship-borne aircraft طائرة محمولة على متن سفينة
*ṭāʾira maḥmūla ʿala matn safīna*
shipborne capability إمكانية الحمل بالسفية
*imkānīyat al-ḥaml bis-safīna*
ship fired اطلاق من السفينة
*iṭlāq min as-safīna*
ship-launch إطلاق السفينة
*iṭlāq as-safīna*
ship target هدف سفينة
*hadaf safīna*
ship-to-shore bombardment قصف من السفن إلى الساحل
*qaṣf min as-sufun ilas-sāḥil*
shipyard ورشة بناء السفن
*warshat bināʾ as-sufun*
Shir tank دبابة « شير »
*dabbābat shir*
shock absorber ممتص الصدمات
*mumtaṣṣ aṣ-ṣadamāt*
Shoet armoured carrier حاملة مدرعة « شوت »
*ḥāmila mudarraʿa shūt*
shore base قاعدة برية
*qāʿida barrīya*
shore-based air cover حماية جوية من البر
*ḥimāya jawwīya min al-barr*
shore-based helicopter طائرة عمودية برية
*ṭāʾira ʿamūdīya barrīya*
shore bombardment قصف ساحلي
*qaṣf sāḥilī*
Shorland armoured car عربة مدرعة « شورلاند »
*ʿaraba mudarraʿa shūrland*
short-burn rocket صاروخ قصير الاشتعال
*ṣārūkh qaṣīr al-ishtiʿāl*
Short Horn radar رادار « شورت هورن »
*rādār shūrt hūrn*
short-range قصير المدى
*qaṣīr al-mada*
Short-Range Ballistic Missile صاروخ بالستي قصير المدى
*ṣārūkh bālistī qaṣīr al-mada*
short-span wing جناح قصير الباع
*janāḥ qaṣīr al-bāʿ*
shot simulator جهاز محاكاة الطلقات
*jihāz muḥākāt aṭ-ṭalaqāt*
shoulder arms! « علق سلاح ! »
*ʿalliq silāḥ*
shoulder strap سير الكتف
*sayr al-katif*
Shrike AGM صاروخ جو - أرض « شرايك »
*ṣārūkh jaww-arḍ shrāyk*
Shrike Commander aircraft طائرة « شرايك كوماندور »
*ṭāʾirat shrāyk kumāndar*
Siai-Marchetti (Co) شركة « سياي - مارشيتي »
*sharikat syāy marṣhiti*
sick مريض
*marīḍ*
sick bay حجرة المرضى
*ḥujrat al-marḍa*

S

sick leave إجازة مرضية
*ijāza marḍīya*
sick parade تفتيش المرضى
*taftīsh al-marḍa*
side-cap غطاء جانبي
*ghiṭā' jānibī*
Side Globe ESM تدابير دعم إلكترونية « ساید . جلوب »
*tadābīr da'm iliktrūnīya sāyd glūb*
side-looking airborne radar رادار جوي جانبي الرؤية
*rādār jawwī jānibī ar-ru'ya*
side-mounted camera آلة تصوير مركبة على الجنب
*ālat taṣwīr murakkaba 'alal-janb*
Side Net radar رادار « ساید نیت »
*rādār sāyd nit*
Sidewinder AIM صاروخ اعتراض جوي « ساید ویندر »
*ṣārūkh i'tirāḍ jawwī sāyd wāyndar*
siege حصار
*ḥiṣār*
sight جهاز تسديد . مهداف
*jihāz tasdīd · mihdāf*
sighting تصويب . تسديد
*taṣwīb · tasdīd*
sighting system جهاز التسديد
*jihāz at-tasdīd*
sighting telescope تلسكوب التسديد
*talskūb at-tasdīd*
sightline خط التسديد
*khaṭṭ at-tasdīd*
signal cartridge خرطوشة إشارات
*kharṭūshat ishārāt*
signal processor جهاز تحليل الاشارات
*jihāz taḥlīl al-ishārāt*
signals! اشارات !
*ishārāt*
Sikorsky (Co) شركة « سيكورسكي »
*sharikat sikūrski*
silence of operation صموت التشغيل
*ṣumūṭ at-tashghīl*
silent operation تشغيل صامت . عملية صامتة
*tashghīl ṣāmit · 'amalīya ṣāmita*
silhouette خيال . مظهر جانبي
*khayyāl · maẓhar jānibī*
silo صومعة
*ṣawma'a*
Silver Dog grenade قنبلة يدوية « سيلڤر دوج »
*qunbula yadawīya silvar dug*
silver-zinc cell خلية الفضة والزنك
*khalīyat al-fiḍḍa waz-zink*
simulator جهاز محاكاة
*jihāz muḥākāh*
Singapore سنغافورة
*singhāfūra*
single mount تركيب مفرد
*tarkīb mufrad*
single round طلقات مفردة
*ṭalaqāt mufrada*
single seater طائرة بمقعد واحد
*ṭā'ira bi-maq'ad wāḥid*
single-shot طلقة مفردة
*ṭalaqa mufrada*
single-stage مرحلة واحدة
*marḥala wāḥida*
Sir Bedivere landing ship سفينة إنزال « سير بديڤير »
*safīnat inzāl sir badivīr*
siren بوق الانذار . صفار
*būq al-indhār · ṣafāra*
Sirena series radar رادار من سلسلة « سيرينا »
*rādār min silsilat sāyrīna*
Sir Lancelot landing ship سفينة إنزال « سير لانسلوت »
*safīnat inzāl sir lānsalūt*
site depot مخزن الموقع
*makhzan al-mawqi'*
six-blade سداسي الأرياش
*sidāsī al-aryāsh*
Sjoormen submarine غواصة «سيورمين »
*ghawwāṣat syūrmin*
SK-105 light tank دبابة خفيفة « اس كيه ـ ١٠٥ »
*dabbāba khafīfa is kayy-khamsa wa mi'a*
skid landing gear جهاز الحط الانزلاقي
*jihāz al-ḥaṭṭ al-inzilāqī*
skid-steered توجيه انزلاقي
*tawjih inzilāqī*
ski-jump ممر منحدر الاقلاع
*mamarr munḥadir lil-iqlā'*
Skima-12 hovercraft حوامة « سكيما ـ ١٢ »
*ḥawwāmat skīma - ithnata 'ashar*
Skin Head radar رادار « سكين هيد »
*rādār skin hid*
Skipjack submarine غواصة « سكيپجاك »
*ghawwāṣat skipjāk*
Skip Spin radar رادار « سكيب سپين »
*rādār skip spin*
skirmish مناوشة . مصادمة
*munāwasha · muṣādama*

SKN 2602 navigation نظام الملاحة « اس كيه ان ٢٦٠٢ »
*niẓām al-milāḥa is kayy in alfayn wa sitt mi'a wa ithnayn*
Skorpion sub-machine gun رشاش قصير « سكورپيون »
*rashshāsh qaṣīr skurpyūn*
Skory destroyer مدمرة « سكوري »
*mudammirat skūri*
SKS carbine بندقية قصيرة « اس كيه اس »
*bunduqīya qaṣīra is kayy is*
Skycrane helicopter طائرة عمودية « سكايكرين »
*ṭā'ira ʿamudīya skāykrayn*
Skyflash AAM صاروخ جو ـ جو « سكايفلاش »
*ṣārūkh jaww-jaww skāyflash*
Skyfox aircraft طائرة سكايفوكس
*ṭā'irat skāyfuks*
Skyguard cannon مدفع هاون سكايچارد
*midfaʿ hāwun skāygārd*
Skyguard launcher قاذفة سكايچارد
*qādhifat skāygārd*
Skyguard system نظام « سكايچارد »
*niẓām skāygārd*
Skyhawk bomber طائرة قاذفة « سكايهوك »
*ṭā'ira qādhifa skāyhūk*
Skyvan air transport طائرة نقل « سكايڤان »
*ṭā'irat naql skāyvān*
slaved متابع
*mutābiʿ*
sleeping accommodation مهجع
*mahjaʿ*
sleeping bag كيس النوم
*kīs an-nawm*
sleeve insignia شارة الكم
*shārat al-kumm*
slide زلق . إنزلاق . مزلقة
*zalaqa · inzilāq · mizlaqa*
sliding wedge إسفين منزلق
*isfīn munzaliq*
Slim Net radar رادار « سليم نيت »
*rādār slim nit*
sling arms! علق سلاح !
*ʿalliq silāḥ*
slipway رصيف منحدر للسفن
*raṣīf munḥadir lis-sufun*
slope arms! تنكب سلاح !
*tanakkab silāḥ*
slotted-waveguide antenna هوائي توجيه موجي مشقوب
*hawā'ī tawjīh mawjī mashqūb*
slow march خطوة الاستعراض
*khuṭwat al-istiʿrāḍ*

SLQ-29 ESM تدابير دعم إلكترونية « اس ال كيو ـ ٢٩ »
*tadābīr daʿm iliktrūnīya is il kyū - tisʿa wa ʿishrin*
SLQ-32(V)2 ESM تدابير دعم إلكترونية « اس ال كيو ـ ٣٢ (ڤي) ـ ٢ »
*tadābīr daʿm iliktrūnīya is il kyū - ithnayn wa thalāthīn (vī) ithnayn*
SLQ(V)-1 ESM تدابير دعم إلكترونية « اس ال كيو (ڤي) ـ ١ »
*tadābīr daʿm iliktrūnīya is il kyū (vī)-wāhid*
SLR-20 ECM تدابير مضادة إلكترونية « اس ال آر ـ ٢٠ »
*tadābīr muḍādda iliktrūnīya is il ār - ʿishrīn*
small arms أسلحة صغيرة
*asliḥa ṣaghīra*
smallpox جُدَري
*judarī*
SMI-ER SAM صاروخ سطح ـ جو « اس ام ١ ـ ئي آر »
*ṣārūkh saṭḥ-jaww is im waḥid - ī ār*
SM2-ER SAM صاروخ سطح ـ جو « اس ام ١ ـ ئي آر »
*ṣārūkh saṭḥ-jaww is im ithnayn - ī ār*
smoke ammunition ذخيرة دخان
*dhakhīrat dukhān*
smoke bomb قنبلة دخان
*qunbulat dukhān*
smoke candle شمعة دخان
*shamʿat dukhān*
smoke canister علبة دخان
*ʿulbat dukhān*
smoke cloud سحابة دخان
*saḥābat dukhān*
smoke-discharger جهاز اطلاق الدخان
*jihāz iṭlāq ad-dukhān*
smoke grenade قنبلة دخان يدوية
*qunbulat dukhān yadawīya*
smoke hand grenade قنبلة دخان يدوية
*qunbulat dukhān yadawīya*
smokelaying equipment معدات توجيه الدخان
*muʿaddāt tawjīh ad-dukhān*
smoke projectile قذيفة دخان
*qadhīfat dukhān*
smoke trail أثر الدخان
*athar ad-dukhān*
smoke warhead رأس قذيفة دخان
*ra's qadhīfa dukhān*
smoky trail أثر داخن
*athar dākhin*
smooth-bore gun مدفع أملس الجوف
*mifdaʿ amlas al-jawf*

S

"snail drum" magazine خزنة على شكل حلزوني
*khaznat ʿala shakl ḥalazūnī*
Snapper ATM صاروخ مضاد للدبابات « سنابر »
*ṣārūkh muḍādd lid-dabbābāt snapar*
SNEB rocket صاروخ « اس ان ئي بي »
*ṣārūkh is in ī bī*
sniper قناص
*qannāṣ*
sniper rifle بندقية القناص
*bunduqīyat al-qannāṣ*
Snoop Group radar رادار « سنوب جروب »
*rādār snūp grūp*
Snoop Tray radar رادار « سنوب تريه »
*rādār snūp trayy*
snorkel منشاق : سنوركل
*minshāq · snūrkal*
snorkeling submarine غواصة استنشاق
*ghawwāṣat istinshāq*
snort induction mast صاري حثي للمنشاق
*ṣārī hathī lil-minshāq*
snorting استنشاق تحت الماء
*istinshāq taḥt al-māʾ*
SO-1 patrol craft سفينة خفر سواحل « اس اوه ـ ١ »
*safīnat khafar sawāḥil is aw-wāḥid*
Soko (Co) شركة سوكو
*sharikat sūkū*
soldier جندي . عسكري
*jundī · ʿaskarī*
solid-fuel وقود جاف
*wuqūd jāff*
solid fuel cooker جهاز طهي بالوقود الجاف
*jihāz ṭuhan bil-wuqūd al-jāff*
solid fuel tablet قرص وقود جاف
*qurṣ wuqūd jāff*
solid motor محرك صلب
*muḥarrik ṣulb*
solid propellant دافع جاف
*dāfiʿ jāff*
solid-propellant missile صاروخ بدافع جاف
*ṣārūkh bi-dāfiʿ jāff*
solid-state حالة الصلابة
*ḥālat aṣ-ṣalāba*
Soltam L-33 gun مدفع « سولتام ال ـ ٣٣ »
*midfaʿ sultam il-thalātha wa thalāthīn*
Somali صومالي
*sūmālī*
Somalia الصومال
*aṣ-ṣūmāl*
Soman nerve gas غاز الأعصاب « سومان »
*ghāz al-aʿṣāb sūmān*
sonar سونار
*sūnār*
sonar array مجموعة سونار
*majmūʿat sūnar*
sonar coupler قارن سونار
*qārin sūnār*
sonar search pattern نمط البحث للسونار
*namaṭ al-baḥth lis-sūnār*
sonobuoy طافية صوتية رادارية
*ṭāfīya ṣawtīya rādārīya*
sonobuoy launcher قاذفة طافيات صوتية رادارية
*qādifat ṭāfīyāt ṣawtīya rādārīya*
sonobuoy stowage تخزين الطافية الصوتية الرادارية
*takhzīn aṭ-ṭāfīyā aṣ-ṣawtīya ar-rādārīya*
sophisticated حديث . متطوّر
*ḥadīth · mutaṭawwar*
Soptac 23 FCS نظام التحكم في الطيران « سوپتاك ٢٣ »
*niẓām at-taḥakkum fiṭ-ṭayarān suptak thalātha wa ʿishrīn*
sortie غارة
*ghāra*
SOS-23 sonar سونار « اس اوه اس ـ ٢٣ »
*sūnār is aw is thalātha wa ʿishrīn*
SOS-505 sonar سونار « اس اوه اس ـ ٥٠٥ »
*sūnār is aw is khams miʾa wa khamsa*
sound and flash shock grenade قنبلة صدمة بالصوت والوميض
*qunbulat ṣadma biṣ-ṣawṭ wal-wamīḍ*
sound proofing عزل الصوت
*ʿazl aṣ-ṣawt*
South جنوب
*janūb*
South Africa جنوب أفريقيا
*janūb afrīqya*
South African جنوب أفريقي
*janūb afrīqī*
southern command القيادة الجنوبية
*al-qiyāda al-janūbīya*
South Korea جنوب كوريا
*janūb kūrya*

S

South Yemen — اليمن الجنوبية
*al-yaman al-janūbīya*

Soviet-manned — بقيادة رجال سوفييت
*bi-qiyādat rijāl sūfyīt*

Soviet marines — جنود البحرية السوفياتية
*junūd al-baḥrīya as-sūfyātīyā*

Soviet Union — الاتحاد السوفياتي
*al-ittiḥād as-sūfyātī*

SP-70 howitzer — مدفع هاوتزر « اس پي - ٧٠ »
*midfa' hāwitsar is pī sab'īn*

SP-73 howitzer — مدفع هاوتزر « اس پي - ٧٣ »
*midfa' hāwitsar is pī thalātha wa sab'īn*

Space and Defence system — نظام الفضاء والدفاع
*niẓām al-faḍā' wal-difā'*

Space Defence Operation — عملية دفاع في فضاء
*'amalīyat difā' fil-faḍā'*

Space Surveillance System — نظام الاستطلاع الفضائي
*niẓām al-istiṭlā' al-faḍā'ī*

Spacetrack BMEWS — نظام الانذار المبكر بالصواريخ البالستية سپيستراك
*niẓām al-indhār al-mubakkir biṣ-ṣawārīkh al-bālistīya spaystrak*

Spada SAM — صاروخ « سطح -جو سپادا »
*ṣārūkh saṭḥ-jaww spāda*

Spain — اسبانيا
*isbānya*

Spandrel ATM — صاروخ مضاد للدبابات « سپاندريل »
*ṣārūkh muḍādd lid-dabbābāt spandril*

Spanish — اسباني
*isbānī*

spare parts — قطع غيار
*qiṭa' ghiyār*

spares — قطع غيار . قطع احتياطية
*qiṭa' ghiyār · qiṭa' iḥtiyāṭīya*

Sparklet gas cylinder — اسطوانة غاز سپاركليت
*usṭuwānat ghāz spārklit*

Sparrow AIM — صاروخ اعتراض جوي « سپارو »
*ṣārūkh i'tirāḍ jawwī spārū*

Spartan personnel carrier — ناقلة جنود « سپارتان »
*nāqilat junūd spārtan*

Sparviero missile — صاروخ « سپارڤيرو »
*ṣārūkh spārvīrū*

SPB-35A landing aid — معين انزال « اس پي بي -٣٥ ايه »
*mu'īn inzāl is pī bī - khamsa wa thalāthīn ayy*

spearhead — رأس المقدمة
*ra's al-muqaddima*

Spear patrol craft — سفينة خفر سواحل « سپير »
*safīnat khafar as-sawāḥil spīr*

special forces — قوات خاصة
*qūwāt khāṣṣa*

specialist unit — وحدة اختصاصيين
*wiḥdat ikhtiṣāṣiyīn*

special mission — مهمة خاصة
*muhimma khāṣṣa*

special service vessel — سفينة خدمة خاصة
*safīnat khidma khāṣṣa*

speech transmission mask — قناع ارسال المحادثات
*qinā' irsāl al-muḥādathāt*

speed — سرعة
*sur'a*

spent cartridge case — ظرف الطلقة الفارغة
*ẓarf aṭ-ṭalaqa al-fārigha*

Sperry computer — كومبيوتر سپيري
*kumbyūtar spīri*

SPG-9 gun — مدفع « اس پي جي - ٩ »
*midfa' is pī jī - tis'a*

SPG-34 radar — رادار « اس پي جي - ٣٤ »
*rādār is pī jī - arba'a wa thalāthīn*

SPG-49 radar — رادار « اس پي جي - ٤٩ »
*rādār is pī jī - tis'a wa arba'īn*

SPG-50 radar — رادار « اس پي جي - ٥٠ »
*rādār is pī jī - khamsīn*

SPG-51 radar — رادار « اس پي جي - ٥١ »
*rādār is pī jī - wāḥid wa khamsīn*

SPG-53A radar — رادار « اس پي جي - ٥٣ ايه »
*rādār is pī jī - thalātha wa khamsīn ayy*

SPG-55A radar — رادار « اس پي جي - ٥٥ ايه »
*rādār is pī jī - khamsa wa khamsīn ayy*

SPG-60 radar — رادار « اس پي جي - ٦٠ »
*rādār is pī jī - sittīn*

SPG self-propelled gun — مدفع ذاتي الحركة « اس پي جي »
*midfa' dhātī al-ḥaraka is pī jī*

Spica torpedo boat — زورق طوربيد « سپيكا »
*zawraq ṭūrbīd spīka*

Spigot ATM — صاروخ مضاد للدبابات « سپيجوت »
*ṣārūkh muḍādd lid-dabbābāt spigut*

spike — مسمار . غارز
*mismār · ghāriz*

Spin Scan radar — رادار « سپين سكان »
*rādār spīn skān*

S

spin-stabilized موازن بالتدويم
*muwāzan bit-tadwīm*
spin-stabilized grenade قنبلة يدوية موازنة بالتدويم
*qunbula yadawī muwāzana bit-tadwīm*
Spin Trough radar رادار « سبين تروف »
*rādār spin trūf*
Spiral ATM صاروخ مضاد للدبابات « سبايرال »
*ṣārūkh muḍādd lid-dabbābāt spāyral*
splinterproof glass زجاج منيع للشظايا
*zujāj manīᶜ lish-shaẓāya*
SPN-10 landing aid معين الانزال « اس بي ان ـ ١٠ »
*muᶜīn al-inzāl is pī in - ᶜashara*
SPN-43 landing aid معين الانزال « اس بي ان ـ ٤٣ »
*muᶜīn al-inzāl is pī in - thalātha wa arbaᶜīn*
Spoon Rest radar رادار « سبون ريست »
*rādār spūn rist*
spot charges شحنات موضعية
*shaḥnāt mawḍᶜīya*
SPQ-9A radar رادار « اس بي كيو ـ ٩ ايه »
*rādār is pī kyū - tisᶜa ayy*
sprag locking brake مكبح تثبيت دولاب المركبة
*mikbaḥ tathbīt dūlāb al-markaba*
Springfield rifle بندقية « سبرينج فيلد »
*bunduqīyat springfīld*
spring loaded محمّل بنابض . ملقم بنابض
*muḥammal bi-nābiḍ · mulaqqam bi-nābiḍ*
Spruance destroyer مدمرة « سبرونس »
*mudammirat spruwans*
SPS-10 radar رادار « اس بي اس ـ ١٠ »
*rādār is pī is - ᶜashara*
SPS-33 radar رادار « اس بي اس ـ ٣٢ »
*rādār is pī is - thalātha wa thalāthīn*
SPS-49 radar رادار « اس بي اس ـ ٤٩ »
*rādār is pī is - tisᶜa wa arbaᶜīn*
SPS-55 radar رادار « اس بي اس ـ ٥٥ »
*rādār is pī is khamsa wa khamsīn*
SPS-703 radar رادار « اس بي اس ـ ٧٠٣ »
*rādār is pī is - sabᶜ miᵓa wa thalātha*
Sputnik satellite قمر صناعي « سبتنيك »
*qamr ṣināᶜī sputnik*
SPW-2 radar رادار « اس بي دبليو ـ ٢ »
*rādār is pī dablyū - ithnayn*
spy جاسوس
*jāsūs*
SPY-1A radar رادار « اس بي واي ـ ١ ايه »
*rādār is pī āyy - wāḥid ayy*
SQQ-23 sonar سونار « اس كيو كيو ـ ٢٣ »
*sūnār is kyū kyū - thalātha wa ᶜishrīn*
SQR-19 sonar سونار « اس كيو أر ـ ١٩ »
*sūnār is kyū ār - tisᶜata ᶜashar*
SQS-17 sonar سونار « اس كيو اس ـ ١٧ »
*sūnār is kyū is - sabᶜata ᶜashar*
SQS-53 sonar سونار « اس كيو اس ـ ٥٣ »
*sūnar is kyū is - thalātha wa khamsīn*
squad حضيرة
*ḥaḍīra*
squad leader قائد الحضيرة
*qāᶜid al-ḥaḍīra*
squadron سرية . سرب
*sarīya · sirb*
square ميدان الاستعراض . مربع
*maydān al-istiᶜrāḍ · murabᶜ*
Square Head radar رادار « سكوير هيد »
*rādār skwīr hid*
Square Pair radar رادار « سكوير پير »
*rādār skwīr payr*
Square Tie radar رادار « سكوير تاي »
*rādār skwīr tāyy*
squash head رأس مهروس
*raᵓs mahrūs*
Squatt Eye radar رادار « سكوات أي »
*rādār skwat āyy*
Squint Eye radar رادار « سكوينت أي »
*rādār skwīnt āyy*
SR-71 aircraft طائرة « اس آر ـ ٧١ »
*ṭāᵓirat is ār - wāḥid wa sabᶜīn*
SRAAM AAM صاروخ جو ـ جو قصير المدى
*ṣārūkh jaww-jaww qaṣīr al-mada*
SRAM AGM صاروخ جو ـ أرض « اس ار اي ام »
*ṣārūkh jaww-arḍ is ār ayy im*
SRBoc chaff launcher قاذفة شرائح التشويش « اس ار بي اوه سي »
*qādhifat sharāᶜī at-tashwīsh is ār bī aw sī*
SRE-M5 radar رادار « اس آرئي ـ ام ٥ »
*rādār is ār ī - im khamsa*
Sri Lanka سري لانكا
*srī lānkā*

SR-N-6 hovercraft — حوامة «اس آر ـ ان ـ ٦»
*ḥawwāma is ār - in - sitta*

SS-1 SSM — صاروخ سطح ـ سطح «اس اس ـ ١»
*ṣārukh saṭḥ-saṭḥ is is wāḥid*

SS-4 SSM — صاروخ سطح ـ سطح «اس اس ـ ٤»
*ṣārukh saṭḥ-saṭḥ is is arbaʿa*

SS-5 SSM — صاروخ سطح ـ سطح «اس اس ـ ٥»
*ṣārukh saṭḥ-saṭḥ is is khamsa*

SS-9 SSM — صاروخ سطح ـ سطح «اس اس ـ ٩»
*ṣārukh saṭḥ-saṭḥ is is tisʿa*

SS-10 SSM — صاروخ سطح ـ سطح «اس اس ـ ١٠»
*ṣārukh saṭḥ-saṭḥ is is ʿashara*

SS-11 SSM — صاروخ سطح ـ سطح «اس اس ـ ١١»
*ṣārukh saṭḥ-saṭḥ is is aḥaha ʿashar*

SS-12 SSM — صاروخ سطح ـ سطح «اس اس ـ ١٢»
*ṣārukh saṭḥ-saṭḥ is is ithnata ʿashar*

SS-13 SSM — صاروخ سطح ـ سطح «اس اس ـ ١٣»
*ṣārukh saṭḥ-saṭḥ is is thalāthata ʿashar*

SS-14 SSM — صاروخ سطح ـ سطح «اس اس ـ ١٤»
*ṣārukh saṭḥ-saṭḥ is is arbaʿata ʿashar*

SS-15 SSM — صاروخ سطح ـ سطح «اس اس ـ ١٥»
*ṣārukh saṭḥ-saṭḥ is is khamsata ʿashar*

SS-16 ICBM — صاروخ بالستي عابر للقارات «اس اس ـ ١٦»
*ṣārukh bālistī ʿābir lil-qārāt is is - sittata ashar*

SS-17 ICBM — صاروخ بالستي عابر للقارات «اس اس ـ ١٧»
*ṣārukh bālistī ʿābir lil-qārāt is is sabʿata ashar*

SS-18 ICBM — صاروخ بالستي عابر للقارات «اس اس ـ ١٨»
*ṣārukh bālistī ʿābir lil-qārāt is is thamānyata ashar*

SS-19 ICBM — صاروخ بالستي عابر للقارات «اس اس ـ ١٩»
*ṣārukh bālistī ʿābir lil-qārāt is is tisʿata ashar*

SS-20 IRBM — صاروخ بالستي متوسط المدى «اس اس ـ ٢٠»
*ṣārukh bālistī mutawassiṭ al-mada is is - ʿishrīn*

SS-21 SSM — صاروخ سطح ـ سطح «اس اس ـ ٢١»
*ṣārukh saṭḥ-saṭḥ is is wāḥid wa ʿishrīn*

SS-22 SSM — صاروخ سطح ـ سطح «اس اس ـ ٢٢»
*ṣārukh saṭḥ-saṭḥ is is ithnayn wa ʿishrīn*

SS-23 missile — صاروخ «اس اس ـ ٢٣»
*ṣārūkh is is - thalātha wa ʿishrīn*

SSB submarine — غواصة «اس اس بي»
*ghawwāṣat is is bī*

SSBN nuclear submarine — غواصة نووية «اس اس بي ان»
*ghawwāṣa nawawīya is is bī in*

SS-C-1B SSM — صاروخ سطح ـ سطح «اس اس ـ سي ـ ١ بي»
*ṣārukh saṭḥ-saṭḥ is is - sī - wāḥid bī*

SSG submarine — غواصة «اس اس جي»
*ghawwāṣat is is jī*

SSGN nuclear submarine — غواصة نووية «اس اس جي ان»
*ghawwāṣat nawawīya is is jī in*

SSM launcher — قاذفة صواريخ «اس اس ام»
*qādhifat ṣawārīkh is is im*

SSN nuclear submarine — غواصة نووية «اس اس ان»
*ghawwāṣa nawawīya is is in*

SS-N-1 SSM — صاروخ سطح ـ سطح «اس اس ـ ان ـ ١»
*ṣārukh saṭḥ-saṭḥ is is - in - wāḥid*

SS-N-2 SSM — صاروخ سطح ـ سطح «اس اس ـ ان ـ ٢»
*ṣārukh saṭḥ-saṭḥ is is - in - ithnayn*

SS-N-2A SSM — صاروخ سطح ـ سطح «اس اس ـ ان ـ ٢ ايه»
*ṣārukh saṭḥ-saṭḥ is is - in - ithnayn ayy*

SS-N-3 SSM — صاروخ سطح ـ سطح «اس اس ـ ان ـ ٣»
*ṣārukh saṭḥ-saṭḥ is is - in - thalātha*

SS-N-4 SSM — صاروخ سطح ـ سطح «اس اس ـ ان ـ ٤»
*ṣārukh saṭḥ-saṭḥ is is - in - arbaʿa*

SS-N-5 SSM — صاروخ سطح ـ سطح «اس اس ـ ان ـ ٥»
*ṣārukh saṭḥ-saṭḥ is is - in - khamsa*

SS-N-6 SLBM — صاروخ بالستي منطلق من الغواصة «اس اس ـ ان ـ ٦»
*ṣārukh bālistī munṭaliq min al-ghawwāṣa is is - in - sitta*

SS-N-7 SSM — صاروخ سطح ـ سطح «اس اس ـ ان ـ ٧»
*ṣārukh saṭḥ-saṭḥ is is - in - sabʿa*

SS-N-8 SSM — صاروخ سطح ـ سطح «اس اس ـ ان ـ ٨»
*ṣārukh saṭḥ-saṭḥ is is - in - thamānya*

SS-N-9 SSM — صاروخ سطح ـ سطح «اس اس ـ ان ـ ٩»
*ṣārukh saṭḥ-saṭḥ is is - in - tisʿa*

SS-N-11 SSM — صاروخ سطح ـ سطح «اس اس ـ ان ـ ١١»
*ṣārukh saṭḥ-saṭḥ is is - in - aḥada ʿashar*

SS-N-12 SSM صاروخ سطح ـ سطح
*ṣārukh saṭḥ-saṭḥ is is - in - ithnata ʿashar* « اس اس ـ ان ـ ١٢ »

SS-N-14 SSM صاروخ سطح ـ سطح
*ṣārukh saṭḥ-saṭḥ is is - in - arbaʿata ʿashar* « اس اس ـ ان ـ ١٤ »

SS-N-15 SSM صاروخ سطح ـ سطح
*ṣārukh saṭḥ-saṭḥ is is - in - khamsata ʿashar* « اس اس ـ ان ـ ١٥ »

SS-N-16 SSM صاروخ سطح ـ سطح
*ṣārukh saṭḥ-saṭḥ is is - in - sittata ʿashar* « اس اس ـ ان ـ ١٦ »

SS-N-17 SSM صاروخ سطح ـ سطح
*ṣārukh saṭḥ-saṭḥ is is - in - sabʿata ʿashar* « اس اس ـ ان ـ ١٧ »

SS-N-18 SSM صاروخ سطح ـ سطح
*ṣārukh saṭḥ-saṭḥ is is - in - thamānyata ʿashar* « اس اس ـ ان ـ ١٨ »

SS-N-19 SSM صاروخ سطح ـ سطح
*ṣārukh saṭḥ-saṭḥ is is - in - tisʿata ʿashar* « اس اس ـ ان ـ ١٩ »

SS-N-21 SSM صاروخ سطح ـ سطح
*ṣārukh saṭḥ-saṭḥ is is - in - wāḥid wa ʿishrīn* « اس اس ـ ان ـ ٢١ »

SS-N-22 SSM صاروخ سطح ـ سطح
*ṣārukh saṭḥ-saṭḥ is is - in - ithnayn wa ʿishrīn* « اس اس ـ ان ـ ٢٢ »

SS-NX-13 missile صاروخ « اس اس ـ ان اكس ١٣ »
*ṣārūkh is is - in iks - thalāthata ʿashar*

SS-NX-17 ICBM صاروخ بالستي عابر للقارات « اس اس ـ ان اكس ـ ١٧ »
*ṣārukh bālistī ʿābir lil-qārat is is - in iks - sabʿata ʿashar*

SS-NX-20 missile صاروخ « اس اس ـ ان اكس ـ ٢٠ »
*ṣārūkh is is - in iks - ʿishrīn*

SSR-1 receiver مستقبل « اس اس أر ـ ١ »
*mustaqbil is is ar - wāhid*

SST4 torpedo طوربيد « اس اس تي ٤ »
*ṭūrbīd is is tī arbaʿa*

SS-X-23 SSM صاروخ سطح ـ سطح « اس اس ـ اكس ـ ٢٣ »
*ṣārukh saṭḥ-saṭḥ is is - iks - thalātha wa ʿishrīn*

SS-X-28 missile صاروخ « اس اس ـ اكس ـ ٢٨ »
*ṣārūkh is is - iks - thamānya wa ʿishrīn*

stability استقرار
*isitqrār*

stabilization system نظام موازنة
*niẓām muwāzana*

stabilized gun مدفع متوازن
*midfaʿ mutawāzan*

stabilized monocular sight مهداف متوازن أحادي العين
*mihdāf mutawāzan uḥādī al-ʿayn*

stabilized sight مهداف متوازن
*mihdāf mutawāzan*

stabilizer blade ريشة الموازن
*rīshat al-muwāzin*

staff أركان
*arkān*

staff officer ضابط ركن
*ḍābiṭ rukn*

stainless steel فولاذ لا يصدأ
*fūlādh lā yaṣdaʾ*

stand موضع . منصة . حامل
*mawḍiʿ · minaṣṣa · ḥāmil*

Standard ARM missile صاروخ ايه ار ام ستاندارد مضاد للرادار
*ṣārūkh ayy ār im stāndārd muḍādd lir-rādār*

standard bearer حامل العلم
*ḥāmil al-ʿalam*

standard fuel وقود اعتيادي
*wuqūd iʿtiyādī*

standard launcher قاذفة اعتيادية
*qādhifa iʿtiyādīya*

standard model طراز اعتيادي
*ṭirāz iʿtiyādī*

Standard SAM صاروخ سطح ـ جو « ستاندارد »
*ṣārukh saṭḥ-jaww stāndārd*

Standard SM-1 missile صاروخ ستاندارد « اس ام ـ ١ »
*ṣārūkh stāndārd is im - wāḥid*

Standard SM-2 missile صاروخ ستاندارد « اس ام ـ ٢ »
*ṣārūkh stāndārd is im - ithnayn*

stand at attention! قف في وضع انتباه
*qiff fī waḍʿ intibāh*

stand at ease! استرح !
*istariḥ*

stand-by إحتياطي
*ihtiyāṭī*

stand-down! الحرس ـ بدل !
*al-ḥaras - baddil*

stand easy! راحة !
*rāḥa*

standing orders أوامر دائمة
*awāmir dāʾima*

stand-off ASW سلاح للهجوم عن بعد مضاد للغواصات
*silāḥ lil-hujūm ʿan buʿd muḍādd lil-ghawwāṣat*

stand-off interceptor طائرة معترضة للهجوم عن بعد
*ṭāʾira muʿtarida lil-hujūm ʿan buʿd*

stand-off weapon سلاح للهجوم عن بعد
*silāḥ lil-hujūm ʿan buʿd*
S-tank دبابة « اس »
*dabbābat is*
starboard ميمنة
*maymana*
starboard bin صندوق الميمنة
*ṣundūq al-maymana*
starboard island جزيرة الميمنة
*jazīrat al-maymana*
Starfighter aircraft طائرة « ستارفايتر »
*ṭāʾirat stārfāytar*
Starlifter air-transporter طائرة نقل « ستارلفتر »
*ṭāʾirat naql stārliftar*
start up! انطلق
*inṭaliq*
state of alert حالة الانذار
*ḥālat al-indhār*
state of emergency حالة الطوارىء
*ḥālat aṭ-ṭawāriʾ*
state security أمن الدولة
*amn ad-dawla*
static ساكن . متوقف
*sākin · mutawaqqaf*
static thrust قوة الدفع الساكن
*qūwat ad-dafʿ as-sākin*
stationary ثابت . ساكن
*thābit · sākin*
stationary target هدف ثابت
*hadaf thābit*
steam catapult منجنيق بخاري
*manganīq bukhārī*
steam turbine تربين بخاري
*turbīn bukhārī*
steel فولاذ . صُلب
*fūlādh · ṣulb*
steel deck سطح فولاذي
*saṭḥ fūlādhī*
steel helmet خوذة فولاذية
*khūdha fūlādhīya*
steer أدار . قاد
*adāra · qāda*
steering إدارة . تسيير . توجيه
*idāra · tasyīr · tawjīh*
stellar-inertial navigation system نظام بالقصور الذاتي للملاحة النجمية
*niẓām bil-quṣūr adh-dhātī lil-milāḥa an-najmīya*
stem ساق . جذع
*sāq · jidhʿ*
Stenka torpedo boat زورق طوربيد « ستينكا »
*zawraq ṭūrbīd stīnka*
Sten gun مدفع « ستن »
*midfaʿ stin*
Sten Gun sub-machine gun رشاش قصير « ستن جن »
*rashshāsh qaṣīr stin gan*
step faster! خطوة - سريعة !
*khuṭwa - sarīʿa*
step out! أسرع - الخطى !
*asriʿ - al-khuṭā*
step short! خطوة - قصيرة !
*khuṭwa - qaṣīra*
step slower! خطوة - بطيئة !
*khuṭwa - baṭīʾa*
sterile dressing ضمادة معقمة
*ḍimāda muʿaqqama*
Sterling sub-machine gun رشاش قصير « ستيرلينج »
*rashshāsh qaṣīr stirling*
stern مؤخرة السفينة
*muʾakhkharat as-safīna*
stern door باب المؤخرة
*bāb al-muʾakhkhara*
sterngate بوابة المؤخرة
*bawwābat al-muʾakhkhara*
Steyr AUG rifle بندقية « شتير ايه يو جي »
*bunduqīya shtayr ayy yū jī*
stick عصا . قضيب .
*ʿaṣa · qaḍīb*
Stinger SAM صاروخ سطح - جو « ستينجر »
*ṣārukh saṭḥ-jaww stingar*
Stinger missile صاروخ « ستينجر »
*ṣārūkh stingar*
Stingray torpedo طوربيد « ستينجراى »
*ṭūrbīd stingrayy*
stock مؤونة . بضاعة . تموين
*muʾna · baḍāʿa · tamwīn*
Stockholm class فئة « ستوكهولم »
*fiʾat stuk-hulm*
STOL operations عمليات الاقلاع والحط القصير
*ʿamaliyāt al-iqlāʿ wal-ḥaṭṭ al-qaṣīr*
stop! قف !
*qiff*
Stop Light ESM تدبير دعم الكتروني « ستوب لايت »
*tadbīr daʿm iliktrūnīya stup lāyt*
stop firing! الرمي - أوقف !
*ar-ramī awqif*
storable liquid سائل قابل للتخزين
*sāʾil qābil lit-takhzīn*

storage خزن . تخزين
*khazn · takhzīn*
store مخزن
*makhzan*
store dump مستودع تخزين
*mustawdaʿ takhzīn*
stores مخازن . تموينات
*makhāzin · tamwīnāt*
stores issue صرف التموينات
*ṣarf at-tamwīnāt*
stores-transfer نقل التموينات
*naql at-tamwīnāt*
STOVL اقلاع قصير وحط عمودي
*iqlāʿ qaṣīr wa ḥaṭṭ ʿamūdī*
straggler متخلف
*mutakhallif*
Straight Flush radar رادار « ستريت فلاش »
*rādār strayt flash*
stranded vehicle عربة معطلة
*ʿaraba muʿaṭṭala*
strap-on booster جهاز تعزيز مربوط
*jihāz taʿziz marbūṭ*
Strategic Air Command القيادة الجوية الاستراتيجية
*al-qiyāda al-jawwīya al-istrātījīya*
strategic bombing قصف استراتيجي
*qaṣf istrātījī*
strategic capacity سعة استراتيجية
*siʿa istrātījīya*
strategic missile submarine غواصة صواريخ استراتيجية
*ghawwāṣat ṣawārīkh istrātījīya*
strategic missile system شبكة صواريخ استراتيجية
*shabakat ṣawārīkh istrātījīya*
Strategic Nuclear Forces القوات النووية الاستراتيجية
*al-qūwāt an-nawawīya al-istrātījīya*
strategic parts أجزاء استراتيجية
*ajzāʾ istrātījīya*
strategic potential امكانيات استراتيجية
*imkānīyāt istrātījīya*
strategic reconnaissance استطلاع استراتيجي
*istiṭlāʿ istrātījī*
strategic reconnaissance aircraft طائرة استطلاع استراتيجي
*ṭāʾirat istiṭlāʿ istrātījī*
strategic rocket forces قوات الصواريخ الاستراتيجية
*qūwāt aṣ-ṣawārīkh al-istrātījīya*

strategic target هدف استراتيجي
*hadaf istrātījī*
strategy استراتيجية
*istrātījīya*
stratosphere طبقة الجو العالية
*ṭabaqat al-jaww al-ʿālīya*
stratospheric aircraft طائرة الجو العالي
*ṭāʾirat al-jaww al-ʿālī*
Stratotanker طائرة نقل « ستراتوتانكر »
*ṭāʾirat naql strātūtankar*
Streaker vehicle مركبة « ستريكر »
*markabat strīkar*
streamlining خط انسيابي
*khaṭṭ insiyābi*
street fighting قتال الشوارع
*qitāl ash-shawāriʿ*
strength شدة . قوة
*shidda · qūwa*
stretcher نقالة .
*naqqāla*
stretcher bearer حامل نقالة
*ḥāmil naqqāla*
stretcher case جريح واجب نقلة
*jarīḥ wājib naqqāla*
stretcher casualty مصاب النقالة
*muṣāb an-naqqāla*
Stridsvagn 103 tank دبابة « ستريدز ڤاجن ١٠٣ »
*dabbābat strīdz vāgan miʾa wa thalātha*
strike ضربة . إضراب
*ḍarba · iḍrāb*
strike aircraft طائرة هجوم
*ṭāʾirat hujūm*
Strike Command قيادة الهجوم
*qiyādat al-hujūm*
strike fighter طائرة مقاتلة مهاجمة
*ṭāʾira muqātila muhājima*
Strikemaster aircraft طائرة « سترايكماستر »
*ṭāʾirat strāykmāstar*
Striker vehicle مركبة « سترايكر »
*markabat strāykar*
Strikemaster trainer طائرة تدريب « سترايكماستر »
*ṭāʾirat tadrīb strāykmāstar*
strike squadron سرب هجوم
*sirb hujūm*
STRIM-89 rocket launcher قاذفة صواريخ « ستريم ـ ٨٩ »
*qādhifat ṣawārīkh strim - tisʿa wa thamānīn*
string of grenades سلسلة قنابل يدوية
*silsilat qanābil yadawīya*

Stromboli ship — سفينة « سترومبولي »
*safīnat strumbūlī*

stronghold — حصن
*ḥiṣn*

Strut Curve radar — رادار « سترات كيرف »
*rādār strat kurv*

Sturgeon submarine — غواصة « سترجن »
*ghawwāṣat starjan*

Styrofoam closure — مختوم بستايروفوم
*makhtūm bi-stāyrufūm*

Styx missile — صاروخ ستيكس
*ṣārūkh stiks*

Su-7 aircraft — طائرة « إس يو ـ ٧ »
*ṭā'irat is yū - sab'a*

Su-7UMK aircraft — طائرة « إس يو ـ ٧ يو ام كيه »
*ṭā'irat is yū im kayy*

Su-9 fighter — طائرة مقاتلة « إس يو ـ ٩ »
*ṭā'ira muqātila is yū - tis'a*

Su-11 fighter — طائرة مقاتلة « إس يو ـ ١١ »
*ṭā'ira muqātila is yū - aḥada 'ashar*

Su-15 fighter — طائرة مقاتلة « إس يو ـ ١٥ »
*ṭā'ira muqātila is yū - khamsata 'ashar*

Su-17 aircraft — طائرة « إس يو ـ ١٧ »
*ṭā'irat is yū sab'ata 'ashar*

Su-19 combat aircraft — طائرة حربية « إس يو ـ ١٩ »
*ṭā'ira ḥarbīya is yū tis'ata 'ashar*

Su-20 aircraft — طائرة « إس يو ـ ٢٠ »
*ṭā'irat is yū 'ishrīn*

Su-22 aircraft — طائرة « إس يو ـ ٢٢ »
*ṭā'irat is yū ithnayn wa 'ishrīn*

Su-24 Fencer — طائرة « إس يو ـ ٢٤ » فنسر
*ṭā'irat is yū arba'a wa 'ishrīn finsar*

Su-25 aircraft — طائرة « إس يو ـ ٢٥ »
*ṭā'irat is yū khamsa wa 'ishrīn*

Su-27 fighter — طائرة مقاتلة « إس يو ـ ٢٧ »
*ṭā'ira muqātila is yū sab'a wa 'ishrīn*

sub-calibre mortar — هاون مصغر العيار
*hāwun muṣaghghar al-'iyār*

Sub-Harpoon missile — صاروخ « صب ـ هاربون »
*ṣārūkh ṣab-harpūn*

sub-machine gun — رشاش قصير
*rashshāsh qaṣīr*

submarine — غواصة
*ghawwāṣa*

submarine base — قاعدة غواصات
*qā'idat ghawwāṣāt*

submarine-based — مقرها الغواصة
*maqarruhā al-ghawwāṣa*

submarine battery — بطارية غواصات
*baṭṭārīyat ghawwāṣat*

submarine launched — منطلق من الغواصة
*munṭaliq min al-ghawwāṣa*

submarine mine — لغم مغمور
*lughm maghmūr*

submariner — غواص
*ghawwāṣ*

submarine rocket — صاروخ غواصات
*ṣārūkh ghawwāṣāt*

submarine salvage vessel — سفينة انقاذ الغواصات
*safīnat inqād al-ghawwāṣāt*

submerged — مغمور . غاطس
*maghmūr · ghāṭis*

submerged bridge — جسر غاطس
*jisr ghāṭis*

submerged launch — إطلاق مغمور
*iṭlāq maghmūr*

submerged speed — السرعة تحت الماء
*as-sur'a taḥt al-mā'*

submerged voyage — رحلة تحت الماء
*raḥla taḥt al-mā'*

suborbital warhead-carrier — حاملة رأس قذيفة شبه مداري
*ḥāmilat ra's qadhīfa shibh madārī*

subordinate — مرؤوس . تابع
*mar'ūs · tābi'*

subordination — تبعية . خضوع
*taba'īya · khuḍū'*

Subroc missile — صاروخ « سبروك »
*ṣārūkh sabrūk*

SUBSAFE features — خصائص أمان الغواصة
*khaṣā'iṣ amān al-ghawwāṣa*

subsonic cruise armed decoy — صاروخ كروز نوع شرك مسلح ذو سرعة دون الصوت
*ṣārūkh krūz naw' sharak musallaḥ dhu sur'a dūn aṣ-sawtīya*

subsonic speed — سرعة دون الصوتية
*sur'a dūn aṣ-ṣawtīya*

sub tender — سفينة مموّنة للغواصة
*safīna mumawwina lil-ghawwāṣa*

sub-unit — وحدة فرعية
*wihda far'īya*

subversive — هدام
*haddām*

S

subversive group مجموعة هدامة
*majmūʿa haddāmīya*
Sudan السودان
*as-sūdān*
Suffren destroyer مدمرة « سفرن »
*mudammirat sufran*
suicide squad فرقة انتحارية
*firqa intiḥārīya*
Sukhoi (Co) شركة « سوخوي »
*sharikat sūkhuwi*
Sukhoi-built aircraft طائرة من صنع « سوخوي »
*ṭāʾira min ṣunʿ sūkhuwi*
Sultan vehicle مركبة « سلطان »
*markabat salṭan*
summer camp معسكر صيفي
*muʿaskar ṣayfī*
sunk غاطس . غرق
*ghātis · ghariq*
sunshade واقية الشمس
*wāqiyat ash-shams*
sunstroke ضربة شمس
*ḍarbat shams*
Sun Visor radar رادار « صن قايزر »
*rādār ṣan vāyzar*
Super 530 AAM صاروخ جو ـ جو « سوبر ٥٣٠ »
*ṣārūkh jaww-jaww sūpar khams miʾa wa thalathīn*
Super Bazooka M20 مدفع مضاد للدبابات « سوبر بازوكا ام ٢٠ »
*midfaʿ muḍādd lid-dabbābāt sūpar bāzūkā im ʿishrīn*
super-carrier حاملة ضخمة
*ḥāmila ḍakhma*
Super Cub aircraft طائرة « سوبر كب »
*ṭāʾirat sūpar kab*
Super Etendard strike fighter طائرة مقاتلة مهاجمة « سوبر إتيندارد »
*ṭāʾira muqātila muhājima sūpar aytandārd*
Super Falcon AAM صاروخ جو ـ جو « سوبر فالكون »
*ṣārukh jaww-jaww sūpar falkan*
Super Frelon helicopter طائرة عمودية « سوبر فريلون »
*ṭāʾira ʿamūdīya sūpar frilun*
superheating boiler مرجل فرط تسخين
*mirjal farṭ taskhīn*
Super King Air aircraft طائرة « سوبر كينج اير »
*ṭāʾirat sūpar king ayr*
Super Mini Signal Cartridge خرطوشة إشارات « سوبر ميني »
*kharṭūshat ishārāt sūpar mini*

Super Mirage 4000 aircraft طائرة « سوبر ميراج ٤٠٠٠ »
*ṭāʾirat sūpar mīrāj arbaʿa alāf*
Super Puma helicopter طائرة عمودية « سوبر پيوما »
*ṭāʾira ʿamudīya sūpar pyūma*
Super R530 AAM صاروخ جو ـ جو « سوبر آر ٥٣٠ »
*ṣārūkh jaww-jaww sūpar ār khams miʾa wa thalāthīn*
Super RBOC chaff launcher قاذفة شرائح تشويش « سوبر أربي اوه سي »
*qādhifat sharāʾī tashwīsh sūpar ār bī aw sī*
Super Sabre aircraft طائرة « سوبر سيبر »
*ṭāʾirat sūpar saybar*
Super Skywagon aircraft طائرة « سوبر سكايواجون »
*ṭāʾirat sūpar skāywagan*
supersonic أسرع من الصوت
*asraʿ min aṣ-ṣawt*
supersonic endurance تحمل فوق سرعة الصوت
*taḥmīl fawqa surʿat aṣ-ṣawt*
supersonic tactical missile صاروخ تكتيكي أسرع من الصوت
*ṣārūkh taktīkī asraʿ min aṣ-ṣawt*
Super Standard fighter طائرة مقاتلة « سوبر ستاندرد »
*ṭāʾira muqātila sūpar stāndard*
superstructure إنشاءات علوية للسفينة
*inshāʾāt ʿulwīya lis-safīna*
supervision unit وحدة مراقبة
*wiḥdat murāqaba*
supplies إمدادات . تموين
*imdādāt · tamwīn*
supply agency وكالة تموين
*wakalat tamwīn*
supply base قاعدة تموين
*qāʿidat tamwīn*
supply depot مستودع التموينات
*mustawdaʿ at-tamwīnāt*
supply drop إسقاط التموينات
*isqāṭ at-tamwīnāt*
supply line خط الامدادات
*khaṭṭ al-imdādāt*
support دعم . تعزيز
*daʿm · taʿzīz*
support element عنصر الدعم
*ʿunṣur ad-daʿm*
support operation عملية التعزيز
*ʿamalīyat at-taʿzīz*
support squadron سرية تعزيز . سرب تعزيز
*sarīya taʿzīz · sirb taʿzīz*

support unit — وحدة دعم
*wiḥdat daʿm*
supreme command — قيادة عليا
*qiyāda ʿulyā*
Sura rocket — صاروخ « سورا »
*ṣārūkh sūra*
surface combatants — مقاتلون بريّون
*muqātilūn barrīyūn*
surfaced — صعد إلى السطح
*ṣaʿada ilas-saṭḥ*
surface engagements — إشتباكات سطحية
*ishtibākāt saṭḥīya*
surface-search radar — رادار كشف سطحي
*rādār kashf saṭḥī*
surface threat — تهديد سطحي
*tahdīd saṭḥī*
surface-to-air missile — صاروخ سطح - جو
*ṣārūkh saṭḥ-jaww*
surface-to-surface missile — صاروخ سطح - سطح
*ṣārukh saṭḥ-saṭḥ*
surgeon — جراح
*jarrāḥ*
surplus store — مخزن الفائض
*makhzan al-fāʾiḍ*
surprise assault — انقضاض مباغت
*inqiḍāḍ mubāghit*
surprise attack — هجوم مباغت
*hujūm mubāghit*
surrender — تسليم . استسلام
*taslīm · istislām*
surveillance — إستطلاع
*istiṭlāʿ*
surveillance equipment — معدات الاستطلاع
*muʿaddāt al-istiṭlāʿ*
surveillance fighter — طائرة مقاتلة استطلاعية
*ṭāʾira muqātila istiṭlāʿīya*
surveillance radar — رادار استطلاع
*rādār istitlāʿ*
survey — مسح . مساحة
*masḥ · misāḥa*
surviving — يبقى حياً
*yabqā ḥayyan*
survivor — على قيد الحياة
*ʿala qayd al-ḥayāh*
Susa patrol craft — سفينة خفر سواحل « سوزا »
*safīnat khafar sawāḥil sūza*
SUSAT sight — مهداف « سوسات »
*mihdāf sūsāt*
sustainer — مداوم
*mudāwim*
sustainer burning — حرق مداوم
*ḥarq mudāwim*
sustainer motor — محرك مداومة
*muḥarrik mudāwima*
sustainer nozzle — فوهة مداومة
*fūhat mudāwima*
Sutjeska submarine — غواصة « سوتجيسكا »
*ghawwāṣat sūtjiska*
SUU20 dispenser — موزع « اس يو يو ٢٠ »
*muwazziʿ is yū yū ʿishrīn*
SUW-N-1 ASW launcher — قاذفة صواريخ مضادة للغواصات « اس يو دبليو ان - ١ »
*qādhifat sawārīkh mudādda lil-ghawwāṣāt is yū dablyū in wāḥid*
SVD rifle — بندقية « اس ڤي دي »
*bunduqīyat is vī dī*
Sverdlov cruiser — طرادة « سڤردلوف »
*ṭarrādat svirdluf*
Swatow craft — سفينة « سواتو »
*safīnat swatū*
Swatter ATM — صاروخ مضاد للدبابات « سواتر »
*ṣārūkh muḍādd lid-dabbābāt swatar*
Sweden — السويد
*as-suwīd*
Swedish — سويدي
*suwīdī*
sweep position — وضع الكسح
*waḍʿ al-kasḥ*
Swiftsure submarine — غواصة « سويفت شور »
*ghawwāṣat swift-shūr*
swimmer delivery vehicle — مركبة تسليم عائمة
*markabat taslīm ʿāʾima*
Swingfire ATGW — سلاح موجه مضاد للدبابات « سوينج فاير »
*silāḥ muwajjah muḍādd lid-dabbābāt swingfāyr*
Swiss — سويسري
*swīsarī*
switch — مفتاح
*miftāḥ*
switchboard operator — عامل الهاتف
*ʿāmil al-hātif*
Switch Off! — اقفل !
*iqfil*
Switzerland — سويسرة
*swīsara*
sword — سيف
*sayf*
Sycamore HC14 helicopter — طائرة عمودية « سيكامور اتش سي ١٤ »
*ṭāʾira ʿamūdīya sikamūr itsh sī arbaʿata ʿashar*

S

Syllex ECM rocket launcher قاذفة صواريخ « سايلكس ئي سي ام »
*qādhifat sawārīkh sāyliks ī sī im*

symmetrical flow تدفق متماثل
*tadaffuq mutamāthil*

synchronisation data بيانات التزامن
*bayānāt at-tazāmun*

Synthetic Aperture Radar رادار « سينثاتك اپاتشر »
*rādār sinthitik apatshar*

Syria سوريا
*sūrya*

Syrian سوري
*sūrī*

syringe محقنة
*miḥqana*

system نظام . جهاز . شبكة
*niẓām · jihāz · shabaka*

S

# T

T-class submarine — غواصة « طراز ـ تي »
*ghawwāṣa ṭirāz tī*

T-1 trainer aircraft — طائرة تدريب « تي ـ ١ »
*ṭā'irat tadrīb tī - wāḥid*

T-10 tank — دبابة « تي ـ ١٠ »
*dabbābat tī - ʿashara*

T-12 gun — مدفع « تي ـ ١٢ »
*midfaʿ tī-ithnata ʿashar*

T-42 aircraft — طائرة « تي ـ ٤٢ »
*ṭā'irat tī - ithnayn wa arbaʿīn*

T-43 minesweeper — كاسحة الغام « تي ـ ٤٣ »
*kāsiḥat alghām tī - thalātha wa arbaʿīn*

T-53-L-701 turboprop — طائرة بمحرك مروحي تربيني « تي ـ ٥٣ ـ ال ـ ٧٠١ »
*ṭā'ira bi-muḥarrik mirwaḥī turbīnī tī - thalātha wa khamsīn - il-sabʿa mi'a wa wāḥid*

T-54 tank — دبابة « تي ـ ٥٤ »
*dabbābat tī - arbaʿa wa khamsīn*

T-55 aircraft — طائرة « تي ـ ٥٥ »
*ṭā'irat tī - khamsa wa khamsīn*

T-55 tank — دبابة « تي ـ ٥٥ »
*dabbābat tī - khamsa wa khamsīn*

T-58 engine — محرك « تي ـ ٥٨ »
*muḥarrik tī - thamānya wa khamsīn*

T-62 tank — دبابة « تي ـ ٦٢ »
*dabbābat tī - ithnayn wa sittīn*

T-64 tank — دبابة « تي ـ ٦٤ »
*dabbābat tī - arbaʿa wa sittīn*

T-66 fighter — طائرة مقاتلة « تي ـ ٦٦ »
*ṭā'ira muqātila tī - sitta wa sittīn*

T-69 tank — دبابة « تي ـ ٦٩ »
*dabbābat tī - tisʿa wa sittīn*

T-72 tank — دبابة « تي ـ ٧٢ »
*dabbābat tī - ithnayn wa sabʿīn*

T-72K tank — دبابة « تي ـ ٧٢ كيه »
*dabbābat tī - ithnayn wa sabʿīn kayy*

T-80 tank — دبابة « تي ـ ٨٠ »
*dabbābat tī - thamānīn*

TA-4J aircraft — طائرة « تي ايه ـ ٤ جيه »
*ṭā'irat tī ayy - arbaʿa jayy*

Tacamo aircraft — طائرة تاكامو
*ṭā'irat takāmū*

TACAN navigation — نظام ملاحة تاكان
*niẓām milāḥa tākān*

TAC-EWS — نظام انذار مبكر « تي ايه سي »
*niẓām indhār mubakkir tī ayy sī*

tachometer — عداد دورات المحرك · تاكومتر
*ʿaddād dawrat al-muḥarrik · takūmitar*

tactical — تكتيكي
*taktīkī*

Tactical Air Command — قيادة الطيران التكتيكي
*qiyādat aṭ-ṭayarān at-taktīkī*

tactical aircraft — طائرة تكتيكية
*ṭā'ira taktīkīya*

tactical crew — طقم تكتيكي
*ṭaqm taktīkī*

Tactical Data System — نظام البيانات التكتيكية
*niẓām al-bayānāt at-taktīkīya*

Tactical Flag Command Centre — مركز القيادة الجوية التكتيكية
*markaz al-qiyāda al-jawwīya at-taktīkīya*

tactical helicopter — طائرة عمودية تكتيكية
*ṭā'ira ʿamūdīya taktīkīya*

T

tactical missile صاروخ تكتيكي
*ṣarūkh taktīkī*
tactical missile system شبكة صواريخ تكتيكية
*shabakat ṣawārīkh taktīkīya*
tactical nuclear نووي تكتيكي
*nawawī taktīkī*
tactical radio لاسلكي تكتيكي
*lā-silkī taktīkī*
tactical reconnaissance إستطلاع تكتيكي
*istiṭlāᶜ taktīkī*
tactical reconnaissance aircraft طائرة استطلاع تكتيكي
*tāʾirat istiṭlāᶜ taktīkī*
tactical sensor جهاز احساس تكتيكي
*jihāz iḥsās taktīkī*
tactical situation موقف تكتيكي
*mawqif taktīkī*
tactical stores مخزونات تكتيكية
*makhzūnāt taktīkīya*
tactical support دعم تكتيكي
*daᶜm taktīkī*
tactics تكتيك : فن التعبئة العسكرية
*taktīk: fann at-taᶜbiʾa al-ᶜaskarīya*
tailboom دعامة الذيل
*diᶜāmat adh-dhayl*
tail rotor دوّار الذيل
*dawwār adh-dhayl*
tailwheel landing gear جهاز الحط لدولاب الذيل
*jihāz al-ḥaṭṭ li-dūlāb adh-dhayl*
Taiwan تايوان
*tāywān*
take a bearing حدد الاتجاه الزاوي
*ḥaddad al-ittjāh az-zāwī*
take aim! صوّب !
*ṣawwib*
take cover! استتر
*istatirr*
take into custody أسر . اعتقل
*asara · iᶜtaqala*
take into service ضم الى الخدمة
*ḍamma ilal-khidma*
take-off إقلاع . إنطلاق
*iqlāᶜ · inṭilāq*
take-off distance مسافة الاقلاع
*masāfat al-iqlāᶜ*
take-off weight الوزن عند الاقلاع
*al-wazn ᶜind al-iqlāᶜ*
take up arms! ارفع السلاح
*irfaᶜ as-silāḥ*

Tall King radar رادار « طول كينج »
*rādār ṭūl king*
Talon cannon مدفع هاون « تالون »
*midfaᶜ hāwun tālūn*
Talos fire-control نظام السيطرة على الرمي « تالوس »
*niẓam as-sayṭara ᶜalar-ramī tālūs*
TAM tank دبابة « تي ايه ام »
*dabbābāt tī ayy īm*
tandem seat مقعد مترادف
*maqᶜad mutarādif*
tandem-wheel دولاب ترادفي
*dūlāb tarādufī*
Tango submarine غواصة تانجو
*ghawwāṣat tāngū*
tank battalion كتيبة دبابات
*katībat dabbābāt*
tank bridge جسر دبابات
*jisr dabbābāt*
tank-carrier ناقلة دبابات
*nāqilat dabbābāt*
tank crew طقم الدبابة
*ṭaqm ad-dabbāba*
tank destroyer قانصة دبابات
*qāniṣat dabbābāt*
tank division فرقة دبابات
*firqat dabbābāt*
tanker سفينة صهريجية . ناقلة نفط
*safīna ṣihrījīya · nāqilat nafṭ*
tank fire control السيطرة على رمي الدبابة
*as-sayṭara ᶜala ramī ad-dabbāba*
tank laser ليزر الدبابة
*layzar ad-dabbāba*
Tank Laser Sight مهداف ليزر للدبابات
*mihdāf layzar lid-dabbābāt*
tank-on-tank engagement إشتباك بين الدبابات
*ishtibāk bayn ad-dabbābāt*
tank platoon فصيلة دبابات
*faṣīlat dabbābāt*
tank regiment فوج دبابات
*fawj dabbābāt*
tank support دعم الدبابات
*daᶜm ad-dabbābāt*
tank-tested مجرب بالدبابة
*mujarrab bil-dabbāba*
tank training تدريب الدبابات
*tadrīb ad-dabbābāt*
tank trap مصيدة دبابات
*miṣyadat dabbābāt*

T

tank unit وحدة دبابات
*wiḥdat dabbābāt*
TAN SAM صاروخ سطح ـ جو « تان »
*ṣārūkh saṭḥ-jaww tān*
Tanzania تنزانيا
*tanzānya*
Tarantul rocket ship سفينة صواريخ « تارانتيل »
*safīnat ṣāwārīkh tarantīl*
Tarawa assault ship سفينة انقضاض تاراوا
*safīnat inqiḍāḍ tarāwa*
target هدف . نقطة التسديد
*hadaf · nuqṭat at-tasdīd*
target acquisition إكتساب الهدف
*iktisāb al-hadaf*
target-acquisition phase طور اكتساب الهدف
*ṭawr iktisāb al-hadaf*
target acquisition sight مهداف اكتساب الهدف
*mihdāf iktisāb al-hadaf*
target bearing الاتجاه الزاوي للهدف
*al-ittijāh az-zāwī lil-hadaf*
target category فئة الهدف
*fi'at al-hadaf*
target data receiver مستقبل بيانات الهدف
*mustaqbil bayānāt al-hadaf*
target data transmission system نظام ارسال بيانات الهدف
*niẓām irsāl bayānat al-hadaf*
target designation sight مهداف تعيين الهدف
*mihdāf taʿyīn al-hadaf*
target designation system نظام تعيين الهدف
*niẓām taʿyīn al-hadaf*
target designator معين الهدف
*muʿayyin al-hadaf*
target-detection performance أداء كشف الهدف
*adā' kashf al-hadaf*
target displacement إزاحة الهدف
*izāḥat al-hadaf*
target engagement إشتباك مع هدف
*ishtibāk maʿa hadaf*
target identified! « الهدف ـ معيَّن ! »
*al-hadaf – muʿayyan*
target illuminating radar رادار اضاءة الهدف
*rādār iḍā'at al-hadaf*
target illumination إضاءة الهدف
*iḍā'at al-hadaf*
target information معلومات عن الهدف
*maʿlūmāt ʿan al-hadaf*
targeting إتخاذ الهدف
*ittikhādh al-hadaf*
target location موقع الهدف
*mawqiʿ al-hadaf*
target-location data بيانات موقع الهدف
*bayānāt mawqiʿ al-hadaf*
target not understood! الهدف لم يتعين !
*al-hadaf lam yataʿayyan*
target practice تدريب على الرمي
*tadrīb ʿalar-ramī*
target range ميدان الرمي . مدى الرمي
*maydān ar-ramī · madā ar-ramī*
target range rate معدل مدى الرمي
*muʿaddal madā ar-ramī*
target surveillance إستطلاع الهدف
*istiṭlāʿ al-hadaf*
target-tracking تتبع الهدف
*tatabbuʿ al-hadaf*
target tracking beam شعاع تتبع الهدف
*shuʿāʿ tatabbuʿ al-hadaf*
target tracking computer كومبيوتر تتبع الهدف
*kumbyūtar tatabbuʿ al-hadaf*
target training تدريب الرمي
*tadrīb ar-ramī*
target understood! تعيّن الهدف !
*taʿayyana al-hadaf*
Tartar SAM صاروخ سطح ـ جو « تارتر »
*ṣārūkh saṭḥ-jaww tārtar*
task force قوة واجب معين
*qūwat wājib muʿayyan*
taxiway مدرج
*madraj*
taxying-out درجان
*darajān*
teamwork تعاون . عمل جماعي
*taʿāwun · ʿamal jamāʿī*
tear gas غاز مسيل للدموع
*ghāz musīl lid-dumūʿ*
tear gas grenade قنبلة غاز مسيل للدموع
*qunbulat ghāz musīl lid-dumūʿ*
tear gas throwing tube ماسورة قذف الغاز المسيل للدموع
*masūrat qadhf al-ghāz al-musīl lid-dumūʿ*
technical stores تموينات فنية
*tamwīnāt fannīya*
technology علم التقنية تكنولوجيا
*ʿilm at-taqniya · taknulūjiya*
telegraph مبرقة . تلغراف
*mibraqa · talighrāf*
telephone cable كبل هاتفي
*kabl hātifī*

T

telephone call مكالمة هاتفية
*mukālama hātifīya*
teleprinter طابعة عن بعد
*ṭābiʿa ʿan buʿd*
teleprocessing support دعم التحليل عن بعد
*daʿm at-taḥlīl ʿan buʿd*
telescope مقراب . تلسكوب
*miqrāb · talskūb*
telescopic butt عقب بندقية متداخل
*ʿuqb bunduqīya mutadākhil*
telescopic hangar door باب حظيرة متداخل
*bāb ḥaẓīra mutadākhil*
telescopic helicopter hangar حظيرة طائرات عمودية متداخلة
*ḥaẓīrat ṭāʾirāt ʿamūdīya mutadākhila*
telescopic mast صاري متداخل
*ṣārī mutadākhil*
telescopic sight مهداف تلسكوبي
*mihdāf talskūbī*
television monitor جهاز مراقبة تلفزيوني
*jihāz murāqaba talafizyūnī*
telex machine جهاز تلكس . مبرقة كاتبة
*jihāz tiliks · mibraqa kātiba*
temporary camp معسكر مؤقت
*muʿaskar muʾaqqat*
temporary deck سطح مؤقت
*saṭḥ muʾaqqat*
tent خيمة
*khayma*
Tercom guidance system نظام توجيه « تيركوم »
*niẓām tawjīh tirkum*
terminal attack height ارتفاع هجومي ختامي
*irtifāʿ hujūmī khitāmī*
terminal homing missile صاروخ موجّه ختامي
*ṣārūkh muwajjah khitāmī*
terrain تربة . تراب . أرض
*turba · turāb · arḍ*
terrain contour matching ملاءمة كنتور التضاريس
*mulāʾamat kuntūr at-taḍārīs*
terrain-following radar رادار متتبع للأرض
*rādār mutatabbiʿ lil-arḍ*
Terrier SAM صاروخ سطح ـ جو « تيريار »
*ṣārūkh saṭḥ-jaww tiryar*
Territorial Militia حرس وطني اقليمي
*ḥaras waṭanī iqlīmī*
terrorist إرهابي
*irhābī*
terrorist weapon سلاح ارهابي
*silāḥ irhabī*
Teruel rocket صاروخ « تريل »
*ṣārūkh tiril*
Teseo launcher قاذفة « تيسيو »
*qādhifat tisayū*
Teseo SSM صاروخ سطح ـ سطح « تيسيو »
*ṣārūkh saṭḥ-saṭḥ tisayū*
test إختبار . تجربة . فحص
*ikhtibār · tajriba · faḥṣ*
test-bed فرشة اختبار
*farshat ikhtibār*
test firing رمي تجريبي
*ramī tajrībī*
test gear أدوات الاختبار
*adawāt al-ikhtibār*
tetanus كُزاز
*kuzāz*
TG-2 command guidance توجيه قيادي « تي جي ـ ٢ »
*tawjīh qiyādī tī jī – ithnayn*
TG 125 turret برج « تي جي ١٢٥ »
*burj tī jī miʾa wa khamsa wa ʿishrīn*
TH-55 helicopter طائرة عمودية « تي اتش ـ ٥٥ »
*ṭāʾira ʿamūdīya tī itsh khamsa wa khamsīn*
Thailand تايلاند
*tāyland*
theatre area missile صاروخ مسرح العمليات
*ṣārūkh masraḥ al-ʿamalīyāt*
theatre missile system شبكة صواريخ مسرح العمليات
*shabakat sawārīkh masraḥ al-ʿamalīyāt*
theatre target هدف بمسرح العمليات
*hadaf bi-masraḥ al-ʿamalīyāt*
thermal battery بطارية حرارية
*baṭṭārīya ḥarārīya*
thermal imager مصور حراري
*muṣawwir ḥarārī*
thermal imagery periscope منظار أفق تصويري حراري
*minẓār ufuq taṣwīrī ḥarārī*
thermal imaging تصوير حراري
*taṣwīr ḥarārī*
thermal powered بالطاقة الحرارية
*biṭ-ṭāqa al-ḥarārīya*
thermal sight مهداف حراري
*mihdāf ḥarārī*
thermal sleeve كم حراري
*kumm ḥarārī*
thermonuclear warhead رأس قذيفة نووية حرارية
*raʾs qadhīfa nawawīya ḥarārīya*

T

Thin Skin radar — رادار « ثين سكين »
*rādār thin skin*

Thiokol rocket — صاروخ « ثيوكول »
*ṣārūkh thiyukūl*

Thomaston sea transporter — ناقلة بحرية « توماستون »
*nāqila baḥrīya tumastun*

Thomson-CSF radar — رادار « تومسون ـ سي اس اف »
*rādār tumsun sī is if*

Thorn-EMI (Co) — شركة « ثورن ـ ئي ام اي »
*sharikat thūrn ī im āyy*

Thornycroft patrol craft — سفينة خفر السواحل « ثورنيكروفت »
*safīnat khafar as-sawāḥil thūrnikruft*

Thor ramjet — محرك نفاث ضغاطي « ثور »
*muḥarrik naffāth ḍughāṭī thūr*

threat — تهديد . إنذار
*tahdīd · indhār*

threat evaluation system — نظام تقييم الانذارات
*niẓām taqyīm al-indhārāt*

threat library — مكتبة انذارات
*maktabat indhārāt*

threat-warning ESM — إجراء دعم إلكتروني للانذار التهديدي
*ijrā' da'm iliktrūnī lil-indhār at-tahdīdī*

three-round burst — دفعة ثلاثية الطلقات
*daf'a thulāthīyat aṭ-ṭalaqāt*

Thresher submarine — غواصة « ثريشر »
*ghawwāṣat thrishar*

through-deck — سطح بيني
*saṭḥ baynī*

through-deck cruiser — طرادة بسطح بيني
*ṭarrāda bi-saṭḥ baynī*

thrust reverser — عاكس الدفع
*'ākis ad-daf'*

thrust vectoring — توجيه الدفع
*tawjīh ad-daf'*

thrust/weight ratio — نسبة الدفع الى الوزن
*nisbat ad-daf' ilal-wazn*

thumb-controlled — محكوم بالابهام
*maḥkūm bil-ibhām*

Thunderbird SAM — صاروخ سطح ـ جو « ثندربيرد »
*ṣārūkh saṭḥ-jaww thandarbird*

Thunderbolt 11 fighter — طائرة مقاتلة « ثندربولت ١١ »
*ṭā'ira muqātila thandarbūlt aḥada 'ashar*

Thunderflash missile — صاروخ « ثندرفلاش »
*ṣārūkh thandarflāsh*

Tica Communications — نظام الاتصالات « تيكا »
*niẓām al-ittiṣālāt tīka*

Ticonderoga cruiser — طرادة « تيكوندروجا »
*ṭarrādat tikundirūga*

Tiger 11 fighter — طائرة مقاتلة « تايجر ١١ »
*ṭā'ira muqātila tāygar aḥada 'ashar*

Tigercat Sam — صاروخ سطح ـ جو « تايجركات »
*ṣārūkh saṭḥ-jaww tāygarkāt*

Tigereye aircraft — طائرة « تايجر أي »
*ṭā'ira tāygar āyy*

Tiger fighter — طائرة مقاتلة « تايجر »
*ṭā'ira muqātila tāygar*

Tigerfish torpedo — طوربيد « تايجرفش »
*ṭūrbīd tāygarfish*

Tiger-shark fighter — طائرة مقاتلة « تايجر ـ شارك »
*ṭā'ira muqātila tāygar-shārk*

tilt cab truck — شاحنة بكابينة قلابة
*shāḥina bi-kābīna qallāba*

time — وقت . زمن
*waqt · zaman*

time delayed — معوق زمنياً
*mu'awwaq zamanīyan*

time-domain analysis — تحليل المجال الزمني
*taḥlīl al-majāl az-zamanī*

time slot — فاصل زمني
*fāṣil zamanī*

Timsah patrol boat — سفينة خفر سواحل « تمسا »
*safīnat khafar sawāḥil timsā*

tip station — محطة طرفية
*maḥaṭṭa ṭarafīya*

Tirailleur AAM — صاروخ جو ـ جو « تيرايار »
*ṣārūkh jaww-jaww tirāyar*

Tiseo EO sensor — جهاز احساس « تيسايو ئي اوه »
*jihāz iḥsās tisayū ī aw*

Titan 11 missile — صاروخ « تايتن ١١ »
*ṣārūkh tāytan aḥada 'ashar*

titanium alloy — سبيكة تيتانيوم
*sabīkat tītānyūm*

titanium hub — صُرة تيتانيوم
*ṣurrat tītānyūm*

TM 1226 radar — رادار « تي ام ١٢٢٦ »
*rādār tī im alf wa mi'atayn wa sitta wa 'ishrīn*

TMS-65 vehicle — مركبة « تي ام اس ـ ٦٥ »
*markabat tī im is – khamsa wa sittīn*

TN21 spotlight — ضوء كشاف تي ان ٢١
*ḍaw' kashshāf tī in wāḥid wa 'ishrīn*

TN37 automatic transmission — نظام آلي لنقل الحركة « تي ان ٣٧ »
*niẓām ālī li-naql al-ḥaraka tī in sab'a wa thalāthīn*

TNC-45 craft — سفينة « تي ان سي - ٤٥ »
*safīnat tī in sī – khamsa wa arbaʿīn*

TNT — ت . ن . ت
*tī in tī*

Togo — توغو
*tūghū*

Tokarev rifle — بندقية « توكاريف »
*bunduqīyat tūkariv*

Token radar — رادار « توكين »
*rādār tūkin*

TOMAK sonar — سونار « توماك »
*sūnār tūmāk*

Tomcat fighter — طائرة مقاتلة « تومكات »
*ṭāʾira muqātila tumkat*

Tomahawk Cruise missile — صاروخ كروز « توماهوك »
*ṣārūkh krūz tumahūk*

Tong Feng missile — صاروخ « تونج فينج »
*ṣārūkh tung fing*

Ton minesweeper — كاسحة ألغام « طن »
*kāsiḥat alghām ṭan*

tool box — صندوق العدة
*ṣundūq al- ʿidda*

tool kit — حقيبة أدوات
*ḥaqībat adawāt*

tools — عدد و أدوات
*ʿudad wa adawāt*

toothed belt — سير مسنن
*sayr musannan*

Top Bow radar — رادار « توپ بو »
*rādār tup buw*

Top Hat ECM — إجراء مضاد الكتروني « توپ هات »
*ijrāʾ muḍādd iliktrūnī tup hat*

Top Knot navigation — ملاحة « توپ نوت »
*milāḥa tūp nūt*

Top Pair 3D radar — رادار « توپ پير ٣ دي »
*rādār tup payr thalātha dī*

top priority — أولوية قصوى
*awlawīya quṣwā*

Top Sail 3D radar — رادار « توپ سيل ٣ دي »
*rādār tup sayl thalātha dī*

top secret — سرّي للغاية
*sirrī lil-ghāya*

top speed — السرعة القصوى
*as-surʿa al-quṣwā*

Top Steer 3D radar — رادار « توپ ستير ٣ دي »
*rādār tup stīr thalātha dī*

Top-Trough radar — رادار « توپ تروف »
*rādār tup truf*

Tornado aircraft — طائرة « تورنيدو »
*ṭāʾirat turnaydū*

Tornado system — نظام « تورنيدو »
*niẓām turnaydū*

torpedo — طوربيد
*ṭūrbīd*

torpedo attack craft — سفينة هجوم بالطوربيد
*safīnat hujūm bit-ṭūrbīd*

torpedo battery — بطارة طوربيد
*baṭṭārīyat ṭūrbīd*

torpedo boat — زورق طوربيد
*zawraq ṭūrbīd*

torpedo fire-control system — نظام السيطرة على قذف الطوربيد
*niẓām as-sayṭara ʿala qadhf aṭ-ṭūrbīd*

torpedo tube — ماسورة طوربيد
*māsūrat ṭūrbīd*

torsion bar — قضيب التوائي
*qaḍīb iltiwāʾī*

total radiation — إشعاع كامل
*ishʿāʿ kāmil*

total strength — قوة كاملة  متانة كاملة
*qūwa kāmila · matāna kāmila*

Totem optronic fire control — جهاز بصري الكتروني توتم للتحكم باطلاق النار
*jihāz basarī iliktrūni tūtam lit-taḥakkum bi-iṭlāq an-nār*

towed — مقطور
*maqṭūr*

towed artillery — مدفعية مقطورة
*midfaʿīya maqṭūra*

towed buoy — عوامة مقطورة
*ʿawwāma maqṭūra*

towed sonar — سونار مقطور
*sūnār maqṭūr*

towing gear — معدات القطر
*muʿaddāt al-qaṭr*

towing hook — خطاف القطر
*khaṭṭāf al-qaṭr*

towing rig — تجهيزات القطر
*tajhīzāt al-qaṭr*

TOW launcher — قاذفة « تو »
*qādhifat tū*

TOW missile — صاروخ « تو »
*ṣārūkh tū*

toxic — سام
*sāmm*

toxic agent — مادة سامة
*mādda sāmma*

toxic fumes — دخان سام
*dukhān sāmm*

toxic gas — غاز سام
*ghāz sāmm*

TP-61 torpedo طوربيد « تي پي ـ ٦١ »
*ṭūrbīd tī pī – wāḥid wa sittīn*
TPQ-36 radar رادار « تي پي كيو ـ ٣٦ »
*rādār tī pī kyū – sitta wa thalāthīn*
TPQ 37 radar رادار « تي پي كيو ٣٧ »
*rādār tī pī kyū sabʿa wa thalāthīn*
TR-1A aircraft طائرة « تي أر ـ ١ ايه »
*ṭāʾirat tī ār – wāḥid ayy*
TR-1400 submarine غواصة « تي أر ـ ١٤٠٠ »
*ghawwāṣat tī ār – alf wa arbaʿ miʾa*
TR-1700 submarine غواصة « تي أر ـ ١٧٠٠ »
*ghawwāṣat tī ār – alf wa sabʿ miʾa*
tracer طلقة خطاطة
*ṭalaqa khaṭṭāṭa*
track درب . سكة . أثر
*darb · sikka · athar*
tracked amphibious vehicle مركبة برمائية مجنزرة
*markaba barmaʾīya mujanzara*
tracked carrier ناقلة مجنزرة
*nāqila mujanzara*
Tracked Rapier system نظام صواريخ « ريپيار » المتتبعة
*niẓām ṣawārīkh raypyar al-mutatabbaʿa*
Tracker aircraft طائرة « تراكر »
*ṭāʾirat trākar*
Tracker patrol craft سفينة خفر سواحل « تراكر »
*safīnat khafr sawāḥil trākar*
track file مسار تتبع
*masār tatabbuʿ*
tracking تتبع . تعقب
*tatabbuʿ · taʿaqqub*
tracking adjunct system نظام تتبع مساعد
*niẓām tatabbuʿ musāʿid*
tracking equipment معدات المتابعة
*muʿaddāt al-mutābaʿa*
tracking processor جهاز تحليل التتبع
*jihāz taḥlīl at-tatabbuʿ*
tracking radar رادار تتبع . رادار متابعة
*rādār tatabbuʿ · rādār mutābaʿa*
tracking sight مهداف متابعة
*mihdāf mutābaʿa*
tracking station محطة تتبع
*muḥaṭṭat tatabbuʿ*
Trader transport aircraft طائرة نقل « تريدر »
*ṭāʾirat naql traydar*
Trafalgar submarine غواصة « ترافالجر »
*ghawwāṣat trafālgar*
traffic control مراقبة المرور
*murāqabat al-murūr*
trail badge شارة الجر
*shārat al-jarr*
trailer-mounted مركب على مقطورة
*murakkab ʿala maqṭūra*
trained مُدَرَّب . متمرس
*mudarrab · mutamarras*
trainee جندي تحت التدريب
*jundī taḥt at-tadrīb*
trainer مُدَرِّبٌ
*mudarrib*
trainer aircraft طائرة تدريب
*ṭāʾirat tadrīb*
training تدريب
*tadrīb*
training aid معين تدريب
*muʿīn tadrīb*
training alert إنذار تدريب
*indhār tadrīb*
training base قاعدة تدريب
*qāʿidat tadrīb*
training battalion كتيبة تدريب
*katībat tadrīb*
training camp معسكر تدريب
*muʿaskar tadrīb*
training centre مركز تدريب
*markaz tadrīb*
training company سرية تدريب
*sarīyat tadrīb*
training cost تكلفة التدريب
*taklifat at-tadrīb*
training development تطوير التدريب
*taṭwīr at-tadrīb*
training device أداة تدريب
*adāt tadrīb*
training exercise مناورة تدريبية
*munāwara tadrībīya*
training ground أرض التدريب
*arḍ at-tadrīb*
training mission مهمة تدريبية
*muhimma tadrībīya*
training of recruits تدريب المجندين
*tadrīb al-mujannadīn*
training ship سفينة تدريب
*safīnat tadrīb*
training sortie هجوم تدريبي
*hujūm tadrībī*

T

training system نظام التدريب
*niẓām at-tadrīb*
training unit وحدة تدريب
*wiḥdat tadrīb*
trajectory مسار المقذوف
*masār al-maqdhūf*
trajectory mode نمط مسار المقذوف
*namaṭ masār al-maqdhūf*
transceiver جهاز ارسال و استقبال
*jihāz irsāl wa istiqbāl*
transfer نقل . ترحيل . تحويل
*naql · tarḥīl · taḥwīl*
transit case مريض عابر
*marīḍ ʿābir*
transit hospital مستشفى ترحيل
*mustashfa tarḥīl*
transmission تحويل . نقل .
*taḥwīl · naql*
transmit أرسل . حول . أذاع . نقل
*arsāla · ḥawwala · adhāʿa · naqala*
transmitted power طاقة منقولة
*ṭāqa manqūla*
transmitter مرسل . جهاز ارسال
*mursil · jihāz irsāl*
transonic acceleration تسارع حول الصوتية
*tasāruʿ ḥaw laṣ-ṣawtīya*
transonic speed سرعة حول الصوتية
*surʿat haw laṣ-ṣawtīya*
transponder-code position وضع شفرة الجهاز المرسل المستجيب
*wadʿ shifrat al-jihāz al-mursil al-mustajīb*
transport نقل . إنتقال
*naql · intiqāl*
transport duty مهمة النقل
*muhimmat an-naql*
transporter ناقلة . طائرة نقل
*nāqila · ṭāʾirat naql*
transport helicopter طائرة نقل عمودية
*ṭāʾirat naql ʿamūdīya*
transport/launching container حاوية نقل / إطلاق
*ḥāwīyat naql/iṭlāq*
transport squadron سرب نقل
*sirb naql*
transport submarine غواصة نقل
*ghawwāṣat naql*
Trap Door SSM صاروخ سطح ـ سطح « تراپ دور »
*ṣārūkh saṭḥ saṭḥ trāp dūr*
trapped وقع في شرك
*waqaʿa fi sharak*

travel allowance بدل سفر
*badal safar*
travelling lock قفل الحركة
*qifl al-ḥaraka*
travelling-wave tube أنبوب الموجة المتنقلة
*unbūb al-mawja al-mutanaqqila*
traverse عارضة . معترضة . واقية شظايا
*ʿāriḍa · muʿtariḍa · wāqīyat shaẓāya*
tread of tyre مداس الاطار
*madās al-iṭār*
treason خيانة
*khiyāna*
treatment معالجة . معاملة
*muʿālaja · muʿāmala*
treaty معاهدة . إتفاق
*muʿāhada · ittifāq*
trench خندق . حفرة
*khandaq · ḥufra*
trench warfare حرب الخنادق
*ḥarb al-khanādiq*
Triad سياسة دفاع ثلاثي أمريكية
*siyāsat difāʿ thulāthī amrīkīya*
trial تجربة . إختبار
*tajriba · ikhtibār*
trial unit وحدة تجريبية
*wiḥda tajrībīya*
tricycle landing gear مهبطة ثلاثية العجلات
*mihbaṭa thulāthīyat al-ʿajalāt*
Trident missile صاروخ « ترايدنت »
*ṣārūkh trāydant*
trigger زناد
*zinād*
trigger actuator محرك الزناد
*muḥarrik az-zinād*
trigger group مجموعة الزناد
*majmūʿat az-zinād*
trigger mechanism آلية الزناد
*ālīyat az-zinād*
Trilux sight مهداف « ترايلوكس »
*mihdāf trāyluks*
trim-boards ألواح تهذيب
*alwāḥ tahdhīb*
Trinidad and Tobago ترنداد وطوباغو
*trinīdād wa ṭubāghū*
tripartite ثلاثي . ثلاثي الأطراف
*thulāthī · thulāthī al-aṭrāf*
tripartite mine launcher قاذفة ألغام ثلاثية
*qādhifat alghām thulāthīya*

triple-channel قناة ثلاثية
*qanāh thulāthīya*
triple-ejector rack حامل القاذف الثلاثي
*ḥāmil al-qādhif ath-thulāthī*
triple launcher قاذفة ثلاثية
*qādhifa thulāthīya*
triple turret برج ثلاثي
*burj thulāthī*
trip wire سلك فصل
*silk faṣl*
Triton radar رادار ترايتن
*rādār trāytan*
TRMS radar رادار « تي أر ان اس »
*rādār tī ār īm is*
TROIJA system نظام « ترويجا »
*niẓām truwija*
Tromp destroyer مدمرة « ترومپ »
*mudammirat trump*
troop جماعة
*jamāʿa*
troop accommodation ثكنة الجنود
*thuknat al-junūd*
troop carrier ناقلة جنود
*nāqilat junūd*
troop concentration حشد الجنود
*hashd al-junūd*
troop deployment نشر الجنود
*nashr al-junūd*
trooping the colour تحية العلم
*taḥīyat al-ʿalam*
troop movements تحركات الجنود
*taḥarrukāt al-junūd*
troop review تفقد الجنود
*tafaqqud al-junūd*
troop-to-vehicle ratio نسبة الجنود إلى المركبة
*nisbat al-junūd ilal-markaba*
troop transport نقل الجنود
*naql al-junūd*
troop transport vessel سفينة نقل الجنود
*safīnat naql al-junūd*
trouser سروال بنطلون
*sirwāl · banṭalūn*
truce هدنة . مهادنة
*hudna · muhādana*
truck شاحنة
*shāḥina*
truck-mounted ramp رصيف مركب على شاحنة
*raṣīf murakkab ʿala shāḥina*
trumpeter بواق . بوقي
*bawwāq · būqī*
trunnion cant ميل مركز الدوران
*mayl markaz ad-dawarān*
trunnion tilt إنحدار مركز الدوران
*inḥidār markaz ad-dawarān*
Truxtun cruiser طرادة « تروكستون »
*ṭarrādat trukstan*
Try Add radar رادار « تراي أد »
*rādār trāyy ād*
T-shirt قميص خارجي
*qamīṣ khārijī*
TSR333 radar رادار « تي اس أر ٣٣٣ »
*rādār tī is ār thalāth miʾa wa thalāth wa thalāthīn*
Tu-16 bomber طائرة قاذفة « تي يو - ١٦ »
*ṭāʾira qādhifa tī yū – sittata ʿashar*
Tu-20 aircraft طائرة « تي يو - ٢٠ »
*ṭāʾirat tī yū – ʿishrīn*
Tu-22 bomber طائرة قاذفة « تي يو - ٢٢ »
*ṭāʾira qādhifa tī yū – ithnayn wa ʿishrīn*
Tu-26 bomber طائرة قاذفة « تي يو - ٢٦ »
*ṭāʾira qādhifa tī yū – sitta wa ʿishrīn*
Tu-28P fighter طائرة مقاتلة « تي يو - ٢٨ بي »
*ṭāʾira mūqatila tī yū thamānya wa ʿishrīn pī*
Tu-95 bomber طائرة قاذفة « تي يو - ٩٥ »
*ṭāʾira qādhifa tī yū – khamsa wa tisʿīn*
Tu-124 aircraft طائرة « تي يو - ١٢٤ »
*ṭāʾirat tī yū – miʾa wa arbaʿa wa ʿishrīn*
Tu-126 AWAC aircraft طائرة « تي يو - ١٢٦ ايه دبليو ايه سي »
*ṭāʾirat tī yū miʾa wa sitta wa ʿishriṇ – ayy dablyū ayy sī*
Tu-128 aircraft طائرة « تي يو - ١٢٨ »
*ṭāʾirat tī yū – miʾa wa thamānya wa ʿishrīn*
Tu-142 aircraft طائرة « تي يو - ١٤٢ »
*ṭāʾirat tī yū – miʾa wa ithnayn wa arbaʿīn*
tube cutter مقطِّع أنابيب
*muqaṭṭiʿ anābīb*
Tullibee submarine غواصة « تولبي »
*ghawwāṣat tulibī*
tunic سترة قصيرة
*sitra qaṣīra*
Tunisia تونس
*tūnis*

T

Tunisian تونسي
*tūnisī*

tunnel نفق
*nafaq*

tunnel vision رؤية نفقية
*ru'ya nafaqīya*

Tupolev (Co) شركة توبولف
*sharikat tūpuliv*

turbine تربين
*turbīn*

turbine powered يعمل بالتربين
*yā'mal bit-turbīn*

Turbo-commander air transporter طائرة نقل « توربوكومّاندر »
*ṭā'irat naql turbū kumāndar*

turboelectric كهروتربيني
*kahrū turbīnī*

turbofan مروحة تربينية
*mirwaḥa turbīnīya*

turbojet طائرة نفاثة تربينية
*ṭā'ira naffātha turbīnīya*

turbojet propulsion دفع تربيني نفاث
*daf' turbīnī naffāth*

Turbomèca engine محرك « تيربوسيكا »
*muḥarrik turbūmika*

Turbo-Porter aircraft طائرة « توربو - بورتر »
*ṭā'irat turbū-pūrtar*

turbo-prop محرك مروحي تربيني
*muḥarrik mirwaḥī turbīnī*

turbo-ramjet engine محرك نفاث ضغاطي تربيني
*muḥarrik naffāth ḍughāṭī turbīnī*

turbo-trainer طائرة تدريب نفاثة تربينية
*ṭā'irat tadrīb naffātha turbīnīya*

Turkey تركيا
*turkiya*

Turkish تركي
*turkī*

turn-around time زمن الاعْداد لدورة تالية
*zaman al-i'dād li-dawra tālīya*

turntable منضدة دوارة
*minḍada dawwāra*

turret برج
*burj*

turret roof سطح برجي
*saṭḥ burjī*

Turya ship سفينة « تريا »
*safīnat tarya*

TV3-117A turboshaft عمود إدارة تربيني « تي في ٣ - ١١٧ ايه »
*'amūd idāra turbīnī – tī vī thalātha – mi'a wa sab'ata 'ashar ayy*

TV camera آلة تصوير تلفزيوني
*ālat taṣwīr talafizyūnī*

TV gun director موجه مدفع تلفزيوني
*muwajjih midfa' talafizyūnī*

TV homing نظام توجيه تلفزيوني
*niẓām tawjīh talafizyūnī*

TV sensor جهاز احساس تلفزيوني
*jihāz iḥsās talafizyūnī*

twin-barrel ماسورة مزدوجة
*māsūra muzdawija*

twin-cockpit حجرة طيار مزدوجة
*ḥujrat ṭayyār muzdawija*

twin-disc drive محرك مزدوج القرص
*muḥarrik muzdawij al-qurṣ*

twin-engine محرك مزدوج
*muḥarrik muzdawij*

twin-engined مزدوج المحركات
*muzdawij al-muḥarrikat*

twin-jet ذات محركين نفاثين
*dhāt muḥarrikayn naffāthayn*

twin launcher قاذفة مزدوجة
*qādhifa muzdawija*

Twin Otter aircraft طائرة « توين أوتر »
*ṭā'irat twin utar*

twin shaft مزدوج أعمدة الادارة
*muzdawij a'midat al-idāra*

twist فتل . برم . لوى
*fatala · barama · lawa*

two-man crew طقم من فردين
*ṭaqm min fardayn*

two seat trainer طائرة تدريب بمقعدين
*ṭā'irat tadrīb bi-maq'adayn*

two-stage مزدوج المرحلة
*muzdawij al-marḥala*

Tyne cruising gas turbine تربين غازي للابحار « تاين »
*tūrbīn ghāzī lil-ibḥār tāyn*

Type 21 frigate فرقاطة طراز ٢١
*firqāṭa ṭirāz wāḥid wa 'ishrīn*

Type 22 frigate فرقاطة طراز ٢٢
*firqāṭa ṭirāz ithnayn wa 'ishrīn*

Type 50 sub-machine gun رشاش قصير طراز ٥٠
*rashshāsh qaṣīr ṭirāz khamsīn*

Type 54 sub-machine gun رشاش قصير طراز ٥٤
*rashshāsh qaṣīr ṭirāz arbaʿa wa khamsīn*

Type 56 rifle بندقية طراز ٥٦
*bunduqīya ṭirāz sitta wa khamsīn*

Type 60 rifle بندقية طراز ٦٠
*bunduqīya ṭirāz sittīn*

Type 61 tank دبابة طراز ٦١
*dabbāba ṭirāz wāḥid wa sittīn*

Type 63 tank دبابة طراز ٦٣
*dabbāba ṭirāz thalātha wa sittīn*

Type 74 tank دبابة طراز ٧٤
*dabbāba ṭirāz arbaʿa wa sabʿīn*

Type 75 howitzer مدفع هاوتزر طراز ٧٥
*midfaʿ hāwitsar ṭirāz khamsa wa sabʿīn*

Type 82 destroyer مدمرة طراز ٨٢
*mudammira ṭirāz ithnayn wa thamānīn*

Type 143 patrol boat سفينة خفر سواحل طراز ١٤٣
*safīnat khafar sawāḥil ṭirāz miʾa wa thalātha wa arbaʿīn*

Type 184 sonar سونار طراز ١٨٤
*sūnār ṭirāz miʾa wa arbaʿa wa thamānīn*

Type 197 sonar سونار طراز ١٩٧
*sūnār tirāz miʾa wa sabʿa wa tisʿīn*

Type 205 submarine غواصة طراز ٢٠٥
*ghawwāṣa ṭirāz miʾatayn wa khamsa*

Type 206 submarine غواصة طراز ٢٠٦
*ghawwāṣa ṭirāz miʾatayn wa sitta*

Type 207 submarine غواصة طراز ٢٠٧
*ghawwāṣa ṭirāz miʾatayn wa sabʿa*

Type 209 submarine غواصة طراز ٢٠٩
*ghawwāṣa ṭirāz miʾatayn wa tisʿa*

Type 963 radar رادار طراز ٩٦٣
*rādār ṭirāz tisʿ miʾa wa thalātha wa sittīn*

Type 993 radar رادار طراز ٩٩٣
*rādār ṭirāz tisʿ miʾa wa thalātha wa tisʿīn*

Type 1006 radar رادار طراز ١٠٠٦
*rādār ṭirāz alf wa sitta*

Type 2001 sonar سونار طراز ٢٠٠١
*sūnār ṭirāz alfayn wa wāḥid*

Type 2016 sonar سونار طراز ٢٠١٦
*sūnār ṭirāz alfayn wa sittata ʿashar*

Type 2019 sonar سونار طراز ٢٠١٩
*sūnār ṭirāz alfayn wa tisʿata ʿashar*

Type 2020 sonar سونار طراز ٢٠٢٠
*sūnār ṭirāz alfayn wa ʿishrīn*

Type 2024 towed sonar سونار مقطور طراز ٢٠٢٤
*sūnār maqṭūr ṭirāz alfayn wa arbaʿa wa ʿishrīn*

Type 2400 submarine غواصة طراز ٢٤٠٠
*ghawwāṣa ṭirāz alfayn wa arbaʿ miʾa*

Typhon تايفون
*tāyfun*

Typhoon submarine غواصة « تايفون »
*ghawwāṣat tāyfūn*

tyre إطار
*iṭār*

tyre-pressure regulation تنظيم ضغط الاطار
*tanẓīm ḍaghṭ al-iṭār*

T

# U

U-2 aircraft — طائرة « يو ـ ٢ »
*ṭā'irat yū-ithnayn*

U-21 aircraft — طائرة « يو ـ ٢١ »
*ṭā'irat yū-wāḥid wa ʿishrīn*

U206 Station Air aircraft — طائرة « يو ـ ٢٠٦ ستيشن أير »
*ṭā'irat yū mi'atayn wa sitta stayshin ayr*

U-206C aircraft — طائرة « يو ـ ٢٠٦ سي »
*ṭā'irat yū-mi'atayn wa sitta sī*

UBC-40 armoured car — عربة مدرعة « يو بي سي ـ ٤٠ »
*ʿaraba mudarraʿa yū bī sī arbaʿīn*

Udaloy cruiser — طرادة اودالو ي
*ṭarrādat ūdaluwi*

Uganda — أوغندا
*ūghanda*

UGM-27 missile — صاروخ « يو جي ام ـ ٢٧ »
*ṣārūkh yū jī im sabʿa wa ʿishrīn*

UGM-73 missile — صاروخ « يو جي ام ـ ٧٣ »
*ṣārūkh yū jī im thalātha wa sabʿīn*

UGM-84 missile — صاروخ « يو جي ام ـ ٨٤ »
*ṣārūkh yū jī im arbaʿa wa thamānīn*

UGM-93 missile — صاروخ « يو جي ام ـ ٩٣ »
*ṣārūkh yū jī im thalātha wa tisʿīn*

Ugra ship — سفينة « يوجرا »
*safīnat yūgra*

UH-1 helicopter — طائرة عمودية « يو اتش ـ ١ »
*ṭā'ira ʿamūdīya yū itsh – wāḥid*

UH-1H aircraft — طائرة « يو اتش ـ ١ اتش »
*ṭā'ira ʿamūdīya yū itsh – wāḥid itsh*

UH-2A helicopter — طائرة عمودية « يو اتش ـ ٢ ايه »
*ṭā'ira ʿamūdīya yū itsh – ithnayn ayy*

UH-12E helicopter — طائرة عمودية « يو اتش ـ ١٢ ئي »
*ṭā'ira ʿamūdīya yū itsh – ithnata ʿashar ī*

UH-46 helicopter — طائرة عمودية « يو اتش ـ ٤٦ »
*ṭā'ira ʿamūdīya yū itsh – sitta wa arbaʿīn*

UH-60 helicopter — طائرة عمودية « يو اتش ـ ٦٠ »
*ṭā'ira ʿamūdīya yū itsh – sittīn*

UHF — تردد فوق العالي
*taraddud fawq al-ʿālī*

UHF homer — موجّه بالتردد فوق العالي
*muwajjih bit-taraddud fawq al-ʿālī*

UHF radio — لاسلكي بالتردد فوق العالي
*lā-silkī bit-taraddud fawq al-ʿālī*

ultrafast camera — آلة تصوير عالية السرعة
*ālat taṣwīr ʿālīyat as-surʿa*

ultra-high frequency — تردد فوق العالي
*taraddud fawq al-ʿālī*

ultra-rapid — عالي السرعة
*ʿālī as-surʿa*

ultra-sonic — فوق الصوتي
*fawq aṣ-ṣawtī*

unarmed — اعزل . غير مسلح
*aʿzal · ghayr musallaḥ*

unarmed combat — قتال أعزل
*qitāl aʿzal*

unauthorized — محظور . غير جائز
*maḥẓūr · ghayr jā'iz*

unconditional surrender — إستسلام بلا شروط
*istislām bilā shurūṭ*

undercarriage — المهبطة
*al-mihbaṭa*

under escort — تحت الحراسة
*taḥt al-ḥirāsa*

under fire — تحت النار
*taḥt an-nār*

underfuselage أسفل جذع الطائرة
*asfal judhʿ aṭ-ṭāʾira*
underfuselage hardpoint النقطة الصلبة أسفل جذع الطائرة
*an-nuqṭa aṣ-ṣaliba asfal judhʿ aṭ-ṭāʾira*
under-ground تحت الأرض
*taḥt al-arḍ*
underground cable كبل ممدود تحت الأرض
*kabl mamdūd taḥt al-arḍ*
underwater تحت الماء
*taḥt al-māʾ*
underwater communication اتصال تحت الماء
*ittiṣāl taḥt al-māʾ*
underwater demolition نسف تحت الماء
*nasf taḥt al-māʾ*
underwater demolition team فريق النسف تحت الماء
*farīq an-nasf taḥt al-māʾ*
underwater disposal system نظام التصريف تحت الماء
*niẓām at-taṣrīf taḥt al-māʾ*
underwater fire control system نظام السيطرة على الرمي تحت الماء
*niẓām as-sayṭara ʿalar-ramī taḥt al-māʾ*
underwater launch إطلاق تحت الماء
*iṭlāq taḥt al-māʾ*
underwater noise ضجيج تحت الماء
*ḍajīj taḥt al-māʾ*
underwater radiated noise ضجيج مشع تحت الماء
*ḍajīj mushiʿʿ taḥt al-māʾ*
underwater telephone هاتف تحت الماء
*hātif taḥt al-māʾ*
underwater threat تهديد تحت الماء
*tahdīd taḥt al-māʾ*
underway replenishment تموين جاري
*tamwīn jārī*
underwing تحت الجناح
*taḥt al-janāḥ*
undetected غير مستبان
*ghayr mustabān*
undisciplined عديم الانتظام
*ʿadīm al-intiẓām*
unexploded bomb قنبلة غير متفجرة
*qunbula ghayr munfajira*
unfix bayonets! حراب - إنزع
*ḥirāb – inzaʿ*
unfriendly معادٍ
*muʿādi*
unguided rocket صاروخ غير موجه
*ṣārūkh ghayr muwajjah*

unit وحدة . مجموعة . جهاز
*wiḥda · majmūʿa · jihāz*
United Arab Emirates الامارات العربية المتحدة
*al-imārāt al-ʿarabīya al-muttaḥida*
United States الولايات المتحدة الأمريكية
*al-wilāyāt al-muttaḥida al-amrīkīya*
unit training تدريب الوحدة
*tadrīb al-wiḥda*
universal عام . شامل . عالمي
*ʿāmm · shāmil · ʿālamī*
unload أنزل . فرغ
*anzala · farragha*
unoccupied غير مشغول . غير محتل
*ghayr mashghūl · gahyr muḥtal*
unrefuelled sortie غارة غير معاد تزويدها بالوقود
*ghāra ghayr muʿād tazwīdiha bil-wuqud*
unsinkable لا تغرق
*lā yughraq*
unsophisticated بسيط
*basīṭ*
update تجديد
*tajdīd*
up-engined version طراز محسن المحرك
*ṭirāz muḥassan al-muḥarrik*
up-grading رفع الكفاية
*rafʿ al-kifāya*
Upholder submarine غواصة « أپهولدر »
*ghawwāṣat aphawldar*
upper deck السطح العلوي
*as-saṭḥ al-ʿulwī*
upper-surface blowing نفخ بالسطح الأعلى
*nafkh bis-saṭḥ al-aʿla*
up-to-date حديث
*ḥadīth*
Ural-375 truck شاحنة « يورال - ٣٧٥ »
*shāḥinat yūral – thalāth miʾa wa khamsa wa sabʿīn*
uranium fuel وقود يورانيوم
*wuqūd yūrānyum*
URN 6 navigation نظام الملاحة « يو آر ان ٦ »
*niẓām al-milāḥa yū ār in sitta*
URN-29 navigation نظام الملاحة « يو آر ان - ٢٩ »
*niẓām al-milāḥa yū ār in tisʿa wa ʿishrīn*

Uruguay اورغواي
*urughwāyy*
Urutu armoured carrier حاملة مدرعة « يوروتو »
*ḥāmila mudarrᶜa yurūtū*
US Air Force القوات الجوية الأمريكية
*al-qūwāt al-jawwīya al-amrīkīya*
USSR اتحاد الجمهوريات السوفيتية الاشتراكية
*ittiḥād al-jumhūrīyāt as-sufyitīya al-ishtirākīya*
utilities منافع . مرافق .
*manāfiᶜ · marāfiq*
utility helicopter طائرة عمودية للأغراض العامة
*ṭāʾira ᶜamūdīya lil-aghrāḍ al-ᶜāmma*
UV-18A aircraft طائرة « يو ڤي - ١٨ ايه »
*ṭāʾirat yū vī – thamānyata ᶜashar ayy*
UZI sub-machine gun رشاش قصير « يو زد آي »
*rashshāsh qaṣīr yū zid āyy*
Uzushio submarine غواصة « يوزوشو »
*ghawwāṣat uzūshū*

# V

6V-53T diesel — ديزل « ٦ ڤي ـ ٥٣ تي »
*dīzl sitta vī – thalātha wa khamsīn tī*

V-class submarine — غواصة طراز « ڤي »
*ghawwāṣa ṭirāz vī*

V3 Kukri AAM — صاروخ جو ـ جو « ڤي ٣ كوكري »
*sārūkh jaww-jaww vī thalātha kukri*

V-12 diesel engine — محرك ديزل « ڤي ـ ١٢ »
*muḥarrik dīzl vī – ithnata ʿashar*

V-14 helicopter — طائرة عمودية « ڤي ـ ١٤ »
*ṭāʾira ʿamūdīya vī – arbaʿata ʿashar*

V-150 gun — مدفع « ڤي ـ ١٥٠ »
*midfaʿ vī-miʾa wa khamsīn*

VAB personnel carrier — ناقلة أفراد ڤي ايه بي
*nāqilat afrād vī ayy bī*

VAB vehicle — مركبة « ڤي ايه بي »
*markabat vī ayy bī*

vaccinate — طعم
*taʿʿama*

vaccination — تطعيم
*taṭʿīm*

Valiant submarine — غواصة « ڤاليانت »
*ghawwāṣat valyant*

Valmet rifle — بندقية « ڤالمت »
*bunduqīyat valmit*

valve — صمام
*ṣimām*

vanguard — مقدمة القوات
*muqaddimat al-qūwāt*

Vanya minesweeper — كاسحة ألغام « ڤانيا »
*kāsiḥat alghām vānya*

variable camber — احديداب متنوع
*iḥdīdāb mutanawwiʿ*

variable camber wing — جناح متغير الاحديداب
*janāh mutaghayyir al-iḥdīdāb*

variable-depth — عمق متنوع
*ʿumq mutanawwiʿ*

variable depth sonar — سونار أعماق متنوعة
*sūnār aʿmāq mutanawwiʿa*

variable-geometry — ذو اجنحة متغيرة
*dhū ajniḥa mutaghayyira*

v-belt — سير مخروطي المقطع
*sayr makhrūṭī al-maqṭaʿ*

VC 10 airtransport — طائرة نقل « ڤي سي ١٠ »
*ṭāʾirat naql vī sī ʿashara*

VCC-1 vehicle — مركبة « ڤي سي سي ١ »
*markabat vī sī sī – wāḥid*

VDS housing — إطار « ڤي دي اس »
*iṭār vī dī is*

VDS system — نظام « ڤي دي اس »
*niẓām vī dī is*

vectored — موجه
*muwajjah*

vectoring thrust — دفع توجيهي
*dafʿ tawjīhī*

vehicle — مركبة . عربة
*markaba · ʿaraba*

vehicle deck — سطح العربات
*saṭḥ al-ʿarabāt*

vehicle fuel — وقود السيارات
*wuqūd as-sayyārāt*

vehicle parking area — منطقة وقوف المركبات
*minṭaqat wuqūf al-markabāt*

velocity — سرعة
*surʿa*

Veltro 2 aircraft — طائرة « ڤيلترو ٢ »
*ṭāʾirat viltrū ithnayn*

venereal disease — مرض تناسلي
*maraḍ tanāsulī*

Venezuela — ڤنزويلا
*vinzwīla*

Venezuelan — ڤنزويلي
*vinzwīlī*

ventilating system — نظام تهوية
*niẓam tahwiya*

V

ventral — بطني
*baṭnī*
ventral fin — زعنفة بطنية
*zi'nifa baṭnīya*
vertical aircraft — طائرة عمودية
*ṭā'ira 'amūdīya*
vertical camera — آلة تصوير عمودية
*ālat taṣwīr 'amūdīya*
vertical landing — حط عمودي
*ḥaṭṭ 'amūdī*
vertical launch — إنطلاق عمودي
*inṭilāq 'amūdī*
vertical obstacle — عائق عمودي
*'ā'iq 'amūdī*
vertical replenishment — تموين عمودي
*tamwīn 'amūdī*
vertical take-off — إقلاع عمودي
*iqlā' 'amūdī*
vertical thrust — دفع عمودي
*daf' 'amūdī*
vertical tube — أنبوب عمودي
*unbūb 'amūdī*
Vertol 107 — طائرة « ڤيرتول ١٠٧ »
*ṭā'irat virtūl mi'a wa sab'a*
vessel — سفينة . مركب
*safīna · markab*
VHF — تردد عالي جداً
*taraddud 'ālī jiddan*
Vickers tank — دبابة « ڤيكرز »
*dabbābat vikarz*
Victor air tanker — طائرة نقل وقود « ڤيكتر »
*ṭā'irat naql wuqūd viktar*
Victor submarine — غوّاصة « ڤيكتر »
*ghawwāṣat viktar*
Vietnam — ڤيتنام
*vītnām*
Vietnamese — ڤيتنامي
*vītnāmī*
view finder — مصورة . معين النظر
*muṣawwira · mu'ayyin an-naẓar*
viewing element — عنصر المشاهدة
*'unṣur al-mushāhada*
Viggen fighter — طائرة مقاتلة « ڤيجن »
*ṭā'ira muqātila vigin*
Vigilant ATGW — سلاح موجه مضاد للدبابات « ڤيجيلانت »
*silāḥ muwajjaḥ muḍādd lid-dabbābāt vijilant*
Viking aircraft — طائرة « ڤايكينج »
*ṭā'irat vāyking*
Vikrant carrier — حاملة « ڤيكرانت »
*ḥāmilat vikrant*
violation — إنتهاك . إخلال . خرق
*intihāk · ikhlāl · kharq*
violet smoke — دخان بنفسجي
*dukhān banafsajī*
Viper 632 engine — محرك « ڤايبر ٦٣٢ »
*muḥarrik vāypar sitt mi'a wa ithnayn wa thalāthīn*
Viper turbojet — طائرة نفاثة تربينية « ڤيبر »
*ṭā'ira naffātha turbīnīya vāypar*
VIP ferrying — نقل الأشخاص البارزين
*naql al-ashkhāṣ al-bārizīn*
Virginia cruiser — طرادة « ڤيرجينيا »
*ṭarrādat virjinya*
visible — واضح . ظاهر . مرئي
*wāḍiḥ · ẓāhir · mar'ī*
visitors' book — سجل الزوار
*sijill az-zuwwār*
visual — بصري . نظري
*baṣarī · naẓarī*
visual aid — معين بصري
*mu'īn baṣarī*
visual conditions — ظروف الابصار
*ẓurūf al-ibṣār*
visual contact — تلامس بصري
*talāmus basārī*
visual inspection — تفتيش بصري
*taftīsh baṣarī*
visual scan — مسح بصري
*masḥ baṣarī*
visual sighting — تصويب بصري
*taṣwīb basarī*
Vittorio Veneto cruiser — طرادة « ڤيتوريو ڤينيتو »
*tarrādat vituryu vinitū*
VK-1F turbojet — طائرة نفاثة تربينية « ڤي كيه ـ ١ اف »
*ṭā'ira naffātha turbīnīya vī kayy-wāḥid if*
Volvo (Co) — شركة « ڤولڤو »
*sharikat vulvū*
Volvo Flygmotor (Co) — شركة محركات « ڤولڤو فلايج موتور »
*sharikat muḥarrikāt vulvū flīg mutūr*
Voodoo fighter — طائرة مقاتلة ڤودو
*ṭā'ira muqātila vūdū*
Vosper frigate — فرقاطة « ڤوسپر »
*firqāṭat vuspar*
Vought (Co) — شركة « ڤوت »
*sharikat vūt*

voyage رحلة . سفر
*riḥla · safar*
VR-55 nerve gas agent عنصر غاز الأعصاب « ڤي آر ـ ٥٥ »
*ʿunṣur ghāz al-aʿṣāb vī ār-khamsa wa khamsīn*
V/STOL aircraft طائرة « ڤي/ستول »
*ṭāʾirat vī/stūl*
VTOL aircraft طائرة « ڤيتول »
*ṭāʾirat vītūl*
VTOL platform منصة « ڤيتول »
*minaṣṣat vītūl*
Vulcan ADS tank دبابة ڤولكان ايه دي اس
*dabbābat valkan ayy dī is*
Vulcan bomber طائرة قاذفة « ڤالكن »
*ṭāʾira qādhifa valkan*
Vulcan cannon مدفع هاون « ڤالكن »
*midfaʿ hāwun valkan*
VX agent عنصر « ڤي اكس »
*ʿunṣur vī iks*
VZ 52 rifle بندقية « ڤي زد ٥٢ »
*bunduqīyat vī zid ithnayn wa khamsīn*
VZ 61 sub-machine gun رشاش قصير « ڤي زد ٦١ »
*rashshāsh qaṣīr vī zid wāḥid wa sittīn*

W-class submarine — غواصة طراز « دبليو »
*ghawwāṣa ṭirāz dablyū*
Wadi corvette — سفينة حراسة صغيرة « وادي »
*safīnat ḥirāsa ṣaghīra wādi*
Wahoday geared turbine — تربين مسنن « واهودي »
*turbīn mussann wahudayy*
Walid carrier — حاملة « وليد »
*ḥāmilat walīd*
Walker Bulldog tank — دبابة « ووكر بولدوج »
*dabbābat wūkar buldug*
walking-out dress — بزة المدينة
*bizzat al-madīna*
Walleye AGM — صاروخ جو - أرض « وولاي »
*ṣārūkh jaww-ard wūlāyy*
Walrus submarine — غواصة « وولرس »
*ghawwāṣat wūlras*
Walther pistol — مسدس « والثر »
*musaddas walthar*
war — حرب
*ḥarb*
war complement — مجموعة حرب كاملة
*majmūʿat ḥarb kāmila*
war correspondent — مراسل حربي
*murāsil ḥarbī*
warfare — حرب
*ḥarb*
war gas — غاز القتال
*ghāz al-qitāl*
War Hawks aircraft — طائرة « وور هوكس »
*ṭāʾirat wūr huks*

warhead — رأس مقذوف
*raʾs maqdhūf*
warhead bus — حافلة رأس المقذوف
*ḥāfilat raʾs al-maqdhūf*
warhead type — نوع رأس المقذوف
*nawʿ raʾs al-maqdhūf*
warhead weight — وزن رأس المقذوف
*wazn raʾs al-maqdhūf*
war machine — آلة حربية
*āla ḥarbīya*
war material — معدات حربية
*muʿaddāt ḥarbīya*
warning — تحذير إنذار
*taḥdhīr · indhār*
warning system — نظام الانذار
*jihāz al-indhār · niẓām al-indhār*
warrant officer — ضابط صف . نائب ضابط
*ḍābiṭ ṣaff · nāʾib ḍābiṭ*
Warsaw Pact — حلف وارسو
*ḥilf wārsū*
Warsaw Pact allies — حلفاء حلف وارسو
*ḥulafāʾ ḥilf wārsū*
Warsaw Pact countries — دول حلف وارسو
*duwal ḥilf wārsū*
wartime — زمن الحرب
*zaman al-ḥarb*
wartime operation — عملية في زمن الحرب
*ʿamalīya fī zaman al-ḥarb*
war zone — منطقة حربية
*minṭaqa ḥarbīya*
Wasp Head radar — رادار « واسپ هيد »
*rādār wasp hīd*
Wasp helicopter — طائرة عمودية « واسپ »
*ṭāʾira ʿamūdīya wasp*
waste incineration — حرق النفاية
*ḥārq an-nufāya*
Watch Dog ECM — إجراء الكتروني مضاد « ووتش دوج »
*ijrāʾ iliktrūnī muḍādd wutsh dug*
watchtower — برج المراقبة
*burj al-murāqaba*
water/alcohol spray — مرش ماء/كحول
*mirashsh māʾ/kuḥūl*
waterborne range — مدى المحمول بطريق البحر
*mada al-maḥmūl bi-ṭariq al-baḥr*

water cooled reactor مفاعل يبرد بالماء
*mufāʿil yubarrad bil-māʾ*
water dam سد ماء
*sadd māʾ*
waterjet نافورة ماء
*nāfūrat māʾ*
water-proof cape معطف صامد للماء
*miʿṭaf ṣāmid lil-māʾ*
water purification تنقية الماء
*tanqīyat al-māʾ*
water supply إمداد الماء
*imdād al-māʾ*
water tanker ناقلة صهريجية للماء
*nāqila ṣihrījīya lil-māʾ*
wave موجة
*mawja*
wave crest قمة الموجة
*qimmat al-mawja*
waveguide دليل موجي
*dalīl mawjī*
wavelength طول الموجة
*ṭūl al-mawja*
Wavell data-processing nets شبكات تحليل البيانات « ويفل »
*shabakāt taḥlīl al-bayānāt wayval*
weapon سلاح
*silāḥ*
weapon-aiming system نظام تصويب الأسلحة
*niẓām taṣwīb al-asliḥa*
weapon delivery system نظام تسليم الأسلحة
*niẓām taslīm al-asliḥa*
weapon handling room غرفة تسليم الأسلحة
*ghurfat taslīm al-asliḥa*
weapon launch إطلاق الأسلحة
*iṭlāq al-asliḥa*
weapons bay مخزن الأسلحة
*makhzan al-asliḥa*
weapons load حمل الأسلحة
*ḥiml al-asliḥa*
weapon space حيز الأسلحة
*ḥayyiz al-asliḥa*
weapon system نظام الأسلحة
*niẓām al-asliḥa*
weapon/wheel nacelle كنّة السلاح / الدولاب
*kinnat as-silāḥ/ad-dūlāb*
weather balloon منطاد الأحوال الجوية
*minṭād al-aḥwāl al-jawwīya*
weather conditions الأحوال الجوية
*al-aḥwāl al-jawwīya*

weather forecast تنبؤات جوية
*tanabuʾāt jawwīya*
weather officer ضابط التنبؤات الجوية
*ḍābit at-tanabuʾāt al-jawwīya*
weather report نشرة جوية
*nashra jawwīya*
webbing أحزمة
*aḥzima*
Wegmann discharge تفريغ « ويجمان »
*tafrīgh wigman*
weight ثقل . وزن
*thuql · wazn*
weight loaded الوزن المحمول
*al-wazn al-maḥmūl*
welding torch مشعل لحام
*mishʿal liḥām*
Wessex helicopter طائرة عمودية « واسيكس »
*ṭāʾira ʿamūdīya wasiks*
West غرب
*gharb*
West Germany ألمانيا الغربية
*almānya al-gharbīya*
Westinghouse (Co) شركة واسنجهاوس
*sharikat wastinghaws*
Westland شركة ويستلاند
*sharikat wistland*
Westland Sea King helicopter طائرة عمودية « ويستلاند سي كينج »
*ṭāʾira ʿamudīya wistland sī king*
WG 30 helicopter طائرة عمودية « دبليو جي ٣٠ »
*ṭāʾira ʿamūdīya dablyū jī thalāthīn*
wheeled tricycle دراجة بعجلات ثلاثة
*darrāja bi-ʿajalāt thalātha*
wheeled truck شاحنة بعجلات
*shāḥina bi-ʿajalāt*
Whidbey Island ship سفينة « ويدبي آيلند »
*safīnat widbi āyland*
Whiff radar رادار « ويف »
*rādār wif*
whip سوط . ارتجاج المدفع
*sawṭ · irtijāj al-midfaʾ*
Whirlwind helicopter طائرة عمودية « ويرلويند »
*ṭāʾira ʿamūdīya wirlwind*
Whiskey Long-Bin submarine غواصة « ويسكي لونج -بن »
*ghawwāṣat wiski lung bin*
Whiskey submarine غواصة « ويسكي »
*ghawwāṣat wiski*

Whiskey Twin Cylinder submarine — غواصة « ويسكي » مزدوجة الاسطوانة
*ghawwāṣat wiski muzdawijat al-usṭuwāna*

Whitby frigate — فرقاطة ويتبي
*firqāṭat witbi*

white light — ضوء أبيض
*ḍaw' abyaḍ*

white-light searchlight — منوار كشاف بضوء أبيض
*minwār kashshāf bi-ḍaw' abyaḍ*

white smoke — دخان أبيض
*dukhān abyaḍ*

who goes there! — من هناك !
*man hunāk*

Wiesel weapon carrier — حاملة أسلحة « ويزل »
*ḥamilat asliḥa wīzl*

Wildcat fighter — طائرة مقاتلة « وايلدكات »
*ṭā'ira muqātila wāyld kat*

Wild Weasel aircraft — طائرة « وايلد ويزل »
*ṭā'irat wāyld wīzl*

winch — ملفاف . مرفاع
*milfāf · mirfā'*

Winchester hovercraft — حوامة « وينتشيستر »
*ḥawwāmat wintshistar*

wind direction — اتجاه الريح
*ittijāh ar-rīḥ*

windmill turbogenerator — مولد تربيني بطاحونة هوائية
*muwallid turbīnī bi-ṭāḥūna hawā'īya*

windscreen — حاجب الريح
*ḥājib ar-rīḥ*

wing area — مساحة الجناح
*masāḥat al-janāḥ*

wing hardpoint — النقطة الصلبة للجناح
*an-nuqta aṣ-ṣaliba lil-janāḥ*

wingspan — باع الجناح
*bā' al-janāḥ*

wire-guided — موجه بالسلك
*muwajjah bis-silk*

wire-guided weapon — سلاح موجه بالسلك
*silāḥ muwajjah bis-silk*

withdraw (to) — سحب . انسحب
*saḥaba · insaḥaba*

withdrawal — انسحاب . تراجع
*insiḥāb · tarāju'*

within range — في حدود المدى
*fi ḥudūd al-mada*

WM20 radar — رادار « دبليو ام ٢٠ »
*rādār dablyū im 'ishrīn*

WM28 radar — رادار « دبليو ام ٢٨ »
*rādār dablyū im thamānya wa 'ishrīn*

Wolf rocket launcher — قاذفة صواريخ « وولف »
*qādhifat ṣawārīkh wulf*

wooded terrain — أرض مشجرة
*arḍ mushajjara*

work capacity — سعة العمل
*si'at al-'amal*

working dress — بزة العمل
*bizzat al-'amal*

workshop — ورشة . معمل اصلاح
*warsha · ma'mal iṣlāḥ*

worldwide — عالمي
*'ālamī*

wound (to) — جرح
*jaraḥa*

wounded — جريح
*jariḥ*

WSC-3 transceiver — جهاز ارسال واستقبال « دبليو اس سي ـ ٣ »
*jihāz irsāl wa istiqbāl dablyū is sī – thalātha*

X 1A2 tank — دبابة « اكس ١ ايه ٢ »
*dabbābat iks wāḥid ayy ithnayn*

Xavante aircraft — طائرة « زاڤانتي »
*ṭā'irat zavānti*

X-band — نطاق الترددات السينية
*niṭāq at-tarradudāt as-sīnīya*

XH-40 helicopter — طائرة عمودية « اكس اتش ـ ٤٠ »
*ṭā'ira ʿamūdīya iks itsh – arbaʿīn*

Xia submarine — غواصة « زيا »
*ghawwāṣat ziya*

Xingu aircraft — طائرة « زينجو »
*ṭā'irat zingū*

XL70E3 grenade — قنبلة يدوية « اكس ال ٧٠ ئي ٣ »
*qunbula yadawīya iks il sabʿīn ī thalātha*

XM1 tank — دبابة « اكس ام ١ »
*dabbābat iks im wāḥid*

XM-58 sight system — جهاز تسديد « اكس ام ـ ٥٨ »
*jihāz tasdīd iks im thamānya wa khamsīn*

XM723 vehicle — مركبة « اكس ام ٧٢٣ »
*markabat iks im sabʿ mi'a wa thalātha wa ʿishrīn*

X-Ray — أشعة سينية
*ashiʿʿa sīnīya*

X-ray room — غرفة الأشعة السينية
*ghurfat al-ashiʿa as-sīnīya*

# Y

| | |
|---|---|
| Y-1 submarine<br>*ghawwāṣat wāyy-wāḥid* | غواصة « واي ١ » |
| Y-5 transporter<br>*ṭā'irat naql wayy-khamsa* | طائرة نقل « واي ـ ٥ » |
| Y-7 transporter<br>*ṭā'irat naql wayy-sabʿa* | طائرة نقل واي ـ ٧ » |
| Y-8 air transporter<br>*ṭā'irat naql wayy-thamānya* | طائرة نقل « واي ـ ٨ » |
| Yagi antenna<br>*hawā'ī yāgi* | هوائي « ياجي » |
| Yak-28P<br>*ṭā'irat yak-thamānya wa ʿishrin' pī* | طائرة « ياك ـ ٢٨ پي » |
| Yak-36MP aircraft<br>*ṭā'irat yak-sitta wa thalāthīn im pī* | طائرة « ياك ـ ٣٦ ام پي » |
| Yakovlev (Co)<br>*sharikat yākūv liv* | شركة « ياكوڤلڤ » |
| Yankee submarine<br>*ghawwāṣat yankī* | غواصة « يانكي » |
| yellow smoke<br>*dukhān aṣfar* | دخان أصفر |
| Yemen Arab Republic<br>*al-jumhūrīya al-ʿarabīya al-yamanīya* | الجمهورية العربية اليمنية |
| Yemen People's Democratic Republic<br>*jumhūrīyat al-yaman ad-dīmuqrāṭīya ash-shaʿbīya* | جمهورية اليمن الديمقراطية الشعبية |
| Yeugeuya minesweeper<br>*kāsiḥat alghām yugūya* | كاسحة الغام « يوجويا » |
| Youth Labour Army<br>*jaysh al-ʿummāl ash-shabāb* | جيش العمال الشباب |
| Yo-Yo radar<br>*rādār yū yū* | رادار « يو ـيو » |
| YRP 765 vehicle<br>*markabat wāyy ār pī sabʿ mi'a wa khamsa wa sittīn* | مركبة « واي آر پي ٧٦٥ » |
| Yugoslav<br>*yughuslāvī* | يوغسلاڤي |
| Yugoslavia<br>*yughuslāvya* | يوغوسلاڤيا |
| Yurka minesweeper<br>*kāsiḥat alghām yurka* | كاسحة ألغام « يوركا » |
| Yuushio submarine<br>*ghawwāṣat yushiyū* | غواصة « يوشيو » |

# Z

Z-5 helicopter طائرة عمودية « زد - ٥ »
*ṭā'ira ʿamūdīya zid-khamsa*
Z-6 helicopter طائرة عمودية « زد - ٦ »
*ṭā'ira ʿamūdīya zid sitta*
Z-9 helicopter طائرة عمودية « زد - ٩ »
*ṭā'ira ʿamūdīya zid-tisʿa*
Z-504M boat زورق « زد - ٥٠٤ ام »
*zawraq zid-khams mi'a wa arbaʿa*
Zaire زائير
*zā'īr*
Zairean زائيري
*zā'īrī*
Zambia زامبيا
*zāmbya*
Zambian زامبي
*zāmbī*
Ze'eu rocket launcher قاذفة صواريخ « زايو »
*qādhifat ṣawārīkh zayū*
zero visibility انعدام الرؤية
*inʿidām ar-ru'ya*
ZF manual box صندوق يدوي « زد إف »
*ṣundūq yadawī zid if*
Zhuk craft سفينة « زوك »
*zafīnat zuk*
ZIL-131 erector-launcher قاذفة ـ ناصبة « زيل - ١٣١ »
*qādhifa nāṣiba zil – mi'a wa wāḥid wa thalāthīn*
ZIL-135 wheeled launcher قاذفة بعجلات « زيل - ١٣٥ »
*qādhifa bi-ʿajalāt zil – mi'a wa khamsa wa thalāthīn*
ZIL truck شاحنة « زيل »
*shāḥinat zil*
Zimbabwe زمبابوي
*zimbābwī*
Zlin (Co) شركة « زلين »
*sharikat zalin*
Zlin trainer طائرة تدريب « زلين »
*ṭā'irat tadrīb zalin*
zone منطقة
*minṭaqa*
zoom optics بصريات تزويم
*baṣarīyāt tazwīm*
ZSU-23-4 gun مدفع « زد اس يو - ٢٣ - ٤ »
*midfaʿ zid is yū – thalātha wa ʿishrīn – arbaʿa*
ZSU-24 gun مدفع « زد اس يو - ٢٤ »
*midfaʿ zid is yū – arbaʿa wa ʿishrīn*
ZSU-57 gun مدفع « زد اس يو - ٥٧ »
*midfaʿ zid is yū – sabʿa wa khamsīn*
ZU-23 gun مدفع « زد يو ٢٣ »
*midfaʿ zid yū – thalātha wa ʿishrīn*
Zubov ship سفينة « زوبوف »
*safīnat zubūf*
Zulu IV submarine غواصة « زولو ٤ »
*ghawwāṣat zūlū arbaʿa*
ZW-01 radar رادار « زد دبليو - ٠١ »
*rādār zid dablyu – ṣifr wāḥid*
ZW-06 radar رادار « زد دبليو - ٠٦ »
*rādār zid dablyu – ṣifr sitta*
Zwaardis submarine غواصة « زواردیس »
*ghawwāṣat zwārdis*

Z

# تمهيد

تم تجميع المصطلحات العلمية والفنية التي يضمها هذا المعجم ليستعملها الأفراد العسكريون وجميع المهتمين بالتقنية العسكرية ، سواءً بصورة مباشرة أو غير مباشرة . إنه معجم عملي في المقام الأول ، يضم المصطلحات المستخدمة في التعامل اليومي سواءً بالميدان أو بالقيادة ، ويتحاشى التعريفات الايضاحية على افتراض أن هؤلاء الذين يستعملون المصطلح يعرفون معناه .

وتمتد التغطية الفنية للمعجم لتشمل جميع فروع القوات المسلحة والتقنيات العسكرية شاملة القوات المسلحة لدول العالم ، والأسلحة والذخائر ، والأسلحة والمعدات البرية بما في ذلك الدبابات ، والصواريخ ، والطائرات المقاتلة وطائرات الاستطلاع ، والطائرات العمودية (الهليكوبتر) ، والسفن الحربية شاملة الغواصات والملاحة البحرية والمواصلات والتدريب .

إنه أول معجم من نوعه للمصطلحات العسكرية ، ولذا فهو يعتبر سلاحا ضروريا لجميع المرتبطين بالقوات المسلحة سواءً أكانوا من المقاتلين بالميدان أو العاملين بالقيادات أو المشرفين على حفظ الأمن . ونظراً لتغطيته الشاملة للموضوع ، فسوف يجده جميع المرتبطين - بصورة أو بأخرى - بالأنشطة العسكرية بما في ذلك العاملون في مجال تصنيع أو توريد الأسلحة والمعدات للقوات المسلحة معجماً قيماً . كما سيجده المعلمون وطلاب الاستراتيجيات والتكتيكات الحربية بالمعاهد والكليات والجامعات العسكرية وجميع المضطلعين بمسؤولية توفير المصطلحات العربية المعادلة للمصطلحات الانكليزية مرجعاً لا غنى عنه .

لقد تم انتقاء المصطلحات بعناية بغرض الاحتفاظ بالمعجم في حجم مناسب ، وفي عديد من الحالات تم إدراج المصطلح كجزء من عبارة أو جملة يتكرر استعمالها بكثرة . هذا وقد تم حذف بعض المصطلحات عن عمد لأنها شائعة الاستعمال ومدرجة بالمعاجم العامة ، وإذا سهونا عن بعضها الآخر فنحن نرحب بالانتقادات البناءة التي من شأنها رفع مستوى الطبعات التالية .

# عربي - انكليزي

# ARABIC - ENGLISH

# أ

| | |
|---|---|
| إبادة الحشرات | disinfestation |
| إبتعاث | emission |
| إبتعاث ثانو ي | secondary emission |
| إبتعاث موجي بالنبضات | pulsed wave emission |
| إبتعاث موجي مستمر | continuous wave emission |
| أبرق | cable |
| إبطال الذخيرة | munition deactivation |
| أبو ظبي | Abu Dhabi |
| أبي هيل | Abbey Hill |
| « اتبعوني ! » | follow me! |
| إتجاه | direction, bearing |
| اتجاه الريح | wind direction |
| الاتجاه الزاو ي للهدف | target bearing |
| الاتحاد السوفياتي | Soviet Union |
| اتحاد الجمهوريات السوفيتية الاشتراكية | USSR |
| إتخاذ الهدف | targeting |
| إتزان اصطناعي | artificial stability |
| إتزان اوتوماتيكي | auto-stabilization |
| إتصال | communication |
| اتصال تحت الماء | underwater communication |
| إتصال طليق | floating communication |
| إتصالات | communications |
| إتصالات بالقمر الصناعي | satellite communications |
| إتفاق | treaty |
| إتفاقية الحد من الأسلحة الاستراتيجية | SALT Agreement |
| إتلاف ذاتي | self-destruct |
| إثبات الهو ية | identification |
| أثر داخن | smoky trail |
| أثر الدخان | smoke trail |
| إثيو بيا | Ethiopia |
| إجازة | leave |
| إجازة خاصة | compassionate leavc |
| إجازة مرور | pass |
| اجازة سنو ية | annual leave |
| إجازة مرضية | sick leave |
| إجراء | action |
| إجراء الكتروني مضاد « ووتش دوج » | Watch Dog ECM |
| إجراء دعم إلكتروني للانذار التهديدي | threat-warning ESM |
| إجراء دفاعي | defensive action |
| إجراء مضاد الكتروني « توپ هات » | Top Hat ECM |
| إجراء معياري | modular action |
| إجراءات إستطلاع إلكتروني | electronic surveillance measures |
| إجراءات تدعيم إلكتروني | electronic support measures |
| اجراءات مضادة فعالة | active countermeasures |
| أجزاء استراتيجية | strategic parts |
| إجلاء | evacuation |
| أجهزة | hardware |
| أجهزة إحساس | sensors |
| أجهزة رسم الخلايا | cytographic equipment |
| أجهزة العرض بحجرة الطيار | cockpit display |

| | |
|---|---|
| أحادي السكة | monorail |
| أحاط | encircle |
| إحتفال | ceremonial |
| إحتكاك السحب | pull friction |
| إحتكاك سهل المسك | easygrip friction |
| إحتلال | occupation |
| إحتمالية الهجوم الأول | first-strike probability |
| إحتياطات الأمان | safety precautions |
| إحتياطي | reserve, stand-by |
| إحتياطي القوات الجوية | Air Force Reserve |
| احديداب متنوع | variable camber |
| أحرق | burn |
| أحزمة | webbing |
| أحزمة المظلة | parachute harness |
| الأحوال الجوية | weather conditions |
| إختبار | test, examination, trial |
| إختبار الطيران | flight test |
| إختبار المعايرة | calibration test |
| إختراق من ارتفاع منخفض | low-altitude penetration |
| إختراق من مستوى منخفض | low-level penetration |
| إختلاس السمع | eavesdropping |
| إختلاف المحاذاة | misalignment |
| إختيار الفاصمة | fuse option |
| اخرج ! | dismiss! |
| إخلاء | evacuation |
| إخلاء طبي | medevac |
| إخلاء المصابين | casualty evacuation |
| أخمص قابل للطي | folding butt |
| الأداء خارج الطرق | cross-country performance |
| أداء الرادار | radar performance |
| أداء فائق | high performance |
| أداء كشف الهدف | target-detection performance |
| أداة إشعاع أمواج دقيقة | microwave radiation device |
| أداة بارزة | protruding device |
| أداة بالأشعة دون الحمراء | infra-red device |
| أداة « پدرسين » | Pedersen Device |
| أداة تدريب | training device |
| أداة الشرب | drinking device |
| أداة للقدح اثناء الطيران | inflight cocking device |
| أداة محرقة | incendiary device |
| أدار | steer |
| إدارة | steering, administration |
| إدارة ديزل كهربائية | diesel-electric drive |
| إدارة المساحة | ordnance survey |
| أدوات الاختبار | test gear |
| أدوات التحويل | conversion kit |
| أدوات تضميد الحروق | burn dressing kit |
| أدوات النظافة | cleaning kit |
| أذاع | transmit |
| أذكر اشارة النداء ! | give your call sign! |
| إذن | leave |
| إذن ركوب | embarkation leave |
| أذن إلكترونية | electronic ear |
| أذى | injury |
| إراقة الدم | bloodshed |
| أربض | bring into action |
| أربعة رجال | four-man |
| ارتجاج المدفع | whip |
| إرتفاع | height |
| إرتفاع | elevation |
| إرتفاع الاعتراض الأدنى | minimum interception height |
| الأرتفاع الأقصى الفعال | effective ceiling |
| إرتفاع السحاب | cloud height |
| إرتفاع عالٍ | high altitude |
| الارتفاع العملي الاقصى | service ceiling |
| إرتفاع منخفض | low altitude |
| ارتفاع هجومي ختامي | terminal attack height |
| الأرجنتين | Argentina |
| ارجنتيني | Argentine |

| | |
|---|---|
| الأردن | Jordan |
| اردني | Jordanian |
| أرسل | transmit |
| إرسال | dispatch |
| إرسال تشويش | jamming transmission |
| إرسالية عسكرية | military consignment |
| إرشاد | guidance |
| إرشاد قيادي | command guidance |
| أرض | land, terrain |
| أرض الاستعراض | parade ground |
| « أرضاً ـ سلاح ! » | ground arms! |
| أرض التدريب | training ground |
| أرض جبلية | mountainous terrain |
| أرض مجزأة | broken terrain |
| أرض المدافن | burial ground |
| أرض مشجرة | wooded terrain |
| أرض المعركة | battleground |
| أرض مكشوفة | open country |
| أرضي | land-based |
| أرضية غير ملائمة | adverse terrain |
| ارفع السلاح | take up arms! |
| أركان | staff |
| أركان حرب | battle staff |
| أركان الطيران | aviation staff |
| الأركان العامة | general staff |
| اركب ! | mount! |
| إرهابي | terrorist |
| أرياش الدوامة | rotor blades |
| إزاحة | displacement |
| إزاحة الحمل الكامل | full load displacement |
| إزاحة الهدف | target displacement |
| إزالة الألغام | mine clearing |
| إزالة التلوث | decontamination |
| إزالة العوائق | obstacle clearing |
| إزعاج العدو | harass the enemy |
| اسباني | Spanish |
| اسبانيا | Spain |
| إستأنف الارسال ! | resume transmitting! |
| استتر | take cover! |
| إستجابة | response |
| إستجواب | interrogation |
| إستجوب | interrogate (to) |
| إستخبار إلكتروني | Elint |
| إستخبار إلكتروني | electronic intelligence |
| إستخبارات | intelligence |
| إستخبارات الاتّصالات | communications intelligence |
| إستدعاء الاحتياطي | bring up reserves |
| استراتيجية | strategy |
| استرالي | Australian |
| أستراليا | Australia |
| استرح ! | stand at ease! |
| إسترداد | recapture |
| استسلام | surrender |
| إستسلام بلاشروط | unconditional surrender |
| إستطلاع | surveillance, reconnaissance, reconnoitering |
| إستطلاع أرضي | ground surveillance |
| استطلاع استراتيجي | strategic reconnaissance |
| إستطلاع بأجهزة احساس متعددة | multi-sensor reconnaissance |
| إستطلاع بحري | maritime surveillance |
| إستطلاع بري | overland surveillance |
| إستطلاع بالقمر الصناعي | satellite reconnaissance |
| إستطلاع تصويري | photographic reconnaissance |
| إستطلاع تكتيكي | tactical reconnaissance |
| إستطلاع جليدي | ice reconnaissance |
| إستطلاع جوي | airborne surveillance |
| استطلاع جوي | aerial reconnaissance |
| إستطلاع جوي بحري | naval air surveillance |
| إستطلاع ساحة المعركة | battlefield surveillance |
| إستطلاع مضاد للسفن | anti-ship surveillance |
| إستطلاع الهدف | target surveillance |
| إستعادة | recapture |
| إستعد ! | ready! |
| الاستعداد للقتال | combat readiness |

| | |
|---|---|
| إستعراض | parade, review |
| إستعراض التفتيش | inspection parade |
| إستعراض الصيانة | maintenance parade |
| إستقبال | reception |
| استقرار | stability |
| استقرار قذيفي | ballistic stability |
| إستقصاء | investigation |
| استكشاف | reconnoitering |
| إستكمل | interpolate |
| إستكمل بالاستقراء أو القياس | extrapolate |
| استنشاق تحت الماء | snorting |
| إستيقاظ | reveille |
| أسر | take into custody |
| أسر | capture |
| اسرائيل | Israel |
| اسرائيلي | Israeli |
| أسرع ـ الخطى ! | step out! |
| أسرع من الصوت | supersonic |
| أسطوانة أكسجين | oxygen cylinder |
| أسطوانة الغاز | gas cylinder |
| اسطوانة غاز سپاركليت | Sparklet gas cylinder |
| أسطول البحر الأسود | Black Sea Fleet |
| أسطول بحر البلطيق | Baltic Fleet |
| أسطول الشمال | Northern Fleet |
| أسطول صغير | flotilla |
| أسطول قتال | battle fleet |
| أسطول المحيط الهادىء | Pacific Fleet |
| إسعاف أولي | first aid |
| أسفل جذع الطائرة | underfuselage |
| إسفين منزلق | sliding wedge |
| إسقاط بالمظلات | parachute drop |
| إسقاط التموينات | supply drop |
| إسقاط جوي | airborne drop, air-dropping |
| إسقاط الطوارىء | emergency drop |
| إسكات لاسلكي | radio silence |
| أسلحة الجيش | army weapons |
| أسلحة الحفر | dibber weapon |
| أسلحة صغيرة | small arms |
| أسلحة نارية | firearms |
| أسلوب التدريب | drill technique |
| إسهال | dysentery |
| أسير | prisoner |
| أسير الحرب | prisoner of war |
| اشارات ! | signals! |
| إشارات بأطوال موجية طويلة | long-wavelength signals |
| إشارة استغاثة | distress signal |
| إشارة ذات تردد عالٍ | high-frequency signal |
| إشارة ذراع | armband |
| إشارة عدائية | hostile signal |
| إشارة كهربائية | electrical signal |
| إشارة النداء | call signal |
| إشتباك | engagement |
| إشتباك بين الدبابات | tank-on-tank engagement |
| اشتباك جوي | dogfight |
| اشتباك جوي متلاحم | close-combat dogfight |
| إشتباك مع هدف | target engagement |
| إشتباكات سطحية | surface engagements |
| إشتعال خلفي | backfire |
| إشعار الاستدعاء | call-up notice |
| إشعاع | radiation |
| إشعاع حراري | heat radiation |
| إشعاع كامل | total radiation |
| إشعاع كهرومغنطيسي | electromagnetic radiation |
| إشعاع مرتد | returning radiation |
| إشعاع منعكس | reflected radiation |
| إشعاعي | radiological |
| إشعال المحرك المعزز | boost motor ignition |
| أشعة سينية | X-Ray |
| أشعل | ignite |
| إصابة | hit |
| إصابة مباشرة | direct hit |
| إصدار | emission |
| أصدر | issue |
| إصطدام | collision, crash |

| | |
|---|---|
| إصلاح | repair, refit |
| إضاءة | illumination |
| إضاءة ليزر | laser light |
| إضاءة الهدف | target illumination |
| إضرب | strike |
| إضطراري | emergency |
| أضواء الاقتراب | approach lights |
| إطار | tyre |
| إطار الرفع | elevating frame |
| إطار « ڤي دي اس » | VDS housing |
| إطار مطاط | rubber tyre |
| إطعام | messing |
| إطفاء الأنوار | blackout |
| إطفائي | fireman |
| أطفيء الأنوار ! | lights out! |
| أطلق | discharge |
| اطلاق | launch |
| إطلاق أرضي | ground launch |
| إطلاق أرضي للنيران | ground fire |
| إطلاق الأسلحة | weapon launch |
| إطلاق بارد | cold-launch, cold type launch |
| إطلاق بمدى ومسار | range and bearing launch |
| إطلاق تحت الماء | underwater launch |
| إطلاق سريع للنيران | rapid firing |
| إطلاق السفينة | ship-launch |
| إطلاق عشوائي | blind launching |
| اطلاق ليزر لنظام ريپيار | Rapier laserfire |
| إطلاق مباشر | fire point blank |
| إطلاق مغمور | submerged launch |
| إطلاق مقيد للنيران | captive firing |
| اطلاق من السفينة | ship fired |
| إطلاق من نوع ساخن | hot type launch |
| إطلاق نيران اوتوماتيكي | automatic fire |
| أطلق وتناسى | fire and forget |
| اطلق وجدد | fire-and-update |
| أطوال موجية للاشعة دون الحمراء | infra-red wavelengths |
| إعادة انتشار | redeploy |
| إعادة تجنيد | re-enlistment |
| إعادة التزود بالوقود بالذراع الطائر | flying-boom refuelling |
| إعادة التسخين | reheat |
| اعادة التسليح | re-arming |
| إعادة تلقيم | reload (to) |
| اعادة تلقيم سريع | rapid reload |
| إعتراض | interception |
| اعترض | intercept (to) |
| إعتزال | retire |
| اعتقل | take into custody |
| إعتقال | internment |
| اعزل | unarmed |
| إعطاء التعليمات | briefing |
| أعمال الأمن | security work |
| أعمال الدورية | patrol work |
| أغار | invade (to) |
| إغلاق | closure |
| افتح النار | open fire |
| أفراد أرضيون | ground staff |
| أفراد البحرية | naval personnel |
| أفراد عسكريون بعقود أجنبية | foreign contract military personnel |
| أفراد المهمة | mission crew |
| أفغانستان | Afghanistan |
| أفق الرادار | radar horizon |
| إقامة | establishment |
| إقتحام على الشاطىء | assault over the beach |
| إقتراب اوتوماتي | auto-approach |
| أقرب الأقارب | next of kin |
| إقفال | closure |
| « إقفز ! » | jump |
| اقفل ! | Switch Off! |
| إقلاع | take-off |
| إقلاع عمودي | vertical take-off |

| | |
|---|---|
| اقلاع قصير وحط عمودي | STOVL |
| اكتساب | acquisition |
| إكتساب الهدف | target acquisition |
| اكتسب | acquire |
| إكتشف | detect |
| اكثر من المقرر | above establishment |
| الاكوادور | Ecuador |
| إكوادورى | Ecuadorean |
| ألات السطح | deck machinery |
| ألباني | Albanian |
| الألبانية | Albania |
| ألبسة واقية | protective clothing |
| آلة تحديد الاتجاه « بارك لامب » | Park Lamp direction finder |
| آلة تصوير « اوميرا » | OMERA camera |
| آلة تصوير باطار مائل | oblique frame camera |
| آلة تصوير بانورامية | panoramic camera |
| آلة تصوير تلفزيوني | TV camera |
| آلة تصوير عالية السرعة | ultrafast camera |
| آلة تصوير عمودية | vertical camera |
| آلة تصوير « كيه اس - ٩٢ ايه » | KS-92A camera |
| آلة تصوير للرصد الأمامي | forward-looking camera |
| آلة تصوير مائلة | oblique camera |
| آلة تصوير مركبة على الجنب | side-mounted camera |
| آلة حربية | war machine |
| آلة مقاتلة | fighting machine |
| الالتحاق بالطائرة والاقلاع مباشرة | scramble |
| إلتفاف | envelopment |
| إلتهاب معدي معوي | gastroenteritis |
| التواء | distortion |
| إلحاق | attachment |
| القم | load (to) |
| القم ! | load! |
| الكتروني | electronic |
| إلكترونيات | electronics |
| إلكترونيات الرادار | radar electronics |
| إلكترونيات الطيران | avionics |
| إلكترونات طيران لجميع الأجواء | all-weather avionics |
| إلكترونيات طيران محسنة | improved avionics |
| ألماني | German |
| المانيا الشرقية | East Germany |
| ألمانيا الغربية | West Germany |
| ألواح تهذيب | trim-boards |
| ألومنيوم | aluminium |
| الى الوراء ـ در ! | reverse!, about turn! |
| إلى اليسار ـ در ! | left turn! |
| إلى اليمين ـ در ! | right turn! |
| آلي | mechanized, automatic |
| ألياف زجاجية | glass-fibre |
| آلية التأخير | delay mechanism |
| آلية اطلاق النار | firing mechanism |
| آلية الانتخاب | selector mechanism |
| آلية انكماش هوائي دوار مقبب | rotodome retraction mechanism |
| آلية داخلية | internal mechanism |
| آلية الزناد | trigger mechanism |
| الامارات العربية المتحدة | United Arab Emirates |
| أماكن الاطعام | mess accommodation |
| أمامي | fore |
| أمبولة | ampoule |
| إمتياز جوي | air supremacy |
| إمداد خارجي | external supply |
| إمداد الماء | water supply |
| إمداد الهواء | air supply |
| إمدادات | supplies |
| امدادات الطاقة | power supply |
| إمدادات طبية | medical supplies |
| آمر | commandant |
| أمر | command, instruction |
| أمر تغيير مسار الطائرة | jet-deflection order |

| | |
|---|---|
| أمر التوجيه | guidance command |
| أمر لاسلكي | radio command |
| إمكانيات الاستخدام في جميع الأجواء | all-weather capability |
| امكانيات استراتيجية | strategic potential |
| إمكانيات التجاوز | override capability |
| إمكانيات التعرض | offensive capability |
| إمكانيات قتالية | fighting capability |
| إمكانيات ليلية | night capability |
| إمكانيات مضادة لاهداف سطحية | anti-surface capability |
| إمكانيات الهجوم الثانوي | secondary attack capability |
| إمكانية الاختراق | penetration capability |
| إمكانية الاطلاق البارد | cold launch capability |
| إمكانية إعادة تلقيم مدمجة | integral reload capability |
| إمكانية انتشار | deployment capability |
| إمكانية الحمل بالسفينة | shipborne capability |
| إمكانية الغوص العميق | deep diving capability |
| إمكانية محسنة | improved capability |
| إمكانية مزدوجة | dual capability |
| إمكانية النظر / الاطلاق للأسفل | Look-down/shoot-down potential |
| أمل | Amal |
| أمن | security |
| أمن الدولة | state security |
| أمهل | delay |
| أمين الصندوق | paymaster |
| انا استقبلك | am receiving |
| إنارة | illumination |
| أنبوب أشعة كثود | cathode-ray tube |
| أنبوب تهوية تحت الماء | schnorkel |
| أنبوب عمودي | vertical tube |
| أنبوب عود قابل للنفخ | inflatable buoyancy tube |
| أنبوب الموجة المتنقلة | travelling-wave tube |
| أنبوبة الصاروخ | missile tube |
| أنبوبة القذف | launch tube, launcher tube |
| أنبوبة نافورية | jetpipe |
| إنتباه ! | attention!, pay attention! |
| انتشار | deployment |
| انتشار خارجي | overseas deployment |
| « انتشار ـ شكل ! » | form extended line! |
| انتشار عالمي | global deployment |
| إنتقال | transport |
| إنتهاك | violation |
| انتيتكسين | anti-toxin |
| انجز | carry out |
| إنحدار | gradient |
| إنحدار مركز الدوران | trunnion tilt |
| إنحراف زاوي | angular deviation |
| إنحراف الصاروخ | missile deviation |
| إنحلال | disintegration |
| اندونيسي | Indonesian |
| اندونيسيا | Indonesia |
| إنذار | alarm, threat, warning |
| إنذار تدريب | training alert |
| إنذار زائف | false alarm |
| إنذار مبكر | early warning |
| إنذار مبكر محمول جواً | airborne early warning |
| إنذار مسموع | audible alarm |
| إنذار مقدم | forewarn |
| إنزال | landing |
| إنزال بالحاملة | carrier landing |
| إنزال الحبال | hauldown |
| أنزل | land (to) |
| أنزل | unload, disembark |
| أنزل ! | dismount! |
| انسحاب | withdrawal |
| انسحب | withdraw (to) |
| إنشاء | construction |
| الانشاء الاساسي للمؤخرة | aft superstructure |
| إنشاءات علوية للسفينة | superstructure |
| انضباط | discipline |
| إنضغاط الذبذبة | pulse-compression |
| إنطلاق | lift-off, take-off |

| | |
|---|---|
| إنطلاق جوي | air launch |
| إنطلاق عمودي | vertical launch |
| انطلق | start up! |
| انظر يساراً | eyes left! |
| انظر يميناً | eyes right! |
| أنظمة | regulations |
| انعدام الرؤية | zero visibility |
| إنعكس | reflect (to) |
| أنغولا | Angola |
| أنغولي | Angolan |
| إنفجار | blast, explosion |
| إنفجار ثانوي | secondary explosion |
| إنفجار جوي نووي | nuclear airburst |
| إنفجار للداخل | implosion |
| إنفجار نووي | nuclear explosion |
| انفجر | blow up (to), burst (to) |
| إنقاذ | salvage |
| انقضاض | dive |
| انقضاض مباغت | surprise assault |
| إنقضاض من مستوى منخفض | low-level strike |
| إهجم | charge! |
| أهلية | capacity |
| اوامر اطلاق النار | firing orders |
| أوامر دائمة | standing orders |
| اوتوماتيكي | automatic |
| أوتوماتيكياً | automatically |
| اوتوماتية | automation |
| اورغواي | Uruguay |
| أوسمة القتال | battle honours |
| أوغندا | Uganda |
| أولوية قصوى | high-priority; top priority |
| أوهن العزيمة | demoralize |
| ايران | Iran |
| ايراني | Iranian |
| ايرلندة | Ireland |
| ايرلندي | Irish |
| الايطالي | Italian |
| ايطاليا | Italy |
| ايقاف شديد | close-arrest |
| إيواء | accommodation |

| | |
|---|---|
| باب حظيرة متداخل | telescopic hangar door |
| باب دائري | circular hatch |
| باب دخول | access hatch |
| باب القنابل | bomb door |
| باب المؤخرة | stern door |
| باب مقدمة السفينة | bow door |
| بابوا غيني الجديدة | Papua New Guinea |
| باتفاق | in concert |
| باحث بالأشعة دون الحمراء | infra-red seeker |
| باحث راداري | radar seeker |
| باحث راداري « ايه دي ايه سي » | ADAC radar seeker |
| باحث راداري فعال | active radar seeker |
| باحث صاروخي | missile seeker |
| باحث كهربائي بصري | electro-optical seeker |
| باحث ليزر عن الهدف | laser target seeker |
| باحث مضاد للاشعاع | anti-radiation seeker |
| باحث هدف مميز/معين مدى بالليزر | laser ranger/marked-target seeker |
| باراغواي | Paraguay |
| بارود الذخيرة | ball powder |
| بارامتر | parameter |
| باع الجناح | wingspan |
| باعات « فستبروكا » للجسور العائمة | Festbrucke Spans for flooding bridge |
| باعث معادي | hostile emitter |
| الباكستان | Pakistan |
| باكستاني | Pakistani |
| باناما | Panama |
| بانسجام | in concert |

| | |
|---|---|
| بانغلاديش | Bangladesh |
| بانورامي | panoramic |
| بتوجيه راداري تلقائي | automatically homing |
| بثرة | blister |
| بحار | sailor |
| بحث | investigation |
| البحث والانقاذ | search-and-rescue |
| البحث والتدمير | search and destroy |
| البحث والتعيين | search and find |
| بحر | sea |
| البحر الأبيض المتوسط | Mediterranean |
| البحر الأسود | Black Sea |
| بحر قزوين | Caspian Sea |
| بحر المانش | English Channel |
| بحر هائج | rough sea |
| بحري | maritime, seagoing |
| البحرين | Bahrain |
| بدائل | replacements |
| بدل إجازة | leave allowance |
| بدل سفر | travel allowance |
| بدل طعام | messing allowance, ration allowance |
| بدل ملابس | clothing allowance |
| بدل يومي | daily allowance |
| بدن السفينة | hull |
| بدن المغلاق | breech block, locking block |
| بر | land |
| البرازيل | Brazil |
| برازيلي | Brazilian |

ب

| | |
|---|---|
| البرتغال | Portugal |
| برتغالي | Portuguese |
| برج | turret |
| برج « اتش ام جي » | HMG turret |
| برج « اس ٢٠ » | S20 turret |
| برج « اس ٣٦٥ » | S365 turret |
| برج « اس ٥٣٠ اف » | S530F turret |
| برج « اس ايه ـ ٩٠ » | SA-90 turret |
| برج « اس ايه ام ام اس ٥٣٠ » | SAMM S530 turret |
| برج « اوتو ـ ميلارا » | OTO-Melara turret |
| برج « بي » | B-turret |
| برج تذبذبي | oscillating turret |
| برج « تي جي ١٢٥ » | TG 125 turret |
| برج ثلاثي | triple turret |
| برج جاتلينج | Gatling turret |
| برج جهاز احساس أمامي | forward sensor turret |
| برج « جيات تي اس ـ ٩٠ » | GIAT TS-90 turret |
| برج « سرڤال » | Serval turret |
| برج « لينكس ٩٠ » | Lynx 90 turret |
| برج مدرع | armoured turret |
| برج مدفع أمامي | forward gun turret |
| برج مدفع « دي پي » | DP gun turret |
| برج مراقبة | lookout tower |
| برج المراقبة | watchtower, control tower |
| برج مصوب عن بعد | remotely-aimed turret |
| برج الملاحة | pilot house |
| برج ملحوم بأكمله | all-welded turret |
| برغي دوار | rotating bolt, rotary bolt |
| برغي ذو اذن لسحب دوار | rotary lug bolt |
| برغي مضلع | ribbed bolt |
| برقية | cablegram |
| برقية | dispatch |
| برقية بالشفرة | cypher telegram |
| بركينافاسو | Burkina Faso |
| برمائي | amphibious |
| برمجة اوتوماتيكية | automatic programming |
| برنامج إعادة دخول قذيفي | ballistic re-entry programme |
| برنامج « پايڤويه » | Paveway programme |
| برنامج التجديد | refit programme |
| برنامج معونة الدفاع | Defense Aid Program |
| بري | land-based |
| « بريسكوب » | periscope |
| بريطاني | British |
| بريطانيا | Britain |
| بريطانيا العظمى | Great Britain |
| بريوني | Brunei |
| بزة الاستعراض | parade dress |
| بزة العمل | overall, working dress |
| بزة القتال | combat dress |
| بزة المدينة | walking-out dress |
| بزة المراسم | ceremonial dress, full dress |
| بزة معتادة | everyday dress |
| بزة واقية مدرعة | armoured body suit |
| بسيط | unsophisticated |
| بصري | visual |
| بصريات تزويم | zoom optics |
| بصريات « كاسجرين » | Cassegrain Optics |
| بصريات متوازنة جيروسكوبيا | gyro-stabilized optics |
| بضغط الغاز | gas-pressured |
| بطارية | battery |
| بطارية حرارية | thermal battery |
| بطارية طوربيد | torpedo battery |
| بطارية غواصات | submarine battery |
| بطارية كهربائية | electric battery |
| بطاقة | label |
| بطاقة السجل | record card |
| بطاقة هوية | identity card |
| بالطاقة الحرارية | thermal powered |
| بالطاقة النووية | nuclear powered |
| بطن الطائرة | aircraft belly |
| بطني | ventral |
| بعثة استطلاع مسلحة | armed reconnaissance mission |

ب

| | |
|---|---|
| بعثة حفظ الأمن | peacekeeping mission |
| بعثة عبور | ferry mission |
| بقيادة رجال سوفييت | Soviet-manned |
| بكرة وحبل | block and tackle |
| بلاستيك مقوى بالألياف الزجاجية | glassfibre-reinforced plastic |
| بلاط لاصدي | anechoic tiles |
| بلجيكا | Belgium |
| بلجيكي | Belgian |
| بلد جبلي | mountainous country |
| بلطيقي | Baltic |
| بلغ | reach |
| بلغارى | Bulgarian |
| بلغاريا | Bulgaria |
| بلى الماسورة | barrel wear |
| بندقية | rifle, gun |
| بندقية « اتش كيه پي - ٧ » | HKP-7 rifle |
| بندقية « اتش كيه ٣٣ » | HK 33 rifle |
| بندقية « اس سي ٧٠ » | SC70 rifle |
| بندقية « اس ڤي دي » | SVD rifle |
| بندقية « اف اف ڤي ٨٩٠ سي » | FFV 890C rifle |
| بندقية « إف إن إف ايه إل » | FN FAL rifle |
| بندقية « اف ايه ام ايه إس » | FAMAS rifle |
| بندقية اقتحام | assault rifle |
| بندقية « ال ١ ايه ١ » | L1A1 rifle |
| بندقية آلية | automatic rifle |
| بندقية آلية خفيفة | light automatic rifle |
| بندقية « ام ١ » | M1 rifle |
| بندقية « ام ١ ايه ١ » | M1A1 rifle |
| بندقية « ام ٢ » | M2 rifle |
| بندقية « ام ٣ » | M3 rifle |
| بندقية « ام ١٤ » | M14 rifle |
| بندقية « ام ١٦ » | M16 rifle |
| بندقية « ام ١٦ ايه ١ » | M16A1 rifle |
| بندقية « ام ٦٢ » | M62 rifle |
| بندقية « ام ٦٧ » | M67 rifle |
| بندقية « ام ايه اس ٣٦ » | MAS 36 rifle |
| بندقية « ام پي ٤٤ » | MP44 rifle |
| بندقية « ام پي اي كيه ام » | MPiKM rifle |
| بندقية « آي دبليو اكس إل ٧٠ ئي ٣ » | IW XL70E3 rifle |
| بندقية « ايه آر - ١٥ » | AR-15 rifle |
| بندقة « ايه آر - ١٨ » | AR-18 rifle |
| بندقية « ايه آر ٧٠ » | AR70 rifle |
| بندقية « ايه كيه ٤٧ » | AK-47 rifle |
| بندقية « ايه كيه إس - ٧٤ » | AKS-74 rifle |
| بندقية « ايه كيه إم » | AKM rifle |
| بندقية « ايه يو جي » | AUG rifle |
| بندقية « توكاريف » | Tokarev rifle |
| بندقية « جي ٣ » | G3 rifle |
| بندقية « جي ٣ ايه ٤ » | G3A4 rifle |
| بندقية « جي ١١ » | G11 rifle |
| بندقية رقم ٤ | number 4 rifle |
| بندقية « روجر ميني ١٤ » | Ruger Mini-14 rifle |
| بندقية « سبرينج فيلد » | Springfield rifle |
| بندقية سيتمي | Cetme rifle |
| بندقية « شتير ايه يو جي » | Steyr AUG rifle |
| بندقية طراز ٤٩ | model 49 rifle |
| بندقية طراز ٥٦ | Type 56 rifle |
| بندقية طراز ٦٠ | Type 60 rifle |
| بندقية عديمة الارتداد | recoilless rifle |
| بندقية فدائي « كولت » | Colt commando rifle |
| بندقية « ڤالمت » | Valmet rifle |
| بندقية « ڤي زد ٥٢ » | VZ 52 rifle |
| بندقية قتال ليلي | night-action rifle |
| بندقية قصيرة | carbine |
| بندقية قصيرة « اس كيه اس » | SKS carbine |
| بندقية القناص | sniper rifle |
| بندقية المظلى | para version rifle |

ب

| | |
|---|---|
| بنزين الطائرات | aviation gasoline |
| بنطلون | trouser |
| البنين | Benin |
| بالهواء المضغوط | pneumatically |
| بوابة المؤخرة | stern gate |
| بواق | trumpeter |
| بوتسوانا | Botswana |
| بورما | Burma |
| بوروندي | Burundi |
| بوصلة | compass |
| بوصلة الجيب | pocket compass |
| بوق | horn |
| بوق الانذار | siren |
| بوقي | trumpeter |
| بولندة | Poland |
| بولندي | Polish |
| بوليڤي | Bolivian |
| بوليڤيا | Bolivia |
| بوينج | Boeing |
| البيئة البرية للدفاع الجوي لمنظمة ناتو | NATO Air Defence Ground Environment |
| بيان عملي | demonstration |
| بيان الهدف المتحرك | moving target indication |
| بيانات استخبارات | intelligence information |
| بيانات التزامن | synchronisation data |
| بيانات الحرس | guard data |
| بيانات خارجية | extraneous data |
| بيانات الدخل | in-put data |
| بيانات العمليات | operational information |
| بيانات موقع الهدف | target-location data |
| البيانات الواردة | in-coming data |
| بيرو | Peru |
| بيضوي | oval |
| بين السفن | intership |

| | |
|---|---|
| تأثير الانفجار | blast effect |
| تأثير مميت | lethal effect |
| تأثيرات صوتية | acoustical effects |
| تأهب ! | on guard! |
| تابع | subordinate |
| تايفون | Typhon |
| تايلاند | Thailand |
| تايوان | Taiwan |
| تبدد | scatter |
| تبعية | subordination |
| تتبع | tracking |
| تتبع الهدف | target-tracking |
| تثبيت سقاطة الأمان | apply safety-catches! |
| تجارب الرمي | firing trials |
| تجديد | refit, update |
| تجديد شامل | major refit |
| تجربة | trial |
| تجربة بحرية | sea trial |
| تجربة طيران | flight trial |
| تجسس | espionage |
| « تجمع ! » | fall in! |
| تجميد | immobilization |
| تجند | enlist |
| تجنيد | conscription |
| تجنيد انتقائي | selective conscription |
| تجهيز | fitting out |
| تجهيزات شخصية | personal equipment |
| تجهيزات القطر | towing rig |
| تجويف | cavitation |
| تجويف متقارن | coupled-cavity |
| تجوف | cavitation |
| تحت الأرض | under-ground |
| تحت الجناح | underwing |
| تحت الحراسة | under escort |
| تحت قيادتي | at my command! |
| تحت الماء | underwater |
| تحت النار | under fire |
| تحديد | demarcation |
| تحديد التحركات الفردية | individual movements, identify |
| تحديد مسافة الهدف من الجو | air-to-surface ranging |
| تحذير | warning |
| تحركات الجنود | troop movements |
| تحركات الطائرات | aircraft movements |
| تحرك تفاضلي | move differentially |
| تحرير | liberation |
| تحصين | immunization, fortification |
| تحصينات | defences |
| تحصينات الميدان | field fortifications |
| تحقيق | investigation |
| تحكم | control |
| تحكم ايروديناميكي | aerodynamic control |
| تحكم عن بعد | remote control |
| التحكم في الطائرة | flight-control |
| تحلية ماء البحر | sea water desalination |
| تحليل البيانات | data handling |
| تحليل مجال التردد | frequency-domain analysis |
| تحليل المجال الزمني | time-domain analysis |

ت

| | |
|---|---|
| تحمل فوق سرعة الصوت | supersonic endurance |
| تحويل | transmission, transfer |
| تحويل السرعة اليدوي | manual transmission |
| تحية | salute |
| تحية العلم | trooping the colour |
| تخريب ذاتي | self-destruct |
| تخريب سري | sabotage |
| تخزين | storage |
| تخزين الطافية الصوتية الرادارية | sonobuoy stowage |
| تخصيص | designation |
| تخطيط الحدود | demarcation |
| تخندق | dig in (to) |
| تدابير الانذار المبكر | EW provisions |
| تدابير دعم إلكترونية « اس ال كيو ـ ٢٩ » | SLQ-29 ESM |
| تدابير دعم إلكترونية « اس ال كيو ـ ٣٢ (في) ـ ٢ » | SLQ-32(V)-2 ESM |
| تدابير دعم إلكترونية « اس ال كيو (في) ـ ١ » | SLQ(V)-1 ESM |
| تدابير دعم الكترونية « بريك پمپ » | Brick Pump ESM |
| تدابير دعم الكترونية « بريك سپليت » | Brick Split ESM |
| تدبير دعم الكترونية « رام تاب » | Rum Tub ESM |
| تدبير دعم الكترونية « ستوپ لايت » | Stop Light ESM |
| تدابير دعم الكترونية سلبية الاعتراض | passive intercept ESM |
| تدابير دعم إلكترونية « سايد جلوب » | Side Globe ESM |
| تدابير مضادة | counter-measure |
| تدابير مضادة إلكترونية | electronic counter-measures |
| تدابير مضادة إلكترونية « اس ال آر ـ ٢٠ » | SLR-20 ECM |
| تدابير مضادة إلكترونية « إلتا ام ان ـ ٥٣ » | Elta MN-53 ECM |
| تدابير مضادة الكترونية « ايه ال آر ـ ٦٩ » | ALR-69 ECM |
| تدابير مضادة الكترونية « ايه ال كيو ـ ١٣١ » | ALQ-131 ECM |
| تدابير مضادة الكترونية « بل تاب » | Bell Tap ECM |
| تدابير مضادة الكترونية « بل سكوات » | Bell Squat ECM |
| تدابير مضادة الكترونية « بل سلام » | Bell Slam ECM |
| تدابير مضادة الكترونية « بل شراود » | Bell Shroud ECM |
| تدابير مضادة الكترونية « بل كلوت » | Bell Clout ESM |
| تدابير مضادة إلكترونية لنظام الانذار المبكر « ئي دبليو اس ٩٠٥ » | EWS905 ECM |
| تداخل إنعكاسات الموجات الرادارية | clutter |
| تداخل راداري من الارض | ground clutter |
| تداخل راداري من البحر | sea clutter |
| تداخل لاسلكي | radio interference |
| تداخل من جانب العدو | enemy-introduced interference |
| تدخل عسكري | military intervention |
| تدخل مسلح | armed intervention |
| تدريب | instruction, training, exercise, drill |
| تدريب أساسي | basic training |
| تدريب بالأسلحة | arms drill |
| تدريب بحري | sea training |
| تدريب الدبابات | tanks training |
| تدريب الرمي | target training |
| تدريب عسكري | military training |
| تدريب عقابي | pack drill |
| تدريب على الاستطلاع | reconnaissance training |
| تدريب على اطلاق النار | firing exercise |
| تدريب على الرمي | target practice |
| تدريب على رمي المدفعية | gunnery training |
| تدريب على القتال | combat training |

|  |  |
| --- | --- |
| تدريب عملي | drill instruction |
| تدريب فردي | individual training |
| تدريب لاحق على التعبئة | post-mobilization training |
| تدريب مائي | aquatic training |
| تدريب المجندين | training of recruits |
| تدريب ميداني | field exercise |
| تدريب الوحدة | unit training |
| تدريع | armour plating |
| تدريع قضيبي | bar armour |
| تدفق متماثل | symmetrical flow |
| تدمر | destroy |
| تدمير | demolition |
| تراجع | fall back (to), retire (to), retreat, withdrawal |
| تراصف كامل | dressed overall |
| ترامز | ciphering, coding |
| تربة | terrain |
| تربين | turbine |
| تربين بخاري | steam turbine |
| تربين بخاري مسنن | geared steam turbine |
| تربين دائر في اتجاه معاكس | contra-rotating turbine |
| تربين غاز « اوليمپوس » | Olympus gas turbine |
| تربين غازي | gas turbine |
| تربين غازي « ال ام ٢٥٠٠ » | LM2500 gas turbine |
| تربين غازي « براون بوفري » | Brown Boveri gas turbine |
| تربين غازي « پروتيوس » | Proteus gas turbine |
| تربين غازي للابحار « تاين » | Tyne cruising gas turbine |
| تربين مسنن | geared turbine |
| تربين مسنن « واهودي » | Wahoday geared turbine |
| ترتيب الاشعال | firing order |
| ترجم | interpret (to) |
| ترجمة | interpretation |
| ترحيل | transfer |
| ترخيص | authorization |
| تردد اطلاق النار | firing frequency |
| تردد تكرار النبضات | pulse repetition frequency |
| تردد عالي جداً | VHF |
| تردد فوق العالي | UHF, ultra-high frequency |
| تردد متوسط | medium frequency |
| ترددات منخفضة | low frequency |
| ترس تخفيض السرعة | reduction gear |
| ترس وسيط | idler |
| تركي | Turkish |
| تركيا | Turkey |
| ترقية | promotion |
| تركيب | installation, mounting |
| تركيب الصواريخ : منشأة صواريخ | missile installation |
| تركيب مفرد | single mount |
| تركيبات حساسة | sensitive installations |
| تركيز | concentration |
| ترميم | repair |
| ترميم منتصف العمر | mid-life refit |
| ترنداد وطوباغو | Trinidad and Tobago |
| ترياق | antidote |
| تزود بالوقود | refuelling |
| تزود بالوقود أثناء الطيران | inflight refuelling |
| التزويد بالوقود اثناء الطيران | buddy refuelling |
| تسارع | accelerate |
| تسارع حول الصوتية | transonic acceleration |
| تسارع عالٍ | high acceleration |
| تسديد | aim |
| تسديد بصري | optical sighting |
| تسرب | infiltration |
| تسريح | demobilization |
| تسريح من الجيش | discharge from army |
| تسلل | infiltration |
| تسليح | fitting out |

| | |
|---|---|
| تسليح أساسي | primary armament |
| تسليح ثقيل | heavy armament |
| تسليح رئيسي | main armament |
| تسليح كامل | full armament |
| تسليم | surrender |
| تسليم على متن الحاملة | carrier onboard delivery |
| تسهيلات الاتصال | communication facilities |
| تسهيلات الاصلاح | repair facility |
| تسهيلات تحليل الاستخبارات | intelligence analysis facility |
| تسهيلات الصيانة | maintenance facilities |
| تسهيلات القاعدة الرئيسية | main base facilities |
| تسهيلات القيادة | command facilities |
| تسهيلات مراقبة | control facilities |
| تسهيلات معيارية | modular facility |
| تشاد | Chad |
| تشتت | scatter, breakaway |
| تشظية | fragmentation |
| تشظية شديدة الانفجار | HE fragmentation |
| تشغيل | operation |
| تشغيل آلي | automation |
| تشغيل صامت | silent operation |
| تشغيل يدوي | manual operation |
| تشغيلي | operational |
| تشكيل | formation |
| تشكيل المعركة | battle formation |
| تشكيل مفتوح | open formation, open out! |
| تشكيل منضم | close formation |
| تشويش إلكتروني | electronic jamming |
| تشويش رقمي | digital jamming |
| تشويش فعال | active jamming |
| تشويه | distortion |
| تشيكوسلوفاكي | Czech |
| تشيكوسلوفاكيا | Czechoslovakia |
| تشيلي | Chile |
| تصادم | collision |
| تصحيح أمام الهدف | aim-off |
| تصحيح التوجيه | guidance correction |
| تصحيح للرياح | correction for wind |
| تصريح إجازة | leave pass |
| تصفيح | armour plating |
| تصفية | liquidation |
| تصميم الصواريخ | missile design |
| تصنيف الأمن | security classification |
| تصويب | aim, sighting |
| تصويب بصري | visual sighting |
| تصوير | photography |
| تصوير جوي | aerial photography |
| تصوير حراري | thermal imaging |
| تضخيم الضوء | light-amplification |
| تطعيم | innoculation |
| تطعيم | vaccination |
| تطهير | clearing, disinfection |
| تطهير الألغام | mine clearance |
| تطور المعركة | combat development |
| تطوير التدريب | training development |
| تطويق العدو | containing the enemy |
| تعاظم قوة الدفاع الساحلي | coastal force build-up |
| تعاون | collaboration, teamwork |
| تعبئة | mobilization |
| تعبئة متقدمة | pre-mobilization |
| تعزيز | reinforcement, support |
| تعزيز حركي | logistics support |
| تعزيز رأس الساحل | consolidate a beachhead |
| تعزيز لاحق | post-boost |
| تعزيز مستمر للمقاتلات | continuous fighter support |
| تعزيزات دفاعية | defensive reinforcement |
| تعقب | tracking |
| تعليق هوائي سائلي | hydro-pneumatic suspension |
| تعليق هيدروغازي | hydrogas suspension |
| تعليم | instruction |
| تعويق الاشتعال | ignition delay |
| تعويق البيانات | data delay |

| | |
|---|---|
| تعويق المفجر | detonator delay |
| تعيين | designation |
| تعيّن الهدف ! | target understood! |
| تعيين الاتجاه | direction-finding |
| تغذية | messing |
| تغطية | covering |
| تغطية ٣٦٠ درجة | 360 degrees coverage |
| تغليف | covering |
| تغليف لاحق | after casing |
| تغيب بدون إذن | absent without leave |
| تغير التردد | frequency change |
| تغير سريع | rapid shift |
| تغير سريع للتردد | frequency-agile |
| تغيير السير | change course |
| تغيير الموقع | change location |
| تغيير الوضع | change of position |
| تفادى العدو | evade the enemy |
| تفتيت | disintegration |
| تفتيش | inspection, review |
| تفتيش أمتعة | kit inspection |
| تفتيش بصري | visual inspection |
| تفتيش ظاهري | external inspection |
| تفتيش طبي | medical inspection |
| تفتيش عام | general inspection |
| تفتيش المرضى | sick parade |
| تفجير | detonation, burst (to), detonate |
| تفجير تشظية | blast-fragmentation |
| تفرع | bypass |
| « تفرق ! » | fall out! |
| تفريغ « ويجمان » | Wegmann discharge |
| تفسير | interpretation |
| تفصيل | detail |
| تفقد الجنود | troop review |
| تفوق جوي | air superiority, air supremacy |
| تفويض | authorization, commission |
| تقاطع | intersection |
| تقاطع سكة مع طريق | level-crossing |
| تقاطع طرق | road junction |
| تقدم ! | advance! |
| تقدم بالقوة | advance in force |
| تقدم للتماس | advance to contact |
| تقدير خسائر القذف | bomb damage assessment |
| تقدير المدى | range estimation |
| تقرير استخبارات | intelligence report |
| تقرير حادث | accident report |
| تقنية المتقفي البصري | Optical Seeker Technique |
| تقهقر | fall back |
| تقويض الخيام | break camp |
| تكبير | magnification |
| تكتيك | tactics |
| تكتيكي | tactical |
| تكلفة التدريب | training cost |
| تكنولوجيا | technology |
| تكوين | formation |
| تل | hill |
| تلامس بصري | visual contact |
| تلسكوب | telescope |
| تلسكوب بالأشعة دون الحمراء | IR telescope |
| تلسكوب بصري | optical telescope |
| تلسكوب التسديد | sighting telescope |
| تلسكوب التصويب | aiming telescope |
| تلسكوب تصويب ليلي | night-sighting telescope |
| تلسكوب وحيد العين | monocular telescope |
| تلغراف | telegraph |
| تلف | damage |
| تلقائياً | automatically |
| تلقيح | inoculation |
| تلقيم آلي | automatic loading |
| تلقيم اوتوماتي | automatic feed |
| تلقيم منفصل | separate-loading |
| تلقيم يدوي | manual loading |
| تلقين | indoctrination |
| تلوث | contamination |

ت

| | |
|---|---|
| تلوث بكتيري | bacterial contamination |
| تلوث نووي | nuclear contamination |
| تمديدات جذر حافة المتقدمة للجناح | leading-edge root extensions |
| تمرد | insubordination, insurrection, mutiny |
| تموين جاري | underway replenishment |
| تموين ذخيرة | ammunition supply |
| تموين عمودي | vertical replenishment |
| تموينات | stores |
| تموينات غذائية | food supplies |
| تموينات فنية | technical stores |
| تمويه | camouflage |
| تمويه طبيعي | natural camouflage |
| تمييز | identification |
| تمييز الصديق والعدو « هاي پول » | High Pole IFF |
| تنبؤات جوية | weather forecast |
| تنبيه عام | general alert |
| ت . ن . ت | TNT |
| تنزانيا | Tanzania |
| تنظيف | clearing |
| تنظيم ضغط الاطار | tyre-pressure regulation |
| تنفسي | respiratory |
| تنقلية | mobility |
| تنقية الماء | water purification |
| تنكب سلاح ! | slope arms! |
| تنكيس العلم | flag at half mast |
| تهديد | threat |
| تهديد تحت الماء | underwater threat |
| تهديد جوي | air threat |
| تهديد سطحي | surface threat |
| توازن عسكري | military equilibrium |
| توافقات المحرك | engine harmonics |
| توجيه | azimuth, direction, guidance, guideline, steering |
| توجيه آلي ذاتي | self-homing |
| توجيه آلي راداري نصف فعال | semi-active radar homing |

| | |
|---|---|
| توجيه آلي طرفي بالأشعة دون الحمراء | infra-red terminal homing |
| توجيه آلي طرفي نصف فعال | semi-active terminal homing |
| توجيه انزلاقي | skid-steered |
| توجيه بالقصور الذاتي | inertial guidance |
| توجيه بالقصور الذاتي/تيركوم | inertial/Tercom guidance |
| توجيه بالليزر توجيه الدفع | laser guidance, laser homing |
| توجيه راداري | thrust vectoring |
| توجيه راداري | radar homing |
| « اس ايه آر اتش » | SARH homing |
| توجيه راداري فعال | active radar homing |
| توجيه قيادي « تي جي ـ ٢ » | TG-2 command guidance |
| توجيه لنصف المسافة | mid-course guidance |
| توجيه مزدوج | dual guidance |
| توجيه ملاحي بالقصور الذاتي | inertial navigation guidance |
| توجيه ميكانيكي | mechanical steering |
| توزيع | deployment |
| توزيع الطاقة | power distribution |
| توزيع للقوات العسكرية | service delivery |
| توزيع مشترك للمعلومات التكتيكية | joint tactical information distribution |
| توصيل البيانات | data link |
| توصيل البيانات الرقمية | digital data link |
| توصيلات كهربائية | electrical connections |
| توصيلة بيانات أرض ـ جو | ground-air data link |
| توضيح شعاعي دوپلر | doppler beam-sharpening |
| توغو | Togo |
| توقيع الكتروني لجهاز الاحساس | sensor signature |
| تونس | Tunisia |
| تونسي | Tunisian |
| تيار النيران | firing current |
| تيتانيوم مطروق | forged titanium |

ث

| | |
|---|---|
| ثابت | stationary |
| ثبات الترجّح | pitch stability |
| ثرمومتر مسجل | recording thermometer |
| ثقب | drill (to) |
| ثقل | weight |
| ثكنات | barracks |
| ثكنة | quarters, barrack |
| ثكنة الجنود | troop accommodation |
| ثلاثي | tripartite |
| ثلاثي الأطراف | tripartite |
| دراجة بعجلات ثلاثة | wheeled tricycle |
| ثورة | insurrection, rebellion |

# ج

| | |
|---|---|
| جاجوار | Jaguar |
| جاجوار سيپيكات | Sepecat Jaguar |
| جاسوس | spy |
| جاسوسية | espionage |
| جامايكا | Jamaica |
| جاهز للاطلاق | ready-to-launch |
| جبهة | front |
| جُدَري | smallpox |
| جراب الطلقات | bandolier |
| جراب المسدس | holster |
| جراب المؤونة | haversack |
| جراح | surgeon |
| جرار « ايه تي -تي » | AT-T tractor |
| جرار المدفع | gun tractor |
| جرار مدفعية « ايه تي - اس » | AT-S artillery tractor |
| جرار مدفعية ثقيلة | heavy artillery tractor |
| جرار مهندس قتال | combat engineer tractor |
| جرح | wound (to) |
| جرد | inventory |
| جرد البحرية | navy inventory |
| جرد عسكري | army inventory |
| جرد من السلاح | disarm |
| جرد « ناتو » | NATO inventory |
| جرعة قاتلة | lethal dose |
| جريح | wounded, casualty |
| جريح واجب نقله | stretcher case |
| الجزء الأساسي | main component |
| جزء الرادار | radar component |
| الجزائر | Algeria |
| جزائري | Algerian |
| جزيرة الميمنة | starboard island |
| جسر | bridge |
| جسر « اس ئي » | SE bridge |
| جسر « بيلي » | Bailey bridge |
| جسر جاهز للتركيب | prefabricated bridge |
| جسر جوي | airlift |
| جسر دبابات | tank bridge |
| جسر عائم | floating bridge |
| جسر على المقص | scissors bridge |
| جسر غاطس | submerged bridge |
| جسر قابل للفك | demountable bridge |
| جسر متحرك | draw-bridge |
| جسر مراقبة الطائرات العمودية | helicopter control bridge |
| جسر مشاة | foot bridge |
| جسر نقالي خفيف | light portable bridge |
| جسم الطائرة | fuselage |
| جسم غريب | foreign object |
| جماعة | company, troop |
| جماعة العلم | flag group |
| جماعة مغيرة | raiding party |
| جمّد | immobilise (to) |
| جمع استخبارات سلبي | passive intelligence-gathering |
| جمع اوتوماتي | auto-gather |
| جمع المدفعية | gun gathering |
| جمل | camel |

ج

| | |
|---|---|
| جمنازيوم | gymnasium |
| جمهورية أفريقيا الوسطى | Central African Republic |
| جمهورية المانيا الاتحادية | German Federal Republic |
| جمهورية المانيا الديمقراطية | German Democratic Republic |
| جمهورية الدومينيكان | Dominican Republic |
| الجمهورية العربية اليمنية | Yemen Arab Republic |
| جمهورية كوريا الديمقراطية الشعبية | Democratic People's Republic of Korea |
| جمهورية اليمن الديمقراطية الشعبية | Yemen People's Democratic Republic |
| جناح | flank |
| جناح أبتر جانبي | lateral stub wing |
| جناح إضافي ـ مزدوج الشقوق | double-slotted flap |
| جناح ثابت | fixed-wing |
| جناح جوي | air wing |
| الجناح الجوي للشرطة | Police Air Wing |
| جناح العزل | isolation ward |
| جناح قصير الباع | short-span wing |
| جناح متحرك | moving wing |
| جناح متغير الاحديداب | variable camber wing |
| جناح مثلثي | delta wing |
| جناح المستشفى | hospital ward |
| جناح مقاتل | combat wing |
| جناح الميسرة | left flank |
| جناح نظام « اواك » | AWAC Wing |
| جنباً سلاح ! | order arms! |
| جند ! | enlist |
| جنَّد | recruit (to) |
| جند الاقتحام | assault troops |
| جند الجو | airborne troops |
| جند القتال | combat troops |
| جُند المشاة | infantry |
| جندي | soldier, private, serviceman |
| جندي تحت التدريب | trainee |
| جندي جديد | recruit |
| جندي مدفعية هاون | mortarman |
| جندي مرتزق | mercenary |
| جنوب | south |
| جنوب أفريقي | South African |
| جنوب أفريقيا | South Africa |
| جنوب كوريا | South Korea |
| جنود الأمن | security troops |
| جنود الانشاءات | construction troops |
| جنود البحرية السوفياتية | Soviet marines |
| جنود الصحراء | desert troops |
| جنود صواريخ | rocket troops |
| جنود غير مقاتلين | non-combat troops |
| جنود مترجلون | disembarked troops |
| جنيح | fin |
| جنيح قلابة حافة المتقدمة للجناح | leading-edge flap |
| جنيح متدلي | drooping aileron |
| جنيح مساعد | canard |
| جنيح ممتد | extended foil |
| جنيحات | ailerons |
| جهاز إحساس | sensor |
| جهاز احساس آيبول | Eyeball sensor |
| جهاز الاحساس بالارتفاع | elevation sensor |
| جهاز احساس بالأشعة دون الحمراء | infra-red sensor |
| جهاز احساس بالأشعة دون الحمراء للرصد الأمامي | forward looking infra-red sensor |
| جهاز احساس بصري | optical sensor |
| جهاز احساس تكتيكي | tactical sensor |
| جهاز احساس تلفزيوني | TV sensor |
| جهاز احساس تلفزيوني منخفض الاضاءة | low-light TV sensor |
| جهاز احساس « تيسايو ئي اوه » | Tiseo EO sensor |
| جهاز إحساس كهرومغنطيسي | electromagnetic sensor |

| | |
|---|---|
| جهاز احساس للحرب المضادة للغواصات | ASW sensor |
| جهاز ارسال | transmitter |
| جهاز الارسال بالقيادة | command transmitter |
| جهاز ارسال البيانات « لينك » | Link data transmission |
| جهاز إرسال المعطيات « ايه جي ١٥ » | AG 15 data link |
| جهاز ارسال معطيات الطائرة | aircraft data link |
| جهاز إرسال واستقبال | duplexer |
| جهاز ارسال واستقبال | transceiver |
| جهاز ارسال واستقبال « دبليو اس سي ـ ٣ » | WSC-3 transceiver |
| جهاز اطلاق | launcher |
| جهاز اطلاق الدخان | smoke-discharger |
| جهاز الأمان | safety device |
| جهاز الانذار | warning system |
| جهاز انعاش | life-support system |
| جهاز الايقاف | arrester gear |
| جهاز باحث | seeker |
| جهاز بصري الكتروني توتم للتحكم باطلاق النار | Totem optronic fire control |
| جهاز تحليل الاشارات | signal processor |
| جهاز تحليل البيانات « آي پي إن ١٠ » | IPN 10 data processing |
| جهاز تحليل التتبع | tracking processor |
| جهاز تدابير مضادة للألغام | mine countermeasure gear |
| جهاز التزود بالوقود أثناء الطيران | inflight refuelling gear |
| جهاز تسديد | sight |
| جهاز التسديد | sighting system |
| جهاز تسديد « اكس ام ـ ٥٨ » | XM-58 sight system |
| جهاز تسديد مزدوج العينين | binocular sight |
| جهاز تشويش ذاتي الاسقاط | self-projection jammer |
| جهاز تصويب القنابل | bomb sight |
| جهاز التطهير « ايه آر اس ـ ١٢ يو » | ARS-12U decontamination |
| جهاز تعزيز مربوط | strap-on booster |
| جهاز تلكس | telex machine |
| جهاز تنفس | respirator |
| جهاز جمع اوتوماتي | auto-gathering device |
| جهاز الحط الانزلاقي | skid landing gear |
| جهاز الحط لدولاب الذيل | tailwheel landing gear |
| جهاز سائل ومجيب لتمييز الصديق والعدو / لخاصية التمييز الانتقائي | IFF/SIF transponder |
| جهاز السيطرة على الرمي « داردو » | Dardo fire control |
| جهاز طهي بالوقود الجاف | solid fuel cooker |
| جهاز طيران تلقائي | autopilot |
| جهاز طيران تلقائي لتثبيت وضع الطيران | attitude-hold autopilot |
| جهاز لاسلكي عقابي | pack radio |
| جهاز لاسلكي « لينك ١١ » | Link 11 wireless |
| جهاز مؤازر | servo |
| جهاز محاكاة | simulator |
| جهاز محاكاة الطائرة | flight simulator |
| جهاز محاكاة الطلقات | shot simulator |
| جهاز مراقبة | monitor |
| جهاز مراقبة تلفزيوني | television monitor |
| جهاز مستقل للتنفس تحت الماء | scuba |
| جهاز مسح | scanner |
| جهاز مسح بالأشعة دون الحمراء « اس ايه تي سايكلوپ ١٦٠ ايه تي » | SAT Cyclope 160 AT IR linescan |
| جهاز مسح دوار | rotating scanner |
| جهاز هبوط رباعي العجلات | quadricycle landing gear |
| جهاز وضع الرموز | coder |
| الجو | atmosphere |

ج

| | |
|---|---|
| جو | air |
| جو سيء | bad-weather |
| جو عاصف | rough weather |
| جو قاسي | severe weather |
| جيبوتي | Djibouti |
| الجيران العرب | Arab neighbours |
| جيروسكوب | gyro |
| جيروسكوب ليزر حلقي | ring laser gyro |
| جيش | army |
| جيش التحرير الشعبي | People's Liberation Army |
| الجيش الشعبي | people's army |
| جيش الطيران | aviation army |
| جيش العمال الشباب | Youth Labour Army |
| الجيل الأول | first-generation |
| جيني | Guinea |

# ح

| | |
|---|---|
| حاجب | orderly |
| حاجب الريح | windscreen |
| حاجبة الوميض | flash hider |
| حاجز مستطيل | rectangular block |
| حادث مميت | fatal accident |
| حارس | guardsman, guard, sentry |
| حارفة | deflector |
| حارق لاحق | afterburner |
| حاسبة رقمية | digital computer |
| حاسبة نسبية | analogue computer |
| حاضن امامي | forestock |
| حاضن قابل للطي | folding stock |
| حافة | chine |
| حافة أمامية ساقطة | drooped leading edge |
| حافظ على الخطوة ! | keep step! |
| حافلة رأس المقذوف | warhead bus |
| حاكمات باشارات كهربائية | electrically signalled controls |
| حاكمات الطيران بالسلك | fly-by-wire controls |
| حالة الانذار | state of alert |
| حالة البحر ٤ | Sea State 4 |
| حالة البحر ٦ | Sea State 6 |
| حالة التدخل | intervention situation |
| حالة الصلابة | solid-state |
| حالة طوارىء | alert |
| حالة الطوارىء | state of emergency |
| حالة مثالية | optimum condition |
| حام | hover |
| حامل جاهز | ready-use rack |
| حامل الذخيرة « ليزي سوزان » | Lazy Susan ammunition rack |
| حامل ذو ساقين | bipod |
| حامل الرشاش | machine-gun mounting |
| حامل العلم | standard bearer |
| حامل القاذف الثلاثي | triple-ejector rack |
| حامل قنطري | gantry |
| حامل نقالة | stretcher bearer |
| حاملة | carrier |
| حاملة أسلحة « ويزل » | Wiesel weapon carrier |
| حاملة « إنتربرايز » | Enterprise carrier |
| حاملة بالطاقة النووية | nuclear-powered carrier |
| حاملة « پي ايه ـ ٧٥ » | PA-75 carrier |
| حاملة « جاندارك » | Jeanne d'Arc carrier |
| حاملة جنود مدرعة | armoured personnel carrier (APC) |
| حاملة جنود مدرعة « بي تي آر ـ ٤٠ » | BTR-40 APC |
| حاملة جنود مدرعة « بي تي آر ـ ٥٠ » | BTR-50 APC |
| حاملة جنود مدرعة « بي تي ار ـ ٦٠ » | BTR-60 APC |
| حاملة جنود مدرعة « بي تي آر ـ ٧٠ » | BTR-70 APC |
| حاملة جنود مدرعة « بي تي آر ـ ١٥٢ » | BTR-152 APC |
| حاملة « جيوسيپى جاريبالدي » | Giueseppe Garibaldi carrier |
| حاملة حراسة | escort carrier |

| | |
|---|---|
| حاملة « ديدالو ايه اس دبليو » | Dedalo ASW carrier |
| حاملة رأس قذيفة شبه مداري | suborbital warhead-carrier |
| حاملة ضخمة | super-carrier |
| حاملة طائرات | aircraft carrier |
| حاملة الطائرات « أمريكا » | America aircraft carrier |
| حاملة طائرات « جون إف كنيدي » | John F. Kennedy carrier |
| حاملة طائرات خفيفة | light aircraft carrier |
| حاملة الطائرات ٢٥ دي مايو | 25 de Mayo aircraft carrier |
| حاملة طائرات عمودية | helicopter carrier |
| حاملة طائرات عمودية جاريبالدي | Galibaldi helicopter carrier |
| حاملة طائرات « كليمانصو » | Clemenccau aircraft carrier |
| حاملة طائرات « كييف » | Kiev carrier |
| حاملة طائرات نووية « سي ڤي ان » | CVN nuclear powered aircraft carrier |
| حاملة « فوريستال » | Forrestal carrier |
| حاملة « ڤيكرانت » | Vikrant carrier |
| حاملة « كولوسوس » | Colossus carrier |
| حاملة « كيتي هوك » | Kitty Hawk carrier |
| حاملة مدرعة « شوت » | Shoet armoured carrier |
| حاملة مدرعة « يوروتو » | Urutu armoured carrier |
| حاملة « نيميتس » | Nimitz carrier |
| حاملة « هانكوك » | Hancock carrier |
| حاملة هاون « ام ـ ١٠٦ ايه ٢ » | M-106A2 mortar carrier |
| حاملة هاون « ام ـ ١٢٥ ايه ٢ » | M-125 A2 mortar carrier |
| حاملة « هيرميز » | Hermes carrier |
| حاملة « وليد » | Walid carrier |
| حاوية | container |
| حاوية ـ قاذفه | container-launcher |
| حاوية نقل / إطلاق | transport/launching container |
| حبل القلع | halyard |
| حبل نجاة | life-line |
| حجاب دخان | screening smoke |
| حجاب المفاعل | reactor shielding |
| حجر صحي | quarantine |
| حجرة الاحتراق | combustion chamber |
| حجرة السطح | deckhouse |
| حجرة الطاقم | crew compartment |
| حجرة الطيار | cockpit |
| حجرة طيار مزدوجة | twin-cockpit |
| حجرة المحرك | engine compartment |
| حجرة المرضى | sick bay |
| حجرة المنوبين | orderly-room |
| حجز في الثكنة | confined to barracks |
| حجز في الغرفة | confined to quarters |
| حجز في محل مأمون | safe custody |
| حجم داخلي | internal volume |
| حد الأمان | safety line |
| حدد الاتجاه الزاوي | take a bearing |
| حدود الانقضاض | dive limit |
| حدود حساسة | sensitive border |
| حديث | up-to-date, modern, sophisticated |
| حذاء الجندي | boot |
| حراب ـ إنزع | unfix bayonets! |
| « الحراب ركب » | fix bayonets! |
| حراسة | escort |
| حراسة الجناح | flank guard |
| حرب | war, warfare |
| حرب إلكترونية | electronic warfare |
| حرب أهلية | civil war |
| حرب برمائية | amphibious warfare |
| حرب الجراثيم | bacteriological warfare |
| حرب الخنادق | trench warfare |
| حرب إشعاعية | radiological warfare |
| حرب ضد الغواصات | anti-submarine warfare (ASW) |
| حرب عالمية | global war |
| حرب كيماوية | chemical warfare |
| حرب نووية | nuclear warfare |

ح

| | |
|---|---|
| حربة | bayonet |
| حربة مدمجة | integral bayonet |
| حربة مركبة | fixed bayonet |
| حرس | Guards, escort |
| « الحرس ـ أخرج » | guard-turn out! |
| الحرس ـ بدل ! | stand-down! |
| حرس جمهوري | Republican Guard |
| الحرس الجوي الوطني | Air National Guard |
| حرس الحاملة | carrier escort |
| حرس الحدود | frontier guard, border guard |
| حرس الحدود « كيه جي بي » | KGB border guards |
| حرس خاص | body guard |
| حرس سواحل | coastguard |
| حرس الصحراء | desert guard |
| حرس قبلي للحدود | Border Tribal Militia |
| حرس لبنان الحر | Free Lebanese Militia |
| حرس المؤخرة | rear guard |
| حرس مرافق | convoy |
| حرس وطني | militia |
| الحرس الوطني | Home Guard |
| حرس وطني خصوصي | private militia |
| حرس وطني اقليمي | Territorial Militia |
| حرق | burn |
| حرق مداوم | sustainer burning |
| حرق من الدرجة الاولى | first degree burn |
| حرق من الدرجة الثانية | second degree burn |
| حرق النفاية | waste incineration |
| حرق ومضي | flash burn |
| حركة التدريب | drill movement |
| حركة الرتاج | bolt action |
| حركة كماشية | pincer movement |
| حركية | mobility |
| حركيات سفن الانزال | landing ships logistics |
| حزام | belt |
| حزام الذخيرة | ammunition belt |
| حزام المعدات | equipment belt |
| حزام وشريط كتف للضباط | Sam Browne |
| حزمة استمرار | holding beam |
| حزمة إلكترونية | electron beam |
| حزمة طاقة | beam of energy |
| حزمة ليزر مضمنة | modulated laser beam |
| حساس للحرارة | heat-sensitive |
| حشد | concentration |
| حشد الجنود | troop concentration |
| حشد الجنود في الجبهة الأمامية | forward troop concentration |
| حشد القوات الاحتياطية | reserve troop concentration |
| حشد المدفعية | gun concentration |
| حصار | blockade, siege |
| حصن | barricade, stronghold |
| حضور لأداء الواجب | report for duty |
| حضيرة | squad |
| حط عمودي | vertical landing |
| حظيرة | hangar |
| حظيرة صندوقية | box hangar |
| حظيرة الطائرات | aircraft hangar |
| حظيرة الطائرات العمودية | helicopter hangar |
| حظيرة طائرات عمودية متداخلة | telescopic helicopter hangar |
| حفار خنادق « ام دي كيه » | MDK ditching machine |
| حفار خنادق « بي تي ام ـ تي ام جي » | BTM-TMG trench digger |
| حفر | drill |
| حفرة المناوشة | fox hole |
| حقل ألغام | minefield |
| حقل الرمي | firing range |
| حقن | injection |
| حقن الوقود | fuel injection |
| حقيبة أدوات | tool kit |
| حقيبة الاسعاف الأولي | first aid kit |
| حقيبة بالأشعة دون الحمراء | infra-red suitcase |

| | |
|---|---|
| حقيبة كهرومغنطيسية | electro-magnetic suitcase |
| حقيبة متاع الجندي | pack |
| حُكم بعقوبة | sentence |
| حكومة عسكرية | military administration |
| حل | disband |
| حل الرموز | decipher (to) |
| حل الشفرة | break a code, decoding |
| حلاّل الرموز | cryptoanalyst |
| حلف وارسو | Warsaw Pact |
| حلفاء حلف وارسو | Warsaw Pact allies |
| حلقة اتصال لاسلكي | radio link |
| حمالة الأجهزة | harness rig sling |
| حمالة البندقية | rifle sling |
| حمالة رافعة « هاي » | Hi-liftloader |
| حمالة المصابين | casualty litter |
| حماية | defence |
| حماية جوية | air-cover |
| حماية جوية من البر | shore-based air cover |
| حمل الأسلحة | weapons load |
| الحمل الأقصى المسموح | maximum permissible load |
| حمل التخلص | disposable load |
| حمل كامل | full load |
| حمل المهمة | mission load |
| حملة | expedition |
| حمولة | cargo |
| حمى | defend |
| حمّى | fever |
| حوامة « هوفركرافت » | hovercraft |
| حوامة « اس آر ـ ان ـ ٦ » | SR-N-6 hovercraft |
| حوامة « ايست » | Aist hovercraft |
| حوامة « سكيما ـ ١٢ » | Skima-12 hovercraft |
| حوامة « ليبيد » | Lebed hovercraft |
| حوامة « وينتشيستر » | Winchester hovercraft |
| حوض | bath |
| حوض سفن الانزال | landing ships dock |
| حوض عائم | floating dock |
| حوض منصة الانزال | landing platform dock |
| حوض نقل برمائي | amphibious transport dock |
| حول | transmit |
| حياة عسكرية | military life |
| حيدان التصويب الصحيح | correct laying offset |
| حيز الأسلحة | weapon space |

# خ



| | |
|---|---|
| خارج المدى | out of range |
| خارج مدى البصر | beyond visual range |
| خارجي | overseas |
| خارطة | chart |
| خارق للدروع | armour-piercing |
| خاكي | khaki |
| خبرة قتالية | battle experience |
| خدعة | decoy |
| خدمة | service |
| خدمة عاملة | active service |
| خدمة عسكرية | military service |
| خدمة فعلية | active duty, active service |
| الخدمة في الجبهة | front-line service |
| خذ أوضاع القتال ! | battle stations! |
| خرب | destroy |
| خرج نظام الملاحة | navigation-system output |
| خرطوشة | cartridge |
| خرطوشة إشارات | signal cartridge |
| خرطوشة إشارات « سوبر ميني » | Super Mini Signal Cartridge |
| خرطوشة إضاءة | illuminating cartridge |
| خرطوشة « ام ١٩٣ » | M193 cartridge |
| خرطوشة خلبية | blank cartridge |
| خرطوشة مشعل إنذار | alarm flare cartridge |
| خرطوشة مضيئة | flare |
| خرطوشة « ناتو » | NATO cartridge |
| خرطوشة ومضية للتصوير | photoflash cartridge |
| خرق | breach (to), breakthrough |
| خروج من المستشفى | discharge from hospital |
| خريطة | map |
| خريطة أركان | ordnance map |
| خريطة الملاحة الجوية | aeronautical chart |
| خزان الاسقاط | drop tank |
| خزان حصى الرصف | ballast tank |
| خزان مركزي | central container |
| خزان الوقود | fuel tank |
| خزانة أجهزة | console |
| خزانة عرض | display console |
| خزفي | ceramic |
| خزن | storage |
| خزنة الذخيرة | magazine |
| خزنة ذخيرة اسطوانية | drum magazine |
| خزنة ذخيرة صندوقية | box magazine |
| خزنة على شكل حلزوني | "snail drum" magazine |
| خزنة مختومة | sealed magazine |
| خسائر | losses, casualties |
| خسائر فادحة | heavy casualties |
| خسارة | damage, casualty |
| خصائص أمان الغواصة | SUBSAFE features |
| خصائص التشغيل | operating characteristics |
| خصم | enemy, foe |
| خصوصي | private |
| خضوع | subordination |
| خط الاقتحام | assault line |
| خط الامدادات | supply line |
| خط انسيابي | streamlining |
| خط التسديد | sightline, line of sight |

خ

|  |  |
|---|---|
| خط تسديد بالليزر | laser sight line |
| خط ساحلي | coastline |
| خطأ التراصف | misalignment |
| خطاف القطر | towing hook |
| خطاف كمح السرعة | arrester hook |
| خطاف المرساة | grappling hook |
| خطاف نقل البضائع | cargo hook |
| خطر | danger |
| خطر الحريق | fire hazard |
| « الخطوة ـ أترك ! » | break step! |
| خطوة الاستعراض | slow march |
| خطوة ـ بطيئة ! | step slower! |
| خطوة ـ سريعة ! | step faster!, quicken step! |
| خطوة عكسية | reverse-pitch |
| خطوة ـ قصيرة ! | step short! |
| خطوة المراسم | ceremonial step |
| خطوط الاتصال | lines of communication |

|  |  |
|---|---|
| خطوط الاتصالات البحرية | Sea Lines Of Communication |
| خطير | serious |
| خفير | sentry |
| خفيف الوزن | light-weight |
| خلط الذخيرة | ammunition mix |
| خلوص الارتفاع | height clearance |
| خلية الفضة و الزنك | silver-zinc cell |
| الخليج العربي | Arab Gulf, Persian Gulf |
| خندق | trench |
| خوذة | helmet |
| خوذة فولاذية | steel helmet |
| خوّل | authorize (to) |
| خيال | silhouette |
| خيانة | treason |
| خيمة | tent |
| خيمة الاسعاف الطبي | medical care tent |
| خيوط متصالبة | cross hairs |

# د



| | |
|---|---|
| داء | disease |
| داء مُعْدٍ | infectious disease |
| دائرة مطبوعة | printed circuit |
| دائرة المفجر | detonator circuit |
| دافع | propellant |
| دافع جاف | solid propellant |
| دافع عن | defend |
| الدانمرك | Denmark |
| دانمركي | Danish |
| « داوم ! » | carry on! |
| دبابة « ابرامز » | Abrams tank |
| دبابة « اس » | S-tank |
| دبابة اصلاح « ايه إم إكس ـ ٣٠ دي » | AMX-30D recovery tank |
| دبابة « اف ڤي ٤٢٠١ » | FV4201 tank |
| دبابة « اكس ١ ايه ٢ » | X 1A2 tank |
| دبابة « اكس ام ١ » | XM1 tank |
| دبابة « ام ١ » | M1 tank |
| دبابة « ام ٤١ » | M41 tank |
| دبابة « ام ٤٧ » | M47 tank |
| دبابة « ام ٤٨ » | M48 tank |
| دبابة « ام ٦٠ » | M60 tank |
| دبابة « ام ٦٠ ايه ١ » | M60A1 tank |
| دبابة « ام ٦٠ ايه ٢ » | M60A2 tank |
| دبابة « ام ٦٠ ايه ٣ » | M60A3 tank |
| دبابة « ام ٥٥١ » | M551 tank |
| دبابة « ام/تي أر ـ ٧٧ » | M/TR-77 tank |
| دبابة « أي كيه ڤي ٩١ » | IK V 91 tank |
| دبابة « ايه ٤١ » | A41 tank |
| دبابة « ايه إم إكس ـ ١٠ أرسي » | AMX-10RC tank |
| دبابة « اوه اف ـ ٤٠ » | OF-40 tank |
| دبابة « پانتسر ييجر كيه » | Panzerjäger K tank |
| دبابة برمائية خفيفة | amphibious light tank |
| دبابة « پي تي ـ ٧٦ » | PT-76 tank |
| دبابة « پي زد ٦٨ » | PZ 68 tank |
| دبابة « تشالينجر » | Challenger tank |
| دبابة تشرشل | Churchill tank |
| دبابة « تشيفتاين » | Chieftain tank |
| دبابة « تي ـ ١٠ » | T-10 tank |
| دبابة « تي ـ ٥٤ » | T-54 tank |
| دبابة « تي ـ ٥٥ » | T-55 tank |
| دبابة « تي ـ ٦٢ » | T-62 tank |
| دبابة « تي ـ ٦٤ » | T-64 tank |
| دبابة « تي ـ ٦٩ » | T-69 tank |
| دبابة « تي ـ ٧٢ » | T-72 tank |
| دبابة « تي ـ ٧٢ كيه » | T-72K tank |
| دبابة « تي ـ ٨٠ » | T-80 tank |
| دبابة « تي ايه ام » | TAM tank |
| دبابة « خالد » | Khalid tank |
| دبابة خفيفة | light tank |
| دبابة خفيفة « اس كيه ـ ١٠٥ » | SK-105 light tank |
| دبابة خفيفة « ايه إم إكس ـ ١٣ » | AMX-13 light tank |
| دبابة « ساراسن » | Saracen tank |
| دبابة « ستريدز ڤاجن ١٠٣ » | Stridsvagn 103 tank |

| | |
|---|---|
| دبابة سفينة الانزال | landing ships tank |
| دبابة « سنتيوريون » | Centurion tank |
| دبابة « سيزر » | Caesar tank |
| دبابة « شير » | Shir tank |
| دبابة شيرمان | Sherman tank |
| دبابة « شيريدان » | Sheridan tank |
| دبابة طراز ٦١ | Type 61 tank |
| دبابة طراز ٦٣ | Type 63 tank |
| دبابة طراز ٧٤ | Type 74 tank |
| دبابة طويلة المدى | long-range tank |
| دبابة ڤولكان ايه دي اس | Vulcan ADS tank |
| دبابة « ڤيكرز » | Vickers tank |
| دبابة « لايون » | Lion tank |
| دبابة « ليپارد » | Leopard tank |
| دبابة « ليپارد آي ايه ٤ » | Leopard IA4 tank |
| دبابة « مركاڤا » | Merkava tank |
| دبابة معارك رئسية | main battle tank |
| دبابة معارك رئيسية « ايه ام اكس ـ ٣٠ » | AMX-30 MBT |
| دبابة معارك رئيسية « ايه ام اكس ـ ٣٢ » | AMX-32 MBT |
| دبابة « ووكر بولدوج » | Walker Bulldog tank |
| دبابة ياكت بانتسر كانونة | Jagdpanzer Kanone tank |
| دبي | Dubai |
| دثار | jacket |
| دحاريج عودة | return rollers |
| دخان أبيض | white smoke |
| دخان أحمر | red smoke |
| دخان أخضر | green smoke |
| دخان أزرق | blue smoke |
| دخان أسود | black smoke |
| دخان أصفر | yellow smoke |
| دخان برتقالي | orange smoke |
| دخان بنفسجي | violet smoke |
| دخان رمادي | grey smoke |
| دخان سام | toxic fumes |
| دراجة نارية | motor cycle |
| درّب | drill (to) |
| درب | track |
| درجان | taxying-out |
| درجة التحمل القصوى | maximum endurance |
| درجة حرارة الذخيرة | ammunition temperature |
| درجة حرارة الشحن | charge temperature |
| درجة حرارة الغرفه | chamber temperature |
| درجة الحرارة المحيطة | ambient temperature |
| درجة الميل | gradient |
| درع | armour |
| درع « بورون » | boron armour |
| درع « تشوبام » | Chobham armour |
| درع حاجب | screen armour |
| درع خزفي | ceramic armour |
| الدَّرَكْ | Gendarmerie |
| الدروز | Druze |
| دفاع | defence |
| دفاع الاسطول | fleet-defence |
| دفاع بالصواريخ المضادة للسفن | anti-ship missile defence |
| دفاع تخصصي | layered defence |
| دفاع جوي | air defence |
| الدفاع الجوي الأمريكي الشمالي | North American Air Defence |
| دفاع ساحلي | coastal defence |
| دفاع الطوق الخارجي | outer-ring defence |
| دفاع عن النفس | self-defence |
| دفاع مدني | civil defence |
| دفاع مضاد للطائرات | anti-aircraft defence |
| دفة | rudder |
| دفع | propulsion |
| دفع احتراق لاحق | afterburning thrust |
| دفع أمامي | forward thrust, frontal thrust |
| دفع بالطاقة النووية | nuclear propulsion |
| دفع تربيني نفاث | turbojet propulsion |
| دفع توجيهي | vectoring thrust |
| دفع صاروخي | rocket propulsion |

د

| | |
|---|---|
| دفع عكسي | reverse-thrust |
| دفع عمودي | vertical thrust |
| دفع « هايبريد » | Hybrid propulsion |
| دفعة ثلاثية الطلقات | three-round burst |
| دفعة نيران | burst |
| دعامة الذيل | tailboom |
| دعم | support |
| دعم إلكتروني | electronic support |
| دعم التحليل عن بعد | teleprocessing support |
| دعم تكتيكي | tactical support |
| دعم جوي | air support |
| دعم الدبابات | tank support |
| دعم المدفعية | artillery support |
| دعم النيران | fire support |
| دليل | handbook, instruction book |
| دليل موجي | waveguide |
| دمر | destroy |
| دهان للتمويه | camouflage paint |
| دواء | medicine |
| دوار | rotating |
| دوار الجو | air sickness |
| دوّار الذيل | tail rotor |
| دوار رئيسي جاسيء | rigged main rotor |
| دوار عديم المفصلة | hingeless rotor |
| دوار مفصلي | hinged rotor |
| دوارات متحدة المحور | coaxial rotors |
| دوامة جيروسكوبية | gyro rotor |
| دوامة رئيسية قابلة للطي | folding main rotor |
| دوامة رباعية الشفرات | four-blade rotor |
| دوران جوي | air slew |
| دورة | cycle |
| دورة تجديد المعلومات | refresher course |
| دورية | patrol |
| دورية حراسة السواحل | coastal patrol |
| دورية حراسة الصيد | fishery patrol |
| دورية مراقبة الحدود | border patrol |
| دورية الفجر | dawn patrol |
| دولاب | road wheel |
| دولاب ترادفي | tandem-wheel |
| دول حلف وارسو | Warsaw Pact countries |
| دول منظمة ناتو | NATO nations |
| دون الحمراء | infra red |
| ديزل | diesel |
| ديزل « ٦ في -٥٣ تي » | 6V-53T diesel |
| ديزل احتياطي | reserve diesel |
| ديزل « ام ٥٠ » | M50 diesel |
| ديزل « ام تي يو » | MTU diesel |
| ديزل فيات | Fiat diesel |
| ديزل « مان » | MAN diesel |
| ديز نظاريا | dysentery |
| ديناميت | dynamite |

د

ذ

| | |
|---|---|
| ذات محركين نفاثين | twin-jet |
| ذاتي التلقيم | self-loading |
| ذاتي الحركة | self-propelled |
| ذاكرة الميكرو بروسسور | microprocessor memory |
| ذبذبة | pulse |
| ذخيرة | ammunition |
| ذخيرة احتياطية | reserve ammunition |
| ذخيرة إضاءة | illuminating ammunition |
| ذخيرة « ام ١٩٣٧ » | M-1937 ammunition |
| ذخيرة حية | live ammunition |
| ذخيرة خطّاطة متعددة الأغراض | multi-purpose tracer |
| ذخيرة خلبية | blank ammunition |
| ذخيرة دخان | smoke ammunition |
| ذخيرة سائبة | caseless ammunition |
| ذخيرة شديدة الانفجار | HE ammunition |
| ذخيرة غير نووية | conventional munition |
| ذخيرة في شريط | belted ammunition |
| ذخيرة محرقة | incendiary ammunition |
| ذخيرة المسدس | pistol ammunition |
| ذخيرة مضادة للدبابات شديدة الانفجار | HEAT ammunition |
| ذراع امتداد جانبي | lateral outrigger |
| ذراع القيادة | joystick |
| ذراع المغلاف المقفل | locked-breech arm |
| ذو اجنحة متغيرة | variable-geometry |
| ذو راس قذيفة نووي | nuclear-tipped |
| ذو قطبين | dipole |
| ذيل قابل للطي | folding tail |

ر

| | |
|---|---|
| رئاسة المراقبة | control headquarters |
| رأس الباحث | seeker head |
| رأس التوجيه الراداري | homing head |
| رأس الجسر | bridgehead |
| رأس الشاطىء | beach head |
| رأس قذيفة اف زد | FZ warhead |
| رأس قذيفة « ام آر في » | MR V warhead |
| رأس قذيفة تدريب | practice warhead |
| رأس قذيفة دخان | smoke warhead |
| رأس قذيفة شديدة الانفجار | HE warhead |
| رأس قذيفة شديدة الانفجار | high explosive warhead |
| رأس قذيفة شظايا / انفجار مستدير | annular blast/ fragmentation warhead |
| رأس قذيفة كيماوية | chemical warhead |
| رأس قذيفة محرقة | incendiary warhead |
| رأس قذيفة مخترق للأرض | earth penetrator warhead |
| رأس قذيفة نووية حرارية | thermonuclear warhead |
| رأس قذيفة وقود هواء | fuel-air explosive warhead |
| رأس المقدمة | spearhead |
| رأس مقذوف | warhead |
| رأس مقذوف « اوه ـ ٢ كيه تي » | O-2KT warhead |
| رأس مقذوف بحشوة مفرغة | hollow-charge warhead |
| رأس مقذوف منخفض العيار | low yield warhead |
| رأس مقذوف نووي | nuclear warhead |

| | |
|---|---|
| رأس مقذوف نووي ينفجر في الجو | air-burst nuclear warhead |
| رأس مهروس | squash-head |
| رأس مهروس شديد الانفجار | high-explosive squash-head |
| رؤوس حربية منتشرة | dispersion warhead |
| رؤية ليلية | night vision |
| رؤية ليلية بالأشعة دون الحمراء | IR night-vision |
| رؤية نفقية | tunnel vision |
| رئيس الأركان | chief of staff |
| رئيس أركان الحرب | chief of battle staff |
| رئيس رقباء | sergeant major |
| رائد | major |
| رائد فضاء | cosmonaut |
| الراتب والعلاوات | pay and allowances |
| راحة ! | stand easy! |
| رادار | radar |
| رادار اتجاه الطائرات العمودية | helicopter direction radar |
| رادار « اتش اس ايه ـ ريبورتر » | HSA Reporter radar |
| رادار « اتش اف ٢٠٠ » | HF 200 radar |
| رادار أجاف | Agave radar |
| رادار « آر ام ٧ » | RM7 radar |
| رادار « ار اي ال » | RIL radar |
| رادار « آر ايه ان ٣ ال ٣ دي » | RAN 3L 3D radar |
| رادار « آر ايه ان ١٠ اس » | RAN 10S radar |

| | |
|---|---|
| رادار « آر ايه تي ٣١ » | RAT 31 radar |
| رادار « آر ايه تي ٣١ اس » | RAT 31s radar |
| رادار « آر تي إن ـ ١٠ اكس » | RTN-10X radar |
| رادار « آر تي ان ٢٠ اكس » | RTN-20X radar |
| رادار « آر تي ان ٣٠ اكس » | RTN-30X radar |
| رادار « آر دي آي » | RDI radar |
| رادار أرضي | ground radar |
| رادار أرضي | ground-based radar |
| رادار إريكسون جيراف | Ericsson Giraffe radar |
| رادار « اس آر ئي ـ ام ٥ » | SRE-M5 radar |
| رادار « اس ايه آر » | SAR radar |
| رادار « اس پي اس ـ ١٠ » | SPS-10 radar |
| رادار « اس پي اس ـ ٣٢ » | SPS-33 radar |
| رادار « اس پي اس ـ ٤٩ » | SPS-49 radar |
| رادار « اس پي اس ـ ٥٥ » | SPS-55 radar |
| رادار « اس پي اس ـ ٧٠٣ » | SPS-703 radar |
| رادار « اس پي جي ـ ٣٤ » | SPG-34 radar |
| رادار « اس پي جي ـ ٤٩ » | SPG-49 radar |
| رادار « اس پي جي ـ ٥٠ » | SPG-50 radar |
| رادار « اس پي جي ـ ٥١ » | SPG-51 radar |
| رادار « اس پي جي ـ ٥٣ ايه » | SPG-53A radar |
| رادار « اس پي جي ـ ٥٥ ايه » | SPG-55A radar |
| رادار « اس پي جي ـ ٦٠ » | SPG-60 radar |
| رادار « اس پي دبليو ـ ٢ » | SPW-2 radar |
| رادار « اس پي كيو ـ ٩ ايه » | SPQ-9A radar |
| رادار « اس پي واي ـ ١ ايه » | SPY-1A radar |
| رادار استطلاع | surveillance radar |
| رادار استطلاع ثانوي | secondary-surveillance radar |
| رادار استطلاع جوي | air-surveillance radar |
| رادار استكشاف جوي | air search radar |
| رادار استكشاف مركزي | central search radar |
| رادار « اس جي آر ـ ١٠٩ » | SGR-109 radar |
| رادار اضاءة الهدف | target illuminating radar |
| رادار اعتراضي محمول جواً | airborne-interception radar |
| رادار الاقتراب | approach radar |
| رادار اكتساب بموجات مستمرة | continuous wave acquisition radar |
| رادار « ال ان ٦٦ » | LN66 radar |
| رادار « ال ان ٦٦ اتش پي » | LN66HP radar |
| رادار « إلتا ٢٠٠ ١ بي » | Elta 200 1B radar |
| رادار « ألتأير ٣ » | Altair III radar |
| رادار « ال دبليو ـ ٠١ » | LW-01 radar |
| رادار « ال دبليو ـ ٠٢ » | LW-02 radar |
| رادار « ال دبليو ـ ٠٥ » | LW-05 radar |
| رادار « ال دبليو ـ ١٠ » | LW-10 radar |
| رادار « ال دبليو ـ ١١ » | LW-11 radar |
| رادار « ام پي كيو ـ ٤٩ » | MPQ-49 radar |
| رادار أول سكريتش | Owl Screech radar |
| رادار « اوه آربي ٣١ هركليز ١ » | ORB 31 Héraclès I radar |
| رادار « اوه آربي ٣٢ هركليز ٢ » | ORB 32 Héraclès II radar |
| رادار « اوه آربي ٣١ دبليو » | ORB 31W radar |
| رادار « اوه پي اس ـ ٩ » | OPS-9 radar |
| رادار « اوه پي اس ـ ١٤ » | OPS-14 radar |

ر

| | |
|---|---|
| رادار « اوه بي اس ـ ١٦ » | OPS-16 radar |
| رادار « آيباول » | Eye Bowl radar |
| رادار « إيج بول » | Egg Bowl radar |
| رادار « إيج كاپ » | Egg Cup radar |
| رادار « ايجيس » | AEGIS radar |
| رادار « ايه آر ـ ٣ دي » | AR-3D radar |
| رادار « ايه اس ـ ٣٧ » | AS-37 radar |
| رادار « ايه إن/اس بي اس ـ ٤٨ » | AN/SPS-48 radar |
| رادار « ايه ان/اس بي اس ٥٠٣ » | AN/SPS-503 radar |
| رادار « ايه إن/اس بي كيو ـ ١١ » | AN-SPQ-11 radar |
| رادار ايه إن/ايه اس آر ـ ٥ » | AN/ASR-5 radar |
| رادار « ايه إن/ايه اس اس ـ ٢ » | AN/ASS-2 radar |
| رادار « ايه إن/إيه إس دي ـ ٥ » | AN/ASD-5 radar |
| رادار « ايه إن/ايه إل إتش ـ ٤٦ » | AN/ALH-46 radar |
| رادار « ايه إن/ايه إل إم ـ ١٦٦ » | AN/ALM-166 radar |
| رادار « ايه إن/ايه إل ايه ـ ٦ » | AN/ALA-6 radar |
| رادار « ايه إن/ايه إل دي ـ ٥١ » | AN-ALD-51 radar |
| رادار « ايه ان/ايه ال كيو ـ ٥٢ » | AN/ALQ-52 radar |
| رادار « ايه ان/ايه ال كيو ـ ٦٣ » | AN/ALQ-63 radar |
| رادار « ايه ان/ايه ال كيو ـ ١١٩ » | AN/ALQ-119 radar |
| رادار « ايه ان/ايه ال كيو ـ ١٦١ » | AN/ALQ-161 radar |
| رادار « ايه إن/إيه إل ئي ـ ٥ » | AN/ALE-5 radar |
| رادار « ايه إن/ايه ايه آر ـ ٣٨ » | AN/AAR-38 radar |
| رادار « ايه إن/ايه ايه إس ـ ١٨ » | AN-AAS-18 radar |
| رادار « ايه إن/ايه بي آر ـ ١٧ » | AN/APR-17 radar |
| رادار « ايه إن/ايه بي اس ـ ٨٢ » | AN/APS-82 radar |
| رادار « ايه إن ـ ايه بي إس ـ ١١٨ » | AN/APS-118 radar |
| رادار « ايه إن/ايه بي إم ـ ٨٣ » | AN/APM-83 radar |
| رادار « ايه إن/ايه بي جي ـ ٦٣ » | AN/APG-63 radar |
| رادار « ايه إن/ايه بي جي ـ ٦٧ » | AN/APG-67 radar |
| رادار « ايه إن/ايه واي إتش ـ ١ » | AN/AYH-1 radar |
| رادار « ايه ان/يواس آر ـ ١ » | AN/USR-1 radar |
| رادار « ايه ان/يو ال ايه ـ ٢ » | AN/ULA-2 radar |
| رادار « ايه ان/يو ايه اس ـ ٤ » | AN/UAS-4 radar |
| رادار « ايه ان/يو واي كيه ـ ٢١ » | AN/UYK-21 radar |
| رادار « ايه بي آر ـ ٣٩ » | APR-39 radar |
| رادار « ايه بي اس ـ ١٢٤ » | APS-124 radar |
| رادار « ايه بي جي ـ ٦٣ » | APG-63 radar |
| رادار « ايه بي جي ـ ٦٦ » | APG-66 radar |
| رادار « ايه بي واي ـ ١ » | APY-1 radar |
| رادار « ايه دبليو جي ـ ٩ » | AWG-9 radar |
| رادار « پات هاند » | Pat Hand radar |
| رادار باحث | search radar |
| رادار باحث « سكانتر ٠٠٩ » | Scanter 009 search radar |
| رادار « بارلوك » | Bar Lock radar |
| رادار « پاف پول » | Puff Ball radar |
| رادار باك سكاتر | Backscatter radar |
| رادار باك نيت | Back Net radar |

ر

| | |
|---|---|
| Palm Frond radar | رادار « پام فروند » |
| Band Stand radar | رادار « باند ستاند » |
| Pave Paws radar | رادار « پايڤ پوز » |
| frequency-agile radar | رادار بتغير سريع للتردد |
| Searchwater radar | رادار بحري جو ـ سطح « سيرتشووتر » |
| Prisma radar | رادار « پريزما » |
| Pluto radar | رادار « پلوتو » |
| Blue Fox radar | رادار « پلوفوكس » |
| Blue Kestrel radar | رادار « بلوكستريل » |
| Plinth Net radar | رادار « پلينث نيت » |
| phased-array radar | رادار بمجموعة عناصر مشعة |
| Pop Group radar | رادار « پوپ جروپ » |
| Pot Drum radar | رادار « پوت درم » |
| Boat Sail radar | رادار « بوت سيل » |
| Pot Head radar | رادار « پوت هيد » |
| Post Lamp radar | رادار « پوست لامپ » |
| Pollux radar | رادار « پولكس » |
| P-50 radar | رادار « پي ـ ٥٠ » |
| PS7p/R radar | رادار « پي اس ٧ پي / آر » |
| Big Bar radar | رادار « بيج بار » |
| Big Bulge radar | رادار « بيج بالج » |
| Big Fred radar | رادار « بيج فريد » |
| Big Mesh radar | رادار « بيج ميش » |
| Big Nose radar | رادار « بيج نوز » |
| Big Net radar | رادار « بيج نيت » |
| Bass Tilt radar | رادار « بيس تيلت » |
| Peel Group radar | رادار « پيل جروپ » |
| Bee Hind radar | رادار « بي هايند » |
| tracking radar | رادار تتبع |
| Try Add radar | رادار « تراي آد » |
| Triton radar | رادار ترايتن |
| Cheese Cake radar | رادار « تشيز كيك » |
| IFF radar | رادار تمييز الصديق والعدو |
| Top Bow radar | رادار « توپ بو » |
| Top Pair 3D radar | رادار « توپ پير ٣ دي » |
| Top-Trough radar | رادار « توپ تروف » |
| Top Steer 3D radar | رادار « توپ ستير ٣ دي » |
| Top Sail 3D radar | رادار « توپ سيل ٣ دي » |
| navigation direction radar | رادار توجيه ملاحي |
| Token radar | رادار « توكين » |
| Thomson-CSF radar | رادار « تومسون ـ سي اس اف » |
| TRMS radar | رادار « تي آر ان اس » |
| TSR333 radar | رادار « تي اس آر ٣٣٣ » |
| TM 1226 radar | رادار « تي ام ١٢٢٦ » |
| TPQ-36 radar | رادار « تي پي كيو ـ ٣٦ » |
| TPQ-37 radar | رادار « تي پي كيو ٣٧ » |
| Thin Skin radar | رادار « ثين سكين » |
| Gun Dish radar | رادار « جن ديش » |
| airborne radar | رادار جوي |
| side-looking airborne radar | رادار جوي جانبي الرؤية |
| Gage radar | رادار « جيج » |
| GWS22 radar | رادار « جي دبليو اس ٢٢ » |
| Giraffe radar | رادار « جيراف » |
| Gemini radar | رادار « جيمني » |
| Jay Bird radar | رادار « جيه بيرد » |
| WM20 radar | رادار « دبليو ام ٢٠ » |
| WM28 radar | رادار « دبليو ام ٢٨ » |
| Drum Tilt radar | رادار « درُم تيلت » |
| Doppler radar | رادار « دوپلر » |
| Dog House radar | رادار « دوج هاوس » |
| Don-2 radar | رادار « دون ـ ٢ » |
| Don Kay radar | رادار « دون كيه » |
| D1280 radar | رادار « دي ١٢٨٠ » |
| DRBR 32C radar | رادار « دي آر بي آر ٣٢ سي » |
| DRBR 51 radar | رادار « دي آر بي آر ٥١ » |

ر

| | |
|---|---|
| رادار « دي آر بي آي ١٠ » | DRBI 10 radar |
| رادار « دي آر بي آي ١٠ دي » | DRBI 10D radar |
| رادار « دي آر بي ٣١ » | DRB 31 radar |
| رادار « دي آر بي سي ٣١ » | DRBC 31 radar |
| رادار « دي آر بي سي ٣٢ » | DRBC 32 radar |
| رادار « دي آر بي ان ٣٢ » | DRBN 32 radar |
| رادار « دي آر بي ڤي ٢٠ » | DRBC 20 radar |
| رادار « دي آر بي ڤي ٢٠ سي » | DRBC 20C radar |
| رادار « دي آر بي ڤي ٢٢ دي » | DRBV 22D radar |
| رادار « دي آر بي ڤي ٢٣ سي » | DRBC 23C radar |
| رادار « دي آر بي ڤي ٥٠ » | DRBV 50 radar |
| رادار « دي آر يو ايه ٢٣ » | DRUA 23 radar |
| رادار « دي ان ١٨١ » | DN181 radar |
| رادار « دي ايه ـ ٠٢ » | DA-02 radar |
| رادار « دي ئي ار بي ڤ ٢٣ بي » | DERBV 23B radar |
| رادار « ديكا » | Decca radar |
| رادار « ديكا آر ام ٤١٦ » | Decca RM 416 radar |
| رادار « رابيدز » | Rapids radar |
| رادار « رايثيون ١٩٠٠ » | Raytheon 1900 radar |
| رادار « رمسيس » | Rameses radar |
| رادار « روك كيك » | Rock Cake radar |
| رادار « ريد بارون » | Red Baron radar |
| رادار « زددبليو ـ ٠١ » | ZW-01 radar |
| رادار « زددبليو ـ ٠٦ » | ZW-06 radar |
| رادار ساحة المعركة | battlefield radar |
| رادار « سايد نيت » | Side Net radar |
| رادار « سبون ريست » | Spoon Rest radar |

| | |
|---|---|
| رادار « سپين تروف » | Spin Trough radar |
| رادار « سپين سكان » | Spin Scan radar |
| رادار « ستريت فلاش » | Straight Flush radar |
| رادار « سترات كيرڤ » | Strut Curve radar |
| رادار « سكان اود » | Scan Odd radar |
| رادار « سكان ثري » | Scan Three radar |
| رادار سكان فيكس | Scan Fix radar |
| رادار « سكوات آي » | Squatt Eye radar |
| رادار « سكوپ پير » | Scoop Pair radar |
| رادار « سكور بورد » | Score Board radar |
| رادار « سكوير پير » | Square Pair radar |
| رادار « سكوير تاي » | Square Tie radar |
| رادار « سكوير هيد » | Square Head radar |
| رادار « سكوينت آي » | Squint Eye radar |
| رادار « سكيپ سپين » | Skip Spin radar |
| رادار « سكين هيد » | Skin Head radar |
| رادار « سلسلة ٨٢ » | 82 series radar |
| رادار « سليم نيت » | Slim Net radar |
| رادار سليندر هيد | Cylinder Head radar |
| رادار « سلينيا اورايون » | Selenia Orion radar |
| رادار « سنوپ تريه » | Snoop Tray radar |
| رادار « سنوپ جروپ » | Snoop Group radar |
| رادار « سي ـ جل » | Sea Gull radar |
| رادار « سي دبليو آي » | CWI radar |
| رادار سيرانو | Cyrano radar |
| رادار « سي سپريه » | Seaspray radar |
| رادار « سي سيرتشر » | Sea Searcher radar |
| رادار السيطرة على الرمي | fire-control radar |
| رادار « سي فاير » | Seafire radar |
| رادار « سينثاتك اپاتشر » | Synthetic Aperture Radar |
| رادار « شورت هورن » | Short Horn radar |
| رادار « صن ڤايزر » | Sun Visor radar |
| رادار ضخم | giant radar |
| رادار طائرة مقاتلة احادي النبضة ـ نطاق « آي » | I-band monopulse fighter radar |
| رادار طراز ٩٦٣ | Type 963 radar |

ر

| | |
|---|---|
| رادار طراز ٩٩٣ | Type 993 radar |
| رادار طراز ١٠٠٦ | Type 1006 radar |
| رادار « طول كينج » | Tall King radar |
| رادار العدو | enemy radar |
| رادار عسكري | military radar |
| رادار « فان تيل » | Fan Tail radar |
| رادار « فان سونج - ئي » | Fan Song-E radar |
| رادار « فايركان » | Fire Can radar |
| رادار « فايرويل » | Fire Wheel radar |
| رادار « فريسكان » | FRESCAN radar |
| رادار فعال | active radar |
| رادار « فلاپ ليد » | Flap Lid radar |
| رادار « فلاپ ويل » | Flap Wheel radar |
| رادار « فلات جاك » | Flat Jack radar |
| رادار « فلات سپين » | Flat spin radar |
| رادار « فلات فيس » | Flat Face radar |
| رادار فوق الأفق | over-the-horizon radar |
| رادار « فوكسهنتر » | Foxhunter radar |
| رادار « كات هاوس » | Cat House radar |
| رادار « كاستور » | Castor radar |
| رادار كاستور يعمل عن بعد | Castor stand-off radar |
| رادار « كايت سكريتش » | Kite Screech radar |
| رادار « كايزر » | Kaiser radar |
| رادار كسب الذبذبة | pulse acquisition radar |
| رادار كشف سطحي | surface-search radar |
| رادار « كلام شل » | Clam Shell radar |
| رادار « كوبرا - جودي » | Cobra-Judy radar |
| رادار « كوجاك » | Kojak radar |
| رادار كور | Corps radar |
| رادار « كويك لوك ٢ » | Quick Look II radar |
| رادار « كيك سيريز » | Cake Series radar |
| رادار « كيو آرسي - ٣٣٤ » | QRC-334 radar |
| رادار « لاند رول » | Land Roll radar |
| رادار للرصد الامامي | fore-see radar |
| رادار « لو بلو » | Low Blow radar |
| رادار « لو سيف » | Low Sieve radar |
| رادار « لوك تو » | Look Two radar |
| رادار « لونج پو » | Long Bow radar |
| رادار « لونج تراك » | Long Track radar |
| رادار « ليرودز » | Lirods radar |
| رادار « ماشروم » | Mushroom radar |
| رادار « ماف كوب » | Muff Cob radar |
| رادار متابعة | tracking radar |
| رادار متتبع للأرض | terrain-following radar |
| رادار متعدد الأوضاع | multi-mode radar |
| رادار محكوم من الحاملة | carrier-controlled radar |
| رادار محمول جواً عن بعد | airborne stand-off radar |
| رادار مُخبر | reporter radar |
| رادار مُدافع | defending radar |
| رادار مدى فقط | range-only radar |
| رادار ملاحة | navigation radar |
| رادار ملاحي ئي اس دي | ESD navigational radar |
| رادار من سلسلة « سيرينا » | Sirena series radar |
| رادار « نايساسي » | Nysa C radar |
| رادار « نايف ريست » | Knife Rest radar |
| رادار نبتيون | Neptune radar |
| رادار نبضات « دوپلر » | pulse-Doppler radar |
| رادار نصف الكرة في المقدّمة | nose-hemisphere radar |
| رادار « هاف بو » | Half Bow radar |
| رادار « هاي سيف » | High Sieve radar |
| رادار « هاي فيكس » | High Fix radar |
| رادار « هاي لارك » | High Lark radar |
| رادار « هاي لون » | High Lune radar |
| رادار « هن إيج » | Hen Egg radar |
| رادار « هن روست » | Hen Roost radar |
| رادار « هن نست » | Hen Nest radar |
| رادار « هن هاوس » | Hen House radar |
| رادار « هورن سبون » | Horn Spoon radar |
| رادار « هوك سكريتش » | Hawk Screech radar |

| | |
|---|---|
| رادار هولاندزه | Hollandse radar |
| رادار « هيد لايت » | Head Light radar |
| رادار « هيد نت ـ ايه » | Head Net-A radar |
| رادار « هيد نت ـ سي » | Head Net-C radar |
| رادار « هيرنت » | Hair Net radar |
| رادار « واسپ هيد » | Wasp Head radar |
| رادار « ويف » | Whiff radar |
| رادار « يو ـ يو » | Yo-Yo radar |
| رادع | deterrent |
| رادوم | radome |
| راصد | observer |
| راصد جوي | aerial spotter |
| راصد فوق الأفق | over-the-horizon spotter |
| رافعة الطيران | fly off lever |
| رافعة هيدرولية | hydraulic jack |
| رافق | escort |
| رام ماهر | marksman |
| رامي حاذق | sharp shooter |
| راوح ! | mark time! |
| راية | flag, ensign |
| رباعي الماسورات | four-barrel |
| رباعي المقاعد | four-seat |
| ربط الاتصالات | communication liaison |
| ربط الاسطول | fleet liaison |
| رتاج مغلاق محوري | pivoted locking piece |
| رتبه | rank |
| رتل آلي | mechanized column |
| رجال | men |
| رجال صيانة اللاسلكي | radio maintenance men |
| رجل واحد | one-man |
| رحلة | voyage |
| رحلة تحت الماء | submerged voyage |
| رخمار | balaclava |
| رداء سروالي صامد للنار | fireproof overall |
| رسالة | message |
| رسالة عاجلة | dispatch |
| رسول | envoy |
| رشاش | machine-gun |
| رشاش « اس جي ام تي » | SGMT machine-gun |
| رشاش « ام ٢ » | M2 machine-gun |
| رشاش « ام ٢ اتش بي » | M2HB machine-gun |
| رشاش « ام ٦٠ » | M60 machine-gun |
| رشاش « ام ـ ٢٤٠ » | M-240 machine-gun |
| رشاش « ام جي ٣ » | MG3 machine-gun |
| رشاش « براونينج ٥٠ » | Browning 50 machine-gun |
| رشاش « پي كيه تي » | PKT machine-gun |
| رشاش ثقيل | heavy machine-gun |
| رشاش خفيف | light machine-gun |
| رشاش « دي إس اتش كيه ـ ٣٨ » | DShK-38 machine-gun |
| رشاش دي إس اتش كيه إم | DShKM machine-gun |
| رشاش قصير | sub-machine gun |
| رشاش قصير « اف ١ » | F1 sub-machine gun |
| رشاش قصير « ال ٢ ايه ٣ » | L2A3 sub-machine gun |
| رشاش قصير « ام ٣ ايه ١ » | M3A1 sub-machine gun |
| رشاش قصير « ام ١٩٢٨ ايه ١ » | M1928A1 sub-machine gun |
| رشاش قصير « ام ايه تي ٤٩ » | MAT 49 sub-machine gun |
| رشاش قصير « ام پي ٤٠ » | MP40 sub-machine gun |
| رشاش قصير « پي پي اس اتش ٤١ » | PP Sh41 sub-machine gun |
| رشاش قصير « ستن جن » | Sten Gun sub-machine gun |
| رشاش قصير « ستيرلينج » | Sterling sub-machine gun |
| رشاش قصير « سكورپيون » | Skorpion sub-machine gun |
| رشاش قصير طراز ٥٠ | Type 50 sub-machine gun |
| رشاش قصير طراز ٥٤ | Type 54 sub-machine gun |
| رشاش قصير « ڤي زد ٦١ » | VZ 61 sub-machine gun |

| | |
|---|---|
| رشاش قصير « كارل غوستاف » | Carl Gustav sub-machine gun |
| رشاش قصير « يو زد أي » | UZI sub-machine gun |
| رشاش « كيه بي قي » | KPV machine-gun |
| رشاش مضاد للطائرات | anti-aircraft machine-gun |
| رشاش « مينيمي » | Minimi machine-gun |
| رشاقة المناورة | agility |
| رشق متتابع | sequential salvo |
| رشقة مدفعية | salvo |
| رصاصة « دم ـ دم » | Dum-Dum bullet |
| رصد | lookout |
| رصيف مركب على شاحنة | truck-mounted ramp |
| رصيف منحدر للسفن | slipway |
| رفع | hoist (to) |
| رفع | lift |
| رفع ثقيل | heavy-lift |
| رفع الكفاية | up-grading |
| رقابة | control |
| رقابة عسكرية | military censorship |
| رقمي | digital |
| رقيب | censor, sentry, sergeant |
| الرقيب الأحدث | junior sergeant |
| الرقيب الأقدم | senior sergeant |
| ركب الحربة | bayonets fix! |

| | |
|---|---|
| ركوب | embarkation |
| رمث | pontoon |
| رمث نجاة قابل للنفخ | inflatable liferaft |
| رمز النداء | call sign |
| رموز | code |
| رموز مسبقة الاعداد | pre-arranged code |
| رموز « مورس » | morse code |
| رمي | fire |
| رمي أمامي | forward firing |
| رمي انتقائي | selective fire |
| الرمي ـ أوقف ! | stop-firing! |
| رمي بناره | bring fire to bear |
| رمي تجريبي | test firing |
| رمي سريع | rapid fire |
| رهينة | hostage |
| رواندة | Rwanda |
| روسي | Russian |
| روسيا | Russia |
| روماني | Romanian |
| رومانيا | Romania |
| رياضة بدنية | physical training |
| ريح معترضة | cross wind |
| ريشة تطوى | folding blade |
| ريشة دوامة رئيسية معقودة | kinked main-rotor blade |
| ريشة الموازن | stabilizer blade |

ر

| | |
|---|---|
| زائير | Zaire |
| زائيري | Zairean |
| زارعة الغام | minelayer |
| زارعة ألغام « جي ام زد » | GMZ minelayer |
| زامبي | Zambian |
| زامبيا | Zambia |
| زاوية الارتفاع | elevation |
| زاوية الاصطدام | angle of impact |
| زاوية الاقتراب | angle of approach |
| زاوية الانحرام | deflection angle |
| زاوية التسديد | angle of sight |
| زاوية الرؤية | angle of view |
| زاوية الشعاع | beam angle |
| زاوية القذف | dropping angle |
| زاوية الهبوب | angle of attack |
| زجاج أمان | safety glass |
| زجاج لا يخرقه الرصاص | bullet-proof glass |
| زجاج ليفي | fibreglass |
| زجاج منيع للشظايا | splinterproof glass |
| زجاجة زيت | oil bottle |
| زجاجة مخلوط « مولوتوف » | Molotov cocktail |
| زحف | march |
| زرع ألغام | mine laying |
| زعامة | leadership |
| زعانف خلفية صليبية | cruciform rear fins |
| زعنفة | fin |
| زعنفة بطنية | ventral fin |
| زعيم | leader |
| زلق | slide |
| زمبابوي | Zimbabwe |
| زمن | time |
| زمن الاحتراق | burn time |
| زمن الاعداد لدورة تالية | turn-around time |
| زمن التباطؤ | loiter time |
| زمن التعويق | delay time |
| زمن الحرب | wartime |
| زمن حقيقي | real-time |
| زمن السلم | peacetime |
| زمن الطيران | flight time |
| زناد | trigger |
| زوج من الصاروخ التموجي | ripple missile in pairs |
| زورق أغراض عامة | general purpose craft |
| زورق إنزال | landing craft |
| زورق إنزال « ال سي ام - ٦ » | LCM-6 landing craft |
| زورق إنزال « سي - ١٠٧ » | C-107 landing craft |
| زورق برمائي | amphibious boat |
| زورق بسطح انسيابي | aerofoil boat |
| زورق « جيمني » | Gemini boat |
| زورق حراسة بالصواريخ | missile patrol boat |
| زورق حراسة « جيهان » | Jihan patrol craft |
| زورق حراسة ساحلية | inshore patrol craft |
| زورق حراسة « كيث نيلسون » | Keith Nelson patrol craft |

| | |
|---|---|
| زورق حراسة لدعم الاقتحام | assault support patrol boat |
| زورق حراسة مجهز بصواريخ موجهة | guided missile patrol boat |
| زورق حراسة نهرية | river patrol craft |
| زورق حرس السواحل | coastguard cutter |
| زورق حرس سواحل « كومباتانت » | Combattante patrol boat |
| زورق حرس سواحل هجومي | attack patrol boat |
| زورق خفر السواحل | patrol boat |
| زورق خفر السواحل | coastal patrol craft |
| زورق دورية | patrol craft |
| زورق دورية مسلحة بالمدافع | patrol gun-boat |
| زورق « ريجيد رايدر » | Rigid Raider boat |
| زورق « زد ـ ٥٠٤ ام » | Z-504M boat |
| زورق « سي وولف » | Seawolf boat |
| زورق صواريخ | missile boat |
| زورق صواريخ « زار » | Saar missile boat |
| زورق صواريخ « ماترا » | Matra missile boats |
| زورق طوربيد | torpedo boat |
| زورق طوربيد « پي ٤ » | P4 torpedo boat |
| زورق طوربيد « پي ٦ » | P6 torpedo boat |
| زورق طوربيد « ستينكا » | Stenka torpedo boat |
| زورق طوربيد « سپيكا » | Spica torpedo boat |
| زورق طوربيد « شيرشن » | Shershen torpedo boat |
| زورق « كومار » | Komar boat |
| زورق « كوموران » | Cormoran boat |
| زورق « لي فوجيه » | Le Fougeux craft |
| زورق مسلح | gunboat |
| زورق مسلح « مارانون » | Maranon gunboat |
| زورق نهري مسلح | river gunboat |
| زورق « هايداو » | Haidau craft |
| زورق « هايكو » | Haikou craft |
| زورق هجوم سريع | fast strike craft, fast attack craft |
| زورق هجوم « سيميتار » | Scimitar |
| زورق هجوم « شانج هاي » | Shanghai attack craft |
| زورق هجوم « لا كومبتانت » | La Combattante attack craft |
| زورق « هوكو » | Hoku craft |
| زورق « هولا » | Hola craft |

# س

| | |
|---|---|
| سائق | driver |
| سائل قابل للتخزين | storable liquid |
| سائل مزيل التلوث | liquid decontaminant |
| ساتر طبيعي | natural cover |
| ساتر نيران | curtain of fire |
| ساحة المعركة | field of battle |
| ساحة القتال | battlefield |
| ساحل | coast |
| ساحل العاج | Ivory Coast |
| ساحلي | coastal |
| ساعٍ راكب | dispatch rider |
| ساعات الخدمة | hours on station |
| ساعات النهار | hours of daylight |
| ساق | leg, stem |
| ساكن | stationary, static |
| « سالت » : مفاوضات الحد من الأسلحة الاستراتيجية | SALT (Strategic Arms Limitation Talks) |
| السالڤادور | El Salvador |
| سام | toxic |
| ساماريتان | Samaritan |
| سبر بالصدى | echo-sounding |
| سبيكة تيتانيوم | titanium alloy |
| سبيكة خفيفة | light alloy |
| ستار | mask |
| سترة قصيرة | tunic |
| سترة نجاة قابلة للنفخ | inflatable life jacket |
| سجل كهدف ! | record as target! |
| سجل الزوار | visitors' book |
| سجل السفينة أو الطائرة | log book |
| سجلات طبية | medical records |
| سجن | prison |
| سجين | prisoner |
| سحاب | cloud |
| سحابة دخان | smoke cloud |
| سحب | withdraw |
| سحق | overwhelm |
| سد ماء | water dam |
| سداسي الأرياش | six-blade |
| سرب | squadron |
| سرب إستطلاع | reconnaissance squadron |
| سرب تعزيز | support squadron |
| سرب طائرات عمودية | helicopter squadron |
| سرب طائرات معترضة | interceptor squadron |
| سرب مقاتلات | fighter squadron |
| سرب نقل | transport squadron |
| سرب هجوم | attack squadron, strike squadron |
| سرب هجوم أرضي | ground-attack squadron |
| سرح | disband |
| سرعة | speed, velocity |
| سرعة التباطؤ | loiter speed |
| السرعة تحت الماء | submerged speed |
| سرعة التطاوف | cruise speed |
| السرعة التطاوفية | cruising speed |
| سرعة حول الصوتية | transonic speed |
| السرعة ـ خفض ! | reduce speed! |
| سرعة الدورية | patrol speed |

| | |
|---|---|
| سرعة دون الصوتية | subsonic speed |
| سرعة الرمي | rate of fire |
| سرعة الطائرة | aircraft velocity |
| سرعة عالية | high-speed |
| السرعة الفوهية | muzzle velocity |
| السرعة القصوى | top speed, maximum speed |
| السرعة المفرطة | hypervelocity |
| سروال | trouser |
| سريّ للغاية | top secret |
| سرية | squadron |
| سرية اتصالات | communications squadron |
| سرية إستطلاع | reconnaissance squadron |
| سرية اقتحام | assault squadron |
| سرية تدريب | training company |
| سرية تعزيز . سرب تعزيز | support squadron |
| سرية عربات مدرعة | armoured car squadron |
| سرية الفرسان | cavalry squadron |
| سرية مدفعية | battery, artillery battery |
| سرية مدفعية هاون | mortar battery |
| سرية مراقبة | control squadron |
| سرية مشاة | infantry company |
| سرية مظلات | parachute company |
| سرية هجوم | attack squadron |
| سرير مرن | elastic cradle |
| سريع الاشتعال | highly-inflammable |
| سريع الالتهاب | inflammable |
| سري لانكا | Sri Lanka |
| سطح انسيابي رافع | aerofoil |
| سطح برجي | turret roof |
| سطح بيني | through-deck |
| سطح الحظيرة | hangar deck |
| سطح ذيل ثابت | fixed tailplane |
| سطح رامغ عاطف | elevon |
| سطح زاوي | angled deck |
| سطح الطائرات العمودية | helicopter deck |
| سطح طيران | flight deck |
| سطح طيران زاوي | angled flight deck |
| سطح الطيران للطائرات العمودية | helicopter flightdeck |
| سطح العربات | vehicle deck |
| السطح العلوي | upper deck |
| سطح فولاذي | steel deck |
| سطح مؤقت | temporary deck |
| سطح متساطح | flush deck |
| سطح مقدم السفينة | foredeck |
| سعة | capacity |
| سعة استراتيجية | strategic capacity |
| سعة التحكم | control capacity |
| سعة الذاكرة | memory capacity |
| سعة العمل | work capacity |
| سعة الوقود | fuel capacity |
| سعر منخفض | low price |
| سعودي | Saudi Arabian |
| سفينة | vessel |
| سفينة اقتحام برمائية مجهزة بطائرات عمودية | amphibious helicopter assault ship |
| سفينة « اكتوبر ـ ٦ » | October-6 craft |
| سفينة اليجايتور | Alligator vessel |
| سفينة أليشا | Alesha ship |
| سفينة « أمجا » | Amga ship |
| سفينة انقاذ « أنتيو » | Anteo rescue ship |
| سفينة إنزال « باترال » | Batral landing ship |
| سفينة إنزال « پولنوكني » | Polnocny landing ship |
| سفينة إنزال « پي اس ـ ٧٠٠ » | PS-700 landing craft |
| سفينة إنزال « راپوتشا » | Rapucha landing ship |
| سفينة إنزال « رالي » | Raleigh landing ship |
| سفينة انزال « روپيتشا » | Ropucha landing ship |
| سفينة إنزال « سير بديڤير » | Sir Bedivere landing ship |
| سفينة إنزال « سير لانسلوت » | Sir Lancelot landing ship |

س

| | |
|---|---|
| سفينة إنزال مركبات وأفراد | LCVP |
| سفينة انقاذ الغواصات | submarine salvage vessel |
| سفينة انقاذ مقاتلة | combat salvage boat |
| سفينة انقضاض تاراوا | Tarawa assault ship |
| سفينة انقضاض طراز « ليرسن » | Lürssen-type attack craft |
| سفينة انقضاض مضاد | counter-ambush vessel |
| سفينة « ايڤان روجوڤ » | Ivan Rogov ship |
| سفينة ايواء مساعدة | auxiliary barrack ship |
| سفينة « ايوا جيما » | Iwo Jima ship |
| سفينة « پتيا » | Petya ship |
| سفينة بحرية | seagoing vessel |
| سفينة « بدزينا » | Bedezine ship |
| سفينة برمائية « أتسيومي » | Atsiumi amphibious vessel |
| سفينة « پروڤينس » | Province craft |
| سفينة « پريموري » | Primorye ship |
| سفينة بضائع برمائية | amphibious cargo ship |
| سفينة « بلو ريدج » | Blue Ridge vessel |
| سفينة « بنينا » | Benina craft |
| سفينة « بوريس تشيليكين » | Boris Chilikin ship |
| سفينة « پوك » | Pauk ship |
| سفينة « پوليشات » | Poluchat craft |
| سفينة « بي إم ـ ٢١ » | BM-21 craft |
| سفينة « پي جي جي ـ ١ » | PGG-1 craft |
| سفينة « بيدرو تيكسيرا » | Pedro Teixeira ship |
| سفينة تجارية | merchant ship |
| سفينة تدابير مضادة للألغام | mine countermeasure ship |
| سفينة تدريب | training ship, school ship |
| سفينة « تريا » | Turya ship |
| سفينة تزويد بالوقود | refuelling craft |
| سفينة تموين « أبديل » | Abdiel supply ship |
| سفينة تموين الاسطول | fleet supply ship |
| سفينة تموين دي ٩٥ | D95 supply ship |
| سفينة « تي ان سي ـ ٤٥ » | TNC-45 craft |
| سفينة « جس » | Gus ship |
| سفينة الحراسة | escort ship |
| سفينة حراسة « بوكسينا » | Boxina patrol craft |
| سفينة حراسة سواحل « ديورا » | Duora patrol craft |
| سفينة حراسة سواحل « رايجا » | Riga patrol ship |
| سفينة حراسة صغيرة « اسبانيا » | España corvette |
| سفينة حراسة صغيرة « أسد » | Assad corvette |
| سفينة حراسة صغيرة « إسميرالدا » | Esmeralda corvette |
| سفينة حراسة صغيرة « پي سي جي ـ ١ » | PCG-1 corvette |
| سفينة حراسة صغيرة « جريشا » | Grisha corvette |
| سفينة حراسة صغيرة « ديسكو بييرتا » | Descubierta corvette |
| سفينة حراسة صغيرة مجهزة بالصواريخ | Missile corvette |
| سفينة حراسة صغيرة « نانوتشكا » | Nanuchka corvette |
| سفينة حراسة صغيرة « وادي » | Wadi corvette |
| سفينة حربية برمائية | amphibious warfare ship |
| سفينة حربية « ريڤرين » | Riverine warfare vessel |
| سفينة حربية مضادة للغواصات | anti-submarine warfare vessel |
| سفينة خدمة خاصة | special service vessel |
| سفينة خفر السواحل « اراوكا » | Arauca patrol craft |
| سفينة خفر سواحل « اس اوه ـ ١ » | SO-1 patrol craft |
| سفينة خفر السواحل « اوسا » | Osa patrol boat |
| سفينة خفر السواحل « پي بي آر » | PBR patrol craft |

| | |
|---|---|
| سفينة خفر السواحل « پيكوك » | Peacock patrol craft |
| سفينة خفر سواحل « تراكر » | Tracker patrol craft |
| سفينة خفر سواحل « تمسا » | Timsah patrol boat |
| سفينة خفر السواحل « ثورنيكروفت » | Thornycroft patrol craft |
| سفينة خفر سوائل « جاريان » | Garian patrol craft |
| سفينة خفر السواحل « دابور » | Dabur patrol craft |
| سفينة خفر سواحل « راتشاريت » | Ratcharit patrol boat |
| سفينة خفر سواحل « سپير » | Spear patrol craft |
| سفينة خفر سواحل سريعة | fast patrol craft |
| سفينة خفر سواحل « سوزا » | Susa patrol craft |
| سفينة خفر سواحل طراز ١٤٣ | Type 143 patrol boat |
| سفينة خفر سواحل « هوك » | Hawk patrol craft |
| سفينة دعم الاقتحام | assault support ship |
| سفينة دعم حركي | logistic support vessel |
| سفينة « دون » | Don ship |
| سفينة دورية | patrol vessel |
| سفينة دورية « پي سي اف » | PCF patrol craft |
| سفينة « روraيما » | Roraima ship |
| سفينة « ريشاف » | Reshaf craft |
| سفينة « زوبوف » | Zubov ship |
| سفينة « زوك » | Zhuk craft |
| سفينة « سترومبولي » | Stromboli ship |
| سفينة « سواتو » | Swatow craft |
| سفينة صهريجية | tanker |
| سفينة صواريخ | rocket ship, missile craft |
| سفينة صواريخ « تارانتيل » | Tarantul rocket ship |
| سفينة طراز « أنكوراج » | Anchorage class ship |
| سفينة طراز « هاينان » | Hainan Class ship |
| سفينة فروش | Frosch ship |
| سفينة « فيرلس » | Fearless ship |
| سفينة القيادة | mother ship, parent ship, flagship |
| سفينة قيادة القوات البرمائية | Amphibious Command ship |
| سفينة القيادة والمراقبة | command and control boat |
| سفينة كاسحة جليد | icebreaker |
| سفينة كانين | Kanin ship |
| سفينة كورموران | Cormoran craft |
| سفينة « كيلدين » | Kildin ship |
| سفينة « لاما » | Lama ship |
| سفينة مجهزة بالمدافع « تشونبوري » | Chonburi gun boat |
| سفينة مجهزة بالمدافع « لوريتو » | Loreto gunboat |
| سفينة مضادة لاهداف سطحية | anti-surface vessel |
| سفينة موّنة للغواصة | sub tender |
| سفينة من طراز « أشقيل » | Asheville class ship |
| سفينة نقل « اوستن » | Austin transport ship |
| سفينة نقل « تشارلستون » | Charleston cargo ship |
| سفينة نقل الجنود | troop transport vessel |
| سفينة نهرية مزودة بالمدافع « برنكيلا » | Baranquilla river gunboat |
| سفينة « نيوبورت » | Newport ship |
| سفينة هجوم برمائي | amphibious assault vessel |
| سفينة هجوم بالطوربيد | torpedo attack craft |
| سفينة « هيوميتا » | Humaita ship |
| سفينة « ويدبي أيلند » | Whidbey Island ship |
| سفينة « يوجرا » | Ugra ship |
| سقاطة | ratchet |
| سقف | roof |
| سقوط | crash |
| سقوط حر | free fall |
| سُكان الارتفاع | elevator |
| سكان التوجيه | rudder |

س

|  |  |
|---|---|
| سكن | accommodation |
| سكيني الشكل | knife-type |
| سلاح | weapon, armament |
| سلاح احساس المدرعات وتدميرها | Sense and Destroy Armour |
| سلاح ارهابي | terrorist weapon |
| سلاح اطلاق عن بعد للحرب المضادة للغواصات | ASW Stand-off Weapon |
| سلاح آلي | automatic weapon |
| سلاح « ام ٧٢ ايه ١ » | M72A1 weapon |
| سلاح « ام ٧٢ ايه ٢ » | M72A2 weapon |
| سلاح باحث عن الحرارة | heat-seeking weapon |
| سلاح تحديد المدى | ranging weapon |
| سلاح تعزيز خفيف | light support weapon |
| سلاح تقليدي يطلق عن بعد | conventional stand-off weapon |
| سلاح خفيف | light weapon |
| سلاح خفيف مضاد للدبابات | light anti-tank weapon |
| سلاح الدفاع عن النفس | self-defence weapon |
| سلاح ذو اجنحة صليبية الشكل | cruciform-wing weapon |
| سلاح شخصي | individual weapon |
| سلاح الطائرات | aviation weapon |
| سلاح الفرسان | cavalry |
| سلاح « لانتسا بي زد ٤٤ » | Lanze PZ44 weapon |
| سلاح لجميع الأغراض | all-purpose weapon |
| سلاح للهجوم عن بعد | stand-off weapon |
| سلاح للهجوم عن بعد مضاد للغواصات | stand-off ASW |
| سلاح متحرك | mobile weapon |
| سلاح المدفعية | gun armament |
| سلاح المدرعات | armoured branch |
| سلاح موجه | guided weapon |
| سلاح موجه بالسلك | wire-guided weapon |
| سلاح موجه مضاد للدبابات | anti-tank guided weapon |
| سلاح موجّه مضاد للدبابات « پيكيت » | Picket ATGW |
| سلاح موجه مضاد للدبابات « سوينج فاير » | Swingfire ATGW |
| سلاح موجه مضاد للدبابات « ڤيجيلانت » | Vigilant ATGW |
| سلاح مضاد للطائرات | anti-aircraft armament |
| سلاح مضاد للغواصات | anti-submarine weapon, anti-submarine armament |
| سلاح مضاد للغواصات « إيكارا » | Ikara ASW |
| سلاح نووية | nuclear weapon |
| سلاسل صاروخية | pyrotechnical chains |
| سلام | salute |
| سلامة | security |
| سلبي | passive |
| سلسلة رادار « نادج » | Nadge radar chain |
| سلسلة قنابل يدوي | string of grenades |
| سلسلة القيادة | chain of command |
| سلطات تأديبية | disciplinary powers |
| سلطة التصديق | approving authority |
| سلك أمن | security wire |
| سلك الايقاف | arrester wire |
| سلك التفجير | detonating cord |
| سلك دقيق | fine wire |
| سلك شائك | barbed wire |
| سلك فصل | trip wire |
| سلك قطر | hawser |
| سلك واق | protective wire |
| سلوك | conduct |
| سلّم ـ سلاح | present arms! |
| السماح بالاقتراب | allow to approach |
| سماعتا الرأس | headset |
| سمت | azimuth |
| سمعي | acoustic |
| سناد الشكيمة | cheek-rest |
| سند مباشر | close-support |
| سنغافورة | Singapore |

س

| | |
|---|---|
| السنغال | Senegal |
| سنوركل | snorkel |
| سهولة المناورة | manoeuvrability |
| سوء الرؤية | bad visibility |
| السودان | Sudan |
| سوري | Syrian |
| سوريا | Syria |
| سوط | whip |
| سونار | sonar |
| سونار « اس اوه اس - ٢٣ » | SOS-23 sonar |
| سونار « اس اوه اس - ٥٠٥ » | SOS-505 sonar |
| سونار « اس كيو آر - ١٩ » | SQR-19 sonar |
| سونار « اس كيو اس - ١٧ » | SQS-17 sonar |
| سونار « اس كيو اس - ٥٣ » | SQS-53 sonar |
| سونار « اس كيو كيو - ٢٣ » | SQQ-23 sonar |
| سونار أعماق متنوعة | variable depth sonar |
| سونار « اف سي اس » | FCS sonar |
| سونار « ال اف » | LF sonar |
| سونار « ام اف » | MF sonar |
| سونار « پاريس » | PARIS sonar |
| سونار بحث عن الألغام « ام ايه آر ار ٢٤ » | MAR R24 minehunting sonar |
| سونار بدن السفينة ذو تردد عالي | high-frequency hull sonar |
| سونار « بنديكس » | Bendix sonar |
| سونار « بي كيو آر - ٧ » | BQR-7 sonar |
| سونار « بي كيو اس - ٤ » | BQS-4 sonar |
| سونار « بي كيو اس - ٦ » | BQS-6 sonar |
| سونار « بي كيو كيو - ٢ » | BQQ-2 sonar |
| سونار « بي كيو كيو - ٥ » | BQQ-5 sonar |
| سونار تحديد مدى سلبي | passive ranging sonar |
| سونار تحديد مدى واعتراض | range and intercept sonar |
| سونار « توماك » | TOMAK sonar |
| سونار « دي اس يو ڤي ٢٢ » | DSUV 22 sonar |
| سونار « دي ئي ١١٦٠ » | DE 1160 sonar |
| سونار « دي يوُيو اكس ٢ » | DUUX 2 sonar |
| سونار طراز ١٨٤ | Type 184 sonar |
| سونار طراز ١٩٧ | Type 197 sonar |
| سونار طراز ٢٠٠١ | Type 2001 sonar |
| سونار طراز ٢٠١٦ | Type 2016 sonar |
| سونار طراز ٢٠١٩ | Type 2019 sonar |
| سونار طراز ٢٠٢٠ | Type 2020 sonar |
| سونار غاطس ألكاتل | Alcatel dipping sonar |
| سونار غمس | dipping sonar |
| سونار فعال | active sonar |
| سونار فنيكس | Feniks sonar |
| سونار قنص الغام | minehunting sonar |
| سونار مراقبة الرمي | fire-control sonar |
| سونار المقدمة | bow sonar |
| سونار مقطور | towed sonar |
| سونار مقطور طراز ٢٠٢٤ | Type 2024 towed sonar |
| سونار منخفض التردد مركب في مقدمة السفينة | low-frequency bow sonar |
| سونار « ئي ال ايه سي » | ELAC sonar |
| سونار « ئي دي اوه » | EDO sonar |
| السويد | Sweden |
| سويدي | Swedish |
| سويسرة | Switzerland |
| سويسري | Swiss |
| سيارة استطلاع « فريت » | Ferret scout car |
| سيارة إسعاف الميدان | field ambulance |

س

| | |
|---|---|
| سيارة اصلاح « اف ڤي ٤٣٤ » | FV434 repair vehicle |
| سيارة تدريب السائقين | driver training vehicle |
| سيارة تدعيم النيران | fire-support vehicle |
| سيارة شحن | cargo vehicle |
| سيارة « فوكس » | Fox vehicle |
| سيارة قابلة للانزال بالمظلة | parachutable vehicle |
| سيارة « كاسكاڤيل » | Cascavel vehicle |
| سيارة لاند روڤر | Land Rover |
| سيارة مدرعة « اف يو جي - ٧٠ » | FUG-70 armoured vehicle |
| سيارة مدرعة « ئي آر سي - ٩٠ » | ERC-90 armoured vehicle |
| سيارة المهندسين | engineer vehicle |
| سياسة دفاع ثلاثي أمريكية | Triad |
| سيانيد | cyanide |
| سيانيد البوتاسيوم | potassium cyanide |
| سيانيد هيدروجيني | hydrogen cyanide |
| سير الكتف | shoulder strap |
| سير مخروطي المقطع | v-belt |
| سير مسنن | toothed belt |
| سير الناقلة | conveyor belt |
| سير وصل « ام ١٣ » | M13 link belt |
| السيطرة على الرمي | fire control |
| السيطرة على رمي الدبابة | tank fire control |
| السيطرة على الاطلاق باجهزة بصرية الكترونية | optronic fire control |
| سيطرة مزدوجة . قيادة مزدوجة | dual-control |
| سيف | sword |

س

# ش



| | |
|---|---|
| شاحن بطاريات | battery charger |
| شاحنة | lorry, truck |
| شاحنة إزالة التلوث | decontamination bowser |
| شاحنة اعادة التزويد بالصورايخ | missile resupply truck |
| شاحنة بعجلات | wheeled truck |
| شاحنة بكابينة قلابة | tilt cab truck |
| شاحنة « بومباردير » | Bombardier truck |
| شاحنة تزويد بالوقود | refuelling truck |
| شاحنة « زيل » | ZIL truck |
| شاحنة صهريج للوقود | fuel bowser |
| شاحنة صهريجية | bowser |
| شاحنة لرفع الاثقال ونقلها | lift truck |
| شاحنة المقدمة | follow me truck |
| شاحنة « يورال - ٣٧٥ » | Ural-375 truck |
| شاخص التصويب | aiming post |
| شاذ | off beat |
| شارة | badge, ensign |
| شارة الجر | trail badge |
| شارة الرتبة | badge of rank |
| شارة الكم | sleeve insignia |
| شاشة الرادار | radar scope |
| شاطىء | coast |
| شبكة | grid, network |
| شبكة أحادية السكة | monorail system |
| شبكة الايقاف | arrester net |
| شبكات تحليل البيانات « ويڤل » | Wavell data-processing nets |
| شبكة دفاع | defence system |
| شبكة الدفاع | defence network |
| شبكة دفاع جوي | air defence system, ADS |
| شبكة دفاع جوي متحركة | mobile air-defence system |
| شبكة مربعات | graticule |
| شبكة صواريخ استراتيجية | strategic missile system |
| شبكة صواريخ تكتيكية | tactical missile system |
| شبكة صواريخ الدفاع الجوي | air defence missile system |
| شبكة صواريخ خفيفة الوزن متعددة الأغراض ستنبجر المقذوفة جواً | MLMS (Air-Launched Stinger) |
| شبكة صواريخ مسرح العمليات | theatre missile system |
| شبكة قوة نيران متحركة | mobile firepower |
| شبه عسكري | paramilitary |
| شبه قابل للنقل | semi-transportable |
| شحن ثانياً | recharge |
| شحنات موضعية | spot charges |
| شحنة | cargo |
| شحنة متفجرة | explosive charge |
| شدة | strength |
| شديدة الانفجار | high explosive, HE |
| شرائح تشويش | chaff |
| شرطة بحرية | Marine Police |
| شرق | east |
| شرك | decoy, booby trap |

| | |
|---|---|
| شرك بالأشعة دون الحمراء | infra-red decoy |
| شرك مضاد للصواريخ « داجاي » | Dagaie anti-missile decoy |
| شركة « اف ام ايه » | FMA (Co) |
| شركة اليوشين | Ilyushin (Co) |
| شركة إمبراير | Embraer (Co) |
| شركة اوتونوك | Autonoc (Co) |
| شركة « اوجاستا » | Augusta (Co) |
| شركة « آيرماكي » | Aermacchi (Co) |
| شركة آيروسباسيال | Aérospatiale (Co) |
| شركة إيرو فودوشودي | Aero Vodochody (Co) |
| شركة « آيريتاليا » | Aeritalia (Co) |
| شركة « ايه أي دي سي » | AIDC (Co) |
| شركة « باناڤيا » | Panavia (Co) |
| « شركة پرات اند ويتني » | Pratt & Whitney (Co) |
| شركة بريتش ايروسپيس | British Aerospace (Co) |
| شركة « بريجيه » | Breguet (Co) |
| شركة بل للطائرات | Bell (Co) |
| شركة پياجيو | Piaggo (Co) |
| شركة بيتش | Beech (Co) |
| شركة « پي زد إل ميليك » | PZL Mielec (Co) |
| شركة پيلاتوس | Pilatus (Co) |
| شركة تشينكول | Chincul (Co) |
| شركة توپوليف | Tupolev (Co) |
| شركة « ثورن ـ ئي ام آي » | Thorn-EMI (Co) |
| شركة جرومان | Grumman (Co) |
| شركة جنرال الكتريك | General Electric (Co) |
| شركة جنرال ديناميكس | General Dynamics (Co) |
| شركة « داسو ـ بريجيه » | Dassault-Breguet (Co) |
| شركة دوجلاس | Douglas (Co) |
| شركة ديڤيد براون | David Brown (Co) |
| شركة دي هاڤيلاند | de Havilland (Co) |
| شركة « روكويل » | Rockwell (Co) |
| شركة « روكويل انترناشيونال » | Rockwell International (Co) |
| شركة « رولز ـ رويس » | Rolls-Royce (Co) |
| شركة « زلين » | Zlin (Co) |
| شركة ساب | Saab (Co) |
| شركة « سوخوي » | Sukhoi (Co) |
| شركة سوكو | Soko (Co) |
| شركة « سياي ـ مارشيتي » | Siai-Marchetti (Co) |
| شركة سيپيكات | Sepecat (Co) |
| شركة سيسنا | Cessna (Co) |
| شركة « سيكورسكي » | Sikorsky (Co) |
| شركة « شين ميه وا » | Shin Meiwa (Co) |
| شركة « شينيانج » | Shenyang (Co) |
| شركة فرانتي | Ferranti (Co) |
| شركة « ڤوت » | Vought (Co) |
| شركة فوجي | Fuji (Co) |
| شركة « فوكر » | Fokker (Co) |
| شركة « ڤولڤو » | Volvo (Co) |
| شركة فيات | Fiat (Co) |
| شركة فيرتشايلد | Fairchild (Co) |
| شركات كاسا | Casa (Co) |
| شركة كامان | Kaman (Co) |
| شركة كاموف | Kamov (Co) |
| شركة كاواساكي | Kawasaki (Co) |
| شركة كناديان | Canadian (Co) |
| شركة « لوكهيد » | Lockheed (Co) |
| شركة « ماكدونل دوجلاس » | McDonnell Douglas (Co) |
| شركة « ماياسيتشيف » | Myasishchev (Co) |
| شركة محركات « ڤولڤو فلايج موتور » | Volvo Flygmotor (Co) |
| شركة مصانع الطائرات الاسرائيلية | Israel Aircraft Industries (Co) |
| شركة « ميتسوبيشي » | Mitsubishi (Co) |
| شركة « ميكويان ـ جوريڤيتش » | Mikoyan-Gurevich (Co) |
| شركة « ميل » | Mil (Co) |

| | |
|---|---|
| شركة « نانتشانج » | Nanchang (Co) |
| شركة نورث اميريكان | North American (Co) |
| شركة نورثروپ | Northrop (Co) |
| شركة « نيڤا » | Neiva (Co) |
| شركة هكْلَرْ اند كوخ | Heckler and Koch (Co) |
| شركة هندوستان | Hindustan (Co) |
| شركة هيوز | Hughes (Co) |
| شركة واسنجهاوس | Westinghouse (Co) |
| شركة ويستلاند | Westland (Co) |
| شركة « ياكوڤلڤ » | Yakovlev (Co) |
| شريط | belt |
| شظية القذيفة | shell splinter |
| شعار | badge |
| شعارات | insignia |
| شعاع | beam |
| شعاع إرشاد | guidance beam |
| شعاع تتبع الهدف | target tracking beam |
| شعاع هبوط | landing beam |
| شفرة | cipher |
| شكل الجنيحات المساعدة | canard configuration |
| شل الحركة | immobilise (to) |
| شمال | north |
| شمعة دخان | smoke candle |
| شن هجوماً | launch an attack |
| شن هجوم مضاد | launch a counter-attack |
| شهادة طبية | doctor's certificate |
| شهادة اللياقة | fitness certificate |
| شهادة وفاة | death certificate |
| شوش | jam (to) |

# ص

| | |
|---|---|
| صائد الذباب | fly catcher |
| صاروخ | rocket |
| صاروخ | missile |
| صاروخ ابطال الدفاع الجوي | air defence suppression missile |
| صاروخ احتياطي | reserve missile |
| صاروخ « آر ٤٤٠ » | R440 missile |
| صاروخ « آر ـ ٥٥٠ » | R-550 missile |
| صاروخ « آربي اس ١٥ » | RBS 15 missile |
| صاروخ « آربي اس ـ ٥٦ » | RBS-56 missile |
| صاروخ « آربي ٠٨ ايه » | RB08 A missile |
| صاروخ « آربي يو ٢٥٠٠ » | RBU 2500 rocket |
| صاروخ « آرجي ام ـ ٨٤ ايه » | RGM-84A missile |
| صاروخ « اس اس ـ ٢٣ » | SS-23 missile |
| صاروخ « اس اس ـ اكس ـ ٢٨ » | SS-X-28 missile |
| صاروخ « اس اس ـ ان اكس ١٣ » | SS-NX-13 missile |
| صاروخ « اس اس ـ ان اكس ـ ٢٠ » | SS-NX-20 missile |
| صاروخ « اس ان ئي بي » | SNEB rocket |
| صاروخ اعتراض جوي « سايد ويندر » | Sidewinder AIM |
| صاروخ اعتراض جوي « سپارو » | Sparrow AIM |
| صاروخ اعتراض جوي « فينيكس » | Phoenix AIM |
| صاروخ اعتراض محمول جواً « جيني » | Genie AIR |
| صاروخ اعتراضي محمول جواً | airborne-interception rocket |
| صاروخ « إف ار ايه اس ـ ١ » | FRAS-1 rocket |
| صاروخ افلات | escape rocket |
| صاروخ « اكسوست اس ام ٣٩ » | Exocet SM39 missile |
| صاروخ « إكسوست إم إم ٣٨ » | Exocet MM38 missile |
| صاروخ « اكسوست إم إم ٤٠ » | Exocet MM40 missile |
| صاروخ « ام ـ ١ » | M-1 missile |
| صاروخ « ام ـ ٢ » | M-2 missile |
| صاروخ « ام ـ ٤ » | M-4 missile |
| صاروخ « ام ٧٢ » | M72 missile |
| صاروخ ام ٦٠١ تو | M-901 TOW |
| صاروخ « ام آربي ام » | MRBM missile |
| صاروخ « ايه آر إم » | ARM missile |
| صاروخ ايه ار ام ستاندارد مضاد للرادار | Standard ARM missile |
| صاروخ « ايه اس ام ـ ١ » | ASM-1 missile |
| صاروخ « ايه اس تي ـ ١٢٢٨ » | AST-1228 missile |
| صاروخ « ايه أي آر ـ ٢ ايه » | AIR-2A |
| صاروخ « ايه بي ام ـ ١ بي » | ABM-1B missile |

| | |
|---|---|
| صاروخ « باراك » | Barak missile |
| صاروخ بالستي عابر للقارات | ICBM, inter-continental ballistic missile |
| صاروخ بالستي عابر للقارات « اس اس ـ ١٦ » | SS-16 ICBM |
| صاروخ بالستي عابر للقارات « اس اس ـ ١٧ » | SS-17 ICBM |
| صاروخ بالستي عابر للقارات « اس اس ـ ١٨ » | SS-18 ICBM |
| صاروخ بالستي عابر للقارات « اس اس ـ ١٩ » | SS-19 ICBM |
| صاروخ بالستي عابر للقارات « اس اس ـ ان اكس ـ ١٧ » | SS-NX-17 ICBM |
| صاروخ عابر للقارات « ام جي ام ـ ١١٨ (ام اكس) » | MGM-118 (MX) ICBM |
| صاروخ بالستي عابر للقارات « إيڤايدر » | Evader ICBM |
| صاروخ بالستي عابر للقارات « پيسكيپر » | Peacekeeper ICBM |
| صاروخ بالستي عابر للقارات « مينتمان » | Minuteman ICBM |
| صاروخ بالستي قصير المدى | Short-Range Ballistic Missile |
| صاروخ بالستي قصير المدى « پرشينج ٢ » | Pershing SRBM |
| صاروخ بالستي متوسط المدى | medium-range ballistic missile |
| صاروخ بالستي متوسط المدى | intermediate-range ballistic missile (IRBM) |
| صاروخ بالستي متوسط المدى « اس اس ـ ٢٠ » | SS-20 IRBM |
| صاروخ بالستي متوسط المدى « پرشينج ٢ » | Pershing II MRBM |
| صاروخ بالستي منطلق من الغواصة « اس اس ـ ان ـ ٦ » | SS-N-6 SLBM |
| صاروخ « بانتام » | Bantam missile |
| صاروخ بحشوة مفرغة | hollow-charge rocket |
| صاروخ بدافع جاف | solid-propellant missile |
| صاروخ « پلوتون » | Pluton missile |
| صاروخ « پوسيدون » | Poseidon missile |
| صاروخ « پولاريس » | Polaris missile |
| صاروخ « بي جي إم ـ ١٠٩ جي » | BGM-109G missile |
| صاروخ « تايتن ١١ » | Titan 1·1 missile |
| صاروخ تدريب | practice missile |
| صاروخ « ترايدنت » | Trident missile |
| صاروخ « تريل » | Teruel rocket |
| صاروخ تضاغطي | ram-rocket |
| صاروخ تكتيكي | tactical missile |
| صاروخ تكتيكي أسرع من الصوت | supersonic tactical missile |
| صاروخ « تو » | TOW missile |
| صاروخ تو محسن | Improved TOW |
| صاروخ « تونج فينج » | Tong Feng missile |
| صاروخ « ثندرفلاش » | Thunderflash missile |
| صاروخ « ثيوكول » | Thiokol rocket |
| صاروخ « جالوش » | Galosh missile |
| صاروخ جو ـ أرض | air-to-ground missile, AGM |
| صاروخ جو ـ أرض « ـ ١٢ » | AGM-12 |
| صاروخ جو ـ أرض « ـ ٢٨ » | AGM-28 |
| صاروخ جو ـ أرض « ـ ٤٥ » | AGM-45 |
| صاروخ جو ـ أرض « ـ ٥٣ » | AGM-53 |
| صاروخ جو ـ أرض « ـ ٦٢ » | AGM-62 |
| صاروخ جو ـ أرض « ـ ٦٥ » | AGM-65 |
| صاروخ جو ـ أرض « ـ ٦٩ » | AGM-69 |
| صاروخ جو ـ أرض « ٦٩ ايه ـ اس آر ايه إم » | AGM-69A SRAM |
| صاروخ جو ـ أرض « ـ ٧٨ » | AGM-78 |

| | |
|---|---|
| صاروخ جو ـ أرض « ٨٣ » | AGM-83 |
| صاروخ جو ـ أرض « ـ ٨٤ ايه » | AGM-84A |
| صاروخ جو ـ أرض « ـ ٨٦ » | AGM-86 |
| صاروخ جو ـ أرض « ـ ٨٦ بي ـ ايه ال سي إم » | AGM-86B ALCM |
| صاروخ جو ـ أرض « ـ ٨٨ » | AGM-88 |
| صاروخ جو ـ أرض « اس ار اي ام » | SRAM AGM |
| صاروخ جو ـ أرض « بولپاپ » | Bullpup AGM |
| صاروخ جو ـ أرض « بولدوج » | Bulldog AGM |
| صاروخ جو ـ أرض « شرايك » | Shrike AGM |
| صاروخ جو ـ أرض « كوندور » | Condor AGM |
| صاروخ جو ـ أرض « ماڤريك » | Improved Hawk AGM |
| صاروخ جو ـ أرض محسّن « هوك » | Maverick AGM |
| صاروخ جو ـ ارض « هوند ـدوج » | Hound-dog AGM |
| صاروخ جو ـ أرض « وولاي » | Walleye AGM |
| صاروخ جو ـ جو | air-to-air missile |
| صاروخ جو ـ جو « ـ ١ » | AAM-1 |
| صاروخ جو ـ جو « ـ ٢ » | AAM-2 |
| صاروخ جو ـ جو « أبيكس » | Apex AAM |
| صاروخ جو ـ جو « أتول » | Atoll AAM |
| صاروخ جو ـ جو « أتول » متقدم | Advanced Atoll AAM |
| صاروخ جو ـ جو « آر ـ ٥٣٠ » | R-530 AAM |
| صاروخ جو ـ جو اعتراضي متقدم | Advanced Intercept AAM |
| صاروخ جو ـ جو « أفيد » | Aphid AAM |
| صاروخ جو ـ جو « أكريد » | Acrid AAM |
| صاروخ جو ـ جو ألكالي | Alkali AAM |
| صاروخ جو ـ جو « أناب » | Anab AAM |
| صاروخ جو ـ جو « اناب » متقدم | Advanced Anab AAM |
| صاروخ جو ـ جو « أول » | Awl AAM |
| صاروخ جو ـ جو « ايه ايه ـ ١ » | AA-1 AAM |
| صاروخ جو ـ جو « ايه ايه ـ ٢ » | AA-2 AAM |
| صاروخ جو ـ جو « ايه ايه ٢ ـ ٢ » | AA-2-2 AAM |
| صاروخ جو ـ جو « ايه ايه ـ ٣ » | AA-3 AAM |
| صاروخ جو ـ جو « ايه ايه ـ ٣ ـ ٢ » | AA-3-2 AAM |
| صاروخ جو ـ جو « ايه ايه ـ ٤ » | AA-4 AAM |
| صاروخ جو ـ جو « ايه ايه ـ ٥ » | AA-5 AAM |
| صاروخ جو ـ جو « ايه ايه ـ ٦ » | AA-6 AAM |
| صاروخ جو ـ جو « ايه ايه ـ ٧ » | AA-7 AAM |
| صاروخ جو ـ جو « ايه ايه ـ ٨ » | AA-8 AAM |
| صاروخ جو ـ جو « ايه ايه ـ ٩ » | AA-9 AAM |
| صاروخ جو ـ جو « ايه ايه ـ اكس ـ ٩ » | AA-X-9 AAM |
| صاروخ جو ـ جو « ايه ايه ـ اكس ـ ١٠ » | AA-X-10 AAM |
| صاروخ جو ـ جو « ايه ايه ـ اكس پي ـ ١ » | AA-XP-1 AAM |
| صاروخ جو ـ جو « ايه ايه ـ اكس پي ـ ٢ » | AA-XP-2 AAM |

| | |
|---|---|
| صاروخ جو - جو « ايه إم آر » | AMRAAM |
| صاروخ جو - جو « پايثون » | Python AAM |
| صاروخ جو - جو « تيرايار » | Tirailleur AAM |
| صاروخ جو - جو « رد توپ » | Red Top AAM |
| صاروخ جو - جو « سكايفلاش » | Skyflash AAM |
| صاروخ جو - جو « سوپر ٥٣٠ » | Super 530 AAM |
| صاروخ جو - جو « سوپر آر ٥٣٠ » | Super R530 AAM |
| صاروخ جو - جو « سوپر فالكون » | Super Falcon AAM |
| صاروخ جو - جو « شافرير ٢ » | Shafrir 2 AAM |
| صاروخ جو - جو « فاير ستريك » | Firestreak AAM |
| صاروخ جو - جو « ڤي ٣ كوكري » | V3 Kukri AAM |
| صاروخ جو - جو قصير المدى | SRAAM AAM |
| صاروخ جو - جو « ماترا آر ٥٣٠ » | Matra R530 AAM |
| صاروخ جو - جو « ماترا آر ٥٥٠ ماجيك » | Matra R550 Magic AAM |
| صاروخ جو - جو « ماترا سوبر آر ٥٣٠ » | Matra Super R530 AAM |
| صاروخ جو - جو « ماجيك » | Magic AAM |
| صاروخ جو - جو متقدم قصير المدى | ASRAAM |
| صاروخ جو - سطح | air-to-surface missile |
| صاروخ جو - سطح « آربي ٠٤ » | RB04 ASM |
| صاروخ جو - سطح « آربي ٠٥ » | RB05 ASM |
| صاروخ جو - سطح « آش » | Ash ASM |
| صاروخ جو - سطح « اوتومات » | Otomat ASM |
| صاروخ جو - سطح « ايه اس - ١ » | AS-1 ASM |
| صاروخ جو - سطح « ايه اس - ٢ » | AS-2 ASM |
| صاروخ جو - سطح « ايه اس - ٢ ال » | AS-2L ASM |
| صاروخ جو - سطح « ايه اس - ٣ » | AS-3 ASM |
| صاروخ جو - سطح « ايه اس - ٤ » | AS-4 ASM |
| صاروخ جو - سطح « ايه اس - ٥ » | AS-5 ASM |
| صاروخ جو - سطح « ايه اس - ٦ » | AS-6 ASM |
| صاروخ جو - سطح « ايه اس - ٧ » | AS-7 ASM |
| صاروخ جو - سطح « ايه اس - ٨ » | AS-8 ASM |
| صاروخ جو - سطح « ايه اس - ١١ » | AS-11 ASM |
| صاروخ جو - سطح « ايه اس - ١٢ » | AS-12 ASM |
| صاروخ جو - سطح « ايه اس - ١٥ » | AS-15 ASM |
| صاروخ جو - سطح « ايه اس - ١٥ تي تي » | AS-15TT ASM |
| صاروخ جو - سطح « ايه اس - ٢٠ » | AS-20 ASM |
| صاروخ جو - سطح « ايه اس - ٣٠ » | AS-30 ASM |
| صاروخ جو - سطح « ايه اس - ٣٠ إل » | AS-30L ASM |
| صاروخ جو - سطح « ايه اس - ٣٩ » | AS-39 ASM |
| صاروخ جو - سطح « ايه اس - اكس - ٩ » | AS-X-9 ASM |
| صاروخ جو - سطح « ايه اس - اكس - ١٠ » | AS-X-10 ASM |
| صاروخ جو - سطح « ايه اس ام پي » | ASMP ASM |
| صاروخ جو - سطح « پيسكادور » | Pescador ASM |

ص

| | |
|---|---|
| صاروخ جو ـ سطح « پينجوين » | Penguin ASM |
| صاروخ جو ـ سطح « جي بي يو ـ ١٥ » | GBU-15 ASM |
| صاروخ جو ـ سطح « دور اندال » | Durandal ASM |
| صاروخ جو ـ سطح « سي سكيوا » | Sea Skua ASM |
| صاروخ جو ـ سطح « كاركرا » | Carcara ASM |
| صاروخ جو ـ سطح « كانجارو » | Kangaroo ASM |
| صاروخ جو ـ سطح « كورموران » | Kormoran ASM |
| صاروخ جو ـ سطح « كيپر » | Kipper ASM |
| صاروخ جو ـ سطح « كيتشن » | Kitchen ASM |
| صاروخ جو ـ سطح « كيري » | Kerry ASM |
| صاروخ جو ـ سطح « كيلت » | Kelt ASM |
| صاروخ جو ـ سطح « كينال » | Kennel ASM |
| صاروخ جو ـ سطح « كينجفيش » | Kingfish ASM |
| صاروخ جو ـ سطح « لوث » | Luz ASM |
| صاروخ جو ـ سطح « مارتيل » | Martel ASM |
| صاروخ جو ـ سطح « مالفور » | Malafor ASM |
| صاروخ جو ـ سطح « هوبوز » | Hobos ASM |
| صاروخ « جبرييل ١ » | Gabriel 1 missile |
| صاروخ « جبرييل ٢ » | Gabriel 2 missile |
| صاروخ « جبرييل ٣ » | Gabriel 3 missile |
| صاروخ « جولف » | Golf missile |
| صاروخ خادع | decoy missile |
| صاروخ « دراجون » | Dragon missile |
| صاروخ دعم ساحة المعركة | battlefield support missile |
| صاروخ دفاعي للقاذفات | bomber defense missile |
| صاروخ ذو توجيه آلي نصف فعال | semi-active homing missile |
| صاروخ ذو جنيحات | fin rocket |
| صاروخ « ريجيولوس ١ » | Regulus I missile |
| صاروخ « سپارقيرو » | Sparviero missile |
| صاروخ « سبروك » | Subroc missile |
| صاروخ ستاندارد « اس ام ـ ١ » | Standard SM-1 missile |
| صاروخ ستاندارد « اس ام ـ ٢ » | Standard SM-2 missile |
| صاروخ ستيكس | Styx missile |
| صاروخ « ستينجر » | Stinger missile |
| صاروخ سطح ـ جو | surface-to-air missile, SAM |
| صاروخ سطح ـ جو « آر بي ٦٨ » | RB 68 SAM |
| صاروخ سطح ـ جو « آر بي اس ٧٠ » | RBS 70 SAM |
| صاروخ سطح ـ جو « اس ام ١ ـ ئي آر » | SM1-ER SAM |
| صاروخ سطح ـ جو « اس ام ١ ـ ئي آر » | SM2-ER SAM |
| صاروخ سطح ـ جو « اس ايه ـ ١ » | SA-1 SAM |
| صاروخ سطح ـ جو « اس ايه ـ ٢ » | SA-2 SAM |
| صاروخ سطح ـ جو « اس ايه ـ ٣ » | SA-3 SAM |
| صاروخ سطح ـ جو « اس ايه ـ ٤ » | SA-4 SAM |
| صاروخ سطح ـ جو « اس ايه ـ ٥ » | SA-5 SAM |
| صاروخ سطح ـ جو « اس ايه ـ ٦ » | SA-6 SAM |
| صاروخ سطح ـ جو « اس ايه ـ ٧ » | SA-7 SAM |
| صاروخ سطح ـ جو « اس ايه ـ ٨ » | SA-8 SAM |
| صاروخ سطح ـ جو « اس ايه ـ ٨ بي » | SA-8B SAM |
| صاروخ سطح ـ جو « اس ايه ـ ٩ » | SA-9 SAM |

ص

| | |
|---|---|
| صاروخ سطح ـ جو « اس ايه ـ ١٠ » | SA-10 SAM |
| صاروخ سطح ـ جو « اس ايه ـ ١١ » | SA-11 SAM |
| صاروخ سطح ـ جو « اس ايه ـ ١٢ » | SA-12 SAM |
| صاروخ سطح ـ جو « اس ايه ـ ١٣ » | SA-13 SAM |
| صاروخ سطح ـ جو « اس ايه ـ ان ـ ١ » | SA-N-1 SAM |
| صاروخ سطح ـ جو « اس ايه ـ ان ـ ٢ » | SA-N-2 SAM |
| صاروخ سطح ـ جو « اس ايه ـ ان ـ ٣ » | SA-N-3 SAM |
| صاروخ سطح ـ جو « اس ايه ـ ان ـ ٤ » | SA-N-4 SAM |
| صاروخ سطح ـ جو « اس ايه ـ ان ـ ٥ » | SA-N-5 SAM |
| صاروخ سطح ـ جو « اس ايه ـ ان ـ ٦ » | SA-N-6 SAM |
| صاروخ سطح ـ جو « اس ايه ـ ان ـ ٧ » | SA-N-7 SAM |
| صاروخ سطح ـ جو « اسپيد » | Aspide SAM |
| صاروخ سطح ـ جو أستر | Aster SAM |
| صاروخ سطح ـ جو « اف آي ام ـ ٩٢ ايه » | FIM-92A SAM |
| صاروخ سطح ـ جو ألباتروس | Albatross SAM |
| صاروخ سطح ـ جو « ام آي ام ـ ٨ بي ٤ » | MIM-8P4 SAM |
| صاروخ سطح ـ جو « ام آي ام ـ ٢٣ » | MIM-23 SAM |
| صاروخ سطح ـ جو « انديجو » | Indigo SAM |
| صاروخ سطح ـ جو « پاتريوت » | Patriot SAM |
| صاروخ سطح ـ جو بلوبايب | Blowpipe missile |
| صاروخ سطح ـ جو « بلودهاوند » | Bloodhound SAM |
| صاروخ سطح ـ جو « تارتر » | Tartar SAM |
| صاروخ سطح ـ جو « تان » | TAN SAM |
| صاروخ سطح ـ جو « تايجركات » | Tigercat SAM |
| صاروخ سطح ـ جو « تيريار » | Terrier SAM |
| صاروخ سطح ـ جو « ثندربيرد » | Thunderbird SAM |
| صاروخ سطح ـ جو جاسكين | Gaskin SAM |
| صاروخ سطح ـ جو « جامون » | Gammon SAM |
| صاروخ سطح ـ جو « جانيف » | Ganef SAM |
| صاروخ سطح ـ جو « جريل » | Grail SAM |
| صاروخ سطح ـ جو « جوا » | Goa SAM |
| صاروخ سطح ـ جو « جوبلت » | Goblet SAM |
| صاروخ سطح ـ جو « جي دبليو دي ٣٠ » | GWD30 SAM |
| صاروخ سام « جيكو » | Gecko SAM |
| صاروخ سطح ـ جو « جيلد » | Guild SAM |
| صاروخ سطح ـ جو « جينفول » | Gainful SAM |
| صاروخ سطح ـ جو « راپيار » | Rapier SAM |
| صاروخ سطح ـ جو « رد آي » | Redeye SAM |
| صاروخ سطح ـ جو « رد فلاج » | Red Flag SAM |
| صاروخ سطح ـ جو « رولاند » | Roland SAM |
| صاروخ سطح ـ جو « رومب » | Romb SAM |
| صاروخ سطح ـ جو « ساملیت » | Samlet SAM |
| صاروخ سطح ـ جو « سپادا » | Spada SAM |
| صاروخ سطح ـ جو « ستاندارد » | Standard SAM |

ص

| | |
|---|---|
| صاروخ سطح ـ جو « ستينجر » | Stinger SAM |
| صاروخ سطح ـ جو « سي ـ دارت » | Sea Dart SAM |
| صاروخ سطح ـ جو « سيسلج » | Seaslug SAM |
| صاروخ سطح ـ جو « سيكات » | Seacat SAM |
| صاروخ سطح ـ جو « شابارال » | Chaparral SAM |
| صاروخ سطح ـ جو « شاهين » | Shahine SAM |
| صاروخ سطح ـ جو كاكتوس | Cactus SAM |
| صاروخ سطح ـ جو « كروتال » | Crotale SAM |
| صاروخ سطح ـ جو « لايتويت سيوولف » | Lightweight Seawolf SAM |
| صاروخ سطح ـ جو « مازوركا » | Masurca SAM |
| صاروخ سطح ـ جو « نايكي هاركيوليز » | Nike Hercules SAM |
| صاروخ سطح ـ جو « هونجي ـ ٢ » | Honggi-2 SAM |
| صاروخ سطح ـ سطح | surface-to-surface missile |
| صاروخ سطح ـ سطح « آر اس ـ ١٤ » | RS-14 SSM |
| صاروخ سطح ـ سطح « آر اس ـ ١٦ » | RS-16 SSM |
| صاروخ سطح ـ سطح « آر اس ـ ١٨ » | RS-18 SSM |
| صاروخ سطح ـ سطح « آر اس ـ ٢٠ » | RS-20 SSM |
| صاروخ سطح ـ سطح « اس اس ـ ١ » | SS-1 SSM |
| صاروخ سطح ـ سطح « اس اس ـ ٤ » | SS-4 SSM |
| صاروخ سطح ـ سطح « اس اس ـ ٥ » | SS-5 SSM |
| صاروخ سطح ـ سطح « اس اس ـ ٩ » | SS-9 SSM |
| صاروخ سطح ـ سطح « اس اس ـ ١٠ » | SS-10 SSM |
| صاروخ سطح ـ سطح « اس اس ـ ١١ » | SS-11 SSM |
| صاروخ سطح ـ سطح « اس اس ـ ١٢ » | SS-12 SSM |
| صاروخ سطح ـ سطح « اس اس ـ ١٣ » | SS-13 SSM |
| صاروخ سطح ـ سطح « اس اس ـ ١٤ » | SS-14 SSM |
| صاروخ سطح ـ سطح « اس اس ـ ١٥ » | SS-15 SSM |
| صاروخ سطح ـ سطح « اس اس ـ ٢١ » | SS-21 SSM |
| صاروخ سطح ـ سطح « اس اس ـ ٢٢ » | SS-22 SSM |
| صاروخ سطح ـ سطح « اس اس ـ اكس ـ ٢٣ » | SS-X-23 SSM |
| صاروخ سطح ـ سطح « اس اس ـ ان ـ ١ » | SS-N-1 SSM |
| صاروخ سطح ـ سطح « اس اس ـ ان ـ ٢ » | SS-N-2 SSM |
| صاروخ سطح ـ سطح « اس اس ـ ان ـ ٢ ايه » | SS-N-2A SSM |
| صاروخ سطح ـ سطح « اس اس ـ ان ـ ٣ » | SS-N-3 SSM |
| صاروخ سطح ـ سطح « اس اس ـ ان ـ ٤ » | SS-N-4 SSM |
| صاروخ سطح ـ سطح « اس اس ـ ان ـ ٥ » | SS-N-5 SSM |
| صاروخ سطح ـ سطح « اس اس ـ ان ـ ٧ » | SS-N-7 SSM |
| صاروخ سطح ـ سطح « اس اس ـ ان ـ ٨ » | SS-N-8 SSM |
| صاروخ سطح ـ سطح « اس اس ـ ان ـ ٩ » | SS-N-9 SSM |
| صاروخ سطح ـ سطح « اس اس ـ ان ـ ١١ » | SS-N-11 SSM |
| صاروخ سطح ـ سطح « اس اس ـ ان ـ ١٢ » | SS-N-12 SSM |
| صاروخ سطح ـ سطح « اس اس ـ ان ـ ١٤ » | SS-N-14 SSM |
| صاروخ سطح ـ سطح « اس اس ـ ان ـ ١٥ » | SS-N-15 SSM |

|  |  |
|---|---|
| SS-N-16 SSM | صاروخ سطح ـ سطح « اس اس ـ ان ـ ١٦ » |
| SS-N-17 SSM | صاروخ سطح ـ سطح « اس اس ـ ان ـ ١٧ » |
| SS-N-18 SSM | صاروخ سطح ـ سطح « اس اس ـ ان ـ ١٨ » |
| SS-N-19 SSM | صاروخ سطح ـ سطح « اس اس ـ ان ـ ١٩ » |
| SS-N-21 SSM | صاروخ سطح ـ سطح « اس اس ـ ان ـ ٢١ » |
| SS-N-22 SSM | صاروخ سطح ـ سطح « اس اس ـ ان ـ ٢٢ » |
| SS-C-1B SSM | صاروخ سطح ـ سطح « اس اس ـ سي ـ ١ بي » |
| Exocet SSM | صاروخ سطح ـ سطح « اكسوست » |
| MGM-31s SSM | صاروخ سطح ـ سطح « ام جي ام ـ ٣١ اس » |
| MGM-52C SSM | صاروخ سطح ـ سطح « ام جي ام ـ ٥٢ سي » |
| Honest John SSM | صاروخ سطح ـ سطح « اونست جون » |
| AM-39 SSM | صاروخ سطح ـ سطح « ايه ام ٣٩ » |
| Penguin SSM | صاروخ سطح ـ سطح « بينجوين » |
| Trap Door SSM | صاروخ سطح ـ سطح « تراپ دور » |
| Teseo SSM | صاروخ سطح ـ سطح « تيسيو » |
| Savage SSM | صاروخ سطح ـ سطح « ساڤيج » |
| Sandbox SSM | صاروخ سطح ـ سطح « ساندبوكس » |
| Scud-A SSM | صاروخ سطح ـ سطح « سكاد ـ ايه » |
| Scud-B SSM | صاروخ سطح ـ سطح « سكاد ـ بي » |
| Scarp SSM | صاروخ سطح ـ سطح « سكارپ » |
| Scapegoat SSM | صاروخ سطح ـ سطح « سكايبجوت » |
| Scaleboard SSM | صاروخ سطح ـ سطح « سكايلبورد » |
| Scrubber SSM | صاروخ سطح ـ سطح « أسكرابر » |
| Scrag SSM | صاروخ سطح ـ سطح « سكراج » |
| Scrooge SSM | صاروخ سطح ـ سطح « أسكروج » |
| CSS-1 SSM | صاروخ سطح ـ سطح « سي اس اس ـ ١ » |
| CSS-2 SSM | صاروخ سطح ـ سطح « سي اس اس ـ ٢ » |
| CSS-3 SSM | صاروخ سطح ـ سطح « سي اس اس ـ ٣ » |
| CSS-5 SSM | صاروخ سطح ـ سطح « سي اس اس ـ ٥ » |
| CSS-X-4 SSM | صاروخ سطح ـ سطح « سي اس اس ـ اكس ـ ٤ » |
| Sea Eagle SSM | صاروخ سطح ـ سطح « سي ايجل » |
| Sepal SSM | صاروخ سطح ـ سطح « سيپال » |
| Lance SSM | صاروخ سطح ـ سطح « لانس » |
| Luna SSM | صاروخ سطح ـ سطح « لونا » |
| Shaddock SSM | صاروخ سطح ـ سطح « شادوك » |
| Sandal SSM | صاروخ سطح ـ سطح « صندل » |
| Hai Ying SSM | صاروخ سطح ـ سطح « هاي ينج » |
| Sura rocket | صاروخ « سورا » |
| CRV7 rocket | صاروخ « سي آر ڤي ٧ » |
| CSS-NX-4 missile | صاروخ « سي اس اس ـ ان اكس ـ ٤ » |
| Saber missile | صاروخ « سيبر » |
| Sea Sparrow missile | صاروخ « سي سپارو » |
| Sea Killer missile | صاروخ « سي كيلر » |
| Hsiung Feng missile | صاروخ سيونج فينج |
| Seawolf missile | صاروخ « سي وولف » |
| Chevaline missile | صاروخ « شاڤالين » |
| Shillelagh missile | صاروخ شيليهلي |

ص

| | |
|---|---|
| صاروخ « صب ـ هاربون » | Sub-Harpoon missile |
| صاروخ العطوف | roll rocket |
| صاروخ غواصات | submarine rocket |
| صاروخ غير موجه | unguided rocket |
| صاروخ « فروج ـ ٧ » | FROG-7 missile |
| صاروخ « فروج ـ ٩ » | FROG-9 missile |
| صاروخ قانص مضاد للأقمار الصناعية | anti-satellite hunter missile |
| صاروخ قذفي | ballistic missile |
| صاروخ قصير الاشتعال | short-burn rocket |
| صاروخ كابح | retro-rocket |
| صاروخ « كوبرا » | Cobra missile |
| صاروخ « كيه ـ ١٣ ايه » | K-13A missile |
| صاروخ « كيه ايه ام ٩ » | KAM 9 missile |
| صاروخ كروز | cruise missile |
| صاروخ كروز « بي إم جي ـ ١٠٩ » | BMG-109 cruise missile |
| صاروخ كروز « توماهوك » | Tomahawk Cruise missile |
| صاروخ « كروز » لا استراتيجي | non-strategic cruise missile |
| صاروخ كروز نوع شرك مسلح ذو سرعة دون الصوتية | subsonic cruise armed decoy |
| صاروخ كروز يطلق من الجو | air-launched cruise missile |
| صاروخ كوني | global missile |
| صاروخ « كينجفيشر » | Kingfisher missile |
| صاروخ « ماثاجو » | Mathago missile |
| صاروخ « مارت » | Marte missile |
| صاروخ « مامبا » | Mamba missile |
| صاروخ متصل بالجو « هيديز » | Hades ACM |
| صاروخ مسرح العمليات | theatre area missile |
| صاروخ « موسكيتو » | Mosquito missile |
| صاروخ مضاد للدبابات | anti-tank missile |
| صاروخ مضاد للدبابات « ايه تي ـ ١ » | AT-1 ATM |
| صاروخ مضاد للدبابات « ايه تي ـ ٢ » | AT-2 ATM |
| صاروخ مضاد للدبابات « ايه تي ـ ٣ » | AT-3 ATM |
| صاروخ مضاد للدبابات « ايه تي ـ ٤ » | AT-4 ATM |
| صاروخ مضاد للدبابات « ايه تي ـ ٥ » | AT-5 ATM |
| صاروخ مضاد للدبابات « ايه تي ـ ٦ » | AT-6 ATM |
| صاروخ مضاد للدبابات « ساجر » | Sagger ATM |
| صاروخ مضاد للدبابات « سپاندريل » | Spandrel ATM |
| صاروخ مضاد للدبابات « سپايرال » | Spiral ATM |
| صاروخ مضاد للدبابات « سپيجوت » | Spigot ATM |
| صاروخ مضاد للدبابات « سناپر » | Snapper ATM |
| صاروخ مضاد للدبابات « سواتر » | Swatter ATM |
| صاروخ مضاد للدبابات « هوت » | HOT ATM |
| صاروخ مضاد للرادار | anti-radar missile |
| صاروخ مضاد للرادار « هارم » | HARM ARM |
| صاروخ مضاد للسفن | anti-ship missile |
| صاروخ مضاد للغواصات | anti-submarine missile |
| صاروخ مضاد للغواصات « ام بي يو ٦٠٠ » | MBU 600 ASW rocket |
| صاروخ مضاد للمدرعات | anti-armour missile |
| صاروخ معادي | hostile missile |
| صاروخ موجه | guided missile |
| صاروخ موجه بالأشعة دون الحمراء | IR-homing missile |
| صاروخ موجه بالليزر | laser guided missile |
| صاروخ موجّه ختامي | terminal homing missile |
| صاروخ موجه يطلق من الجو | air-launched guided missile |

ص

| | |
|---|---|
| صاروخ ميداني فايروس | Firos field rocket |
| صاروخ « ميلان » | Milan missile |
| صاروخ نووي يطلق عن بعد | nuclear stand-off missile |
| صاروخ هاربون | Harpoon missile |
| صاروخ « هلفاير » | Hellfire missile |
| صاروخ يطير فوق سطح البحر | sea-skimming missile |
| صاروخ « يو جي ام - ٢٧ » | UGM-27 missile |
| صاروخ « يو جي ام - ٧٣ » | UGM-73 missile |
| صاروخ « يو جي ام - ٨٤ » | UGM-84 missile |
| صاروخ « يو جي ام - ٩٣ » | UGM-93 missile |
| صاروخ « يوروميسايل » | Euromissile |
| صاري | mast |
| صاري حثي للمنشاق | snort induction mast |
| صاري الرادار | radar mast |
| صاري شبكي | lattice mast |
| صاري متداخل | telescopic mast |
| صاري « ئي اس ام » | ESM mast |
| صالح للابحار | seaworthy |
| صالح للاستخدام | serviceable |
| صانع ماهر | artificer |
| صحراء | desert |
| صحن الرادار | radar dish |
| صحن فرعي مكافؤ السطح مقعّر | convex hyperboloid sub-dish |
| صحية الميدان | field hygiene |
| صدرة دعم دفاعية | defensive support vest |
| صدرة صامدة للرصاص | bullet-proof vest |
| صدرة نجاة | life jacket |
| صدمة | impact |
| صدى النبضات | pulse echo |
| صديق | friend |
| صراع | fight |
| صراع نووي | nuclear conflict |
| صُرة تيتانيوم | titanium hub |
| صرف التموينات | stores issue |
| صعد إلى السطح | surfaced |
| صف | array |
| صف هوائيات | antenna array |
| « صف واحد ـ شكل ! » | form single rank! |
| « صفان .. شكل ! » | form two ranks! |
| صفيحة هوية | dog tags |
| صلاحية الطيران | air worthiness |
| صُلب | steel |
| صليبي الشكل | cruciform |
| صمام | valve |
| صمام تخفيف الضغط | pressure reducing valve |
| صمام الغاز | gas tube |
| صمامة تقاربية | proximity fuse |
| صمامة تقاربية كهرومغنطيسية | electromagnetic proximity fuse |
| صمامة تقاربية رادارية | radar proximity fuse |
| صمامة صدمية | impact fuse |
| صموت التشغيل | silence of operation |
| صنبور | nozzle |
| صندوق أدوات | kit |
| صندوق توصيل | junction box |
| صندوق جهاز الاطلاق | launcher bin |
| صندوق جهاز إطلاق الصواريخ | missile-launcher bin |
| صندوق الذخيرة | ammunition box |
| صندوق صواريخ مقطور | quad missile box |
| صندوق العدة | tool box |
| صندوق مظلي | parachute container |
| صندوق الميمنة | starboard bin |
| صندوق يدوي « زد إف » | ZF manual box |
| صهاريج وقود قابلة للاسقاط | long-range drop tanks |
| صوّب ! | take aim! |
| صوتي | acoustic |

ص

| | |
|---|---|
| صورة فوتوغرافية | photographic image |
| صورة محسنة | enhanced image |
| الصومال | Somalia |
| صومالي | Somali |
| صومعة | silo |
| صومعة مصلدة | hardened silo |
| صياد | hunter |
| صيانة | service |
| صيانة معتادة | routine maintenance |
| صيدلية | pharmacy |
| الصين | China |
| صيني | Chinese |

ص

| | |
|---|---|
| ضابط | officer |
| ضابط إداري | administrative officer |
| ضابط الاسكان | billeting officer |
| ضابط الاعاشة | catering officer |
| الضابط الاقدم | senior officer |
| ضابط تحقيقات | investigating officer |
| ضابط تقدير الخسائر | damage assessment officer |
| ضابط التموين والامدادات | quartermaster |
| ضابط التنبؤات الجوية | weather officer |
| ضابط تنفيذي | administrator |
| ضابط الخفر | orderly officer |
| ضابط ركن | staff officer |
| ضابط صف | non-commissioned officer, warrant officer |
| ضابط صف بحري | petty officer |
| ضابط قائد | officer commanding |
| ضابط مسؤول | officer in charge |
| الضابط المسؤول | duty officer |
| ضابط مساعد للقائد | adjutant |
| ضابط مقلد | commissioned officer |
| ضابط ميدان | field officer |
| ضاغط | compressor |
| ضاغط هواء ميكرو | Micro turbo |
| ضبط | regulate |
| ضبط | discipline |
| ضبط النيران | adjustment of fire |
| ضجيج تحت الماء | underwater noise |
| ضجيج مشع | radiated noise |
| ضجيج مشع تحت الماء | underwater radiated noise |
| ضجيج ايروديناميكي | aerodynamic noise |
| ضرب تحريم | interdiction strike |
| ضربة | hit, strike |
| ضربة شمس | sunstroke |
| ضغط الهواء | air pressure |
| ضغط هيدروستاتي | hydrostatic pressure |
| ضم الى الخدمة | take into service |
| ضمادة | bandage |
| ضمادة مطهرة | antiseptic dressing |
| ضمادة معقمة | sterile dressing |
| ضمادة ميدان | field dressing |
| ضوء أبيض | white light |
| ضوء أسود بالأشعة دون الحمراء | black light IR |
| ضوء كشاف تي ان ٢١ | TN21 spotlight |
| ضوء موجه بالأشعة دون الحمراء | infra-red driving light |
| ضوء النهار | daylight |
| ضوضاء المكنات | machinery noise |

# ط

| | |
|---|---|
| طائرة « إبسيلون » | Epsilon aircraft |
| طائرة « اتش زد ـ ٥ » | HZ-5 aircraft |
| طائرة « آر اف ـ ٤ » | RF-4 aircraft |
| طائرة « آر اف ـ ٥ ئي » | RF-5E aircraft |
| طائرة « آر اف ـ ٣٥ » | RF-35 aircraft |
| طائرة « آر اف ـ ١٠١ » | RF-101 aircraft |
| طائرة « آر ايه ام ـ ام » | RAM-M aircraft |
| طائرة « ارايون » | Orion aircraft |
| طائرة « آرسي ـ ١٢ دي » | RC-12 D aircraft |
| طائرة « آرسي ـ ١٣٥ ڤي » | RC-135V aircraft |
| طائرة أرصاد جوية | meteorological aircraft |
| طائرة « آريو ـ ٢١ » | RU-21 aircraft |
| طائرة « آريو ـ ٢١ جيه » | RU-21J aircraft |
| طائرة « اس ـ ٣ ايه » | S-3A aircraft |
| طائرة « اس ٣٥ ئي » | S35E aircraft |
| طائرة « اس آر ـ ٧١ » | SR-71 aircraft |
| طائرة « اس اف ٣٧ » | SF 37 |
| طائرة « اس اف ـ ٢٦٠ » | SF-260 aircraft |
| طائرة « اس سي ـ ٧ » | SC-7 aircraft |
| طائرة استطلاع استراتيجي | strategic reconnaissance aircraft |
| طائرة الاستطلاع « اواكس » | AWACS |
| طائرة استطلاع « بيردي » | Bear D surveillance aircraft |
| طائرة استطلاع « بيرئي » | Bear E surveillance aircraft |
| طائرة استطلاع تكتيكي | tactical reconnaissance aircraft |
| طائرة « اس يو ـ ٧ » | Su-7 aircraft |
| طائرة « إس يو ـ ام كيه » | Su-7UMK aircraft |
| طائرة « إس يو ـ ١٧ » | Su-17 aircraft |
| طائرة « إس يو ـ ٢٠ » | Su-20 aircraft |
| طائرة « إس يو ـ ٢٢ » | Su-22 aircraft |
| طائرة « إس يو ـ ٢٤ » فنسر | Su-24 Fencer |
| طائرة « إس يو ـ ٢٥ » | Su-25 aircraft |
| طائرة اطلاق | launch aircraft |
| طائرة « أطلنتيك » | Atlantic aircraft |
| طائرة اعتراض | interceptor |
| طائرة اعتراض « اف ـ ١٠٦ » | F-106 interceptor |
| طائرة اعتراض « دلتا دارت » | Delta Dart interceptor |
| طائرة اعتراض نفاثة | jet interceptor |
| طائرة اعتراضية لجميع الأجواء | all-weather interceptor |
| طائرة اعتراضية « ميراج إف ١ سي » | Mirage F-IC interceptor |
| طائرة « اف ـ ٤ جي » | F-4G aircraft |
| طائرة « اف ـ ١٤ ايه » | F-14A aircraft |
| طائرة « اف ـ ١٥ ايجال » | F-15 Eagle aircraft |
| طائرة « اف ـ ١٦ » | F-16 aircraft |
| طائرة « اف ـ ٢٧ ـ ٦٠٠ » | F-27 600 aircraft |
| طائرة « اف ـ ١٠٠ » | F-100 aircraft |

| | |
|---|---|
| طائرة أڤينجر | Avenger aircraft |
| طائرة « أڤيوجيت » | Aviojet trainer |
| طائرة « أڤيوكار » | Aviocar aircraft |
| طائرة « ال ـ ٢٩ دلفين » | L-29 Delfin aircraft |
| طائرة « إل ـ ١٤ » | IL-14 aircraft |
| طائرة « إل ـ ١٨ » | IL-18 aircraft |
| طائرة « إل ـ ٢٨ » | IL-28 aircraft |
| طائرة « إل ـ ٣٨ ايه اس دبليو » | IL-38 ASW aircraft |
| طائرة « ألفاجيت » | Alpha Jet aircraft |
| طائرة أليزيه | Alizé aircraft |
| طائرة « ام ـ ١٢ » | M-12 aircraft |
| طائرة « أندوڤر » | Andover aircraft |
| طائرة انذار مبكر « شاكلتون ايه ئي دبليو ـ ٢ » | Shackleton AEW-2 |
| طائرة انقضاض للهجوم الأرضي | ground-attack strike aircraft |
| طائرة انقضاض نووي | nuclear strike aircraft |
| طائرة « اواك إل ـ ٧٦ » | IL-76 AWAC |
| طائرة « أواكس سنتري » | Sentry AWACS |
| طائرة أواكس ئي ـ ٣ ايه | E-3A AWACS |
| طائرة « أوراو » | Orao aircraft |
| طائرة « اوه ڤي ـ ١ » | OV-1 aircraft |
| طائرة « اوه ڤي ـ ١ دي » | OV-1D aircraft |
| طائرة « اوه ڤي ـ ١٠ » | OV-10 aircraft |
| طائرة « إيجل » | Eagle aircraft |
| طائرة ايجال المحسنة | Enhanced Eagle aircraft |
| طائرة ايرباص | airbus |
| طائرة « ايه ـ ٤ ئي إتش » | A-4EH aircraft |
| طائرة « ايه ـ ٧ ئي » | A-7E aircraft |
| طائرة ايه اوه پي ـ ٩ | AOP-9 aircraft |
| طائرة « ايه جيه ٣٧ » | AJ-37 aircraft |
| طائرة « بافالو » | Buffalo aircraft |
| طائرة « پاناڤياتورنادو » | Panavia Tornado aircraft |
| طائرة بجناح ثابت | fixed wing aircraft |
| طائرة بحرية شين ميه وا | Shin Meiwa flying boat |
| طائرة بدون طيار | pilotless aircraft |
| طائرة « پراولر » | Prowler aircraft |
| طائرة « برونكو » | Bronco aircraft |
| طائرة « بكانير » | Buccaneer aircraft |
| طائرة « بلاك بيرد » | Blackbird aircraft |
| طائرة بمحرك مروحي تربيني « ايه ١ ـ ٢٠ » | A1-20 turboprop |
| طائرة بمحرك مروحي تربيني « تي ـ ٥٣ ـ ال ـ ٧٠١ » | T-53-L-701 turboprop |
| طائرة بمقعد واحد | single seater |
| طائرة « پوكارا » | Pucara aircraft |
| طائرة « بي ـ ٥٢ جي » | B-52G aircraft |
| طائرة « بي ـ ٥٢ إتش » | B-52H aircraft |
| طائرة « پي ـ ٢ جيه » | P-2J aircraft |
| طائرة « پي ـ ٣ سي » | P-3C aircraft |
| طائرة « بي ار ١١٥٠ » | Br 1150 aircraft |
| طائرة « پي اف ام » | PFM aircraft |
| طائرة « بي ايه سي ١٤٥ » | BAC 145 aircraft |
| طائرة « بيسون » | Bison aircraft |
| طائرة « پي سي ـ ٧ » | PC-7 aircraft |
| طائرة « بيڤر » | Beaver aircraft |
| طائرة « پيلاتوس » | Pilatus aircraft |
| طائرة « بي ئي ـ ١٢ » | Be-12 aircraft |
| طائرة « تايجر آي » | Tigereye aircraft |
| طائرة تاكامو | Tacamo aircraft |
| طائرة تجميع الاتصالات | communications-gathering aircraft |
| طائرة تدريب | trainer aircraft |
| طائرة تدريب « اس اف ـ ٢٦٠ ام » | SF-260M trainer |
| طائرة تدريب « اس اف ـ ٢٦٠ دبليو ال » | SF-260WL trainer |
| طائرة تدريب « ال ـ ٣٩ زد اوه » | L-39ZO trainer |
| طائرة تدريب « ام بي بي ـ ٢٢٣ » | MBB-223 trainer |

ط

| | |
|---|---|
| طائرة تدريب « أميت » | Amit training aircraft |
| طائرة تدريب « براڤو » | Bravo trainer |
| طائرة تدريب « بروسار » | Broussard trainer |
| طائرة تدريب بقيادة مزدوجة | dual-control trainer |
| طائرة تدريب بمقعدين | two-seat trainer |
| طائرة تدريب « بولدوج » | Bulldog trainer |
| طائرة تدريب « تي ـ ١ » | T-1 trainer aircraft |
| طائرة تدريب « جاليب » | Galeb trainer |
| طائرة تدريب « جمهورية » | Gomhouria training aircraft |
| طائرة تدريب « جيه جيه ـ ٤ » | JJ-4 trainer |
| طائرة تدريب « دي اوه ـ ٢٨ دي » | DO-28D trainer |
| طائرة تدريب « زلين » | Zlin trainer |
| طائرة تدريب « سافير » | Safir trainer |
| طائرة تدريب « سترايكماستر » | Strikemaster trainer |
| طائرة تدريب « سي جيه ـ ٥ » | CJ-5 trainer |
| طائرة تدريب « فلامينجو » | Flamingo trainer |
| طائرة تدريب مزدوجة | dual trainer |
| طائرة تدريب الملاحين | crew trainer |
| طائرة تدريب « مونجول » | Mongol trainer |
| طائرة تدريب نفاثة تربينية | turbo-trainer |
| طائرة « تراكر » | Tracker aircraft |
| طائرة « تشيبمونك » | Chipmunk aircraft |
| طائرة تطوير | development aircraft |
| طائرة تكتيكية | tactical aircraft |
| طائرة « توربو ـ بورتر » | Turbo-Porter aircraft |
| طائرة « تورنيدو » | Tornado aircraft |
| طائرة « توين أوتر » | Twin Otter aircraft |
| طائرة « تي ـ ٤٢ » | T-42 aircraft |
| طائرة « تي ـ ٥٥ » | T-55 aircraft |
| طائرة « تي أر ـ ١ ايه » | TR-1A aircraft |
| طائرة « تي ايه ـ ٤ جيه » | TA-4J aircraft |
| طائرة « تي يو ـ ٢٠ » | Tu-20 aircraft |
| طائرة « تي يو ـ ١٢٤ » | Tu-124 aircraft |
| طائرة « تي يو ـ ١٢٦ ايه دبليو ايه سي » | Tu-126 AWAC aircraft |
| طائرة « تي يو ـ ١٢٨ » | Tu-128 aircraft |
| طائرة « تي يو ـ ١٤٢ » | Tu-142 aircraft |
| طائرة « جاسترب » | Jastreb aircraft |
| طائرة « جرين نايتس » | Green Knights aircraft |
| طائرة « جراي هاوند » | Greyhound aircraft |
| طائرة الجو العالي | stratospheric aircraft |
| طائرة « جي ٢٢٢ ڤي إس » | G222VS aircraft |
| طائرة « جيت بروڤوست » | Jet Provost aircraft |
| طائرة « جيتستار » | Jetstar aircraft |
| طائرة « جيتستريم » | Jetstream aircraft |
| طائرة « جيه ٣٥ » | J35 aircraft |
| طائرة « جيه زد ـ ٦ » | JZ-6 aircraft |
| طائرة حرب إلكترونية | electronic-warfare aircraft |
| طائرة حرب ضد الغواصات | ASW aircraft |
| طائرة الحرب ضد الغواصات « اورورا » | Aurora ASW aircraft |
| طائرة حربية « إس يو ـ ١٩ » | Su-19 combat aircraft |
| طائرة « دراجونفلاي » | Dragonfly aircraft |
| طائرة « دلفين ال ـ ٢٩ » | Delfin L-29 aircraft |
| طائرة دورية « اس ـ ٢ ئي » | S-2E patrol aircraft |
| طائرة دورية مقاتلة | combat air patroller |
| طائرة « دي ـ ٥ اكس » | D-5X aircraft |
| طائرة « دي اوه ـ ٢٧ » | DO-27 aircraft |
| طائرة « دي اوه ـ ٢٨ » | DO-28 aircraft |
| طائرة ذات الأجنحة الدوارة | rotary winged aircraft |
| طائرة « زاڤانتي » | Xavante aircraft |

ط

|  |  |
|---|---|
| Xingu aircraft | طائرة « زينجو » |
| Saab aircraft | طائرة « ساب » |
| Citation aircraft | طائرة « سايتيشن » |
| Starfighter aircraft | طائرة « ستارفايتر » |
| Strikemaster aircraft | طائرة « سترايكماستر » |
| Skyfox aircraft | طائرة سكايفوكس |
| close-support aircraft | طائرة السند المباشر |
| Super Skywagon aircraft | طائرة « سوبر سكايواجون » |
| Super Sabre aircraft | طائرة « سوبر سيبر » |
| Super Cub aircraft | طائرة « سوبر كب » |
| Super King Air aircraft | طائرة « سوبر كينج اير » |
| Super Mirage 4000 aircraft | طائرة « سوبر ميراج ٤٠٠٠ » |
| C-2A aircraft | طائرة « سي ـ ٢ ايه » |
| C-5A airtransporter | طائرة نقل « سي ـ ٥ ايه » |
| C-12A aircraft | طائرة « سي ـ ١٢ ايه » |
| C-130 aircraft | طائرة « سي ـ ١٣٠ » |
| CF-101 aircraft | طائرة « سي إف ـ ١٠١ » |
| CM-170 aircraft | طائرة « سي ام ١٧٠ » |
| CP-140 aircraft | طائرة « سي بي ـ ١٤٠ » |
| Sea Devon aircraft | طائرة « سي ديڤن » |
| Sea Scan aircraft | طائرة « سي سكان » |
| Cessna aircraft | طائرة « سيسنا » |
| Sea Harrier aircraft | طائرة « سي هارير » |
| Sea Heron aircraft | طائرة « سي هيرون » |
| Shrike Commander aircraft | طائرة « شرايك كوماندور » |
| Ka-6D tanker aircraft | طائرة صهريج « كيه ايه ـ ٦ دي » |
| KC-10 tanker aircraft | طائرة صهريج « كيه سي ـ ١٠ » |
| KC-135 tanker aircraft | طائرة صهريج « كيه سي ـ ١٣٥ » |
| KC-707 air tanker | طائرة صهريج « كيه سي ـ ٧٠٧ » |
| intruder tanker aircraft | طائرة صهريجية اقتحامية |

|  |  |
|---|---|
| missile aircraft | طائرة صواريخ |
| low-flying aircraft | طائرة طيران منخفض |
| helicopter, vertical aircraft | طائرة عمودية |
| 206B helicopter | طائرة عمودية « ٢٠٦ بي » |
| 500 MD helicopter | طائرة عمودية ٥٠٠ إم دي |
| Apache helicopter | طائرة عمودية « اباتشي » |
| HH-3E helicopter | طائرة عمودية « اتش اتش ـ ٣ ئي » |
| HH-3F helicopter | طائرة عمودية « اتش اتش ـ ٣ اف » |
| HH-65A helicopter | طائرة عمودية « اتش اتش ٦٥ ايه » |
| HHS-2 helicopter | طائرة عمودية « اتش اتش اس ـ ٢ » |
| HAS Mk 1 helicopter | طائرة عمودية « اتش ايه اس ماركة ١ » |
| HAS Mk2 helicopter | طائرة عمودية « اتش ايه اس ماركة ٢ » |
| HAS Mk 5 helicopter | طائرة عمودية « اتش ايه اس ماركة ٥ » |
| HU Mk 5 helicopter | طائرة عمودية « اتش يو مارك ٥ » |
| R4 helicopter | طائرة عمودية أر ٤ |
| RH-3 helicopter | طائرة عمودية « أر اتش ـ ٣ » |
| RH-53 helicopter | طائرة عمودية « أر اتش ـ٥٣ » |
| S-61/H-3 helicopter | طائرة عمودية « اس ـ ٦١/اتش ـ ٣ » |
| S-65/H-53 helicopter | طائرة عمودية « اس ـ ٦٥/اتش ـ٥٣ » |
| SH-2 helicopter | طائرة عمودية « اس اتش ـ ٢ » |
| SH-2F helicopter | طائرة عمودية « اس اتش ـ ٢ اف » |
| SH-3 helicopter | طائرة عمودية « اس اتش ـ ٣ » |
| SH-60 helicopter | طائرة عمودية « اس اتش ـ ٦٠ » |

ط

طائرة عمودية « اس ايه ٣١٦ سي » SA 316C helicopter

طائرة عمودية « اس ايه ٣١٩ بي » SA 319B helicopter

طائرة عمودية « اس ايه ٣٢١ جي » SA 321G helicopter

طائرة عمودية « اس ايه ٣٤١ اف » SA 341F helicopter

طائرة عمودية « اس ايه ٣٤٢ ام » SA 342M helicopter

طائرة عمودية « اس ايه ٣٦٠ سي » SA 360C helicopter

طائرة عمودية « اس ايه ٣٦٥ اف » SA 365F helicopter

طائرة عمودية « اس ايه ٣٦٥ إن » SA 365N helicopter

طائرة عمودية « اس ايه ٣٦٦ جي » SA 366G helicopter

طائرة عمودية « اس ايه أر » SAR helicopter

طائرة عمودية « اس ئي ٣١٣ بي » SE313B helicopter

طائرة عمودية « اكس اتش ـ ٤٠ » XH-40 helicopter

طائرة عمودية « إكورايه » Ecureuil helicopter

طائرة عمودية ألباتروس Albatross helicopter

طائرة عمودية « ألويت » Alouette helicopter

طائرة عمودية « ام اي ـ ٤ » Mi-4 helicopter

طائرة عمودية « ام اي ـ ٦ » Mi-6 helicopter

طائرة عمودية « ام اي ـ ٨ » Mi-8 helicopter

طائرة عمودية « ام اي ـ ١٤ » Mi-14 helicopter

طائرة عمودية « ام اي ـ ٢٤ » Mi-24 helicopter

طائرة عمودية « ام اي ـ ٢٦ » Mi-26 helicopter

طائرة عمودية « ام اي ـ ٢٩ » Mi-29 helicopter

طائرة عمودية « اوفيليا » Orphelia helicopter

طائرة عمودية « اوه اتش ـ ٦ » OH-6 helicopter

طائرة عمودية « اوه اتش ـ ٢٣ اف » OH-23F helicopter

طائرة عمودية « اوه اتش ـ ٥٨ ايه » OH-58A helicopter

طائرة عمودية « ايه ١٠٩ » A-109 helicopter

طائرة عمودية « ايه ١٢٩ » A-129 helicopter

طائرة عمودية « ايه إتش ـ ١ » AH-1 helicopter

طائرة عمودية « ايه إتش ـ ١ اس » AH-1S helicopter

طائرة عمودية « ايه إتش ـ ١ جي » AH-1G helicopter

طائرة عمودية « ايه اتش ـ ١٥ » AH-15 helicopter

طائرة عمودية « ايه إتش ـ ٥٦ » AH-56 helicopter

طائرة عمودية « ايه إتش ـ ٦٤ » AH-64 helicopter

طائرة عمودية « ايه إتش ـ أي تي » AH-IT helicopter

طائرة عمودية « ايه اس ـ ٣٣٢ بي » AS-332B helicopter

طائرة عمودية « ايه اس ـ ٣٥٠ بي » AS-350B helicopter

طائرة عمودية « ايه اس ـ ٣٦٥ ان » AS-365N helicopter

طائرة عمودية « ايه بي ـ ٤٧ » AB-47 helicopter

طائرة عمودية « ايه بي ٢٠٤ » AB-204 helicopter

طائرة عمودية « ايه بي ٢٠٤ بي » AB-204 B helicopter

طائرة عمودية « ايه بي ٢٠٥ » AB-205 helicopter

طائرة عمودية « ايه بي ـ ٢١٢ » AB-212 helicopter

طائرة عمودية « ايه بي ـ ٤١٢ » AB-412 helicopter

ط

| | |
|---|---|
| طائرة عمودية « بادجر » | Badger helicopter |
| طائرة عمودية بحرية | naval helicopter, maritime helicopter, shore-based helicopter |
| طائرة عمودية « بل ٢٠٦ » | Bell-206 helicopter |
| طائرة عمودية « بل - ٢٠٩ » | Bell-209 helicopter |
| طائرة عمودية « بل ٢١٤ اس تي » | Bell-214ST helicopter |
| طائرة عمودية « بل ايه إتش - ١ اس » | Bell AH-1S helicopter |
| طائرة عمودية « بلاك هوك » | Black Hawk helicopter |
| طائرة عمودية « پليكان » | Pelican helicopter |
| طائرة عمودية « بي اوه ١٠٥ » | BO 105 helicopter |
| طائرة عمودية « پي ايه اتش - ١ » | PAH-1 helicopter |
| طائرة عمودية « بي كيه ١١٧ » | BK 117 helicopter |
| طائرة عمودية « پيوما » | Puma helicopter |
| طائرة عمودية « تشينوك » | Chinook helicopter |
| طائرة عمودية تكتيكية | tactical helicopter |
| طائرة عمودية « تي اتش - ٥٥ » | TH-55 helicopter |
| طائرة عمودية « جازيل » | Gazelle helicopter |
| طائرة عمودية « جريفون » | Grifon helicopter |
| طائرة عمودية « جريه ويلز » | Grey Whales helicopter |
| طائرة عمودية « جو لي جرين جاينت » | Jolly Green Giant helicopter |
| طائرة عمودية « جيت رينجر » | Jet Ranger helicopter |
| طائرة عمودية « دبليو جي ٣٠ » | WG 30 helicopter |
| طائرة عمودية « دفيندر » | Defender helicopter |
| طائرة عمودية « دوفين » | Dauphin helicopter |
| طائرة عمودية « دولفين » | Dolphin helicopter |
| طائرة عمودية « زد - ٥ » | Z-5 helicopter |
| طائرة عمودية « زد - ٦ » | Z-6 helicopter |
| طائرة عمودية « زد - ٩ » | Z-9 helicopter |
| طائرة عمودية « سكايكرين » | Skycrane helicopter |
| طائرة عمودية « سكوت » | Scout helicopter |
| طائرة عمودية « سكوت ايه اتش » | Scout AH helicopter |
| طائرة عمودية « سكوت ديفيندر » | Scout Defender helicopter |
| طائرة عمودية « سوپر پيوما » | Super Puma helicopter |
| طائرة عمودية « سوپر فريلون » | Super Frelon helicopter |
| طائرة عمودية « سي اتش ٤٦ » | CH-46 helicopter |
| طائرة عمودية « سي اتش - ٤٧ » | CH-47 helicopter |
| طائرة عمودية « سي اتش - ٤٧ سي » | CH-47C helicopter |
| طائرة عمودية « سي اتش ٤٧ دي » | CH-47D helicopter |
| طائرة عمودية « سي اتش - ٥٣ » | CH-53 helicopter |
| طائرة عمودية « سي اتش - ٥٤ » | CH-54 helicopter |
| طائرة عمودية « سي سپرايت » | Seasprite helicopter |
| طائرة عمودية « سي ستاليون » | Sea Stallion helicopter |
| طائرة عمودية « سيكامور اتش سي ١٤ » | Sycamore HC14 helicopter |
| طائرة عمودية « سي كوبرا » | Sea Cobra helicopter |

ط

|  |  |
|---|---|
| Sea King helicopter | طائرة عمودية « سي كينج » |
| Sea Knight helicopter | طائرة عمودية « سي نايت » |
| military helicopter | طائرة عمودية عسكرية |
| V-14 helicopter | طائرة عمودية « في ـ ١٤ » |
| Kaman helicopter | طائرة عمودية « كامان » |
| Cobra helicopter | طائرة عمودية « كوبرا » |
| Quick-fix helicopter | طائرة عمودية « كويك فيكس » |
| K9-25 helicopter | طائرة عمودية « كيه ٩ ـ ٢٥ » |
| Ka-25 helicopter | طائرة عمودية « كيه ايه ـ ٢٥ » |
| Ka-27 helicopter | طائرة عمودية « كيه ايه ـ ٢٧ » |
| Ka-32 helicopter | طائرة عمودية « كيه ايه ـ ٣٢ » |
| KV-107 helicopter | طائرة عمودية « كيه في ـ ١٠٧ » |
| aerial scout helicopter | طائرة عمودية للاستطلاع الجوي |
| utility helicopter | طائرة عمودية للأغراض العامة |
| LAMPS helicopter | طائرة عمودية « لامپس » |
| mine countermeasures helicopter | طائرة عمودية للتدابير المضادة للالغام |
| battlefield helicopter | طائرة عمودية لساحة المعركة |
| ship-based helicopter | طائرة عمودية للسفن |
| minesweeping helicopter | طائرة عمودية لكسح الألغام |
| observation helicopter | طائرة عمودية للمراقبة |
| commando assault helicopter | طائرة عمودية للهجوم الفدائي |
| Lynx helicopter | طائرة عمودية « لينكس » |
| Mastiff helicopter | طائرة عمودية « ماستيف » |

|  |  |
|---|---|
| multi-role helicopter | طائرة عمودية متعددة المهام |
| compound helicopter | طائرة عمودية مركبة |
| gunship helicopter | طائرة عمودية مسلحة هجومية |
| anti-tank helicopter | طائرة عمودية مضادة للدبابات |
| anti-submarine helicopter | طائرة عمودية مضادة للغواصات |
| combat helicopter | طائرة عمودية مقاتلة |
| Advanced Attack Helicopter | طائرة عمودية مهاجمة متقدمة |
| Mil Miz helicopter | طائرة عمودية « ميل ميز » |
| NATO helicopter | طائرة عمودية « ناتو » |
| Harke helicopter | طائرة عمودية « هارك » |
| Hound A helicopter | طائرة عمودية « هاوند ايه » |
| Hound C helicopter | طائرة عمودية « هاوند سي » |
| Hind helicopter | طائرة عمودية « هايند » |
| Hoop helicopter | طائرة عمودية« هوپ » |
| Hoplite helicopter | طائرة عمودية « هوپلايت » |
| Hormone helicopter | طائرة عمودية « هورمون » |
| Hook helicopter | طائرة عمودية « هوك » |
| Hip-C helicopter | طائرة عمودية « هيپ ـ سي » |
| Hare helicopter | طائرة عمودية « هير » |
| Haze helicopter | طائرة عمودية « هيز » |
| Helix helicopter | طائرة عمودية « هيلكس » |
| Halo helicopter | طائرة عمودية « هيلو » |
| Huey Cobra helicopter | طائرة عمودية « هيوي كوبرا » |
| Wasp helicopter | طائرة عمودية « واسپ » |
| Wessex helicopter | طائرة عمودية « واسيكس » |

| | |
|---|---|
| طائرة عمودية « ويرلويند » | Whirlwind helicopter |
| طائرة عمودية « ويستلاند سي كينج » | Westland Sea King helicopter |
| طائرة عمودية « ئي اتش ـ ٦٠ ايه » | EH-60A helicopter |
| طائرة عمودية « ئي اتش ـ ١٠١ » | EH-101 helicopter |
| طائرة عمودية « يو اتش ـ ١ » | UH-1 helicopter |
| طائرة « يو اتش ـ ١ اتش » | UH-1H aircraft |
| طائرة عمودية « يو اتش ـ ٢ ايه » | UH-2A helicopter |
| طائرة عمودية « يو اتش ـ ١٢ ئي » | UH-12E helicopter |
| طائرة عمودية « يو اتش ـ ٤٦ » | UH-46 helicopter |
| طائرة عمودية « يو اتش ـ ٦٠ » | UH-60 helicopter |
| طائرة « فالكون » | Falcon aircraft |
| طائرة « فايربار » | Firebar aircraft |
| طائرة « ڤايكينج » | Viking aircraft |
| طائرة « فروجفوت » | Frogfoot aircraft |
| طائرة « فلاجون ـ اف » | Flagon-F aircraft |
| طائرة « فورجر » | Forger aircraft |
| طائرة « فوكسبات » | Foxbat aircraft |
| طائرة « فوكسهاوند » | Foxhound fighter |
| طائرة « فيتر ـ جيه » | Fitter-J aircraft |
| طائرة « فيتر اف » | Fitter-F aircraft |
| طائرة « ڤيتول » | VTOL aircraft |
| طائرة « ڤيرتول ١٠٧ » | Vertol 107 |
| طائرة « ڤي/ستول » | V/STOL aircraft |
| طائرة فيشبوت | Fishpot aircraft |
| طائرة « ڤيلترو ٢ » | Veltro 2 aircraft |
| طائرة « فينسر » | Fencer aircraft |
| طائرة قاذفة « اف ـ ١١ » | F-11 bomber |
| طائرة قاذفة « اف بي ـ ١١١ » | FB-111 bomber |
| طائرة قاذفة « ايه ـ ٤ » | A-4 bomber |
| طائرة قاذفة « ايه ـ ٤ إتش » | A-4H bomber |
| طائرة قاذفة « ايه ـ ٤ إم » | A-4M bomber |
| طائرة قاذفة « ايه ـ ٦ ئي » | A-6E bomber |
| طائرة قاذفة « ايه ـ ٧ » | A-7 bomber |
| طائرة قاذفة « بادجر » | Badger bomber |
| طائرة قاذفة « باك فاير » | Backbire bomber |
| طائرة قاذفة « بلايندر » | Blinder bomber |
| طائرة قاذفة « بي ـ ١ بي » | B-1B bomber |
| طائرة قاذفة « بي ـ ٥٢ » | B-52 bomber |
| طائرة قاذفة « تي يو ـ ١٦ » | Tu-16 bomber |
| طائرة قاذفة « تي يو ـ ٢٢ » | Tu-22 bomber |
| طائرة قاذفة « تي يو ـ ٢٦ » | Tu-26 bomber |
| طائرة قاذفة « تي يو ـ ٩٥ » | Tu-95 bomber |
| طائرة قاذفة « سكايهوك » | Skyhawk bomber |
| طائرة قاذفة « ڤالكن » | Vulcan bomber |
| طائرة قاذفة « كورسأير » | Corsair bomber |
| طائرة قاذفة للانقضاض من مستوى منخفض | low-level strike bomber |
| طائرة قاذفة « ميج ـ ٢٣ » | MiG-23 bomber |
| طائرة قتال | combat aircraft |
| طائرة قذف من مستوى منخفض | low-level bomber |
| طائرة قيادة ومراقبة عمودية | command and control helicopter |
| طائرة « كانبيريا » | Canberra |
| طائرة كشافة | pathfinder |
| طائرة « كفير » | Kfir aircraft |
| طائرة « كوت ايه » | Coot A aircraft |

| | |
|---|---|
| طائرة « كودفيش » | CODfish aircraft |
| طائرة « كورڤيت » | Corvette aircraft |
| طائرة « كوين آير » | Queen Air aircraft |
| طائرة « كينج آير » | King Air aircraft |
| طائرة « ليهزن » | Liason aircraft |
| طائرة « ماتدور » | Matador aircraft |
| طائرة « ماجيستر » | Magister aircraft |
| طائرة « مايا » | Mya aircraft |
| طائرة « مايه » | May aircraft |
| طائرة محمولة على متن سفينة | ship-borne aircraft |
| طائرة مدنية | civilian aircraft |
| طائرة معادية | hostile aircraft |
| طائرة معادية | enemy aircraft |
| طائرة معترضة للهجوم عن بعد | stand-off interceptor |
| طائرة مقاتلة | fighter aircraft |
| طائرة مقاتلة « إتيندارد » | Etendard fighter |
| طائرة مقاتلة « أر اف ـ ٥ » | RF-5 fighter |
| طائرة مقاتلة « أر اف ـ ١٠٤ جي » ستار فايتر | RF-104G Starfighter |
| طائرة مقاتلة استطلاعية | surveillance fighter |
| طائرة مقاتلة « إس يو ـ ٩ » | Su-9 fighter |
| طائرة مقاتلة « إس يو ـ ١١ » | Su-11 fighter |
| طائرة مقاتلة « إس يو ـ ١٥ » | Su-15 fighter |
| طائرة مقاتلة « إس يو ـ ٢٧ » | Su-27 fighter |
| طائرة مقاتلة « اف ـ ١ » | F-1 fighter |
| طائرة مقاتلة « اف ١ ـ سي » | F-1C fighter |
| طائرة مقاتلة « اف ـ ٤ » | F-4 fighter |
| طائرة مقاتلة « اف ـ ٥ اف » | F-5F fighter |
| طائرة مقاتلة « اف ـ ٥ ئي » | F-5E fighter |
| طائرة مقاتلة « اف ـ ٦ » | F-6 fighter |
| طائرة مقاتلة « اف ـ ٦ بيس » | F-6 bis fighter |
| طائرة مقاتلة « اف ـ ٧ » | F-7 fighter |
| طائرة مقاتلة « اف ـ ٨ » | F-8 fighter |
| طائرة مقاتلة « اف ـ ١٤ » | F-14 fighter |
| طائرة مقاتلة « اف ـ ١٥ ئي » | F-15E fighter |
| طائرة مقاتلة « اف ـ ١٦ اكس إل » | F-16XL fighter |
| طائرة مقاتلة « اف ـ ١٦ ئي » | F-16E fighter |
| طائرة مقاتلة « اف ـ ١٨ » | F-18 fighter |
| طائرة مقاتلة « اف ـ ٢٠ » | F-20 fighter |
| طائرة مقاتلة « اف ـ ٥٣ » | F-53 fighter |
| طائرة مقاتلة « اف ـ ٧٠ » | F-70 fighter |
| طائرة مقاتلة « اف ١٠١ » | F-101 fighter |
| طائرة مقاتلة « اف ـ ١٠٤ » | F-104 fighter |
| طائرة مقاتلة « اف ١٠٤ اس » | F-104S fighter |
| طائرة مقاتلة « اف/ايه ـ ١٨ ايه هورنيت » | F/A-18A Hornet fighter |
| طائرة مقاتلة « ال ٣٩ دي » | L39D fighter |
| طائرة مقاتلة ألباتروس | Albatross fighter |
| طائرة مقاتلة « إمپالا » | Impala fighter |
| طائرة مقاتلة « ام بي ٣٢٦ » | MB326 fighter |
| طائرة مقاتلة « ام پي ٣٣٩ كيه » | MB339K fighter |
| طائرة مقاتلة انقضاضية « لاڤي » | Lavi strike fighter |
| طائرة مقاتلة « ايه ـ ٧ دي » | A-7D fighter |
| طائرة مقاتلة « ايه إم ـ اكس » | AM-X fighter |

| | |
|---|---|
| AV-8B fighter | طائرة مقاتلة « ايه ڤي - ٨ بي » |
| sea-based fighter | طائرة مقاتلة بحرية |
| land-based fighter | طائرة مقاتلة برية |
| Tiger fighter | طائرة مقاتلة « تايجر » |
| Tiger 11 fighter | طائرة مقاتلة « تايجر ١١ » |
| Tiger-shark fighter | طائرة مقاتلة « تايجر - شارك » |
| light tactical fighter | طائرة مقاتلة تكتيكية خفيفة |
| Tomcat fighter | طائرة مقاتلة « تومكات » |
| T-66 fighter | طائرة مقاتلة « تي - ٦٦ » |
| Tu-28P fighter | طائرة مقاتلة « تي يو - ٢٨ بي » |
| Thunderbolt 11 fighter | طائرة مقاتلة « ثندربولت ١١ » |
| G91R fighter | طائرة مقاتلة « ٩١ آر » |
| G91Y fighter | طائرة مقاتلة « جي ٩١ واي » |
| J-4 fighter | طائرة مقاتلة « جيه - ٤ » |
| J-5 fighter | طائرة مقاتلة « جيه - ٥ » |
| J-6 fighter | طائرة مقاتلة « جيه - ٦ » |
| J-7 fighter | طائرة مقاتلة « جيه - ٧ » |
| JA37 fighter | طائرة مقاتلة « جيه ايه ٣٧ » |
| Dagger fighter | طائرة مقاتلة داجر |
| Saab 35 fighter | طائرة مقاتلة « ساب ٣٥ » |
| Super Standard fighter | طائرة مقاتلة « سوپر ستاندرد » |
| Seahawk fighter | طائرة مقاتلة « سي هوك » |
| Farmer fighter | طائرة مقاتلة « فارمر » |
| Fantan A fighter | طائرة مقاتلة « فانتان ايه » |
| Phantom II fighter | طائرة مقاتلة « فانتوم ٢ » |
| Fighting Falcon fighter | طائرة مقاتلة « فايتنج فالكون » |
| Fresco fighter | طائرة مقاتلة « فريسكو » |
| Flanker fighter | طائرة مقاتلة فلانكر |
| Flogger F fighter | طائرة مقاتلة « فلوجر اف » |
| Flogger D fighter | طائرة مقاتلة « فلوجر دي » |
| Voodoo fighter | طائرة مقاتلة ڤودو |
| Fulcrum fighter | طائرة مقاتلة « فولكروم » |
| Fitter-A fighter | طائرة مقاتلة « فيتر - ايه » |
| Viggen fighter | طائرة مقاتلة « ڤيجن » |
| Fiddler fighter | طائرة مقاتلة « فيدلر » |
| Fishbed fighter | طائرة مقاتلة « فيشبيد » |
| fighter/bomber | طائرة مقاتلة/قاذفة |
| Crusader fighter | طائرة مقاتلة « كروسيدر » |
| Cobra fighter | طائرة مقاتلة « كوبرا » |
| Q-5 fighter | طائرة مقاتلة « كيو - ٥ » |
| Lightning fighter | طائرة مقاتلة « لايتنينج » |
| low-visibility fighter | طائرة مقاتلة للرؤية المنخفضة |
| Marut fighter | طائرة مقاتلة « ماروت » |
| multi-role fighter | طائرة مقاتلة متعددة المهام |
| strike fighter | طائرة مقاتلة مهاجمة |
| Super Etendard strike fighter | طائرة مقاتلة مهاجمة « سوپر إتيندارد » |
| MiG-19 fighter | طائرة مقاتلة « ميج - ١٩ » |
| MiG-21 fighter | طائرة مقاتلة « ميج - ٢١ » |
| MiG-21MF fighter | طائرة مقاتلة « ميج - ٢١ ام اف » |

ط

| | |
|---|---|
| طائرة مقاتلة « ميج ـ ٢٣ اس » | MiG-23S fighter |
| طائرة مقاتلة « ميج ـ ٢٥ ام » | MiG-25M fighter |
| طائرة مقاتلة « ميج ـ ٢٩ » | MiG-29 fighter |
| طائرة مقاتلة « ميج ـ ٣١ » | MiG-31 fighter |
| طائرة مقاتلة « ميراج » | Mirage fighter |
| طائرة مقاتلة « ميراج ٣ » | Mirage III fighter |
| طائرة مقاتلة « ميراج ٣ ئي » | Mirage IIIE fighter |
| طائرة مقاتلة « ميراج ٣ ئي إل » | Mirage IIIEL fighter |
| طائرة مقاتلة« ميراج ٤ » | Mirage IV fighter |
| طائرة مقاتلة « ميراج ٥ » | Mirage 5 fighter |
| طائرة مقاتلة « ميراج ٥ دي » | Mirage 5D fighter |
| طائرة مقاتلة « ميراج ٥ ئي ٢ » | Mirage 5E2 fighter |
| طائرة مقاتلة « ميراج ٢٠٠٠ » | Mirage 2000 fighter |
| طائرة مقاتلة « ميراج ٢٠٠٠ إن » | Mirage 2000N fighter |
| طائرة مقاتلة « ميراج اف ١ » | Mirage F1 fighter |
| طائرة « ميراج إف ـ ١ ايه » | Mirage F-1A fighter |
| طائرة مقاتلة « ميراج إف ١ سي آر » | Mirage F-ICR fighter |
| طائرة مقاتلة « نات » | Gnat fighter |
| طائرة مقاتلة « هال أجيت » | HAL Ajeet fighter |
| طائرة مقاتلة « هانتر » | Hunter fighter |
| طائرة مقاتلة « وايلدكات » | Wildcat fighter |
| طائرة من صنع « سوخوي » | Sukhoi-built aircraft |
| طائرة منقولة على الحاملة | carrierborne aircraft |
| طائرة مهاجمة | attack aircraft |
| طائرة مهاجمة « ايه ـ ١٠ ايه » | A-10A attack aircraft |
| طائرة مقاتلة « ايه ـ ١٨ » | A-18 fighter |
| طائرة مقاتلة « ايه ـ ٣٧ بي » | A-37B fighter |
| طائرة موجهة | director aircraft |
| طائرة « موجيك » | Moujik aircraft |
| طائرة « موهوك » | Mohawk aircraft |
| طائرة « ميج ـ ١٥ » | MiG-15 aircraft |
| طائرة « ميج ـ ٢١ آر » | MiG-21R aircraft |
| طائرة « ميج ـ ٢٣ ام اف » | MiG-23MF aircraft |
| طائرة « ميج ـ ٢٣ بي إن » | MiG-23BN aircraft |
| طائرة « ميج ـ ٢٣ يو » | MiG-23U aircraft |
| طائرة « ميج ـ ٢٥ » | MiG-25 aircraft |
| طائرة « ميج ـ ٢٥ آر » | MiG-25R aircraft |
| طائرة « ميج ـ ٢٧ » | MiG-27 aircraft |
| طائرة « ميراج ٥-٥٠ » | Mirage 5-50 aircraft |
| طائرة « ميستير فالكون » | Mystère-Falcon aircraft |
| طائرة « ميل » | Mail aircraft |
| طائرة نفاثة بالاحتراق اللاحق | afterburning turbojet |
| طائرة نفاثة تربينية | turbojet |
| طائرة نفاثة تربينية « جيه ٥٢ ـ پي ٤٠٨ » | J52-P-408 turbojet |
| طائرة نفاثة تربينية « جيه ٧٩-١٧ » | J79-17 turbojet |
| طائرة نفاثة تربينية « جيه ٧٩ ـ جيه ١ ئي » | J79-J1E turbojet |
| طائرة نفاثة تربينية « جيه ٧٩ ـ جي ئي ـ ١٥ » | J79-GE-15 turbojet |
| طائرة نفاثة تربينية « جيه ٨٥-٢١ ئي » | J85-21A turbojet |
| طائرة نفاثة تربينية « ڤيپر » | Viper turbojet |
| طائرة نفاثة تربينية « ڤي كيه ـ ١ اف » | VK-1F turbojet |

| | |
|---|---|
| طائرة نفاثة تربينية « ليولكا » | Lyulka turbojet |
| طائرة نقل | airlifter, transporter |
| طائرة نقل « إف ـ ٢٧ » | F-27 airtransporter |
| طائرة نقل « إل ـ ٧٦ » | IL-76 airtransporter |
| طائرة نقل « إل ـ ٨٦ » | IL-86 airtransporter |
| طائرة نقل « أي ايه ـ ٥٠ » | IA-50 airtransport |
| طائرة نقل « ايه إن ـ ١٢ » | An-12 airtransporter |
| طائرة نقل « ايه إن ـ ١٤ » | An-14 airtransporter |
| طائرة نقل « ايه إن ـ ٢٢ » | An-22 airtransporter |
| طائرة نقل « ايه إن ـ ٢٦ » | An-26 airtransporter |
| طائرة نقل « ايه إن ـ ٢٨ » | An-28 airtransporter |
| طائرة نقل « ايه إن ـ ٧٢ » | An-72 airtransporter |
| طائرة نقل « بي ايه سي ـ ١٧٦ » | BAC-167 airtransport |
| طائرة نقل « تريدر » | Trader transport aircraft |
| طائرة نقل « توربوكومّاندر » | Turbo-commander airtransporter |
| طائرة نقل « جالاكسي » | Galaxy airtransporter |
| طائرة نقل « جلف ـ ستريم » | Gulf-stream airtransport |
| طائرة نقل « جي ٢٢٢ » | G222 airtransporter |
| طائرة نقل « جيوراني » | Guarani airtransport |
| طائرة نقل « دوڤ » | Dove airtransporter |
| طائرة نقل « دي اتش سي ـ ٥ دي » | DHC-5D transporter |
| طائرة نقل « دي اتش سي ـ ٦ » | DHC-6 airtransporter |
| طائرة نقل الركاب | airliner |
| طائرة نقل « ستارلفتر » | Starlifter airtransporter |
| طائرة نقل « ستراتوتانكر » | Stratotanker |
| طائرة نقل « سكايڤان » | Skyvan airtransport |
| طائرة نقل « سي ـ ١٣٠ اتش | C-130H transporter |
| طائرة نقل « سي ١٣٠ بي/اتش » | C130 B/H airtransporter |
| طائرة نقل « سي ـ ١٣٥ » | C-135 airtransporter |
| طائرة نقل « سي ـ ١٤١ » | C-141 airtransporter |
| طائرة نقل « سي ـ ٢١٢ ايه » | C-212A airtransporter |
| طائرة نقل « سيبر لاينر » | Sabreliner airtransport |
| طائرة نقل عمودية | transport helicopter |
| طائرة نقل « ڤي سي ١٠ » | VC 10 airtransport |
| طائرة نقل كارڤيل » | Caravelle airtransporter |
| طائرة نقل « كانديد » | Candid airtransporter |
| طائرة نقل « كوب » | Cub airtransporter |
| طائرة نقل « كوك » | Cock airtransport |
| طائرة نقل كيرل | Curl transporter |
| طائرة نقل « ليرجيت » | Learjet airtransport |
| طائرة نقل « هركيوليز » | Hercules airtransporter |
| طائرة نقل « واي ـ ٥ » | Y-5 transporter |
| طائرة نقل « واي ـ ٧ » | Y-7 transporter |
| طائرة نقل « واي ـ ٨ » | Y-8 airtransporter |
| طائرة نقل وقود « ڤيكتر » | Victor air tanker |
| طائرة نقل « ئي سي ـ ١٣٠ » | EC-130 airtransporter |
| طائرة « نيشر » | Nesher aircraft |
| طائرة « نيمرود ايه ئي دبليو ٣ » | Nimrod AEW 3 aircraft |
| طائرة « هارير » | Harrier aircraft |
| طائرة « هارير ايه ڤي ـ ٨ ايه » | AV-8A Harrier |
| طائرة « هارير ڤي استول » | Harrier V/STOL aircraft |
| طائرة هجوم | strike aircraft |
| طائرة هجوم أرضي | ground-attack aircraft |
| طائرة هجومية « كيانج ـ جيجي ٥ » | Qiang-jiji 5 attack aircraft |
| طائرة « هورنيت » | Hornet aircraft |
| طائرة « هوك » | Hawk aircraft |

| | |
|---|---|
| طائرة « هوكأي » | Hawkeye aircraft |
| طائرة « وايلد ويزل » | Wild Weasel aircraft |
| طائرة « وورهوكس » | War Hawks aircraft |
| طائرة « ئي ـ ٢ » | E-2 aircraft |
| طائرة « ئي ـ ٢ سي هوكاي » | E-2C Hawkeye aircraft |
| طائرة « ئي ـ ٤ بي » | E-4B aircraft |
| طائرة « ئي ـ ٦ ايه » | E-6A aircraft |
| طائرة « ئي اف ـ ١١١ » | EF-111 aircraft |
| طائرة « ئي ام بي ـ ١٢١ » | EMB-121 aircraft |
| طائرة « ئي ام بي ـ ٣٢٦ » | EMB-326 aircraft |
| طائرة « ئي ايه ـ ٦ بي » | EA-6B aircraft |
| طائرة « ئي سي ـ ١٣٥ إن » | EC-135N aircraft |
| طائرة « ياك ـ ٢٨ پي » | Yak-28P |
| طائرة « ياك ـ ٣٦ ام پي » | Yak-36MP aircraft |
| طائرة « يو ـ ٢ » | U-2 aircraft |
| طائرة « يو ـ ٢١ » | U-21 aircraft |
| طائرة « يو ـ ٢٠٦ ستيشن آير » | U-206 Station Air aircraft |
| طائرة « يو ـ ٢٠٦ سي » | U-206C aircraft |
| طائرة « يو ڤي ـ ١٨ ايه » | UV-18A aircraft |
| طائرة يقودها انسان | manned aircraft |
| طائفة العصابات | guerrilla faction |
| طابعة عن بعد | teleprinter |
| طابعة عن بعد « كوكليه » | Coquelet teleprinter |
| طابعة عن بعد « لينك ١٤ » | Link 14 teleprinter |
| طابق المسكن (في سفينة) | accommodation deck |
| طارد الدخان | fume extractor |
| طارىء | emergency |
| طاف | buoyant |
| طافية صوتية رادارية | sonobuoy |
| طافية صوتية رادارية سلبية « ديفار » | Difar passive sonobuoy |
| طافية صوتية رادارية فعالة « ديكاس » | Dicass active sonobuoy |
| طاقة | energy |
| طاقة ترددات لاسلكية | radio frequency energy |
| طاقة حركة | kinetic energy |
| طاقة منقولة | transmitted power |
| طاقة نووية | nuclear energy |
| طاقم | crew |
| طالب عسكري | cadet |
| طالب في كلية بحرية | naval cadet |
| طالب في كلية عسكرية | officer cadet |
| طاه | cook |
| طب | medicine |
| طباخ | cook |
| طبقة الجو العالية | stratosphere |
| طبقة جوية ذات نشاط كهربائي ضوئي | chemosphere |
| طبلة | kettledrum |
| طرادة | cruiser |
| طرادة الباني | Albany cruiser |
| طرادة « أندريا دوريا » | Andrea Doria cruiser |
| طرادة « إنڤينسابل » | Invincible cruiser |
| طرادة اودالوي | Udaloy cruiser |
| طرادة أيووا | Iowa cruiser |
| طرادة بسطح بيني | through-deck cruiser |
| طرادة بالطاقة النووية | nuclear-powered cruiser |
| طرادة « بلاك ـ كوم ١ » | Black-Com 1 cruiser |
| طرادة « بلناپ » | Belknap cruiser |
| طرادة « بينبريدج » | Bainbridge cruiser |
| طرادة « تروكستون » | Truxtun cruiser |
| طرادة « تيكوندروجا » | Ticonderoga cruiser |
| طرادة « سڤردلوف » | Sverdlov cruiser |
| طرادة « سي جي إن » | CGN cruiser |
| طرادة صواريخ | rocket cruiser |
| طرادة صواريخ موجهة | guided missile cruiser |
| طرادة « ڤنيتوريو ڤينيتو » | Vittorio Veneto cruiser |
| طرادة « ڤيرجينيا » | Virginia cruiser |
| طرادة « كارا » | Kara cruiser |

| | |
|---|---|
| طرادة « كاليفورنيا » | California cruiser |
| طرادة « كراسينا » | Krasina cruiser |
| طرادة « كريستا » | Kresta cruiser |
| طرادة « كولبير » | Colbert cruiser |
| طرادة « كيروف » | Kirov cruiser |
| طرادة « كيندا » | Kynda cruiser |
| طرادة للحراسة | escort cruiser |
| طرادة « لونج بيتش » | Long Beach cruiser |
| طرادة « ليهي » | Leahy cruiser |
| طرادة « موسكفا » | Moskva cruiser |
| طراز بدائي | prototype |
| طراز اعتيادي | standard model |
| طراز انتربيد | Intrepid class |
| طراز محسن المحرك | up-engined version |
| طراز نووي | nuclear class |
| طرف المؤخرة | after end |
| طرف المؤخرة . موقع الضباط | quarter-deck |
| طرق التعليم أو التدريب | methods of instruction |
| طريق العوائق | obstacle course |
| طريق مفتوح | road clear |
| طعام | food |
| طعم | vaccinate |
| طقم تكتيكي | tactical crew |
| طقم الدبابة | tank crew |
| طقم من فردين | two-man crew |
| طلاب بحرية | midshipmen |
| طلب تعزيز النيران | request fire support |
| طلقات | rounds |
| طلقات ذخيرة | rounds of ammunition |
| طلقات في الدقيقة | rounds per minute |
| طلقات مفردة | single round |
| طلقة خطاطة | tracer |
| طلقة المسدس | pistol cartridge |
| طلقة مطاط | rubber bullet |
| طلقة مفردة | single-shot |
| طهر | disinfect |
| طور الاشارات | phase of signals |
| طور اكتساب الهدف | target-acquisition phase |
| طوربيد | torpedo |
| طوربيد ٥٣٣ إم إم | 533-MM torpedo |
| طوربيد « اس اس تي ٤ » | SST4 torpedo |
| طوربيد « ام كيه ٣٢ » | MK32 torpedo |
| طوربيد « ايه اس » | AS torpedo |
| طوربيد « ايه اس ٢٤٤/اس » | AS-244/S torpedo |
| طوربيد بالتوجيه الراداري | homing torpedo |
| طوربيد « تايجرفش » | Tigerfish torpedo |
| طوربيد « تي پي ـ ٦١ » | TP-61 torpedo |
| طوربيد حرب ضد الغواصات | ASW torpedo |
| طوربيد « ستينجراي » | Stingray torpedo |
| طوربيد صاروخي بالتوجيه الراداري مضاد للغواصات | ASROC |
| طوربيد طراز « سيل » | Seal Type torpedo |
| طوربيد كياسيو ـ اس | Ciacio-S torpedo |
| طوربيد مضاد للغواصات | anti-submarine torpedo |
| طوربيد نووي | nuclear torpedo |
| طوزلق | leggings |
| طوف قابل للنفخ | inflatable pontoon |
| طوف | pontoon, dinghy |
| طوف نجاة | life-raft |
| طوف هولپلاتا | Hohlplatte pontoon |
| طوق | encircle |
| طول | length |
| طول جسم الطائرة | fuselage length |
| طول الصاروخ | missile length |
| طول الماسورة | length of barrel |
| طول الموجة | wavelength |
| طول موجي كهرومغنطيسي | electromagnetic wavelength |
| الطول الموجي للعمليات | operation wavelength |
| طويل المدى | long-range |

ط

| | |
|---|---|
| **طي آلي للأرياش** | automatic blade folding |
| **طيار** | pilot, airman |
| **طيران** | flying |
| **طيران بالغ الدقة** | precision flying |
| **طيران بالتوجيه نحو الهدف** | homing |
| **طيران بمحرك** | powered-flight |
| **طيران تجريبي** | shakedown flying |
| **طيران حر** | free flight |
| **طيران كنتوري** | contour flying |
| **طيف كهرومغنطيسي** | electro-magnetic spectrum |

| | |
|---|---|
| ظرف الخرطوشة | empty case |
| ظرف خرطوشة قابل للاحتراق | combustible cartridge case |
| ظرف الطلقة الفارغة | spent cartridge case |
| ظرف القذيفة | shell case |
| ظروف الابصار | visual conditions |
| ظروف التشغيل | operating conditions |
| الظروف الصحية | sanitary conditions |
| ظروف الميدان | field conditions |
| ظلة | awning |

ظ

# ع

| | |
|---|---|
| عائق اصطناعي | artificial obstacle |
| عائق طبيعي | natural obstacle |
| عائق عمودي | vertical obstacle |
| عائمة الاتصالات | communications buoy |
| عاجز | bogged down |
| عادم الصاروخ | missile exhaust |
| عادم كبت بالأشعة دون الحمراء | IR-suppressing exhaust |
| عارض | opposing |
| عارضة | traverse |
| عاص | insurgent |
| عاكس | reflector |
| عاكس بمواجهة المؤخرة | rear-facing reflector |
| عاكس الدفع | thrust reverser |
| عالمي | worldwide |
| عالياً ـ احمل ! | port arms! |
| عالي السرعة | ultra-rapid |
| عام | general, universal |
| عامل الأمان | safety factor |
| عامل تحميل | loader |
| عامل تركيب | erector |
| عامل تسجيل الاتصالات | record communications operator |
| عامل تنشيط | activating agent |
| عامل الدم | blood agent |
| عامل الرادار | radar operator |
| عامل لاسلكي | radio operator |
| عامل المواصلات | communications operator |
| عامل الهاتف | switchboard operator |
| عاملاً | in action |
| عبر الضواحي والحقول | cross-country |
| عبور انقضاضي | assault crossing |
| عبور الأنهار | river crossing |
| عبور الجسر | bridge crossing |
| عتاد | equipment |
| عتلة القدح | cocking lever |
| عجل | accelerate |
| عجلة بطنية | belly-wheel |
| عجلة الدرجان | bogie wheel |
| عد تنازلي | count-down |
| عداد دورات المحرك | tachometer |
| عداد « جيجر » | Geiger counter |
| عدد كامل | complement |
| عدد كامل للطائرات | aircraft complement |
| عدد المقاعد | seating capacity |
| عدد وأدوات | tools |
| عدو | enemy, foe |
| عدواني | hostile |
| عديم الانتظام | undisciplined |
| عديم الصيانة | non-serviceable |
| العراق | Iraq |
| عراقي | Iraqi |
| عربة | vehicle |
| عربة استكشاف | scout car |
| عربة اسعاف | ambulance |
| عربة اصلاح العطل الطارىء | recovery vehicle |
| عربة اصلاح مدرعة | armoured recovery vehicle |

| | |
|---|---|
| عربة انزال مجنزرة للافراد | LVTP |
| عربة « جرايف » | Greif vehicle |
| عربة جيب « تشيروكي » | Cherokee jeep |
| عربة مجنزرة « كوبرا » | Cobra tracked vehicle |
| عربة مجنزرة متعددة المهام | multi-role tracked vehicle |
| عربة مدرعة | armoured car |
| عربة مدرعة « ايه ام ال ـ ٩٠ » | AML-90 armoured car |
| عربة مدرعة « پانهارد » | Panhard armoured car |
| عربة مدرعة « جراراراكا » | Jararaca armoured car |
| عربة مدرعة « رييم » | Re'em armoured vehicle |
| عربة مدرعة « ساراسن » | Saracen armoured car |
| عربة مدرعة « ساكسون » | Saxon armoured car |
| عربة مدرعة « سالادين » | Saladin armoured car |
| عربة مدرعة « شارلاند » | Sharland armoured car |
| عربة مدرعة « شورلاند » | Shorland armoured car |
| عربة مدرعة « كاسكاڤيل » | Cascavel armoured car |
| عربة مدرعة « ئي ئي ـ ٣ » | EE-3 armoured car |
| عربة مدرعة « ئي ئي ـ ٩ » كاسكاڤل | EE-9 Cascavel armoured car |
| عربة مدرعة « ئي ئي ـ ١١ » | EE-11 armoured car |
| عربة مدرعة « يو بي سي ـ ٤٠ » | UBC-40 armoured car |
| عربة معطلة | stranded vehicle |
| عربة نقل منخفضة | bogie |
| العربية السعودية | Saudi Arabia |
| عرض | parade |
| عرض بيانات الطيران على واقي الريح | head-up display |
| عرض جوي | flypast |
| عرض خرائط إلكتروني | electronic map display |
| عرض في حجرة الطيار | head-down display |
| عرض ليزر | laser display |
| عريف | corporal |
| عزّز | reinforce (to) |
| عزل | isolation |
| عزل الصوت | sound proofing |
| عسكري | soldier, serviceman |
| عصا | stick |
| عصابات | guerrilla |
| عصر | epoch |
| عصري | modern |
| عصيان | rebellion, insubordination, mutiny |
| عطل | breakdown |
| عقاب | punishment |
| عقب البندقية | butt |
| عقب بندقية متداخل | telescopic butt |
| عقوبة | punishment |
| عقيد | colonel |
| عكس | reflect |
| علاج بالمستشفى | hospital treatment |
| علاج طارىء | emergency treatment |
| علامات | insignia |
| علامة | marker |
| علبة | canister |
| علبة البوصلة | compass case |
| علبة توزيع | junction box |
| علبة حاوية قاذفة | container-launcher box |
| علبة دخان | smoke canister |
| علبة طافية | buoyant canister |
| علبة القذف | launching canister |
| علق سلاح ! | sling arms!, shoulder arms! |
| علم | flag |
| علم الالكترونيات | electronics |
| علم التقنية | technology |
| علم المتفجرات وصناعتها | pyrotechnics |
| علوي | overhead |

ع

| | |
|---|---|
| على شكل المعين | lozenge fashion |
| على قيد الحياة | survivor |
| على الهدف | on target |
| عُمان | Oman |
| عمق التغلغل | depth of penetration |
| عمق الغوص | diving depth |
| عمق متنوع | variable-depth |
| عمل جماعي | teamwork |
| عمليات الاقلاع والحط القصير | STOL operations |
| عمليات تطهير | mopping-up operations |
| عمليات دفاعية | defensive operations |
| عمليات طيران | flying operations |
| عمليات طيران مستمر | continuous flight operation |
| عمليات مشتركة | combined operations |
| عملية | operation |
| عملية برمائية | amphibious operation |
| عملية بعيدة المدى | long-range operation |
| عملية التحميل | roll-on operation |
| عملية تطهير | clearing operation |
| عملية تعرضية | offensive operation |
| عملية التعزيز | support operation |
| عملية التفريغ | roll-off operation |
| عملية دفاع في فضاء | Space Defence Operation |
| عملية سرية | clandestine operation |
| عملية ضد الدبابات | anti-tank operation |
| عملية على متن سفينة | ship-board operation |
| عملية في زمن الحرب | wartime operation |
| عملية في زمن السلم | peacetime operation |
| عملية في الماء الضحل | shallow-water operation |
| عملية ليلية | night operation |
| عملية نهارية | day operation |
| عملية واسعة النطاق | large scale operation |
| عمود | pylon |
| عمود إدارة | shaft |
| عمود الادارة | joystick |
| عمود ادارة تربيني « ٢٥٠ ـ سي ٢٠ بي » | 250-C20B turboshaft |
| عمود إدارة تربيني « تي في ٣-١١٧ ايه » | TV3-117A turboshaft |
| عمود ادارة تربيني « جي تي دي ـ ٣ بي ام » | GTD-3BM turboshaft |
| عمود ادارة تربيني « جيم ٤١ » | Gem 41 turboshaft |
| عمود ادارة تربيني « نوم » | Gnome turboshaft |
| عمود إدارة تربيني « نيمباص » | Nimbus turboshaft |
| عمود بدن الطائرة | fuselage pylon |
| عمود الجناح الطرفي | outer wing pylon |
| عمود زورق خارجي | outboard pylon |
| عميد | brigadier, colonel-general |
| عميل استخبارات | intelligence agent |
| عن قرب | close-up, close-in |
| عناصر الاتهام | charges |
| عناصر قتالية | fighting elements |
| عناصر هوائي اضافية | directors |
| عنبر أمامي للبحارة | forecastle |
| عند الاطلاق | at launch |
| عنصر اعصاب | nerve agent |
| عنصر الدعم | support element |
| عنصر غاز الأعصاب « قي آر ـ ٥٥ » | VR-55 nerve gas agent |
| عنصر غاز تابون جي اي | GA (Tabun) agent |
| عنصر غاز سارين جي بي | GN (Sarin) agent |
| عنصر غاز سومان جي دي | GD (Soman) agent |
| عنصر « قي اكس » | VX agent |
| عنصر المشاهدة | viewing element |
| عنصر مشع | radiating element |
| عنق الزجاجة | bottleneck |
| عوامة مقطورة | towed buoy |
| عوامل التنفط | blistering agent |
| عوق | delay |
| عيار | calibre |
| عين إلكترونية | electronic eye |
| عيون بعيدة المدى | long-range eyes |

ع

# غ

| | |
|---|---|
| غارة | foray, sortie, invasion, raid |
| غارة غير معاد تزويدها بالوقود | unrefuelled sortie |
| غارز | spike |
| غاز | gas |
| غاز أعصاب | nerve gas |
| غاز الأعصاب « سومان » | Soman nerve gas |
| غاز الخردل | mustard gas |
| غاز داسر | propellant gas |
| غاز سام | poisonous gas, toxic gas |
| غاز القتال | war gas |
| غاز مسيل للدموع | tear gas |
| غازات الدفع الصاروخي | efflux |
| غازات العادم | exhaust gases |
| غاز | invader |
| غاطس | sunk, submerged |
| غاطس السفينة | draft, draught |
| غانا | Ghana |
| غايانا | Guyana |
| غرب | west |
| غرض عام | general purpose |
| غرفة | chamber |
| غرفة إزالة التلوث | decontamination chamber |
| غرفة استعلامات | information room |
| غرفة الأشعة السينية | X-ray room |
| غرفة التأقلم | acclimatization room |
| غرفة تخفيف الانضغاط | decompression chamber |
| غرفة الترامز | coding room |
| غرفة تسليم الأسلحة | weapon handling room |
| غرفة الحرس | guardroom |
| غرفة طب الأسنان | dentistry room |
| غرفة العمليات | operating room |
| غرفة عمليات الاقتحام | assault operations room |
| غرفة عمليات معيارية | modular operations room |
| غرفة الغاز | gas chamber |
| غرفة المحركات | engine room |
| غرفة مراقبة | control room |
| غزا | invade (to) |
| غزو | invasion |
| غزوة | foray |
| غطاء | cap |
| غطاء أمان | safety cap |
| غطاء انسيابي | fairing |
| غطاء جانبي | side-cap |
| غطاء الرأس | headgear |
| غطاء الزعنفة | fin cap |
| غطاء كانتين | canteen cover |
| غطاء الكوة | hatch cover |
| غطاء منزلق شفاف | bubble canopy |
| غطاس | diver |
| غطس | dive |
| غلاف | jacket |
| غلاية بنار الزيت | oil-fired boiler |
| غلب | overwhelm |
| غمد الحربة | bayónet scabbard |
| غنيمة | capture |
| غواتيمالا | Guatemala |

| | |
|---|---|
| غواص | submariner, diver |
| غواصة | submarine |
| غواصة « ابتو » | Abtao submarine |
| غواصة « أبهولدر » | Upholder submarine |
| غواصة « أجوستا » | Agosta submarine |
| غواصة « أريثيوز » | Arethuse submarine |
| غواصة « اس اس بي » | SSB submarine |
| غواصة « اس اس جي » | SSG submarine |
| غواصة استنشاق | snorkeling submarine |
| غواصة ألفا | Alfa submarine |
| غواصة « ألفا » | Alpha submarine |
| غواصة « إنريكو توتي » | Enrico Toti submarine |
| غواصة « اوبرون » | Oberon submarine |
| غواصة « اوسكار » | Oscar submarine |
| غواصة « اوشيو » | Ooshio submarine |
| غواصة « اوهايو » | Ohio submarine |
| غواصة « ئي ـ ٢ » | E-11 submarine |
| غواصة « ايثان ألن » | Ethan Allen submarine |
| غواصة « أيكو ٢ » | Echo II submarine |
| غواصة « أي كيه ال ٥٤٠ » | IKL 540 submarine |
| غواصة « ايه جي اس اس » | AGSS submarine |
| غواصة « بابا » | Papa submarine |
| غواصة بادارة ديزل كهربائية | diesel-electric submarine |
| غواصة « باربيل » | Barbel submarine |
| غواصة « بالاو » | Balao submarine |
| غواصة « برميت » | Permit submarine |
| غواصة « بلارك » | PLARK submarine |
| غواصة « بوربويس » | Porpoise submarine |
| غواصة تانجو | Tango submarine |
| غواصة « تايفون » | Typhoon submarine |
| غواصة « ترافالجر » | Trafalgar submarine |
| غواصة « تشارلي » | Charlie submarine |
| غواصة تشرشل | Churchill submarine |
| غواصة « تولبي » | Tullibee submarine |
| غواصة « تي آر ـ ١٤٠٠ » | TR-1400 submarine |
| غواصة « تي آر ـ ١٧٠٠ » | TR-1700 submarine |
| غواصة « ثريشر » | Thresher submarine |
| غواصة « جريه باك » | Grayback submarine |
| غواصة « جلنارد بي ليبسكم » | Glenard P Lipscomb submarine |
| غواصة « جوبي ٣ » | Guppy III submarine |
| غواصة « جورج واشنطن » | George Washington submarine |
| غواصة « جولف » | Golf submarine |
| غواصة « جولييت » | Juliett submarine |
| غواصة الخط الأمامي | front-line submarine |
| غواصة « دارتر » | Darter submarine |
| غواصة « دافني » | Daphné submarine |
| غواصة « دراكن » | Draken submarine |
| غواصة « دريدنوت » | Dreadnought submarine |
| غواصة « دلتا » | Delta submarine |
| غواصة دلفينن | Delfinen submarine |
| غواصة دورية | patrol submarine |
| غواصة دولفيجن | Dolfijn submarine |
| غواصة « دي ـ ٣ » | D-III submarine |
| غواصة « روبيس » | Rubis submarine |
| غواصة « روميو » | Romeo submarine |
| غواصة « ريزولوشن » | Resolution submarine |
| غواصة « زوارديس » | Zwaardis submarine |
| غواصة « زولو ٤ » | Zulu IV submarine |
| غواصة « زيا » | Xia submarine |
| غواصة « ساڤا » | Sava submarine |
| غواصة « سترجن » | Sturgeon submarine |
| غواصة « سكيبجاك » | Skipjack submarine |
| غواصة « سوتجيسكا » | Sutjeska submarine |
| غواصة « سورو » | Sauro submarine |
| غواصة « سويفت شور » | Swiftsure submarine |
| غواصة « سي ـ ١ » | C-1 submarine |
| غواصة « سيورمين » | Sjoormen submarine |
| غواصة صغيرة | midget submarine |

غ

| | |
|---|---|
| غواصة صواريخ استراتيجية | strategic missile submarine |
| غواصة صواريخ بالستية بالطاقة النووية | nuclear-powered ballistic missile submarine |
| غواصة صواريخ قذفية | ballistic missile submarine |
| غواصة صواريخ كروز | cruise-missile submarine |
| غواصة طراز ٢٠٥ | Type 205 submarine |
| غواصة طراز ٢٠٦ | Type 206 submarine |
| غواصة طراز ٢٠٧ | Type 207 submarine |
| غواصة طراز ٢٠٩ | Type 209 submarine |
| غواصة طراز ٢٤٠٠ | Type 2400 submarine |
| غواصة « طراز ـ آر » | R-class submarine |
| غواصة طراز « اف » | F-class submarine |
| غواصة « طراز ـ اوه » | O-class submarine |
| غواصة « طراز ايه » | A-class submarine |
| غواصة « طراز پي » | P-class submarine |
| غواصة « طراز ـ تي » | T-class submarine |
| غواصة طراز « جي » | G-class submarine |
| غواصة « طراز جيه » | J-class submarine |
| غواصة طراز « دبليو » | W-class submarine |
| غواصة طراز « ڤي » | V-class submarine |
| غواصة « ڤاليانت » | Valiant submarine |
| غواصة فرانكلين | Franklin submarine |
| غواصة فوكستروت | Foxtrot submarine |
| غواصة « ڤيكتر » | Victor submarine |
| غواصة « كويبيك » | Quebec submarine |
| غواصة « كيلو » | Kilo submarine |
| غواصة « لافاييت » | Lafayette submarine |
| غواصة « لوس انجيليز » | Los Angeles submarine |
| غواصة ليپسكام | Lipscomb submarine |
| غواصة « لي ريدوتابل » | Le Redoutable submarine |
| غواصة « مالا » | Mala submarine |
| غواصة « نارڤال » | Narval submarine |
| غواصة « ناروال » | Narwhal submarine |
| غواصة « نازاريو ساورو » | Nazario Sauro submarine |
| غواصة « ناكين » | Nacken submarine |
| غواصة نقل | transport submarine |
| غواصة « نوڤمبر » | November submarine |
| غواصة نووية | nuclear submarine |
| غواصة نووية « اس اس ان » | SSN nuclear submarine |
| غواصة نووية « اس اس بي ان » | SSBN nuclear submarine |
| غواصة نووية « اس اس جي ان » | SSGN nuclear submarine |
| غواصة « هان » | Han submarine |
| غواصة هجوم نووية | nuclear attack submarine |
| غواصة هجومية | attack submarine |
| غواصة « هوتيل » | Hotel submarine |
| غواصة « هو لي ستون » | Holy Stone submarine |
| غواصة « هيروج » | Hcroj submarine |
| غواصة « واي ١ » | Y-1 submarine |
| غواصة « وولرس » | Walrus submarine |
| غواصة « ويسكي » | Whiskey submarine |
| غواصة « ويسكي لونج ـ بن » | Whiskey Long-Bin submarine |
| غواصة « ويسكي » مزدوجة الاسطوانة | Whiskey Twin Cylinder submarine |
| غواصة « ئي ـ ١ » | E-1 submarine |
| غواصة « يانكي » | Yankee submarine |
| غواصة « يوزوشو » | Uzushio submarine |
| غواصة « يوشيو » | Yuushio submarine |
| غوص | dive |
| غير جائز | unauthorized |
| غير فعال | passive |
| غير كامل العدد | below strength |
| غير محتل | unoccupied |
| غير مستبان | undetected |
| غير مسلح | unarmed |
| غير مشغول | unoccupied |
| غير مقاتل | non-combatant |
| غيم | cloud |

غ

# ف

| | |
|---|---|
| فئة « ستوكهولم » | Stockholm class |
| فئة الهدف | target category |
| فاصل زمني | time slot |
| فاصل اطلاق النار | firing interval |
| فاصمة | fuse |
| فاصمة تماسية | contact fuse |
| فتاحة زجاجات | bottle cap opener |
| فتل | twist |
| فتيل يدوي | hand fuse |
| فجر | detonate |
| فحص | inspection, examination |
| فحص الدم | blood test |
| فحص طبي | medical examination |
| فخاري | ceramic |
| فدائي | commando |
| فدائي بحري | naval commando |
| فرشة اختبار | test-bed |
| فرضة الغلاف | jacket slot |
| فرغ | unload |
| فرقاطة | frigate |
| فرقاطة « اف ـ ٢٠٠٠ » | F-2000 frigate |
| فرقاطة « أمازون » | Amazon frigate |
| فرقاطة « اوليڤر هازارد پيرى » | Oliver Hazard Perry frigate |
| فرقاطة « برود سورد » | Broadsword frigate |
| فرقاطة « بروك » | Brooke frigate |
| فرقاطة « برونستين » | Bronstein frigate |
| فرقاطة « بلاك سوان » | Black Swan frigate |
| فرقاطة « تشيكوجو » | Chikugo frigate |
| فرقاطة « تشينجدو » | Chengdu frigate |
| فرقاطة « جارسيا » | Garcia frigate |
| فرقاطة « جلوڤر » | Glover frigate |
| فرقاطة « جانج دونج » | Jiangdong frigate |
| فرقاطة « جانج نان » | Jiangnan frigate |
| فرقاطة « جينغو » | Jianghu frigate |
| فرقاطة « ديستيين دورڤ » | D'Estienne d'Orves frigate |
| فرقاطة رمضان | Ramadan frigate |
| فرقاطة « روثسي » | Rothesay frigate |
| فرقاطة « ريڤر » | River frigate |
| فرقاطة « ساڤيج » | Savage frigate |
| فرقاطة « سنتشان » | Cinchan frigate |
| فرقاطة صواريخ موجهة | guided missile frigate |
| فرقاطة طراز ٢١ | Type 21 frigate |
| فرقاطة طراز ٢٢ | Type 22 frigate |
| فرقاطة « ڤوسپر » | Vosper frigate |
| فرقاطة « كريڤاك » | Krivak frigate |
| فرقاطة « كورتينايِر » | Kortenaer frigate |
| فرقاطة « كولن » | Köln frigate |
| فرقاطة « كوني » | Koni frigate |
| فرقاطة « لوپو » | Lupo frigate |
| فرقاطة « لياندر » | Leander frigate |
| فرقاطة « ميسترال » | Maestrale frigate |
| فرقاطة « نوكس » | Knox frigate |
| فرقاطة « هانت » | Hunt frigate |
| فرقاطة ويتبي | Whitby frigate |
| فرقة | regiment, division |
| فرقة اقتحام جوي | air assault division |

| | |
|---|---|
| فرقة انتحارية | suicide squad |
| فرقة بحرية | marine division |
| فرقة البنادق | rifle division |
| فرقة بنادق آلية | motor-rifle division |
| فرقة جنود قابلة للنقل جواً | airmobile brigade |
| فرقة الحراسة | guards division |
| فرقة دبابات | tank division |
| فرقة محمولة جواً | airborne division |
| فرقة مدرعات | armoured division |
| فرقة مسلحة | armed division |
| فرقة مشاة | infantry division |
| فرغ | discharge |
| فرنسا | France |
| فرنسي | French |
| فريق | lieutenant general, detail |
| فريق الاستطلاع | recce party |
| فريق الانزال | landing team |
| فريق النسف تحت الماء | underwater demolition team |
| فسجين | phosgene |
| فسر | interpret (to) |
| فسفور | phosphorus |
| فصل | disengage |
| فصل | isolation |
| فصيلة | platoon |
| فصيلة دبابات | tank platoon |
| فصيلة مضادة للدبابات | anti-tank platoon |
| فعالية | potency |
| فعل التفادي | evasive action |
| فعل العدو | enemy action |
| فعل معوق | delayed action |
| فك | dismantle |
| الفلبين | Philippines |
| فلبيني | Philippine |
| فم | mouth |
| ڤنزويلا | Venezuela |
| ڤنزويلي | Venezuelan |
| فنلندة | Finland |
| فنلندي | Finnish |
| فني جوي | airborne technician |
| فوج | regiment |
| فوج بنادق آلية | motor-rifle regiment |
| فوج دبابات | tank regiment |
| فوج قاذفات | bomber regiment |
| فوّض | authorize (to) |
| فوق الصوتي | ultra-sonic |
| فوق الماء | overwater |
| فولاذ | steel |
| فولاذ لا يصدأ | stainless steel |
| فولاذ منقى | refined steel |
| فوهة | nozzle, mouth |
| فوهة البندقية او المدفع | muzzle |
| فوهة الحارق اللاحق | afterburner nozzle |
| فوهة قابلة للدوران | rotatable nozzle |
| فوهة مداومة | sustainer nozzle |
| فوهة مزدوجة المحور | gimballed nozzle |
| في الاحتياط | in reserve |
| في حدود المدى | within range |
| في الخدمة | in service |
| في قبضة العدو | enemy-held |
| في وسط السفينة | amidships |
| ڤيتنام | Vietnam |
| ڤيتنامي | Vietnamese |
| فيلق | corps |

ف

# ق

| | |
|---|---|
| قائد | commandant, commander, leader, officer commanding |
| قائد الاسطول | fleet command officer |
| قائد أسطول صغير | flotilla leader |
| قائد الحضيرة | squad leader |
| قائد الطائرة | captain |
| قائد الطابور | column leader |
| القائد العام | commander-in-chief |
| قائد القافلة | convoy leader |
| قائد القوات | force commander |
| قائد وحدة | commanding officer |
| قائمة | list |
| قائمة سوداء | blacklist |
| قابل للبرمجة | reprogrammable |
| قابل للتفريغ | jettisonable |
| قابل للطي | retractable |
| قابل للنقل الجوي | air-portable, air-transportable |
| قابلية الطفو | buoyancy |
| قاتل | killer, deadly |
| قاد | steer |
| قاذفة | launcher |
| قاذفة اعتيادية | standard launcher |
| قاذفة ألغام ثلاثية | tripartite mine launcher |
| قاذفة « ال ايه يو - ٧ » | LAU-7 launcher |
| قاذفة « ام - ٢٠ » | M-20 launcher |
| قاذفة « ام ٧٢٧ اس پي هوك » | M727SP Hawk launcher |
| قاذفة بازوكا | bazooka launcher |
| قاذفة بالأشعة دون الحمراء | infra-red launcher |
| قاذفة بعجلات « زيل - ١٣٥ » | ZIL-135 wheeled launcher |
| قاذفة « تو » | TOW launcher |
| قاذفة « تيسيو » | Teseo launcher |
| قاذفة ثلاثية | triple launcher |
| قاذفة خرطوشة لهب يدوية | hand flame cartridge launcher |
| قاذفة رباعية | quadruple-launcher |
| قاذفة سكايجارد | Skyguard launcher |
| قاذفة شرائح التشويش | chaff launcher |
| قاذفة شرائح التشويش « اس اربي اوه سي » | SRBOC chaff launcher |
| قاذفة شرائح تشويش « سوپر أربي اوه سي » | Super RBOC chaff launcher |
| قاذفة شرائح التشويش « كوڤوس » | Corvus chaff launcher |
| قاذفة صندوقية | box-type launcher |
| قاذفة صواريخ | rocket-launcher |
| قاذفة صواريخ « آربي يو ٦٠٠٠ ايه اس دبليو » | RBU 6000 ASW rocket launcher |
| قاذفة صواريخ « آرپي يو - ١٤ » | RPU-14 rocket launcher |
| قاذفة صواريخ « اس اس ام » | SSM launcher |
| قاذفة صواريخ « بوفورز ايه/اس » | Bofors A/S rocket launcher |
| قاذفة صواريخ « بي - ٣٠٠ » | B-300 rocket launcher |
| قاذفة صواريخ « بي إم - ٢١ » | BM-21 rocket launcher |
| قاذفة صواريخ « بي إم - ٢٤ » | BM-24 rocket launcher |

| | |
|---|---|
| قاذفة صواريخ « بي إم ـ ٢٥ » | BM-25 rocket launcher |
| قاذفة صواريخ « بي إم دي » | BMD rocket launcher |
| قاذفة صواريخ « زايو » | Ze-eu rocket launcher |
| قاذفة صواريخ « سايلكس ئي سي ام » | Syllex ECM rocket launcher |
| قاذفة صواريخ « ستريم ـ ٨٩ » | STRIM-89 rocket launcher |
| قاذفة صواريخ سطح ـ جو | SAM launcher |
| قاذفة صواريخ متعددة | multiple rocket launcher |
| قاذفة صواريخ مضادة للغواصات « اس يو دبليو ـ ان ـ ١ » | SUW-N-1 ASW launcher |
| قاذفة صواريخ « وولف » | Wolf rocket launcher |
| قاذفة طافيات صوتية رادارية | sonobuoy launcher |
| قاذفة طراز ١٠٥٥ | class 1055 launcher |
| قاذفة عديمة الارتداد | recoilless launcher |
| قاذفة قنابل « بادجر جي » | Badger G bomber |
| قاذفة قنابل البندقية | rifle grenade launcher |
| قاذفة قنابل يدوية | grenade launcher |
| قاذفة قنابل يدوية « آر بي جي ـ ٧ » | RPG-7 grenade launcher |
| قاذفة قنابل يدوية آلية | automatic grenade launcher |
| قاذفة قنابل يدوية « ام ٧٩ » | M79 grenade launcher |
| قاذفة قنابل يدوية « ام ٢٠٣ » | M203 grenade launcher |
| قاذفة « لايران » | Lyran launcher |
| قاذفة لهب | flamethrower |
| قاذفة « لو ـ ٨٠ » | Law-80 launcher |
| قاذفة متحركة | mobile launcher |
| قاذفة مزدوجة | twin launcher |
| قاذفة مشاعل | flare launcher |
| قاذفة مشاعل آلية | automatic flare launcher |
| قاذفة مشتركة | combined launcher |
| قاذفة مقاتلة « دراكن » | Draken fighter-bomber |
| قاذفة ـ ناصبة « زيل ـ ١٣١ » | ZIL-131 erector-launcher |
| قارب | dinghy |
| قارب نجاة | lifeboat |
| قارب إنقاذ | lifeboat |
| قارب يطوى | collapsible boat |
| قارن سونار | sonar coupler |
| قاري | continental |
| قاعة الطعام | dining hall |
| قاعدة « اوتو ميلارا كومپاكت » | OTO Melara Compact mount |
| قاعدة بحرية | naval base |
| قاعدة برية | shore base |
| قاعدة تثبيت | mount |
| قاعدة تدريب | training base |
| قاعدة ترابية | earth bank |
| قاعدة تموين | supply base |
| قاعدة جوية | air base |
| قاعدة غواصات | submarine base |
| قاعدة ماسورة طوربيد الحرب ضد الغواصات | ASW torpedo tube mounting |
| قاعدة مدفع صغيرة | compact gun-mount |
| قاعدة المهدف الامامي | fore-sight base |
| قاعدة المهداف الخلفي | rear sight base |
| قاعدة الهجوم | attack base |
| قافلة | convoy |
| قانصة دبابات | tank destroyer |
| قانون عرفي | martial law |
| القانون والنظام | law and order |
| قاوم | hold out against |
| قبة | dome, cupola |
| قبة رادارية للتدابير الالكترونية المضادة | ECM dome |
| قبة هوائي الرادار | radome |
| قبرص | Cyprus |
| قبضة المسدس | pistol grip |
| قبطان | captain |

ق

| | |
|---|---|
| قبعة الدغل | jungle hat |
| قبعة المغاور | ranger hat |
| قتال | combat, fight |
| قتال أعزل | unarmed combat |
| قتال بري | land combat |
| قتال بالسلاح الأبيض | hand to hand fighting |
| قتال الخنادق | ditch battle |
| قتال الشوارع | street fighting |
| قتال المؤخرة | rear guard action |
| قتال متلاحم | close combat |
| قتال « مرتفع ـ منخفض ـ مرتفع » | hi-lo-hi combat |
| قتال مسلح | armed combat |
| قتيل | casualty |
| قتيل المعركة | killed in action |
| قدح الزناد | cock the hammer |
| قدرة تربين الغاز | gas-turbine power |
| قدرة قتالية | fighting efficiency |
| قدرة النظر للأسفل | look-down capability |
| قدم الصاروخ | missile shoe |
| قذف | cast |
| قذف | dart |
| قذف بالقنابل | bomb (to) |
| قذف جوي | air drop, airborne drop |
| قذف قنابل | bombardment |
| قذف القنابل | bomb drop |
| قذف القنابل أثناء الانقضاض | dive bombing |
| قذف قنابل جوية | aerial bombing |
| قذيفة | missile, projectile |
| قذيفة اعتراضية جوية | AIM, air-interception missile |
| قذيفة اعتراضية جوية « ايه أي ام ـ ٤ » | AIM-4 |
| قذيفة اعتراضية جوية « ايه أي ام ـ ٧ » | AIM-7 |
| قذيفة اعتراضية جوية « ايه أي ام ـ ٩ » | AIM-9 |
| قذيفة اعتراضية جوية « ايه أي ام ـ ٢٦ » | AIM-26 |
| قذيفة اعتراضية جوية « ايه أي ام ـ ٤٧ » | AIM-47 |
| قذيفة اعتراضية جوية « ايه أي ام ـ ٥٤ » | AIM-54 |
| قذيفة اعتراضية جوية « ايه أي ام ـ ١٢٠ ايه ايه ام » | AIM-120 AAM |
| قذيفة أعماق | depth charge |
| قذيفة بحشوة مفرغة | hollow-charge projectile |
| قذيفة تشظية شديدة الانفجار | high explosive fragmentation projectile |
| قذيفة خارقة للدروع | armour-piercing shell |
| قذيفة دخان | smoke projectile |
| قذيفة شديدة الانفجار | HE projectile |
| قذيفة قاتلة مضادة للأقمار الصناعية | anti-satellite killer missile |
| قذيفة كيماوية | chemical shell |
| قذيفة متوازنة بزعانف خارقة للمدرعات | APFSDS, Armour-Piercing Fin-Stabilised Discarding Sabot |
| قذيفة مخترقة للمدرعات « اتش في ايه بي ـ تي » | HVAP-T shot |
| قذيفة مدفعية | artillery rocket |
| قذيفة مصغرة العيار ذات مدى بعيد | extended-range sub-calibre projectile |
| قذيفة مضادة للدبابات شديدة الانفجار | HEAT projectile |
| قذيفة مضادة للدبابات شديدة الانفجار متعددة الأغراض | HEAT multi-purpose |
| قذيفة مضادة للدبابات شديدة الانفجار موزونة بالرياش | HEAT fin-stabilized |
| قذيفة معانة بالصاروخ | rocket-assisted shell |
| قذيفة موجهة ذات مدى بعيد | extended-range guided projectile |
| قرص دوار | rotary disc |

ق

| | |
|---|---|
| قرص وقود جاف | solid fuel tablet |
| القسم الأكبر | main body |
| قسيس | chaplain |
| قصير المدى | short-range |
| قصف | bomb |
| قصف استراتيجي | strategic bombing |
| قصف ساحلي | shore bombardment |
| قصف مضاد | counter-bombardment |
| قصف من ارتفاع منخفض | low-altitude bombing |
| قصف من السفن إلى الساحل | ship-to-shore bombardment |
| قصف منطقة | area bombing |
| قضاء عسكري | military justice |
| قضيب الاطلاق | launch rail |
| قضيب التوائي | torsion bar |
| قطاع طريق جسري على اطواف | pontoon causeway section |
| قطاع المقدمة | nose section |
| قطاعة سلك شائك | barbed wire cutter |
| قطبي جنوبي | Antarctic |
| قطر | Qatar |
| قطر | diameter |
| قطر داخلي | calibre |
| قطر الدوامة | rotor diameter |
| قطري | Qatari |
| قطع | break off |
| قطع ساحة المعركة | battlefield interdiction |
| قطع احتياطية | spares |
| قطع غيار | spares, spare parts |
| قطن البارود | gun cotton |
| « قف ! » | halt!, stop! |
| قف في وضع انتباه | stand at attention! |
| قفز معوق | delayed jump |
| قفص | crate |
| قفل الحركة | travelling lock |
| قلب المفاعل | reactor core |
| قلس | hawser |
| قلنسوة جليدية قطبية | polar icecap |
| قماش القنب | canvas |
| قمة الموجة | wave crest |
| قمر الاتصالات | communications satellite |
| قمر إستطلاع | reconnaissance satellite |
| قمر صناعي | satellite |
| قمر صناعي « بيج بيرد » | Big Bird satellite |
| قمر صناعي « سبتنيك » | Sputnik satellite |
| قمر صناعي فعال | active satellite |
| قمر صناعي للملاحة البحرية « ناف سات » | NavSat satellite |
| قمع | funnel |
| قميص خارجي | T-shirt |
| قناة | channel |
| قناة ثلاثية | triple-channel |
| قناص | sniper, hunter |
| قناصة ألغام | mine hunter |
| قناع | mask |
| قناع ارسال المحادثات | speech transmission mask |
| قناع واق من الغاز | gas mask |
| قناع واقي من الغاز | anti-gas cape |
| قنبلة | bomb |
| قنبلة إشعال يدوية | igniter grenade |
| قنبلة إيروسول | aerosol bomb |
| قنبلة بالثقل | gravity bomb |
| قنبلة بمكبح | braked bomb |
| قنبلة تمرين | dummy bomb |
| قنبلة جوية | aerial bomb |
| قنبلة « جيه بي - ٢٣٣ » | JP-233 bomb |
| قنبلة دخان | smoke bomb |
| قنبلة دخان يدوية | smoke grenade |
| قنبلة دخان يدوية | smoke hand grenade |
| قنبلة دخان ملون يدوية | coloured smoke grenade |
| قنبلة ذرية | atomic bomb |
| قنبلة شديدة الانفجار | HE bomb |
| قنبلة صدمة بالصوت والوميض | sound and flash shock grenade |

ق

| | |
|---|---|
| قنبلة عنقودية | cluster bomb |
| قنبلة عنقودية « بي ال ٧٥٥ » | BL 755 cluster bomb |
| قنبلة غاز | gas bomb |
| قنبلة غاز مسيل للدموع | tear gas grenade |
| قنبلة غير متفجرة | unexploded bomb |
| قنبلة كيماوية | chemical bomb |
| قنبلة مؤخرة الانفجار | retarded bomb |
| قنبلة محرقة | incendiary bomb |
| قنبلة مقذوفة من بندقية « ام ٢٢ » | M22 rifle grenade |
| قنبلة من نوع « بايڤويه » | Paveway-series bomb |
| قنبلة موجهة بالليزر | laser-guided bomb |
| قنبلة نابام | napalm bomb |
| قنبلة نووية | nuclear bomb |
| قنبلة نووية « ايه إن ـ ٥٢ » | AN52 nuclear bomb |
| قنبلة « نيوترون » | neutron bomb |
| قنبلة هاون | mortar bomb |
| قنبلة هيدروجينية | hydrogen bomb |
| قنبلة يدوية | grenade |
| قنبلة يدوية | hand grenade |
| قنبلة يدوية « أرجي دي ـ ٥ » | RGD-5 grenade |
| قنبلة يدوية « أركيه جي ـ ٣ » | RK-3 grenade |
| قنبلة يدوية « اكس ال ٧٠ ئي ٣ » | XL70E3 grenade |
| قنبلة يدوية « ام ٤٣ ايه ١ » | M43A1 grenade |
| قنبلة يدوية انحلالية | decay grenade |
| قنبلة يدوية ايه پي ـ ٣٢ زد | AP-32Z grenade |
| قنبلة يدوية بالأشعة دون الحمراء | infra-red grenade |
| قنبلة يدوية تطلق بالبندقية | rifle grenade |
| قنبلة يدوية « سيلڤر دوج » | Silver Dog grenade |
| القنبلة اليدوية الصدمية | concussion grenade |
| قنبلة يدوية للبلاغ | reports grenade |
| قنبلة يدوية متشظية | fragmentation grenade |
| قنبلة يدوية متشظية محرقة | incendiary frangible grenade |
| قنبلة يدوية مضادة للأفراد | anti-personnel grenade |
| قنبلة يدوية موازنة بالتدويم | spin-stabilized grenade |
| قنبلة يدوية « هوت دوج » | Hot Dog grenade |
| قوائم الحامل | bipod legs |
| قوات | forces |
| قوات الاحتياط | reservists |
| قوات احتياطية | reserves |
| قوات أرضية | ground forces |
| القوات الأمريكية | American Forces |
| قوات الأمن | security force |
| قوات الأمن العام | Public Security Force |
| قوات انقضاض نووي | nuclear strike force |
| قوات تدعيم | reinforcements |
| القوات الجوية | Air Force, air arm |
| القوات الجوية الأمامية | Frontal Aviation Force |
| القوات الجوية الأمريكية | US Air Force |
| القوات الجوية البحرية | naval air force, Naval Aviation Force |
| القوات الجوية للاسطول | fleet air force |
| القوات الجوية المركزية | Central Air Force |
| القوات المحمولة جوا | airborne forces |
| قوات حفظ الأمن | peace-keeping force |
| قوات خاصة | special forces |
| قوات الدفاع الجوي | Air Defence Force |
| قوات الدفاع الجوي الوطنية | national air defence troops |
| قوة الدفاع الذاتي الجوية | air self-defence force |
| قوات الدفاع الكيماوي | chemical defence troops |
| قوات الدفاع المدني | Civil Defence Force |
| قوات دفاعية | defence force |

ق

| | |
|---|---|
| قوات شبه عسكرية | para-military force |
| قوات الصواريخ | missile forces |
| قوات الصواريخ الاستراتيجية | strategic rocket forces |
| قوات العدو | enemy forces |
| قوات العصابات | guerrilla force |
| قوات في الخارج | forces abroad |
| قوات « كيه جي بي » | KGB troops |
| قوات محولة بحراً | seaborne force |
| قوات مسلحة | armed forces |
| قوات النقل الجوي | Air Transport Force |
| القوات النووية الاستراتيجية | Strategic Nuclear Forces |
| قوات الهجوم | attack force |
| قوات واجب ذرية بالكامل | all-nuclear task force |
| قواعد | bases |
| قوة | strength |
| قوة أرضية | ground force |
| قوة جوية طويلة المدى | Long-Range Aviation Force |
| قوة الحاملة | carrier force |
| قوة الدفاع الذاتي الأرضية | ground self-defence force |
| قوة الدفع الساكن | static thrust |
| القوة الرئيسية | main force |
| قوة الردع | deterrent force |
| قوة سرية | covert force |
| قوة كاملة | total strength |
| قوة النيران | fire power |
| قوة واجب معين | task force |
| قوى عاملة | manpower |
| قيادة | command, leadership |
| القيادة الأمامية | forward headquarters |
| قيادة جند الجو | Airborne Command |
| القيادة الجنوبية | southern command |
| القيادة الجوية الاستراتيجية | Strategic Air Command |
| قيادة الدفاع الجوي | Air Defence Command |
| القيادة الشرقية | eastern command |
| القيادة الشمالية | northern command |
| قيادة الطيران التكتيكي | Tactical Air Command |
| قيادة طيران الجيش | army aviation command |
| قيادة عليا | supreme command |
| قيادة القاذفات | bomber command |
| قيادة القوات البرمائية | Amphibious Command |
| قيادة المراقبة | control command |
| القيادة المركزية | central command |
| القيادة العليا | high command |
| قيادة مزدوجة | dual-control |
| قيادة معارك جند الجو | Airborne Battlefield Command |
| قيادة المقاتلات | fighter command |
| قيادة النقل البحري العسكري | military sealift command |
| قيادة النقل الجوي العسكري | military airlift command |
| قيادة الهجوم | Strike Command |
| قياس المدى | rangefinding |

ق

# ك

| | |
|---|---|
| كائن محلياً | home-based |
| كاتب | clerk |
| كاتب رواتب | pay clerk |
| كارثة | disaster |
| كاسحة ألغام | minesweeper |
| كاسحة ألغام اجوتنت | Adjutant minesweeper |
| كاسحة ألغام « ام اس سي ـ ٣٢٢ » | MSC-322 minesweeper |
| كاسحة ألغام « بوشار » | Bouchard mine-sweeper |
| كاسحة ألغام « تي ـ ٤٣ » | T-43 minesweeper |
| كاسحة ألغام دورية | patrol mine-sweeper |
| كاسحة ألغام « طن » | Ton minesweeper |
| كاسحة ألغام عدائية | aggressive minesweeper |
| كاسحة ألغام « ڤانيا » | Vanya minesweeper |
| كاسحة ألغام « ناتيا » | Natya minesweeper |
| كاسحة ألغام « يوجويا » | Yeugeuya minesweeper |
| كاسحة ألغام « يوركا » | Yurka minesweeper |
| كاشف | detector |
| كاشف ألغام « آي ام بي » | IMP mine detector |
| كاملة الرتاج | bolt cam |
| كامل | overall |
| كامل الرؤية | panoramic |
| كاهن عسكري | padre |
| كبّاس مقوّى بالرتاج | bolt-assist plunger |
| كبت بالأشعة دون الحمراء | IR-suppressing |
| كبت داخلي | internal damping |
| كبسولة | cap, capsule |
| كبسولة تفجير | detonator |
| كبسولة تفجير صاروخية | pyrotechnical detonator |
| كبل | cable |
| كبل التحكم | control cable |
| كبل التردد | frequency cable |
| كبل معلق | overhead cable |
| كبل ممدود تحت الأرض | underground cable |
| كبل الميدان | field cable |
| كبل هاتفي | telephone cable |
| الكتائب | Phalange |
| كتاب الميدان | field manual |
| كتابة بالرموز | coding |
| كتيب | handbook |
| كتيّب تشغيل | instruction book |
| كتيبة | battalion |
| كتيبة برمائية | amphibious detachment |
| كتيبة بنادق آلية | motor-rifle battalion |
| كتيبة تأديب | punishment battalion |
| كتيبة تدريب | training battalion |
| كتيبة جند الهجانة | camel corps battalion |
| كتيبة دبابات | tank battalion |
| كتيبة صواريخ | missile regiment |
| كتيبة طائرات عمودية مسلحة | armed helicopter battalion |
| كتيبة طيران الجيش | army aviation battalion |
| كتيبة فرسان الصحراء | desert cavalry battalion |
| كتيبة مدفعية | artillery battalion |
| كتيبة مدفعية مضادة للطائرات | anti-aircraft artillery battalion |

ك

| | |
|---|---|
| كتيبة مشاة | infantry battalion |
| كتيبة مضادة للدبابات | anti-tank regiment |
| كتيبة مغاوير | ranger battalion |
| كثيب رملي | sand dune |
| كرية خاملة | inert pellet |
| كرسي تحميل | bearing |
| كُزاز | tetanus |
| كسح الغام | minesweeping |
| كشف | detect |
| كشف راداري | radar detection |
| كشف راداري عن الهدف | radar target detection |
| الكل موجود وصحيح | all present and correct |
| كلابة | grapnel |
| كلب حراسة | guard dog |
| كلور | chlorine |
| كلية عسكرية | military academy |
| كم حراري | thermal sleeve |
| « كما كنت ! » | as you were! |
| كمامة | respirator |
| كمبوتشيا | Kampuchea |
| كمبوديا | Cambodia |
| الكميرون | Cameroon |
| كمين | ambush |
| كنّة السلاح / الدولاب | weapon/wheel nacelle |
| كنتور | contour |
| كندا | Canada |
| كندي | Canadian |
| الكنغو | Congo |
| كهروتربيني | turboelectric |
| كوبا | Cuba |
| كوبي | Cuban |
| كوة الصالب | keel hatch |
| كوة الملء | loading hatch |
| كوة النجاة | escape hatch |
| كوخ | hut |
| كوري | Korean |
| كوريا | Korea |
| كوريا الشمالية | North Korea |
| كوستاريكا | Costa Rica |
| كولومبي | Colombian |
| كولومبيا | Colombia |
| كوليرا | cholera |
| كومبيوتر « ايه ان/يو واي كيه ـ ٧ » | AN-UYK-7 computer |
| كومبيوتر « ايه ان/يو واي كيه ـ ٢٠ » | AN-UYK-20 computer |
| كومبيوتر بطارية « ديڤيد » | DAVID battery computer |
| كومبيوتر تتبع الهدف | target tracking computer |
| كومبيوتر سبيري | Sperry computer |
| كومبيوتر السيطرة على الرمي | fire-control computer |
| كومبيوتر السيطرة على الرمي « ديلكو » | Delco fire-control computer |
| كومبيوتر على متن | on-board computer |
| كومبيوتر قذفي بالستيك | ballistic computer |
| كومبيوتر مركزي | central computer |
| كومبيوتر ملاحي | navigation computer |
| كومبيوتر المهمة | mission computer |
| كومبيوتر « ميج ـ ١٧ » | MiG-17 computer |
| الكويت | Kuwait |
| كويتي | Kuwaiti |
| كيروسين | kerosene |
| كيس الخرطوشة | cartridge bag |
| كيس الدخان المستخلص | fume-extracted bag |
| كيس رفع جوي قابل للنفخ | inflatable air lifting bag |
| كيس الرمل | sand bag |
| كيس من قماش القنب | canvas bag |
| كيس مهمات | kit bag |
| كيس النوم | sleeping bag |
| كيلو متر | kilometre |
| كيماوي | chemical |
| كيني | Kenyan |
| كينيا | Kenya |
| كينين | quinine |

ك

# ل

| | |
|---|---|
| لاسلكي بالتردد فوق العالي | UHF radio |
| لاسلكي تكتيكي | tactical radio |
| لا يخترق | impenetrable |
| لا يخرقه الرصاص | bullet-proof |
| لا يغرق | unsinkable |
| للأمام ـ تقدم ! | advance! |
| « للأمام ـ سر ! » | forward! |
| لأوس | Laos |
| لايبيري | Liberian |
| لايبيريا | Liberia |
| لباس الغواص | diver's suit |
| لباس الميدان | field dress |
| لبنان | Lebanon |
| لبناني | Lebanese |
| للتفتيش « عالياً احمل ! » | for inspection, port arms! |
| اللجنة الطبية | medical board |
| لغم | mine |
| لغم أرضي | ground mine |
| لغم أعماق | bottom mine |
| لغم « ام ١٦ ايه ١ » | M16A1 mine |
| لغم « ام أر ٨٠ مانتا » | MR 80 Manta mine |
| لغم « ايه إم دي - ١٠٠٠ » | AMD-1000 mine |
| لغم راسي | moored mine |
| لغم « سي ارتشن » | Sea Urchin mine |
| لغم « مانتا » | Manta mine |
| لغم مضاد للدبابات | anti-tank mine |
| لغم مغمور | submarine mine |
| لغم الميدان | field mine |
| لغم ينفجر بالأمر | command-detonated mine |
| لفافة ساق | leggings |
| لواء | major-general, brigade |
| لواء أسلحة موجه مضادة للدبابات | anti-tank guided weapon brigade |
| لواء اقتحام جوي | air assault brigade |
| لواء آلي | mechanized brigade |
| لواء آليات ثقيلة | heavy motor brigade |
| لواء صاعقة | commando brigade |
| لواء الصحراء | Sahara brigade |
| لواء في الجيش | army general |
| لواء « مارادا » | Marada brigade |
| لواء مدرعات | armoured brigade |
| لواء مشاة | infantry brigade |
| لواء مظلات | parachute brigade |
| لوازم تجديد الطاقة | repower-modernization kit |
| لوح تكتيف | bracing plate |
| لوح منحدر مقابل | glacis plate |
| لوحة التحكم متعددة الأغراض | multi-purpose console |
| لوحة التفتيش | inspection panel |
| لوحة عقب البندقية | buttplate |
| لوحة مستوية | flat-plate |
| اللوكسمبورغ | Luxembourg |
| ليبي | Libyan |
| ليبيا | Libya |
| ليزر | laser |
| ليزر الدبابة | tank laser |

| | |
|---|---|
| ليزر الدبابة « آر اس آي » | RSI tank laser |
| ليزر صغير | mini laser |
| ليزر نصف فعال | semi-active laser |
| لليسار - در ! | bear left! |
| لليمين - در ! | bear right! |
| لينة إرتداد | recoil pad |

ل

| | |
|---|---|
| مؤخرة | rear |
| مؤخرة السفينة | stern |
| مؤخرة السفينة | aft |
| مؤسسة | establishment |
| مؤشر مسافة عدم اصابة | miss distance indicator |
| مؤشر المناورة | manoeuvre indicator |
| مؤشر الوضع المستوي | plan position indicator |
| مؤونة | stock, food |
| مأوى | shelter |
| مأوى | billet |
| ما بعد التعبئة | post-mobilization |
| ما بعد الحرب | post-war |
| ما قبل الاطلاق | pre-launch |
| ما قبل بدء التشغيل | pre-commissioning |
| ما وراء البحار | overseas |
| ماترا ماجيك | Matra Magic |
| ماخ | Mach |
| مادة خام | raw material |
| مادة سامة | toxic agent |
| مادة لا معدنية | non-metallic material |
| ماسك الفوهة | muzzle-brake |
| ماسورة | barrel |
| ماسورة بندقية مطلية بالكروم | chromed bore |
| ماسورة دوارة | rotary-barrel |
| ماسورة طوربيد | torpedo tube |
| ماسورة طوربيد الحرب ضد الغواصات | ASW torpedo tube |
| ماسورة قذف الغاز المسيل للدموع | tear gas throwing tube |
| ماسورة مدفع ساخنة | hot gun barrel |
| ماسورة مزدوجة | twin-barrel |
| مالطا | Malta |
| مالي | Mali |
| ماليزيا | Malaysia |
| مانع للجليد | anti-ice |
| مانع للعفونة | antiseptic |
| مانع الوميض | flash-suppressor |
| مباغتة بالقنابل اليدوية | grenade surprise |
| مبدل حراري | heat exchanger |
| مبرد بغاز أو سائل التبريد | cyrogenically cooled |
| مُبرد بالهواء | air-cooled |
| مبرقة | telegraph |
| مبرقة كاتبة | telex machine |
| مبعوث | envoy |
| المبنى الدائري | round house |
| مبيت | built-in |
| مبيد حشري | insecticide |
| متابع | slaved |
| متابعة الهدف بالرادار اوتوماتيكياً | lock-on |
| متحد المحور | coaxial |
| متحرك | on the move |
| متحرك بصورة كبيرة | highly mobile |
| متخلف | straggler |
| متر | metre |
| متراس | barricade |
| متراس الطريق | road block |
| مترجم | interpreter |

| | |
|---|---|
| مترسة للمدافع | pillbox |
| متطوّر | sophisticated |
| متطوع « باسج » | Bassej volunteer |
| متعاون | collaborator |
| متعدد | multiple |
| متعدد الأغراض | multi-purpose |
| متعدد الانماط | multi-mode |
| متعدد المهام | multi-role |
| متعدد المهام | multi-mission |
| متعدد المواسير | multi-barrel |
| متعقب بالليزر | laser tracker |
| متعلق بالمحيط الهادىء | Pacific |
| متعلق باجهزة الملاحة اللاسلكية | radio-navaid related |
| متفجرات بلاستيك | plastic explosive |
| متقدم | fore |
| متقفي | seeker |
| متقفي بصري | optical tracker |
| متلوف ذاتيا | self-destructed |
| متماثل للشفاء | convalescent |
| متمرد | insurgent |
| متمرس | trained |
| متناوب | rotating |
| متوازن جيروسكوبيا | gyrostabilized |
| متوقف | static |
| مثقاب | auger, drill |
| مجابهة | encounter |
| مجال جوي | air space |
| مجال جوي معادي | hostile airspace, enemy airspace |
| مجال الصواريخ | missile field |
| مجال المسؤولية | area of responsibility |
| مجال النظر | field of vision |
| مجاهد في سبيل الحرية | Freedom Fighter |
| المجر | Hungary |
| مجراف إرتدادي | recoil spade |
| مجرب بالدبابة | tank-tested |
| مجري | Hungarian |
| مجرى السحب | drag chute |
| مجرى منحدر | ramp |
| مجرى الهروب | escape chute |
| مجلس اتصالات الدفاع | DCB |
| مجلس تحقيق | investigating board |
| مجلس الحرب | council of war |
| مجمع العلب الفارغة | collector for spent cases |
| مجمع هوائيات | antenna complex |
| مجموعة الأنوار الأمامية | headlight group |
| مجموعة توليد | power pack |
| مجموعة جيوش | army group |
| مجموعة حرب كاملة | war complement |
| مجموعة الرتاج | bolt group |
| مجموعة رجال | body of men |
| مجموعة الرجعة | re-entry package |
| مجموعة الزناد | trigger group |
| مجموعة سونار | sonar array |
| مجموعة صاعقة | commando group |
| مجموعة علب | canister grouping |
| مجموعة عناصر هوائي ياجي رباعية | quad Yagi array |
| مجموعة قتال | Battle Group |
| مجموعة قطع تبديل « ام ـ ٦٠ ايه ٣ » | M-60A3 conversion kit |
| مجموعة مرتبة | array |
| مجموعة هدامة | subversive group |
| مجند | conscript |
| مجهز بخرطوم | hose-equipped |
| مجهز تماماً | fully equipped |
| مجهز ثانية | re-equipped |
| محارب | belligerent |
| محارب قديم | ex-serviceman |
| المحافظة على الصحة الشخصية | personal hygiene |
| محجب | masked |
| محجر صحي | quarantine |
| محدد موقع بالأشعة دون الحمراء | infra-red localizer |

م

| | |
|---|---|
| محرك | engine, mover |
| محرك آر ـ ٩ بي اف ـ ٨١١ | R-9BF-811 engine |
| محرك « اف ١٠٣ » | F103 engine |
| محرك « ايه جي تي ـ ١٥٠٠ » | AGT-1500 engine |
| محرك بتربين غازي | gas turbine engine |
| محرك بنزين | petrol engine |
| محرك تربيني نفاث فرعي « ام ٥٣-٥ » | M53-5 bypass turbojet |
| محرك تعزيز | booster motor |
| محرك « تي ـ ٥٨ » | T-58 engine |
| محرك « تيربوسيكا » | Turbomèca engine |
| محرك جوي | aerospace motor |
| محرك « جيم ٢ » | Gem 2 engine |
| محرك « جيه ٥٨ » | J58 engine |
| محرك « جيه تي ٩ دي » | JT9D engine |
| محرك دفعي | propulsion motor |
| محرك « ديترويت » | Detroit engine |
| محرك ديزل | diesel engine |
| محرك ديزل « ايه ڤي دي اس ـ ١٧٩٠ ـ ٢ ايه » | AVDS-1790-2A diesel engine |
| محرك ديزل « ڤي ـ ١٢ » | V-12 diesel engine |
| محرك ديزل « كومينز » | Cummins diesel |
| محرك الزناد | trigger actuator |
| محرك زورق خارجي | outboard motor |
| محرك صلب | solid motor |
| محرك صاروخي | rocket motor |
| محرك صاروخي بوقود سائل | liquid-fuel rocket-engine |
| محرك صاروخي معزز | booster rocket engine |
| محرك الطائرة | flygmotor |
| محرك عالي النبضات | high-impulse motor |
| محرك « ڤايپر ٦٣٢ » | Viper 632 engine |
| محرك كهربائي | electric motor |
| محرك « كيه ٦٠ » | K60 engine |
| محرك مؤازر | servo motor |
| محرك مداومة | sustainer motor |
| محرك المرحلة الأولى | first-stage motor |
| محرك المرحلة الثانية | second-stage motor |
| محرك مروحي تربيني | turbo-prop |
| محرك مزدوج | twin-engine |
| محرك مزدوج القرص | twin-disc drive |
| محرك نفاث تضاغطي | ramjet |
| محرك نفاث ضغاطي تربيني | turbo-ramjet engine |
| محرك نفاث ضغاطي « ثور » | Thor ramjet |
| محرك نفاث « لارزاك » | Larzac jet engine |
| محرك « هيسبانو ـ سويزا » | Hispano-Suiza engine |
| محرك يعمل بوقود متعدد | multi-fuel engine |
| محطة إسعاف طبي | medical aid station |
| محطة تتبع | tracking station |
| محطة رادار | radar station |
| محطة طرفية | tip station |
| محطة كهرباء نووية | nuclear plant |
| محظور | unauthorized, forbidden |
| محظور على الجند | out of bounds |
| محفوظ في حاويات | containerized |
| محفوظ في مكان واق | mothballed |
| محقنة | syringe |
| محكمة عسكرية | military tribunal, court-martial |
| محكوم بالابهام | thumb-controlled |
| محلل غازي بالامتصاص الكيماوي | chemical absorption gas analyser |
| محمل | bearing |
| مُحمل | loader |
| محمّل بنابض | spring loaded |
| محمول على الحاملة | carrierborne |
| محمول على متن السفينة | shipborne |
| محمول على الهيكل | hullborne |
| محول التردد | frequency converter |
| محول عزم هيدرولي | hydraulic torque-converter |

م

| | |
|---|---|
| المحيط الأطلسي | Atlantic |
| مخازن | stores |
| مخالف للأوامر | contrary to orders |
| مخبر | informer |
| مختبر معمل | laboratory |
| مخترق الحصار | blockade runner |
| مختوم بستايروفوم | Styrofoam closure |
| مخرب | saboteur |
| مخرج العادم | exhaust outlet |
| مخزن | depot, store |
| مخزن الأسلحة | weapons bay |
| مخزن الامدادات الطبية | medical store room |
| مخزن التموين والامدادات | quartermaster store |
| مخزن ذخيرة | ammunition store |
| مخزن الفائض | surplus store |
| مخزن مبرد | cold store |
| مخزن ملابس | clothing store |
| مخزن الموقع | site depot |
| مخزن وقود | bunker |
| مخزون ذخيرة | ammunition stowage |
| مخزون الذ خيرة | ammunition dump |
| مخزونات تكتيكية | tactical stores |
| مخزونات على منصات نقالة | palletized stores |
| مخزونات / مصنع أسلحة | arsenal |
| مخطط استخبارات | intelligence planner |
| مخطط الشؤون الحركية | logistics planner |
| مخطط عسكري | military planner |
| مخطط العمليات | operations planner |
| مخفر أمامي | outpost |
| مخفر الحدود | frontier post |
| مخفف إرتدادي | recoil absorber |
| مخفي | concealed |
| مخمد صدمات هيدرو لي | hydraulic shock absorber |
| مخندق | entrenched |
| مد الأنابيب | pipelaying |
| مدار بالكهرباء | electric powered |
| مدار كهربائيا | electrically operated |
| مداس الاطار | tread of tyre |
| مداوم | sustainer |
| مدة الخدمة | length of service |
| مدخل | inlet |
| مدخل بطني ثابت | fixed ventral inlet |
| مدخل الهواء | air intake |
| مدخنة | funnel |
| مُدَرَّب | trained |
| مُدَرِّبُ | trainer |
| مدرب القفز بالمظلات | parachute jumping instructor |
| مدرب كلاب | dog handler |
| مدرج | taxiway |
| مدرج هبوط مؤقت | landing strip |
| مدرسة التدريب العسكري | army training school |
| مدرسة عسكرية | service school |
| مدّرع « خفيفاً » | lightly armoured |
| مدغشقر | Madagascar |
| مدفع | gun |
| مدفع « ٢ اس ٣ » | 2S3 gun |
| مدفع « ٢٥ اس اوه - ١٢٢ » | 25 SO-122 gun |
| مدفع أبت | Abbot gun |
| مدفع « آر بي كيه » | RPK gun |
| مدفع « اس بي جي - ٩ » | SPG-9 gun |
| مدفع « اس دي - ٤٤ » | SD-44 gun |
| مدفع « اف في ٤٣٣ » | FV433 gun |
| مدفع اقتحام منقول جواً | airborne assault gun |
| مدفع « ال ٧ ايه ١ » | L7A1 gun |
| مدفع « ال ٧ ايه ٣ » | L7A3 gun |
| مدفع « ال ١١ ايه ٥ » | L11A5 gun |
| مدفع « ال - ٣٣ » | L-33 gun |
| مدفع « ام ٦٨ » | M68 gun |
| مدفع « ام ١٠٧ » | M107 gun |

م

| | |
|---|---|
| مدفع « ام ١١٣ » | M113 gun |
| مدفع « ام ١٦٣ » | M163 gun |
| مدفع « ام ١٦٧ » | M167 gun |
| مدفع « ام ـ ١٩٤٣ » | M-1943 gun |
| مدفع « ام ـ ١٩٥٥ » | M-1955 gun |
| مدفع أملس الجوف | smooth-bore gun |
| مدفع « اوتو ـ ميلارا » | OTO-Melara gun |
| مدفع « اوريليكون ـ اوتو » | Oerlikon/Oto gun |
| مدفع « آي اس يو ـ ١٢٢ » | ISU-122 gun |
| مدفع « ايه اس يو ٥٧ » | ASU-57 gun |
| مدفع « ايه اس يو ـ ٨٥ » | ASU-85 gun |
| مدفع « ايه إم إكس » | AMX gun |
| مدفع « ايه ام اكس ـ ٣٠ دي سي ايه » | AMX-30 DCA gun |
| مدفع « ايه دبليو ـ إكس » | AW-X gun |
| مدفع « باندكانون » | Bandkanon gun |
| مدفع « بوفورز » | Bofors gun |
| مدفع « بي » | B gun |
| مدفع تحية | saluting gun |
| مدفع « تي ـ ١٢ » | T-12 gun |
| مدفع جاتلينج | Gatling gun |
| مدفع « جول كيبر » | Goalkeeper gun |
| مدفع « جي اس اتش ـ ٢٣ » | GSh-23 gun |
| مدفع « جيه پي زد اس كيه ـ ١٠٥ » | JPzSK-105 gun |
| مدفع حربي عام | army universal gun |
| مدفع خفيف | light gun |
| مدفع « دي ـ ٤٤ » | D-44 gun |
| مدفع « دي ـ ٥٦ تي » | D-56T gun |
| مدفع « دي ـ ٧٤ » | D-74 gun |
| مدفع « دي پي » | DP gun |
| مدفع « دي ئي اف ايه ٥٥٢ » | DEFA 552 gun |
| مدفع ذاتي الحركة | self-propelled gun |
| مدفع ذاتي الحركة « اس پي جي » | SPG self-propelled gun |
| مدفع « زد اس يو ـ ٢٣-٤ » | ZSU-23-4 gun |
| مدفع « زد اس يو ـ ٢٤ » | ZSU-24 gun |
| مدفع « زد اس يو ـ ٥٧ » | ZSU-57 gun |
| مدفع « زد يو ٢٣ » | ZU-23 gun |
| مدفع « ستن » | Sten gun |
| مدفع سلسلي | chain gun |
| مدفع « سولتام ال ـ ٣٣ » | Soltam L-33 gun |
| مدفع « سي ام ـ ٦٠ » | CM-60 gun |
| مدفع صغير | mini-gun |
| مدفع طراز ١٠١٠ | class 1010 gun |
| مدفع طراز ١٠١٥ | class 1015 gun |
| مدفع عديم الارتداد | recoilless gun |
| مدفع « ڤي ـ ١٥٠ » | V-150 gun |
| مدفع « كوراسييه » | Kuerassier gun |
| مدفع « كوك ريل » | Cockerill gun |
| مدفع ماركة اف ٣ | Mk F3 gun |
| مدفع « ماوزر » | Mauser gun |
| مدفع متوازن | stabilized gun |
| مدفع مزدوج | twin gun |
| مدفع محلزن « دي ـ ١٠ تي » | D-10T rifle gun |
| مدفع مضاد للدبابات | anti-tank gun |
| مدفع مضاد للدبابات « سوپر بازوكا ام ٢٠ » | Super Bazooka M20 |
| مدفع مضاد للطائرات | AA gun, anti-aircraft gun |
| مدفع مضاد للطائرات « اس ـ ٦٠ » | S-60 AA-gun |
| مدفع مضاد للطائرات « بريدا » | Breda AA gun |
| مدفع مفرد | single gun |
| مدفع المقدمة | nose gun |
| مدفع الميدان | field gun |
| مدفع ميدان « اس ـ ٢٣ » | S-23 field gun |
| مدفع الميدان « ام ـ ٤٦ » | M-46 field gun |

| | |
|---|---|
| مدفع هاوتزر | howitzer |
| مدفع هاوتزر « ٢ اس ١ » | 2S1 howitzer |
| مدفع هاوتزر « اس پي - ٧٠ » | SP-70 howitzer |
| مدفع هاوتزر « اس پي - ٧٣ » | SP-73 howitzer |
| مدفع هاوتزر « اف إتش - ٧٠ » | FH-70 howitzer |
| مدفع هاوتزر « ام ٤٤ » | M44 howitzer |
| مدفع هاوتزر « ام ٥٢ » | M52 howitzer |
| مدفع هاوتزر إم ١٠١ ايه ١ | M101A1 howitzer |
| مدفع هاوتزر « ام ١٠٢ » | M102 howitzer |
| مدفع هاوتزر « ام ١٠٩ » | M109 howitzer |
| مدفع هاوتزر « ام ١١٠ » | M110 howitzer |
| مدفع هاوتزر « ام ١١٤ » | M114 howitzer |
| مدفع هاوتزر « ام ١٩٨ » | M198 howitzer |
| مدفع هاوتزر « ام ١٩٧٣ » | M1973 howitzer |
| مدفع هاوتزر « ام ١٩٧٤ » | M1974 howitzer |
| مدفع هاوتزر « پالماريا » | Palmaria howitzer |
| مدفع هاوتزر « جي اتش ان - ٤٥ » | GHN-45 howitzer |
| مدفع هاوتزر « دانا » | DANA howitzer |
| مدفع هاوتزر « دي - ٢٠ » | D-20 howitzer |
| مدفع هاوتزر ذاتي الحركة | self-propelled howitzer |
| مدفع هاوتزر طراز ٧٥ | Type 75 howitzer |
| مدفع هاوتزر ميداني « دي - ٣٠ » | D-30 field howitzer |
| مدفع هاون | cannon |
| مدفع هاون | mortar |
| مدفع هاون « آر اتش ٢٠٢ » | Rh 202 cannon |

| | |
|---|---|
| مدفع هاون « اريز » | ARES cannon |
| مدفع هاون « أڤينجر » | Avenger cannon |
| مدفع هاون « ام ٢٩ » | M29 mortar |
| مدفع هاون « ام ٦١ » | M61 cannon |
| مدفع هاون « ام ٦١ ايه » | M61A cannon |
| مدفع هاون « ام - ١٦٠ » | M-160 mortar |
| مدفع هاون « ام ٢٢٤ » | M224 mortar |
| مدفع هاون « ان آر - ٢٣ » | NR-23 cannon |
| مدفع هاون « انداترا » | Ondatra mortar |
| مدفع هاون « اورليكون » | Oerlikon cannon |
| مدفع هاون « أيدن » | Aden cannon |
| مدفع هاون « تالون » | Talon cannon |
| مدفع هاون « جي ايه يو -٨/ايه » | GAU-8/A cannon |
| مدفع هاوتزر « جي سي تي » | GCT howitzer |
| مدفع هاون « جي ئي ام ١٩٧ » | GE M197 cannon |
| مدفع هاون خفيف | lightweight mortar |
| مدفع هاون « دي ئي اف ايه » | DEFA cannon |
| مدفع هاون سكايچارد | Skyguard cannon |
| مدفع هاون « ڤالكن » | Vulcan cannon |
| مدفع هاون « كيه بي ايه -بي » | KBA-B cannon |
| مدفع هاون « كيه سي ايه » | KCA cannon |
| مدفع هاون متعدد المواسير | multi-barrel cannon |
| مدفع هاون متوسط « ان آر ٨٤٧٥ ايه ١ » | NR8475A1 medium mortar |
| مدفع هاون مضاد للدبابات | anti-tank cannon |
| مدفع هاون « مينون » | Menon mortar |
| مدفعي | gunner |
| مدفعية سواحل | coastal artillery |
| مدفعية مقطورة | towed artillery |

| | |
|---|---|
| مدفن | cemetry |
| مدفوع بالطاقة النووية | nuclear-propelled |
| مدفوع كهربائياً | electrically propelled |
| مدمج | built-in |
| مدمرة | destroyer |
| مدمرة أدمز | Adams destroyer |
| مدمرة إراكوا | Iroquois destroyer |
| مدمرة « أنشان » | Anshan destroyer |
| مدمرة « اوداس » | Audace destroyer |
| مدمرة « ترومپ » | Tromp destroyer |
| مدمرة « جورج ليج » | Georges Leygues destroyer |
| مدمرة « جوردي » | Gordy destroyer |
| مدمرة « جيرينج » | Gearing destroyer |
| مدمرة « دي دي ٢٨٠ » | DD 280 destroyer |
| مدمرة « دي دي جي » | DDG destroyer |
| مدمرة « ديكاتور » | Decatur destroyer |
| مدمرة « سپرونس » | Spruance destroyer |
| مدمرة « سفرن » | Suffren destroyer |
| مدمرة « سكوري » | Skory destroyer |
| مدمرة « شفيلد » | Sheffield destroyer |
| مدمرة صواريخ موجهة | guided missile destroyer |
| مدمرة طراز ٨٢ | Type 82 destroyer |
| مدمرة « فاراجوت » | Farragut destroyer |
| مدمرة « فورست شيرمان » | Forrest Sherman destroyer |
| مدمرة « كاشين » | Kashin destroyer |
| مدمرة « كونتس » | Coontz destroyer |
| مدمرة « كيد » | Kidd destroyer |
| مدمرة « لوتا » | Luta destroyer |
| مدمرة « ليدا » | Lüda destroyer |
| مدمرة مجهّزة بصواريخ سطح ـ جو « كوتلين » | Kotlin SAM destroyer |
| مدمرة « ميكو » | Meko destroyer |
| مدمرة « هارونا » | Haruna destroyer |
| مدمرة « هامبورج » | Hamburg destroyer |
| مدى | range |
| المدى الأدني | minimum range |
| مدى الاعتراض | interception range |
| المدى الأقصى | maximum range |
| المدى بين القارات | intercontinental range |
| مدى تنازلي | down-range |
| مدى العبور | ferry range |
| مدى القتال المعتاد | normal combat range |
| مدى قصير | close-range |
| مدى الكشف | detection range |
| مدى الكشف الأقصى | maximum detection range |
| مدى الكشف الراداري | radar-detection range |
| المدى المؤثر | effective range |
| مدى متوسط | medium range |
| مدى المحمول بطريق البحر | waterborne range |
| مدى النظر للأسفل | look-down range |
| مدى النظر للأعلى | look-up range |
| مدير | administrator |
| مدير الاجهزة البصرية الالكترونية | optronic director |
| مدير مدفعية | gun director |
| مدينة عسكرية | military city |
| مراجعة | review |
| مراسل حربي | war correspondent |
| مراسلات رسمية | official correspondence |
| مراسيم | protocol |
| مرافق | utilities |
| مراقب | censor, observer |
| مراقب الاتصالات | communications controller |
| مراقب بالكومبيوتر | computer controlled |
| مراقب جوي | air controller, aerial spotter |
| مراقب العمليات | operations controller |
| مراقبة | lookout, observation |
| مراقبة تسديد إشعاعية | radiation-pointing control |
| مراقبة رادارية | radar monitoring |
| مراقبة الكومبيوتر | computer control |
| مراقبة المرور | traffic control |
| مراقبة المرور الجوي | air traffic control |
| مربع | square |
| مُرجع | recuperator |

م

| | |
|---|---|
| مرجل | boiler |
| مرجل فرط تسخين | superheating boiler |
| المرحلة الاولى | first stage |
| المرحلة الثانية | second stage |
| مرحلة السير نحو الهدف | cruise phase |
| مرحلة واحدة | single-stage |
| مرساة | grapnel |
| مرسال | batman |
| مُرسل | dispatcher, transmitter |
| مرسل بالليزر | laser transmitter |
| مُرسل ثنائي القطب | dipole emitter |
| مرسل راداري | radar transmitter |
| مرسل شعاع الارشاد | guidance beam transmitter |
| مُرسل عالي القدرة | high-power transmitter |
| مرسل لاسلكي | radio transmitter |
| مرش ماء/كحول | water/alcohol spray |
| مرشد | pilot |
| مرض | disease |
| مرض تناسلي | venereal disease |
| مرض مُعد | contagious disease |
| مرفاع | crane, winch |
| مرفاع إنقاذ | rescue hoist |
| مرفاع برج الحفر | derrick crane |
| مرفاع ظهر المركب | deck crane |
| مرفاع كسح ألغام | minesweeping winch |
| مرفاع مركبة « هايويما » | Hywema vehicle lift |
| مرفاع هيدرولي | hydraulic crane |
| مركام | Markham |
| مركب | vessel |
| مركب شراعي | sailer |
| مركب على محور | pintle-mounted |
| مركب على مقطورة | trailer-mounted |
| مركب في مأوى | shelter-mounted |
| مركب مع | co-mounted |
| مركبة | vehicle |
| مركبة إستطلاع | reconnaissance vehicle |
| مركبة استطلاع برمائية | amphibious reconnaissance vehicle |
| مركبة الاطلاق | launch vehicle |
| مركبة « اكس ام ٧٢٣ » | XM723 vehicle |
| مركبة « ام ٨٨ ايه ١ » | M88A1 vehicle |
| مركبة « ام ٥٧٨ » | M578 vehicle |
| مركبة « ام ايه زد - ٧٣٥ » | MAZ-357 vehicle |
| مركبة « ام ايه زد - ٥٤٣ » | MAZ-543 vehicle |
| مركبة « ام تي - ال بي » | MT-LB vehicle |
| مركبة الانزال | landing vehicle |
| مركبة انقاذ عميقة الغوص | deep-submergence rescue vehicle |
| مركبة « ايه إم إكس - ١٠ پي » | AMX-10P vehicle |
| مركبة برمائية | amphibious vehicle |
| مركبة برمائية بوسادة هوائية | amphibious air cushion vehicle |
| مركبة برمائية مجنزرة | tracked amphibious vehicle |
| مركبة بوسادة هوائية | ACV, air cushion vehicle |
| مركبة « بي آردي ام - ١ » | BRDM-1 vehicle |
| مركبة بي آردي ام - ٢ » | BRDM-2 vehicle |
| مركبة « پي جاسو » | Pegaso vehicle |
| مركبة « پيرانا » | Piranha vehicle |
| مركبة « پينتس جاور » | Pinzgauer vehicle |
| مركبة تحت مائية « پي اي پي ١٠٤ » | PAP 104 underwater vehicle |
| مركبة تسليم عائمة | swimmer delivery vehicle |
| مركبة تعزيز لاحق | post boost vehicle |
| مركبة « تي أم أس - ٦٥ » | TMS-65 vehicle |
| مركبة حركية | kinematic vehicle |
| مركبة الرجعة | re-entry vehicle |
| مركبة رادارية | radar vehicle |
| مركبة « رولاند » | Roland vehicle |
| مركبة « سامسون » | Samson vehicle |
| مركبة « سترايكر » | Striker vehicle |

| | |
|---|---|
| مركبة « ستريكر » | Streaker vehicle |
| مركبة سكامپ | Scamp vehicle |
| مركبة « سكورپيون » | Scorpion vehicle |
| مركبة « سلطان » | Sultan vehicle |
| مركبة « شارك » | Shark vehicle |
| مركبة « ڤي ايه بي » | VAB vehicle |
| مركبة « ڤي سي سي ١ » | VCC-1 vehicle |
| مركبة قتال « برادلي » | Bradley combat vehicle |
| مركبة قتال للمشاة | infantry combat vehicle, infantry fighting vehicle |
| مركبة قتال للمشاة الآلية | mechanized infantry combat vehicle |
| مركبة قتال مدرعة « ام - ١١٣ » | M-113 AFV |
| مركبة قتال مدرعة « ام ٥٧٧ » | M557 AFV |
| مركبة قتال مدرعة « ام - ٩٠١ » | M-901 AFV |
| مركبة قتالية للمشاة الآلية « ام ٢ » | M2 MICV |
| مركبة قتالية للمشاة الآلية « ام ٣ » | M3 MICV |
| مركبة قيادة | command vehicle |
| مركبة قيادة واستطلاع مدرعة | ACRV, armoured command/reconnaissance vehicle |
| مركبة « كاماز » | KAMAZ vehicle |
| مركبة « كيه ار ايه زد - ٢١٤ » | KrAZ-214 vehicle |
| مركبة « لوكس » | Luchs vehicle |
| مركبة مركز القيادة | command post vehicle |
| مركبة مشاة | infantry vehicle |
| مركبة مهندس قتال | combat engineer vehicle |
| مركبة مهندسين مدرعة | armoured engineer vehicle |
| مركبة موجة « أر بي ڤي » | RPV drone |
| مركبة نقل وتحميل | loader-transporter vehicle |
| مركبة « واي أر پي ٧٦٥ » | YRP 765 vehicle |
| مركز الاتصالات | communications centre |
| مركز البحوث والتنمية | research and development centre |
| مركز بيانات المعركة | combat information centre |
| مركز التحكم في الطائرة | flight-control station |
| مركز تحليل | analysis centre |
| مركز تدريب | training centre |
| مركز تسمع | listening post |
| مركز التصنيف | classification centre |
| مركز التصنيف والتحليل | Classification and Analysis Centre |
| مركز تنسيق عسكري | military co-ordinating centre |
| مركز الحارس | sentry post |
| مركز الدعم | back-up centre |
| مركز طبي | medical centre, medical post |
| مركز عمليات القتال | combat operations centre |
| مركز قيادة | command post |
| مركز القيادة الجوية التكتيكية | Tactical Flag Command Centre |
| مركز القيادة الجوية للطوارىء الوطنية | National Emergency Airborne Command Post |
| مركز القيادة والمراقبة | command and control centre |
| مركز متقدم | advance post |
| مركز المراقبة | control centre |
| مركز مراقبة | control post, lookout post, observation post |
| مركز مراقبة الاطلاق | launch control centre, launch control post |
| مركز مراقبة السرية | Battery Control Centre |
| مركز ميداني | field station |
| مركز الهدف | bull's eye |
| مروحة | propeller |
| مروحة تربينية | turbofan |
| مروحة تربينية « أدور » طراز ١٠٤ | Adour Mk 104 turbofan |
| مروحة تربينية « آر ام ٨ بي » | RM8B turbofan |
| مروحة تربينية « آر بي - ١٩٩ » | RB-199 turbofan |
| مروحة تربينية « اف ١٠٠ - پي دبليو - ١٠٠ » | F100-PW-100 turbofan |

م

| | |
|---|---|
| مروحة تربينية بالدفع الموجه « پيجاسوس ماركة ١٠٤ » | Pegasus Mk 104 vectored-thrust turbofan |
| مروحة ثابتة الخطوة | fixed pitch propeller |
| مرور تجاري | commercial traffic |
| مرور الطائرات | airline traffic |
| مرور عسكري | military traffic |
| مرؤوس | subordinate |
| مريض | sick |
| مريض عابر | transit case |
| مزدوج أعمدة الادارة | twin shaft |
| مزدوجة التحكم | dual control |
| مزدوج المحركات | twin-engined |
| مزدوج المرحلة | double-stage, two stage |
| مزود بالرجال « ناتو » | NATO manned |
| مزودة | haversack |
| مزيل الجليد | de-icer |
| مساحة | survey |
| مساحة الجناح | wing area |
| مساحة قرص الدوامة | rotor disc area |
| مسار الاصطدام | collision course |
| مسار باليستي مستوى | flat trajectory |
| مسار تتبع | track file |
| مسار المقذوف | trajectory |
| مساعد | adjutant |
| مساعد طيار | co-pilot |
| مسافة الاقلاع | take-off distance |
| مسافة الهبوط | landing distance |
| مسافر بحراً | seagoing |
| مساكن المتزوجين | married quarters |
| مسامير متفجرة | explosive bolt |
| مسبار التزود بالوقود أثناء الطيران | inflight refuelling probe |
| مسبار حساس البيانات الجوية | air-data sensor probe |
| مسبق التشظية | pre-fragmented |
| مستجوب | interrogator |
| مسترجع | recuperator |
| مستشفى | hospital |
| مستشسفى ترحيل | transit hospital |
| مستشفى العزل | isolation hospital |
| مستشفى الميدان | field hospital |
| مستقبل | receiver |
| مستقبل « اس اس أر ـ ١ » | SSR-1 receiver |
| مستقبل انذار راداري | radar warning receiver |
| مُستقبل بالأشعة دون الحمراء | infra-red receiver |
| مستقبل بيانات الهدف | target data receiver |
| مستقبل حراري | heat receiver |
| مستقبل راداري | radar receiver |
| مستقبل المرشد اللاسلكي | beacon receiver |
| مستقل | self-contained |
| مستندات | documents |
| مستودع | depot |
| مستودع أسلحة | arms depot |
| مستودع تخزين | store dump |
| مستودع التموينات | supply depot |
| مستودع جثث | mortuary |
| مستودع ذخيرة | munition depot |
| مستودع طبي | medical store |
| مستودع معدات حربية | ordnance magazine |
| مستودع الوقود | fuel dump |
| مستور | concealed |
| مستوى اضاءة منخفض | low-light-level |
| مستوى سطح البحر | sea level |
| مستوى الضجيج | noise-level |
| مستوى عالٍ | high-level |
| مستوى الغوص | diving plane |
| مستوى القيادة | level of command |
| مستوى منخفض | low level |
| مسح | survey |
| مسح إلكتروني | electronic scanning |
| مسح بصري | visual scan |
| مسح بالليزر | laser scanning |
| مسح ثابت | fixed scan |

م

| | |
|---|---|
| مسح خطي بالأشعة دون الحمراء | IR linescan |
| مسح خطي بالأشعة دون الحمراء | infra-red linescan |
| مسح راداري | radar scan |
| مسح زاوي | angular scan |
| مسح الطريق | route survey |
| مسح على شكل وردي | rosette scan |
| مسح هين | easy scanning |
| مسخن متقدم | pre-heater |
| مسددة خلفية . موجه خلفي | backsight |
| مسددة مدفع عاكسة | reflector gun sight |
| مسدس | gun |
| مسدس « ام ١٩١١ ايه ١ » | M1911A1 pistol |
| مسدس « ايه ٨٠ » | A 80 pistol |
| مسدس « باراكودا » | Barracuda revolver |
| مسدس « بريتا ٨٤ » | Beretta 84 pistol |
| مسدس « بريتا ٩٢ اس » | Beretta 92S pistol |
| مسدس خرطوشة | cartridge revolver |
| مسدس « دي ايه - ١٤٠ » | DA 140 pistol |
| مسدس ذاتي التلقيم | self-loading pistol |
| مسدس رشاشة | machine-pistol |
| مسدس « زاور » | Sauer pistol |
| مسدس طراز ٨٤ | model 84 pistol |
| مسدس طراز ٩٢ | model 92 pistol |
| مسدس طراز ١٩١١ ايه ١ | model 1911A1 pistol |
| مسدس عالي القدرة | high power pistol |
| مسدس مزدوج الفعل | double action pistol |
| مسدس « والثر » | Walther pistol |
| مسدس يعمل بالقدح | percussion revolver |
| مسلح بالصواريخ | missile armed |
| مسلح بصواريخ سطح -جو | SAM-armed |
| مسلح بمدفع | gun-armed |
| مسمار | spike |
| مسمار تثبيت | locking pin |
| مسماع الاذن | earphones |
| المسنن الرئيسي | main gear |
| مسننة سلسلة الادارة | drive sprocket |
| مسؤول طبي | medical officer |
| مسيحي | Christian |
| مسيحي ماروني | Maronite Christian |
| مشاة البحرية | naval infantry |
| مشاة خفاف | light infantry |
| مشاة منقولة بالسيارات | motorized infantry |
| مشبك | clip |
| مشبوك | clip-on |
| مشترك | collaborator |
| مشط ذخيرة | clip |
| مشعل | flare |
| مشعل خادع | decoy flare |
| مشعل قنبلة يدوية | grenade flare |
| مشعل لحام | welding torch |
| المشغّل | operator |
| مُشغل | actuator |
| مُشغل الانذار المبكر | EW operator |
| مشهد | scene! |
| مشوّش | jammer |
| مشوّش التوجيه الراداري | home-on jammer |
| مشوش عالي القدرة | high-powered jammer |
| مشير | marshal, field marshal |
| المشير الأعلى | chief marshal |
| مصاب النقالة | stretcher casualty |
| مصابون | casualties |
| مصادر الأشعة دون الحمراء | IR sources |
| مصادمة | skirmish |
| مصباح أمامي | headlamp |
| مصباح مضيء | illuminator |
| مصباح مضيء مستمر الموجة | continuous wave illuminator |
| مصباح وماض | flashing lamp |

م

| | |
|---|---|
| مصر | Egypt |
| مصروفات الدفاع | defence expenditure |
| مصروفات المطعم | mess expenses |
| مصري | Egyptian |
| مصعد | elevator |
| مصعد الطائرة | aircraft elevator |
| مصنع حربي | armament factory |
| مصهر | fuse |
| مصهر « دي ام ٢٤ » | DM24 fuse |
| مصهر « دي ام ٣٤ » | DM34 fuse |
| مصهر « دي ام ٥٤ » | DM54 fuse |
| مصهر « كيه ايه زد » | KAZ fuse |
| مصوبة بصرية | optical sight |
| مصوبة ليلية | night sight |
| مصور حراري | thermal imager |
| مصورة | view finder |
| مصيدة دبابات | tank trap |
| مضاء | illuminated |
| مضابط قتال | combat controls |
| مضاد | anti- |
| مضاد حيوي (للجراثيم) | antibiotic |
| مضاد للأفراد | anti-personnel |
| مضاد للتجسس | counter-espionage |
| مضاد للدبابات | anti-tank |
| مضاد للسفن | anti-ship |
| مضاد للصواريخ | anti-missile |
| مضاد للطائرات | anti-aircraft |
| مضاد للعصيان | counter-insurgency |
| مضاد الغنغرينا | anti-gangrene |
| مضاد للكزاز | anti-tetanus |
| مضادة | counteraction |
| مضادة للدبابات شديدة الانفجار | HEAT |
| مضاعف | multiple |
| مضبوط على هدف بصورة مستقلة | independently targeted |
| مضبوط مقدماً | pre-set |
| مضخة جوف المركب | bilge pump |
| مضخم | amplifier |
| مطابقة الخرائط | map watching |
| مطار | airfield |
| مطبخ متنقل ميداني | mobile kitchen |
| مطبخ الميدان | field kitchen |
| مطر | rain |
| مطرقة | hammer |
| مطعم الضباط | officers' mess |
| مطعم للضباط | mess |
| مطلق التدابير المضادة ايه ال ئي ـ ٤٠ | ALE-40 countermeasures dispenser |
| مطهر | disinfectant, antiseptic |
| مظاهرة | demonstration |
| مظلة | parachute |
| مظلة الحارس | sentry box |
| مظلة كبح من النوع الشريطي | ribbon type braking parachute |
| مظلي | paratroop, parachutist |
| مظهر جانبي | silhouette |
| مع صدور أمري ! | on my order! |
| معادٍ | hostile |
| معاد | unfriendly |
| معالجة | treatment |
| معالجة « بايتس » | BATES processing |
| معالجة بالكلور | chlorination |
| معالجة البيانات اوتوماتيكياً | automatic information processing |
| معالجة البيانات بالكومبيوتر | computerised data-processing |
| معاملة | treatment |
| مُعان بالطاقة الآلية | power-assisted |
| معان بالكومبيوتر | computer-assisted |
| معاهدة | treaty |
| معاهدة سلام | peace treaty |
| معتاداً ـ سر ! | quick march! |
| معتد | aggressor |
| معتدل السعر | cost-effective |

م

| | |
|---|---|
| معترض | intercepted |
| مُعدٍ | infectious, contagious |
| معدات | equipment |
| معدات الاتصال | communication equipment |
| معدات إرساء | mooring equipment |
| معدات إزالة التلوث | decontamination equipment |
| معدات إزالة القمل | de-lousing equipment |
| معدات الاستطلاع | surveillance equipment |
| معدات إطلاق رافعة | erector launcher |
| معدات اعتراض جوي | air-interception equipment |
| معدات الانزال | landing equipment |
| معدات البحث | search equipment |
| معدات التوجيه | guidance equipment |
| معدات توجيه الدخان | smokelaying equipment |
| معدات الثكنات | barrack equipment |
| معدات حربية | war material |
| معدات الرادار | radar equipment |
| معدات رفض التداخل الراداري | radar-clutter rejection equipment |
| معدات الرؤية الليلية | night vision equipment |
| معدات رؤية ليلية بالأشعة دون الحمراء | infra-red night-vision equipment |
| معدات السيطرة على الرمي | fire control equipment |
| معدات غير مغنطيسية | amagnetic equipment |
| معدات قتالية | fighting equipment |
| معدات القطر | towing gear |
| معدات القياس | measuring equipment |
| معدات كسح الألغام | minesweeping equipment |
| معدات كشف | detection equipment |
| معدات ليزر | laser equipment |
| معدات مانعة لفرط الاحماء | anti-overheating equipment |
| معدات المتابعة | tracking equipment |
| معدات مدفعية | ordnance |
| معدات مرفاع ظهر المركب | deck crane equipment |
| معدات مغتنمة | captured equipment |
| معدات ملاحية | navigation equipment |
| معدات نظام البيانات التكتيكية البحرية | NTDS equipment |
| معدات هجوم | attack equipment |
| معدات هيدرولية | hydraulic equipment |
| معدات وأجهزة المكاتب | office equipment |
| معدل | modified, rate |
| معدل التسلق | climb rate |
| معدل سرعة المدى | range-rate |
| معدل مدى الرمي | target range rate |
| المعدل النظري للرمي | cyclic rate of fire |
| معركة | action, combat |
| معركة بيضاء | bloodless battle |
| معركة دفاعية | defensive battle |
| معزز | booster |
| معزول حرارياً | heat-insulated |
| معسكر | camp |
| معسكر تدريب | training camp |
| معسكر صيفي | summer camp |
| معسكر للاقامة المؤقتة | overnight camp |
| معسكر مؤقت | temporary camp |
| معطف | greatcoat |
| معطف صامد للماء | water-proof cape |
| معطيات صوتية | acoustic data |
| معقب ليزر آلي | automatic laser tracker |
| معقد | seat |
| معلق | overhead |
| معْلَم | parameter |
| معلومات | information |
| معلومات الاستطلاع | recce information |
| معلومات سرية | classified information |
| معلومات عن الهدف | target information |
| معلومات متقدمة | advance information |
| معمل اصلاح | workshop |
| معمل فوتوغرافي | photographic laboratory |
| معوق زمنياً | time delayed |
| معيار بالكيلوطن | kiloton yield |
| معين الاختراق | penetration aid |

م

| | |
|---|---|
| معين اختراق شرائح التشويش | chaff penetration aid |
| معين إختراق الشرك | decoy penetration aid |
| معين الانزال « اس بي ان ـ ١٠ » | SPN-10 launching |
| معين انزال « اس بي بي ـ ٣٥ ايه » | SPB-35A launching aid |
| معين الانزال « اس بي ان ـ ٤٣ » | SPN-43 launching aid |
| معين بصري | visual aid |
| معين تدريب | training aid |
| معين هبوط | landing aid |
| معين الهبوط « ان آر بي ايه » | NRBA landing aid |
| مُعين الاتجاه | direction finder |
| معين الارتفاع | height-finder |
| معين المدى | range finder |
| معين بالليزر | laser rangefinder |
| معين مدى ليزر « سلينيا » | Selenia laser rangefinder |
| معين الهدف | target designator |
| معينات ملاحية | navaids |
| مغادر | defector |
| المغرب | Morocco |
| مغربي | Moroccan |
| مغلاق | breech |
| مغلاق برغي دوار | rotating-bolt breech |
| مغمور | submerged |
| مغير أطوار | phase shifter |
| مفاعل « اس ٥ جي » | S5G reactor |
| مفاعل « اس ٥ دبليو » | S5W reactor |
| مفاعل « دي ٢ جي » | D2G reactor |
| مفاعل ذري يبرد بالماء المضغوط | pressurized-water reactor |
| مفاعل نووي | nuclear reactor |
| مفاعل يبرد بالماء | water cooled reactor |
| مفتاح | switch |
| مفتاح الأمان | safety switch |
| مفتوح | open-ended |
| مفجر | detonator |
| مفرزة | detachment |
| مفرزة تنفيذ الاعدام | firing party |
| مفرزة الحرس | guard detail |
| مفرزة الرمي | firing party |
| مفرزة متقدمة | advance detachment |
| مفرزة مضادة للواشي | anti-tattletale escort |
| مفرّغ | jettisoned |
| مفرقعات إشعال | igniter squibs |
| مفسر | interpreter |
| مفسر صور | photo-interpreter |
| مفهوم « هوتاس » | HOTAS concept |
| مقاتل | combatant |
| مقاتلون بريّون | surface combatants |
| مقاوم | anti- |
| مقاوم للتدابير المضادة الالكترونية | ECM-resistant |
| مقاومة مخابرات العدو | counter-intelligence |
| مقبرة | cemetery |
| مقبس اطلاق النار الكهربائي | electrical firing socket |
| مقبض أمامي | foregrip |
| مقبض القدح | cocking handle |
| مقبض كلابي لمد الكبلات | cable grip |
| مقبض يدوي | hand-grip |
| مقتلع | extractor |
| مقدم | lieutenant colonel |
| المقدمة | advance guard |
| مقدمة السفينة | bow |
| مقدمة القوات | vanguard |
| مقذوف | projectile |
| مقذوف « ام ١١٠ ايه ٢ » | M110A2 projectile |
| مقذوف خارق للدروع | armour-piercing projectile |
| مقذوف « كيلر جونيور » | Killer Junior projectile |
| مقذوف « كيلر سنيور » | Killer Senior projectile |
| مقذوف كيماوي | chemical projectile |

م

| | |
|---|---|
| مقذوف محرق | incendiary projectile |
| مقذوف مدفعي نووي | nuclear shell |
| مقذوف معان بالصاروخ | rocket-assisted projectile |
| مقذوف نخروبي | beehive projectile |
| مقذوف نووي | nuclear projectile |
| مقر | headquarters |
| مقر جماعة الاقتحام | assault group headquarters |
| مقر القيادة | command headquarters |
| مقر المجموعة | group headquarters |
| مقر محلي | home base |
| مقرها الغواصة | submarine-based |
| مقراب | telescope |
| مقرنة هوائيات | antenna coupler |
| مقطع | section |
| مقطِّع أنابيب | tube cutter |
| مقطور | towed |
| مقطورة الذخيرة | ammunition trailer |
| مقطورة « شيڤرتون » | Cheverton tender |
| مقعد قذفي | ejection seat |
| مقعد مترادف | tandem seat |
| مقعد ينطوي | jump seat |
| مقنّع | masked |
| مقياس ارتفاع راداري | radar altimeter |
| مقياس ارتفاع راداري | height-radar |
| مقياس ارتفاع لاسلكي | radio altimeter |
| مقياس ليزر لارتفاع السحاب | laser ceilograph |
| مقيم | resident |
| مكابح ايروديناميكية | aerodynamic brakes |
| مكافأة | gratuity |
| مكافحة الحريق | fire-fighting |
| مكالمة هاتفية | telephone call |
| مكبح تثبيت دولاب المركبة | sprag locking brake |
| مكبح الطوارىء | emergency brake |
| مكبح هوائي | airbrake |
| مكتب | office |
| مكتب المراقبة | control desk |
| مكتبة انذارات | threat library |
| مُكثف | condensor |
| مكثف شدة الصورة | image intensifier |
| مكثف شدة الصورة الالكتروني | electronic image intensifier |
| مكثف شدة صورة داخلي | internal image intensifier |
| المكسيك | Mexico |
| مكسيكي | Mexican |
| مكشاف | detector |
| مكشاف « ام ايه دي » | MAD detector |
| مكشاف حريق معلق | fire overhead detector |
| مكشاف ظاهرات مغنطيسية شاذة | magnetic anomaly detector |
| مكيف الضغط | pressurized |
| مكيف الهواء | air-conditioned |
| ملاءمة كنتور التضاريس | terrain contour matching |
| ملابس مدنية | civilian clothes |
| ملاح | mariner, navigator |
| ملاح جوي | airman |
| ملاح فضائي | astronaut |
| ملاحة | navigation |
| ملاحة بالجمود الفلكي | astro-inertial navigation |
| ملاحة « توب نوت » | Top Knot navigation |
| ملاحة نسبية | relative navigation |
| ملاحو السفينة أو الطائرة | crewmen |
| ملاحو الطائرة | flight crew |
| ملاحي | maritime |
| ملازم أول | lieutenant |
| ملاك القتال | fighting strength |
| ملاوي | Malawi |
| ملجأ | shelter |
| ملجأ خرساني | concrete shelter |
| ملحوم بأكمله | all-welded |
| ملغم | booby trapped |
| ملفاف | winch |
| ملقّم آلي | automatic loader |
| ممتص الصدمات | shock absorber |

م

| | |
|---|---|
| ممددة الجسر | bridgelayer |
| ممدة جسور « بيبر » | Biber bridge layer |
| ممر | pass |
| ممر جبلي | mountain pass |
| ممر جوي | air corridor |
| ممر طيران | apron |
| ممر فرعي | bypass |
| ممر منحدر الاقلاع | ski-jump |
| ممر منحدر هيدرولي | hydraulically operated ramp |
| ممرض | medical orderly |
| ممساك آمان | safety catch |
| ممسوك باليد | hand held |
| ممنوع | forbidden |
| ممنوع التجاوز | no overtaking |
| ممنوع الدخول | no entry |
| ممنوع الوقوف | no parking |
| مموّه | camouflaged |
| مميت | deadly |
| مميز برمز سري | security-coded |
| مميزات مقاومة الارتطام | crash-resistant features |
| من نوع دوار | rotary type |
| من نوع متشظي | fragmentation type |
| من نوع مروحي | helix-type |
| من اليمين الى اليسار ! | from right to left! |
| من هناك ! | who goes there! |
| منارة بالاشعة دون الحمراء | infra-red beacon |
| منارة وماضة | flashing beacon |
| مناعة ضد التشويش | immunity to jamming |
| منافع | utilities |
| مناورة | exercise, manoeuvre |
| مناورات | manoeuvres |
| مناورات بحري | naval exercise |
| مناورة بالنيران | manoeuvre-by-fire |
| مناورة تدريبية | training exercise |
| مناوشة | skirmish |
| منتجات إلاستومير | elastomer products |
| منتخب الرمي | fire selector |
| منجنيق | catapult |
| منجنيق بخاري | steam catapult |
| منحة | gratuity |
| منحدر شاهق | cliff |
| منحرف المحاذاة | out of line |
| منزعة | extractor |
| منزوعة الألغام | cleared of mines |
| منشاق | snorkel |
| منصة الاطلاق | launch pad, launching pad |
| منصة أمامية | forward pad |
| منصة تركيب | pedestal mount |
| منصة التوجيه بالقصور الذاتي | inertial guidance platform |
| منصة جوية | airborne platform |
| منصة الطائرات العمودية | helicopter platform |
| منصة « ڤيتول » | VTOL platform |
| منصة المدفع | gun sponson |
| منصة مدفع بحري | naval gun mount |
| منضدة دوارة | turntable |
| منطقة | zone |
| منطقة إسناد | reference area |
| منطقة انتشار | deployment area |
| منطقة التلوث | contamination area |
| منطقة حربية | warzone |
| منطقة الدفاع الأمامية | forward defence area |
| منطقة دفاعية | defensive zone |
| منطقة ركوب القطار أو تحميله | entrainment area |
| منطقة السطح الجوي | air surface zone |
| منطقة السقوط | dropping zone |
| منطقة عسكرية | military region |
| منطقة العمليات | area of operations |
| منطقة القطب الشمالي | Arctic |
| منطقة مأهولة | populated area |
| منطقة محرمة | prohibited area |
| منطقة محظورة | restricted area |

م

| | |
|---|---|
| منطقة المعركة | battle area, combat zone |
| منطقة المعركة الفرعية | secondary battle zone |
| منطقة ملوثة | contaminated area |
| منطقة ملوثة بالجراثيم | infected zone |
| منطقة ممنوعة | restricted area |
| منطقة الميناء | port area |
| منطقة الهبوط | landing zone |
| منطقة وقوف المركبات | vehicle parking area |
| منطاد | balloon |
| منطاد الأحوال الجوية | weather balloon |
| منطاد مضاد للطائرات | barrage balloon |
| منطلق من الغواصة | submarine launched |
| منظار أفق تصويري حراري | thermal imagery periscope |
| منظار ثنائي العينية | binoculars |
| منظمة استخبارات | intelligence organization |
| منظمة التحرير الفلسطينية | Palestine Liberation Organisation (P.L.O.) |
| منظمة حلف شمال الأطلنطي « ناتو » | NATO (North Atlantic Treaty Organisation) |
| منعطف | detour |
| منغوليا | Mongolia |
| منفتح للدبابات | accessible to tanks |
| منفذ | inlet |
| منقول جواً | airborne |
| منقولة بالسيارات | motorized |
| منوب | orderly |
| منورا كشاف بضوء أبيض | white-light searchlight |
| مهادنة | truce |
| مهبط طائرات | airstrip |
| مهبط الطائرة | landing gear |
| المهبطة | undercarriage |
| مهبطة ثلاثية العجلات | tricycle landing gear |
| مهجع | sleeping accommodation |
| مهجور | obsolescent |
| مهداف | sight |
| مهداف اكتساب الهدف | target acquisition sight |
| مهداف بريسكوبي | periscope sight |
| مهداف « ترايلوكس » | Trilux sight |
| مهداف التسديد | gunner's sight |
| مهداف تصويب امامي | foresight |
| مهداف تعيين الهدف | target designation sight |
| مهداف تلسكوبي | telescopic sight |
| مهداف حراري | thermal sight |
| مهداف « سوسات » | SUSAT sight |
| مهداف القنابل اليدوية | grenade sight |
| مهداف للملاحة | navigation sight |
| مهداف ليزر للدبابات | Tank Laser Sight |
| مهداف متابعة | tracking sight |
| مهداف متوازن | stabilized sight |
| مهداف متوازن أحادي العين | stabilized monocular sight |
| مهداف مدرج | graticule sight |
| مهداف المدفع | gunsight |
| مهداف مدفع « فيرو ـ زد ١٣ » | Fero-Z 13 gunsight |
| مهداف مركب على السقف | roof-mounted sight |
| مهداف مركب على صاري فوق دوامة الطائرة العمودية | mast-mounted sight |
| مهداف هبوط مرآوي | mirror landing sight |
| مهداف وحيد العين | monocular sight |
| مهاجم | hit man |
| مهام الحصار | blockade duties |
| مهرّبات | contraband |
| مهمة | duty, mission |
| مهمة اخلاء المصابين | casevac role |
| مهمة استرداد | recovery task |
| مهمة إستطلاع | reconnaissance mission |
| مهمة اصلاح | recovery task |
| مهمة بحرية | naval duty |
| مهمة تدريبية | training mission |
| مهمة ثانوية | secondary role |
| مهمة جمع الاستخبارات | intelligence-gathering mission |
| مهمة حراسة | guard duty |

| | |
|---|---|
| مهمة الحراسة | escort duty |
| مهمة خاصة | special mission |
| مهمة الدفاع | defence role |
| مهمة دورية | patrol mission |
| مهمة كبرى | major task |
| مهمة كسح الألغام | minesweeping duty |
| مهمة النقل | transport duty |
| مهمة هجومية | attack mission |
| مهنة | occupation |
| مهندس | engineer |
| مهندس عسكري | sapper |
| مهندس قتال | combat engineer |
| مواجة للخارج | outward-facing |
| مواجه للمؤخرة | aft-facing |
| موازن بالتدويم | spin-stabilized |
| موازن بجنيحات | fin-stabilized |
| مواصلات | communications |
| مواصلات لاسلكية | radio communication |
| مواضع دفاعية | defensive positions |
| موالي | partisan |
| موجة | wave |
| موجة مستمرة | continuous wave |
| موجّه بالتردد فوق العالي | UHF homer |
| موجه مدفع تلفزيوني | TV gun director |
| موجه | vectored |
| موجه بالسلك | wire-guided |
| موجه بالكامل | fully guided |
| موجه بالليزر | laser-guided |
| موجّه قيادياً | command-guided |
| موجود بالحاملة | carrier-based |
| موريتانيا | Mauritania |
| موزع « اس يو يو ٢٠ » | SUU20 dispenser |
| موزع التدابير المضادة | counter-measures dispenser |
| موزع شرائح التشويش والمشاعل | chaff and flare dispenser |
| موزمبيق | Mozambique |
| موضع | stand |
| موضع أمامي | forward position |
| موضع المدفع | gun position |
| موضع مكشوف | exposed position |
| موقع | location |
| موقع محصن | prepared position |
| موقع الهدف | target location |
| موقف تكتيكي | tactical situation |
| موقف السطح | deck park |
| مولد تربيني بطاحونة هوائية | windmill turbogenerator |
| مولد ديزل | diesel generator |
| مولد طاقة « كوندور » | Condor power pack |
| مولد كهرباء | generator |
| مولد كهربائي | electrical generator |
| مياه ساحلية | coastal waters |
| ميدان الاستعراض | square |
| ميدان الاقتحام | assault course |
| ميدان الثكنات | barrack square |
| ميادان رمي | butts |
| ميدان الرمي | target range |
| ميزان القوة | balance of power |
| ميزة الردع | deterrence value |
| ميسرة | port |
| ميكروبروسسور | microprocessor |
| ميكروفون | microphone |
| ميل | gradient |
| ميل مركز الدوران | trunnion cant |
| ميل | mile |
| ميل بحري | nautical mile |
| ميلان | list |
| ميليشا | militia |
| ميليشا المرابطون | Mourabitoun Militia |
| ميليشا مسلحة | armed militia |
| ميمنة | starboard |
| ميناء | port |

م

# ن

| | |
|---|---|
| نائب ضابط | warrant officer |
| نائب مدير الخدمات الاجتماعية بالجيش (المملكة المتحدة) | ADAWS |
| ناپام | napalm |
| نابض مسطح | flat spring |
| نابض لولبي | coil spring |
| « نادج » : البيئة البرية للدفاع الجوي لمنظمة ناتو | Nadge (Nato Air Defence Ground Environment) |
| نار | fire |
| نازع | extractor |
| نافذة احراز | acquisition window |
| نافورة ماء | waterjet |
| ناقلة | transporter |
| ناقلة أفراد ڤي ايه بي | VAB personnel carrier |
| ناقلة آلية | motor carrier |
| ناقلة بحرية « توماستون » | Thomaston sea transporter |
| ناقلة بضائع | cargo carrier |
| ناقلة جنود | personnel carrier |
| ناقلة جنود الاقتحام | assault troop carrier |
| ناقلة جنود « ام ۱۱۳ ايه ۲ » | M113A2 personnel carrier |
| ناقلة جنود « بي إم پي » | BMP personnel carrier |
| ناقلة جنود « سپارتان » | Spartan personnel carrier |
| ناقلة جنود مدرعة | armoured troop carrier |
| ناقلة جنود مدرعة « ال ايه ڤي ـ ٢٥ » | LAV-25 APC |
| ناقلة دبابات | tank-carrier |
| ناقلة صهريجية للماء | water tanker |
| ناقلة القاذفة | launcher transporter |
| ناقلة مجنزرة | tracked carrier |
| ناقلة هجومية | assault carrier |
| ناقلة وقود | fuel tanker |
| نايلونيت | nylonite |
| نبضة | pulse |
| نتروجليسرين | nitro-glycerine |
| نتوءات | bulges |
| نتوءات جانبية للهوائي | antenna sidelobes |
| نداء الحضور | roll call |
| نرويجي | Norwegian |
| نزاع مسلح | armed conflict |
| نزع السلاح | disarm |
| نزل | land |
| نسبة الاحديداب | camber |
| نسبة التحويل | bypass ratio |
| نسبة الجنود إلى المركبة | troop-to-vehicle ratio |
| نسبة الدفع الى الوزن | thrust/weight ratio |
| نسبة القدرة الى الوزن | power-to-weight ratio |
| نسف تحت الماء | underwater demolition |
| نسف للهدم | demolition blasting |
| نسق | echelon |
| نشاط عسكري | military activity |
| نشاط العصابات | guerrilla activities |
| نشاط المعركة | combat activity, battle activity |
| نشر | deployment |
| نشر الجنود | troop deployment |

| | |
|---|---|
| نشرة جوية | weather report |
| نشرة دعائية | propaganda leaflet |
| نصف الرحلة | mid-flight |
| نصف قطر الدورية | patrol radius |
| نصف قطر القتال | combat radius |
| نصف كروي | hemispherical |
| نصف المسافة | mid-course |
| نصف مغمور | semi-submerged |
| نصل التراكتور | dozer blade |
| نصل مركب | composite blade |
| نطاق التردد | frequency band |
| نطاق الترددات السينية | X-band |
| نظارات واقية | goggles |
| نظافة شخصية | personal cleansing |
| نظام | system |
| نظام اتصالات بالقمر الصناعي | satellite communication system |
| نظام اتصال بالقمر الصناعي « اوه ئي ـ ٨٢ » | OE-82 satellite communication |
| نظام اتصال صاروخي | rocket communications system |
| نظام الاتصالات « تيكا » | Tica Communications |
| نظام الاخلاء | evacuation system |
| نظام ارسال بيانات الهدف | target data transmission system |
| نظام الاستطلاع الفضائي | Space Surveillance System |
| نظام الاستعلامات | information system |
| نظام الأسلحة | weapon system |
| نظام أسلحة الاشتباك (برج بحري مضاد للطائرات) | close-in weapon system (CIWS) |
| نظام أسلحة الاشتباك (برج بحري مضاد للطائرات) ايه دي جي ٦ ـ ٣٠ | ADG-6-30 CIWS |
| نظام أسلحة الحاويات | container weapon system |
| نظام اسناد الوضع | attitude reference system |
| نظام أشعة دون الحمراء « سايكلوب » | Cyclope IR system |
| نظام اطفاء الحريق | fire extinguishing system |
| نظام الكتروني حديث | modern electronic system |
| نظام آلي لنقل الحركة « تي ان ٣٧ » | TN37 automatic transmission |
| نظام « ام ٢٢ » | M22 system |
| نظام الأمان | safety system |
| نظام أمن القيادة | command buffer system |
| نظام « ان بي سي » | NBC system |
| نظام الانذار | warning system |
| نظام الانذار المبكر | early warning system |
| نظام انذار مبكر « ايه ال ـ كيو ٩٩ » | ALQ-99 E W |
| نظام انذار مبكر « ايه ان/ايه اس كيو ـ ١٨ » | AN-ASQ-18 EWS |
| نظام انذار مبكر « ايه ان/ايه ال آر ـ ٤٦ » | AN/ALR-46 EWS |
| نظام انذار مبكر « ايه ان/ايه ال آر ـ ٥٤ » | AN/ALR-54 EWS |
| نظام انذار مبكر « ايه ان/ايه بي آر ـ ٣٨ » | AN/APR-38 EWS |
| نظام انذار مبكر بالصواريخ البالستية « ٤٧٤ إل » | 474L BMEWS |
| نظام انذار مبكر بالصواريخ البالستية « ٤٩٦ إل » | 496L BMEWS |
| نظام الانذار المبكر بالصواريخ البالستية سبيستراك | Spacetrack BMEWS |
| نظام انذار مبكر « تي ايه سي » | TAC-EWS |
| نظام اوتوماتيكي تماماً | fully automatic system |
| نظام بحري متكامل | integrated naval system |
| نظام بصري للسيطرة على الرمي | optical fire-control |
| نظام بالقصور الذاتي « اس دي ـ ٥١٠ » | SD-510 inertial system |
| نظام بالقصور الذاتي للملاحة النجمية | stellar-inertial navigation system |
| نظام بيانات « ايه ان/يو اس دي ـ ٧ » | AN/USD-7 |

ن

|  |  |
|---|---|
| AN/UXD-1 data system | نظام بيانات « ايه ان/يو اكس دي ـ ١ » |
| Tactical Data System | نظام البيانات التكتيكية |
| SENIT-2 data system | نظام البيانات « سينيت ـ ٢ » |
| action information system | نظام بيانات القتال |
| cooling system | نظام تبريد |
| cyrogenic system | نظام التبريد |
| seeker cooling system | نظام تبريد الباحث |
| tracking adjunct system | نظام تتبع مساعد |
| infra-red gathering system | نظام تجميع بالأشعة دون الحمراء |
| ranging and sighting system | نظام تحديد المدى والتسديد |
| AN/FPS warning system | نظام تحذير ايه إن/اف پي اس |
| AEW | نظام تحذير مبكر محمول جواً |
| Mainstay AWAC | نظام التحذير والمراقبة الجوي « مينستاي » |
| Moss AWAC | نظام التحذير والمراقبة المحمول جواً « موس » |
| control system | نظام التحكم |
| Mepsy system | نظام تحكم بالميكروبروسسور « ميپسى » |
| flight-control system | نظام التحكم في الطائرة |
| Soptac 23 FCS | نظام التحكم في الطيران سوپتاك ٢٣ » |
| Naval Intelligence Processing System | نظام تحليل الاستخبارات البحرية |
| data-processing system | نظام تحليل البيانات |
| advanced radar processing system | نظام تحليل راداري متقدم |
| training system | نظام التدريب |
| TROIJA system | نظام « ترويجا » |
| weapon delivery system | نظام تسليم الأسلحة |
| jammer system | نظام تشويش الكتروني |
| underwater disposal system | نظام التصريف تحت الماء |
| weapon-aiming system | نظام تصويب الأسلحة |
| retargeting system | نظام تعديل الهدف |

|  |  |
|---|---|
| target designation system | نظام تعيين الهدف |
| threat evaluation system | نظام تقييم الانذارات |
| air conditioning system | نظام تكييف بالهواء |
| mines identification & neutralization system | نظام تميز الألغام وابطالها |
| IFF, Identification, Friend or Foe | نظام تمييز الصديق والعدو |
| Dead Duck IFF | نظام تمييز الصديق والعدو « ديد داك » |
| gas regulation system | نظام تنظيم الغاز |
| machinery quieting system | نظام تهدئة ضوضاء المكنات |
| ventilating system | نظام تهوية |
| guidance system | نظام التوجيه |
| inertial guidance system | نظام التوجيه بالقصور الذاتي |
| Tercom guidance system | نظام توجيه « تيركوم » |
| TV homing | نظام توجيه تلفزيوني |
| radar homing and warning system | نظام التوجيه والانذار الراداري |
| Tornado system | نظام « تورنيدو » |
| data link system | نظام توصيل البيانات |
| gas generator system | نظام توليد الغاز |
| Gould Ocean System | نظام « جولد اوشن » |
| receiver simulator system | نظام حاكي المستقبل |
| anti-satellite weapon system | نظام حربي مضاد للأقمار الصناعية |
| sensor system | نظام حساس |
| Bear Trap | نظام حط على السطح للطائرات العمودية البحرية |
| engine silencing system | نظام خفت صوت المحرك |
| ground-based air defence system | نظام دفاع جوي أرضي |
| PIVADS air defense system | نظام الدفاع الجوي « پيڤادز » |
| Chaparral ADS | نظام دفاع جوي « شاپارال » |
| Sea Chaparral ADS | نظام دفاع جوي « سي شاپارال » |

ن

| | |
|---|---|
| نظام دفاعي ضد الصواريخ البالستية | anti-ballistic missile system |
| نظام الدفاع النقطي | point defence system |
| نظام دفع بالطاقة النووية | nuclear propulsion system |
| نظام دفعي | propulsion system |
| نظام راداري « كوبرا دين » | Cobra Dane radar system |
| نظام « رايبيار » | Rapier system |
| نظام رمي قارىء للسهم | arrow read firing system |
| نظام الرؤية الليلية « بادجر » | Badget night vision system |
| نظام الرؤية الليلية للطيار | pilot's night vision system |
| نظام السيطرة على الرمي | fire control system |
| نظام السيطرة على الرمي « ارايون » | Orion fire control |
| نظام السيطرة على الرمي « اف ال تي » | FLT fire control system |
| نظام السيطرة على الرمي « ان ايه ١٠ » | NA10 fire control |
| نظام السيطرة على الرمي « ان ايه ٣٠ » | NA30 fire control |
| نظام السيطرة على الرمي « بي سي كيو ـ ٤ » | BCQ-4 fire control |
| نظام السيطرة على الرمي « تالوس » | Talos fire control |
| نظام السيطرة على الرمي تحت الماء | underwater fire control system |
| نظام السيطرة على الرمي « دي أر بي سي ٣٢ ايه » | DRBC 32A FCS |
| نظام السيطرة على الرمي « جي اف سي اس أي » | GFCSI fire control system |
| نظام السيطرة على الرمي « سابكا » | SABCA fire control |
| نظام السيطرة على الرمي « سافاير » | Sapphire fire control system |
| نظام السيطرة على رمي الصواريخ | missile fire control system |
| نظام السيطرة على الرمي « كوبلدا » | COBELDA fire control |
| نظام السيطرة على الرمي « كوتاك » | COTAC FCS |
| نظام السيطرة على رمي المدفعية | gun fire control system |
| نظام السيطرة على قذف الطوربيد | torpedo fire control system |
| نظام الشبكة | grid system |
| نظام شفري | cipher code |
| نظام شعاع بصري للسيطرة على الصواريخ الموجهة | optical beam ride |
| نظام صواريخ | missile system |
| نظام صواريخ « ريبيار » المتتبعة | Tracked Rapier system |
| نظام صواريخ متعددة | multiple rocket system |
| نظام طرد الهواء | air extractor system |
| نظام عرض | display system |
| نظام عرض المدفع | gun display system |
| نظام عرض المدفع « رفائيل » | Rafael gun display system |
| نظام غير عُقدي | non-nodal system |
| نظام الفضاء والدفاع | Space and Defence system |
| نظام « ڤي دي اس » | VDS system |
| نظام قصور ذاتي | inertial system |
| نظام قفل المغلاق | breech-locking system |
| نظام القناع والمرشح | mask & filter system |
| نظام كشف | detection system |
| نظام كشف سلبي | passive detection system |
| نظام متكامل للسيطرة على الرمي | integrated fire control system |
| نظام محلل | analyser system |
| نظام مراقبة وانذار جوي | airborne warning and control system |
| نظام مضاد للدبابات للدفاع الجوي | ADATS |
| نظام مضاد للصواريخ بالخندق الأخير | last ditch anti-missile system |
| نظام مضاد للطائرات « جيبارد » | Gepard anti-aircraft system |

ن

| | |
|---|---|
| نظام معاونة هيدروستاتي | hydrostatic assistance system |
| نظام المعركة | order of battle |
| نظام معياري | modular system |
| نظام الملاحة | navigation system |
| نظام الملاحة « اس كيه ان ٢٦٠٢ » | SKN 2602 navigation |
| نظام الملاحة « پانتش بول » | Punch Bowl navigation system |
| نظام الملاحة بالقصور الذاتي « اوميجا » | Omega inertial navigation system |
| نظام ملاحة تاكان | TACAN navigation |
| نظام ملاحة للحرب ضد الغواصات | ASW navigation system |
| نظام الملاحة « يو آر ان ٦ » | URN 6 navigation |
| نظام الملاحة « يو آر ان ـ ٢٩ » | URN-29 navigation |
| نظام موازنة | stabilization system |
| نظام موازنة اوتوماتيكي | auto-stabilization system |
| نظام موازنة المدفع | gun-stabilization system |
| نظام موجات دقيقة تبادلي | reciprocal microwave system |
| نظام هجوم بموقع محدد بدقة | precision location strike system |
| نظام الهوائي | antenna system |
| نظام الوقود | fuel system |
| نظام يعمل بدفع الغاز | blowback system |
| نظري | visual |
| نظم | regulate |
| نعل القذيفة | sabot |
| نعل المنظم | adapter shoe |
| نفخ بالسطح الأعلى | upper-surface blowing |
| نفذ | carry out |
| نفطة | blister |
| نفق | tunnel |
| نفاث مضخة | pump-jet |
| نفاث موازنة الترجّح | pitch stabilizer jet |
| نفاثة بالضغط الهوائي | aerojet |
| نفاثة تربينية « أتار ٨ كيه ٥٠ » | Atar 8K50 turbojet |
| نفاثة تربينية « آر ـ ١١ » | R-11 turbojet |
| نفاثة تربينية « آر ـ ١٣ اف » | R-13F turbojet |
| نفاثة تربينية « آر ـ ٢٥ » | R-25 turbojet |
| نفاثة تربينية « آر ـ ٢٩ بي » | R-29B turbojet |
| نفاثة تربينية « آر ـ ٣١ » | R-31 turbojet |
| نفاثة تربينية « آر ام ٦ سي » | RM6C turbojet |
| نفاثة تربينية « إيه إل ـ ٢١-٣ » | AL-21-3 turbojet |
| نقالة | stretcher, litter |
| نقالي | portable |
| نقص الضبط | lack of discipline |
| نقطة الأساس لنظام الصواريخ الدفاعية | BPDMS |
| نقطة التجمع | assembly point |
| نقطة تحميل | hardpoint |
| نقطة التسديد | target |
| نقطة رادارية | radar blip |
| النقطة السوداء | bulls-eye |
| النقطة الصلبة أسفل جذع الطائرة | underfuselage hardpoint |
| النقطة الصلبة للجناح | wing hardpoint |
| نقطة الفحص | check point |
| نقطة الميل | dip point |
| نقل | transmit |
| نقل | transmission, transport, transfer |
| نقل الأشخاص البارزين | VIP ferrying |
| نقل اوتوماتيكي | automatic transmission |
| نقل بحري | sea transport |
| نقل بري | road transport |
| نقل بالسيارات | motor transport |
| نقل البضائع | cargo transport |

ن

| | |
|---|---|
| نقل بموجة مستمرة | continuous wave transmission |
| نقل البيانات | data transmission |
| نقل البيانات اوتوماتيكيا | automatic data transmission |
| نقل التموينات | stores-transfer |
| نقل الجنود | troop transport |
| نقل جوي | air transport |
| نقل الحيوانات | animal transport |
| نقل خفيف | light freighting |
| نقل الدم | blood transfusion |
| نقل الركاب | passenger transport |
| نقل مدني | civil transport |
| النمسا | Austria |
| نمساوي | Austrian |
| نمط البحث للسونار | sonar search pattern |
| نمط تتبع راداري | radar tracking mode |
| نمط الحراسة | patrol pattern |
| نمط الرادار | radar mode |
| نمط مسار المقذوف | trajectory mode |
| نمط منطقة التقارب | convergence-zone mode |
| نموذج أولي . طراز بدائي | prototype |
| نموذج بالحجم الطبيعي | mock-up |
| نور كاشف | searchlight |
| نور كاشف بالاشعة دون الحمراء | infra-red search light |
| النرويج | Norway |
| نوط | medal |
| نوع الذخيرة | ammunition type |
| نوع رأس المقذوف | warhead type |
| نووي | nuclear |
| نووي تكتيكي | tactical nuclear |
| نياط القوارب | davits |
| نيبال | Nepal |
| نيجاير | Niger |
| نيجيري | Nigerian |
| نيجيريا | Nigeria |
| نيران الانسحاب | draw off fire |
| نيران البندقية | rifle fire |
| نيران التغطية | covering fire |
| نيران الرشاش | machine-gun fire |
| نيران متقاطعة | cross-fire |
| نيران مدفعية مضادة للطائرات | flak |
| نيران مكثفة | intensive fire |
| نيكاراغوا | Nicaragua |
| نيكاراغوي | Nicaraguan |
| نيوزيلندة | New Zealand |

ن

|  |  |
|---|---|
| هاتف تحت الماء | underwater telephone |
| هاتف « كريبتاسيك ٨٠ » | Cryptacec 80 telephone |
| هاتف لاسلكي | radio telephone |
| هاتف الميدان | field telephone |
| هاجم | attack |
| هارب من الجندية | deserter |
| هاون دوار | rotary cannon |
| هاون متعدد | multi-cannon |
| هاون مصغر العيار | sub-calibre mortar |
| هاييتي | Haiti |
| هبوط | landing |
| هبوط دون المشاعل | no-flare landing |
| الهبوط على السطح | deck landing |
| هبوط مبرمج | programmed descent |
| هجوم | assault, attack |
| هجوم أرضي | ground-attack |
| هجوم بحري | naval strike |
| هجوم برشق مدفعية | salvo attack |
| هجوم برمائي | amphibious assault |
| هجوم بالصواريخ المضادة للسفن | anti-ship missile attack |
| هجوم تدريبي | training sortie |
| هجوم جبهي | frontal attack |
| هجوم جناحي | flank attack |
| هجوم جوي | air attack, aerial attack |
| هجوم خفيف | light attack |
| هجوم ساحلي | over-the-beach assault, coastal strike |
| هجوم عام | general offensive |
| هجوم ليلي | night attack |
| هجوم مباشر | head-on attack |
| هجوم مباغت | surprise attack |
| هجوم مضاد | counter-offensive, counter-attack |
| هجوم مضلل | diversionary attack |
| هجوم معاكس فجائي | combat sortie |
| هجوم منسق | co-ordinated attack |
| هجوم واسع | attack in force |
| هجومي | offensive |
| هداف | marksman |
| هدام | subversive |
| هداية جهاز الطيران التلقائي | autopilot guidance |
| هدف | target |
| هدف أرضي | ground target |
| هدف استراتيجي | strategic target |
| هدف بمسرح العمليات | theatre target |
| هدف ثابت | stationary target |
| هدف ثابت | fixed target |
| هدف جوي | aerial target |
| هدف راداري رئيسي | primary radar target |
| هدف زائف | false target |
| هدف ساحة المعركة | battlefield target |
| هدف سفينة | ship target |
| الهدف لم يتعين ! | target not understood! |
| هدف متحرك | moving target |
| هدف متعدد ثلاثي الأبعاد | 3-dimension Multi-Target |
| هدف مجوّف | cavitating target |

| | |
|---|---|
| « الهدف ـ معين ! » | target identified! |
| هدف مموّه | camouflaged target |
| هدف « ناتو » | NATO target |
| هدم | demolition |
| هدنة | truce, cease fire |
| هدير | boom |
| هرول ! | at the double!, double march! |
| هزيمة | defeat |
| هلام متفجر | blasting gelatine |
| الهند | India |
| هندوراس | Honduras |
| هندي | Indian |
| هواء | air |
| هواء تهوية ساخن | hot bleed air |
| هوائي | antenna |
| هوائي إرشاد | guidance aerial |
| هوائي « اس اتش اف دي اف » | SHF DF antenna |
| هوائي « إلف » | ELF antenna |
| هوائي ايه پي ايه ـ ١٧١ | APA-171 antenna |
| هوائي « پارك لامپ » | Park Lamp antenna |
| هوائي « بلبورد » | Billboard antenna |
| هوائي توجيه موجي مشقوب | slotted-waveguide antenna |
| هوائي دوار مقبب | rotodome aerial |
| هوائي ذو لوحة مستوية | flat-plate antenna |
| هوائي الرادار | radar antenna |
| هوائي طبقي | dish antenna |
| هوائي طليق | floating antenna |
| هوائي ظهري ريشي | dorsal blade aerial |
| هوائي « فيشبون » | fishbone antenna |
| هوائي قابل للتكيف اثناء الطيران | inflight adaptable antennae |
| هوائي قابل للطي | retractable aerial |
| هوائي قطع مكافيء | paraboloid antenna |
| هوائي « كاسجرين » مقلوب | inverted-cassegrain antenna |
| هوائي لوحي | plate aerial |
| هوائي مجموعة مشعة | phased-array antenna |
| هوائي المستقبل | receiver aerial |
| هوائي مستقبل سلبي | passive receiver antenna |
| هوائي مضغوط | pneumatic |
| هوائي مواصلات | communication antenna |
| هوائي نظام الكشف السلبي | passive-detection system antenna |
| هوائي « ياجي » | Yagi antenna |
| « هوقركرافت » | hovercraft |
| هولندة | Netherlands |
| هيئة التدريب العسكري المدني | civilian military training organisation |
| هيئة الحرس الثوري | Revolutionary Guard Corps |
| هيدروكهربائي | hydro-electric |
| هيكل أمامي للطائرة | forward fuselage |
| هيكل السفينة الظاهر من الماء | freeboard hull |
| هيكل الطائرة | airframe |
| هيكل القيادة | command structure |
| هيكل « ماردر » | Marder chassis |
| هيكل نقل بضائع | cargo chassis |

هـ

# و

| | |
|---|---|
| وابل من الرصاص | hail of bullets |
| واجب | duty |
| واجه | encounter |
| واجهة | front |
| واشي | informer |
| واضح | visible |
| واقية شظايا | traverse |
| واقية الشمس | sunshade |
| وباء | epidemic |
| وثائق | documents |
| وحدات متنوعة | miscellaneous units |
| وحدة | unit, contingent |
| وحدة احراز | acquisition unit |
| وحدة اختصاصيين | specialist unit |
| وحدة استجواب لتمييز الصديق والعدو | IFF interrogator unit |
| وحدة إستطلاع | reconnaissance unit |
| وحدة الاقتحام | assault unit |
| وحدة انقضاض سريع | fast attack unit |
| وحدة تجريبية | trial unit |
| وحدة تحويل العمليات | operations conversion unit |
| وحدة تدريب | training unit |
| وحدة تصويب | aiming unit |
| وحدة تصوير | camera unit |
| وحدة تلفزيونية منخفضة الاضاءة | LLTV unit |
| وحدة حاوية قاذفة | container-launcher unit |
| وحدة الحرب ضد الغواصات | ASW unit |
| وحدة حل الرموز | decipherer |
| وحدة الخط الأمامي | front-line unit |
| وحدة دبابات | tank unit |
| وحدة دعم | support unit |
| وحدة الدفاع الجوي « پي ڤي اوه » | PVO air-defence unit |
| وحدة دفاع ساحلي | coastal defence unit |
| وحدة دفعية | propulsion plant, propulsion unit |
| وحدة رد الارهابيين | counter-terrorist unit |
| وحدة الرمي | firing unit |
| وحدة شواطىء برمائية | amphibious beach unit |
| وحدة صاعقة | commando unit |
| وحدة طاقة | powerplant |
| وحدة طاقة مساعدة | auxiliary power unit |
| وحدة طبية | medical unit |
| وحدة عرض بيانات الطيران على واقي الريح | HUD unit |
| وحدة عسكرية | military unit, service unit |
| وحدة غير مقاتلة | non-combatant unit |
| وحدة فدائية بحرية | Marine Commando unit |
| وحدة فرعية | sub-unit |
| وحدة محمولة جواً | airborne unit |
| وحدة مدرعة | armoured unit |
| وحدة مراقبة | supervision unit, monitoring unit |
| وحدة مستشفى عسكرية | hospital unit |
| وحدة مظلات | paratroop unit |
| وحدة منقولة بالسيارات | motorized unit |
| وحيد النبضة | monopulse |

و

| | |
|---|---|
| ودي | friendly |
| ورشة | workshop |
| ورشة اصلاح | repair shop |
| ورشة بناء السفن | shipyard |
| ورشة الصيانة | maintenance workshop |
| ورشة فحص | inspection workshop |
| ورشة مكنات | machine workshop |
| وزارة الدفاع | Department of Defense, Ministry of Defence |
| وزن | weight |
| وزن الاقلاع الأقصى | maximum take-off weight |
| وزن الصاروخ | missile weight |
| وزن رأس المقذوف | warhead weight |
| وزن عند الاطلاق | launch weight |
| الوزن عند الاقلاع | take-off weight |
| الوزن المجهز فارغاً | empty equipped weight |
| الوزن المحمول | weight loaded |
| وزن الملاحين والآلات | payload |
| وزير الدفاع | defence minister |
| وسام | medal |
| وسام عسكري | military honour |
| وسيلة انذار مبكر | EW device |
| وسيلة التفجير | detonating device |
| وسيلة غلق رتاجية | bolt closure device |
| وسيلة كشف | detection device |
| وسيلة مراقبة | control device |
| وصل الى | reach |
| وصلة فوهة زاويّة | angled muzzle attachment |
| وضع الارتداد السفلي | bottom-bounce mode |
| وضع الاطلاق | launch mode |
| وضع الاطلاق الأمامي | bow launch position |
| وضع بصري | optical mode |
| الوضع الحالي | present position |
| وضع دفاعي رئيسي | main defensive position |
| وضع شفرة الجهاز المرسل المستجيب | transponder-code position |
| وضع عدم اصلاء | disarmed state |
| وضع العمليات | operational status |
| وضع الكسح | sweep position |
| وظيفة تعقب الصواريخ | missile-tracking function |
| وعاء | container |
| وقاية بالدروع | armour protection |
| وقت | time |
| وقف إطلاق النار | cease fire |
| وقود | fuel |
| وقود اعتيادي | standard fuel |
| وقود جاف | solid-fuel |
| وقود « جيه پي ٧ » | JP-7 fuel |
| وقود داخلي | internal fuel |
| وقود دفعي | propellant |
| وقود دفعي سائل | liquid propellant |
| وقود سائل | liquid-fuel |
| وقود السيارات | vehicle fuel |
| وقود الطائرات | aircraft fuel, aviation fuel |
| وقود متعدد | multi-fuel |
| وقود يورانيوم | uranium fuel |
| وقع في شرك | trapped |
| وكالة استخبارات | intelligence agency |
| وكالة تموين | supply agency |
| وكالة المخابرات المركزية | Central Intelligence Agency |
| الولايات المتحدة الأمريكية | United States |
| ومض الفوهة | muzzle flash |

و

# ى

|  |  |
|---|---|
| Japan | اليابان |
| Japanese | ياباني |
| pressurized-water cooled | يبرد بالماء المضغوط |
| surviving | يبقى حياً |
| adopt a ready position | يتخذ وضع الاستعداد |
| infiltrate (to) | يتسرب |
| infiltrate (to) | يتسلل |
| establish contact | يحقق الاتصال |
| decode | يحل الشفرة |
| man-portable | يحمله إنسان |
| hands on throttle and stick | اليدين على الخانق والذراع |
| left dress! | يساراً تراصف ! |
| reusable | يستعمل ثانية |
| hand over | يسلم إلى |
| obey (to) | يطيع |
| automated | يعمل اوتوماتيكياً |
| peroxide-powered | يعمل بالبيروكسيد |
| turbine powered | يعلم بالتربين |
| gas-operated | يعمل بالغاز |
| computerized | يعمل بالكومبيوتر |
| diesel-powered | يعمل بمحرك ديزل |
| defect (to) | يغادر |
| conquer | يفتح |
| outnumbered | يفوقه عدداً |
| outmanoeuvred | يفوقه براعة |
| kill (to) | يقتل |
| eject | يقذف |
| reveille | يقظة |
| conquer | يقهر |
| South Yemen | اليمن الجنوبية |
| North Yemen | اليمن الشمالية |
| right dress! | يمينا تراصف ! |
| peel-off | ينحرف للانقضاض أو الهبوط |
| Yugoslav | يوغسلافي |
| Yugoslavia | يوغوسلافيا |
| Greece | اليونان |
| Greek | يوناني |